Innovative Research and Applications in Next-Generation High Performance Computing

Qusay F. Hassan
Mansoura University, Egypt

A volume in the Advances in Systems Analysis, Software Engineering, and High Performance Computing (ASASEHPC) Book Series

An Imprint of IGI Global

Published in the United States of America by
Information Science Reference (an imprint of IGI Global)
701 E. Chocolate Avenue
Hershey PA, USA 17033
Tel: 717-533-8845
Fax: 717-533-8661
E-mail: cust@igi-global.com
Web site: http://www.igi-global.com

Library of Congress Cataloging-in-Publication Data

Names: Hassan, Qusay F., 1982- editor.
Title: Innovative research and applications in next-generation high
  performance computing / Qusay F. Hassan, editor.
Description: Hershey : Information Science Reference, 2016. | Includes
  bibliographical references and index.
Identifiers: LCCN 2016007158| ISBN 9781522502876 (hardcover) | ISBN
  9781522502883 (ebook)
Subjects: LCSH: High performance computing.
Classification: LCC QA76.88 .H38 2016 | DDC 004.1/1--dc23 LC record available at https://lccn.loc.gov/2016007158

This book is published in the IGI Global book series Advances in Systems Analysis, Software Engineering, and High Performance Computing (ASASEHPC) (ISSN: 2327-3453; eISSN: 2327-3461)

British Cataloguing in Publication Data
A Cataloguing in Publication record for this book is available from the British Library.

All work contributed to this book is new, previously-unpublished material. The views expressed in this book are those of the authors, but not necessarily of the publisher.

For electronic access to this publication, please contact: eresources@igi-global.com.

Advances in Systems Analysis, Software Engineering, and High Performance Computing (ASASEHPC) Book Series

Vijayan Sugumaran
Oakland University, USA

ISSN: 2327-3453
EISSN: 2327-3461

MISSION

The theory and practice of computing applications and distributed systems has emerged as one of the key areas of research driving innovations in business, engineering, and science. The fields of software engineering, systems analysis, and high performance computing offer a wide range of applications and solutions in solving computational problems for any modern organization.

The **Advances in Systems Analysis, Software Engineering, and High Performance Computing (ASASEHPC) Book Series** brings together research in the areas of distributed computing, systems and software engineering, high performance computing, and service science. This collection of publications is useful for academics, researchers, and practitioners seeking the latest practices and knowledge in this field.

COVERAGE

- Distributed Cloud Computing
- Network Management
- Computer Graphics
- Metadata and Semantic Web
- Computer Networking
- Performance Modelling
- Virtual Data Systems
- Human-Computer Interaction
- Storage Systems
- Parallel Architectures

IGI Global is currently accepting manuscripts for publication within this series. To submit a proposal for a volume in this series, please contact our Acquisition Editors at Acquisitions@igi-global.com or visit: http://www.igi-global.com/publish/.

Titles in this Series

For a list of additional titles in this series, please visit: www.igi-global.com

Developing Interoperable and Federated Cloud Architecture
Gabor Kecskemeti (University of Miskolc, Hungary) Attila Kertesz (University of Szeged, Hungary) and Zsolt Nemeth (MTA SZTAKI, Hungary)
Information Science Reference • copyright 2016 • 398pp • H/C (ISBN: 9781522501534) • US $210.00 (our price)

Managing Big Data in Cloud Computing Environments
Zongmin Ma (Nanjing University of Aeronautics and Astronautics, China)
Information Science Reference • copyright 2016 • 314pp • H/C (ISBN: 9781466698345) • US $195.00 (our price)

Emerging Innovations in Agile Software Development
Imran Ghani (Universiti Teknologi Malaysia, Malaysia) Dayang Norhayati Abang Jawawi (Universiti Teknologi Malaysia, Malaysia) Siva Dorairaj (Software Education, New Zealand) and Ahmed Sidky (ICAgile, USA)
Information Science Reference • copyright 2016 • 323pp • H/C (ISBN: 9781466698581) • US $205.00 (our price)

Modern Software Engineering Methodologies for Mobile and Cloud Environments
António Miguel Rosado da Cruz (Instituto Politécnico de Viana do Castelo, Portugal) and Sara Paiva (Instituto Politécnico de Viana do Castelo, Portugal)
Information Science Reference • copyright 2016 • 355pp • H/C (ISBN: 9781466699168) • US $210.00 (our price)

Emerging Research Surrounding Power Consumption and Performance Issues in Utility Computing
Ganesh Chandra Deka (Regional Vocational Training Institute (RVTI) for Women, India) G.M. Siddesh (M S Ramaiah Institute of Technology, Bangalore, India) K. G. Srinivasa (M S Ramaiah Institute of Technology, Bangalore, India) and L.M. Patnaik (IISc, Bangalore, India)
Information Science Reference • copyright 2016 • 460pp • H/C (ISBN: 9781466688537) • US $215.00 (our price)

Advanced Research on Cloud Computing Design and Applications
Shadi Aljawarneh (Jordan University of Science and Technology, Jordan)
Information Science Reference • copyright 2015 • 388pp • H/C (ISBN: 9781466686762) • US $205.00 (our price)

Handbook of Research on Computational Simulation and Modeling in Engineering
Francisco Miranda (Instituto Politécnico de Viana do Castelo and CIDMA of University of Aveiro, Portugal) and Carlos Abreu (Instituto Politécnico de Viana do Castelo, Portugal)
Engineering Science Reference • copyright 2016 • 824pp • H/C (ISBN: 9781466688230) • US $420.00 (our price)

DISSEMINATOR of KNOWLEDGE

www.igi-global.com

701 E. Chocolate Ave., Hershey, PA 17033
Order online at www.igi-global.com or call 717-533-8845 x100
To place a standing order for titles released in this series, contact: cust@igi-global.com
Mon-Fri 8:00 am - 5:00 pm (est) or fax 24 hours a day 717-533-8661

Editorial Advisory Board

Table of Contents

Section 1
Energy and Performance Optimization

Section 4
Mobile, Cloud, and Internet of Things

Detailed Table of Contents

Section 1
Energy and Performance Optimization

    Arsalan Shahid, HITEC University, Pakistan
    Saad Arif, HITEC University, Pakistan
    Muhammad Yasir Qadri, University of Essex, UK
    Saba Munawar, COMSATS Institute of Information Technology, Pakistan

The scaling of CMOS technology has continued due to ever increasing demand of greater performance with low power consumption. This demand has grown further by the portable and battery operated devices market. To meet the challenge of greater energy efficiency and performance, a number of power optimization techniques at processor and system components level are proposed by the research community such as clock gating, operand isolation, memory splitting, power gating, dynamic voltage and frequency scaling, etc. This chapter reviews advancements in the dynamic power optimization techniques like clock gating and power gating. This chapter also reviews some architectures and optimization techniques that have been developed for greater power reduction without any significant performance degradation or area cost.

    Mohammad Shojafar, Sapienza University of Roma, Italy
    Nicola Cordeschi, Sapienza University of Rome, Italy
    Enzo Baccarelli, Sapienza University of Rome, Italy

The pervasive use of cloud computing and the resulting growing number of Internet data centers have brought forth many concerns, including electrical energy cost, energy dissipation, cooling and carbon emission. Therefore, the need for efficient workload schedulers which are capable of minimizing the consumed energy becomes increasingly important. Green computing, a new trend for high-end computing, attempts to approach this problem by delivering both high performance and reduced energy consumption.

Motivated by these considerations, in this chapter, we propose a joint computation-and-communication adaptive resource-provisioning scheduler for virtualized data centers, e.g., the Internet Data Center (IDC) scheduler, which exploits the DVFS-enabled reconfiguration capability of the underlying virtualized computing/communication platform. Specifically, we present and test a dynamic resource provisioning scheduler, which adaptively controls the execution time and bandwidth usage of each input job, as well as the internal and external switching costs on per-Virtual Machine (VM) basis.

Arsalan Shahid, HITEC University, Pakistan
Maryam Murad, HITEC University, Taxila Cantt, Pakistan
Muhammad Yasir Qadri, University of Essex, UK
Nadia N. Qadri, COMSATS Institute of Information Technology, Pakistan
Jameel Ahmed, HITEC University, Pakistan

The initiation to have a concept of shared memory in processors has built an opportunity for thread level parallelism. In various applications, synchronization or ordering tools are utilized to have an access to shared data. Traditionally, multithreaded programming models usually suggest a set of low-level primitives, such as locks, to guarantee mutual exclusion. Possession of one or more locks protects access to shared data. But, due to some flaws they become a suboptimal solution. The idea of transactional memory is in research presently as an alternative to locks. Among which, one way is hardware transactional memory. Atomicity is well supported by using transactions in hardware. In this chapter, we have focused on hardware transactional memories and the work done on them so far.

Arsalan Shahid, HITEC University, Pakistan
Bilal Khalid, HITEC University, Pakistan
Muhammad Yasir Qadri, University of Essex, UK
Nadia N. Qadri, COMSATS Institute of Information Technology, Pakistan
Jameel Ahmed, HITEC University, Pakistan

Multi-Processor System on Chip (MPSoC) architectures have become a mainstream technology for obtaining performance improvements in computing platforms. With the increase in the number of cores, the role of cache memory has become pivotal. An ideal memory configuration is always desired to be fast and large; but, in fact, striking to balance between the size and access time of the memory hierarchy is considered by processor architect. Design space exploration is used for performance analysis of systems and helps to find the optimal solution for obtaining the desired objectives. In this chapter, we explore two design space parameters, i.e., cache size and number of cores, for obtaining the desired energy consumption. Moreover, previously presented energy models for multilevel cache are evaluated by using cycle accurate full system simulator. Our results show that with the increase in cache sizes, the number of cycles required for application execution decreases, and by increasing number of cores, the throughput improve.

Chapter 5

Yan Li, Intel Labs China, China
Jidong Zhai, Tsinghua University, China
Keqin Li, State University of New York, USA

With the development of high performance computers, communication performance is a key factor affecting the performance of HPC applications. Communication patterns can be obtained by analyzing communication traces. However, existing approaches to generating communication traces need to execute the entire parallel applications on full-scale systems that are time-consuming and expensive. Furthermore, for designers of large-scale parallel computers, it is greatly desired that performance of a parallel application can be predicted at the design phase. Despite previous efforts, it remains an open problem to estimate sequential computation time in each process accurately and efficiently for large-scale parallel applications on non-existing target machines. In this chapter, we will introduce a novel technique for performing fast communication trace collection for large-scale parallel applications and an automatic performance prediction framework with a trace-driven network simulator.

Section 2
Heterogeneous Clusters

Chapter 6

Pedro Valero-Lara, University of Manchester, UK
Abel Paz-Gallardo, Research Center for Energy, Environment and Technology, Spain
Erich L Foster, Università della Svizzera Italiana, Italy
Manuel Prieto-Matías, Universidad Complutense de Madrid, Spain
Alfredo Pinelli, City London University, UK
Johan Jansson, Basque Center for Applied Mathematics, Spain

This chapter presents an overview of the evolution of computer architecture, giving special attention on those advances which have promoted the current hybrid systems. After that, we focus on the most extended programming strategies applied to hybrid computing. In fact, programming is one of the most important challenges for this kind of systems, as it requires a high knowledge of the hardware to achieve a good performance. Current hybrid systems are basically composed by three components, two processors (multicore and manycore) and an interconnection bus (PCIe), which connects both processors. Each of the components must be managed differently. After presenting the particular features of current hybrid systems, authors focus on introducing some approaches to exploit simultaneously each of the components. Finally, to clarify how to program in these platforms, two cases studies are presented and analyzed in deep. At the end of the chapter, authors outline the main insights behind hybrid computing and introduce upcoming advances in hybrid systems.

Xiongwei Fei, Hunan City University, China
Kenli Li, Hunan University, China
Wangdong Yang, Hunan University, China
Keqin Li, State University of New York, USA

Heterogeneous and hybrid computing has been heavily studied in the field of parallel and distributed computing in recent years. It can work on a single computer, or in a group of computers connected by a high-speed network. The former is the topic of this chapter. Its key points are how to cooperatively use devices that are different in performance and architecture to satisfy various computing requirements, and how to make the whole program achieve the best performance possible when executed. CPUs and GPUs have fundamentally different design philosophies, but combining their characteristics could avail better performance in many applications. However, it is still a challenge to optimize them. This chapter focuses on the main optimization strategies including "partitioning and load-balancing", "data access", "communication", and "synchronization and asynchronization". Furthermore, two applications will be introduced as examples of using these strategies.

Hugo Perez, Barcelona Supercomputing Center, Spain
Benjamin Hernandez, Oak Ridge National Laboratory, USA
Isaac Rudomin, Barcelona Supercomputing Center, Spain
Eduard Ayguade, Barcelona Supercomputing Center, Spain

Industry trends in the coming years imply the availability of cluster computing with hundreds to thousands of cores per chip, as well as the use of accelerators. Programming presents a challenge due to this heterogeneous architecture; thus, using novel programming models that facilitate this process is necessary. In this chapter, the case of simulation and visualization of crowds is presented. The authors analyze and compare the use of two programming models: OmpSs and CUDA. OmpSs allows to take advantage of all the resources available per node by combining the CPU and GPU while automatically taking care of memory management, scheduling, communications and synchronization. Experimental results obtained from Fermi, Kepler and Maxwell GPU architectures are presented, and the different modes used for visualizing the results are described, as well.

Section 3
Reliability and Fault Tolerance

Camille Coti, Université Paris 13, France

This chapter gives an overview of techniques used to tolerate failures in high-performance distributed applications. We describe basic replication techniques, automatic rollback recovery and application-based fault tolerance. We present the challenges raised specifically by distributed, high performance computing and the performance overhead the fault tolerance mechanisms are likely to cost. Last, we give an example of a fault-tolerant algorithm that exploits specific properties of a recent algorithm.

Chapter 10

A. Don Clark, West Virginia University, USA

High performance computing (HPC) systems are becoming the norm for daily use and care must be made to ensure that these systems are resilient. Recent contributions on resiliency have been from quantitative and qualitative perspectives where general system failures are considered. However, there are limited contributions dealing with the specific classes of failures that are directly related to cyber-attacks. In this chapter, the author uses the concepts of transition processes and limiting distributions to perform a generic theoretical investigation of the effects of targeted failures by relating the actions of the cyber-enemy (CE) to different risk levels in an HPC system. Special cases of constant attack strategies are considered where exact solutions are obtained. Additionally, a stopped process is introduced to model the effects of system termination. The results of this representation can be directly applied throughout the HPC community for monitoring and mitigating cyber-attacks.

Chapter 11

Qiang Guan, Los Alamos National Laboratory, USA
Nathan DeBardeleben, Los Alamos National Lab, USA
Sean Blanchard, Los Alamos National Lab, USA
Song Fu, University of North Texas, USA
Claude H. Davis IV, Clemson University, USA
William M. Jones, Coastal Carolina University, USA

As the high performance computing (HPC) community continues to push towards exascale computing, HPC applications of today are only affected by soft errors to a small degree but we expect that this will become a more serious issue as HPC systems grow. We propose F-SEFI, a Fine-grained Soft Error Fault Injector, as a tool for profiling software robustness against soft errors. We utilize soft error injection to mimic the impact of errors on logic circuit behavior. Leveraging the open source virtual machine hypervisor QEMU, F-SEFI enables users to modify emulated machine instructions to introduce soft errors. F-SEFI can control what application, which sub-function, when and how to inject soft errors with different granularities, without interference to other applications that share the same environment. We demonstrate use cases of F-SEFI on several benchmark applications with different characteristics to show how data corruption can propagate to incorrect results. The findings from the fault injection campaign can be used for designing robust software and power-efficient hardware.

Chapter 12

J. Pourqasem, University of Guilan, Iran
S.A. Edalatpanah, Ayandegan Institute of Higher Education, Iran

Equal peers in peer-to-peer (P2P) networks are the drawbacks of system in term of bandwidth, scalability and efficiency. The super-peer model is based on heterogeneity and different characteristics of peers in P2P networks. The P2P networks and large- scale distributed systems based on P2P networks use the super-peer model to design the query processing mechanism. This chapter first reviews the query processing methods in P2P networks, in which the authors classify theses query processing approaches in Unstructured and Structured mechanisms. Furthermore, the query processing techniques in distributed systems based on P2P networks are discussed. Afterward, authors concentrate on super-peer model to process the query of peers in P2P networks. Authors present the query processing methods in P2P-based distributed systems using the super node. Finally, the chapter provides some examples of each of the presented query processing techniques, and then illustrates the properties of each of them in terms of scalability and performance issues.

Section 4
Mobile, Cloud, and Internet of Things

Mobile devices are gaining high popularity due to support for a wide range of applications. However, the mobile devices are resource constrained and many applications require high resources. To cater to this issue, the researchers envision usage of mobile cloud computing technology which offers high performance computing, execution of resource intensive applications, and energy efficiency. This chapter highlights importance of mobile devices, high performance applications, and the computing challenges of mobile devices. It also provides a brief introduction to mobile cloud computing technology, its architecture, types of mobile applications, computation offloading process, effective offloading challenges, and high performance computing application on mobile devises that are enabled by mobile cloud computing technology.

Multiple properties of big mobile data, namely volume, velocity, variety, and veracity make the big data analytics process a challenging task. It is desired that mobile devices initially process big data before sending it to big data systems to reduce the data complexity. However, the mobile devices have recourse constraints, and the challenge of processing big mobile data on mobile devices requires further exploration. This chapter presents a thorough discussion about mobile computing systems and their implication for big data analytics. It presents big data analytics with different perspectives involving descriptive, predictive, and prescriptive analytical methods. Moreover, the chapter presents a detailed literature review on mobile and cloud based big data analytics systems, and highlights the future application areas and open research issues that are relevant to big data analytics in mobile cloud environments. Lastly, the chapter provides some recommendations regarding big data processing, quality improvement, and complexity optimization.

This Chapter provides several comparable studies of some of the major evolving and enabling wireless technologies in the Internet of Things (IoT). Particularly, it focuses on the ZigBee, 6lowpan, Bluetooth Low Energy, LTE, and the different versions of Wi-Fi protocols including the IEEE 802.11ah. The studies, reported in this chapter, evaluate the capabilities and behaviors of these technologies in terms of various metrics including the data range and rate, network size, RF Channels and Bandwidth, Antenna design considerations, Power Consumption, and their Ecosystem. It is concluded that the requirements of each IoT application play a significant role in the selection of a suitable wireless technology.

The Internet of Things (IoT) brings connectivity to about every objects found in the physical space. It extends connectivity not only to computer and mobile devices but also to everyday objects. From connected fridges, cars and cities, the IoT creates opportunities in numerous domains. This chapter briefly surveys some IoT applications and the impact the IoT could have on societies. It shows how the various application of the IoT enhances the overall quality of life and reduces management and costs in various sectors.

Preface

BACKGROUND

"To out compete, you must out compute." This is how experts in High Performance Computing (HPC) and science sum up their hearing which was held by the Energy Subcommittee of the US House Science, Space and Technology Committee, on January 28, 2015 in seek of more funding for research for more powerful and efficient HPC systems. This can be seen as the theme of this decade, or even the entire century, not just for the US, but for the entire world. Governments, research labs, academia, and private sector all believe that HPC is crucial for competitiveness and economic growth.

HPC has countless definitions that are sometimes contradictory or irrelevant. Also, HPC is sometimes used interchangeably with supercomputing. While this is not necessarily wrong, we prefer to refer to a wide range of concepts and technologies that distinguish HPC from other computer science terminologies. In this book, HPC can be viewed as the use of enormous computing resources — processors, accelerators, memory, storage, high-speed networks, and software systems —, and parallelization and distributed computing techniques that can handle large and complex workloads. HPC is a key enabling technology for scientific discoveries and innovations, as well as many of the governmental and commercial applications.

With the dawn of the Internet of Things and Big Data, the need to perform more complex computations and analyses will increase radically. Furthermore, HPC community, from all sectors, is eager to employ more sophisticated computer systems to perform far more advanced calculations than what can be handled by today's systems. This increase in use of such sophisticated systems will be accompanied with some requirements such as the right understanding of the HPC concepts, and the utilization of its algorithms and techniques, as well as the awareness of the current and foreseen challenges. It will also entail a necessity to devise some new technologies — both hardware and software —, and innovative applications and practices to cope with the unprecedented complexity and computational needs of such systems.

The amplification of large, structured and unstructured datasets, millions of threads, multi-core and manycore architectures, heterogeneous CPU/GPU computing, remote sensors, and mobile and wireless networks is very complex. Therefore, these areas need further analysis and understanding as they are shaping a new era of HPC.

PURPOSE AND READERSHIP

This book aims at addressing the aforementioned issues by providing 17 well-written chapters that offer detailed and comprehensive discussions on these matters. All chapters were reviewed by at least two expert reviewers during the initial evaluation phase, and then again by the editor after receiving the revised versions before final acceptance. Chapters that did not meet the quality standards set by the editorial board, and those whose focus was beyond the scope of this book's theme were omitted. The editor supervised the evaluation phases, and acted as a reviewer for some chapters as well, to ensure the quality of accepted chapters was achieved.

This book is authored by a number of international experts and researchers with diverse expertise. The book focuses on HPC and related technologies, and strives to provide the readers with a broad range of topics on this field. This includes coverage for a number of the key concepts of HPC, as well as state-of-art research on its techniques and applications. Each chapter covers a specific topic, and hence, readers can focus on the ones of their interest.

This book is an excellent reference for researchers, post graduates, and professionals whom of which are interested in learning more about HPC. It will not only help the readers to grasp the basic knowledge on the common techniques and evolving applications, but it will also address some cutting-edge topics that will allow them to further research HPC. Furthermore, this book can be used by academicians as teaching material for some advanced courses of computer science, applied computational science, computer architecture, distributed computing, and parallel processing.

ORGANIZATION OF THE BOOK

This book is organized into four sections, each of which is devoted to a distinctive area.

Introduction

This book begins with a commentary chapter entitled *An Outlook into Novel Concepts of High Performance Computing* by Qusay F. Hassan, which highlights some of the topics and technologies of the broad and current interest in HPC field. The chapter gives a brief overview on each of the addressed topics by describing its current state, challenges, and potential room of improvement. The chapter starts with a discussion over the relentless race towards exascale computing, and lists some of the main issues that must be solved to achieve this exceptional computing scale. The chapter also talks over some of the technologies that are gaining momentum from HPC community such as accelerators, low-power architectures and mobile SoCs, and memory-based storage. Furthermore, it presents some of the multidisciplinary approaches where HPC converges with other models such as mobile computing, the Internet of Things, and Big Data. Finally, the chapter highlights the negative impacts HPC has had on the environment and the importance of improving this area.

Section 1: Energy and Performance Optimization

Section 1 of this book consists of five chapters that provide various techniques for optimizing two of the most critical elements in HPC systems, i.e., energy and performance.

Chapter 1, *Power Optimization Using Clock Gating and Power Gating: A Revie*, by Arsalan Shahid, Saad Arif, Muhammad Yasir Qadri, and Saba Munawar, reviews the latest advancements in clock gating and power gating techniques. The chapter lists power optimization techniques that are being utilized in CMOS integrated circuits. Then, the chapter discusses how clock gating and power gating techniques can save total dynamic power with minimal effect on the performance.

Chapter 2, *Resource Scheduling for Energy-aware Reconfigurable Internet Data Centers*, by Mohammad Shojafar, Nicola Cordeschi, and Enzo Baccarelli, proposes a new Internet data center scheduler that aims at reducing power consumption incurred by computing and communication in virtualized Internet data centers. The chapter discusses how the proposed model offers energy efficiency while achieving high reliability and availability by utilizing Dynamic Voltage and Frequency Scaling (DVFS) tools, which are widely employed in modern computing models such as cluster computing and supercomputing. The chapter also presents the mathematical approach developed to convert the non-convex resulting energy model into a convex model. Additionally, the chapter presents the testbed and simulator that authors implemented to test the proposed Internet data center scheduler. The chapter then ends with the test results and detailed comparisons between the proposed and standard schedulers.

Chapter 3, *Hardware Transactional Memories: A Survey*, by Arsalan Shahid, Maryam Murad, Muhammad Yasir Qadri, Nadia N. Qadri, and Jameel Ahmed, introduces hardware transactional memories as an efficient technique to synchronize parallel processes in multi-threaded systems. The chapter presents the history of transactional memories and how they are superior to the traditional locks in preserving concurrency and atomicity. Moreover, the chapter presents a detailed review of hardware transactional memories, and lists some of its recent implementations.

Chapter 4, *Design Space Exploration Using Cycle Accurate Simulator*, by Arsalan Shahid, Bilal Khalid, Muhammad Yasir Qadri, Nadia N. Qadri, and Jameel Ahmed, presents a technique for the Design Space Exploration (DSE) of Multi-Processor System on Chip (MPSoC) architectures by using a state-of-the-art full system cycle accurate simulator. The DSE focuses on two-level cache memory hierarchy to obtain the optimal design solutions, namely, cache size and number of cores. Moreover, the chapter evaluates previously presented cache energy models using cycle accurate simulation results.

Chapter 5, *Communication Analysis and Performance Prediction of Parallel Applications on Large-Scale Machines*, by Yan Li, Jidong Zhai, and Keqin Li, proposes a novel technique for fast generation and collection of communication traces for large-scale MPI-based parallel applications on small-scale machines. The chapter demonstrates how the proposed technique saves resources and time by preserving the spatial and volume communication attributes of original programs. The chapter also presents a performance prediction framework that integrates a computation-time acquisition approach with a trace-driven network simulator, which can be used by designers/developers during the design time.

Section 2: Heterogeneous Computing

Section 3 of this book consists of three chapters that discuss the utilization of heterogeneous architectures in HPC implementations. Each of these chapters examines heterogeneous computing from a particular angle.

Chapter 6, *Multicore & Manycore: Hybrid Computing Architectures and Applications*, by Pedro Valero-Lara, Abel Paz-Gallardo, Erich L Foster, Manuel Prieto-Matías, Alfredo Pinelli, and Johan Jansson, provides the readers with an excellent insight on multicore and manycore computing architectures and applications. The chapter starts with a brief discussion about the history of parallel computing architectures, and the advances that have enabled the emergence and evolution of current hybrid systems. The chapter then delves into the features and programming aspects of hybrid computing, and discusses how multicore and many core processors can be utilized simultaneously to achieve a great performance. Afterwards, the chapter presents a case study on each model to demonstrate how it can be implemented and where it best fits. Lastly, the chapter highlights some of the future advances in hybrid systems.

Chapter 7, *CPU-GPU Computing: Overview, Optimization, and Applications*, by Xiongwei Fei, Kenli Li, Wangdong Yang, and Keqin Li, introduces CPU-GPU heterogeneous hardware, and OpenMP-CUDA hybrid software environments. The chapter initially explains the CPU and GPU architectures, and then discusses how OpenMP and CUDA can be utilized to make use of them, respectively. The chapter also offers some optimization techniques as well as performance evaluation methods for applications running on heterogeneous environments. Additionally, the chapter presents two examples that demonstrate how optimization techniques can be implemented on heterogeneous hardware, allowing for the development of efficient hybrid parallel software applications.

Chapter 8, *Task-based Crowd Simulation for Heterogeneous Architectures*, by Hugo Perez, Benjamin Hernandez, Isaac Rudomin, and Eduard Ayguade, addresses the utilization of heterogeneous architectures, where multicore processors and accelerators are employed, for real-time, large-scale crowd simulation and visualization. The chapter discusses the implementation details of the algorithm developed to make use of GPUs in order to save the processing time and computation resources. Specifically, the chapter discusses and evaluates the implementation of crowd simulation using CUDA and OmpSs. Moreover, the chapter provides the evaluation results of this algorithm on various GPU architectures. Finally, the chapter presents a configurable visualization engine that supports various visualization modes.

Section 3: Reliability and Fault Tolerance

Section 3 of this book consists of four chapters that address reliability, robustness and fault tolerance of HPC systems.

Chapter 9, *Fault Tolerance Techniques for Distributed, Parallel Applications*, by Camille Coti, provides a list of fault tolerance techniques that are widely used in distributed and high-performance systems that are necessary to sustain the execution of parallel applications on a large scale. The chapter describes basic replication techniques, automatic rollback and recovery, and application-based fault tolerance. Moreover, it discusses the overhead caused by implementing fault tolerance techniques in distributed and high-performance systems. Lastly, the chapter presents an example of an application that utilizes redundant computations availed by communication-avoiding algorithms for fault-tolerance.

Chapter 10, *A Theoretic Representation of the Effects of Targeted Failures in HPC Systems*, by A. Don Clark, investigates the effects of intentional failures in HPC systems where an abstract representation is proposed that depicts the relationship between the actions of the cyber enemy (CE) and failure risk levels. Next, one and two level consistent attacks are considered where – for one leveled attacks – the impact of failure levels directly depends on the attack strategy. However, for the case of two-leveled constant attacks, it can be shown that the transition between any two risk levels depends on the attack rates, the frequency of transition, and the system failure rate. Finally, a model to describe the effects of system termination is proposed. These results provide the HPC community with a fundamental understanding needed for effective troubleshooting and mitigation against cyber-attacks with highlights on future research developments.

Chapter 11, *Analyzing the Robustness of HPC Applications Using a Fine-grained Soft Error Fault Injection Tool*, by Qiang Guan, Nathan DeBardeleben, Sean Blanchard, Song Fu, Claude H. Davis IV, and William M. Jones, proposes a software tool for profiling the robustness of HPC applications against soft errors. It demonstrates the effect of errors on logic circuits by injecting soft errors into HPC systems. The chapter shows how this tool can be used on virtual machines to modify machine instructions and inject errors with diverse granularities to the targeted application without disturbing other applications on the emulated machine. It also shows how data corruption can lead to incorrect results. The chapter concludes by highlighting how fault injections can be used to design robust and energy-efficient HPC systems.

Chapter 12, *Verification of Super-Peer Model for Query Processing in Peer-to-Peer Networks*, by Javad pourqasem and S.A Edalatpanah, surveys various query processing techniques in peer-to-peer (P2P) networks and P2P-based distributed systems. The chapter then focuses on super-peer query processing model, and highlights the major advances and performance issues of each. The chapter gives a few examples of these techniques alongside their properties, advantages and disadvantages.

Section 4: Mobile, Cloud, and Internet of Things

Section 4 of this book consists of four chapters that present various technologies related to HPC.

Chapter 13, *High Performance Computing on Mobile Devices*, by Atta ur Rehman Khan and Abdul Nasir Khan, introduces cloud and mobile cloud computing technology, and discusses how cloud computing can fulfill the ever increasing demands for computational power on mobile devices. The chapter describes how data and computation can be offloaded to the cloud to allow energy-efficient and high-performance computing for complex processes. Furthermore, the chapter provides a list of high-performance applications on mobile devices which are enabled by the mobile cloud computing technology. Finally, the chapter presents some of the future research directions in this area.

Chapter 14, *Big Data Analytics in Mobile and Cloud Computing Environments*, by M. Habib ur Rehman, Atta ur Rehman Khan, and Aisha Batool, provides a detailed discussion about mobile computing systems and the gigantic amount of data they generate. It describes various methods of big data analytics, and how they are handled in mobile and cloud computing environments. Lastly, the chapter highlights application areas and open research issues of big data analytics in mobile cloud environments.

Chapter 15, *Wireless Enabling Technologies for the Internet of Things*, by Mahmoud Elkhodr, Seyed Shahrestani, and Hon Cheung, surveys the various enabling wireless technologies for the Internet of Things (IoT). Specifically, the chapter presents several comparable studies between ZigBee, 6lowpan, Bluetooth Low Energy, LTE, and Wi-Fi protocols including the latest IEEE 802.11ah technology. These studies assess the capabilities and behaviors of these wireless technologies. The chapter then highlights how the selection of the right wireless technology depends on the requirements of each IoT application.

Chapter 16, *Internet of Things Applications: Current and Future Development*, by Mahmoud Elkhodr, Seyed Shahrestani, and Hon Cheung, examples a number of the IoT applications and the implication that the IoT has on our lives. The chapter discusses the adoption of the IoT in healthcare and how it can improve the overall health services and operations. The chapter also provides visions on how to integrate smart home systems with other areas of the IoT. Additionally, the chapter demonstrates how the IoT is revolutionizing cities by connecting various smart city applications together, which enable intelligence and pervasiveness of services leading to cost reduction, better resource management, and environmental sustainability. Then, the chapter ends with a brief discussion on the challenges that face the global implementation of the IoT.

CONCLUSION

To this end, HPC is witnessing a leap change in its scale, complexity, and applications. This will require researchers, practitioners, and professionals to address the inherent challenges and present groundbreaking solutions. Consequently, this book is written to allow those folks to disseminate and share their knowledge and research findings with their peers. It is believed that the chapters complied in this book will enable the readers to learn more about the recent and foreseen issues, and help them take a step towards next-generation high performance computing.

Qusay F. Hassan
Mansoura University, Egypt

Acknowledgment

Thank you to each and every individual that was involved in this project. Without their support, this book would not have become a reality.

First, I would like to thank each one of the authors for their contributions. Sincere gratitude goes to the chapter's authors who contributed their time and expertise to this book.

Second, I wish to acknowledge the valuable contributions of the editorial advisory board members that managed the improvement of quality, coherence, and content presentation of the chapters. Some of the authors also served as referees; their double task is highly appreciated.

I extend my appreciation to Jorge Gonzalez for his constructive criticism and responsive correspondence on the chapters reviewed. I really appreciate his generous support throughout this project.

Special thanks to Axel Kloth for contributing many hours of his precious time to review the chapters of this book, and help in improving it. I feel that Axel provided expert knowledge and feedback that led to the successful completion of this book.

Lastly, I am grateful to the editorial team at IGI Global for their support through the stages of preparation and production. Thanks to Courtney Tychinski and Meghan Lamb who closely worked with me to make the process smooth and efficient.

Qusay F. Hassan
Mansoura University, Egypt
January 2016

Introduction

AN OUTLOOK INTO NOVEL CONCEPTS OF
HIGH PERFORMANCE COMPUTING

High-performance computing (HPC) refers to the use of many processing units that can range from tens to hundreds of thousands of units to solve complex tasks. These processing units may reside on a single physical computer or numerous clusters of nodes, and are connected with a form of high-bandwidth, low-latency networks. HPC relies on parallelization techniques and algorithms to perform computation on multiple processors and cores faster than a single processing unit.

HPC is widely used by universities, laboratories, government organizations, and enterprises to solve data and computation-intensive tasks that are impossible to process on a single processor. Many industries rely on HPC to meet their computational needs such as pharmaceutical and medical research, aerospace, oil industry, media and entertainment, supply chain management, and telecommunication. Examples of HPC utilization include risk analysis, financial analysis, seismic analysis, climate modeling, product design and modeling, data mining and analysis, simulations and data visualization, mathematical calculations and numerical analysis, as well as animation and 3D rendering. HPC is also heavily used by military forces for modelling, emulation and simulation on warfare, military strategies, and dangerous situations. Likewise, the national intelligence community uses HPC for security-related scenarios and sensitive data processing on a very large scale.

The HPC model has witnessed numerous advances over the last few decades, and further advances and changes are expected in the coming years. These advances will bring some new opportunities as well as challenges that will be of interest to both researchers and professionals. This chapter presents a variety of the concepts, challenges, and potential research areas related to HPC. This chapter does not aim at discussing any of the topics in great detail, but instead, it focuses on highlighting and discussing them briefly. Some of the topics presented are discussed in further detail throughout the chapters of this book. The purpose of this chapter is to provide the readers with a quick, yet valuable overview on some of the recent models, bringing to their attention the current status and prospect on foreseen development.

The rest of this chapter is organized as follows. "Exascale Computing" section defines and highlights the need for exascale computing, and the open issues towards achieving this goal. "Accelerated Computing" section discusses the use of accelerators and its key models in HPC systems. "Low-Power Architectures" section lists various hardware architectures that offer power efficiency over the traditional architectures. "In-Memory Computing" section describes how the use of memory-based storage can replace disk-based storage to improve the performance significantly. "Mobile-Based Models" describes two of most common computing models that integrate mobile devices in HPC systems. "Internet of Things" section introduces this new paradigm as it will have a huge impact on HPC in the near future. Similarly, "Big Data and Next-Generation Analytics" section discusses how today's systems result in an unprecedented data growth and what is needed to handle it. "Green Computing" briefly discusses the negative impacts of HPC systems on the environment and how this could be minimized. Finally, the chapter concludes.

EXASCALE COMPUTING

The evolution of computing power has exponentially increased over the last decade, and it is expected to continue growth in the near future. That is to say, some modern supercomputers can perform 10^{15} (one thousand trillion) floating point operations per second (i.e., PFLOPS). Advances in hardware have assisted in the achievement of this unprecedented computing power, and the advent of multicore/manycore processors has reached new heights in the industry.

Computer scientists and engineers are already discussing exascale supercomputers. Their aim is to produce the first supercomputer that can perform 10^{18} (one million trillion) floating point operations per second (i.e., EFLOPS) in 2018-2019 –30x exceeding the speed of the fastest computer in the world. In the global race to make exascale supercomputers, US President Obama has issued an executive order titled "Creating a National Strategic Computing Initiative" to execute a joint program between the Department of Energy (DOE), the Department of Defense (DOD), and the National Science Foundation (NSF) to deliver an exascale supercomputer –100x faster than the current system (The White House, 2015). The US Department of Commerce has also restrained many of the latest-generation accelerators from selling to China, a country that was planning to use them to upgrade Tianhe-2 (the fastest computer in the world) from 33 PFLOPS to 110 PFLOPS, to curb their progress towards acquiring exascale computing systems[1].

Open Issues and Approaches

Despite these efforts, it seems that building an "efficient" exascale supercomputer within this timeframe is not possible (Simon, 2013). Efficient, in this context, means energy effective, resilient, programmable and a usable HPC system. We can produce an exascale computer by aggregating a massive amount of hardware components that are available in the market today. However, it is not necessary to invest in a huge, power consuming system that would most definitely prove to be expensive to run, cool and could be difficult to use (Hsu, 2014). There are many challenges in this area that need addressing before one can produce an efficient exascale system. We discuss some of the key issues in the following subsections.

Computer Architecture

Moore's Law, which is an economic observation that basically refers to the continuous decline in transistor size and therefore the chip cost, has come to a halt (Moore, 1965; Dubash, 2010). Although the transistor manufacturing cost is almost zero, IC (Integrated Circuit) cost has not followed suit. The cost of the design of a complex semiconductor has ballooned and now vastly overshadows the manufacturing cost. Even though density has continued to increase over the last few years, the exponential growth of the planar transistor density has tapered off. Today's challenge lies in the design cost and not in the production cost. On top of that, the computer and processor architecture itself has not changed fundamentally from the days that today's processors were designed as single-core, single-threaded CPUs. Those design criteria are fundamentally at odds with the requirements of a supercomputer. This challenges the researchers and engineers to come up with novel techniques and design methodologies that would represent a new wave of evolution (more on this in the following point).

Power Consumption

Energy consumption is at the heart of exascale HPC systems for two reasons. First, the challenge to keep the supercomputer and its components at their specified operating temperate, and that requires massive amounts of efficient cooling. An electric stove top gets to about 1500 W/144 cm^2 energy density, or about 10 W/cm^2. A Xeon Phi is about 400 mm^2 and dissipates up to 290 W, or 0.75 W/mm^2 which is 75W/cm^2 (Intel, 2014); that needs to be spread out. Second, the energy costs of such systems. In the US, the (subsidized) cost of 1 KWh is about \$0.21, a MWh therefore costs \$210, and a GWh is \$210,000. A 10 MW system running for 365 days a year and 24 hours a day will consume 87,600 MWh (10 * 365 * 24), or 87.6 GWh. That is a cost of \$18,396,000.00 annually. On the other hand, a 10 MW system is nowhere near the exascale performance level; the current crown goes to Tianhe-2 with 34 PFLOPS at a claimed level of power consumption of 18 MW. Extrapolating this system into an exascale system – by stacking lots of today's supercomputers – will yield a necessary multiplier of 29.4 times the performance at 29.4 times the energy consumed –or even more. If a 10 MW system consumes \$18M in electric energy, then an 18 MW system will need at least \$32.4M to operate in electric energy, and the exascale system will consume 29.4 times that; a staggering \$952.56M just in electric energy, not counting any other operating costs.

The goal is to bring the power consumption of an exascale system down to 20; this is not an easy task. Therefore, researchers need to study and identify exactly where power is consumed, and how it can be reduced. New processor, coprocessor, accelerator and memory architectures and interconnects, as well as novel techniques that reduce the need to access storage are required. Some approaches have been proposed in these areas but they are still not mature enough for commercialization or mainstream use.

Tunneling FET and *spintronics* are two interesting approaches that are being considered by chip manufacturers (Seabaugh, 2013; Phys.org, 2015). Intel predicts that one of these technologies will be used in future generations of processors to lower power consumption (Bourzac, 2016). However, these technologies may affect the level of performance, as performance is decreased in comparison to the traditional silicon transistors (i.e., MOSFET). Also, specialized accelerators that are designed to run specific applications can be a good option since they contain a lower numbers of transistors than what is required in general purpose chips.

Likewise, better attachment of memory to processor and coprocessors as well as better interconnects between processors and cores are needed. Better in this context must mean higher bandwidth and lower latency at lower levels of power consumption. One method to do so is to replace electronics with photonics in those applications where long distances must be spanned or bandwidth requirements are extreme. Modern CML-type high-speed serial links that are trunked together can and should replace wide buses for better performance and lower energy use. Attaching memory directly to the CPU or its cores via Through Silicon Vias (TSVs) in 3D stacking can help, but due to thermal issues, heat must be removed from under the memory dice. Carbon Nanotubes (CNT) may help solve this[2] (Shulaker et al., 2013).

Dark Silicon

Another serious issue is dark silicon, which refers to the gap between the amount of transistors that can be placed on a chip versus the number of transistors that can actually be used simultaneously for a given TDP (thermal design power) (Esmaeilzadeh, Blem, Amant, Sankaralingam & Burger, 2011). Dark silicon is likely –or even inevitable– in today's multicore processors, as the designated TDP aims at protecting them from overheating. However, dark silicon's fraction is increasing and would increase much more if we employ current methodologies for designing exascale systems. Such fraction, would in turn, reduce the efficiency and performance of those systems, and this is a major problem. As mentioned earlier, new architectures and techniques are required to solve this issue.

Cooling

Cooling is also critical for HPC systems to protect nodes and components from overheating, failure or causing entire damage. However, traditional cooling systems, which are mainly based on air cooling and chillers/cooling towers, may not be able to survive the exceptional amount of heat that would generate from exascale systems. Such systems are very expensive, require large space and a complex design, dedicated power infrastructure, and these systems consume a large amount of electricity. Exascale cooling systems should offer end-to-end solutions that are not limited to cooling processors, memory and boards, but also power supplies network infrastructures, etc. Such systems should allow for ideal Power Usage Effectiveness (PUE) as well as ideal Energy Reuse Effectiveness (ERE). The former can be achieved by using hot water resulting from the cooling process that can be used for central heating, for example. The latter can be achieved by relying on liquid and/or refrigerants-based cooling systems instead of traditional air cooling systems in datacenters, for example.

Large technology companies and cloud providers such as Facebook and Google have begun to build datacenters in the Nordic region to take advantage of the cold temperatures and their ability of generating inexpensive renewable energy (Powell, 2016). Microsoft developed another innovative approach in which they have built a datacenter under water to take advantage of the cool temperatures of the deep blue sea (Markoff, 2016; Microsoft Research, 2016). Such approaches are not only cost efficient, but also ecofriendly. Not to mention, the lower latency that is enabled by bringing datacenters closer to the clients.

In addition to datacenter cooling, there should be innovative solutions that allow for on-chip cooling. This will not only act as an extra cooling solution, but will also minimize disruptions that happen when the CPU overheats. An electric stove top gets to about 1500 W/144 cm^2 energy density, or about 10 W/cm^2. A Xeon Phi is about 400 mm^2 and dissipates up to 290 W, or 0.75 W/mm^2 which is 75W/cm^2; that needs to be spread out. Research is being dedicated to this area to sustain system reliability and efficiency. For instance, in (Marcinichen, Wu, Paredes, Thome & Michel, 2014), the authors implemented a two-phase cooling system that allows them to absorb heat from hot-spots by pumping refrigerant vapor into microfluidic channels attached to the chips. In Sarvey et al. (2015), the authors dropped chip temperature by >60% more than the air-cooled device by embedding microfluidic channels into it –a few hundred microns away from where the transistors are. Although these approaches are promising, they are still in their infancy, and thus, more research and practical implementations are a must in order to address their limitations and improve their potentials.

Software Systems

Such skyrocketing computing performance will require newer software methodologies and algorithms to manage and maximize its usage. Current algorithms, libraries, programming models and environments, operating systems, file systems, databases, middleware and networks will not support the expected computing scale. In other words, computer performance may improve, but most of it could be stalled. Extending current programming models and environments is essential to cope with the unprecedented levels of concurrency expected to emerge (Heroux, 2016). Creating massively parallel software that can utilize hundreds of thousands (or maybe millions) of processing units is a serious challenge. Similarly, installing a new supercomputer or even upgrading some components of an existing one proves difficult. Doing so would actually require partial or complete redesign and reprogramming of software algorithms and modules. This may also require the implementers to use new operating systems and/or programming environments, which would incur extra costs, time and effort. Furthermore, programmers do not possess the knowledge or skills needed to write programs that can utilize such a huge number of processors and cores. Hence, new training courses and education programs that focus on this area should be availed.

Resilience

Another challenge that is inherent with the shift from petascale to exascale is fault resilience. With millions of processing units and enormous amounts of threads, exascale systems are expected to have a very high rate of various failures ranging from failed processes, corrupted results, to failed components. Users should be able to replace failed components within minutes instead of days or hours. Therefore, both hardware designers and system developers should collaborate and work hard to improve the current computation environments that can survive and work reliably regardless of some components failing. They should leverage and build on the techniques (e.g., checkpointing, failure prediction, replication, forward recovery, etc.) and lessons learned from petascale (Cappello, 2014).

ACCELERATED COMPUTING

Since the 1970's, HPC model has gone through a number of paradigm shifts and technological evolutions. First, supercomputers relied on local parallelism and a small number of fast vector processors that are connected to large amount of shared memory (e.g., Cray-1). Then, implementers moved to massively parallel (MPP) systems, where a larger number of slower SIMD (Single Instruction, Multiple Data) processors are connected to distributed memory and distributed file systems (e.g., Cray T3E). Then, HPC has gone through a series of architectural changes including the big shift from integrated, highly specialized supercomputers manufactured by the big players like Cray to commodity clusters built by small integrators (such as HP which was a new entrant to HPC market when Cray was the market leader), and dedicated researchers (e.g., Beowulf clusters). In recent times, hybrid computing model which combine multicore CPUs with accelerators has become the *de facto* architecture of modern HPC systems including many supercomputers in the Top 500 list (e.g., tianhe-2) (Top 500, 2016).

Figure 1. High-level architectures of a modern multicore CPU and manycore accelerator

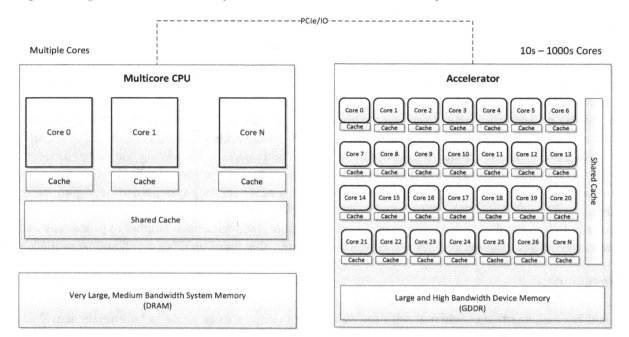

Accelerators

An accelerator (also known as a coprocessor) is manycore hardware with large built-in memory, which is used alongside the CPU to enable faster execution of compute-intensive jobs. In this model, the CPU offloads the complex tasks (as defined in the program) to the accelerator, which in turn, runs them and returns the results back for any further processing. Utilizing hardware accelerators can significantly decrease processing time. As discussed below, there are two main forms of accelerators: GPU and non-GPU.

Figure 1 illustrates the difference between multicore CPUs and manycore accelerators. It is very difficult to show the differences between the architectures of GPU and non-GPU accelerator in one single figure because it widely differs from one product to another, but this figure tries to give an abstract description of the key difference between both architectures.

GPU

GPGPU (**G**eneral-**P**urpose Computing on **G**raphics **P**rocessing **U**nits) is a very common form of accelerated computing, which relies on GPUs (Graphical Processing Units) to perform general-purpose computations. Tesla (by Nvidia) and FirePro (by AMD) are the dominating GPU accelerators in the market (Nvidia, 2016; AMD, 2016). GPU accelerators are massively parallel and highly multi-threaded as they are composed of thousands of small cores (i.e., hardware threads) (e.g., 4,992 CUDA cores on K80, and 2,816 stream processors on FirePro W9100) that are connected to high-speed read/write memory bandwidth (e.g., 480 GB/s on Tesla K80 and 320 GB/s on FirePro W9100). Cores in GPUs are usually referred to as stream processors (SP) which are responsible for executing the created threads. SPs are grouped into a number of streaming multiprocessors (SM) that create, schedule and synchronize threads.

GPUs also integrate large memory on board (e.g., 24 GB Tesla K80 and 16 GB on FirePro W9100, both GDDR5). Thus, using GPUs alongside multicore CPUs (Central Processing Units) can drastically improve the performance of some professional and scientific applications (e.g., Monte Carlo simulations and 3D rendering). High performance is gained by parallelizing and offloading complex computation jobs to the GPU, while running the rest of program (mostly serial jobs) on the CPU. Nevertheless, the entire process is controlled by the host CPU as it is responsible for preparing the jobs and feeding them to the GPU, and then returning the results to the user/system after completion.

Non-GPU

There are also non-GPU accelerators which rely on many cores, local memory and high-speed I/O between the cores (and the host CPUs). Xeon Phi, offered by Intel, is the most popular accelerator in this category (Intel, 2016a). Xeon Phi is based on MIC (Many Integrated Core) architecture which combines many cores on a single chip, allowing for parallel processing for complex jobs (Intel, 2016b). However, it is composed of a much lower number of cores (up to 61 cores) in comparison to GPUs (thousands). Unlike GPUs, Xeon Phi coprocessors do not incur much overhead on CPUs, as they are built using powerful, low-latency cores whose vector size is 512-bit (8 x 64-bit) which offers full double-precision support for floating-point operations, and better support for advanced math. No SMs or SPs in Xeon Phi either, but instead it relies on Pentium-based cores whereby each core supports only four threads. Xeon Phi incorporates high memory bandwidth (up to 352 GB/s), large amount of GDDR5 memory (up to 16 GB), and high-speed bidirectional ring interconnect (Intel, 2016c). Consequently, Xeon Phi offers better performance than GPUs, and consumes less power when used for complex mathematical calculations.

Despite the big names, there are some good accelerators offered by startups. For instance, SSRLabs, a US startup located in Silicon Valley, California, offers two massively parallel accelerators: Neural Net Coprocessor and Floating-Point Coprocessor (SSRLabs, 2016a). Both are sold under the "pScale" name. The former is offered for image and video analysis, graph search and Artificial Intelligence (AI) applications (SSRLabs, 2016b). The latter is for general purpose high-performance computing such as modelling and simulations (SSRLabs, 2016c). Each pScale chip offers great performance (2.867 TFLOPS) as it is composed of large number of cores (1024 cores x 2.8 GFLOPS/core), and incorporates high memory and I/O bandwidth (over 500GB/s) and internal bisection bandwidth (96 TB/s). Although these coprocessors offer better performance over the well-known products, clients are still unaware of them.

Shortcomings and Recommendations

Although accelerated computing is an integral part in many of today's environments, its adoption is still at an early stage. Below, we list some of the challenges that hinder the utilization of accelerated computing:

- **Complex and Hard to Use:** Programming HPC applications that target accelerators is tedious as it imposes sophisticated skills and a lot of programming/compilation tricks. Thus, further studies on such hybrid environments are necessary. This would include: creation of easy-to-use and efficient programming platforms, compilers and debuggers; proposal of new scheduling algorithms; and representation of real-life and hypothetical case-studies.

- **Additional Power Consumption:** Accelerators in general are greener than CPUs as they provide more GFLOPS/W, yet their use incurs additional electricity. Hence, researchers need to tackle this issue and propose some solutions that offer energy saving; maybe by considering new hardware designs, as well as efficient software and scheduling algorithms, to name a few.

- **GPUs vs. Non-GPUs Dilemma:** Educating developers and new entrants to the HPC world about accelerators should not be limited to the programming languages, but it should also teach them about the best tools and algorithms for the job in hand. Some implementers tend to rely on GPGPU for any parallelization opportunity; nevertheless, it is not a silver bullet. For instance, while GPUs offer great performance for Monte Carlo simulations, which are composed of gobs of trivial operations that can be executed concurrently, they do not perform well in numerical analyses or matrix computing as they incur significant communication overheads and data transfers between GPUs and CPUs, and vice versa. Working with an acceleration technology that is unsuitable for the task at hand would lead to more power use and processing time.

- **Portability vs. Performance:** Implementers should also keep the tradeoff between portability and performance in mind. For instance, while open standards like OpenCL offers greater portability for GPU-based applications (i.e., ability to run on various GPUs and operating systems) over proprietary kits like CUDA (offered by Nvidia), this comes at a price: it is slightly slower (Karimi, Dickson, & Hamze, 2010). Choosing the right platform may also require a lot of work experience as well as time and money.

LOW-POWER ARCHITECTURES

As mentioned in the "Exascale Computing" section, HPC community strives to save the power use of their systems. Therefore, they have been exploring different approaches to achieve this goal. Amongst those approaches, implementers have tested various instruction sets and microarchitectures. Here, we present some of these architectures.

Instruction Set Architecture and Energy Efficiency

In the computer architecture field, instruction set architecture (ISA) refers to the basic instructions (e.g., ADD, IN, OUT, JUMP, etc.) that a processor can understand. There are various ISAs, but RISC and CISC are two of the most commonly ones. This section provides further details on ISAs and their role in low-power systems.

RISC

RISC (Reduced Instruction Set Computing) architecture, as the name denotes, uses fewer instructions (i.e., less instructions per cycle), and have simpler architectures (i.e., lower number of transistors). There are many RISC-based ISAs in the market that support both 32-bit and 64-bit address space. This includes, for example, ARM (Advanced RISC Machine) which is widely used in mobiles and handheld devices, MIPS (Microprocessor without Interlocked Pipeline Stages) which is common in embedded systems and video game consoles, and SPARC (Scalable Processor Architecture) which can be found in various servers made by Sun (currently Oracle) and Fujitsu (ARM, 2016; Hennessy, Jouppi, Baskett, & Gill, 1981; SPARC International, 2016).

The simplicity of RISC-based ISAs offers more energy efficiency than x68-64 processors (Blem, Menon, & Sankaralingam, 2013). Moreover, they are lower in cost and smaller in size as they are built with fewer transistors. Due to these advantages, RISC-based processors have been used in some of the fastest supercomputers in the Top 500 list. For example, K Computer and Tianhe-2 use SPARC processors, and IBM Sequoia is built using PowerPC A2 processors. China has also relied on Godson processors, which are based on MIPS architecture, to build its first supercomputer that was entirely created using Chinese components, i.e., Dawning 6000 (Calamia, 2011).

CISC

CISC (Complex Instruction Set Computing) architecture is commonly used in personal computers and commodity servers. On contrary to RISC, CISC is built with a full set of instructions, and hence, it is (technically) more complex than RISC with a higher number of transistors. AMD, Pentium, and Xeon are some popular CISC processors.

In the recent past few years, some simplified CISC-based architectures have been designed for low-power computing. Intel Atom processor is x68 microprocessor in this category, which supports both 32-bit and 64-bit instruction sets. It is optimized for use in small devices with limited access to electricity such as smartphones, tablets, wearables, and embedded systems. Intel also offers Processor C2000 Product Family which can be used to build lightweight servers. Some modern servers are powered by these Atom processors such as the HPE Moonshot system, which was designed with energy efficiency in mind (Hewlett Packard Enterprise, 2016). Moreover, Intel has relied on Atom (Airmont) cores in its second generation MIC architecture, i.e., Knights Landing (Anthony, 2013).

System-on-a-Chip

With the progressing step towards building energy-efficient systems, hardware designers have focused on improving and embedding the aforementioned ISAs into integrated microarchitectures known as System-on-a-Chip (SoC) or mobile SoC. A SoC is more or less like an entire computer on a single chip (Rajsuman, 2000). In other words, a SoC would typically have a (single-core/multicore) microprocessor, memory, USB/SATA ports, audio and graphics processors, communication media, and power management circuits, all integrated on an IC. Further, it includes the software that controls the entire chip.

Due to its compact size and the extremely short wiring between those components, it is believed that a SoC would use significantly less power than the conventional architecture. Furthermore, SoC are cost efficient, yet powerful, and thus, it can be used in datacenters, dedicated for storage, web hosting, streaming, and network and database workloads. Intel, Nvidia, and Samsung are some of the well-known mobile SoC manufacturers in the market. AMD has recently joined SoC market with the launch of Opteron A1100, which is a 64-bit ARM-based processor that target datacenters (AMD, 2016).

Figure 2 illustrates the components of a typical SoC die that can be found in low-power servers.

Figure 2. A SoC die in a low-power server

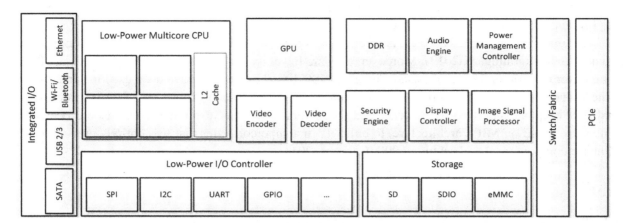

Assessment and Suggested Changes

In the exploration and research to attain low-power, high performance systems, researchers have investigated the use of the aforementioned microarchitectures to determine the fit. Although they have found them promising, as they offer better MFLOPS/Watt ratio than conventional processors, researchers believe that they need further architectural changes as well as software improvements before they pervade compute-intensive and high-performance systems.

In Janapa et al. (2010) the authors compared the performance of Atom Diamondville (1 MB cache, dual-core, 1.6 GHz) against Xeon Harpertown (12 MB cache, quad-core, 2.5 GHz) by running search queries on Bing.com. They discovered that although Atom processors were inexpensive and highly power efficient, they did not perform as well as Xeon processors because Atom processor is not suitable for neural network algorithms (Janapa, Lee, Chilimbi, & Vaid, 2010). They cited that designing octa-core Atom processors with a faster clock speed and more cache memory (which were not available at that time) would mitigate this issue. Thanks to Atom C2750 (4 MB cache, 2.4 GHz), launched late 2013, which meets these criteria without compromising the power efficiency –20 W TDP. Maybe, it is time to evaluate this new microarchitecture for HPC systems.

In Rajovic et al. (2013) the authors evaluated the use of ARM SoCs for HPC. They measured the performance of various ARMv7-A SoCs against i7-2760QM SandyBridge (quad-core, 2.4 GHz), namely, NVIDIA Tegra 2 Cortex-A9 (dual-core, 1.0 GHz), NVIDIA Tegra 3 Cortex-A9 (quad-core, 1.3 GHz), and Samsung Exynos 5250 Intel Core Cortex-A15 (dual-core, 1.7 GHz). The authors cited that although SoC model is promising, there are some issues that need to be addressed before it can be broadly adopted in HPC systems. Namely, lack of support for ECC (Error Checking and Correction) protection in memory controller; slow I/O interfaces; ARMv7 does not support 64-bit architecture, which limits memory to 4 GB/process (thanks to ARMv8 which supports 64-bit architecture); and, high CPU overheads and network latencies due to the absence of hardware support for interconnect protocols, and lack of efficient network interfaces, respectively.

In Maqbool et al. (2015) the authors evaluated the use of ARM SoCs for scientific workload as well as memory-intensive database transactions. The evaluation process took place on both single-node and a cluster of ARMv7-A Cortex-A9s SoCs (with various numbers of cores) against Intel Xeon processors.

To be specific, the authors used Samsung Exynos 4412 (1 MB cache, 1.4 GHz), and Intel Xeon x3430 (1 MB cache, 2.4 GHz) in the evaluation. The researchers cited that although single-core ARM SoCs are slower than multicore ARM SoCs, they deliver more power saving. They also cited that although multi-core ARM SoCs are slower than X86 processors, they can be used for building lightweight, low-power servers as they perform well in I/O bound shared-memory applications. Finally, they cited that ARM SoCs scale well in distributed-memory clusters, which can be used for large-scale scientific simulations. They concluded that the performance of ARM SoCs is linked with a number of factors that need to be considered by both hardware and software makers. Namely, the memory bandwidth, network latency, workload type, application class, and complier –C was 4x faster than Java because of lack of support for double precision floating point in Java.

These are just a few of the studies that have been made on low-power architectures, but they quiet summarize the work that needs to be done in this area.

IN-MEMORY COMPUTING

The dramatic decline in computer memory prices and the relentless needs of organizations to speed up their data processing have helped in the rise of in-memory computing (IMC) as a new HPC paradigm. IMC, in simple terms, refers to storing data in memory (e.g., DRAM, NAND, SSD, non-volatile DIMM and PCI-based flash) rather than hard drives to avoid unnecessary round trips to slow electromagnetic disks. Memory is known for its low latency (in nanoseconds) in comparison to disk latency (in milliseconds), and hence, the speedup in data processing is obvious. In addition, IMC uses massive parallelization techniques to accelerate the data processing rate. The speedup magnitude of IMC depends on the amount of memory and the speed of processing units installed in servers, as well as the size of data being processed. Nevertheless, discussed ahead are results that show a drastic decline in processing time when IMC is in place. Figure 3 illustrates the basic differences between the storage-based storage and memory-based storage.

In 2015, IMC market was worth $5.58 billion. With the continuous drop in memory prices, advent of new memory technologies, and the exponential growth of big data, IMC market is expected to reach $23.15 billion by 2020. Gartner predicted that IMC will become an essential component in the technology stack of organizations that seek efficiency and business growth 2016 (Gartner, 2013).

Typically, the IMC model comprises various technologies such as in-memory data grids, in-memory database management systems, in-memory message queuing, complex-event processing, in-memory servers, and in-memory analytics. Large enterprises like financial firms, telecommunication companies, cloud companies and social media websites have already begun utilizing these technologies in order to process millions of transactions per day. This includes OLTP (e.g., ERP and e-commerce websites) and OLAP (e.g., business intelligence and data analytics) environments, with the ability to manage them both under one single umbrella (Zhang, Chen, Ooi, Tan, & Zhang, 2015).

In addition to the ability to query and process huge, fast-changing datasets in real-time, IMC enables organizations to extend the lifetime of existing computing resources –as they are more powerful than traditional HPC models. This will not only allow organizations to invest in fewer hardware resources and reduce the operational costs and stress, but also minimize the negative impacts of HPC on the environment. In one of its articles, Forbes cited that datacenters with memory-based storage systems could

Figure 3. Disk-based storage vs. memory-based storage

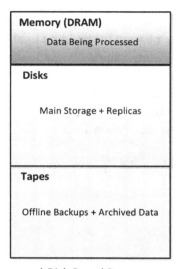
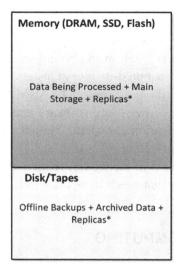

a) Disk-Based Storage
large amount of disks/tapes, and small amount of memory

b) Memory-Based Storage
Large amount of memory, and small amount of disks/tapes.

*Replicas can be stored in memory or disk or both of them

augment 40x storage capacity within the same finite space (Basile, 2013). For example, one shelf of flash-based storage system is capable of creating 1 million input/output operations per second versus four racks of disk-based storage. Forbes also cited that IMC would save around 80% of energy use, as memory-based systems use much less energy and require far less cooling systems.

Technologies and Models

As mentioned earlier, various forms of memory can be used in IMC implementations. Here are the two key approaches that have been proven valid for use in HPC systems.

DRAM

A research team from Stanford proposed and implemented an approach where the entire information is stored in the main memory, i.e., DRAM (Dynamic Random Access Memory). This model is known as RAMCloud in which the main memory of hundreds or thousands of servers in datacenters is combined and used as durable storage for the available data (Ousterhout et al., 2010) –a server often has 32-256 GB of DRAM. DRAM offers ~1000x lower latency and ~1000x higher throughput than the conventional disk-based storage. Reads in RAMCloud take ~5 μs and writes take about 14 μs for 100-byte objects, taking into consideration that written objects are replicated as backup copies on local disks and/or DRAM of two or more other servers (Ousterhout, 2015).

Flash

An alternative approach proposes the use of flash memory (i.e., NAND) for data storage of big-data applications (Kloth, 2014). A group of researchers from MIT and Quanta Research have designed and implemented a system called BlueDBM, which uses racks of flash-based storage that are connected through a very fast inter-controller network, for big-data applications (Jun et al., 2015). Although flash memory is about one tenth slower than DRAM, it is also one tenth cheaper, and consumes about one tenth as much electrical power. Thus, flash-based storage offers a cheap, yet very fast and energy-efficient technology for both high-throughput computing and high-performance computing environments. In fact, results show that BlueDBM sometimes outperforms RAM-based implementations (e.g., RAMCloud). To be specific, the performance of RAMCloud degrades dramatically when access to hard disks is incurred to only 5%-10 (Jun, Chung, & Arvind, 2015).

By connecting each server with a FPGA (Field-Programmable Gate Array), which is a type of electronic chips that can be reprogrammed as needed, data can be processed before being sent to the server, i.e., in-store processing. Performing the data computation on a chip instead of the operating system can improve the performance vastly (Kloth, 2013). Moreover, flash-based storage is much more scalable than its RAM-based counterpart as it can fit into a small cluster, where more flash memory can be easily added, whereas, a modest RAM-based implementation would require tens or hundreds of networked computers. Flash memories are also not volatile, and hence, there is no extra cost, processing time, or complex backup strategies that would be necessary.

Which One to Choose?

Despite the advantages of each model, it would actually make sense to adopt a hybrid architecture whereby disk-based storage is replaced with a combination of RAM and flash-based storage. That is, hot data (i.e., data that is constantly accessed and processed) such as lookups and frequently accessed database tables is stored in RAM. Warm data (i.e., data that is occasionally accessed) such as logs and workflows is stored on flash/SSD storage. Such a hybrid model would allow implementers to get the best of both.

In addition, choosing an efficient model highly depend on the application type. For instance, the former model offers great support for big data applications as it avails real random access memory whereby it does not need a filesystem. On the other hand, the later model is managed by the filesystem so data access is not actually random. Figure 4 illustrates random access and filesystem-based memory attachment.

Challenges and Directions

Despite the aforementioned benefits of IMC, adopters would be challenged to achieve a mainstream adoption. Some of the challenges will require in depth study from the research community, as well as pioneering solutions from the industry in the near future, as discussed in the following:

- **Lack of Knowledge:** Many IT people are still unaware of IMC and/or how it can be implemented in their organizations. Therefore, enterprises and IT professionals require training and education on IMC. This is achievable through conferences and open discussions, presenting case studies and success stories from early adopters. Framing both professional and academic courses that address this model can also help.

Figure 4. Hardware representation of random access and filesystem memory attachment
Courtesy to Axel Kloth.

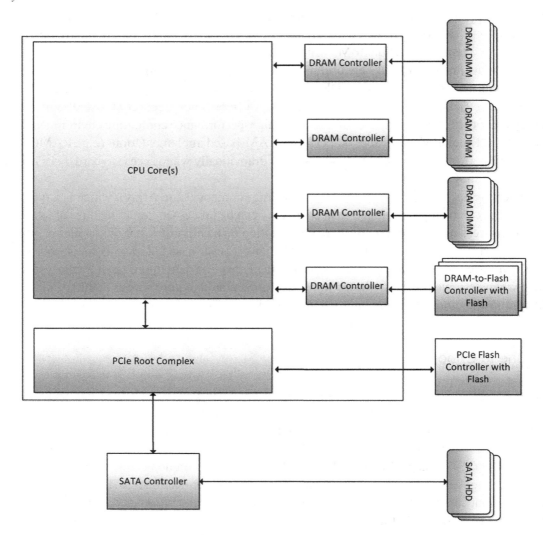

- **Vendor Lock-In:** The severe lack of open standards proves difficult to migrate from one technology to another, especially with the current scarcity of knowledge and skill set. Standardized programming platforms and APIs, as well as protocols, would make it easy and cost efficient to move from one vendor to another. Hopefully, such standards would allow a mixture of solutions, from different vendors, to coexist.
- **Lack of Support from Software Companies:** Most software vendors that offer IMC technologies are of small and medium size –SAP HANA is one of the few exceptions. Gartner expects key software vendors to acquire some small-to-medium companies that offer IMC technologies in the next few years (Gartner, 2013). In the meantime, large organizations are refraining to do so because they feel vulnerable and at risk to migrate to IMC.

- **Complex Backup Strategies:** Data backup and disaster recovery could prove to be problematic to organizations when they transfer to this unusual computing model. Backup tools currently available in the market are designed to backup data and files from hard disks as opposed to memory. To solve this issue, the implementation of some techniques that allows users to move memory content on disks for backup purposes is required. Furthermore, with a sudden power cut, an organization could lose part or all of their data since they are stored in memory. To overcome such situations, IMC-based servers could include optional batteries to solve discrepancies. Adopters may consider redundant power lines to mitigate any unexpected power cuts. As mentioned earlier, they can use non-volatile memory instead of (or in addition to) RAM. They may also implement a checkpointing mechanism that allows part of the data to be periodically saved on disks to minimize data loss when power is lost.

- **Additional Costs:** Some of the IMC technologies require minor or even no changes to non-IMC-based applications when migrating to IMC-based environments. However, to enable non-IMC-based applications to work on in-memory data grids, this requires a mass of work; almost the entire rewriting of code. In-memory data grids technology represents the fastest and ultimate form of in-memory, parallelized data processing. In such cases, adopters should bear in mind the amount and level of work and costs that would be required to rewrite their software applications. Maybe over time there will be automation tools and APIs that can ease the conversion task.

MOBILE-BASED MODELS

Today, the use of mobile devices (e.g., smartphones, tablets, etc.) is ever increasing. This is due to the offered portability, decline in prices, and certainly, the significant progress in their specifications. Some of the mobile devices currently in the market are actually much faster than some supercomputers from the 80's/90's. These features have attracted researchers and engineers to incorporate mobile devices in compute-intensive tasks and complex calculations. Mobile Grid Computing and Mobile Cloud Computing are two of the popular examples where mobile devices are integrated with HPC. We introduce these two models in the following. Although mobile grid computing is relatively an old model, we discuss it here briefly as it represents one of the first models that leveraged mobile devices in HPC systems. Besides, we can say that research on grid computing has pervaded the way for the rise and success of the mobile cloud computing model

Mobile Grid Computing

Grid computing can be defined as a distributed model that aims at combining and coordinating heterogeneous computing resources (e.g., processing cycles, memory, and storage) usually from geographically dispersed locations, to obtain powerful computing capabilities (Foster, 2002). These capabilities can solve computationally-intensive problems in a fast and cost-effective manner. Thus, grid computing is a form of high performance computing where the hardware and software resources are scattered over the network, and are able to communicate with each other through a set of messages.

With the great success of grid computing in the early 2000's, mainly in scientific communities, and the increasing usage of mobile devices, several studies have focused on combining both models together (Litke, Skoutas, & Varvarigou, 2004). Mobile grid computing extends the original grid computing model by adding mobility to it which enables access to the grid on the go. As illustrated in Figure 5, there are two models in which mobile grids can be formed. In the first model, the mobile devices act as service clients to the grid whereby users can tap into it and get access to the offered resources. This allows the users to use their mobile devices to submit complex jobs to the grid, monitor and manage their execution, and then receive the results, without being bound to a physical location. In the second model, mobile devices act as service providers to the grid whereby their data, processing cycles, and storage are contributed to the grid and shared with the other nodes – similar to peer-to-peer (P2P) computing model (Chu & Humphrey, 2004).

Despite the benefits of the mobile grid computing model and with the emergence of competing models, such as cloud computing, we can say that it has lost attraction over the past few years. However, with the leap development in the performance of today's mobile devices, increased storage, diversity of communication protocols, and emergence of 4G mobile networks, HPC community should reconsider it again.

Figure 5. Mobile grid models

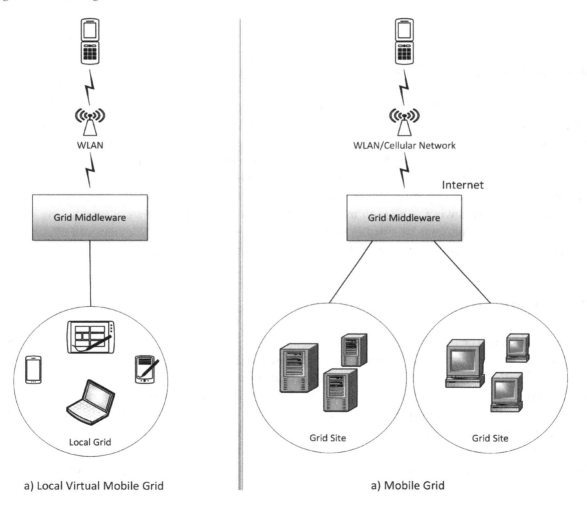

a) Local Virtual Mobile Grid   a) Mobile Grid

Mobile Cloud Computing

Late 2007, cloud computing emerged as a new model that allows both individuals and organizations to make use of the computing resources offered by service providers who offer large pools of computing resources (Hassan, 2011). That is, the user, in this model, does not own the computing resources, but instead, they "rent" them and pay per use –similar to accessing public utilities such as electricity and water. There are three key services in cloud environments: 1) Infrastructure-as-a-Service (IaaS) which provides hardware resources (processing cycles, storage, networking) such as Amazon and Rackspace; 2) Platform-as-a-Service (PaaS) which provides software development and administration platforms such as Windows Azure and Amazon Web Services; 3) Software-as-a-Service (SaaS) which provides software applications and systems such as Microsoft Office 365 and Google Apps.

The maturity of mobile operating systems and applications has made the use of mobile devices necessary to perform day-to-day tasks. Examples include: work (checking calendars and emails, writing documents, preparing presentations, translating texts); health (diets and meal recipes, exercising); lifestyle (ordering taxis, booking hotel rooms and flights, shopping, payments and bank transactions), social networks (Facebook, Twitter, Instagram); multimedia (audio, video, pictures, games). Such applications would generate gigantic amounts of data that are far beyond what is needed for those devices to do their original tasks: make/receive calls, send/receive text messages, and get access to the Internet. That data would require enormous computational resources to process them, and unlimited storage capacities to save them.

Although the performance and storage capacities of modern mobile devices have improved considerably, improving battery life has not progressed at the same pace. This represents a huge constraint on the number of operations and execution time that they can handle. In addition, mobile devices are still limited in what they can do. For instance, using an OCR software to convert a few hundred-page scanned document into text, or performing a simple video editing task such as combining multiple video clips into a single video would take hours to complete on a mobile device. Moreover, due to the inadequacy of built-in storage, saving the files generated from such operations locally would be impossible. Here, mobile cloud computing comes into play as an approach to alleviate these issues.

Mobile cloud computing model can be viewed as the utilization of the resources and systems offered by cloud computing in the mobile environment. In other words, mobile cloud computing enables the actual computation and data storage to take place on the cloud instead of being performed on local resources. Hence, it allows mobile users to perform complex tasks and save large files externally on resourceful environments, while saving the battery life of their devices (Fernando, Loke, & Rahayu, 2013). This is known as computation *offloading* which means moving the job to the cloud to get executed on resourceful and high-performance servers. The granularity of offloaded jobs can vary from system to system: process (small function), component (a task or set of sub-tasks), application (entire application), or virtual machine (the operating system and installed applications). Determining the "offloadable" parts and defining their granularity has huge impact on the overall performance, network utilization, and energy efficiency (Kumar & Lu, 2010; Barbera, Kosta, Mei, & Stefa, 2013).

Similar to mobile grids, there are two forms of mobile clouds (see Figure 6). The first model allows the users to plug their mobile devices into the cloud, through a wireless network (3G/4G or Wi-Fi), and utilize the offered resources and services. Most of us use this model on a daily basis without realizing it. For instance, we watch videos on YouTube, listen to music on Spotify, edit and save Office documents on OneDrive, and play online games. In this model, mobile devices act as thin clients as neither the processing nor the storage of these files occur locally. In the second model, users act as service providers by sharing their mobile devices with others, and collectively forming a (small) local cloud.

Figure 6. Mobile cloud models

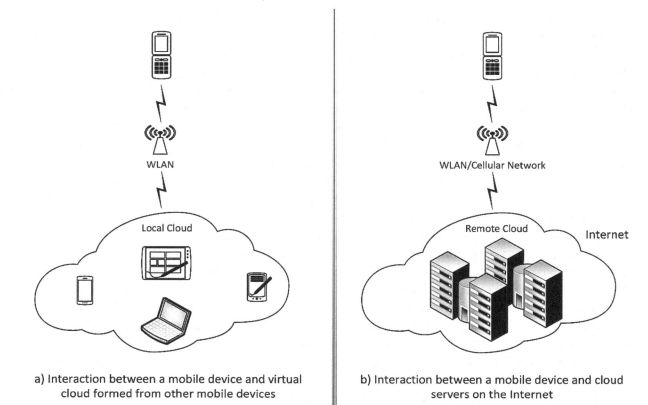

a) Interaction between a mobile device and virtual cloud formed from other mobile devices

b) Interaction between a mobile device and cloud servers on the Internet

Challenges and Directions

In addition to the challenges inherited from the original computing models (grid/cloud) such as security and privacy issues, lack of standards, lack of simulators, availability reliability issues, and complexity of programming environments, mobile grid and cloud computing models come with a set of unique challenges. This includes, but is not limited to:

- **Limited Battery Life:** The use of mobile devices is constrained by short battery life, and thus, researchers need to find techniques to extend it. In addition to the traditional methods such as switching off unused nodes, voltage scaling, and computation offloading, some innovative technologies should be availed to prolong the usage of those devices. Recently, some new technologies have emerged that allow remote charging for batteries. Examples include Po-WiFi, Wi-Charge, and WattUp, which use WiFi streams, infrared light beams, and microwave beams, respectively to carry and deliver electric power to mobile devices and smart objects wirelessly (Talla, 2015; Wi-Charge Technology, 2016; WattUp, 2016). Nonetheless, these technologies need further analysis and improvement because they are still incomplete.

- **Low Bandwidth:** This is another serious limitation to successful implementations of mobile-based models. However, with the increasing deployments of 4G (and soon 5G) networks in the world, this issue will eventually diminish.
- **Intermittent Connectivity:** One of the common issues in mobile environments is the frequent disconnection of devices from the network. Such issues would lead to a high rate of failed jobs. Hence, deploying a local intermediary to which data and computation jobs are offloaded before they migrate to the online environment (i.e., the grid or cloud) can resolve this matter. In this area, some techniques have been developed. For example, in (Park, Ko, & Kim, 2003), the authors have developed a novel job scheduling algorithm that employs an extra layer (on computer(s)) that monitors and executes the jobs, and temporarily stores the results if the mobile device (job sender) gets disconnected during the execution. In mobile cloud computing, *Cloudlets* and *Cloneclouds* can help to solve this problem. A cloudlet is a local cloud datacenter that has some high-end computing resources to which mobile users are connected (Satyanarayanan, Bahl, Caceres, & Davies, 2009). Although this architecture adds an extra layer between the mobile device and the actual cloud, it offers great reliability, and lowers the latency as it brings the cloud closer to the user. A clonecloud is a technology that allows users to make whole copies of their mobile devices on remote servers that are hosted at their cellular service provider (Chun, Ihm, Maniatis, Naik, & Patti, 2011). This approach aims at speeding up the execution of user requests as the actual processing happen on powerful clonecloud instead of the resource-limited mobile devices. It is worth mentioning that although cloudlets and cloneclouds can mitigate the intermittent connectivity, latency, and performance issues, they can only work when the users are within their range. Losing connection with them (e.g., when moving out of range from them) while the job is still being executed, would fail the job and result in errors; thus, this is an open research area.

INTERNET OF THINGS

Interaction between objects like wearable electronics, home appliances, transportation means, energy grids, manufacturing machineries, and healthcare facilities is becoming a reality. This model is known as the Internet of Things (IoT), in which a thing refers to an object that can be anything or anyone with built-in sensors and a unique identifier (i.e., IP) that connects it to the Internet. These objects can communicate and share data from the environment with back-end systems, as well as other objects. Moreover, objects in the IoT are smart as they are embedded with intelligence enabling them to adapt to the environment, and user patterns and preferences.

Indeed, the IoT represents a new generation of the ubiquitous computing that can be found anywhere and everywhere. Additionally, this model is convergent with diverse research areas and technologies. This includes distributed computing, nanotechnology, wireless sensors and actuator networks, mobile computing, location computing, artificial intelligence, context-aware computing, human-computer interaction, and machine-to-machine, to name a few. Each of these areas requires further research from the IoT perspectives.

HPC technologies, both hardware and software, provide the IoT with the environment required for this model to flourish. For instance, it offers a set of great tools (datacenters and cloud computing, many-core and multicore chips, memory storage, parallelization algorithms and software, etc.) for handling the enormous amount of data that is expected to be generated by the IoT objects. Such data will need real-time processing, integration, analysis and visualization.

Challenges and Directions

Gartner expects 26 billion objects to be connected to the Internet by 2020, and the revenues of IoT products and services to exceed $300 billion (Gartner, 2014a). It is likely for IoT to be applied to a wide range of fields such as retail, logistics, pharmaceutical, healthcare, transportation, housing, urban planning and infrastructure monitoring, food and agriculture. However, the IoT is challenged by a number of issues (mostly not HPC related) that need to be explored and resolved. Some of these challenges are discussed in the following:

- **Security and Privacy:** Addressing security and privacy issues in the IoT environment is crucial for widespread acceptance. Namely, the IoT should be sustained with superior security mechanisms and tools that safeguard users against attacks. Also, it should guarantee privacy and confidentiality of user information. Thus, new legislations must be implemented to ensure privacy and security measures are met, and prevent any abuse or misuse of data.
- **Data Structure:** The IoT will generate an enormous amount of data which will need effective methods to handle and organize them. To be specific, new techniques should be designed to allow for efficient transfer, management, storage, real-time processing and visualization of this data. For example, this would include a decentralized processing of data by sending it to the nearest processing clusters. In addition, the use of non-traditional database management systems such as NoSQL/NewSQL databases, as well as HPC facilities and techniques (e.g., accelerated computing) can support in processing non-structured data and scaling up with ease.
- **Lack of Standards:** Formation of open standards for programming, communication and data exchange is vital to prevent future proliferation of architectures, or communication protocols and frequencies, which could hinder the pervasive acceptance of the IoT. Hence, world-leading consortiums and standardization bodies must build some open standards that assure interoperability between different devices.
- **Size and Disposability:** Objects targeting the IoT model should be designed on a nanoscopic scale without compromising the price or processing power in order to allow efficient installation and use. Moreover, as later explored in the "Green Computing" section, these objects should be recyclable or even self-disposable to minimize any negative impacts on the environment.
- **Energy Sources:** The IoT objects should be able to function with the least amount of energy possible. They should even be enriched with ambient renewable sources that enable energy harvesting from the environment. Smart objects that need external power sources should allow for remote and quick charging (as described earlier in the "Mobile-Based Models" section).

BIG DATA AND NEXT-GENERATION ANALYTICS

Over the years, data creation and management methods have gone through some remarkable changes. Firstly, it was limited to organizations and enterprises, but with the advent of the Internet, those entities were enabled to share some of this data with others. Then, with the booming spread of social media, internet users were able to contribute and share data in different formats (e.g., videos on YouTube, tweets on Twitter, images on Instagram, etc.) Similarly, mobile devices exaggerated the amount of data being produced and shared. Add to this, the floods of data generated every day by machines, actuators and sensors (as described earlier in the "Internet of Things" section) and of course, scientific experiments and simulations that yield petabytes of data every day.

All of the aforementioned sources, as well as the diverse amounts of information have led to what we now know as "Big Data". IBM estimates the amount of data being created every day by 2.5 exabytes (2500 petabytes); about 90% of the data we have today has only been created over the last two years (IBM, 2016). IDC also expects the amount of data to reach 40 zettabytes by 2020 –50x the amount of data we have today (Turner, Gantz, Reinsel, & Minton, 2014). As mentioned earlier, this data is accumulated from different sources and in various formats, and in many cases with lots of redundancies. Moreover, the speed at which this data is generated and changed is overwhelming.

The ability to efficiently and effectively use this enormous amount of data is necessary for enterprises that are keen to stay in business. That is why *The Economist* calls it "the new raw material of business (The Economist, 2010). Thus, the ability to monetize this data is critical for success and competitiveness.

Although the data management principles and tools have impressively evolved over the last few decades, those conventional techniques will not be able to manage this ever-growing amount of data. Moreover, most of the data we hold nowadays is unstructured or lacks descriptive metadata that is needed for researching and further analysis. IDC, in 2012, estimated the amount of data that is tagged by 3% of the available data, and only 0.5% of it is analyzed (Gantz & Reinsel, 2012).

Challenges and Directions

Big data poses a vast list of challenges that requires masses of work from various sectors in the coming years. In addition to the classic issues of privacy and data protection, there are challenges that are related to data generation and acquisition, transfer, processing, storage, and certainly visualization and on-the-fly analysis. More details on these issues are provided in the following:

- **Necessity of Parallelism:** Data grows and changes faster than the advances in computing and processing speeds available in the market. As a consequence, the utilization of parallelization techniques, accelerators and HPC solutions is no longer optional. Writing parallel programs is never an easy task, and it requires highly sophisticated skills. This should become easier and allow access to the advantages of the parallelism offered in today's processors and coprocessors. In other words, writing parallel programs should be as easy as writing sequential programs (Asanovic et al., 2009). Likewise, new algorithms and tools should be offered to allow expansion of parallel processing from inter-node parallelism (i.e., between different computing nodes) to intra-node parallelism (i.e., sharing threads and processes across different cores in a single processor).

- **Lack of Metadata:** Large amounts of raw data are being generated every day, but most of it is irrelevant, and hence, there should be ways to enable us to clear data before any further processing. The ability to get rid of unnecessary or noisy data, without affecting the useful data, will have a positive effect on the scalability, storage, processing and management. The ability to automatically describe the generated data is also important. Tagging data would significantly improve our utilization of data, and therefore, metadata generation mechanisms should be integrated with the data recording and acquisition process.

- **Networks Issues:** The existing communication infrastructure and network technologies are not yet capable of dealing with the huge amounts of data streaming between data sources, processing units, storage, and end users. Extensive development needs to be implemented in this sector in order to offer high-bandwidth, low-latency networks that can handle the expected explosion of data efficiently. Moreover, new techniques must be applied to shorten the time needed for data transfer from the source to the processing and storage units. For instance, a non-centralized architecture would allow data to be processed and stored near the generation source. Data "sharddening", where original data is divided into many smaller shards, is one of the techniques that can achieve this goal.

- **Disks Speed:** Due to the necessity of speed in processing, retrieval and analysis of data, traditional storage media (e.g., RAID disks and SANs) are sufficient for big data. However, these storage media options are slow and cause major latencies and bottlenecks. As a result, RAM and flash-based media (as described earlier in the "In-Memory Computing" section) should be utilized at a higher rate in order to allow for radically faster data processing and analysis.

- **RDBS Issues:** The nature of today's data is a considerable challenge; most data is unstructured ranging from textual content to photos, graphs, 3D models, audios and videos. These unusual formats make the traditional RDBMS (relational database management systems) unsuitable for storing and querying big data. As a result, enterprises, on one hand, should rely on new techniques such as key/value data stores, and on the other hand, big software vendors should improve the features of those engines. Many of the available key/value database engines are, in fact, open source and still immature and lagging behind.

- **Lack of Reporting and Presentation Technologies:** Most of the data mining and business intelligence tools currently available on the market are not a good fit for big data. A new generation of analytics is needed to address big data issues. For instance, although current tools allow users to extract and analyze gigabytes (and sometimes terabytes) of data, big data is far larger in size –in petabytes. Moreover, OLAP (Online Analytical Processing) engines are designed to extract and report offline data marts and warehouses. On the other hand, big data users need to be able to analyze online data in real-time –to predict a customer's needs and suggest products on an e-commerce website, for example. Also, traditional reports and presentation formats are not sufficient for big data, and hence, the next-generation analytics should support new formats such as info graphs, paragraphs, pictures and videos.

- **Cloud Computing Issues:** Cloud computing in general allows users to make use of computing resources and services in a cost-effective manner and without an administration overhead. However, cloud computing in the current form may not be suitable for big data due to the need for speed in data processing and analysis. In other words, large cloud computing providers will need to make extreme changes to their infrastructure to fit for big data. Additionally, major improvement to current network infrastructure and internet connectivity is essential to speed up data transfers –for both uploads and downloads. Until this happens, big data adopters should count on dedicated HPC facilities that have high-end specifications.

GREEN COMPUTING

The manufacturing and use of computing resources in general, and the gigantic HPC systems in specific, have negative impacts on the environment. This includes increased greenhouse gas emissions; depletion of natural resources (e.g., fossil fuels); increased use of water, chemicals and electricity; and a generation of masses of toxic waste. Working on alleviating such impacts is crucial for saving our planet.

Again, implementers should focus on developing low-energy hardware and software systems that allow for a drastic saving in electrical use. Cutting on power use, and reliance on renewable energy will not only save the natural resources, but it will also minimize the greenhouse gas emissions, which in turn would slow the pace of global warming. Likewise, some research studies should be conducted on the impact of virtualization and cloud computing on the environment. Cloud vendors and industrial practitioners claim that both virtualization and cloud computing offer energy saving over the non-virtualized and on-premise solutions. These claims need to be validated, as some reports show that cloud solutions are not always greener than their on-premise counterparts, especially when they are used in the same way that traditional models are used (Whitney & Kennedy, 2012). A better understanding of the impact of these technologies on the environment would lead to some new eco-friendly practices and solutions.

The emergence of energy-aware provisioning mechanisms such as DVFS (Dynamic Voltage/Frequency Scaling), and the automatic input of servers into sleep/hibernate mode or switching them on/off in accordance to their utilization, offers some power saving. However, this comes at a cost that jeopardizes overall efficiency and reliability of the offered services (Guenter, Jain & Williams, 2011). In addition, they increase management costs because they require the use of sophisticated and expensive software packages to monitor and control those servers. Also, the frequent on/off cycles speed up the rate at which server components are replaced, which incurs further costs and results in a negative impact on the availability of those servers. Therefore, developing new technologies and algorithms that are able to balance the tradeoff between the systems reliability and power consumption is definitely a must. Similarly, formulating some of the best practices, and presenting case studies in this area would help organizations to better understand, utilize, and improve their systems.

Another point that needs to be addressed is the short lifetime of these resources. The average turnover of computers in enterprises is only three years; some of the HPC components get upgraded every 1.5-2 years, and supercomputers generally retire every 4-5 years. Therefore, some research needs to be devoted on finding ways to reuse or extend the lifetime of these resources. This could save the resources used in the manufacturing process and lessen the carbon footprint.

In addition, novel approaches should be devised to minimize the hazardous impact of "e-waste" resulting from disposing HPC systems. Thus, HPC facilities should be as recyclable as possible. Alternatively, they should be built as self-disposable components from eco-friendly substances such as sustained glass. Xerox PARC has already developed a self-destructing chip for the U.S. Defense Advanced Research Projects Agency (DARPA) using Corning's Gorilla Glass which is used in smartphones' screens (Hsu, 2016). Although data security was the main concern of this innovation, this approach may be leveraged from the sustainability and the environmental friendliness perspective.

CONCLUSION

Since the beginning of the computer era, users have been seeking powerful and high-performance systems that can solve large-scale problems. HPC reigns as the computing paradigm for today's advances and discoveries. In this chapter, we listed a few hot topics that are related to HPC. We started with a discussion on exascale, the next milestone in HPC field, and showed how the journey to get there has many obstacles that must be overcome. Then, we presented the accelerated computing model, and how the use of accelerators is becoming mainstream nowadays. After that, we talked about some of the popular low-energy architectures that could be leveraged in HPC systems to save power consumption. Following this, we introduced in-memory computing as a promising model that can improve systems' performance. In addition, we briefly discussed the utilization of mobile devices in HPC systems and, we dedicated two sections to the Internet of Things and Big Data as two of the influencing and closely-related technologies to HPC. Finally, we spoke over the impacts of HPC on the environment and highlighted the importance of dedicating some work to this area in order to preserve our planet. In fact, most of these technologies have been chosen by Gartner, in various reports, amongst the strategic technologies for the past few years (Gartner, 2009; Gartner, 2010; Gartner, 2011; Gartner, 2012; Gartner, 2014b). These technologies would actually help organizations, but they also come with a set of limitations and challenges that need further research. In the end, we believe that both scientific and industrial communities need to address the new challenges, novel approaches and innovative applications as this would help to envision and adapt to the changing and fast growing HPC ecosystem.

Qusay F. Hassan
Mansoura University, Egypt

ACKNOWLEDGMENT

The author would like to thank Axel Kloth for his dedicated time and effort on improving this chapter. His guidance and expertise has truly been an asset, not to mention the lengthy discussions that have made this possible. The author would also like to thank Mandy Kaur for proofreading this chapter.

REFERENCES

Abate, T. (2014). Stanford Team Combines Logic, Memory to Build a 'High-Rise' Chip. Stanford Engineering. Retrieved from http://engineering.stanford.edu/news/stanford-team-combines-logic-memory-build-high-rise-chip

AMD. (2015). FirePro. Retrieved from http://www.amd.com/en-us/products/graphics/workstation

AMD. (2016). AMD and Key Industry Partners Welcome the AMD Opteron A1100 SoC to the 64-bit ARM Datacenter Arena. Retrieved from http://www.amd.com/en-us/press-releases/Pages/amd-and-key-industry-2015jan14.aspx

Anthony, S. (2013). Intel Unveils 72-core x86 Knights Landing CPU for Exascale Supercomputing. *ExtremeTech*. Retrieved from http://www.extremetech.com/extreme/171678-intel-unveils-72-core-x86-knights-landing-cpu-for-exascale-supercomputing

ARM. (2016). ARM architecturev8-A: Reference Manual. Retrieved from http://infocenter.arm.com/help/topic/com.arm.doc.ddi0487a.h/index.html

Asanovic, K., Bodik, R., Demmel, J., Keaveny, T., Keutzer, K., Kubiatowicz, J., & Yelic, K. et al. (2009). A View of the Parallel Computing Landscape. *Communications of the ACM*, *52*(10), 56–67.

Barbera, M., Kosta, S., Mei, A., & Stefa, J. (2013, April). To offload or not to offload? the bandwidth and energy costs of mobile cloud computing.[IEEE.]. *Proceedings - IEEE INFOCOM*, *13*, 1285–1293.

Basile, D. (2013). IT Revolution: How In Memory Computing Changes Everything. *Forbes*. http://www.forbes.com/sites/ciocentral/2013/03/08/it-revolution-how-in-memory-computing-changes-everything/

Blem, E., Menon, J., & Sankaralingam, K. (2013, February). Power struggles: Revisiting the RISC vs. CISC debate on contemporary ARM and x86 architectures.*Proceedings of the 2013 IEEE 19th International Symposium on High Performance Computer Architecture (HPCA '13)* (pp. 1-12). IEEE.

Bourzac, K. (2016) Intel: Chips Will Have to Sacrifice Speed Gains for Energy Savings. *Technology Review*. Retrieved from https://www.technologyreview.com/s/600716/intel-chips-will-have-to-sacrifice-speed-gains-for-energy-savings/

Calamia, J. (2011). China's Homegrown Supercomputers. *IEEE Spectrum*. Retrieved from http://spectrum.ieee.org/computing/hardware/chinas-homegrown-supercomputers

Cappello, F., Geist, A., Gropp, W., Kale, S., Kramer, B., & Snir, M. (2014). Toward Exascale Resilience: 2014 update. *Supercomputing Frontiers and Innovations*, *1*(1), 5–28.

Chu, D. C., & Humphrey, M. (2004, November). Mobile ogsi. net: Grid computing on mobile devices. *Proceedings of the Fifth IEEE/ACM International Workshop on Grid Computing '04* (pp. 182-191). IEEE.

Chun, B. G., Ihm, S., Maniatis, P., Naik, M., & Patti, A. (2011, April). Clonecloud: elastic execution between mobile device and cloud.*Proceedings of the Sixth Conference on Computer systems* (pp. 301-314). ACM.

Dubash, M. (2010). Moore's Law is dead, says Gordon Moore: Legendary chip man reviews the past, present and future. *TechWorld*. Retrieved from http://www.techworld.com/news/operating-systems/moores-law-is-dead-says-gordon-moore-3576581/

Esmaeilzadeh, H., Blem, E., Amant, R. S., Sankaralingam, K., & Burger, D. (2011, June). Dark silicon and the end of multicore scaling.*Proceedings of the 2011 38th Annual International Symposium on Computer Architecture (ISCA)* (pp. 365-376). IEEE.

Fernando, N., Loke, S. W., & Rahayu, W. (2013). Mobile cloud computing: A survey. *Future Generation Computer Systems*, *29*(1), 84–106.

Foster, I. (2002). What is the grid? A three point checklist. *GRIDtoday*, *1*(6). Retrieve from http://www.mcs.anl.gov/~itf/Articles/WhatIsTheGrid.pdf

Gantz, J., & Reinsel, D. (2012). The digital universe in 2020: Big data, bigger digital shadows, and biggest growth in the far east. *IDC iView*. Retrieved from https://www.emc.com/collateral/analyst-reports/idc-the-digital-universe-in-2020.pdf

Gartner. (2009, October 18-22). Gartner Identifies the Top 10 Strategic Technologies for 2010. Proceedings of Gartner Symposium/ITxpo, Orlando, US. Retrieved from http://www.gartner.com/newsroom/id/1210613

Gartner. (2010, October 17-21). Gartner Identifies the Top 10 Strategic Technologies for 2011. *Proceedings of Gartner Symposium/ITxpo*, Orlando, US. Retrieved from http://www.gartner.com/newsroom/id/1454221

Gartner. (2011, October 16-20). Gartner Identifies the Top 10 Strategic Technologies for 2012. *Proceedings of Gartner Symposium/ITxpo*, Orlando, US. Retrieved from http://www.gartner.com/newsroom/id/1826214

Gartner. (2012, October 21-25). Gartner Identifies the Top 10. *Proceedings of the Strategic Technology Trends for 2013*, Orlando, US. Retrieved from http://www.gartner.com/newsroom/id/2209615

Gartner. (2013). Gartner Says In-Memory Computing Is Racing Towards Mainstream Adoption. Retrieved from http://www.gartner.com/newsroom/id/2405315

Gartner. (2014a). Gartner Says the Internet of Things Will Transform the Data Center. Retrieved from http://www.gartner.com/newsroom/id/2684616

Gartner (2014b, October 5-9). Gartner Identifies the Top 10 Strategic Technology Trends for 2015. *Proceedings of Gartner Symposium/ITxpo 2014*, Orlando, US. Retrieved from http://www.gartner.com/newsroom/id/2867917

Guenter, B., Jain, N., & Williams, C. (2011, April). Managing cost, performance, and reliability tradeoffs for energy-aware server provisioning. *Proceedings of the 2011 Proceedings IEEE INFOCOM* (pp. 1332-1340). IEEE.

Hassan, Q. (2011). Demystifying Cloud Computing. *The Journal of Defense Software Engineering, 2011*, 16–21. Retrieved from http://static1.1.sqspcdn.com/static/f/702523/10181434/1294788395300/201101-Hassan.pdf

Hennessy, J., Jouppi, N., Baskett, F., & Gill, J. (1981). *MIPS: a VLSI processor architecture*. Springer Berlin Heidelberg.

Heroux, M. A. (2016). Exascale Programming: Adapting What We Have Can (and Must) Work. *HPC Wire*. Retrieved from http://www.hpcwire.com/2016/01/14/24151/

Hewlett Packard Enterprise. (2016). HPE Moonshot System. Retrieved from https://www.hpe.com/us/en/servers/moonshot.html

Hsu, J. (2014). When Will We Have an Exascale Supercomputer? 2023 if we do it right; tomorrow if we do it crazy. *IEEE Spectrum*. Retrieved from http://spectrum.ieee.org/computing/hardware/when-will-we-have-an-exascale-supercomputer

Hsu, J. (2016). New U.S. Military Chip Self Destructs on Command. *IEEE Spectrum*. Retrieved from http://spectrum.ieee.org/tech-talk/computing/hardware/us-militarys-chip-self-destructs-on-command

IBM. (2016). What is big data? Retrieved from https://www-01.ibm.com/software/data/bigdata/what-is-big-data.html

Intel. (2014). Intel Xeon Phi Coprocessor x100 Product Family: Datasheet. Retrieved from http://www.intel.com/content/dam/www/public/us/en/documents/datasheets/xeon-phi-coprocessor-datasheet.pdf

Intel. (2016a). Intel Xeon Phi Coprocessors. Retrieved from http://www.intel.com/content/www/us/en/processors/xeon/xeon-phi-coprocessor-overview.html

Intel. (2016b). Intel Many Integrated Core Architecture - Advanced. Retrieved from http://www.intel.com/content/www/us/en/architecture-and-technology/many-integrated-core/intel-many-integrated-core-architecture.html

Intel. (2016c). Intel Xeon Phi Product Family. Retrieved from http://www.intel.com/content/www/us/en/processors/xeon/xeon-phi-detail.html

Janapa Reddi, V., Lee, B. C., Chilimbi, T., & Vaid, K. (2010). Web Search Using Mobile Cores: Quantifying and Mitigating the Price of Efficiency. *ACM SIGARCH Computer Architecture News, 38*(3), 314–325.

Jun, S. W., & Chung, C., Arvind. (2015). Large-Scale High-Dimensional Nearest Neighbor Search Using Flash Memory with In-Store Processing. *Proceedings of the International Conference on Reconfigurable Computing and FPGAs (ReConFig).*

Jun, S. W., Liu, M., Lee, S., Hicks, J., Ankcorn, J., King, M., & Xu, S. (2015, June). BlueDBM: An Appliance for Big Data Analytics.*Proceedings of the 42nd Annual International Symposium on Computer Architecture* (pp. 1-13). ACM.

Karimi, K., Dickson, N. G., & Hamze, F. (2010). A performance comparison of CUDA and OpenCL. arXiv preprint arXiv:1005.2581. Retrieved from http://arxiv.org/ftp/arxiv/papers/1005/1005.2581.pdf

Kloth, A. (2013). Kloth's Observation: Every software library function that has proven to be useful will end up as a piece of hardware. *SSRLabs Official Blog*. Retrieved from http://www.ssrlabs.com/blog.html

Kloth, A. (2014, August). Flash Memory System Redesigned for Big Data. *Proceedings of Flash Memory Summit.* Retrieved from http://www.flashmemorysummit.com/English/Collaterals/Proceedings/2014/20140806_204C_Kloth.pdf

Kogge, P. (2011). Next-Generation Supercomputers. *IEEE Spectrum*. Retrieved from http://spectrum.ieee.org/computing/hardware/nextgeneration-supercomputers

Kumar, K., & Lu, Y. H. (2010). Cloud computing for mobile users: Can offloading computation save energy? *Computer, 4,* 51–56.

Litke, A., Skoutas, D., & Varvarigou, T. (2004, December). Mobile grid computing: Changes and challenges of resource management in a mobile grid environment. *Proceedings of the 5th International Conference on Practical Aspects of Knowledge Management (PAKM 2004).*

Maqbool, J., Oh, S., & Fox, G. C. (2015). Evaluating ARM HPC clusters for scientific workloads. *Concurrency and Computation, 27*(17), 5390–5410.

Marcinichen, J. B., Wu, D., Paredes, S., Thome, J. R., & Michel, B. (2014). Dynamic flow control and performance comparison of different concepts of two-phase on-chip cooling cycles. *Applied Energy, 114*, 179–191.

Markoff, J. (2016). Microsoft Plumbs Ocean's Depths to Test Underwater Data Center. *The New York Times.* Retrieved from http://www.nytimes.com/2016/02/01/technology/microsoft-plumbs-oceans-depths-to-test-underwater-data-center.html?smid=li-share&_r=1

Microsoft Research. (2016). Microsoft's underwater datacenter: Project Natick [YouTube video]. Retrieved from https://youtu.be/L2oJw1a_qEM

Moore, G. E. (1965) Cramming more components onto integrated circuits. Electronics, 38(8).

Nvidia. (2016). Tesla. Retrieved from http://www.nvidia.com/object/why-choose-tesla.html

Ousterhout, J. (2015). A Radical Proposal: Replace Hard Disks With DRAM. *IEEE Spectrum.* http://spectrum.ieee.org/computing/hardware/a-radical-proposal-replace-hard-disks-with-dram

Ousterhout, J., Agrawal, P., Erickson, D., Kozyrakis, C., Leverich, J., Mazières, D., & Stutsman, R. et al. (2010). The case for RAMClouds: Scalable high-performance storage entirely in DRAM. *Operating Systems Review, 43*(4), 92–105.

Park, S. M., Ko, Y. B., & Kim, J. H. (2003). Disconnected operation service in mobile grid computing. In *Service-Oriented Computing-ICSOC 2003* (pp. 499–513). Springer Berlin Heidelberg.

Phys.org. (2015). Beyond silicon: New semiconductor moves spintronics toward reality. *Phys.org.* Retrieved from http://phys.org/news/2015-02-silicon-semiconductor-spintronics-reality.html

Powell, N. (2012). Nordic Countries Increasingly Attractive as Sites for Data Centers. *The New York Times.* Retrieved from http://www.nytimes.com/2012/04/30/business/global/nordic-countries-increasingly-attractive-as-sites-for-data-centers.html

Rajovic, N., Carpenter, P. M., Gelado, I., Puzovic, N., Ramirez, A., & Valero, M. R. (2013, November). Supercomputing with commodity CPUs: are mobile SoCs ready for HPC?*Proceedings of the 2013 International Conference for High Performance Computing, Networking, Storage and Analysis (SC)* (pp. 1-12). IEEE.

Rajsuman, R. (2000). *System-on-a-chip: Design and Test.* Artech House, Inc.

Resarch and Markets. (2015). In-Memory Computing Market by Component (IMDM, IMAP), Sub-Components (IMDB, IMDG), Solutions (OLAP, OLTP), Verticals (BFSI, Retail, Government, & others) - Global Forecast to 2020. Retrieved from http://www.researchandmarkets.com/research/tthjg6/inmemory

Sarvey, T. E., Zhang, Y., Zheng, L., Thadesar, P., Gutala, R., Cheung, C., & Bakir, M. S. et al. (2015, September). Embedded cooling technologies for densely integrated electronic systems.*Proceedings of the IEEE Custom Integrated Circuits Conference.* IEEE.

Satyanarayanan, M., Bahl, P., Caceres, R., & Davies, N. (2009). The case for vm-based cloudlets in mobile computing. *Pervasive Computing*, 8(4), 14–23.

Seabaugh, A. (2013). The Tunneling Transistor. *IEEE Spectrum*. Retrieved from http://spectrum.ieee.org/semiconductors/devices/the-tunneling-transistor

Shulaker, M. M., Hills, G., Patil, N., Wei, H., Chen, H. Y., Wong, H. S. P., & Mitra, S. (2013). Carbon nanotube computer. *Nature, 501*(7468), 526–530.

Simon, H. (2013). "No Exascale for You!" An Interview with Berkely Lab's Horst Simon. *Top 500. org*. Retrieved from http://www.top500.org/blog/no-exascale-for-you-an-interview-with-berkeley-labs-horst-simon/

SPARC International. (2016). Technical Documents. Retrieved from http://sparc.org/technical-documents/

SSRLabs. (2016a). Retrieved from http://ssrlabs.com/index.html

SSRLabs. (2016b). Neural Net Coprocessor. Retrieved from http://ssrlabs.com/neuralnetworkaccelerator.html

SSRLabs. (2016c). Floating-Point Coprocessor. Retrieved from http://ssrlabs.com/floatingpointaccelerator.html

Talla, V., Kellogg, B., Ransford, B., Naderiparizi, S., Gollakota, S., & Smith, J. R. (2015). Powering the Next Billion Devices with Wi-Fi. Retrieved from http://arxiv.org/pdf/1505.06815

The Economist. (2010). Data, data everywhere. Retrieved from http://www.economist.com/node/15557443

The White House. (2015). Executive Order -- Creating a National Strategic Computing Initiative. Retrieved from https://www.whitehouse.gov/the-press-office/2015/07/29/executive-order-creating-national-strategic-computing-initiative

Top500 (2016). Retrieved from http://www.top500.org/lists/

Turner, V., Gantz, J., Reinsel, D., & Minton, S. (2014). "The Digital Universe of Opportunities: Rich Data and the Increasing Value of the Internet of Things". IDC. http://idcdocserv.com/1678

WattUp. (2016). Retrieved from http://www.energous.com/product-overview/

Whitney, J., & Kennedy, J. (2012). The Carbon Emissions of Server Computing for Small-to medium-sized Organizations: A Performance Study of On-Premise vs. The Cloud. *WSP Environment & Energy*. Retrieved from http://www.wspgroup.com/Globaln/USA/Environmental/NRDC-WSP_Cloud_Computing.pdf

Wi-Charge Technology. (2016). Retrieved from http://www.wi-charge.com/technology.php?ID=25

Zhang, H., Chen, G., Ooi, B. C., Tan, K. L., & Zhang, M. (2015). In-Memory Big Data Management and Processing: A Survey. *IEEE Transactions on Knowledge and Data Engineering*. IEEE.

KEY TERMS AND DEFINITIONS

Accelerated Computing: Refers to a computing model that uses manycore accelerators (i.e., coprocessors) together with the processor to speed up the execution of compute-intensive tasks.

Big Data: Refers to enormous, diverse, and very complex datasets that cannot be processed using the traditional tools and algorithms.

Exascale Computing: Refers to a computing system that can perform at least one quintillion (10^{18}) floating point operations per second (i.e., exaFLOPS).

Green Computing: Refers to the practices that should be followed during the design, manufacturing, use, and disposal of computing systems to prevent or minimize any negative impacts on the environment.

High Performance Computing: It means different things to different communities, but it usually refers to the use of supercomputers and parallel processing algorithms to solve complex scientific and engineering problems.

In-Memory Computing: Refers to a computing model that stores data into memory instead of disks in order to improve systems' performance. It usually uses memory that is denser but slower than DRAM such as Phase Change Memory or MLC Flash.

Internet of Things: A network/computing model in which physical objects (e.g., wearables, vehicles, buildings, home appliances, etc.) are connected to the Internet. Each of these objects is embedded with sensors, actuators, and a moderate amount of preprocessing that allow it to collect and exchange data with one another, as well as the backend servers.

Low-Power Architectures: Refers to the use of energy-efficient instruction sets (e.g., RISC and optimized CISC) and microarchitectures (e.g., SoC) to reduce power consumption in datacenters.

Mobile-Based Models: Refers to incorporating mobile devices in HPC systems. This can be either by augmenting many mobile devices and use their computational power to process complex tasks, or by offloading those tasks to powerful servers (on the grid/cloud) where their processing takes place.

Next-Generation Analytics: Refers to a set of analysis, reporting, and presentation technologies that need to be devised to handle big data.

ENDNOTES

[1] The US government believes those computing resources are used in nuclear-related research http://bis.doc.gov/index.php/forms-documents/doc_download/1196-80-fr-8524

[2] A research group Stanford has proposed a technique to build 3D chips that combine logic and memory circuits in a multi-story structure, where memory is layered on top of the logic transistors (Abate, 2014).

Section 1
Energy and Performance Optimization

Chapter 1
Power Optimization Using Clock Gating and Power Gating:
A Review

Arsalan Shahid
HITEC University, Pakistan

Muhammad Yasir Qadri
University of Essex, UK

Saad Arif
HITEC University, Pakistan

Saba Munawar
COMSATS Institute of Information Technology, Pakistan

ABSTRACT

The scaling of CMOS technology has continued due to ever increasing demand of greater performance with low power consumption. This demand has grown further by the portable and battery operated devices market. To meet the challenge of greater energy efficiency and performance, a number of power optimization techniques at processor and system components level are proposed by the research community such as clock gating, operand isolation, memory splitting, power gating, dynamic voltage and frequency scaling, etc. This chapter reviews advancements in the dynamic power optimization techniques like clock gating and power gating. This chapter also reviews some architectures and optimization techniques that have been developed for greater power reduction without any significant performance degradation or area cost.

INTRODUCTION

Recent advances in the field of computer architecture have marked power consumption as one of the major design constraints (Farkas, Jouppi, Ranganathan, & Tullsen, 2015). Power optimization is now a prerequisite for not only portable and mobile computing systems but also for advanced multicore platforms (Hager, Treibig, Habich, & Wellein, 2014). An energy-efficient design strives to deliver optimum throughput while minimizing power consumption (Hanumaiah & Vrudhula, 2014). Current research on energy-efficient processor architectures targets various abstraction levels, spanning from integration technology to algorithmic optimization. Integrated Chip (IC) manufacturing technologies

DOI: 10.4018/978-1-5225-0287-6.ch001

have largely improved during the past decades to cater the greater performance demands, while being energy efficient. Modern multiprocessor systems have billions of transistors with operating frequencies in gigahertz (GHz) range (Daud, Ahmad, & Lynn, 2014). Power optimization in such highly integrated systems is not just an option but a basic requirement. A microprocessor experiences both static and dynamic power consumption; the static power is mainly contributed by leakage current in the device, whereas the dynamic power consumption is a function of toggling frequency. A number of techniques have been developed to control the dynamic power of **C**omplementary **M**etal-**O**xide **S**emiconductor (CMOS) circuits in general, and processors in particular such as clock gating (CG), pre-computation, operand isolation, memory splitting, power gating, body biasing, dynamic voltage-frequency scaling, etc. (Arora et al., 2014; Shah & Ahir, 2013).

This chapter introduces and reviews recent advancements in *clock gating (CG)* and *power gating* (PG) techniques in details. The rest of this chapter is organized as follows: the next section presents a background of power optimization techniques and motivation to use clock gating and power gating among them. Then, a detailed review of clock gating techniques is presented in the next section. After that, power gating techniques to optimize power consumption in a microprocessor are described. Finally, the chapter concludes.

BACKGROUND

Reducing the power consumption has become one of very important research interest and a great challenge in various computing platform for the past decade. In this section we will discuss various techniques used for power optimization. Moreover, we will discuss the advantages of power gating and clock gating techniques over the other available techniques.

Power dissipation has emerged as an important factor in the design phase of a microprocessor. Careful and intelligent design is required at different levels of computer system to obtain optimal power performance. Therefore, it is very important to know the sources of energy consumption at different levels of memory hierarchies. Various energy models have been presented to understand the accurate power consumptions by integration with different cycle accurate simulators. One such example is energy models of multilevel cache memory presented by Qadri et al. (Qadri, M. Y., & McDonald-Maier, K. D., 2010). Energy models can also be subdivided in to three types, i.e., CPU level Energy models (Brooks, D. M. et al, 2000), complete system level models and interconnect level energy models. Hence, energy models do provide a very deep level of energy consumption analysis and result in to power optimization. Then comes the Dynamic Power Measurement (DPM) techniques, which can be classified into three subcategories:

1.   CPU level DPM,
2.   Complete system level DPM, and
3.   Parallel system-level DPM.

These techniques target energy consumption reduction at run-time by selectively turning off or slowing down components when the systems are idle or serving light. DPM techniques can be applied in different ways and are applied at different levels; in accordance to which they lie in the three mentioned categories e.g. dynamic voltage scaling changes the processor's supply voltage and similarly frequency scaling changes the operating frequency at runtime resulting into power optimization. Both of them lies in CPU-level DPM. Clock gating also comes in CPU level DPM. System and parallel level DPM are also further classified into two types:

1. Hardware based DPM, and
2. Software based DPM.

In this chapter, we discuss clock gating and power gating. Clock gating saves power by adding more logic to a circuit to prune the clock tree. Pruning the clock disables portions of the circuitry so that the flip-flops in them do not have to switch states. Clock gating is widely used because it is conceptually simple and a very small additional circuitry is needed to implement it. Moreover, the component can transit from an idle to an active state in only a few cycles. In power gating, reduction in power consumption is obtained by switching off the current to blocks of the circuit that are not in use. In addition to reducing stand-by or leakage power, power gating has the benefit of enabling Iddq testing. Iddq testing is a method for testing CMOS integrated circuits for the presence of manufacturing faults. The following section presents different clock gating techniques along with their design and efficiency.

CLOCK GATING

This technique is based on the concept of powering off the clock to the flip-flops or memory elements which are not taking part in the current processing; therefore, their unnecessary switching is stopped in order to save dynamic power that is required for their speculative toggling (Zhou, Peng, Hou, Wan, & Lin, 2014). This power reduction can also be achieved by minimizing the number of gates used in each stage and hence reducing the operating frequency at the cost of performance degradation.

From 20% to 40% of the total dynamic power consumptions can be saved so performance degradation can be neglected. (Qadri, Gujarathi, & McDonald-Maier, 2009). Therefore, the cost of performance degradation is bearable at this level of power saving and is based on a compromise between these two aspects.

Clock related power accounts for more than 60% of the total dynamic power requirements (Li, Wang, Choi, Park, & Chung, 2010). Clock gating (CG) is most recognized and commonly applied in number of systems. CG is further divided into three subcategories:

1. System level CG,
2. Combinational CG, and
3. Sequential CG (Donno, Ivaldi, Benini, & Macii, 2003).

System level CG requires information of architecture design and works when clock gating is required at system components level like caches, etc. Combinational CG is used at individual register level as shown in Figure 1, where a group or block of registers are gated in parallel through a single gate cell. Sequential CG (SCG) is applicable in components with serial chains of registers as in pipeline stages, etc. Combinational and Sequential CGs are used in industry for ultra-low power processors (Li et al., 2010).

Figure 1. Clock gating scheme
Adapted from Hsu & Lin, 2011.

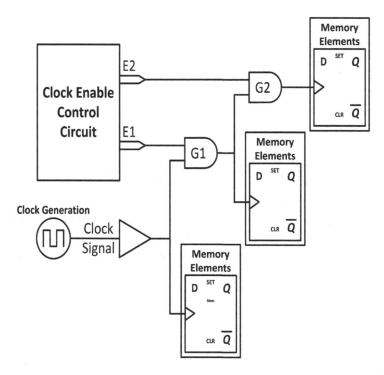

Figure 1 shows a scheme adapted for clock gating in a multi-staged CMOS circuit. Clock control logic block generates the *enable signals* "E1" and "E2" in order to enable clock for multi-staged circuit. "G1" and "G2" are the clock gates which block the clock signal to further stages of flip-flops depending on their usage requirement. Clock control logic decides the depth of stage up to which clock signal is supplied, and unnecessary flip-flops are powered off to avoid speculative toggling, and as a result power saving is achieved.

Huang et al. optimized total power consumption by efficiently designing clock gating circuit (Huang, Tu, & Li, 2012). Control logic used for clock gating has greater circuit area which is also responsible for increased dynamic power consumption. To avoid this, Integer Linear Programming (ILP) is used to optimize both the clock tree and circuit area of clock control logic. In this work, control logic circuit for clock gating is designed by reducing area requirements to 14.5% without loss of performance or increase in power consumption.

Johnson et al. designed a wire-speed power processor SoC (System on Chip) based on IBM 45nm SOI (Silicon on Insulator) technology for inline processing and filtering of data with 2.3GHz core frequency, 16 cores, and 64 threads (Johnson et al., 2010). This chip uses clock gating to achieve AC power saving up to 32% (40W). Brandt et al. developed a technique for identification of speculative or passive executions which are further routed to less power consuming parts through clock gating or operand isolation for low power consumptions (Brandt, Schneider, Ahuja, & Shukla, 2010).

Li et al. introduced Selective Sequential Clock Gating (SeSCG) technique to minimize power consumption in Multimedia Mobile Processor (MMP) designs (Li et al., 2010). SeSCG is used to select optimal sequential clock gating for MMP at Register Transfer (RT) level based on Wasting Toggle Rate

(WTR) analysis. The efficiency of this technique is checked on two real, industrial MMP implementations. Conventional SCG increased total power consumption by 4.77%, while SeSCG reduced it to 23.71% without significant performance degradation.

Hsu et al. described the optimized design of clock gating based on delay-matching technique of gated cells array as compared to the characteristics of type-matching clock gating design (Hsu & Lin, 2011). Their work showed that delay-matching clock gating is much better in achieving better slew and smaller latency with insignificantly changed clock skew and area overhead as compared to type-matching clock gating design. This clock skew is insensitive to process and operating corner variations. The original timing characteristics of the gated tree are preserved by introducing Engineering Change Order (ECO).

Figure 2 shows a clock gating design with type-matching in which all gates at a certain depth level of clock tree are the same. On the other hand, Figure 3 shows clock gating design based on delay-matching in which gated cells are replaced by buffers (inverters) with same timing characteristics.

Koppanalil et al. designed a 1.6GHz dual-core Cortex-A9 processor using 32nm CMOS bulk process (Koppanalil, Yeung, Driscoll, Householder, & Hawkins, 2011). This chip includes power saving schemes like *dynamic voltage-frequency scaling*, *power gating* and *clock gating* for operation at more than GHz frequency and low power. It has all these gates introduced in its all modules to greatly reduce static and dynamic power consumption in this ARM architecture. This Cortex A9 CPU uses Clock Tree Synthesis (CTS) flow for efficient clock distribution in complete tree with hierarchical clock gating schemes.

Figure 2. Type-matching clock gating scheme
Adapted from Hsu & Lin, 2011.

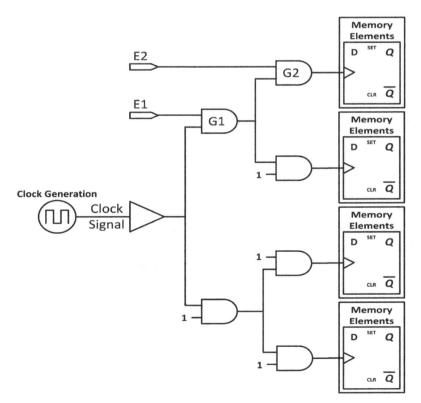

Figure 3. Delay-matching clock gating scheme
Adapted from Hsu & Lin, 2011.

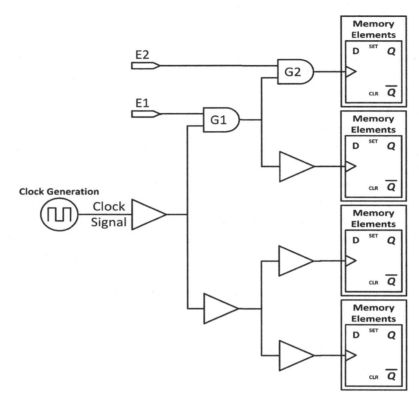

Clock gates are inserted at different levels of clock tree for enhanced power saving. Architecture level blocks like CORE, NEON multimedia, signal processing accelerator, Data Engine (DE) and Snoop Control Unit (SCU) are gated with gates before them. Hence, blocking clock to these in case of idle conditions of processor. Power compiler has also introduced clock gates at register level to achieve enhanced clock gating and hence significantly reduces dynamic power consumptions.

Oliver et al. discussed the experimental results of power consumption measurements of ACTEL's Cyclone III based on 65nm CMOS process and Spartan 6 Field Programmable Gate Arrays (FPGAs) based on 45nm CMOS process (Oliver, Curto, Bouvier, Ramos, & Boemo, 2012). Power saving techniques such as clock gating, clock enable, and blocked inputs, etc., are used to reduce power consumption in standby and active modes. A comparison is performed based on the measurement results of both technologies, in both active and standby modes.

Experimental results showed the trend of power consumption with increasing number of flip-flops in Xilinx Spartan 6 for both active and standby modes. It is clearly evident from the comparison chart that clock gating is the best technique for power reduction in standby mode, and it also behaves well in active mode when compared to clock enable (Oliver et al., 2012). Further results showed the trend of power consumption with increasing number of flip-flops in Cyclone III for both active and standby modes. Here in this case, clock enable is more power saving technique as compared to clock gating. However, clock gating has proved to be the best power optimization technique in standby modes.

Clock gating can also be implemented at gate level rather than RT level. Han et al. developed gate level clock gating using combinational logic (Han & Shin, 2012). This is done by *matching factored forms* in existing combinational logic tree.

Experimental results showed that factored form matching has reduced number of gates used in combinational logic up to 25% as compared to another technique of Boolean division in which this reduction is observed to be only 10%. Consequently, this reduction in gates results in significant dynamic power saving.

Work has also been done on reduction of gate cells in combinational logic for clock gating. Chen et al. developed three phase clock gating technique to generate clock gating tree having minimum number of gate cells and buffers (W.-H. Chen, Chang, Hung, & Hsieh, 2012). Generation of this optimized clock tree is based on clustering and merging algorithms. The proposed scheme is tested on 2GHz Intel Xeon Linux system by using C programming language.

Dillen et al. applied clock gating for power saving in standby mode in Level Sensitive Scan Design (LSSD) with very low area overhead and is implemented on x86 and x64 based AMD microprocessor core called "Bulldozer" (Dillen, Priore, Horiuchi, Naffziger, & others, 2012). The authors of that work presented clock gating scheme for control of flip-flops' scanning operation. This clock gating circuit also provides window transparency. Figure 4 shows field-effect transistor (FET) based complex clock gating circuit with early and late clock gates. The delay between early and late clock signal determines the window transparency time which eventually reduces set-up time, and late arriving data is successfully written to memory elements.

Figure 4. Clock gate for LSSD
Adapted from Dillen et al., 2012.

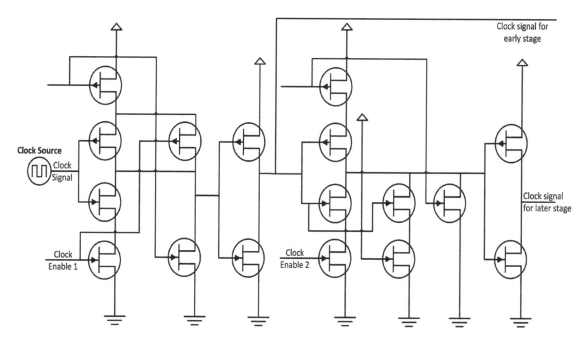

Figure 5. (a) BSCG, (b) LECG, (c) ECG
Adapted from Y. Zhang et al., 2012.

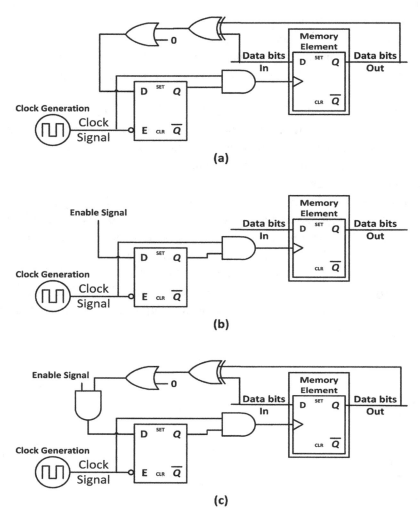

Shelar et al. developed a power optimizing clustering algorithm for power saving in local clock trees for testing on high speed 45nm microprocessor designs (Shelar, 2012). It makes clusters of memory elements and applies clock gating to them. Power reduction up to 14% is achieved by keeping slew and skew factors unchanged. Implementation of this algorithm has achieved up to 32% cost reduction than conventional clock tree synthesis techniques.

Zhang et al. implemented various gate level clock gating optimizations on TSMC 45nm CMOS technology for RT level in Very-large-scale integration (VLSI) designs with effective power reduction (Y. Zhang et al., 2012). *Enable signal* plays an important role in development of number of techniques. Bus Specific Clock Gating (BSCG), Threshold based Clock Gating (TCG) and proposed Optimized Bus Specific Clock Gating (OBSCG) are designed and tested with the absence of *enable signal*. Local Explicit Clock Gating (LECG), Enhanced Clock Gating (ECG), Wasting Toggle Rate (WTR) analysis based clock gating and Single Comparator based Clock Gating (SCCG) are tested when *enable signal* is

Figure 6. SCCG scheme
Adapted from Y. Zhang et al., 2012.

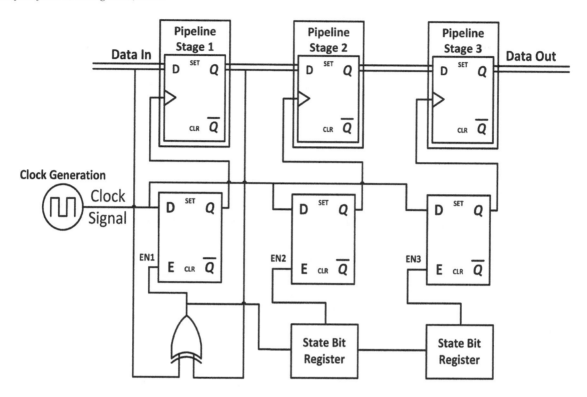

present. Furthermore, new power optimization techniques like *operand isolation* and *memory splitting* are also experimented and tested in this work for above mentioned CMOS technology. Figure 5 shows RT level clock gating schemes for BSCG, LECG and ECG applied on flip-flops. Figure 6 shows clock gating scheme for SCCG in which a single comparator is gating the clock signal to all the stages of pipeline stage registers. OBSCG scheme resulted in power savings up to 26.95% after testing on ISCAS89 bench circuits with Synopsys power compiler (Y. Zhang et al., 2012). Area overhead is increased up to 14.44% while performance degradation in terms of delay incurred is up to 5.77%.

Jotwani et al. designed an AMD x86-64 core implemented in 32nm SOI CMOS technology with a number of design changes and enhancements to improve power requirements which ranges from 2.5W to 25W and hence making the core more suitable for low power mobile devices and products (Jotwani et al., 2010). Enhanced design of clock gating architecture resulted in reduction of clock related power requirement which is now less than 10% of total dynamic power of the chip.

POWER GATING

This technique is based on the concept of powering off the supply voltage to the blocks of flip-flops or memory elements and other system components in idle conditions while system is in standby or sleep mode. Power gating is also applied in active mode for dynamic power reduction as well as static power

Figure 7. Power gating scheme with header/footer switches
Adapted from M. Y. Qadri et al., 2012.

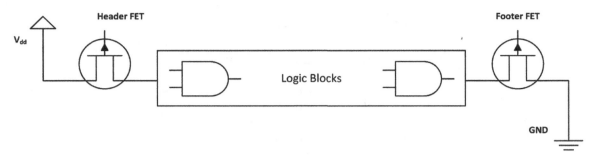

reduction through blocking leakage currents and switching currents while not in use for required results computation. Power switches based on FETs etc. are introduced before and after clusters or logic blocks. Leakage current in active mode heavily takes part in dynamic power consumption which is up to 30% to 40% of total dynamic power consumptions (Seomun, Shin, & Shin, 2010). Figure 7 shows a typical design of power gating circuit with power enabling header and footer switches. State of these switches determines the power supply or blocking to logic block.

Seomun et al. proposed an Active Mode Power Gating (AMPG) scheme to minimize dynamic power consumption because of leakage currents (Seomun et al., 2010). This scheme is a hybrid of power gating and clock gating integrated to actively reduce power consumption due to leakage currents up to 16% in comparison with conventional clock gated schemes, when tested on 45nm CMOS technology. A few constraints like functional, timing and current constraints are also addressed to ensure correct and fast working of the circuit. AMPG is based on power gating with clock gating controls. Figure 8 shows an AMPG scheme layout in which clock gating control signal controls the footer switches which in turn reduces the leakage current of combinational logic. If clock gating controller generates logic to turn off clock transmission, then "EN1" and "EN2" signals become zero, and hence stops clock signal to flip-flops and turns off their unnecessary switching. It also results into disabling of footer switches to stop the leakage currents of combinational logic circuit shown with gates connected by thick power wires. Performance degradation is kept minimized with 6% area overhead due to extra gates and footer switches and 30% wire length overhead due to interleaving wires for combinational logic circuitry, etc. Therefore, AMPG is proved to be a better power saving technique in standby mode as well as active mode for handheld devices like mobile phones and Personal Digital Assistant (PDAs), etc.

Ishihara et al. applied power gating scheme to asynchronous FPGA based on a single two input and one output Look-Up Table (LUT) level fine granularity (Ishihara, Hariyama, & Kameyama, 2011). The proposed scheme for FPGA is designed on ASPLA 90nm CMOS technology. A computer vision technique "Template Matching" is also tested on proposed FPGA design and it also have an added feature of detection of data arrival in order to wake up from sleep mode without delay incurred or unnecessary toggling power consumption. Experimental results of the proposed scheme in comparison with synchronous FPGA and asynchronous FPGA without power gating have showed power reduction up to 38% and 15% respectively at 85oC.

Figure 9 shows the control strategy adopted in proposed scheme. Here, input and output phases of Logic Block (LB) is compared through comparator in phase comparator module. If LB is in operation, then the comparator output will be one which controls the activity switch or FET (power gate) to be

Figure 8. Power gating scheme with clock gating control - AMPG
Adapted from Jun Seomun et al., 2010.

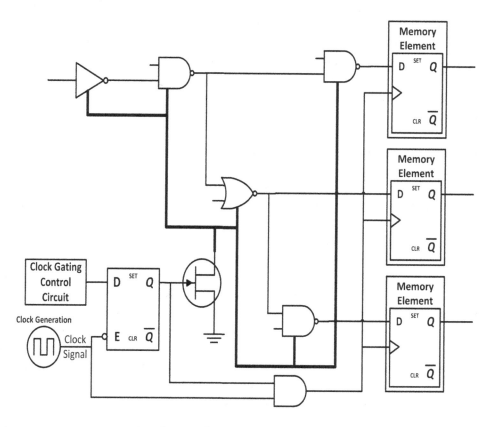

Figure 9. Autonomous power gating for synchronous FPGA (a) circuit, (b) control scheme

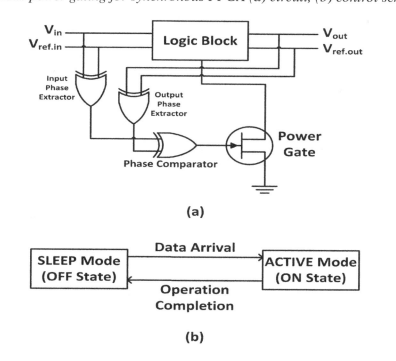

in ON state. This will keep LB working using the applied supply voltage, and if there is no activity or processing in LB, then the phase comparator will generate zero to stop the power gate in order to switch OFF the power supply. Figure 9(b) shows the adopted control scheme that whenever data arrives at LB, the power gate will switch the LB ON in active mode and after completion of operation, LB gets into sleep mode by getting power OFF signal from power gate. The provision of delay occurrence and power consumption in activating and deactivating power gate is more when compared to the saved power. therefore, to avoid this problem, new modified schemes are also discussed such as introducing an interval led checking of activity of LB, which powers OFF the gate if there is no activity observed on LB for a specific time interval, etc. (Ishihara et al., 2011).

Madan et al. have proposed algorithms based on guarded and predictive power gating for multicore settings at intra-core and inter-core level (Madan, Buyuktosunoglu, Bose, & Annavaram, 2012). Algorithms are developed to maintain proper balance of power gating at these levels in order to maximize the power savings at the cost of minimum performance degradation and area overhead. Power gating experimentation at inter-core level resulted in power savings up to 34% with average performance degradation of 4.8% in terms of response time; whereas, intra-core level power gating experimentation yielded maximum power saving up to 20% with a performance loss of 1%.

Chen et al. developed an ARM Cortex-M3 core based millimeter scale sensor system with battery and solar cells (G. K. Chen et al., 2010). Cortex-M3 and SRAM is power gated in order to reduce power consumptions during sleep mode and leakage current losses are reduced up to 20%. This power gating saves energy during sleep mode and provides long lasting battery life during measurement operations.

Kang et al. proposed a software based power saving scheme based on integration of DVFS and power gating by minimizing the leakage currents and chip temperature (Kang, Kim, Yoo, & Kyung, 2010). Proposed scheme is tested with two software applications H.264 Decoder and Ray Tracing with benchmark program Equake and power reduction up to 19.4% to 27.2% is observed in comparison with conventional methods.

Pakbaznia et al. presented a tri-modal Multi Threshold CMOS (MTCMOS) based power gating scheme for power saving in active, drowsy and sleep modes (Pakbaznia & Pedram, 2012). Header and footer power switches are introduced for working in data retentive power gating, multi-drowsy mode structures and dynamic voltage scaling for reduction of dynamic power consumption. Experimental results on IBM 90nm technology with Synopsys power compiler shows power savings due to leakage current stopping is up to 50%, 71% and 91% in proposed drowsy, sleep and active mode circuits. Figure 10 shows the design of footer and header switches used for power gating in drowsy, sleep and active modes. When SLEEP signal is OFF then the gated circuit will be in ACTIVE state irrespective of the state of DROWSY signal. When SLEEP signal is ON and DROWSY signal is OFF then gated circuit will enter in SLEEP mode with power gating in action. When both SLEEP and DROWSY signals are ON then gated circuit will enter in DROWSY mode and hence enabling power saving at an intermediate level.

Yip et al. designed a reconfigurable SAR ADC whose power is scalable with resolution reconfiguration (Yip & Chandrakasan, 2013). Power gating is introduced in it which resulted in improved energy efficiency with reduced complexity and cost. This ADC has reconfigurable resolution of 5 to 10-bit and 0.4 to 1V. Exponential trend is achieved in power reduction with respect to resolution in DAC operation which accounts for 25% of total power consumptions. Leakage current losses are minimized by power gating and now total power is reduced up to 14% which was much higher than this without power gating.

Figure 10. (a) Footer power gate, (b) header power gate, for sleep drowsy and active modes
Adapted from Pakbaznia & Pedram, 2012.

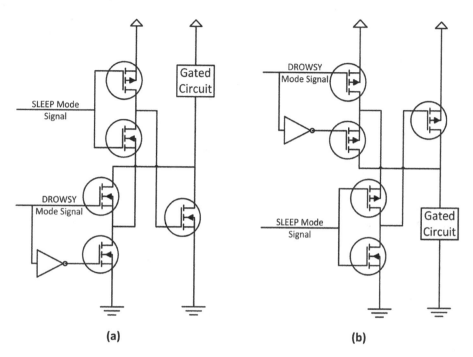

Seok et al. investigated power optimization for ultra-low Vdd CMOS circuits during sleep modes by introducing power gating switches with minimal size (Seok, Hanson, Blaauw, & Sylvester, 2012). SPICE simulations of these proposed minimal sized power gating switches showed 125 times reduction in total power consumptions as compared to those achieved by conventional power saving techniques. Furthermore, this proposed scheme is evaluated and validated by taking measurements from ultra-low power microprocessor.

Jeong et al. introduced a new power optimization technique called Memory Access Power Gating (MAPG), which is used to save power during processor stalls without waiting for thread completion when a number of requests to memory are in progress and hence incurring latency to the system (Jeong, Kahng, Kang, Rosing, & Strong, 2012). Battery operated devices such as mobile phones are mostly prone to this type of problem where limited capacity of battery to be consumed efficiently for increased working span. This scheme has resulted in up to 38.07% power reduction. A counter based power gating is practically implemented resulting in up to 22.57% dynamic power reduction in cores without significant performance degradation and area overhead.

Takeda et al. proposed sleep mode control scheme for dynamic power saving due to leakage current and named it as Opt-Static (Takeda, Miwa, Usami, & Nakamura, 2012a). It uses sleep mode with certain depth level which is reconfigurable according to run-time requirements. Experimentation showed that average power savings by reducing leakage current with simple power gating and proposed multi-mode power gating are 34.4% and 44.1% respectively as compared to consumptions of non-power gated circuits. In various cases, multi-mode power gating resulted in more than 25% power savings in addition to that of conventional power gating scheme. Proposed power gating scheme with depth level has achieved average power saving up to 93.8% as compared to that of ideal multi-mode power gating. Single depth level based power gating has achieved 88.1% power saving without significant degradation.

Wang et al. implemented high speed power gating for reduction of dynamic power consumption due to leakage currents in functional units of CPU MIPS 3000 based cores (Wang, Ohta, Ishii, Usami, & Amano, 2012). Three types of power gating are designed: *cell based, row based* and *ring based*. Experiments and simulation results have shown dynamic power savings up to 28% to 54% at 25°C with much smaller area overhead and design costs.

Chang et al. proposed a new power gating scheme based on balanced rush current for an enhanced active wakeup mode (Chang, Tso, Huang, & Yang, 2012). The proposed scheme is evaluated by implementing a 40-bit ALU on TSMC 0.18m CMOS technology and resulted in 10.23% reduction in wake-up time as compared to other power gating schemes without significant performance or power degradation.

Power optimization techniques for single core processors have been investigated in numerous research works. Some of these power saving schemes are also implemented in multi-core multi-threaded architectures. Zyuban et al. deployed power saving models in IBM POWER7 R processor by introducing design changes at microarchitecture, logic and circuits, etc. level (Zyuban et al., 2011). In another work, Roy et al. investigated power savings in multi-core processors having multi-threaded in-order cores by using power gating of register files with state retention capability (Roy, Ranganathan, & Katkoori, 2011). State retention is a powerful feature enabling register files to retain their data during memory stalls and sleep modes treated with power gating to reduce leakage power losses. A technique is proposed in control unit design of in-order cores with three multi-core configurations named as:

1. Coarse-Grained Multi-Threading (CGMT),
2. Fine-Grained Multi-Threading (FGMT), and
3. Simultaneous Multi-Threading (SMT).

SPEC 2000 integer benchmarks are used to evaluate the proposed technique with the help of simulations. Experiments on 8 core processor with 64 threads execution resulted in average power savings by reducing leakage current up to 42%, 7% and 8% in CGMT, FGMT and SMT configurations, respectively. Simulation results on integer register files showed that power saving is mainly dependent upon number of Thread Context (TC) running (Roy et al., 2011). In CGMT configuration, leakage power saving ranges between 0.9% to 2.9% for 2 TCs, and 22% to 42% for 8 TCs. In FGMT configuration, power saving lies between 0.8% to 2.02% for 3 TCs, and 3.09% to 7.8% for 8 TCs. In SMT configuration, power saving is in the range of 1.02% to 2.23% for 4 TCs and 2.97% to 7.27% for 8 TCs with degradation of 0.023% while each core is executing 8 threads in an 8 core processor.

Takeda et al. proposed a multi-depth based sleep control scheme, which decides the depth of sleep mode during runtime by keeping in view the idle duration, program load and temperature, etc. (Takeda, Miwa, Usami, & Nakamura, 2012b). This sleep control scheme is optimized for better leakage savings with stepwise depth selection of sleep mode. Body biasing technique is used here to effectively reduce leakage savings by putting system in sleep mode. Experiments of proposed scheme with floating point benchmarks of FPAlu at 1.0GHz, 75oC resulted in 43% net power saving by reducing leakage current.

Hong et al. proposed a power model for Graphics Processing Unit (GPU) named as Integrated Power and Performance modelling system (IPP) which saves power by considering core temperature increase and by optimizing number of cores to be used for a specific task according to power consumed by each core (Hong & Kim, 2010). Power saving by power gating of cores in GPUs is also computed here. Experimentation and evaluation resulted in average power savings up to 10.99% in case of optimization of number of cores according to application demand. Power requirements are reduced up to 25.85% by introducing power gating before each core.

Singh et al. presented a power gating scheme with multiple sleep modes for improved leakage reduction in combinational circuits (Singh, Agarwal, Sylvester, & Nowka, 2007). Every sleep mode has unique power and performance level and multi-mode power gating which allows for improved power savings for processors. After simulations, this multilevel sleep mode power gating resulted in 17% extra reduction in leakage losses as compared to single mode power gating results. State retentive mode resulted in 19% reduction of leakage losses with active data retention.

Zhang et al. proposed a new power gating scheme with further improvements in comparison with multiple sleep mode power gating as described in an earlier work (Singh et al., 2007). Analysis of previous scheme of (Singh et al., 2007) resulted in high sensitivity for process changes effecting manufacturing and application level up to only two intermediate sleep levels (Z. Zhang, Kavousianos, Chakrabarty, & Tsiatouhas, 2011). This new multilevel power gating scheme is designed to overcome the drawbacks of previous scheme and allows more than two intermediate sleep levels resulting in increased power savings with lesser complexity and area overhead cost.

Annavaram et al. highlighted few challenges in designing an optimal power management system like negative outcomes and increased performance degradation in terms of response time and area overhead (Annavaram, 2011). Guarded power gating models are proposed in this work to overcome above mentioned challenges. Two proposed schemes are:

1. Idleness-Triggered Per-core Power Gating (IdlePG), and
2. Utilization-based Per-core Power Gating (UtilPG).

IdlePG is based on monitoring of idle state duration in all cores of processor which is very effective in power saving but incurs delay in wakeup duration of cores. So idleness duration threshold should be carefully chosen in this case in order to reduce degradation and negative outcomes. Experimentation showed performance degradation up to 8.4% if wakeup latency is increased up to 100ms. UtilPG is based on sampling system utilization repeatedly in a specific time period and based on this utilization, minimum number of cores required to be active are switched on. This scheme is sensitive to both parameters power saving and system response latency. A maximum performance degradation of 11% is observed with longest utilization sampling time period of 1s during experimentation. Both power gating schemes were tested against a few examples of different workloads for failure analysis, and a guard mechanism is proposed in order to make these schemes fail safe and effective in power saving in all types of workloads and circumstances (Annavaram, 2011).

CONCLUSION

This chapter has reviewed the advancements in power optimization techniques (i.e. clock gating and power gating) being used in a number of systems like multi-core CPUs, CMOS circuits and FPGAs, etc. These techniques have proven to be optimal in achieving static and dynamic power savings without significant performance degradation or additional area overheads. A number of other optimization techniques such as operand isolation, pre-computation, memory splitting and dynamic voltage-frequency scaling are also being developed and implemented with integration of these two techniques to generate hybrid power saving schemes.

Clock gating and power gating proved to be efficient resulting in up to 30% to 40% total dynamic power reduction. These are being used in IBM POWER7 R, ARM (Cortex A9, Cortex M3, Bulldozer), Intel (Xeon), IA and in various other in-order multi-threaded and multi-core processors, and Multi-Mini-Processor (MMPs). Furthermore, power saving techniques for FPGAs such as RT level implementation and gate-based architectures (e.g. type-matching and delay-matching) were discussed.

The power savings schemes discussed in this chapter are widely being used in system-level components like cores, caches, pipelines, buses and memories, etc. They are also being used in advanced multi-core architectures to deliver high grade performance with minimal static and dynamic power consumptions and area overheads.

REFERENCES

Annavaram, M. (2011). A case for guarded power gating for multi-core processors. *Proceedings of the 2011 IEEE 17th International Symposium on High Performance Computer Architecture (HPCA)* (pp. 291–300).

Arora, M., Manne, S., Eckert, Y., Paul, I., Jayasena, N., & Tullsen, D. (2014). A comparison of core power gating strategies implemented in modern hardware. Proceedings of the 2014 ACM international conference on Measurement and modeling of computer systems (pp. 559–560). ACM. doi:doi:10.1145/2591971.2592017 doi:10.1145/2591971.2592017

Brandt, J., Schneider, K., Ahuja, S., & Shukla, S. K. (2010). The model checking view to clock Sgating and operand isolation. *Proceedings of the 2010 10th International Conference on Application of Concurrency to System Design (ACSD)* (pp. 181–190). IEEE.

Chang, C.-Y., Tso, P.-C., Huang, C.-H., & Yang, P.-H. (2012). A fast wake-up power gating technique with inducing a balanced rush current. *Proceedings of the 2012 IEEE International Symposium on Circuits and Systems (ISCAS)* (pp. 3086–3089). IEEE. doi:doi:10.1109/ISCAS.2012.6271972 doi:10.1109/ISCAS.2012.6271972

Chen, G. K., Fojtik, M., Kim, D., Fick, D., Park, J., Seok, M., . . . Blaauw, D. (2010). Millimeter-scale nearly perpetual sensor system with stacked battery and solar cells. Proceedings of ISSCC (Vol. 10, pp. 288–289). doi:doi:10.1109/ISSCC.2010.5433921 doi:10.1109/ISSCC.2010.5433921

Chen, W.-H., Chang, H.-H., Hung, J.-H., & Hsieh, T.-M. (2012). Clock tree construction using gated clock cloning. *Proceedings of the 2012 4th Asia Symposium on Quality Electronic Design (ASQED)* (pp. 54–58). IEEE.

Daud, S., Ahmad, R. B., & Lynn, O. B. (2014). CPU Power Prediction on Modern Multicore Embedded Processor. *International journal of Computer Science and Mobile Computing, 3*(2), 709–715. IJCSMC.

Dillen, S. J., Priore, D., Horiuchi, A. K., & Naffziger, S. D. (2012, September). Design and implementation of soft-edge flip-flops for x86-64 AMD microprocessor modules. *Proceedings of theCustom Integrated Circuits Conference CICC'12* (pp. 1-4). IEEE. doi:doi:10.1109/CICC.2012.6330707 doi:10.1109/CICC.2012.6330707

Donno, M., Ivaldi, A., Benini, L., & Macii, E. (2003). Clock-tree power optimization based on RTL clock-gating. Proceedings of the Design Automation Conference (pp. 622–627). IEEE.

Farkas, R. K. K., Jouppi, N. P., Ranganathan, P., & Tullsen, D. M. (2015). A Multi-Core Approach to Addressing the Energy-Complexity Problem in Microprocessors.*Proceedings of Workshop on Complexity-Effective Design.*

Qadri, M. Y., & McDonald-Maier, K. D. (2010, March). Analytical Evaluation of Energy and Throughput for Multilevel Caches. *Proceedings of the 2010 12th International Conference on Computer Modelling and Simulation (UKSim)* (pp. 598-603). IEEE. doi:10.1109/UKSIM.2010.114

Brooks, D. M., Bose, P., Schuster, S. E., Jacobson, H., Kudva, P. N., Buyuktosunoglu, A., & Cook, P. W. (2000). Power-aware microarchitecture: Design and modeling challenges for next-generation microprocessors. *Micro*, *20*(6), 26–44. doi:10.1109/UKSIM.2010.114

Hager, G., Treibig, J., Habich, J., & Wellein, G. (2014). Exploring performance and power properties of modern multi-core chips via simple machine models. *Concurrency and Computation.*

Han, I., & Shin, Y. (2012). Synthesis of clock gating logic through factored form matching. *Proceedings of the 2012 IEEE International Conference on IC Design & Technology (ICICDT)* (pp. 1–4). IEEE. doi:doi:10.1109/ICICDT.2012.6232835 doi:10.1109/ICICDT.2012.6232835

Hanumaiah, V., & Vrudhula, S. (2014). Energy-efficient operation of multicore processors by DVFS, task migration, and active cooling. *IEEE Transactions on Computers*, *63*(2), 349–360. doi:10.1109/TC.2012.213

Hong, S., & Kim, H. (2010). An integrated GPU power and performance model. In *ACM SIGARCH Computer Architecture News* (Vol. 38, pp. 280–289). ACM. doi:10.1145/1815961.1815998

Hsu, S.-J., & Lin, R.-B. (2011). Clock gating optimization with delay-matching. Proceedings of the Design, Automation & Test in Europe Conference & Exhibition (pp. 1–6). IEEE.

Huang, S.-H., Tu, W.-P., & Li, B.-H. (2012). High-level synthesis for minimum-area low-power clock gating. *Journal of Information Science and Engineering*, *28*(5), 971–988.

Ishihara, S., Hariyama, M., & Kameyama, M. (2011). A low-power FPGA based on autonomous fine-grain power gating. *IEEE Transactions on Very Large Scale Integration (VLSI) Systems*, *19*(8), 1394–1406.

Jeong, K., Kahng, A. B., Kang, S., Rosing, T. S., & Strong, R. (2012). MAPG: Memory access power gating.*Proceedings of the Conference on Design, Automation and Test in Europe* (pp. 1054–1059). EDA Consortium.

Johnson, C., Allen, D.H., Brown, J., Vanderwiel, S., Hoover, R., Achilles, H., Cher, CY., May, G.A., Franke, H., Xenidis, J. & Basso, C. (2010). 5.5 A Wire-Speed PowerTM Processor: 2.3 GHz 45nm SOI with 16 Cores and 64 Threads.

Jotwani, R., Sundaram, S., Kosonocky, S., Schaefer, A., Andrade, V., Constant, G., & Naffziger, S. (2010). An x86-64 core implemented in 32nm SOI CMOS. *Proceedings of the 2010 IEEE International Solid-State Circuits Conference-(ISSCC).* IEEE.

Kang, K., Kim, J., Yoo, S., & Kyung, C.-M. (2010). Temperature-aware integrated DVFS and power gating for executing tasks with runtime distribution. *IEEE Transactions on Computer-Aided Design of Integrated Circuits and Systems, 29*(9), 1381–1394. doi:10.1109/TCAD.2010.2059290

Koppanalil, J., Yeung, G., Driscoll, D. O., Householder, S., & Hawkins, C. (2011). A 1.6 GHz dual-core ARM Cortex A9 implementation on a low power high-K metal gate 32nm process. Proceedings of the 2011 International Symposium on VLSI Design, Automation and Test (VLSI-DAT) (pp. 1–4). IEEE.

Li, L., Wang, W., Choi, K., Park, S., & Chung, M.-K. (2010). SeSCG: Selective sequential clock gating for ultra-low-power multimedia mobile processor design. *Proceedings of the 2010 IEEE International Conference on Electro/Information Technology (EIT)* (pp. 1–6). IEEE.

Madan, N., Buyuktosunoglu, A., Bose, P., & Annavaram, M. (2012). Guarded power gating in a multi-core setting. In *Computer Architecture* (pp. 198–210). Springer.

Oliver, J. P., Curto, J., Bouvier, D., Ramos, M., & Boemo, E. (2012). Clock gating and clock enable for FPGA power reduction. *Proceedings of the 2012 VIII Southern Conference on Programmable Logic (SPL)* (pp. 1–5). IEEE. doi:doi:10.1109/SPL.2012.6211782 doi:10.1109/SPL.2012.6211782

Pakbaznia, E., & Pedram, M. (2012). Design of a tri-modal multi-threshold CMOS switch with application to data retentive power gating. *IEEE Transactions on Very Large Scale Integration Systems, 20*(2), 380–385.

Qadri, M. Y., Gujarathi, H. S., & McDonald-Maier, K. D. (2009). Low Power Processor Architectures and Contemporary Techniques for Power Optimization–A Review. *Journal of Computers, 4*(10), 927–942. doi:10.4304/jcp.4.10.927-942

Roy, S., Ranganathan, N., & Katkoori, S. (2011). State-retentive power gating of register files in multicore processors featuring multithreaded in-order cores. *IEEE Transactions on Computers, 60*(11), 1547–1560. doi:10.1109/TC.2010.249

Seok, M., Hanson, S., Blaauw, D., & Sylvester, D. (2012). Sleep Mode Analysis and Optimization with Minimal-Sized Power Gating Switch for Ultra-Low Operation. *IEEE Transactions on Very Large Scale Integration Systems, 20*(4), 605–615.

Seomun, J., Shin, I., & Shin, Y. (2010). Synthesis and implementation of active mode power gating circuits. *Proceedings of the 2010 47th ACM/IEEE Design Automation Conference (DAC)* (pp. 487–492). IEEE. doi:doi:10.1145/1837274.1837395 doi:10.1145/1837274.1837395

Shah, N. A., & Ahir, D. H. (2013). Power Consumption Reduction using Microarchitecture Techniques for Modern Multicore Microprocessors. *Current Trends in Information Technology, 3*(3), 16–20.

Shelar, R. S. (2012). A fast and near-optimal clustering algorithm for low-power clock tree synthesis. *IEEE Transactions on Computer-Aided Design of Integrated Circuits and Systems, 31*(11), 1781–1786.

Singh, H., Agarwal, K., Sylvester, D., & Nowka, K. J. (2007). Enhanced leakage reduction techniques using intermediate strength power gating. *IEEE Transactions on Very Large Scale Integration Systems*, *15*(11), 1215–1224.

Takeda, S., Miwa, S., Usami, K., & Nakamura, H. (2012a). Efficient leakage power saving by sleep depth controlling for Multi-mode Power Gating. *Proceedings of the 2012 13th International Symposium on Quality Electronic Design (ISQED)* (pp. 625–632). IEEE. doi:doi:10.1109/ISQED.2012.6187558 doi:10.1109/ISQED.2012.6187558

Takeda, S., Miwa, S., Usami, K., & Nakamura, H. (2012b). Stepwise sleep depth control for run-time leakage power saving.*Proceedings of the great lakes symposium on VLSI* (pp. 233–238). ACM. doi:10.1145/2206781.2206838

Wang, W., Ohta, Y., Ishii, Y., Usami, K., & Amano, H. (2012). Trade-off analysis of fine-grained power gating methods for functional units in a CPU. Proceedings of IEEE 2012 Cool Chips XV (COOL Chips), (pp. 1–3). IEEE. doi:doi:10.1109/COOLChips.2012.6216587 doi:10.1109/COOLChips.2012.6216587

Yip, M., & Chandrakasan, A. P. (2013). A resolution-reconfigurable 5-to-10-bit 0.4-to-1 V power scalable SAR ADC for sensor applications. *IEEE Journal of Solid-State Circuits*, *48*(6), 1453–1464. doi:10.1109/JSSC.2013.2254551

Zhang, Y., Tong, Q., Li, L., Wang, W., Choi, K., Jang, J. E., . . . Ahn, S. Y. (2012). Automatic Register Transfer level CAD tool design for advanced clock gating and low power schemes. *Proceedings of the 2012 International SoC Design Conference (ISOCC)* (pp. 21–24). IEEE.

Zhang, Z., Kavousianos, X., Chakrabarty, K., & Tsiatouhas, Y. (2011). A robust and reconfigurable multi-mode power gating architecture. *Proceedings of the 2011 24th International Conference on VLSI Design (VLSI Design)* (pp. 280–285). IEEE. doi:doi:10.1109/VLSID.2011.29 doi:10.1109/VLSID.2011.29

Zhou, Y., Peng, X., Hou, L., Wan, P., & Lin, P. (2014). Clock gating-A power optimization technique for smart card. *Proceedings of the 2014 12th IEEE International Conference on Solid-State and Integrated Circuit Technology (ICSICT)* (pp. 1–3). IEEE. doi:doi:10.1109/ICSICT.2014.7021594 doi:10.1109/ICSICT.2014.7021594

Zyuban, V., Friedrich, J., Gonzalez, C. J., Rao, R., Brown, M. D., Ziegler, M. M., & Culp, J. A. (2011). Power optimization methodology for the IBM POWER7 microprocessor. *IBM Journal of Research and Development*, *55*(3), 7–11. doi:10.1147/JRD.2011.2110410

KEY TERMS AND DEFINITIONS

Clock Gating: A Technique of reducing power consumption by addition of extra logic in the circuit; resulting in pruning the clock tree.

Logic Circuit: A basic building block of a real world computing platform.

Logic Gate: A basic building block of digital system having specific number of inputs and a outputs based on a certain logic.

Multi-Core System: A processor system composed up of multiple central processing units in a form of a single computing package for reading and executing instructions.

Power Gating: A technique to use integrated circuit design for reducing the power consumption by switching off the blocks of circuit which are not being used.

Power Optimization: The process of reducing the power consumption of a digital electronic system by the use of electronic design automation tools.

Chapter 2
Resource Scheduling for Energy–Aware Reconfigurable Internet Data Centers

Mohammad Shojafar
Sapienza University of Roma, Italy

Nicola Cordeschi
Sapienza University of Rome, Italy

Enzo Baccarelli
Sapienza University of Rome, Italy

ABSTRACT

The pervasive use of cloud computing and the resulting growing number of Internet data centers have brought forth many concerns, including electrical energy cost, energy dissipation, cooling and carbon emission. Therefore, the need for efficient workload schedulers which are capable of minimizing the consumed energy becomes increasingly important. Green computing, a new trend for high-end computing, attempts to approach this problem by delivering both high performance and reduced energy consumption. Motivated by these considerations, in this chapter, we propose a joint computation-and-communication adaptive resource-provisioning scheduler for virtualized data centers, e.g., the Internet Data Center (IDC) scheduler, which exploits the DVFS-enabled reconfiguration capability of the underlying virtualized computing/communication platform. Specifically, we present and test a dynamic resource provisioning scheduler, which adaptively controls the execution time and bandwidth usage of each input job, as well as the internal and external switching costs on per-Virtual Machine (VM) basis.

BACKGROUND AND MOTIVATIONS

Green Cloud Computing (GCC) refers to the environmental benefits that Internet-based Information Technology (IT) services may offer. The term combines the words Green – meaning environmentally friendly – and Cloud. GCC aims at providing various models and techniques to seamlessly integrate

DOI: 10.4018/978-1-5225-0287-6.ch002

the management of computing-communication virtualized platforms, which provide Quality of Service (QoS), robustness and reduced energy utilization (Cugola & Margara, 2012; Shamshirband, Petković, Ćojbašić, Nikolić, Anuar, Shuib, & Akib, 2014). The main challenge in GCC is to minimize the energy usage, while still meeting the QoS requirements of the supported applications. For this purpose, an energy-aware scheduler is needed that jointly accounts for the networking and computing resource allocation in the Cloud. In this respect, several works focused on the energy efficiency of Cloud infrastructures, by exploiting (Mishra, Jain, & Durresi, 2012; Baliga, Ayre, Hinton, & Tucker, 2011), and/ or virtualization of the cloud resources (Azodolmolky, Wieder, & Yahyapour, 2013). DVFS is applied in most of the modern computing units, such as cluster computing and supercomputing, in order to reduce power consumption and achieve high reliability and availability. Resource virtualization refers to instantiating several VMs on the same physical server, in order to reduce the number of physical CPUs, while improving the resource utilization. Furthermore, one of the main requirements for Cloud computing environments is the provision of reliable Service Level Agreements (SLAs). SLAs can be managed *globally* or *locally* by the Cloud providers by relying on suitable scheduling policies (Shamshirband, Shojafar, Hosseinabadi, Kardgar, Nasir, & Ahmad, 2015). Another issue of growing concern in Cloud environments is to evenly distribute huge amount of workloads over various servers, which is referred to as *load balancing*. Load balancing algorithms seek to distribute workloads across a number of servers, so that the average executions times are minimized (Warneke & Kao, 2011). Load balancing schemes may be *static* or *dynamic* ones. In static schemes, the current state of the servers is not considered when dispatching the workloads. Examples of such schemes include Random Selection of servers and Round Robin policies. However, dynamic schemes involve direct notification or indirect inference of the servers' states by the load balancer (Warneke & Kao, 2011).

In this chapter, we present and test the performance of a new adaptive resource scheduler. It aims at minimizing the energy consumption induced by the computing, communication and reconfiguration costs in Internet-based virtualized data centers. In such environments, work is performed under hard limits on the execution times of the offered jobs. Our scheduler accounts for the dynamic load balancing, by using online job decomposition. For this purpose, we have developed a framework for the Cloud resource management that considers the optimum joint allocation of VM processing frequencies and link bandwidths. Consider that the resulting energy model is non-convex, so that, we have developed a mathematical approach to turn non-convexity into convexity.

RELATED WORK

Updated surveys of current technologies and open communication challenges about energy-efficient data centers have been recently presented in (Hirzel, Soule´, Schneider, Gedik, & Grimm, 2014; Cordeschi, Shojafar, & Baccarelli, 2013; Cordeschi, Amendola, & Baccarelli, 2014; Cordeschi, Shojafar, Amendola & Baccarelli, 2015; Shojafar, Cordeschi, Amendola & Baccarelli, 2015a; Shojafar, Javanmardi, Abolfazli & Cordeschi, 2015b; Baccarelli & Biagi, 2003a, 2003b). Specifically, power management schemes that exploit DVFS techniques for performing resource provisioning are the focus of (Baliga, Ayre, Hinton, & Tucker, 2011; Azodolmolky, Wieder, & Yahyapour, 2013; Qian, He, Su, Wu, Zhu, Zhang, & Zhang, 2013; Javanmardi, Shojafar, Amendola, Cordeschi, Liu, & Abraham, 2014). Although these contributions consider hard deadline constraints, they do not consider, indeed, the performance penalty and the energy-vs.-delay tradeoff stemming from the finite transmission rate of the utilized network infrastructures. Energy-saving dynamic provisioning of the computing resources in virtualized Green data centers is the topic of (Zaharia, Das, Li, Hunter, Shenker, & Stoica, 2013; Urgaonkar, Kozat, Igarashi, & Neely, 2010; Mathew, Sitaraman, & Shenoy, 2012; Wang, Zhang, Arjona Aroca, Vasilakos, Zheng, Hou, & Liu, 2014; Daliri, Shamshirband, & Besheli, 2011; Khan, Kiah, Madani, Ali, & Shamshirband, 2014; Rababah, & Alqudah, 2005). Specifically, Zaharia, Das, Li, Hunter, Shenker, and Stoica (2013) formulates the optimization problem as a feedback control problem that must converge to an a priori known target performance level. While this approach is suitable for tracking problems, it cannot be employed for energy-minimization problems, where the target values are a priori unknown. Roughly speaking, the common approach pursued by Mathew, Sitaraman, and Shenoy (2012) is to formulate the afforded minimum-cost resource allocation problem as a sequential optimization problem and, then, solve it by using limited look-ahead control. Hence, the effectiveness of this approach relies on the ability to accurately predict the future workload (such as (Rababah, 2008) and (Victoria, Ahmad, Ahmad, & Silviu, 2015)) and the resulting performance degrades when the workload exhibits almost unpredictable time fluctuations. In order to avoid the prediction of future workload, (Urgaonkar, Kozat, Igarashi, & Neely, 2010) resorts to a Lyapunov-based technique that dynamically optimizes the provisioning of the computing resources by exploiting the available queue information. Although the pursued approach is of interest, it relies on an inherent delay-vs.-utility tradeoff, which does not allow us to account for hard deadline constraints. The suitable exploitation of some peculiar features of the network topology of current networked data centers is at the basis of the capacity-planning approach recently proposed in Wang, Zhang, Arjona Aroca, Vasilakos, Zheng, Hou, & Liu (2014). For this purpose, a novel traffic engineering-based framework is developed (inspired by extending Baccarelli, Cordeschi, & Patriarca, 2012) and (Cordeschi, Polli, & Baccarelli, 2012)), which aims at reducing the number of active switches, while simultaneously balancing the resulting communication flows. Although the attained reductions of the energy consumed by the networking infrastructures are, indeed, noticeable, the pursued capacity-planning approach does not consider, by design, the corresponding energy consumed by the computing servers and, which is the most, it subsumes delay-tolerant application scenarios. The joint analysis of the computing-plus-communication energy consumption in virtualized Clouds is, indeed, the focus of (Mishra, Jain, & Durresi, 2012), where delay-tolerant Internet-based applications are considered. Interestingly, the main lesson stemming from these contributions is that the energy consumption due to data communication may represent a large part of the overall energy demand, especially when the utilized network is bandwidth-limited. Overall, these works numerically analyze and test the energy performance of some state-of-the-art schedulers for virtualized Clouds, but do not attempt to optimize it through the dynamic joint scaling of the available communication-plus-computing resources.

The reminder of this chapter is organized as follows. In the following section, we present the model of the considered Internet-based reconfigurable virtualized data center, and the approach leading to the proposed joint scheduler is developed. Then, the implemented testbed is presented and its performance is investigated. Finally, we draw some conclusions in the last section.

THE CONSIDERED IDC INFRASTRUCTURE

An Internet virtualized platform for parallel computing is composed of multiple clustered virtualized processing units (e.g., VMs), which are interconnected by a single-hop virtual local network (VLAN) and managed by a central controller. Each VM executes the currently assigned task by self-managing own

Figure 1. The considered IDC architecture; the data center includes M servers. Each server (e.g., PM) is equipped with a Virtualized layer, a VM, a local controller and a Physical layer. Yellow stars indicate bidirectional controlling path.

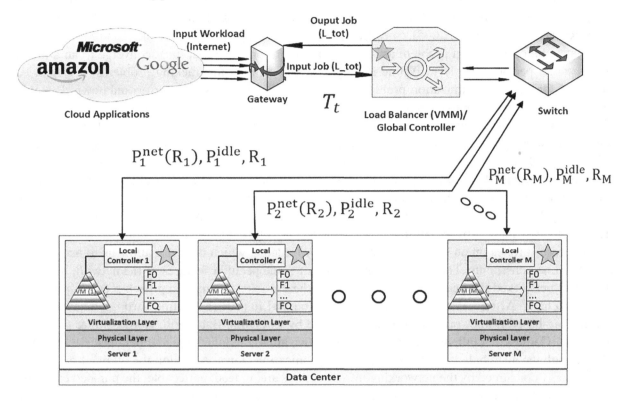

local virtualized storage/computing resources. When a request for a new job is submitted to the networked data center, the resource controller dynamically performs both admission control and allocation of the available virtual resources (Lu, Chen, & Andrew, 2013). Hence, according to the typical architecture recently presented in (Wang, Zhang, Arjona Aroca, Vasilakos, Zheng, Hou, & Liu, 2014), emerging Internet-based Data Centers (IDCs) are composed by three main components, i.e., the data storage unit, the Virtual Machine Manager (VMM) and the switched VLAN (see Figure 1). A new job is initiated by the arrival of a file of size L_{tot} [*bit*]. Due to the real-time nature of the considered application scenario, full processing of the input file must be carried out within an assigned deterministic working time T_t [*s*] (*s* means second). Hence, in our framework, a real-time job is characterized by:

1. The size L_{tot} of the file to be processed;
2. The maximum tolerated processing delay T_t; and,
3. The job granularity, that is, the (integer-valued) maximum number $M_T \geq 1$ of independent parallel tasks embedded into the submitted job.

Let $M \geq 1$ be the maximum number of VMs that are available in Figure 1. In principle, each VM may be modeled as a virtual server, that is capable to process $f(i)$ bits per second (i is the VM identifier and its maximum value is M) (Cordeschi, Shojafar & Baccarelli, 2013), (Drugarin, Ahmad, Ahmad, & Lyashenko, 2015). Depending on the size $L(i)$ [*bit*] of the task to be currently processed by $VM(i)$, the corresponding processing rate $f(i)$ may be adaptively scaled up/down at run-time, and it may assume discrete values over the interval [0, f^{max}], where f^{max} [*bit/s*] is the maximum allowed processing speed of VM [1].

In our approach, the IDC scheduler splits the overall scheduling problem into two smaller sub-problems. These sub-problems are addressed by two controllers, e.g., the *global controller* and the *local controller*. A local controller manages each Physical Machines (PM) (or physical server), in order to optimize the energy consumption by observing its current utilization. Moreover, the architecture has a global controller (e.g., a supervisor), in order to optimize the VM placement sub-problem. Each local controller resides on a PM. It monitors the CPU and VMs utilizations and classifies the PM into one of the Q+1 sets of discrete frequency ranges: {F_0, . . ., $F_Q = f^{max}$} by exploiting the DVFS technology. The global controller collects the states of the PMs from the local controllers and builds up a global best-plan by using the IDC scheduling algorithm, which is described in the next section. The global controller sends commands to the VMM for the optimization of the VM placement. The commands fix which VMs on a source PM should be activated. The VMM performs the dispatching of the VM tasks on the basis of the commands from the local controllers. Due to the real-time nature of the considered application scenario, the time allowed each VM to fully process each submitted task is fixed in advance at $T[s]$, *regardless* of the actual size $L(i)$ of the task currently assigned to $VM(i)$. Our model is able to work under any type of workload distribution. We only assume that each VM is capable to work at some allowed discrete processing frequency. Formally, $t(i)$ is the execution time of $VM(i)$ which works at the processing frequency $f(i)$. Therefore, the workload $L(i)$ to be processed by $VM(i)$ is: $f(i)t(i) = L(i)$.

Offered Workload and VMM

Let L_{tot} be the overall size of the job currently submitted to the IDC of Figure 1. The VMM of Figure 1 must carry out two main operations at run-time, namely, resource management and load balancing. Specifically, goal of the VMM is to adaptively control the Virtualization Layer of Figure 1. In particular, the set of the attributes which characterizes each VM is:

$$VM \triangleq \left\{ T, P_{Idle}, F_{Idle}, f^{max} \right\}, i = 1, ..., M , \tag{1}$$

where T is the maximum allowed execution time (in seconds); P_{Idle} is the power consumed by VM in the idle state (in Watt); F_{Idle} is corresponding idle frequency of the VM (in [*bit/s*]); and f^{max} is the maximum processing frequency allowed the VM (in [*bit/s*]).

Energy Models for the Computing and Reconfiguration Costs

In the following two sub-sections, we detail the adopted energy models, which account for the computing and reconfiguration costs.

Figure 2. The discrete range of frequencies considered for each VM, Case of Q = 9

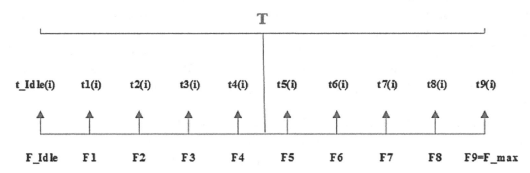

Computational Cost

The adopted model for the computing energy is based on the CPU's energy curve and VM states. DVFS is applied by the host physical servers, in order to stretch the processing times of the tasks and reduce energy consumptions. For this purpose, each server can be operated at multiple voltages which correspond to different processing frequencies (Azodolmolky, Wieder, & Yahyapour, 2013; Shojafar, Cordeschi, Amendola & Baccarelli, 2015a; Shojafar, Javanmardi, Abolfazli & Cordeschi, 2015b). Q is the finite number of discrete processing frequencies allowed each VM. Hence, we can pose:

$$A \triangleq \left\{ F_0 \equiv F_{Idle} < F_1 < F_2 < ... < F_Q \equiv f^{\max} \right\} \tag{2}$$

Figure 2 illustrates the discrete range of frequencies for the dummy case of *Q = 9*.

According to Azodolmolky, Wieder, and Yahyapour (2013), the dynamic power consumption P_{dyn} of the host CPU equates:

$$P_{dyn} = A C_{eff} f v^2, \left[Watt \right] \tag{3}$$

where *A*, C_{eff}, *f*, and *v* represent the active percentage of gates, effective capacitance load, the processor frequency and the supply voltage of the considered CPU, respectively. The frequency and voltage are correlated to each-other as: $f \infty \left(v - vth \right)^2 / v$, where *vth* is the threshold voltage (Azodolmolky, Wieder, & Yahyapour, 2013). Since the VM enters the *idle* mode at P_{Idle} power consumption, the overall energy wasted by the VM is:

$$A C_{eff} f^3 t + P_{Idle} \left(T - t \right), \left[Joule \right] \tag{4}$$

where *f* is the processing frequency, *t* is the computing time, *(T − t)* is the time-duration of the idle mode. By spreading out the working time of each VM over the allowed discrete range of frequencies, we obtain:

$\sum_{l=0}^{Q} t_l = T$, where t_0 is the duration of the idle mode. Therefore, the total energy E_{CPU} wasted by each CPU for sustaining all active VMs equates:

$$E_{CPU} = \sum_{i=1}^{M} \sum_{j=0}^{Q} A\, C_{eff} F_{ij}^{\;3} t_{ij}, [Joule] \tag{5}$$

where t_{ij} is the time interval over which *VM(i)* works at the processing frequency F_{ij} .

Reconfiguration Cost

Switching from the processing frequency f_1 to the processing frequency f_2 entails an energy cost of $E_{REC}\left(f_1;f_2\right)$ (Azodolmolky, Wieder, & Yahyapour, 2013; Qian, He, Su, Wu, Zhu, Zhang, & Zhang, 2013). Although the actual behavior of the function: $E_{REC}\left(f_1;f_2\right)$ may depend on the adopted DVFS technique and the underlying physical CPU (Mathew, Sitaraman, & Shenoy, 2012), any practical $E_{REC}\left(f_1;f_2\right)$ function typically retains the following general properties (Von Laszewski, Wang, Younge, & He, 2009; Kim, Buyya, & Kim, 2007):

1.   It depends on the absolute frequency gap: $\left|f_1 - f_2\right|$;
2. $E_{REC}\left(.\right)$ vanishes at $f_1 = f_2$ and it is not decreasing in $\left|f_1 - f_2\right|$; and,
3.   It is jointly convex in f_1, f_2.

A quite common practical model which retains the aforementioned formal properties is the following quadratic one (Mathew, Sitaraman, & Shenoy, 2012):

$$E_{REC}\left(f_1;f_2\right) = \sum_{i=1}^{M} k_e \left(f_1 - f_2\right)^2, [Joule] \tag{6}$$

where k_e [*Joule/(Hz)²*] dictates the reconfiguration cost induced by a unit-size processing frequency switching. Typical values of k_e for current DVFS-based virtualized computing platforms are limited up to few hundreds of μJs per [*MHz*] (Qian, He, Su, Wu, Zhu, Zhang, & Zhang, 2013). For sake of concreteness, the following analytical developments directly subsume the quadratic model in (6).

ENERGY CONSUMPTION IN TCP/IP-BASED INTERNET DATA CENTERS

We assume that the *i*-th end-to-end connection (e.g., the *i*-th virtual link of Figure 1) is bidirectional, symmetric and operates in a *half-duplex* way (Baliga, Ayre, Hinton, & Tucker, 2011). Furthermore, we also assume that the one-way transmission-plus-switching operation over the *i*-th link drains a (fixed) power of P_i^{net} [*Watt*]. P_i^{net} may be expressed as in: $P_i^{net} = P_T^{net}(i) + P_R^{net}(i)$, where $P_T^{net}(i)$ is the power required by the (one-way) transmission and switching and $P_R^{net}(i)$ is the power demanded by the receive circuit of the i-th virtual link of Figure 1. The actual value of P_i^{net} depends on the switching unit, the noise affecting the i-th link, as well as the demanded reliability (Baccarelli, & Biagi, 2003a, 2004). In the sequel, we assume that the set of link powers: { P_i^{net}, $i = 1, \ldots, M$} are assigned. In principle, the links may be wireless, wired or hybrid, and, furthermore, they may also exhibit heterogeneous transmission capabilities (Baccarelli, Biagi, Bruno, Conti, & Gregori, 2005; Baccarelli, & Biagi, 2003b). A joint analysis of the computing-plus-networking energy consumption in delay-tolerant data centers is performed in (Portnoy, 2012), where the effects of inter and intra-cloud networking infrastructures are evaluated. Two main conclusions arise from (Portnoy, 2012). First, the energy consumption due to data transport may represent a large part of the total energy consumption, especially at medium/high bandwidth usage. Second, the energy consumption of virtualized IDCs needs to be analyzed by simultaneously accounting for data computing and data transport.

Motivated by these considerations and in order to limit the implementation cost, current IDCs utilize off-the-shelf rackmount physical servers which are interconnected by commodity Fast/Giga Ethernet switches. Furthermore, they implement legacy TCP protocol (mainly, the TCP NewReno one) for attaining end-to-end (typically, multi-hop) reliable communication (Mishra, Jain, & Durresi, 2012). In this regard, we note that the data center-oriented versions of the legacy TCP New Reno suite proposed in (Das & Sivalingam, 2013) allow the managed end-to-end transport connections to operate in the Congestion Avoidance state during 99.9% of the overall working time, while assuring the same end-to-end reliable throughput of legacy TCP NewReno protocol. This means, in turn, that the average throughput R_i [*bit/s*] of the i-th virtual link of Figure 1 (i.e., the i-th end-to-end transport connection from/to VMM to/from *VM* (i)) equates (Tamm, Hermsmeyer, & Rush, 2010),

$$R_i = \sqrt{\frac{3}{2v}} \frac{MSS}{RTT_i \sqrt{\overline{P_i}^{Loss}}}, i = 1,...,M ,$$ (7)

where *MSS* [*bit*] is the maximum segment size, $v \in \{1,2\}$ is the number of per-ACK acknowledged segments, $\overline{RTT_i}$ is the average round-trip-time of the i-th end-to-end connection, and $\overline{P_i}^{Loss}$ is the average segment loss probability experienced by the i-th connection. Several studies point out that $\overline{P_i}^{Loss}$ scales down for increasing P_i^{net} as in (Liu, Zhou, & Giannakis, 2004):

$$\overline{P_i}^{Loss} = \left(g_i P_i^{net}\right)^{-d}, i = 1,...,M ,$$ (8)

where g_i [*Watt*]$^{-1}$ is the coding gain-to-receive noise power ratio of the i-th end-to-end connection, while the positive exponent d measures the diversity gain provided by the frequency-time interleaving implemented at the Physical layer. Hence, after introducing (8) in (7), we obtain:

$$P_i^{net} = \Omega_i \left(\overline{RTT_i} R_i\right)^\alpha, i = 1,...,M$$ (9)

with $a \triangleq \left(2/d\right) \geq 1$, and $\Omega_i \equiv \frac{1}{g_i} \left[\frac{1}{MSS} \sqrt{\frac{2v}{3}} \right]^{\alpha}$, $i = 1,...,M$. Hence, the corresponding one-way transmission delay equates: $D\left(i\right) = \left(f\left(i\right)t\left(i\right)/R\left(i\right)\right)$, while the corresponding one-way communication energy E_i^{NET} for all active VMs is:

$$E_i^{NET} = \Omega_i \left(\overline{RTT_i}R_i\right)^{\alpha} D\left(i\right), i = 1,...,M. \tag{10}$$

VIRTUAL-TO-PHYSICAL QOS RESOURCE MAPPING IN VIRTULAIZED IDCS

Due to the hard delay-sensitive feature of the considered services, the Virtualization Layer of Figure 1 *must guarantee* that the demands for the computing $\{F_{ij}\}$ and communication $\{R_i\}$ rates done available by the VMM are mapped onto adequate (i.e., large enough) computing (e.g., CPU cycles) and communication (e.g., link bandwidths) physical supplies. In our setting, efficient QoS mapping of the virtual demands $\{F_{ij}\}$ for the computing resources may be actually implemented by equipping the Virtualization Layer of Figure 1 with a per-VM queue system that implements the (recently proposed) *mClock* scheduling discipline (Gulati, Merchant, & Varman, 2010; Hosseinabadi, Siar, Shamshirband, Shojafar, & Nasir, 2014). Interestingly enough, Table 1 of (Gulati, Merchant, & Varman, 2010) points out that the *mClock* scheduler works on a per-VM basis and provides:

1. Resource isolation;
2. Proportionally fair resource allocation; and,
3. Hard (i.e., absolute) resource reservation.

Table 1. Main taxonomy of the chapter

Symbol	Meaning/Role
$MSS\ [bit]$	Maximum size of a TCP segment
$\overline{RTT}_i\ [s]$	Average round-trip-time of the i-th end-to-end virtual connection
A	Active percentage of the gate of the CPU processor
$C_{eff}\ [Farad]$	Effective capacitance load of the CPU processor
$f^{max}\ [bit\ /\ s]$	Maximum allowed processing frequency
$F_{Idle}\ [bit\ /\ s]$	Computing frequency in the idle mode

continued on following page

Table 1. Continued

Symbol	Meaning/Role
$F_{ij}\ [bit\ /\ s]$	j-th computing frequency of *VM(i)*
$L_{tot}\ [bit]$	Job size (workload size)
$R_i\ [bit\ /\ s]$	Communication rate of the i-th end-to-end virtual connection
$R_t\ [bit\ /\ s]$	Aggregate communication rate of the VLAN of Figure 1
$T\ [s]$	Per-job maximum allowed computing time
$t_{ij}\ [s]$	Computing time of *VM(i)* working at F_{ij}
$T_t\ [s]$	Per-job maximum allowed computing-plus-communication time
$P_{Idle}\ [Watt]$	Idle power
$P_i^{net}\ [Watt]$	Power consumed by the i-th end-to-end virtual connection
$P_i^{idle}\ [Watt]$	Power consumed by the i-th virtual connection in the idle mode
$E_{tot}\ [Joule]$	Total consumed energy
$E_{CPU}\ [Joule]$	Computing energy
$E_{REC}\ [Joule]$	Reconfiguration energy
$E^{NET}\ [Joule]$	Network energy
M	Maximum number of available VMs
$Q+1$	Number of discrete processing frequencies allowed each VM
PMR	Peak-to-Mean Ratio of the offered workload

About the TCP-based networking virtualization, several (quite recent) contributions (Alizadeh, Greenberg, Maltz, Padhye, Patel, Prabhakar, & Sridharan, 2011; Ballani, Costa, Karagiannis, & Rowstron, 2011; Guo, Lu, Wang, Yang, Kong, Sun, &Zhang, 2010; Xia, Cui, Lange, Tang, Dinda, & Bridges, 2012; Ballani, Costa, Karagiannis, & Rowstron, 2011) point out that the most appealing property of emerging data centers for the support of delay-sensitive services is the *agility*, i.e., the capability to assign arbitrary physical server to *any* service *without* experiencing performance degradation. To this end, it is recognized that the virtual network atop the Virtualization Layer should provide a *flat* networking abstraction (Mishra, Jain, & Durresi, 2012). The Middleware layer architecture of the considered IDC in Figure 1 is aligned, indeed, with this requirement and, then, it is *general enough* to allow the implementation of *agile* data centers. Specifically, according to (Mishra, Jain, & Durresi, 2012), the IDC of Figure 1 may work in tandem with *any* Network Virtualization Layer that is capable to map the rate-demands $\{R_i\}$ onto bandwidth-guaranteed end-to-end (possibly, multi-hop) connections over the actually available underlying physical network. Just as examples of practical state-of-the-art Networking Virtualization tools, *Oktopous* (Ballani, Costa, Karagiannis, & Rowstron, 2011) provides a contention-free switched LAN abstraction atop tree-shaped physical network topologies. Furthermore, *SecondNet* (Guo, Lu, Wang, Yang, Kong, Sun, &Zhang, 2010) and *VNET/P* (Xia, Cui, Lange, Tang, Dinda, & Bridges, 2012) provide bandwidth-guaranteed virtualized Ethernet-type contention-free LAN environments atop *any* TCP-based end-to-end connection. For this purpose, *SeconNet* implements Port-Switching based Source Routing (PSSR), while *VNET/P* relies on suitable Layer2 Tunneling Protocols. An updated survey of emerging contention-free virtual networking technologies is provided by (Mishra, Jain, & Durresi, 2012). In all cases, the goal to be pursued is the minimization (on a per-job basis) of the overall resulting communication-plus-computing energy, formally defined as in

$$E_{tot} = E_{CPU} + E_{REC} + E^{NET} [Joule].$$ (11)

This energy depends, in turn, on the (one-way) delays $\{D(i), i = 1, \ldots, M\}$ introduced by the VLAN of Figure 1 and the allowed per-task processing time T. Specifically, since the M virtual connections are typically activated by the Switch Unit in a parallel fashion, the overall two-way communication-plus-computing delay induced by the i-th end-to-end connection of Figure 1 equates: $2D(i) + T$, so that the hard constraint on the overall per-job execution time reads as in:

$$\max_{1 \le i \le M} \left\{ 2D(i) \right\} + T \le T_t.$$ (12)

Table 1 summarizes the main notations of this chapter.

THE OPTIMIZATION PROBLEM AND THE SOLUTION APPROACH

The proposed scheduler we present here aims at minimizing the per-job total energy consumption by selecting the best resource allocation based on the current load level and link states. In detail, it is able to obtain the optimum minimum-energy values for the processing frequencies of the VMs and the transmission rates of the VLAN of Figure 1. Since each VM may move from one of its discrete frequency to another one for performing the assigned task, the overall considered discrete optimization problem assumes the following form:

$$\min_{\{R_i, t_{ij}\}} \left\{ \sum_{i=1}^{M} \sum_{j=0}^{Q} \left[A\, C_{eff} F_{ij}^{\ 3} t_{ij} \right] + E_{REC} + \sum_{i=1}^{M} \sum_{j=1}^{Q} 2 P_i^{net} \left(R_i \right) \left(\frac{F_{ij} t_{ij}}{R_i} \right) \right\},$$ (13.1)

s.t:

$$\sum_{i=1}^{M}\sum_{j=1}^{Q} F_{ij}t_{ij} = L_{tot}, \tag{13.2}$$

$$\sum_{j=0}^{Q} t_{ij} \leq T, i = 1,...M, \tag{13.3}$$

$$\sum_{j=1}^{Q} \frac{2F_{ij}t_{ij}}{R_i} + T \leq T_t, i = 1,...,M, \tag{13.4}$$

$$\sum_{i=1}^{M} R_i \leq R_t. \tag{13.5}$$

The first term in (13.1) accounts for the computing energy of each VM, the second term is the reconfiguration/switching cost, and the last term accounts for the communication cost. Furthermore, Equation (13.2) is the (global) constraint which guarantees that the overall job is decomposed into M parallel tasks. Thus, the product: $F_{ij}t_{ij}$ is the current workload to be processed by $VM(i)$ working at F_{ij}. The total time T for the computation is bounded as in Equation (13.3). From this equation and Figure 1, we understand that the summation of time-quotas for each active VM must be not larger than the allowed computation time. The (global) constraint in (13.4) forces the Cloud to process the overall job within the assigned hard deadline T_t, and, then, it guarantees that the overall communication-computing platform operates in hard real-time. Finally, the inequality in (13.5) ensures that the overall bandwidth wasted by the VLAN of Figure 1 is less than the maximum allowed one R_t.

Remark 1: Computing E_{REC}

The second term in (13.1) can be split into two reconfiguration costs. The first one is the cost incurred when $VM(i)$ changes the processing frequency from F_{ij} to $F_{i(j+k)}$ (i.e., k steps movement to reach to the next active discrete frequency) and spans $t_{i(j+k)}$ seconds. The second cost is the reconfiguration cost for the external-switching from the current final discrete frequency $\left(F_{ij}^0\right)$ to the first discrete frequency for the next incoming job. It is worth nothing that the active discrete frequencies are found based on the related time-quota variables. In other words, we track each active discrete frequency (F_{ij}) while the constraint $t_{ij} > 0$ is met. So, we have a list of active discrete frequencies for each VM on a per-job basis. The switch from the current active discrete frequency to the next active discrete frequency affects the reconfiguration cost. We use the FCFS (First-Come, First-Serve) scheduling policy for visiting each frequency in the active frequency list of each $VM(i)$. It means that, in the $VM(i)$'s active discrete frequency list, we start from the first active discrete frequency (F_{ik}) and, then, move to the second active discrete frequency in the list ($F_{i(k+1)}$). Therefore, we calculate the difference as follows: $\Delta F_{ik} = F_{i(k+1)} - F_{ik}$, and the resulting reconfiguration energy cost as: $k_e \left(\Delta F_{ik}^{\ 2} \right) [Joule]$. We continue until the end of the *VM(i)*'s list. In the (specific) case of homogeneous VMs, the total cost of internal switching for all VMs is: $k_e \sum_{i=1}^{M} \sum_{k=0}^{K} (\Delta F_{ik})^2$, where: $K \leq Q$ is the number of active discrete frequencies allowed *VM(i)*. On the other hand, the external-switching cost: *Ext_Cost* is calculated by multiplying by k_e the quadratic difference between the last active discrete frequency of *VM(i)* for the current job and the first active discrete frequency of *VM(i)* for the next incoming job. In a nutshell, the total reconfiguration energy can be written as:

$$E_{REC} \equiv k_e \sum_{i=1}^{M} \sum_{k=0}^{K} \left(\Delta F_{ik} \right)^2 + k_e \sum_{i=1}^{M} Ext\_Cost .$$

In the worst case of $K = Q$, we need to move Q steps from F_0. Formally speaking, we need to visit all the possible active discrete frequencies of each *VM(i)*, so that: $k_e M \sum_{k=0}^{K} \left(\Delta F_k \right)^2$, and the external-switching cost is: $k_e M \left(F_Q^t - F_Q^{t-1} \right)^2$.

Remark 2: Cache Memory and Cache Miss Rate

The developed model for the VNetDC of Figure 1 subsumes the assumption that each VM is equipped with a local cache memory which stores all data needed for processing the assigned tasks. As a consequence, the resulting per-VM cache miss rates vanish and no delay/energy costs are incurred, in order to access to nonlocal miss memory pages. This assumption may be, indeed, reasonable for streaming applications, which must operate in real-time and require strict limits on the overall in-Cloud processing times (Hirzel, Soulé, Schneider, Gedik & Grimm, 2014). This assumption may be also reasonable in emerging virtualized data centers equipped with Network Attached Storage (NAS) devices, which are uniformly accessible from all the instantiated VMs through dedicated high-speed TenGigabit single-hop LANs (Portnoy, 2012). However, it may be more critical in traditional large-size production data centers which operate under relaxed processing times, process heterogeneous workloads and are not equipped with dedicated NAS devices and dedicated storage LANs. Modeling the time/energy penalty induced by cache memory miss rates and the resulting limitations induced on the maximum allowed switching rate of the processed tasks is, indeed, an interesting topic under investigation by the authors.

The reported version of the problem in (13) is non-convex, due to the non-convexity of the communication terms of the objective function in (13.1). However, it may be turned into an equivalent (possibly, feasible) convex problem, as pointed out by the following *Proposition 1*.

Proposition 1: The expression of E_i^{NET} can be written into the following convex form

$$\sum_{i=1}^{M} \sum_{j=1}^{Q} 2 P_i^{net} \left(R_i \right) \left(\frac{F_{ij} t_{ij}}{R_i} \right) = \left(T_t - T \right) \sum_{i=1}^{M} \sum_{j=1}^{Q} P_i^{net} \left(\frac{2 F_{ij} t_{ij}}{\left(T_t - T \right)} \right), \tag{14}$$

which is convex in the involved variables.

About the feasibility of the resource problem in (13), the following result holds.

Proposition 2: The following set of conditions is necessary and sufficient for the feasibility of the optimization problem in (13.1)-(13.5):

$$L_{tot} \leq R_t \frac{\left(T_t - T\right)}{2},$$ (15.1)

$$L_{tot} \leq \sum_{i=1}^{M} f^{\max} T.$$ (15.2)

The Algorithm 1 presents the steps implemented by the proposed scheduler, in order to allocate the minimum-energy computing-plus-communication resources needed for processing each input job.

TEST RESULTS AND PERFORMANCE COMPARISONS

This section presents the tested energy performance of the proposed IDC scheduler for a set of offered workloads. The tests are carried out by using the simulator we developed, named TEST-DVFS. TEST-DVFS simulates DVFS-enabled data centers by enabling DVFS functionalities not only for the components performance model but also for the offered workloads and energy model.

THE IMPLEMENTED TESTBED

Specifically, the TEST-DVFS tool consists of the following modules:

- **Workload Module:** This module is developed to simulate various types of offered workloads;
- **Component Module:** This module emulates all the considered components of the system, e.g., VMs, links and DVFS platform;
- **Working Module:** The working module implements the energy model, scheduling type and network topology.

TEST-DVFS is applied under two different scenarios. The first scenario focuses on the low number of VMs, incoming workloads, and the second scenario focuses on multiple huge amount of VMs and workloads, as detailed in Table 2 and Table 3, respectively. The main difference between the considered scenarios is the corresponding communication parameters. The second scenario uses Equation (9) for the network cost. Specifically, in order to account for the effects of the reconfiguration costs and time-fluctuations of the offered workload on the energy performance of the tested schedulers, we model the offered workload as an independent identically distributed (i.i.d) random sequence $\left\{ \overline{L}_{tot}(m), m = 0,1,..., \right\}$, whose samples are evenly distributed over the interval $\left[\overline{L}_{tot} - a, \overline{L}_{tot} + a \right]$, with $\overline{L}_{tot} = \{8, 70\}$ [*Gbit*]. Furthermore, we pose *a=2* [*Gbit*] with *PMR = 1.25* and $\overline{L}_{tot}$ = *8* in scenario 1, and: *a=10* [*Gbit*], PMR

Algorithm 1. IDC Algorithm

1. Set $\left(M,T,T_t\right)$ // General SLA parameters

2. Set $\left(Q,F_0,f^{\max},A,C_{eff}\right)$ // Computing parameters

3. Set $\left(k_e,R_t\right)$ // Link parameters

4. Receive L_{tot}

5. Feasibility condition in Proposition 2

6. $b_1=\left(L_{tot}\leq R_t\dfrac{\left(T_t-T\right)}{2}\right)$

7. $b_2=\left(L_{tot}\leq\displaystyle\sum_{i=1}^{M}f^{\max}T\right)$

8. If $\neg\left(b_1,b_2\right)$ then

9. error('Program is not feasible')

10. else

11. Minimize $\left(\varepsilon_{tot}\right)$ //using Equation (13.1)

12. Subject to:

13. Constraints: Equations (13.2)-(13.5)

14. End If

15. Return $\varepsilon_{tot},\varepsilon_{CPU},\varepsilon_{REC},\varepsilon^{NET},\{F_{ij}\},\{R_i\}$.

Table 2. Default values of the main tested parameters under the first scenario

Symbol	Value	Symbol	Value
M	[1…10]	T_t	7 [s]
R_t	100 [Gbit/s]	C_{eff}	1 [Farad]
k_e	0.05 [Joule/ (GHz)²]	A	1
F	F_I [GHz]	Q	4
P_i^{idle}	0.5 [Watt]	F_0	0.15 [GHz]
T	5 [s]	f^{max}	2.688 [GHz]

Table 3. Default values of the main tested parameters under the second scenario

Symbol	Value	Symbol	Value
M	$\{20, 30, 40\}$	$\Omega i, \alpha$	0.5,0.5 [*Watt*]
F	F_2 [*GHz*]	$\bar{L}_{tot}$	70 [*Gbit*]
k_e	0.005 [*Joule/ (GHz)^2*]	f^{max}	0.933 [*GHz*]

$= 1.1428$ and $\bar{L}_{tot} = 70$ in scenario 2. The discrete frequencies for the first scenario are taken from Intel Nehalem Quad-core Processor (Kimura, Sato, Hotta, Boku, & Takahashi, 2006), e.g., $F_1 = \{0.300; 0.533; 0.667; 0.800; 0.933\}$. For the second scenario, we considered the power-scalable real Crusoe cluster with TM-5800 CPU in (Almeida, Almeida, Ardagna, Cunha, Francalanci, & Trubian, 2010), e.g., $F_2 = \{0.15; 1.867; 2.133; 2.533; 2.668\}$. Each tested point has been evaluated by averaging over 1000 independent runs.

In order to evaluate the per-job average communication-plus-computing energy E_{tot} [*Joule*] consumed by the proposed IDC scheduler, we have implemented its prototype under paravirtualized Xen 3.3 Linux 2.6.18 as guest OS kernel (see Figure 1). The adaptive scheduler has been implemented in SW at the driver domain (i.e., Dom0) of the legacy Xen 3.3. Interestingly enough, out of approximately 1100 lines of SW code needed for implementing the proposed scheduler, 45% is directly reused from existing Xen/ Linux code. The reused code includes part of the Linux's TCP New Reno congestion control suite and Xen's I/O buffer management. The tested setup comprises four Dell PowerEdge servers, with 3.06 GHz Intel Xeon CPU and 4GB of RAM. All servers are connected through commodity Fast Ethernet NICs. In all carried out tests, we configure the VMs with 512MB of memory and utilize the TCP New Reno suite for implementing the needed VM-to-VM transport connections.

TEST RESULTS

In this section, we compare the energy performance of the proposed IDC scheduler against the corresponding ones of some state-of-the-art schedulers, namely, the IDEAL and Standard schedulers (Cordeschi, Shojafar, Amendola & Baccarelli, 2014b) and the (more recent) NetDC scheduler (Cordeschi, Shojafar & Baccarelli, 2013). In order to put the reported performance comparisons under the right perspective, we point out that the IDEAL scheduler subsumes the following (quite optimistic) assumptions:

1. All the reconfiguration costs are negligible; and,
2. Each VM operates over a continued (e.g., no discrete) spectrum of processing frequencies.

Hence, its energy performance is the best one and acts as an ultimate benchmark. The Standard scheduler does not employ DVFS-enabled technological platforms and, then, it does not allow to dynamically scale up/down the processing frequencies and the communication rates of the VMs and VLAN of Figure 1. Hence, the Standard scheduler constantly operates at the maximum processing frequencies and communication rates, regardless of the size of the currently submitted job. As a consequence, the

Standard scheduler does not incur reconfiguration costs, but it constantly wastes the maximum computing-plus-communication energy. Finally, the NetDC scheduler adaptively scales up/down the computing frequencies and communication rates and, then, it is affected by the corresponding reconfiguration costs. However, it allows the instantiated VMs to operate over a continued (e.g., no discrete) spectrum of computing frequencies.

Hence, we expect that the energy consumption of the proposed IDC scheduler is larger (resp., smaller) than the one of the IDEAL (resp., Standard) scheduler, while it approaches (from the above) the energy consumption of the NetDC scheduler when the number M of instantiated VMs and/or the number Q of the per-VM allowed processing frequencies increase. The plots of Figures 3-6 confirm, indeed, these expectations. In a nutshell, they point out that the energy gaps suffered by the proposed IDC scheduler with respect to the IDEAL and NetDC ones are quite limited, while the IDC scheduler (largely) outperforms the Standard one.

Specifically, Figures 3-6 present the average values of E_{tot}, E_{CPU}, E_{REC} and E^{NET} under the IDC, IDEAL, Standard, and NetDC schedulers (see Figures 3, 4, 5, 6, respectively). Figure 3 points out that, barring the Standard scheduler, by increasing the VM number, the average total cost for all schedulers decreases. In fact, while the number of VMs is increased, the capability to respond to the offered workloads will be higher, so that less quota of L_{tot} will be assigned to each VM. On the other hand, the Standard scheduler focuses on the next active discrete frequency for each frequency of the $VM(i)$, that means that, for $M = 2$, it goes up, because it works at f^{max} for each $VM(i)$. In Figure 4, although the curves increase for $M > 2$, this does not affect the computing cost too-much, because the proposed scheduler is able to manage the running time for each active discrete frequency even when M is low (e.g., $M < 4$) or

Figure 3. E_{tot} for the four tested schedulers at PMR = 1.25

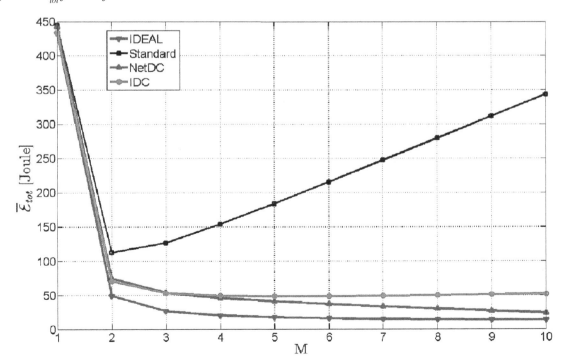

high, (e.g., *M > 20*). Figure 5 points out that the IDC scheduler considers two costs (internal-switching and external-switching) for each *VM(i)* in each incoming workload. So, it suffers from increased reconfiguration costs compared to the NetDC scheduler (Cordeschi, Shojafar & Baccarelli, 2013). Since the IDC scheduler allows only a finite number Q of processing frequencies, we expect that its reconfiguration costs are (somewhat) larger than the corresponding ones of the NetDC scheduler. Figure 5 confirms, indeed, this expectation. However, it also points out that the resulting energy gap is limited up to $2.5 - 3\left[Joule\right]$ and tends to stay constant even for increasing values of M. The reconfiguration costs of the IDEAL and Standard scheduler vanish by design and, then, they are not reported in Figure 5. Lastly, Figure 6 highlights that the communication cost of the NetDC and Standard schedulers are nearly the same. However, the energy consumption of the proposed IDC scheduler is about 10% less than aforementioned schedulers, because the IDC scheduler is capable to compute suitable working times for the active discrete frequencies on a per-job basis.

Figure 7 reports the tested average execution-times at *M = 2* and *M = 10*. Specifically, for increasing M, the matrices in programming increase and the per-VM execution times grow. Figure 8 presents the total average consumed energies in the aforementioned schedulers at *M = 20, 30* and *40*. It points out that, by increasing the number of VMs, the energy decreases and the decrement rate of the IDC scheduler approaches the one of the NetDC scheduler.

Figure 4. E_{CPU} for the four tested schedulers at PMR = 1.25

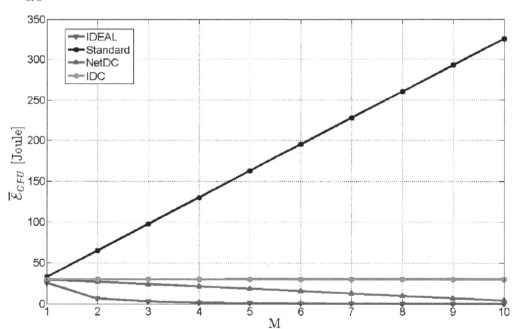

Figure 5. E_{REC} for the four tested schedulers at PMR = 1.25

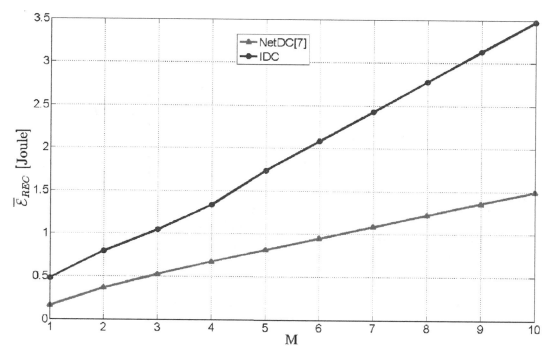

Figure 6. E^{NET} for the four tested schedulers at PMR = 1.25

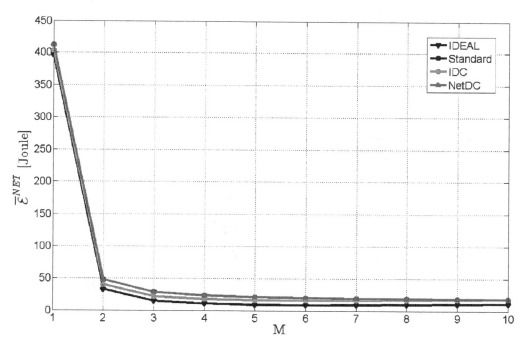

Figure 7. Per-VM average execution times under the first test scenario

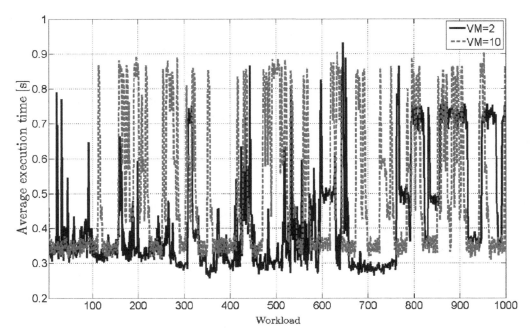

Figure 8. Average total energy in (13.1) for the second test scenario

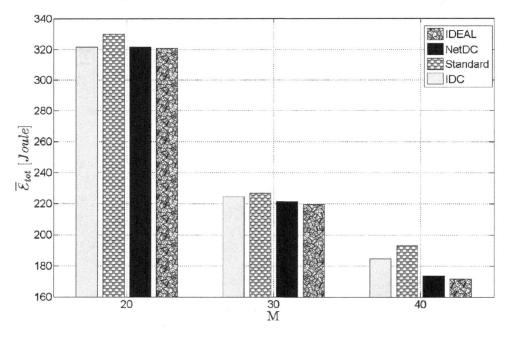

PERFORMANCE COMPARISONS UNDER TIME-CORRELATED REAL-WORLD WORKLOAD TRACES

These conclusions are confirmed by the numerical results of this subsection, that refer to the real-world (e.g., not synthetic) workload trace of Figure 9. This is the same real-world workload trace considered in (Urgaonkar, Kozat, Igarashi, & Neely, 2010). The tests of this subsection refer to the communication-computing infrastructure of Figure 1 at $k_e = 0.5 \; [Joule/(MHz)^2]$ and $T = 1.2 \; [s]$. Furthermore, in order to maintain the peak workload fixed at *16 [Mbit/slot]*, we assume that each arrival of Figure 9 carries out a workload of *0.533 [Mbit]*. Since the (numerically evaluated) PMR of the workload trace of Figure 9 is limited up to *1.526* and the corresponding time-covariance coefficient is large and approaches 0.966, the workload trace of Figure 9 is smoother (e.g., it exhibits less time-variations) than the previously considered ones. Hence, we expect that the corresponding performance gaps of the IDC scheduler over the Standard one is somewhat less than those previously reported for the case of time-uncorrelated workloads. However, according to our tests, even under the (strongly) time-correlated workload trace of Figure 9, the average energy reduction of the proposed IDC scheduler over the Standard one is nearly 40%.

Figure 9. Measured workload trace; the corresponding PMR and covariance coefficient equate 1.526 and 0.966, respectively.

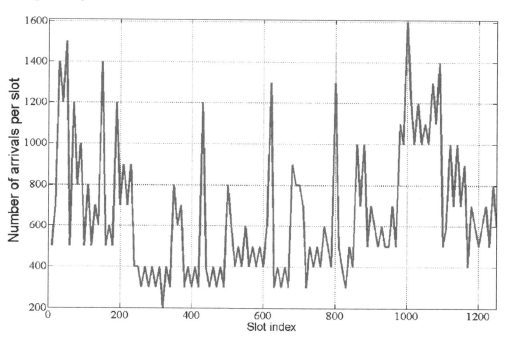

CONCLUSION

The goal of this chapter is to present an online energy-aware resource provisioning scheduler for virtual machines in DVFS-enabled Internet data centers, and highlight the key techniques and formal policies that minimize the data center's energy consumption. In the process, we identified the sources of energy consumptions in data centers and presented high-level solutions.

The carried out tests highlight that the average energy savings provided by the proposed IDC scheduler over the Standard one may approach 85%. This is due to the fact that the IDC scheduler is capable of properly managing not-only the online workload, but also the inter-switching costs among the active discrete frequencies for each VM. The interesting point is that the proposed IDC scheduler is able to approach the performance of the IDEAL one about 10% faster than the NetDC scheduler when the communication cost is also considered. Due to the considered hard real-time constrains, in our framework, the size L_{tot} of the incoming job is measured at the beginning of the corresponding slot and, then, it remains constant over the slot duration T_t. As a consequence, the scheduling policy considered here is of clairvoyant-type, and this implies, in turn, that migrations of VMs are not to be considered. However, under soft delay constraints, intra-slot job arrivals may take place. Hence, the optimal resource provisioning policy could be no longer of clairvoyant-type, so that live migrations and VMs consolidation could become effective means to further reduce the energy costs. The development of adaptive mechanisms for planning at runtime minimum-energy live migrations of VMs is a second research topic of potential interest.

REFERENCES

Alizadeh, M., Greenberg, A., Maltz, D. A., Padhye, J., Patel, P., Prabhakar, B., & Sridharan, M. (2011). Data center tcp (dctcp). *Computer Communication Review*, *41*(4), 63–74.

Almeida, J., Almeida, V., Ardagna, D., Cunha, ´. I., Francalanci, C., & Trubian, M. (2010). Joint admission control and resource allocation in virtualized servers. *Journal of Parallel and Distributed Computing*, *70*(4), 344–362. doi:10.1016/j.jpdc.2009.08.009

Assunc̜, M. D., Calheiros, R. N., Bianchi, S., Netto, M. A., & Buyya, R. (2014). Big data computing and clouds: Trends and future directions. *Journal of Parallel and Distributed Computing*, *79-80*, 3–15. doi:10.1016/j.jpdc.2014.08.003

Azodolmolky, S., Wieder, P., & Yahyapour, R. (2013). Cloud computing networking: Challenges and opportunities for innovations. *Communications Magazine, IEEE*, *51*(7), 54–62. doi:10.1109/MCOM.2013.6553678

Baccarelli, E., & Biagi, M. (2003a). Optimized power allocation and signal shaping for interference-limited multi-antenna "ad hoc" networks. In Personal Wireless Communications, LNCS (Vol. 2775, pp. 138-152). Springer Verlag.

Baccarelli, E., & Biagi, M. (2003b). Error resistant space-time coding for emerging 4G-WLANs. Proceedings of WCNC'03 (pp.72-77).

Baccarelli, E., & Biagi, M. (2004). Power–allocation policy and optimized design of multiple-antenna systems with imperfect channel estimation. *IEEE Transactions on Vehicular Technology, 52*(1), 136–145. doi:10.1109/TVT.2003.822025

Baccarelli, E., Biagi, M., Bruno, R., Conti, M., & Gregori, E. (2005). Broadband wireless access networks: a road map on emerging trends and standards. In *Broadband services: business models and technologies for community networks* (pp. 215–240). John Wiley & Sons. doi:10.1002/0470022515.ch14

Baccarelli, E., Cordeschi, N., & Patriarca, T. (2012). Jointly optimal source-flow, transmit-power, and sending-rate control for maximum-throughput delivery of VBR traffic over faded links. *IEEE Transactions on Mobile Computing, 11*(3), 390–401. doi:10.1109/TMC.2011.68

Baliga, J., Ayre, R. W., Hinton, K., & Tucker, R. (2011). Green cloud computing: Balancing energy in processing, storage, and transport. *Proceedings of the IEEE, 99*(1), 149–167. doi:10.1109/JPROC.2010.2060451

Ballani, H., Costa, P., Karagiannis, T., & Rowstron, A. (2011). Towards predictable datacenter networks. *Computer Communication Review, 41*(4), 242–253. doi:10.1145/2043164.2018465

Cordeschi, N., Amendola, D., & Baccarelli, E. (2014a). Primary-secondary resource-management on vehicular networks under soft and hard collision constraints. *Proceedings of the fourth ACM international symposium on Development and analysis of intelligent vehicular networks and applications* (pp. 161-168). ACM. doi:10.1145/2656346.2656362

Cordeschi, N., Polli, V., & Baccarelli, E. (2012). Traffic engineering for wireless connectionless access networks supporting QoS-demanding media applications. *Computer Networks, 56*(1), 186–197. doi:10.1016/j.comnet.2011.08.016

Cordeschi, N., Shojafar, M., Amendola, D., & Baccarelli, E. (2014b). Energy-efficient adaptive networked datacenters for the QoS support of real-time applications. *The Journal of Supercomputing, 71*(2), 448–478. doi:10.1007/s11227-014-1305-8

Cordeschi, N., Shojafar, M., Amendola, D., & Baccarelli, E. (2015). Energy-Saving QoS Resource Management of Virtualized Networked Data Centers for Big Data Stream Computing. In S. Bagchi (Ed.), *Emerging Research in Cloud Distributed Computing Systems* (pp. 122–155). Hershey, PA, USA: IGI Global. doi:10.4018/978-1-4666-8213-9.ch004

Cordeschi, N., Shojafar, M., & Baccarelli, E. (2013). Energy-saving self-configuring networked data centers. *Computer Networks, 57*(17), 3479–3491. doi:10.1016/j.comnet.2013.08.002

Cugola, G., & Margara, A. (2012). Processing flows of information: From data stream to complex event processing. *ACM Computing Surveys, 44*(3), 15. doi:10.1145/2187671.2187677

Daliri, Z. S., Shamshirband, S., & Besheli, M. A. (2011). Railway security through the use of wireless sensor networks based on fuzzy logic. *Int. J. Phys. Sci, 6*(3), 448–458.

Das, T., & Sivalingam, K. M. (2013). TCP improvements for data center networks. *Proceedings of the 2013 fifth international conference on Communication systems and networks* (pp. 1–10). doi:doi:10.1109/COMSNETS.2013.6465539 doi:10.1109/COMSNETS.2013.6465539

Drugarin, C. V. A., Ahmad, M. A., Ahmad, N. A., & Lyashenko, V. (2015). Algorithmic Research and Application Using the Rayleigh Method. *Int. Journal of Science & Research*, *4*(4), 1669–1671.

Gulati, A., Merchant, A., & Varman, P. J. (2010). mclock: handling throughput variability for hypervisor io scheduling.*Proceedings of the 9th usenix conference on operating systems design and implementation* (pp. 1–7).

Guo, C., Lu, G., Wang, H. J., Yang, S., Kong, C., Sun, P., & Zhang, Y. (2010). Secondnet: a data center network virtualization architecture with bandwidth guarantees.*Proceedings of the 6th international conference* (p. 15). doi:10.1145/1921168.1921188

Hirzel, M., Soulé, R., Schneider, S., Gedik, B., & Grimm, R. (2014). A catalog of stream processing optimizations. *ACM Computing Surveys*, *46*(4), 46. doi:10.1145/2528412

Hosseinabadi, A. A. R., Siar, H., Shamshirband, S., Shojafar, M., & Nasir, M. H. N. M. (2014). Using the gravitational emulation local search algorithm to solve the multi-objective flexible dynamic job shop scheduling problem in Small and Medium Enterprises. *Annals of Operations Research*, *229*(1), 451–474. doi:10.1007/s10479-014-1770-8

Javanmardi, S., Shojafar, M., Amendola, D., Cordeschi, N., Liu, H., & Abraham, A. (2014, January). Hybrid job scheduling algorithm for cloud computing environment.*Proceedings of the Fifth International Conference on Innovations in Bio-Inspired Computing and Applications IBICA 2014* (pp. 43-52). Springer International Publishing. doi:10.1007/978-3-319-08156-4_5

Khan, A. N., Kiah, M. M., Madani, S. A., Ali, M., & Shamshirband, S. (2014). Incremental proxy re-encryption scheme for mobile cloud computing environment. *The Journal of Supercomputing*, *68*(2), 624–651. doi:10.1007/s11227-013-1055-z

Kim, K. H., Buyya, R., & Kim, J. (2007). *Power aware scheduling of bag-of-tasks applications with deadline constraints on dvs-enabled clusters* (Vol. 7, pp. 541–548). Ccgrid. doi:10.1109/CCGRID.2007.85

Kimura, H., Sato, M., Hotta, Y., Boku, T., & Takahashi, D. (2006). Empirical study on reducing energy of parallel programs using slack reclamation by dvfs in a power-scalable high performance cluster. Proceedings of the 2006 IEEE international conference on Cluster computing (pp. 1–10).

Liu, Q., Zhou, S., & Giannakis, G. B. (2004). Cross-layer combining of adaptive modulation and coding with truncated arq over wireless links. *IEEE Transactions on Wireless Communications*, *3*(5), 1746–1755. doi:10.1109/TWC.2004.833474

Lu, T., Chen, M., & Andrew, L. L. (2013). Simple and effective dynamic provisioning for power-proportional data centers. *Parallel and Distributed Systems. IEEE Transactions on*, *24*(6), 1161–1171.

Mathew, V., Sitaraman, R. K., & Shenoy, P. (2012). Energy-aware load balancing in content delivery networks. Proceedings of IEEE INFOCOM '12 (pp. 954–962). doi:doi:10.1109/INFCOM.2012.6195846 doi:10.1109/INFCOM.2012.6195846

Mishra, A., Jain, R., & Durresi, A. (2012). Cloud computing: Networking and communication challenges. *IEEE Communications Magazine*, *50*(9), 24–25. doi:10.1109/MCOM.2012.6295707

Pioro, M., & Medhi, D. (2004). *Routing, flow, and capacity design in communication and computer networks. Elsevier.*

Portnoy, M. (2012). *Virtualization essentials.* John Wiley & Sons.

Qian, Z., He, Y., Su, C., Wu, Z., Zhu, H., Zhang, T., & Zhang, Z. et al. (2013). Timestream: Reliable stream computation in the cloud.*Proceedings of the 8th ACM European conference on computer systems* (pp. 1–14). doi:10.1145/2465351.2465353

Rababah, A. (2008). Bivariate orthogonal polynomials on triangular domains. *Mathematics and Computers in Simulation, 78*(1), 107–111. doi:10.1016/j.matcom.2007.06.006

Rababah, A., & Alqudah, M. (2005). Jacobi-weighted orthogonal polynomials on triangular domains. *Journal of Applied Mathematics, 2005*(3), 205–217. doi:10.1155/JAM.2005.205

Shamshirband, S., Petković, D., Ćojbašić, Ž., Nikolić, V., Anuar, N. B., Shuib, N. L. M., & Akib, S. et al. (2014). Adaptive neuro-fuzzy optimization of wind farm project net profit. *Energy Conversion and Management, 80,* 229–237.

Shamshirband, S., Shojafar, M., Hosseinabadi, A. R., Kardgar, M., Nasir, M. M., & Ahmad, R. (2015). OSGA: Genetic-based open-shop scheduling with consideration of machine maintenance in small and medium enterprises. *Annals of Operations Research, 229*(1), 743–758. doi:10.1007/s10479-015-1855-z

Shojafar, M., Cordeschi, N., Amendola, D., & Baccarelli, E. (2015a). Energy-saving adaptive computing and traffic engineering for real-time-service data centers.*Proceedings of IEEE ICC Workshop on Cloud Computing Systems, Networks, and Applications* (pp. 1800-1806). doi:10.1109/ICCW.2015.7247442

Shojafar, M., Javanmardi, S., Abolfazli, S., & Cordeschi, N. (2015b). FUGE: A joint meta-heuristic approach to cloud job scheduling algorithm using fuzzy theory and a genetic method. *Cluster Computing, 18*(2), 829–844. doi:10.1007/s10586-014-0420-x

Tamm, O., Hermsmeyer, C., & Rush, A. M. (2010). Eco-sustainable system and network architectures for future transport networks. *Bell Labs Technical Journal, 14*(4), 311–327. doi:10.1002/bltj.20418

Urgaonkar, R., Kozat, U. C., Igarashi, K., & Neely, M. J. (2010). Dynamic resource allocation and power management in virtualized data centers. Proceedings of the Network operations and management symposium NOMS '10 (pp. 479–486). IEEE. doi:doi:10.1109/NOMS.2010.5488484 doi:10.1109/NOMS.2010.5488484

Victoria, A. D. C., Ahmad, M. A., Ahmad, N. A., & Silviu, D. (2015). The Mathematical Study of Data Transmission in Digital Electronics. *Int. J. of Advanced Research, 3*(3), 697–702.

Von Laszewski, G., Wang, L., Younge, A. J., & He, X. (2009). Power-aware scheduling of virtual machines in dvfs-enabled clusters. Proceedings of the IEEE international conference on Cluster computing and workshops Cluster '09 (pp. 1–10). doi:doi:10.1109/CLUSTR.2009.5289182 doi:10.1109/CLUSTR.2009.5289182

Wang, L., Zhang, F., Arjona Aroca, J., Vasilakos, A. V., Zheng, K., Hou, C., & Liu, Z. (2014). Greendcn: A general framework for achieving energy efficiency in data center networks. *IEEE Journal on Selected Areas in Communications, 32*(1), 4–15. doi:10.1109/JSAC.2014.140102

Warneke, D., & Kao, O. (2011). Exploiting dynamic resource allocation for efficient parallel data processing in the cloud. *IEEE Transactions on Parallel and Distributed Systems*, *22*(6), 985–997. doi:10.1109/TPDS.2011.65

Xia, L., Cui, Z., Lange, J. R., Tang, Y., Dinda, P. A., & Bridges, P. G. (2012). Vnet/p: Bridging the cloud and high performance computing through fast overlay networking.*Proceedings of the 21st international symposium on high-performance parallel and distributed computing* (pp. 259–270). doi:10.1145/2287076.2287116

Zaharia, M., Das, T., Li, H., Hunter, T., Shenker, S., & Stoica, I. (2013). Discretized streams: Fault-tolerant streaming computation at scale.*Proceedings of the twenty-fourth ACM symposium on operating systems principles* (pp. 423– 438). doi:10.1145/2517349.2522737

KEY TERMS AND DEFINITIONS

Data Center: A facility used to host computer systems and associated components, such as telecommunications and storage systems.

Dynamic Voltage and Frequency Scaling (DVFS): DVFS is applied in most of the modern computing units, such as cluster computing and supercomputing, in order to reduce power consumption and achieve high reliability and availability.

Load Balancing: A technique that aims at distributing workloads across a number of servers, in order to minimize the average execution time.

Network Virtualization: Categorized as either external virtualization, combining many networks or parts of networks into a virtual unit, or internal virtualization, providing network-like functionality to software containers on a single network server.

Reconfiguration Cost: Measured at the Middleware layer of the considered VNetDCs, and refers to the energy cost of scaling up/down the computing and communication rates of the hosted VMs and VLAN.

Virtual Machine Manager (VMM): It allows users to create, edit, start and stop VMs, view and control each of VM's consoles, and see performance and utilization statistics for each VM.

ENDNOTE

[1]   Since L_{tot} is expressed in [*bit*], we express $f(i)$ in [*bit/s*]. However, all the presented analytic developments and formal properties still hold verbatim when L_{tot} is measured in Job and, then, $f(i)$ is measured in [*Job/s*].

Chapter 3
Hardware Transactional Memories:
A Survey

Arsalan Shahid
HITEC University, Pakistan

Muhammad Yasir Qadri
University of Essex, UK

Maryam Murad
HITEC University, Taxila Cantt, Pakistan

Nadia N. Qadri
COMSATS Institute of Information Technology, Pakistan

Jameel Ahmed
HITEC University, Pakistan

ABSTRACT

The initiation to have a concept of shared memory in processors has built an opportunity for thread level parallelism. In various applications, synchronization or ordering tools are utilized to have an access to shared data. Traditionally, multithreaded programming models usually suggest a set of low-level primitives, such as locks, to guarantee mutual exclusion. Possession of one or more locks protects access to shared data. But, due to some flaws they become a suboptimal solution. The idea of transactional memory is in research presently as an alternative to locks. Among which, one way is hardware transactional memory. Atomicity is well supported by using transactions in hardware. In this chapter, we have focused on hardware transactional memories and the work done on them so far.

INTRODUCTION

Two or more threads when needed to access some mutual data, then a proper mechanism is required to accurately make those executions. There were some issues in using locks to handle such flaws like mutual exclusion and debugging. Therefore, idea of transactional memory was presented (Guerraoui & Romano, 2014). Basic problem in programming multithreads is to manage shared states (Alessandrini, 2015). A great difficulty is faced when multithreaded programs are created because then the main problem that arises is to synchronize them and made them being able to access the mutual data properly

DOI: 10.4018/978-1-5225-0287-6.ch003

(A McDonald, 2009). Programming and computer architecture communities are researching in finding ways to improve parallel techniques of accessing data (Navarro, Hitschfeld-Kahler, & Mateu, 2014). Database systems have successfully exploited parallel hardware for decades. Database is accessed by various operations through transaction even with predictable response.

The idea of transactional memory was first presented by Lomet (Lomet, 1985). He proposed an idea of atomic operations, like the one used in database systems, in programming languages. TM is an attractive feature that access parallel shared data by dealing intellectually with certain issues. TM system is based mainly on three major properties:

- **Atomicity:** States that operations within transactions are all finished successfully, or none of them is executed.
- **Consistency:** Means that each transaction initiates its operation with a consistent view of the shared data and exits the system in a consistent state after completion.
- **Isolations:** Concurrently running transactions are not interrupted by each other (Firoozshahian, 2009).

In TM, programmer defines certain regions that are executed at run-time to detect conflicts automatically. And this is done through read-set and write-set by tracking transactions, and checking reads and writes which are taking place within transactions. For atomicity and isolation, these read sets and write sets are compared with sets of other transactions (A McDonald, 2009).

Transaction Pattern

Transactional memory provides the following (see Table 1) special instructions to access memory instead of the simple load and store.

A transaction's read set is defined as the set of locations loaded using LT, write set as the set of locations loaded using LTX or stored using ST, and data set as the union of the two. The following (see Table 2) instructions are also provided to change the transaction state (Tripathi et al., n.d.).

Listing 1 shows a simple transaction style that shows how the above mentioned primitives can be implemented.

Listing 1. Transaction style

```
Repeat {
    Begin Transaction ();                /* initialize transaction */
    <Read input values>
    Success ← Validate ();               /* test if inputs consistent */
If (success)
    {
        <Generate updates>
        Success ← Commit ();             /* attempt permanent update */
        If (! success)
        Abort ();                        /*terminate if unable to commit */
    }
End Transaction ();                      /* close transaction */
}
Until (success);
```

Adapted from "Transactional Memory part 1".

Table 1. TM instructions

LT	Load-transactional	Loads the value of a shared memory location into a register.
LTX	Load-transactional-exclusive	Same as LT but means that the location is likely to be updated.
ST	Store-transactional	Stores the value from the register to the shared memory location tentatively.

Adapted from Tripathi, Kumar, Faruqui, & Chheda, n. d.

Table 2. Transaction state instructions

Validate	Returns true if the present transaction has not been aborted and false otherwise
Commit	Makes the transaction's changes permanent; succeeds only if no updates to its data set have been made by other transactions and no other transaction has accessed its write set.
Abort	All changes to the transaction's write set are discarded.

Adapted from Tripathi et al., n. d.

First read using LT or LTX from a set of locations then VALIDATE to check the consistency of the values. If it fails then read is performed again.ST is for storing to memory locations from register. In last COMMIT to try to make the transactions changes permanent. If it fails have to start again from read step (Tripathi et al., n. d.).

Researchers have implemented the idea of transactions in various ways. These are usually categorized into three classes:

1. **Software Transactional Memory:** Implementing transactions purely in software at run time (Marathe & Dice, 2014; A. Saha, Chatterjee, Pal, Ghosh, & Chaki, 2015);
2. **Hardware Transactional Memory:** Implements transaction semantics in the hardware (Herlihy, 2014; Leis, Kemper, & Neumann, 2014);
3. **Hybrid Transaction:** Rely on few modifications in underlying hardware (Arcas et al., 2012).

This chapter focuses on HTM systems, because they support transactional mechanisms at minimal overheads and make the implementation details transparent to software. The following section presents the history of transactional memories, their need and major advantages. Further sections present the detailed review of HTM and their mechanism. Moreover, implementations of HTM and advancements in the implementation techniques with time have also been presented. Then some future work is discussed and the final section presents the conclusions.

History of Transactional Memories

The concept of parallel process/thread execution has emerged from past decades. With the trend shifting towards parallel programming, several approaches to synchronize parallel processes have been presented. However, thread synchronization becomes quite difficult when shared memory architectures are under consideration. Many techniques have been presented to overcome this need, i.e., Locks (mutex), Lock-free algorithms (Lockless) etc. One of those technique is to use the concept of transactional memory (TM).

Transactional memory is a technology for addressing concurrent thread synchronization. TM simplifies the parallel programming models by extracting instruction groups to atomic transactions. Concurrent threads operate parallel fashion till they start to modify the same memory chunk. The main advantages for using transactional memories are, 1) easy to use 2) no locks and deadlocks 3) level of performance is increased with the improvement in parallelism. The earliest implementation of transactional memory includes gated store buffer ("Transactional memory," 2015) which was used in Transmeta's Crusoe and Efficeon processors ("Transmeta," 2015).

The following section illustrates a brief overview of Hardware transactional memories (HTM) and their mechanism.

HARDWARE TRANSACTIONAL MEMORIES

Hardware transactional memory can be implemented in three flavors:

1. Full transactional implementation in hardware,
2. HTM synchronized with software, and
3. Hardware extension to software to provide speed-up to parts of software TM.

Hardware implementation relies deeply on memory system to provide the following key capabilities:

- **Tracking:** The memory system has to provide mechanisms to keep track of transactions read and write sets.
- **Buffering:** All results should be buffered inside the memory system.
- **Detecting Conflicts:** The memory system has to detect any potential conflict between any two running transactions in the system (Firoozshahian, 2009).

Thus, an HTM system must be able to recognize memory locations for transactional contacts, manage the read-sets and write-sets of the transactions, detecting and resolving data conflicts, managing architectural register states and committing or aborting transactions. In HTM extensions to the instruction set Tracking read sets and buffering write sets is done using caches and buffers. Coherence messages activate conflict detection. Almost all conventional HTM proposals perform eager conflict detection (Minh, 2008).

Figure 1 shows cache implementation for hardware approach. Caches and shared memory are interconnected through shared bus. They snoop and update contents accordingly.

Each cache has address, value and state to which transactional memory adds a tag (see Figure 2). The address and value pair needs to be consistent across other sets of cache. The basic theme is that any proposed protocol that can detect the conflicts to access can also detect transactional conflicts. Essentially, it is a number of small processor cores, each with some private cache, connected through an interconnect implementing the MESI coherence protocol or some derivative. Keeping in view these basic points, various mechanisms have been presented related to implementing transactions on hardware.

Figure 1. Cache implementation
Adapted from Minh, 2008.

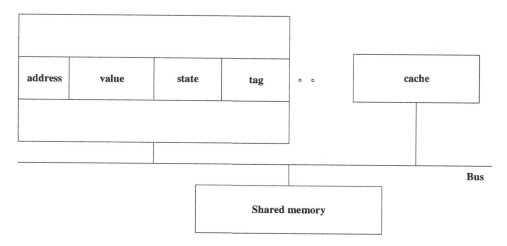

Figure 2. Transactional tag
Adapted from "Architectures for TM," 2009.

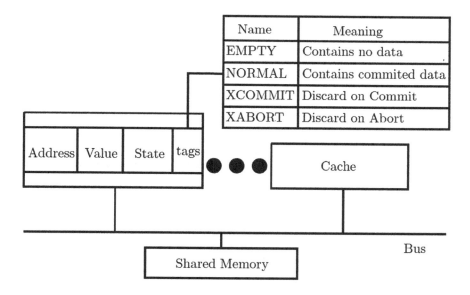

HTM Mechanisms

According to researches and various studies related to HTM, the design paradigm can be as in Figure 3. It shows two mechanisms for the implementation of HTM: Versioning and Conflict Detection (see Table 3) ("Architectures for TM," 2009).

Versioning is to make a transactional code region appear atomic; all its modifications must be stored and kept isolated from other transactions until the commit time. The system does this by implementing a versioning policy. Two versioning paradigms exist: eager and lazy.

Table 3. Implementation approaches

		Versioning	
		Lazy	Eager
Conflict Detection	Optimistic	Storing updates in write buffer, Detecting conflicts at commit time	Not practical; waiting to update memory until commit time but detecting conflicts at access time guarantees wasted work and provide no advantage
	Pessimistic	Storing updates in a write buffer; detecting conflicts at access time	Updating memory, keeping old values in undo log; detecting conflicts at access time, Log TM

Adapted from "Architectures for TM", 2009.

Figure 3. Design space
Adapted from "Architectures for TM, 2009".

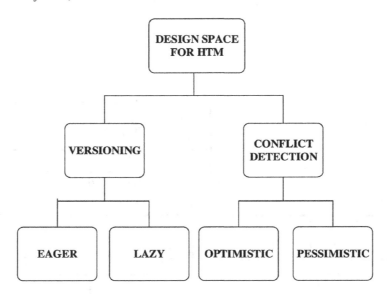

The hardware monitors multiple threads for conflicting memory accesses. Transactions that are not successfully completed are aborted or rolled back. Conflict detection ensures serializability between transactions, conflicts must be detected and resolved. The system detects conflicts by implementing a conflict detection policy, either optimistic or pessimistic. These are the design dimensions that provide choices for HTM designing.

According to some researchers there is also a third type of implementation of HTM, i.e., conflict resolution (Bobba et al., 2007; Yen et al., 2007).

Each TM system needs versioning and conflict detection techniques for implementation. These options give rise to four distinct TM design areas, i.e., Eager-Pessimistic (EA), Eager-Optimistic (EO), Lazy-Pessimistic (LP) and Lazy-Optimistic (LO) (See Figure 4).

These designs provide certain implementation approaches, e.g., Eager-Pessimistic (EP) provides LogTM (K. Moore & others, n. d.; K. E. Moore & Grossman, n. d.), UTM (Akkary, Adl-Tabatabai, Saha, & Rajwar, 2014) and MegaTM (Ramadan et al., 2008); Lazy-Pessimistic (LP) provides LTM and VTM

Figure 4. Design paradigms HTM

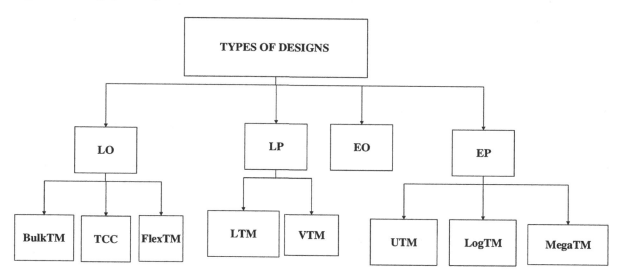

(Scott, 2015) design areas and Lazy-Optimistic (LO) is implemented in FlexTM (Dwarkadas, Shriraman, & Scott, 2014), TCC (Hammond et al., 2004) and BulkTM (Ceze, Tuck, Torrellas, & Cascaval, 2006). All of these design approaches are described in following sections.

Hardware Approaches for Transactional Memory

The full hardware implementation idea for transactional memories was introduced by Knight (Knight, 1986) and Moss. Herlihy and Moss (Herlihy & Moss, 1993) gave description of hardware transactional Memory system by describing lock-free data synchronization mechanism. They showed that by making few changes in cache, those transactions that are completed without using context switching can be well supported. They proposed a protocol that was capable to detect conflicts related to access. Two versions of transactional memory were implemented based on protocols, i.e., Goodman's protocol and chicken directory protocol. Their results showed that transactional memory is more competitive than other lock-based techniques for simple benchmark applications, i.e., counting, producer/consumer and doubly-linked list benchmarks. Moreover, the approach was limited to assumptions like short transactions duration and small data sets. After this, transactional memory has been worked out in various ways.

Rajwar et al. (R. Rajwar & Goodman, 2002) remarked on Herlihy and Moss' proposal that it is not prime because it has certain restrictions as it cannot be accomplished without a well programmer and some extensions to protocols. Lev et al. (Lev & Maessen, 2008) further added Herlihy and Moss work is not that much robust; it can only work for certain transactions with size limitations. They also high-lighted the point that it is based on architecture and is not that suitable. Some of these problems were then tried to overcome in Rajwar et al.'s work that was on Virtualizing Transactional Memory (Ravi Rajwar, Herlihy, & Lai, 2005).

LogTM (K. E. Moore & Grossman, n.d.) Is an eager version management HTM that stores old transactional values in a private software log. This eliminates commit actions because all the changes introduced by transactions are in place, but requires a software handler to restore transactional state in case of abort. LogTM refinements (Moravan et al., 2006; Moss & Hosking, 2006) minimize the hardware resources needed to track transactional state. In its first incarnation, LogTM used RW bits in the cache and in the directory to track the access summary, using line granularity. Later, LogTM-SE (Yen et al., 2007) introduced signatures to decouple RW bits from caches.

A LogTM design is able to read the old line and write the new value in the same cache access. The old line is momentarily stored in a latch, which also contains the modified memory location. Assuming a 64 byte cache line and a 32-bit processor, an undo log entry consists of 64 bytes to keep the old cache line, 26 bits to track its address and 6 bits that identifies it as an undo entry. Notice that a log entry requires 68 bytes, distributed in two different cache lines. This means that log entries are not aligned at cache line boundaries. Moreover, the system has to keep a log pointer that tracks where the entry is located in the software log. This pointer is an address that is incremented by the entry size. Hence, once the old data is placed in the latch, the system can store the undo entry in the log, moving the latch values plus the identifier to the memory hierarchy. These two movements do not need to check the RW bits of other transactions, because they update a memory section that is private to the thread.

Logging has a non-negligible cost, because it requires several movements to memory. For that reason, two different improvements can be implemented to reduce the time spent logging. First, a table can be used to track those addresses that have been written before inside this transaction. These lines are present in the log, so there is no necessity to replicate them. If the address is not in the table, a new undo entry is stored in the log, although the log already contains it. That is not a problem, because, if an abort occurs, the log is restored in reverse order. Figure 5 shows a diagram of the logging process.

Figure 5. Log process in LogTM
Adapted from "Hardware Approaches for Transactional Memory".

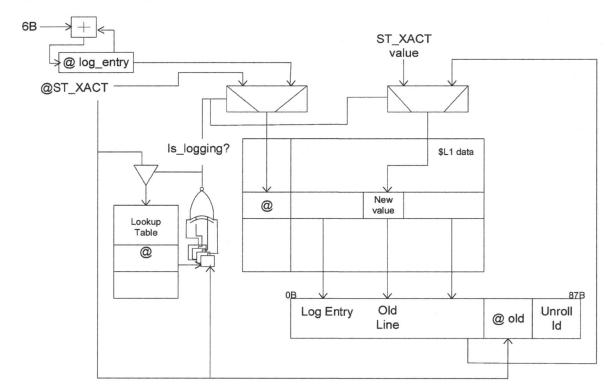

Nested LogTM supports nesting by segmenting the log into a stack of activation records and modestly replicating R/W bits. Open nesting is done by allowing a committing open transaction to release isolation and optionally save commit and compensating actions on the log, and non-transactional escape actions, also with commit and compensating actions (Moravan et al., 2006).

Eager Version Management Transactional Memory (EVM) stores new values in the memory hierarchy and the old values in the buffer. EVM operates identically to LogTM, but it accelerates its version management mechanism with the Transactional Buffer. Figure 6 overviews different operations that are responsible for EVM by using Transactional Buffer. EVM keeps old values in the buffer; whereas, new values are in the memory hierarchy. A transactional store searches if a location is present in the Transactional Buffer. If it is present, no action is performed in the buffer; otherwise the old value is introduced in the buffer, with its own memory address. A commit pushes the valid bits of all the entries of the Transactional Buffer, whereas an abort stores the values from the buffer to the memory hierarchy.

Lazy Version Management Transactional Memory (LVM) uses the Transactional Buffer to store speculative transactional values, keeping old values in the memory hierarchy. LVM operates with the other mechanisms of the LogTM, such as conflict detection or conflict resolution, but the version management approach is slightly different, modifying the commit and abort phase, like Rock (Moir, Moore, & Nussbaum, 2008) or BulkTM (Moir et al., 2008).

Figure 6. EVM using transactional buffer
Adapted from "Hardware Approaches for Transactional Memory".

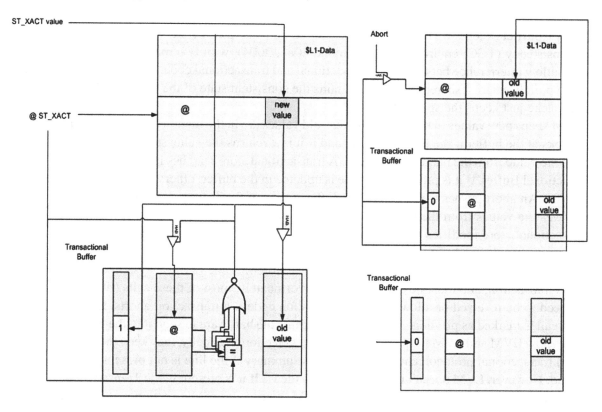

Figure 7. Eager conflict detection in EVM and LVM
Adapted from "Hardware Approaches for Transactional Memory".

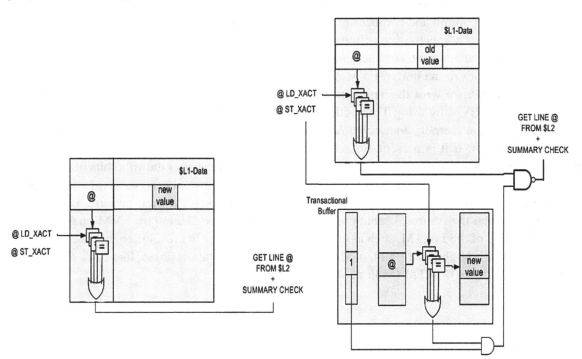

Lazy Conflict Detection Transactional Memory (LCD) emulates a Transactional memory Coherence and Consistency (TCC) environment (Hammond et al., 2004), with two main differences. First, TCC doesn't allow interference between non-transactional and transactional code. Second, TCC uses a write-through policy, where a shared L2 cache contains the consistent state of the committed transactions, so the L1 cache just keeps the speculative state.

LVM keeps new values in the buffer whereas old values are in the memory hierarchy. A transactional load looks at the buffer if the line is present, and if it is it returns the value stored in the buffer. If not, it returns the value from the memory hierarchy. A transactional store searches if a location is present in the Transactional Buffer. If it is present, the value is updated in the buffer; otherwise a new entry is added in the buffer. An abort pushes the valid bits of all the entries of the Transactional Buffer, whereas a commit moves the values from the buffer to the memory hierarchy. However, there is an exception where a transactional store modifies both the memory hierarchy and the Transactional Buffer. System calls usually modify memory locations, and these updates must be done in the memory hierarchy. Otherwise, the Operation System does not know where they are stored. Some of these system calls are executed inside a transaction, and must be done atomically. Fortunately, most of these calls (like malloc or free) don't need to be reversed or allow some compensation code if a transaction aborts. Each store from a system call is marked as privileged store, which permits the hardware to send it to the memory. Figure 7 resumes how EVM and LVM perform eager conflict detection. Basically, they keep the coherency using a MESI transactional protocol, checking the access summary if the line is not present in the cache or if is shared. However, LVM doesn't request the line to the L2 if it is present in the Transactional Buffer, so it reduces the track for evicted lines. EVM and LVM improve LogTM's version management, but they keep its conflict detection philosophy.

Figure 8. Knight's hardware organization
Adapted from Herlihy & Moss, 1993.

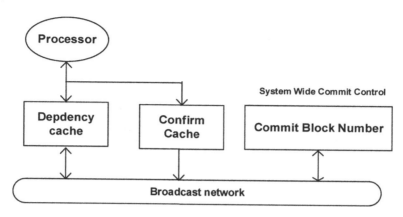

A modified version of coherence protocol was presented in LOGTM (K. Moore & others, n.d.). It allowed transactional phase to escape phase. Whereas, TCC version management keeps new data in a speculative cache until commit, when they are written through to a shared L2 cache, LogTM can operate with writeback caches and generates no traffic at commit. In TCC's lazy conflict detection, other transactions learn about transaction T's conflicting store when T commits, not earlier when the store is executed (Tripathi et al., n.d.).

In Knight's proposal, TCC requires the program to be divided in a series of transactions—either a single threaded program is divided into a series of transactions, or a programmer may specify explicit transactions in a multithreaded environment (see Figure 8) (Herlihy & Moss, 1993).

Like LogTM, LTM keeps new data in cache when it can. However, when a transaction overflows a set in the cache, LTM stores new values in an uncatchable memory hash table (see Figure 9). On commit, LTM copies overflowed data to its new location. In contrast, LogTM allows both old and new versions to be cached (often generating no memory traffic) and never copies data on commit. Whereas, an LTM processor must search a table in uncatchable memory on an incoming request to any set that has overflowed a block during the transaction, a LogTM processor needs to check only local state allowing it to respond immediately to a directory request (Tripathi et al., n.d.).

Ananian et al. (Akkary et al., 2014) proposed an extension where evicted transactional lines in an HTM would be moved by hardware into a dedicated area in local memory without aborting. Their HTM system, called Large Transactional Memory allocates a special uncashed region in local memory to buffer transaction state that spills from the cache. This region is maintained as a hash table. Each cache set has an associated overflow bit (O bit). This bit is set when a transactional cache line (tracked using a T bit) is evicted and moved into the hash table. During this process, the processor responds to incoming snoops with a negative acknowledgment (NACK). The processor does not service incoming snoops until it has checked both the cache and the memory hash table for a conflict (Herlihy & Moss, 1993).

UTM version management stores new values in place and old values in a log. UTM's log is larger, however, because it contains blocks that are targets of both loads and stores, whereas LogTM's log only contains blocks targeted by stores. UTM uses this extra log state to provide more complete virtualization of conflict detection, allowing transactions to survive paging, context switching and thread migration. UTM's conflict detection must, however, walk the log on certain coherence requests, and clean up log

Figure 9. LTM design to overflow cache lines into DRAM
Adapted from (Herlihy & Moss, 1993.

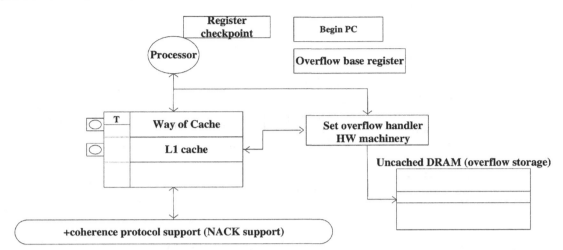

state on commit, while LogTM uses a simple directory protocol extension (that does not even know the location of the log) and uses lazy cleanup to optimize commits (Tripathi et al., n. d.). UTM is an idealized design for HTM that requires significant changes to both the processor and the memory subsystem of current computer architecture. UTM adds two new instructions to a processor's instruction:

- **XBEGIN PC:** Begin a new transaction. The pc argument to XBEGIN specifies the address of an abort handler (e.g., using a PC-relative offset). If at any time during the execution of a transaction the hardware determines that the transaction must fail, it immediately rolls back the processor and memory state to what it was when XBEGIN was executed, then jumps to pc to execute the abort handler.
- **XEND:** End the current transaction. If XEND completes, then the transaction is committed, and all of its operations appear to be atomic with respect to any other transaction (Akkary et al., 2014).

Another HTM design that has improved hardware to handle infinite sized transactions is TM (Moravan et al., 2006). For unbounded transactions it simply focuses on hardware to permit those transactions and to permit unbounded transaction sizes, but it limits the implementation to single unbounded transaction at specific time interval. This is then handled by assigning tokens to blocks of memories that enables them to execute without conflicts. In TM (Dwarkadas et al., 2014), transactions that were not overflowed were not affected by those transactions that were overflowed. Moreover, some schemes were also proposed for hardware implementations to aid software's. Like in METATM (Ramadan et al., 2008), that supports transactional operating system (TXLINUX (Rossbach et al., 2007)) by providing architectural support to run. Another scheme Flex-TM (Dwarkadas et al., 2014) presents a transactional hardware. It decoupled hardware into four components, access tracing, conflict notification, data versioning support and conflict tracking. These properly defined sections make non transactional implementation easy (Navarro et al., 2014).

LogTM-SE (A. Saha et al., 2015), a log-based HTM system that uses eager version management. LogTM-SE decouples transactions from caches using signatures (large bit tables) to store transactional accesses, which permits the elimination of RW bits in the L1 and the sticky states in the L2. Lots of addresses are stored in the signature using hash functions, which might introduce false positives. LogTM-SE requires a signature per nesting level, and they are checked in parallel to detect conflicts. If signatures are not available, they are virtualized.

Saha et al. (B. Saha, Adl-Tabatabai, Hudson, Minh, & Hertzberg, 2006, p. -) proposed a scheme hardware accelerated STM (HASTM).It was a suggested hardware support to reduce the overhead of software transactional memory instrumentation. Performance and even flexibility has been the main focuses in hardware transactional memory related work. To improve the performance and to make things flexible remained the main theme. A research ("Architectures for TM, 2009) compared two different approaches for hardware transactional memories. They compared Eager-Eager and Lazy-Lazy to observe their respective energy utilization and performance. And they concluded that eager approach requires improving their energy consumption.

Figure 10 shows the typical signature operations in LogTM-SE. LogTM-SE supports operations on signatures similar to Bulk: adding an address to a signature, checking whether an address aliases with a signature, and clearing a signature's "O" set. Unlike Bulk, LogTM-SE continues to use the existing cache coherence protocol for conflict detection, rather than relying on separate global broadcasts of signatures or tokens. Conflicts are detected by comparing the address in an incoming coherence request against the local signatures.

The Rock (Dice, Lev, Moir, Nussbaum, & Olszewski, 2009) processor is assumed as the first to include transactional hardware support. A gated buffer is used to store the alterations in transactions and when the store is filled, the system gives an indication through interrupts and software then takes corresponding action.

Figure 10. LogTM-SE signatures
Adapted from Yen et al., 2007.

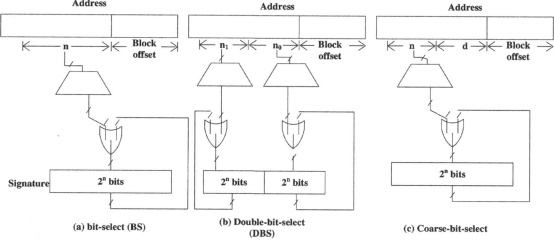

TokenTM (Bobba, Goyal, Hill, Swift, & Wood, 2008) used the idea of tokens to detect the issues related to memory blocks and then implementing them again by a different mechanism. Those mechanisms were either fission or fast token process.to correctly track conflicts on an unrestrained number of memory blocks and implements them with new mechanisms, including metastatic fission/fusion and fast token release. By TokenTM small sized transactions were executed in less time and large transactions were dealt parallel without any conflict. Thus, context switching and paging was dealt in a good manner.

Implementation of speculative lock elision (Ravi Rajwar & Goodman, 2001) in hardware was also proposed to execute lock regions as transactions. It enabled users to use frequent locks to some extent. Speculative lock elision or SLR was extended to Transactional lock removal TLR (Hammond et al., 2004) that used the idea of time stamps to resolve arising conflicts in transactions. Afterwards, HTM system focused SLR by limiting its size of transactions.

To avoid any modifications to the data cache for tracking read sets and write sets, they considered an HTM design with 32 KB 4 way set associative data cache with 64 byte cache lines and found that such an HTM could frequently support transactions up to 30,000 instructions that operate on hundreds of cache line, that was fairly large compared to common perceptions (Minh, 2008).

Zilles and Rajwar (Zilles & Rajwar, 2007) studied the effectiveness of data cache for tracking read sets and write sets. They considered an HTM design with a 32 KB four-way associative set data cache with 64 bit cache lines and found that such system could repeatedly support transactions for about 30,000 instructions that implements on several of cache lines that were equally large compared to common observations. However, in this kind of systems, a transaction must be aborted whenever an overflow occurs.

Khan et al. (Khan et al., 2008) integrate transaction management with the object translation buffer used in processor with an object-based model implementation instead of orthodox cache line model. The Azul (Click, 2009) HTM system uses data cache to track accesses and buffer transactional state. However, it relies on software to perform register recovery. KILO TM (Fung, Singh, Brownsword, & Aamodt, 2011) scheme presents hardware transaction design for GPU's that scales many parallel transactions. It is not dependent on cache coherent hardware. It utilizes conflict detection at word level based on values in order to reduce the storage overhead on chip.

Another proposal by Epifanio et al. (Gaona, Titos-Gil, Acacio, & Fernández, 2012) is implemented on top of a hardware transactional memory system in which eager conflicts manages and detects transactions mechanism. It also serializes conflicting transactions in a dynamic way. Especially when there is a conflict only single conflict is allowed to work out further. In Lazy hardware transactional memory (Negi, Titos-Gil, Acacio, Garcia, & Stenstrom, 2012), which is more competent way, available parallel part is utilized instead of eager one. They computed the issues related to the problem and developed a scheme named π-TM that is early conflict detection and a modified lazy conflict resolution design. This design focuses on how to make extensions to existing directory based protocols and how to utilize the available information to attain the proper parallelism concept.

Tor M. et al. (Fung, Singh, Brownsword, & Aamodt, 2012) explored how transactional memory concept can support GPU systems. The main challenge was to make it easy to write corresponding programming model as it requires very well defined synchronization to cope with several threads. The proposed TM system optimally runs transactions in parallel sequence. In this system, if data race occurs between any transactions, the system restarts any of the transaction in order to insure atomic appearance of transactions. In Fact, eager implementations are relatively simpler to handle in cache coherence architectures as compared to lazy scheme. In view of this fact related to HTM techniques, it was claimed that if stores are properly handled, more challenging design alternatives can be proposed (Titos-Gil, Negi, Acacio, Garcia, & Stenstrom, 2013).

RECENT IMPLEMENTATIONS OF HTM

IBM launched BlueGene/Q processors for Livermore National Labs. It was provided in 2011 and was functionally deployed in 2012. It provides power to the 20 petaflops Sequoia supercomputer ("IBM Sequoia," 2015). They are first commercial processors providing hardware support for transactional memory. The transactional memory has been configured in two modes; one is an unordered and single-version mode, where a write from one transaction causes a conflict with any transactions reading the same memory address. The second mode is for speculative multithreading, providing an ordered, multi-versioned transactional memory. IBM Blue Gene/Q multicore will be 64-bit PowerPC-based system-on-chip based on IBM's four-way multithreaded PowerPC A2 design with 1.47 billion transistor chip TM that will appear in 32 MB level 2 cache 18 cores 16 for running actual computations 1 for the operating system 1 to improve chip reliability.

Intel Haswell launched its Haswell architecture corresponding to transactional memory in 2013. It was supporting hardware for memory transactions. These transactions were named as Transactional Synchronization Extensions (TSX) by Intel. They will be extended in to two parts, Hardware Lock Elision (HLE) and Restricted Transactional Memory (RTM). HLE will enable to convert lock based programs into transactional related programs and that will be in line with present processor. (RTM) will be a full implementation of transactions on memory.

HTM, despite of many limitations, allows for efficient concurrent and atomic operations; which is considered to be very significant in context of databases. Viktor et al. (Leis et al., 2014) presented a mechanism to exploit HTM in main memory databases. Moreover, they evaluated transaction management scheme to transforms a large database transaction into a sequence of elementary and single tuple HTM transactions.

Most recently, Transactional memory support has been added to IBM POWER8 Processors by IBM (Le et al., 2015). The POWER8 transactional memory facility provides a robust capability to execute transactions that can survive interrupts. Moreover, it provides the first implementation of hardware transactional memory that is supported directly by the Power ISA. The architecture also provides Rollback-Only Transactions to permit transactional memory to be used to execute single-thread code.

AMD proposed Advanced Synchronization Facility (ASF), i.e., the x86-64 instruction set architecture that would add hardware transactional memory support ("Advanced Synchronization Facility," 2015). Up till now, none of the released microprocessors included this support. However, it is expected to be launched soon in the upcoming versions.

CONCLUSION

Shared memory architectures have emerged as mainstream processor architectures. Trend shifting towards shared memory systems have motivated researchers for thread level parallelism. Many people have been using locks for synchronization and thread ordering. Transactional memory is an approach to address the same problem as an alternative to locks as it supports atomicity. The design area related to hardware transactional memory systems has been studied widely by researchers. To achieve true optimism is dealt in various policies, ordinary lazy designs are a bit suspicious. Eager designs are pessimistic in cases where they detect conflicts. This chapter presents a survey on researches so far done and some of the proposed schemes related to hardware transactional memories. Moreover, some of the recent implementations of HTM have also been presented.

REFERENCES

Advanced Synchronization Facility. (n. d.). *Wikipedia, the free encyclopedia*. Retrieved from https://en.wikipedia.org/w/index.php?title=Advanced_Synchronization_Facility&oldid=680636378

Akkary, H. H., Adl-Tabatabai, A.-R., Saha, B., & Rajwar, R. (2014). *Unbounded transactional memory systems*. Google Patents.

Alessandrini, V. (2015). *Shared Memory Application Programming: Concepts and strategies in multicore application programming*. Morgan Kaufmann.

Arcas, O., Kirchhofer, P., Sönmez, N., Schindewolf, M., Unsal, O. S., Karl, W., & Cristal, A. (2012). A low-overhead profiling and visualization framework for Hybrid Transactional Memory. *Proceedings of the 2012 IEEE 20th Annual International Symposium on In Field-Programmable Custom Computing Machines* (FCCM) (pp. 1–8). IEEE.

Bobba, J., Goyal, N., Hill, M. D., Swift, M. M., & Wood, D. A. (2008). Tokentm: Efficient execution of large transactions with hardware transactional memory. ACM SIGARCH Computer Architecture News, 36(3), pp. 127–138. IEEE Computer Society.

Bobba, J., Moore, K. E., Volos, H., Yen, L., Hill, M. D., Swift, M. M., & Wood, D. A. (2007). Performance pathologies in hardware transactional memory. In *ACM SIGARCH Computer Architecture News* (Vol. 35, pp. 81–91). ACM.

Ceze, L., Tuck, J., Torrellas, J., & Cascaval, C. (2006). Bulk disambiguation of speculative threads in multiprocessors. ACM SIGARCH Computer Architecture News, 34(2), 227–238). ACM. doi:doi:10.1109/ISCA.2006.13 doi:10.1109/ISCA.2006.13

Click, C. (2009). Azul's experiences with hardware transactional memory. *Proceedings of theTransactional Memory Workshop*.

Dice, D., Lev, Y., Moir, M., Nussbaum, D., & Olszewski, M. (2009). *Early experience with a commercial hardware transactional memory implementation*. Sun Microsystems. doi:10.1145/1508244.1508263

Dwarkadas, S., Shriraman, A., & Scott, M. (2014). *Mechanism to support flexible decoupled transactional memory*. Google Patents.

Firoozshahian, A. (2009). *Smart memories: A reconfigurable memory system architecture*. ProQuest.

Fung, W. W., Singh, I., Brownsword, A., & Aamodt, T. M. (2011). Hardware transactional memory for GPU architectures.*Proceedings of the 44th Annual IEEE/ACM International Symposium on Microarchitecture* (pp. 296–307). ACM.

Fung, W. W., Singh, I., Brownsword, A., & Aamodt, T. M. (2012). *Kilo tm: Hardware transactional memory for gpu architectures* (Vol. 3, pp. 7–16). IEEE Micro.

Gaona, E., Titos-Gil, R., Acacio, M. E., & Fernández, J. (2012). Dynamic Serialization: Improving Energy Consumption in Eager-Eager Hardware Transactional Memory Systems. *Proceedings of the 2012 20th Euromicro International Conference on Parallel, Distributed and Network-Based Processing (PDP)* (pp. 221–228). IEEE.

Guerraoui, R., & Romano, P. (2014). *Transactional Memory. Foundations, Algorithms, Tools, and Applications, LCNS* (Vol. 8913). Springer.

Hammond, L., Wong, V., Chen, M., Carlstrom, B. D., Davis, J. D., Hertzberg, B., & Olukotun, K. (2004). Transactional memory coherence and consistency. In *ACM SIGARCH Computer Architecture News* (Vol. 32, p. 102). IEEE Computer Society.

Hardware Approaches for Transactional Memory. (n. d.). Retrieved from http://arco.e.ac.upc.edu/wiki/images/e/e3/Mlupon_msc.pdf

Herlihy, M. (2014). Fun with hardware transactional memory.*Proceedings of the 2014 ACM SIGMOD international conference on Management of data* (pp. 575–575). ACM. doi:10.1145/2588555.2602132

Herlihy, M., & Moss, J. E. B. (1993). *Transactional memory: Architectural support for lock-free data structures* (Vol. 21). ACM. doi:10.1145/165123.165164

IEEE Transactional memory. (n. d.). *Wikipedia, the free encyclopedia.* Retrieved from https://en.wikipedia.org/w/index.php?title=Transactional_memory

Khan, B., Horsnell, M., Rogers, I., Luján, M., Dinn, A., & Watson, I. (2008). A first insight into object-aware hardware transactional memory.*Proceedings of the twentieth annual symposium on Parallelism in algorithms and architectures* (pp. 107–109). ACM. doi:10.1145/1378533.1378552

Knight, T. (1986). An architecture for mostly functional languages.*Proceedings of the 1986 ACM conference on LISP and functional programming* (pp. 105–112). ACM. doi:10.1145/319838.319854

Le, H. Q., Guthrie, G. L., Williams, D. E., Michael, M. M., Frey, B. G., Starke, W. J., Nakaike, T. (2015). Transactional memory support in the IBM POWER8 processor. *IBM Journal of Research and Development*, 59(1), pp. 8:1–8:14.

Leis, V., Kemper, A., & Neumann, T. (2014). Exploiting hardware transactional memory in main-memory databases. *Proceedings of the 2014 IEEE 30th International Conference on Data Engineering (ICDE)* (pp. 580–591). IEEE. doi:doi:10.1109/ICDE.2014.6816683 doi:10.1109/ICDE.2014.6816683

Lev, Y., & Maessen, J.-W. (2008). Split hardware transactions: true nesting of transactions using best-effort hardware transactional memory. *Proceedings of the 13th ACM SIGPLAN Symposium on Principles and practice of parallel programming* (pp. 197–206). ACM.

Lomet, D. B. (1985). *Process structuring, synchronization, and recovery using atomic actions*. Springer. doi:10.1007/978-3-642-82470-8_21

Marathe, V. J., & Dice, D. (2014). *Lock-clustering compilation for software transactional memory*. Google Patents.

McDonald, A. (2009). *Architectures for Transactional Memory* [Ph.D. Dissertation]. Stanford University, Stanford, USA. Retrieved from http://csl.stanford.edu/~christos/publications/2009.austen_mcdonald.phd_thesis.pdf

Minh, C. C. (2008). *Designing an effective hybrid transactional memory system*. ProQuest.

Moir, M., Moore, K., & Nussbaum, D. (2007). The Adaptive Transactional Memory Test Platform: A tool for experimenting with transactional code for Rock. *Proceedings of the Workshop on Transactional Computing (Transact).* Sun Microsystems.

Moore, K. E., Bobba, J., Moravan, M. J., Hill, M. D., & Wood, D. A. (2006, February). LogTM: log-based transactional memory. Proceedings of HPCA '06 (pp. 254-265). doi:doi:10.1109/HPCA.2006.1598134 doi:10.1109/HPCA.2006.1598134

Moore, K. E., & Grossman, D. Log-based transactional memory. *Proc. of the Twelfth International Symposium on High-Performance Computer Architecture* (pp. 11–15).

Moravan, M. J., Bobba, J., Moore, K. E., Yen, L., Hill, M. D., Liblit, B., & Wood, D. A. (2006). Supporting nested transactional memory in LogTM. In *ACM Sigplan Notices* (Vol. 41, pp. 359–370). ACM.

Moss, J. E. B., & Hosking, A. L. (2006). Nested transactional memory: Model and architecture sketches. *Science of Computer Programming, 63*(2), 186–201. doi:10.1016/j.scico.2006.05.010

Navarro, C. A., Hitschfeld-Kahler, N., & Mateu, L. (2014). A survey on parallel computing and its applications in data-parallel problems using GPU architectures.Communications in Computational Physics, 15(2), 285–329.

Negi, A., Titos-Gil, R., Acacio, M. E., Garcia, J. M., & Stenstrom, P. (2012). π-TM: Pessimistic invalidation for scalable lazy hardware transactional memory. *Proceedings of the 2012 IEEE 18th International Symposium on High Performance Computer Architecture (HPCA)* (pp. 1–12). IEEE.

Rajwar, R., & Goodman, J. R. (2001). Speculative lock elision: Enabling highly concurrent multithreaded execution. *Proceedings of the 34th annual ACM/IEEE international symposium on Microarchitecture* (pp. 294–305). IEEE Computer Society.

Rajwar, R., & Goodman, J. R. (2002). Transactional lock-free execution of lock-based programs. *Operating Systems Review, 36*(5), 5–17. doi:10.1145/635508.605399

Rajwar, R., Herlihy, M., & Lai, K. (2005). Virtualizing transactional memory.*Proceedings of 32nd International Symposium on Computer Architecture ISCA '05* (pp. 494–505). IEEE. doi:10.1109/ISCA.2005.54

Ramadan, H. E., Rossbach, C. J., Porter, D. E., Hofmann, O. S., Bhandari, A., & Witchel, E. (2007). Metatm/txlinux: Transactional memory for an operating system. *ACM SIGARCH Computer Architecture News, 35*(2), 92–103. doi:10.1145/1273440.1250675

Saha, A., Chatterjee, A., Pal, N., Ghosh, A., & Chaki, N. (2015). A Lightweight Implementation of Obstruction-Free Software Transactional Memory. In *Applied Computation and Security Systems* (pp. 67–84). Springer. doi:10.1007/978-81-322-1988-0_5

Saha, B., Adl-Tabatabai, A.-R., Hudson, R. L., Minh, C. C., & Hertzberg, B. (2006). McRT-STM: a high performance software transactional memory system for a multi-core runtime.*Proceedings of the eleventh ACM SIGPLAN symposium on Principles and practice of parallel programming* (pp. 187–197). ACM. doi:10.1145/1122971.1123001

Scott, M. (2015). Transactional Memory Today. *ACM SIGACT News, 46*(2), 96–104. doi:10.1145/2789149.2789166

IBM Sequoia. (2015, August 18). Wikipedia, the free encyclopedia. Retrieved from https://en.wikipedia.org/w/index.php?title=IBM_Sequoia&oldid=676692785

Titos-Gil, R., Negi, A., Acacio, M. E., Garcia, J. M., & Stenstrom, P. (2013). Eager beats lazy: Improving store management in eager hardware transactional memory. *IEEE Transactions on Parallel and Distributed Systems*, *24*(11), 2192–2201. doi:10.1109/TPDS.2012.315

Transmeta. (n. d.). *Wikipedia, the free encyclopedia*. Retrieved from https://en.wikipedia.org/w/index.php?title=Transmeta&oldid=680746415

Yen, L., Bobba, J., Marty, M. R., Moore, K. E., Volos, H., Hill, M. D., & Wood, D. (2007, February). LogTM-SE: Decoupling hardware transactional memory from caches. *Proceedings of the IEEE 13th International Symposium on In High Performance Computer Architecture* (pp. 261-272). IEEE.

Zilles, C., & Rajwar, R. (2007). Transactional memory and the birthday paradox.*Proceedings of the nineteenth annual ACM symposium on Parallel algorithms and architectures* (pp. 303–304). ACM. doi:10.1145/1248377.1248428

KEY TERMS AND DEFINITIONS

Conflict Detection: In transactional memories, Conflict detection ensures serializability between transactions. It is a process to detect conflicts which must be resolved.

FlexTM: Flexible transactional memories provide a 5× speedup over high-quality software TM.

LogTM: Log-based transactional memories make commits fast by storing old values to a per-thread log in cacheable virtual memory and storing new values in place.

Multithreading: The ability of a CPU or a single core in a multicore processor system to execute multiple processes or threads concurrently.

Shared Memory: A memory that may be simultaneously accessed by multiple programs in order to provide communication among them. Efficient way to pass data between programs.

TCC: Transactional memory Coherence and Consistency is a model in which atomic transactions are always the basic unit of parallel work, communication, memory coherence, and memory reference consistency.

Thread Synchronization: The handshaking or join up of multiple processes at a certain point to commit a certain series of actions.

Versioning: In Transactional Memory, versioning means that code region should appear atomic and all its modifications must be stored and kept isolated from other transactions until the commit time.

Chapter 4
Design Space Exploration Using Cycle Accurate Simulator

Arsalan Shahid
HITEC University, Pakistan

Muhammad Yasir Qadri
University of Essex, UK

Bilal Khalid
HITEC University, Pakistan

Nadia N. Qadri
COMSATS Institute of Information Technology, Pakistan

Jameel Ahmed
HITEC University, Pakistan

ABSTRACT

Multi-Processor System on Chip (MPSoC) architectures have become a mainstream technology for obtaining performance improvements in computing platforms. With the increase in the number of cores, the role of cache memory has become pivotal. An ideal memory configuration is always desired to be fast and large; but, in fact, striking to balance between the size and access time of the memory hierarchy is considered by processor architect. Design space exploration is used for performance analysis of systems and helps to find the optimal solution for obtaining the desired objectives. In this chapter, we explore two design space parameters, i.e., cache size and number of cores, for obtaining the desired energy consumption. Moreover, previously presented energy models for multilevel cache are evaluated by using cycle accurate full system simulator. Our results show that with the increase in cache sizes, the number of cycles required for application execution decreases, and by increasing number of cores, the throughput improve.

INTRODUCTION

With the evolution of multicore processor architectures and trend shifting towards parallelism, the role of cache memory has become pivotal (Wei, Shao, Huang, 2016; Geer, 2005; Jacob, Ng & Wang, 2010). Cache memory plays a vital role in modern processor architectures as it reduces the gap between main memory and the processor (González, A., Aliagas, C., & Valero, 2014). It serves to reduce the average time taken by each memory access or in other words cache acts as a buffer between Central Processing Unit (CPU) and main memory. Multi-level cache hierarchy is always beneficial as it bridges processor-

DOI: 10.4018/978-1-5225-0287-6.ch004

memory gap efficiently (Whitham, J., Audsley, N. C., & Davis, 2014). Moreover, this memory hierarchy can reduce up to 50% of the total energy spent by the microprocessor (Segars, 2001). Therefore, cache size has become a critical parameter for a processor architect to choose (Huang, J., Yeluri, S., Frailong, Libby, 2014). This fact has urged researchers to explore cache hierarchy design in terms of energy optimization.

Energy consumption has always been a key concern and desired objective in multicore processor systems (Hennessy & Patterson, 2011). For the processor architect, choice of components to achieve minimum energy consumption is a very important and critical decision to make. Most of the techniques involve verification methodology based on Transaction Level Modeling (TLM) (Ferro, Pierre, Amor, Lachaize, & Lefftz, 2011) or virtualized platforms (Magnusson, Christensson, Eskilson, & others, 2002) to analyze a proposed configuration several times. But, a single configuration can take several hours for complete evaluation. Moreover, the results obtained out of those techniques to explore the optimum design space are not accurate as the simulators are not cycle accurate. Therefore, an efficient technique to propose search/design space parameters using a cycle accurate simulator is required. The problem of exploring configurable parameters to minimize energy consumption is known as Design Space Exploration (DSE) (Silvano, Fornaciari, & Villar, 2014). DSE is used for system optimization, integration and to explore several design parameters. In this paper, we have explored two such parameters:

1. The optimum sizes of cache at different levels of memory hierarchy.
2. The number of cores for best performance with respect to energy consumption.

We focused on the design space parameters for two level cache memory hierarchies (L1 & L2 cache) and improved the cache energy models presented by M.Y Qadri (Qadri & McDonald-Maier, 2010). Moreover, we evaluated cache energy mathematical models by using different standard benchmarks. These models significantly require less number of parameters which have been estimated by using state-of-the-art cycle accurate Micro Architectural and System Simulator (MARSS) for multicore processors (Patel, Afram, & Ghose, 2011). MARSS gives the exact number of cycles required to execute an instruction. Energy per access of the tag array for the L1 and L2 cache were obtained from HP Labs' CACTI, i.e., an integrated cache timing, power, and area model tool (D. Tarjan & N. P. Jouppi, 2006).

The aim of this research is to explore the design space parameters, i.e., cache size and number of cores, to estimate the best point where a benchmark takes minimum number of cycles to execute an instruction. For this purpose, we took different sizes of L1 and L2 cache and observed the number of cycles for various number of cores, i.e., 2, 4, 8, 12 and 16. Modern processor architectures have evolved with a lot of complexities that it becomes too difficult to simulate a whole CPU or just even a core. However, MARSS provide simulation results on cycle by cycle basis for microprocessor architectures. For the sake of simplicity, we have evaluated the results by considering homogeneous cores.

The rest of chapter is divided into six sections. Section 2 presents related work in the field of cache memory hierarchy and different performance estimation techniques along with simulation tools. Cache energy models are discussed in section 3. Design space exploration methodology and results have been shown in section 4. In section 5 discussions are presented on energy estimation and number of cycles for various cache sizes and then the chapter concludes.

RELATED WORK

In the recent past years, drive towards low power processing has challenged the designers and researchers to optimize every component of the processor (Wang & Naffziger, 2008). As cache memory is an integral part in designing of microprocessor, cache energy consumption and throughput models have been the focus of research for some time. Some of the previous works related to cache power estimation along with tools such as full system cycle accurate simulators are presented in this section.

Simunic et al. (Šimunić, Benini, & De Micheli, 1999) proposed analytical models for energy estimation in embedded systems. The per cycle energy model presented in their work comprises components such as energy consumption of processor, memory, interconnects and pins, DC-to-DC converters and level two (L2) cache. The model validation was performed using integrated simulator of ARM SDK (Advanced RISC Machines Limited (ARM) Inc., 1996). These models only analyze the embedded system power but do not estimate energy consumption for individual components of a processor. Li et al. (Y. Li & Henkel, 1998) proposed a full system detailed energy model comprising cache, main memory, and software energy components. Their work includes description of an Avalanche framework for estimating and optimizing energy dissipation of embedded systems. M.B. Kamble et al. (Kamble & K. Ghose, 1998) present analytical models for the energy dissipation in low power cache. The power obtained by these models was compared with that obtained by CAPE (Cache Power Estimator). The models for conventional caches are found to be accurate to within 2% error. A. C. borty et al. (Chakraborty et al., 2010) represents a new cache building that is multi-copy cache (MC2) which gives significant reduction in energy consumption of forceful voltage scaling in caches by producing the multiple copies of each data cache. From the experimental results, they obtain that using MC2 60% reduction in energy can be achieved. Johnson Kin et al. (Kin, Gupta, & Mangione-Smith, 1997) proposed an energy efficient memory structure. According to them L2 cache is placed behind the filter cache (a small memory), which is similar in structure and size to L1 cache in order to improve performance of processors.

C. Long. Su et al. (Su & Despain, 1995) have proposed the power trade-offs in designing of caches and energy reduction using Gray code addressing and cache sub banking. And experimental results show that direct-mapped caches consume less energy than set associative caches. Sheng Li et al. (S. Li et al., 2009) presented Multicore Power, Area, and Timing (McPAT) framework that supports comprehensive design space exploration for multicore processor configurations. At micro architectural level, McPAT includes models for the fundamental components of a chip multiprocessor and at circuit and technology level it supports critical-path timing, area, dynamic, short-circuit and leakage power modeling. McPAT help architects to use new standards combining performance with both area and power. As die cost increases with area, hence area is a critical design constraint. Therefore, good trade-off between performances and cost needs careful design of on-chip resources.

Yourst (2007) developed a full system clock accurate simulator (PTLsim) to simulate each component at instruction level. This simulator features the configurable RTL level architecture and pipelines at the speed of host system. Avadh et al. presented MARSS (Patel et al., 2011) based on PTLsim which is a cycle accurate complete system simulator for x86 and x64 based architectures, especially for multi-core hardware's. MARSS extends the functionality and support of PTLsim including complete user space simulations, unmodified software and OS stack and unmodified kernel. Tarjan et al. (D. Tarjan & N. P. Jouppi, 2006) presented CACTI which is an integrated cache access time, cycle time, area, aspect ratio, and power model. CACTI is intended for use by computer architects so they can better understand the performance tradeoffs inherent in different cache sizes and organizations.

Qadri et al. (Qadri, Gujarathi, & McDonald-Maier, 2009) have presented the techniques for power efficiency at processor core level. They proposed that processor's speed can be improved by adding pipeline stages. Clock frequency, supply voltage and cache can be used efficiently for power reduction. They proposed various techniques such as DVFS, Power and Clock gating for power optimization. In (Qadri & McDonald-Maier, 2010), Qadri et al. also presented mathematical models to calculate consumption of energy for multilevel caches using Ultra SPARC-2 and Power PC750 processors for two level cache. Then they extend their work in (Muhammad Yasir, Klaus D, & others, 2010), by considering the concept of battery powered embedded system, i.e., processor only turns on when required, otherwise it remains in sleep mode. Moreover, they proposed improved energy and throughput models of data caches. These models are suitable for design of optimized cache for processors.

In this paper, we evaluated the energy models presented in (Qadri & McDonald-Maier, 2010) for multilevel cache using MARSSx86 simulator. Being cycle accurate, this simulator has been used for multicore implementation of mathematical models and gives more accurate results as compared to other system simulators. We also explored design space to estimate minimum number of cycles a benchmark takes to execute an instruction. The following section illustrates cache energy models and estimation of cache parameters through cache simulator.

CACHE MEMORY ENERGY MODELS

In (Qadri & McDonald-Maier, 2010), Qadri et al. presented mathematical models to calculate consumption of energy for multilevel caches. The models presented by him analyze the energy consumption for multilevel cache using PowerPC750, and UltraSPARC-II processors. These models are used in various publications of authors (Qadri & Klaus, 2008, 2009, 2010); and are also compared against the results reported by Simics (River, W., 2006). According to the proposed models:

$$E_{total} = E_{ic} + E_{dc} + E_{l2c} \tag{1}$$

E_{ic} = Energy consumed by instruction cache.

E_{dc} = Energy consumed by data cache.

E_{l2c} = Energy consumed by L2 cache.

where:

$$E_{ic} = E_{ic-read} + E_{ic-mp} \tag{2}$$

$$E_{dc} = E_{dc-read} + E_{dc-write} + E_{dc-mp} \tag{3}$$

$$E_{l2c} = E_{l2c-read} + E_{l2c-write} + E_{l2c-mp} \tag{4}$$

E_{x-read}, $E_{x-write}$ are read and write energy for instruction, data or L2 cache, E_{x-mp} is miss penalty energy for corresponding cache.

In this paper, we improve the energy models by evaluating them using full system simulator, i.e., MARSS for multicore processor simulations. MARSS provides number of read/write cache hits and misses for evaluation of models presented above. It has been used in hundreds of research papers in order to obtain cycle accurate results. We have compared results of our models with those of MARSS and the comparison shows a small amount of error for various configurations. CACTI is used to calculate read and write energy and energy per cycle, cache access time is obtained by simple formula of energy given below:

$$E = \frac{V * I}{f} \tag{5}$$

Table 1 shows the data obtained from CACTI for various cache sizes such as 4 KB, 8 KB, 16 KB, 32 KB, 64 KB and 128 KB respectively.

Table 1. CACTI simulator data

Parameters	For 4 KB	For 8 KB	For 16 KB	For 32 KB	For 64 KB	For 128 KB
Line Size [Bytes]	64	64	64	64	64	64
Number of lines	1024	1024	1024	1024	1024	1024
R/W ports	1	1	1	1	1	1
Associativity	2	2	2	2	2	2
Read ports	0	0	0	0	0	0
Write ports	1	1	1	1	1	1
Access time [ns]	0.687433	0.774311	0.776892	0.889597	1.21415	1.365661
Cycle time [ns]	0.350633	0.36339	0.367621	0.41209	0.555608	0.6597919
Read Energy [nJ]	0.018092	0.023574	0.031482	0.0359356	0.0421182	0.0421182
Write Energy [nJ]	0.004482	0.009114	0.0091872	0.0095884	0.0118159	0.0179147

Table 2. Benchmark applications from Splash-2

Benchmarks	Description
Barnes	This benchmark simulates the gravitational forces acting on a galactic cluster using the Barnes-Hut n-body algorithm (Singh, Hennessy, & Gupta, 1995).
Fmm	The FMM application implements a parallel adaptive Fast Multipole Method to simulate the interaction of a system of bodies (N-body problem) (Singh, Holt, Hennessy, & Gupta, 1993).
Water-spatial	It imposes a, 3-D spatial data structure on the cubical domain, resulting in a 3-D, grid of boxes.
Water-nsquared	Evaluated forces and potential that occur over time in a system of water & molecules using predictor -corrector method.

DESIGN SPACE EXPLORATION

In this section, we have presented the methodology to explore design space in order to find the optimal point where a program takes minimum number of cycles to run completely. Moreover, results have also been presented.

Different standard benchmark applications from SPLASH-2 (Woo, Ohara, Torrie, Singh, & Gupta, 1995) benchmarking suite have been used, i.e., Barnes, Fmm, Water-Spatial and water-nsquared. These benchmark applications are described in Table 2.

We have taken different sizes of L1 and L2 caches for 2, 4, 8, 12 and 16 cores. We changed the sizes of L2 cache to 32kB, 64kB, 128kB, 256kB and 512kB in the machine configuration file of MARSS, keeping L1 cache and number cores constant and observed the number of cycles. Table 3 shows cache parameters, we have kept in cache configuration file of MARSS.

Figure 1 shows the number of cycles consumed by benchmark applications for two cores with different L1 & L2 cache sizes. Similarly results for 4, 8, 12, and 16 cores have been shown in Figure 2, 3, 4, and 5 respectively.

For evaluation of energy we kept L1 (instruction and data) cache as 32kB and L2 cache as 64kB. Table 4 illustrates the energy of calculated for different benchmarks on single core machine. Similarly, we evaluated the energy consumption by changing the number of cores, i.e., 2, 4, 8 and 16 shown in Table 5, 6, 7, and 8 respectively.

Figure 1. Number of cycles for 2 cores

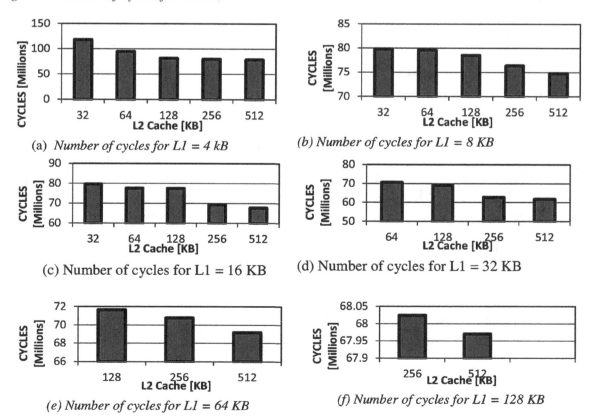

(a) *Number of cycles for L1 = 4 kB*

(b) *Number of cycles for L1 = 8 KB*

(c) Number of cycles for L1 = 16 KB

(d) Number of cycles for L1 = 32 KB

(e) *Number of cycles for L1 = 64 KB*

(f) *Number of cycles for L1 = 128 KB*

Table 3. Cache configuration data

Parameter	Value
Cache Type	Mesi
Associativity	4 for L1, 8 for L2
Latency	2 for L1, 5 for L2
Read ports	2 for L1, 2 for L2
Write ports	1 for L1, 2 for L2
Line Size (Bytes)	64

Table 4. Energy evaluation for single core

Benchmarks	E_{ic} [nJ]	E_{dc} [nJ]	$E_{l\,2\,c}$ [nJ]	E_{total} [nJ]
Barnes	930034.37	1877528.1277	52741139.298	55548701.298
Fmm	1419665.393	23047857.59	49737310.15	74164833.1344
Water-Spatial	1830823.931	24666379.48	63805772.92	90302976.33
Water-nsquared	844077.9734	18740226.11	62852582.11	82436886.1883

Figure 2. Number of cycles for 4 cores

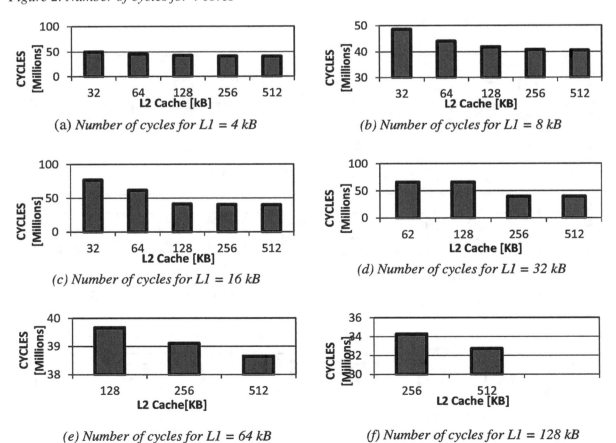

(a) *Number of cycles for L1 = 4 kB*

(b) *Number of cycles for L1 = 8 kB*

(c) *Number of cycles for L1 = 16 kB*

(d) *Number of cycles for L1 = 32 kB*

(e) *Number of cycles for L1 = 64 kB*

(f) *Number of cycles for L1 = 128 kB*

Figure 3. Number of cycles for 8 cores

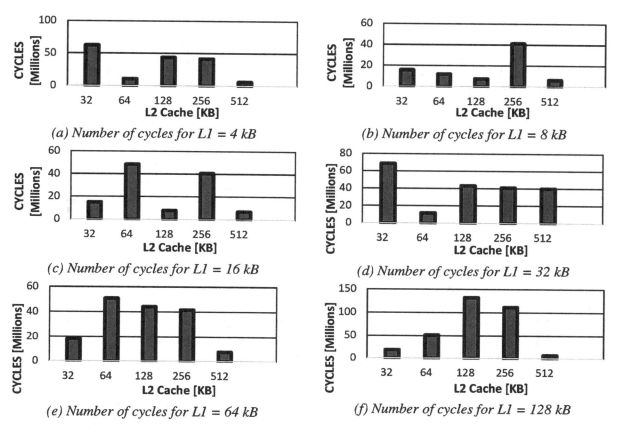

(a) Number of cycles for L1 = 4 kB

(b) Number of cycles for L1 = 8 kB

(c) Number of cycles for L1 = 16 kB

(d) Number of cycles for L1 = 32 kB

(e) Number of cycles for L1 = 64 kB

(f) Number of cycles for L1 = 128 kB

Table 5. Energy evaluation for 2 cores

Benchmarks	E_{ic} (nJ)	E_{dc} (nJ)	E_{l2c} (nJ)	E_{total} (nJ)
Barnes	252064.016	51951.646	728441.298	1032456.96
Fmm	218533.9278	31863.6381	567673.15	818070.7159
Water-Spatial	64791.4625	4337.5904	835757.92	904886.9729
Water-nsquared	1021534.506	6356317.51	796150.11	8174002.126

Table 6. Energy evaluation for 4 cores

Benchmarks	E_{ic} (nJ)	E_{dc} (nJ)	E_{l2c} (nJ)	E_{total} (nJ)
Barnes	118664.457	30981.096	524411.92	674057.473
Fmm	100933.767	10463.9521	319693.11	431090.8291
Water-Spatial	44790.502	6037.0103	305707.92	356535.4323
Water-nsquared	609532.074	37601.16	602440.12	1249573.354

Figure 4. Number of cycles for 12 cores

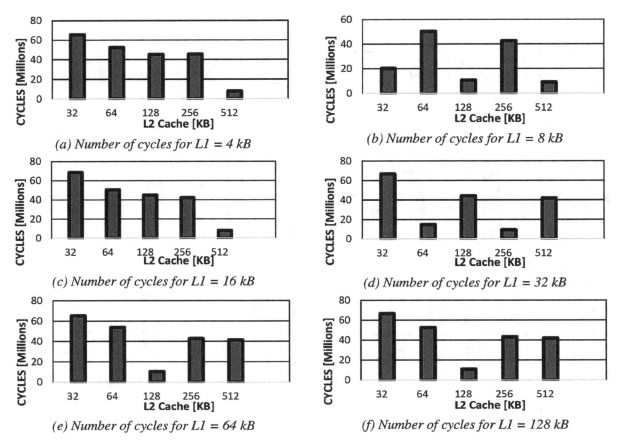

(a) Number of cycles for L1 = 4 kB

(b) Number of cycles for L1 = 8 kB

(c) Number of cycles for L1 = 16 kB

(d) Number of cycles for L1 = 32 kB

(e) Number of cycles for L1 = 64 kB

(f) Number of cycles for L1 = 128 kB

Table 7. Energy evaluation for 8 cores

Benchmarks	E_{ic} (nJ)	E_{dc} (nJ)	$E_{l\,2\,c}$ (nJ)	E_{total} (nJ)
Barnes	92014.223	9551.236	40211.32	141776.779
Fmm	8233.919	6263.385	29093.11	43590.414
Water-Spatial	6594.232	927.5934	65047.70	72569.5254
Water-nsquared	50213.205	9317.51	30440.42	89971.135

Table 8. Energy evaluation for 16 cores

Benchmarks	E_{ic} (nJ)	E_{dc} (nJ)	$E_{l\,2\,c}$ (nJ)	E_{total} (nJ)
Barnes	8064.25	981.6	8169.33	17215.18
Fmm	433.9278	863.8	33410.78	34708.5078
Water-Spatial	491.450	74.5	5773.34	6339.29
Water-nsquared	9534.506	657.49	5582.109	15774.105

Figure 5. Number of cycles for 16 cores

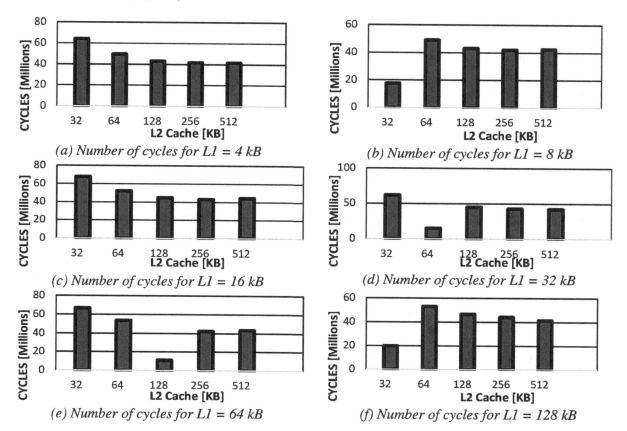

(a) *Number of cycles for L1 = 4 kB*

(b) *Number of cycles for L1 = 8 kB*

(c) *Number of cycles for L1 = 16 kB*

(d) *Number of cycles for L1 = 32 kB*

(e) *Number of cycles for L1 = 64 kB*

(f) *Number of cycles for L1 = 128 kB*

DISCUSSIONS

In order to find out the energy out of proposed model, we used MARSS-x86 (Patel et al., 2011) to run a number of benchmark applications from SPLASH-2 (Woo et al., 1995) benchmarking suite. Simulations have been run on Linux kernel 3.5.7. It is to be noted that MARSS provide cycle accurate simulations for various benchmark applications but parameters such as E_{x-read}, $E_{x-write}$ were obtained using HP labs' CACTI that is an integrated cache timing, power, and area model tool (Tarjan & Jouppi, 2006) (see Table 1.)

Following are the observations made during design space exploration for finding optimum conditions where a program takes minimum number of cycles to run completely.

1. Benchmark takes less number of cycles to execute an instruction, if value of L1 cache increases.
2. Large value of L2 requires less number of cycles to execute an application.
3. Number of cores and energy consumption have inverse relationship. Greater number of cores in a processor architecture will take less energy to complete the task.

CONCLUSION

In this chapter, we had proposed a technique for the design space exploration of multicore processors to explore the optimum search space solutions in the form of number of cores and cache sizes. Furthermore, we evaluated cache memory energy models for various benchmark applications from SPLASH-2 benchmarking suite, i.e., Barnes, Fmm, Water-nsquared and Water-Spatial. For this purpose, a full system cycle accurate simulator had been used. The benchmarks had been run on various number of cores by changing cache sizes as well. For evaluation of mathematical models, parameters such as cache access time were obtained by using cache simulator. For dual core machine, Barnes performed 25.1%, 32.61%, and 32.61% better than Fmm, Water-nsquared and Water-spatial respectively. We observed that with the increase in cache sizes, number of cycles in benchmarks execution decreases. By increasing number of cores, the throughput improved.

We had evaluated the results by considering homogeneous cores. In the future work the presented technique will be improved to explore more design space solutions and will be extended for heterogeneous cores. The design solutions will be applied in real time adaptive memory systems, where an accurate estimate of energy consumption for cache is required for reconfiguration purpose. Moreover, Cache models had been previously used to analyze the multilevel cache using PowerPC750, and UltraSPARC-II processors. In the future, these models would be used to evaluate state-of-the-art Intel Xeon processors.

ACKNOWLEDGMENT

This work was supported by the National ICT R&D Fund, Pakistan through grant numbered: ICTRDF/TR&D/2012/65

REFERENCES

Advanced RISC Machines Limited (ARM) Inc. (1996). *ARM Software Development Toolkit.*

Chakraborty, A., Homayoun, H., Khajeh, A., Dutt, N., Eltawil, A., & Kurdahi, F. (2010). E< MC2: less energy through multi-copy cache.*Proceedings of the 2010 international conference on Compilers, architectures and synthesis for embedded systems* (pp. 237–246). ACM.

Ferro, L., Pierre, L., Amor, Z. B. H., Lachaize, J., & Lefftz, V. (2011). Runtime Verification of Typical Requirements for a Space Critical SoC Platform. In *Formal Methods for Industrial Critical Systems* (pp. 21–36). Springer. doi:10.1007/978-3-642-24431-5_4

Geer, D. (2005). Chip makers turn to multicore processors. *Computer, 38*(5), 11–13. doi:10.1109/MC.2005.160

González, A., Aliagas, C., & Valero, M. (2014, June). A data cache with multiple caching strategies tuned to different types of locality. *Proceedings of the 25th Anniversary International Conference on Supercomputing Anniversary* (pp. 217-226). ACM. doi:doi:10.1145/2591635.2667170 doi:10.1145/2591635.2667170

Hennessy, J. L., & Patterson, D. A. (2011). *Computer architecture: a quantitative approach.* Elsevier.

Huang, J., Yeluri, S., Frailong, J. M., Libby, J. G., Gupta, A. P., & Coelho, P. (2014). *U.S. Patent No. 8,627,007*. Washington, DC: U.S. Patent and Trademark Office.

Jacob, B., Ng, S., & Wang, D. (2010). *Memory systems: cache, DRAM, disk*. Morgan Kaufmann.

Kamble, M. B., & Ghose, K. (1998). Modeling energy dissipation in low power caches. *Proceedings of theInternational Symposium on Low Power Electronics and Design* (pp. 143–148).

Kin, J., Gupta, M., & Mangione-Smith, W. H. (1997). The filter cache: an energy efficient memory structure.*Proceedings of the 30th annual ACM/IEEE international symposium on Microarchitecture* (pp. 184–193). IEEE Computer Society. doi:10.1109/MICRO.1997.645809

Li, S., Ahn, J. H., Strong, R. D., Brockman, J. B., Tullsen, D. M., & Jouppi, N. P. (2009). McPAT: an integrated power, area, and timing modeling framework for multicore and manycore architectures. *Proceedings of the 42nd Annual IEEE/ACM International Symposium on Microarchitecture MICRO-42* (pp. 469–480). IEEE. doi:doi:10.1145/1669112.1669172 doi:10.1145/1669112.1669172

Li, Y., & Henkel, J. (1998). A framework for estimation and minimizing energy dissipation of embedded HW/SW systems.*Proceedings of the 35th annual Design Automation Conference* (pp. 188–193). ACM. doi:10.1145/277044.277097

Magnusson, P. S., Christensson, M., Eskilson, J., Forsgren, D., Hallberg, G., Hogberg, J., & Werner, B. et al. (2002). Simics: A full system simulation platform. *IEEE Computer*, *35*(2), 50–58. doi:10.1109/2.982916

Mittal, M. (1998). *Computer system and method of allocating cache memories in a multilevel cache hierarchy utilizing a locality hint within an instruction*. Google Patents.

Muhammad Yasir, Q., Klaus D, M.-M. (2010). Data cache-energy and throughput models: design exploration for embedded processors. *EURASIP Journal on Embedded Systems*. EURASIP.

Patel, A., Afram, F., & Ghose, K. (2011). Marss-x86: A qemu-based micro-architectural and systems simulator for x86 multicore processors. Proceedings of the 1st International Qemu Users' Forum (pp. 29–30).

Przybylski, S. A. (1990). *Cache and memory hierarchy design: a performance-directed approach*. Morgan Kaufmann.

Qadri, M. Y., Gujarathi, H. S., & McDonald-Maier, K. D. (2009). Low Power Processor Architectures and Contemporary Techniques for Power Optimization–A Review. *Journal of Computers*, *4*(10), 927–942. doi:10.4304/jcp.4.10.927-942

Qadri, M. Y., & McDonald-Maier, K. D. (2010). Analytical Evaluation of Energy and Throughput for Multilevel Caches. *Proceedings of the 2010 12th International Conference on Computer Modelling and Simulation (UKSim)* (pp. 598–603). IEEE. doi:doi:10.1109/UKSIM.2010.114 doi:10.1109/UK-SIM.2010.114

River, W. (2006). Simics Full System Simulator.

Segars, S. (2001). *Low power design techniques for microprocessors*. Tutorial Note of the ISSCC.

Silvano, C., Fornaciari, W., & Villar, E. (2014). *Multi-objective Design Space Exploration of Multiprocessor SoC Architectures*. Springer.

Šimunić, T., Benini, L., & De Micheli, G. (1999). Cycle-accurate simulation of energy consumption in embedded systems.*Proceedings of the 36th annual ACM/IEEE Design Automation Conference* (pp. 867–872). ACM. doi:10.1109/DAC.1999.782199

Singh, J. P., Hennessy, J. L., & Gupta, A. (1995). Implications of hierarchical N-body methods for multiprocessor architectures.*ACM Transactions on Computer Systems, 13*(2), 141–202. doi:10.1145/201045.201050

Singh, J. P., Holt, C., Hennessy, J. L., & Gupta, A. (1993). A parallel adaptive fast multipole method.*Proceedings of the 1993 ACM/IEEE conference on Supercomputing* (pp. 54–65). ACM. doi:10.1145/169627.169651

Smith, A. J. (1982). Cache memories.[CSUR]. *ACM Computing Surveys, 14*(3), 473–530. doi:10.1145/356887.356892

Su, C.-L., & Despain, A. M. (1995). Cache design trade-offs for power and performance optimization: a case study.*Proceedings of the 1995 international symposium on Low power design* (pp. 63–68). ACM. doi:10.1145/224081.224093

D. Tarjan, S. Thoziyoor, & N. P. Jouppi. (2006). CACTI 4.0. *HP Laboratories Palo Alto*.

Wang, A., & Naffziger, S. (2008). *Adaptive techniques for dynamic processor optimization: theory and practice*. Springer Science & Business Media. Springer. doi:10.1007/978-0-387-76472-6

Wei, H., Shao, Z., Huang, Z., Chen, R., Guan, Y., Tan, J., & Shao, Z. (2016). RT-ROS: A real-time ROS architecture on multi-core processors. *Future Generation Computer Systems, 56*, 171–178. doi:10.1016/j.future.2015.05.008

Whitham, J., Audsley, N. C., & Davis, R. I. (2014). Explicit reservation of cache memory in a predictable, preemptive multitasking real-time system. *ACM Transactions on Embedded Computing Systems, 13*(4s), 120. doi:10.1145/2523070

Wilson, A. W. Jr, & Frank, S. J. (1988). *Hierarchical cache memory system and method*. Google Patents.

Woo, S. C., Ohara, M., Torrie, E., Singh, J. P., & Gupta, A. (1995). The SPLASH-2 programs: Characterization and methodological considerations. In ACM SIGARCH Computer Architecture News (Vol. 23, pp. 24–36). ACM.

Yourst, M. T. (2007). PTLsim: A cycle accurate full system x86-64 microarchitectural simulator. *Proceedings of the IEEE International Symposium on Performance Analysis of Systems & Software ISPASS '07* (pp. 23–34). IEEE. doi:doi:10.1109/ISPASS.2007.363733 doi:10.1109/ISPASS.2007.363733

KEY TERMS AND DEFINITIONS

Benchmarks: Standard tools for performance evaluation and comparison.

Cache Memory: A memory used by central processing unit of a computer to reduce the average time to access data from the main memory, i.e., it serves as a bridge between processor and main memory.

Cycle Accurate Simulator: A computer program that simulates a microarchitecture on a cycle-by-cycle basis.

Design Space Exploration: Finding the optimal search space solutions for desired objective.

Multicore Processors: A multicore processor is a processor with multiple processor cores on a single die or multiple dice inside a multi-chip module.

Chapter 5
Communication Analysis and Performance Prediction of Parallel Applications on Large–Scale Machines

Yan Li
Intel Labs China, China

Jidong Zhai
Tsinghua University, China

Keqin Li
State University of New York, USA

ABSTRACT

With the development of high performance computers, communication performance is a key factor affecting the performance of HPC applications. Communication patterns can be obtained by analyzing communication traces. However, existing approaches to generating communication traces need to execute the entire parallel applications on full-scale systems that are time-consuming and expensive. Furthermore, for designers of large-scale parallel computers, it is greatly desired that performance of a parallel application can be predicted at the design phase. Despite previous efforts, it remains an open problem to estimate sequential computation time in each process accurately and efficiently for large-scale parallel applications on non-existing target machines. In this chapter, we will introduce a novel technique for performing fast communication trace collection for large-scale parallel applications and an automatic performance prediction framework with a trace-driven network simulator.

INTRODUCTION

Different applications in the high performance computing (HPC) field exhibit different communication patterns, which can be characterized by three key attributes: volume, spatial and temporal (Chodnekar, et al., 1997; Kim & Lilja, 1998). Proper understanding of communication patterns of parallel applica-

DOI: 10.4018/978-1-5225-0287-6.ch005

tions is important to optimize the communication performance of these applications (Chen et al., 2006; Preissl, et al., 2008a). For example, with the knowledge of spatial and volume communication attributes, MPIPP (Chen, et al., 2006) optimizes the performance of Message Passing Interface (MPI) programs on non-uniform communication platforms by tuning the scheme of process placement. Besides, such knowledge can also help design better communication subsystems. For instance, for circuit-switched networks used in parallel computing, communication patterns are used to pre-establish connections and eliminate the runtime overhead of path establishment. Furthermore, a recent work shows spatial and volume communication attributes can be employed by replay-based MPI debuggers to reduce replay overhead significantly (Xue, et al., 2009).

Previous work on communication patterns of parallel applications mainly relies on traditional trace collection methods (Kim & Lilja, 1998; Preissl et al., 2008b; Vetter & Mueller, 2002). A series of trace collection and analysis tools have been developed, such as ITC/ITA (Intel, 2008; Kerbyson et al., 2001), KOJAK (Mohr & Wolf, 2003), TAU (Shende & Malony,2006), DiP (Labarta et al., 1996) and VAMPIR (Nagel et al., 1996). These tools need to instrument original programs at the invocation points of communication routines. The instrumented programs are executed on full-scale parallel systems and communication traces are collected during the execution. The collected communication trace files record type, size, source and destination etc. for each message. The communication patterns of parallel applications can be easily generated from the communication traces. However, traditional communication trace collection methods have two main limitations: huge resource requirement and long trace collection time. For example, ASCI SAGE routinely runs on 2000-4000 processors (Kerbyson, et al., 2001) and FT program in the NPB consumes more than 600 GB memory for Class E input (Bailey, et al., 1995). Therefore, it is impossible to use traditional trace collection methods to collect communication patterns of large-scale parallel applications without full-scale systems. Moreover, it takes several months to complete even on a system with thousands of CPUs. It is prohibitive long for trace collection and prevents many interesting explorations of using communication traces, such as input sensitivity analysis of communication patterns. Additionally, MPIP (Vetter, et al., 2001) is a lightweight profiling library for MPI applications and only collects statistical information of MPI functions. However, all these traditional trace collection methods require the execution of the entire instrumented programs, which restricts their wide usage for analyzing large-scale applications. Our method adopts the similar technique to capture the communication patterns at runtime as the traditional trace collection methods.

We have two observations on existing communication trace collection and analysis approaches:

1. Many important applications of communication pattern analysis, such as the process placement optimization (Chen, et al., 2006) and subgroup replay (Zhang, et al., 2009), do not require temporal attributes.
2. Most computation and message contents in message-passing parallel applications are not relevant to their spatial and volume communication attributes.

Motivated by the above observations, we describe a novel technique in this chapter, called FACT, which can perform fast communication trace collection for large-scale parallel applications on small-scale systems. Our idea is to reduce the original program to obtain a program slice through static analysis, and to execute the program slice to acquire communication traces. The program slice preserves all the variables and statements in the original program relevant to the spatial and volume attributes, but deletes any unrelated parts. In order to recognize the relevant variables and statements, we propose a live-propagation slicing algorithm (LPSA) to simplify original programs. By solving an inter-procedural data flow equation, it can identify all the variables and statements affecting the communication patterns. We have implemented FACT and evaluated it with 7 NPB programs as well as Sweep3D. The results show that FACT can preserve the spatial and volume communication attributes of original programs and reduce resource consumptions by two orders of magnitude in most cases.

Large-scale parallel computers usually consist of thousands of processor cores and cost millions of dollars which take years to design and implement. For designers of these computers, it is critical to answer the following question at the design phase: What is the performance of application X on a parallel machine Y with 10000 nodes connected by network Z? Accurate answer to the above question enables designers to evaluate various design alternatives and make sure that the design can meet the performance goal. In addition, it also helps application developers to design and optimize applications even before the target machine is available. However, accurate performance prediction of parallel applications is difficult because the execution time of large parallel applications is determined by sequential computation time in each process, the communication time and their convolution. Due to the complex interactions between computation and communications, the prediction accuracy can be hurt significantly if either computation or communication time is estimated with notable errors.

In this chapter, we also focus on how to acquire sequential computation time accurately for large-scale parallel applications. This is because existing approaches address the communication time estimation and the convolution issues fairly well, such as BigNetSim and DIMEMAS (Labarta, et al., 1996; Choudhury, et al., 2005). The bottleneck of current prediction framework is to estimate sequential computation time in each process accurately and efficiently for large-scale parallel applications on non-existing target parallel machines. We illustrate a novel approach based on deterministic replay techniques to solve the problem. There are two main contributions:

1. Employing deterministic replay techniques to measure sequential computation time of strong-scaling applications without full-scale target machines, and
2. Employing representative replay to reduce measurement time.

We have implemented a performance prediction framework, called PHANTOM, which integrates the above computation-time acquisition approach with a trace-driven network simulator. We validate our approach on several platforms. For ASCI Sweep3D, the error of our approach is less than 5% on 1024 processor cores. We compare the prediction accuracy of PHANTOM with a recent regression-based prediction approach. The results show that PHANTOM has better prediction accuracy across different platforms than the regression-based approach. The rest of this chapter is organized as follows. In the following section, we present an overview of our approach followed by our live-propagation slicing algorithm and the implementation of FACT. Then, we describe the framework of PHANTOM. And finally, we conclude this chapter.

COMMUNICATION TRACE COLLECTION

We present an overview of our approach followed by our live-propagation slicing algorithm. The implementation and evaluation are also described in this section.

Design Overview

FACT consists of two primary components, a compilation framework and a runtime environment as shown in Figure 1. The compilation framework is divided into two phases, intra-procedural analysis followed by inter-procedural analysis. The program is sliced based on the results of the inter-procedural analysis. Finally, the communication traces are collected in the runtime environment.

During the intra-procedural analysis phase, FACT parses the source code of an MPI program and identifies the invoked communication routines. The relevant arguments of these routines that determine communication patterns are collected. Information about control dependence, data dependence and communication dependence for each procedure is gathered, which will be explained in detail in the following subsections. During the inter-procedural analysis phase, the program call graph is built based on the information of call sites collected during the intra-procedural phase. LPSA is used to identify all the variables and statements that affects the communication patterns. The output of the compilation framework is the program slice as well as directives for usage at runtime.

Figure 1. Overview of FACT

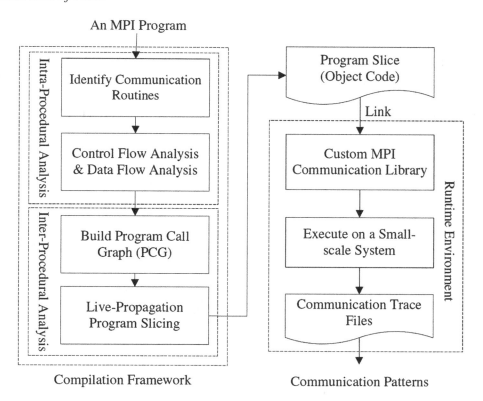

A program slice is a skeleton of the original program that cannot be executed on the system directly. Runtime environment of FACT provides a custom MPI communication library to collect the communication traces from the program slice based on the directives inserted at compile time. The program slice is linked to the custom communication library and executed on a small-scale system. The communication traces of applications are collected during the execution according to the specified problem size, input parameters and number of processes.

Live-Propagation Slicing Algorithm

From a formal point of view, the definition of program slice is based on the concept of slicing criterion (Weiser, et al., 1984). A slicing criterion is a pair (p, V), where p is a program point, and V is a subset of the program variables. A program slice on the slicing criterion (p, V) is a subset of program statements that preserve the behavior of the original program at the program point p with respect to the program variables in V. Therefore, determining the slicing criterion and designing an efficient slicing algorithm according to the actual problem requirements are two key challenges in the compilation framework.

- **Slicing Criterion**: Since our goal is to collect communication traces for analyzing spatial and volume communication attributes, we record the following communication properties in LPSA for a given parallel program:
  - For point-to-point communication, we record message type, message size, message source and destination, message tag and communicator id.
  - For collective communication, we record message type, sending message size, receiving message size, root id (if exist) and communicator id.

Message size, source and destination are used to compute spatial and volume communication attributes, while message type, message tag and communicator id are useful for other communication analysis. In an MPI program, these properties can be acquired directly from the corresponding parameters of the MPI communication routines. For example, in the routine *MPI_Send* in Figure 2, the parameters *count* and *type* determine the message size. The parameters *dest* and *comm* determine the message destination. The message tag and communicator id can be acquired from the parameters tag and comm. The parameter *buf* does not affect the communication patterns directly. However, sometimes it may affect the communication patterns indirectly through data flow propagation and we will analyze it in the following subsections. Comm Variable is defined in this chapter to represent those parameters that determine the communication patterns directly.

Figure 2. Comm variables in the routine for MPI_Send; the variables marked with Comm directly determine the communication patterns of the parallel program.

```
MPI_Send(buf, count, type, dest, tag, comm)
buf : initial address of send buffer
[Comm] count: number of elements in send buffer
[Comm] type : datatype of each buffer element
[Comm] dest : rank of destination
[Comm] tag : uniquely identify a message
[Comm] comm : communication context
```

Definition 1 (Comm Variable): *It is a parameter of a communication routine in a parallel program, the value of which directly determines the communication patterns of the parallel program.*

As MPI is a standard communication interface, we can explicitly mark Comm Variables for each MPI routine. In Figure 2, Comm Variables in the routine for *MPI_Send* are marked. All the parameters, except *buf*, are Comm variables. When a communication routine is identified in the source code, the corresponding Comm Variables are collected. For each procedure P, we use a Comm Set, $C(P)$, to record all the Comm Variables.

$$C(P) = \Big\{ (\ell, v) \mid \ell \text{ is the unique lable of } v, v \text{ is a Comm Variable} \Big\}.$$

The Comm Set $C(P)$ is the slicing criterion for simplifying the original program in LPSA, which will be optimized during the phase of data dependence analysis.

- **Dependence of MPI Programs:** For convenience, we assume that a control flow graph (CFG) is built for each procedure and the program call graph (PCG) is constructed for the whole program. To describe our slicing algorithm easily, we use statement instead of basic block as a node in the CFG. We assume that each statement in the program is uniquely identified by its label 1 and is associated with two sets: DEF[ℓ], a set of variables whose values are defined at ℓ, and USE[ℓ], a set of variables whose values are used at ℓ In an MPI program, there are three main types of dependence for statements and variables that would change the behavior for a given program point, data dependence (dd), control dependence (cd) and communication dependence (md).
- **Data Dependence:** Data dependence between statements means that the program's computation might be changed if the relative order of statements were reversed (Horwitz, et al., 1986). To analyze the data dependence, we must first calculate the reaching definitions for each procedure. We define the *GEN* and *KILL* sets for each node in the CFG. Then we adopt the iterative algorithm presented in (Appel, et al.,1997) to calculate the reaching definitions. The data flow graph (DFG) can be constructed based on the results of the reaching definitions analysis. The node in the DFG is either a statement or a predicate statement. The edge represents the data dependence of the variables. The data dependence information computed by the reaching definitions is stored in the data structures of DU and UD chains (Aho, et al., 1986).

Definition 2 (DU and UD Chain): *Def-use (DU) Chain links each definition of a variable to all of its possible uses.* Use-def (UD) Chain links each use of a variable to a set of its definitions that can reach that use without any other intervening definition.

We can further optimize the Comm Set based on the results of data flow analysis. If there are no other intervening definitions for the consecutive Comm Variables, we keep only the last Comm Variable.

- **Control Dependence:** If a statement X determines whether statement Y is executed, statement Y is control dependent on statement X. The DFG does not include information of control dependence. Control dependence can be computed with the post-dominance frontier algorithm (Ferrante, et al., 1987). In this chapter, we convert the control dependence into data dependence by treating the predicate statement as a definition statement and then incorporating the control dependence into the UD chains.

- **Communication Dependence:** Communication dependence is an inherent characteristic for MPI programs due to message passing behavior. MPI programs take advantage of explicit communication model to exchange data between different processes. For example, sending and receiving routines for the point-to-point communications are usually used in pairs in the programs. Statement X in process i is communication dependent on statement Y in process j, if
  - Process j sends a message to process i through explicit communication routines.
  - Statement X is a receiving operation and statement Y is a sending operation ($X \neq Y$).

In MPI programs, both point-to-point communications and collective communications can introduce communication dependence. Due to limitations of space, we do not list more examples in this chapter.

Communication dependence can be computed through identifying all potential matching communication operations in MPI programs. Although in general, it is a difficult problem for static analysis to determine the matching operations, we find it is sufficient to deal with this problem using simple heuristics in practice. We conservatively connect all potential sending operations with a receiving operation, and adopt some heuristics, such as mismatched tags or data types of message buffer, to prune edges that cannot represent real matches. We will further discuss the communication dependence issues in the following subsections.

In MPI programs, the message is exchanged through the message buffer variable, *buf*. The communication dependence can be represented with the message buffer variable. $msg\_buf(\ell)$ is used to denote the message buffer variable in the communication statement ℓ. Additional considerations for non-blocking communications will be presented in the implementation of runtime environment.

Definition 3 (MD Chain): *Message-Dependence Chain (MD Chain) links each variable of message receiving buffer to all of its sending operations.* The slice set of an MPI program (M) with respect to the slicing criterion $C(M)$, denoted by $C(M)$, consists of all statements ℓ on which the values of variables in $C(M)$ directly or indirectly dependent. More formally:

$$\mathcal{S}(C(M)) = \left\{ \ell \mid v \xrightarrow{d_1} \dots \xrightarrow{d_n} \ell, v \in C(M), n > 0, for 1 \leq i \leq n, d_i \in c\{d, dd, md\} \right\} \qquad (1)$$

We use the symbol $\rightarrow$ to denote the dependence between variables and statements. For computing the program slice with respect to the slicing criterion $C(M)$, we define LIVE Variable to record dependence relationship between the variables of programs. A Comm Variable itself is also a LIVE Variable based on the definition of LIVE Variable.

Definition 4 (LIVE Variable): *A variable x is LIVE, if the change of its value at statement ℓ can affect the value of any Comm Variable v directly or indirectly through dependence of MPI programs, denoted by $v \rightarrow^* (\ell, x)$.* There is a LIVE Set for each procedure P, *LIVE* [P].

$$LIVE[P] = \{ (\ell, x) \mid v \rightarrow^* (\ell, x), v \in C(P) \}. \qquad (2)$$

- **Intra-Procedural Analysis:** During the intra-procedural analysis phase, data dependence, control dependence and communication dependence are collected and put into corresponding data structures. Each procedure P is associated with two sets, $WL[P]$ and LIVE[P]. $WL[P]$ is a worklist that holds the variables waiting to be processed and LIVE[P] holds the LIVE Variables for procedure P. As program slicing in this chapter is a backward data flow problem, we use a worklist algorithm to traverse the UD chains and iteratively find all the LIVE Variables. We put the statements that define LIVE Variables into slice set $\mathbb{S}[P]$ and mark MPI statements that define LIVE Variables or have communication dependence with marked MPI statements. The main body of the analysis algorithm is given in Algorithm 1. *receive_buf* denotes the message buffer variables in the receiving operations. The worklist $WL[P]$ for each procedure is initialized with its Comm Set and LIVE[P] is initialized with null set.

In Algorithm 1, the statements not in slice sets except MPI routines are deleted, while all the MPI routines are retained. For unmarked MPI routines by Algorithm 1, it means that no LIVE Variable is defined or no communication dependence exists in these routines. The retained unmarked MPI routines are served for runtime environment of FACT to collect communication traces. In contrast, for marked MPI routines by Algorithm 1, LIVE Variables are defined or communication dependence exists in these routines. For MPI routines used for message passing, it means that the contents of messages are relevant to the communication patterns. In Figure 3, the LIVE Variable, *num*, is defined in *MPI_Irecv* of Line 5 that is communication dependent on *MPI_Send* of Line 2. Therefore, both MPI routines are marked by the algorithm and will be executed at runtime. Algorithm 1 is sufficient for the MPI program with one function. In the real parallel application, the program is always modularized with several procedures. In the following subsection, we will present additional considerations for inter-procedural analysis.

- **Inter-Procedural Analysis:** Slicing across procedure boundaries is complicated due to the necessity of passing the LIVE Variables into and out of procedures. Because program slicing in this chapter is a backward data flow problem and the slicing criterion can arise either in the calling procedure (caller) or in the called procedure (callee), the LIVE Variable can propagate bidirectionally between the caller and the callee through parameter passing. To obtain a precise program slice, we adopt a two-phase traverse over the PCG, Top-Down phase followed by Bottom-Up phase. Additionally, the UD chains built during the intra-procedural phase are refined to consider the side effects of procedure calls. In this chapter, we assume that all the parameters are passed by reference and our algorithm can be extended to the case where they are passed by value.

Figure 3. Marked MPI point-to-point communication routines by Algorithm 1 (M means marked)

```
1. if(myid == 0){
2. [M] MPI_Send(&num, 1, MPI_INT, 1, 55,...)
3.     MPI_Recv(buf, num, MPI_INT, 1, 66,...)
4. }else{
5. [M] MPI_Irecv(&num, 1, MPI_INT, 0, 55,..., req)
6.     MPI_Wait(req,...)
7.     size = num
8.     MPI_Send(buf, size, MPI_INT, 0, 66,...)
9. }
```

- **MOD/REF Analysis:** To build precise UD chains we use the results of inter-procedural MOD/REF analysis. For example, in Figure 4, before incorporating the information from the MOD/REF analysis, $UD(4, a) = \{2, 3\}$. We compute the following sets in the MOD/REF analysis for each procedure (Banning, et al., 1979): GMOD(P) and GREF(P). GMOD(P) is a set of variables that are modified by an invocation of procedure P, while GREF(P) is a set of variables that are referenced by an invocation of procedure P (Muchnick, et al., 1997). The information from the MOD/REF analysis tells us whether a variable is modified or referenced due to the procedure calls. With these results, we can refine the UD chains built during the intra-procedural analysis. For example, $UD(4, a) = \{3\}$.

- **Extension of MD Chains:** The MD chains collected during the intra-procedural phase do not include inter-procedural communication dependence. During the inter-procedural analysis phase, MD chains are extended to consider cross-procedural dependence. At the same time, Algorithm 1 is extended to Algorithm 2 that will be invoked by Algorithm 3. Only the different parts from Algorithm 1 are listed here. $P' : \ell_j$ denotes the statement ℓ_j in procedure P'.

- **Top-Down Analysis:** The Top-Down phase propagates the LIVE Variables from the caller to the callee over the PCG by binding the actual parameters of the caller to the formal parameters of the callee. As the LIVE Variable can be modified by the called procedure via parameter passing, we need to find the corresponding definition of this variable in the called procedure. For example, in Figure 4 we can compute from the intra-procedural analysis, that $(3, a)$ is a LIVE Variable. This calling context is then passed into the procedure *bar*. The corresponding formal parameter in *bar* is the parameter b. There may be several definitions of b in procedure *bar*, however we only care about the last definitions (it is a set due to the effects of control flow) of variable b due to the property of the backward data flow analysis. This definition appears in statement 9 in *bar*. In addition, we put this statement into slice set and put its USE variables into the worklist of procedure *bar*. Other LIVE Variables in procedure *bar* can be computed iteratively by Algorithm 2. In procedure *foo* the actual parameter $(3, a)$ is no longer put into its worklist. We define the LIVE_Down function to formalize this data flow analysis.

Figure 4. An example of LIVE variable propagation from the caller to the callee

```
1. foo(){
2.    a = 5
3.    call bar(a)
4.    size = a
5.    call MPI_Send(...,size,...)
6. }
7. bar(b){
8.    m = 4
9.    b = m
10. }
```

Definition 5 (LIVE Down): *Procedure P invokes procedure Q, v is a LIVE Variable and also an actual parameter at callsite ℓ in* procedure P, v' is the corresponding formal parameter in procedure Q, $LIVE\_Down(P, \ell, v, Q)$ returns statement set (L is the label set) of the last definitions of v' in procedure $Q : LIVE\_Down(P, \ell, v, Q) = L$.

- **Bottom-Up Analysis:** The Bottom-Up phase is responsible for propagating the LIVE Variables from the callee to the caller. For a LIVE Variable in the called procedure, if its definition is a formal parameter, we need to propagate the LIVE information by binding the formal parameters to the actual parameters. For example, in Figure 5, the formal parameter of *b* in procedure bar is a LIVE Variable computed by the intra-procedure analysis. We need to propagate this information into the calling procedure *foo*. The corresponding actual parameter is the parameter *a* in *foo*. We put this variable into the worklist of procedure *foo* and Algorithm 2 is used for computing other LIVE Variables. The LIVE_Up function is defined as follows.

Definition 6 (LIVE Up): *Procedure Q is invoked by procedure P, v is a LIVE Variable and also a formal parameter (the label of procedure entry point is* ℓ_0 *in* procedure Q, v' is the corresponding actual parameter in procedure P at callsite ℓ', $LIVE\_Up(Q, \ell_0, v, P)$ returns the label of the callsite and the actual parameter pair: $LIVE\_Up(Q, \ell_0, v, P) = (\ell', v')$.

The final algorithm for program slicing based on live-propagation is given in Algorithm 3 that invokes Algorithm 2. The output of LPSA is the program slice set as well as directives for MPI routines. Our experimental results show that LPSA can converge within 3-4 iterations for the outer loop. Let $C(M)$ be the slicing criterion for a given MPI program M; and $\mathbb{S}(M)$ be the slice set computed by LPSA. Then the correctness of the algorithm can be stated by Equation 3.

$$\mathcal{S}(C(M)) = \mathbb{S}(M) \tag{3}$$

Figure 5. An example of LIVE variable propagation from the callee to the caller

```
1. foo(){
2.    n = 5
3.    a = n
4.    call bar(a)
5. }
6. bar(b){
7.    size = b
8.    call MPI_Send(...,size,...)
9.    ...
10. }
```

Algorithm 1. Compute LIVE Set and Mark MPI statements for intra-procedure

1: **procedure** INTRA-LIVE(*P*)

2: **input**: worklist WL[P] and LIVE set LIVE[P]

3: **output**: program slice set of procedure: $\mathbb{S}(P)$

4: Change←False

5: **while** WL[P] ≠∅ **do**

6: Remove an item (ℓ, v) from WL[P]

7: **if** (ℓ, v)∉ LIVE[P] **then**

8: Change←True

9: $LIVE[P] \leftarrow \{(\ell_i,v)\} \cup LIVE[P]$ ▷ Process communication dependence!

10: **if** $\left(\ell_i,v\right) \in receive\_buf$ then

11: **for** $\ell_i \in MD\ (\ell_i,\ v)$ **do**

12: Mark MPI statement ℓ_i

13: $\mathbb{S}(P) = \mathbb{S}(P) \cup \left\{\ell_j\right\}$

14: $WL[P] \leftarrow \left\{\left(\ell_j, msg\_buf\left(\ell_j\right)\right)\right\} \cup WL[P]$

15: **end for**

16: **else** ▷ Process control and data dependence!

17: **for** $\ell_k \in UD\left(\ell_i,v\right)$ do

18: **if** $\ell_k \in MPI\_Routines$ then

19: Mark MPI statement ℓ_k

20: **end if**

21: $\mathbb{S}(P) = \mathbb{S}(P) \cup \{\ell_k\}$

22: **for** $x \in USE[\ell_k]$ do

23: $WL[P] \leftarrow \{(\ell_k,x)\} \cup WL[P]$

24: **end for**

25: **end for**

26: **end if**

27: **end if**

28: **end while**

29: **return** $\mathbb{S}(P)$

30: **end procedure**

Algorithm 2. Extension of INTRA-LIVE(P)

1: **procedure** INTRA-LIVE-EXT(P)

...

12: **for each** $P' : \ell_j \in MD\left(\ell_i, v\right)$ do

13: Mark MPI statement $P' : \ell_j$

14: $\mathbb{S}(P') = \mathbb{S}(P') \cup \{\ell_j\}$

15: $WL[P'] \leftarrow \{(\ell_j, msg\_buf(\ell_j))\} \cup WL[P']$

...

Algorithm 3. Pseudo code for Live-Propagation Slicing Algorithm (LPSA)

1: **input:** An MPI program M

2: **output:** Program slice $\mathbb{S}(M)$ and marked information

3: For each procedure P: Build UD and MD Chains

4: For each procedure P: Build Comm Set $C(P)$

5: MOD/REF analysis over the PCG

6: For each procedure P: Refine UD and MD chains

7: For each procedure P: $WL[P] \leftarrow C(P)$

8: For each procedure P: $LIVE[P] \leftarrow \varnothing$

9: Change←True

10: **while** (Change = True) **do**

11: Change←False ▷Top-Down Phase

12: **for** procedure P in Pre-Order over PCG **do**

13: **call** INTRA-LIVE-EXT(P)

14: **for** $Q \in successor(P)$ do

15: **for** parameter v at callsite ℓ **do**

16: **if** $(\ell, v) \in LIVE[P]$ then

17: $L = LIVE\_Down(P, \ell, v, Q)$

18: **for** $\ell' \in L$ do

19: **if** $\ell' \in MPI\_Routines$ then

20: Mark MPI statement ℓ'

continued on following page

Algorithm 3. Continued

21: **end if**

22: $\mathbb{S}(Q) = \mathbb{S}(Q) \cup \{\ell'\}$

23: **for** $x \in \text{USE}[\ell']$ do

24: $WL[Q] \leftarrow \{(\ell', x)\} \cup WL[Q]$

25: **end for**

26: **end for**

27: **end if**

28: **end for**

29: **end for**

30: **end for**

31: ▷Bottom-Up Phase

32: **for** procedure Q in Post-Order over PCG do

33: **call** INTRA-LIVE-EXT(Q)

34: **for** $P \in predecessor(Q)$ do

35: **for** formal parameter ℓ_0 in Q**do**

36: **if** $\left((\ell_0, v) \in LIVE[Q] \right)$ **then**

37: $(\ell', x) = LIVE\_Up\left(Q, \ell_0, v, P\right)$

38: $WL[P] \leftarrow \{(\ell', x)\} \cup WL[P]$

39: $\mathbb{S}(P) = \mathbb{S}(P) \cup \{\ell'\}$

40: **end if**

41: **end for**

42: **end for**

43: **end for**

44: **end while**

45: For each procedure P: return $\mathbb{S}(P)$

Implementation and Evaluation

We have implemented LPSA for FACT in the production compiler, Open64 (SGI, 2009). Open64 is the open source version of the SGI Pro64 compiler under the GNU General Public License (GPL). As shown in Figure 6, the major functional modules of Open64 are the front end (FE), pre-optimizer (Pre-OPT), inter-procedural analysis, loop nest optimizer (LNO), global scalar optimizer (WOPT) and code generator (CG). To exchange data between different modules, Open64 utilizes a common intermediate representation (IR), called WHIRL. WHIRL consists of five levels of abstraction, from very high level to lower levels. Each optimization module works on a specific level of WHIRL.

FACT is implemented in the PreOPT and inter-procedural analysis modules as shown in Figure 6. In the PreOPT phase, the CFG is created for each procedure. Control dependence analysis is carried out on the CFG in reverse dominator tree order while the data dependence is collected into the DU and UD chains. The inter-procedural analysis module can be further divided into three main phases: Inter-Procedural Local Analysis (IPL), Inter-Procedural Analyzer (IPA), and Inter-Procedural Optimizer (IPO). During the IPL phase, we parse the WHIRL tree and identify the communication routines. Communication dependence is collected into MD chains and Comm Variables are stored in the form of summary data. During the IPA phase, the PCG is constructed. MOD/REF analysis is performed on this and the DU and UD chains built in the IPL phase are refined. MD chains are extended to consider cross-procedural communication dependence. By solving an inter-procedural data flow equation during the IPA phase, we

Figure 6. FACT in the Open64 infrastructure

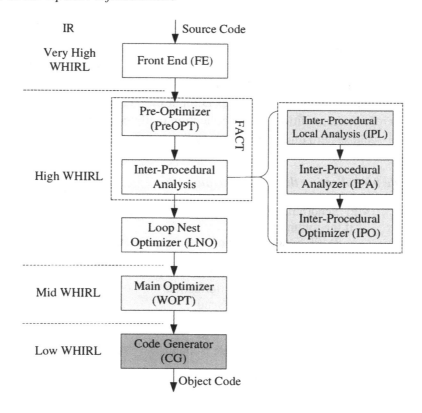

compute the LIVE, sets and slice sets for each procedure and mark necessary MPI statements. During the IPO phase, we delete all the statements that are not in slice sets except MPI routines and remove the variables that are not in the LIVE, sets from the symbol table. The marked information for MPI communication routines are retained in the program slice. Currently, we only support FORTRAN programs in FACT and supporting other languages remains as our future work.

Runtime environment is in charge of collecting communication traces from the program slice. It provides a custom MPI wrapper communication library which differentiates MPI routines based on their functions. For MPI routines used to create and shut down MPI runtime environment, such as *MPI_Init*, *MPI_Finalize*, they are not modified and executed directly in the library. For MPI routines used to manage communication contexts, such as *MPI_COMM_Split*, *MPI_COMM_Dup*, the library requires executing these routines and collecting information about the relation for process translation between different communicators. For MPI routines used for message passing, such as *MPI_Send*, *MPI_Irecv*, *MPI_Bcast*, the library first judges the state of the MPI routine based on the results of LPSA analysis. If the communication routine is marked, we need to execute it and meanwhile collect communication property information. Otherwise only related information is recorded. In addition, for unmarked non-blocking communication routines, the parameters *request* of these routines are set so that the library guarantees that corresponding communication operations are not executed, such as *MPI_Wait* or *MPI_Waitall*.

We use the MPI profiling layer (PMPI) to capture the communication events, record the communication traces to a memory buffer, and eventually write them on local disks. Figure 7 gives an example of collecting the communication traces for *MPI_Send* routine. In Figure 7, *myid* is a global variable computed with *PMPI_Comm_rank*. Our runtime environment also provides a series of communication trace analyzers which can generate the communication profiles of applications, such as the distribution of message sizes, communication topology graph.

To present the advantages of FACT over the traditional trace collection methods, we collect communication traces of NPB programs (Class D) and Sweep3D (150×150×150) with a large date set on a small-scale system, the 4-node *test platform* which has only 32 GB memory in all. The memory requirements of these programs except EP and LU for 512 processes exceed the memory capacity of the *test platform*. For example, the NPB FT with Class D input for 512 processes will consume about 126 GB memory size. Therefore, the traditional trace collection methods cannot collect the communication traces on such a small-scale system due to the memory limitation.

Figure 7. Pseudo code for collecting the communication traces for MPI_Send routine at runtime

```
MPI_Send(buf, count, datatype, dest, tag,comm){
    If the routine is marked by LPSA
        PMPI_Send(buf, count, datatype, dest, tag, comm)
    Endif
    typesize = PMPI_Type_size(datatype)
    Record the following information:
        message type : MPI_Send
        message source : myid
        message destination : dest
        message size : typesize * count
        message tag : tag
        communicator ID : comm
}
```

Our experimental results shown in Figure 8 demonstrate that FACT is able to collect the communication traces for these programs on the *test platform*. Moreover, it consumes very little memory resources. The memory requirements of the original programs are collected on the *validation platform*. In most cases, the memory consumption for collecting the communication traces with FACT is reduced by two orders of magnitude compared to the original programs. For example, Sweep3D only consumes 0.13 GB memory for 64 processes, 1.25 GB memory for 512 processes with FACT while the original program consumes 26.61 GB and 213.83 GB memory respectively.

Figure 9 lists the execution time of FACT when collecting the communication traces on the *test platform*. As the traditional trace collection methods cannot collect the communication traces on the *test platform*, the execution time of the original programs is collected on the *validation platform*. In addition, as the problem size is fixed for each process in the Sweep3D, its execution time increases with the number of processes.

Since FACT deletes irrelevant computations of the original program at compile time and only executes necessary communication operations at runtime, the execution time of the original program can be reduced significantly. For example, FACT just takes 0.28 seconds for collecting the communication traces of BT for 64 processes, while the original program running on the 512-core *validation platform* takes 1175.65 seconds yet. As few of communication operations are used in the EP program, its execution time is negligible after slicing. Overall, the execution time with FACT is acceptable for most developers to study the communication patterns on such a small-scale system. In addition, FACT can benefit when more nodes are available.

Figure 8. The memory consumption (in GigaByte) of FACT for collecting the communication traces of NPB programs (Class D) and Sweep3D (150×150×150) on the test platform; traditional trace collection methods cannot achieve this on the test platform due to the memory limitation. The memory consumption of the original programs is collected on the validation platform.

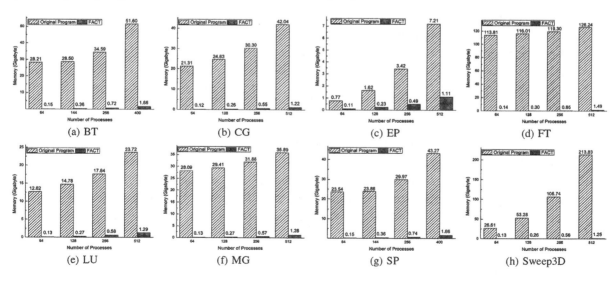

Figure 9. The execution time (in second) of FACT when collecting the communication traces of NPB programs and Sweep3D on the test platform (32 cores); the execution time of original programs are collected on the validation platform (512 cores).

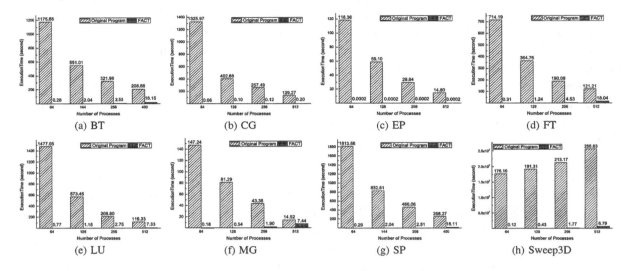

BASE PERFORMANCE PREDICTION FRAMEWORK

We use a trace-driven simulation approach for the performance prediction. In our framework, we split the parallel applications into computation and communication parts, predict computation and communication performance separately and finally use a simulator to convolute them to get the execution time of whole parallel applications. The framework includes the following key steps.

- **Collecting Computation and Communication Traces:** We generate communication traces of parallel applications by intercepting all communication operations for each process, and mark the computation between communication operations as sequential computation units. The purpose of this step is to separate communications and computation in parallel applications to enable us to predict them separately. Figure 11 shows a simple MPI program and its computation and communication traces are given in Figure 10(a).

It should be noted that we only need the communication information (e.g. message type, message size, source and destination etc.) and the interleave of communication / computation in this step. All temporal properties are not used in later steps of performance prediction. A common approach to generating these traces is to execute parallel applications with instrumented MPI libraries. To further reduce the overhead in this step, we employ the FACT technique which can generate traces of large-scale applications on small-scale systems fast.

Figure 10. Base performance prediction framework) when the number of processes is 2 (the elapsed time for the kth computation unit of process x is denoted by CPU_Burst(x,k)

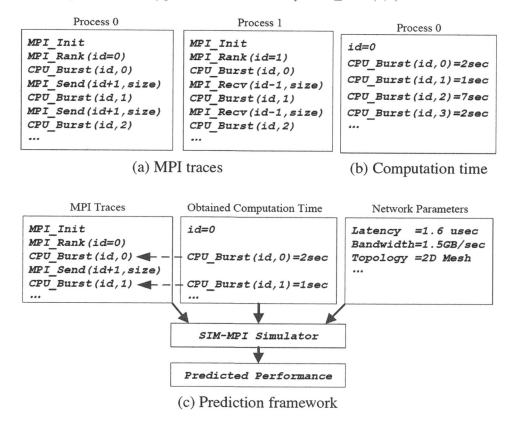

(a) MPI traces   (b) Computation time

(c) Prediction framework

Figure 11. An example of Fortran MPI program

```
real A(MAX,MAX), B(MAX,MAX), C(MAX,MAX),
buf(MAX,MAX)
call MPI_INIT(ierr)
call MPI_COMM_RANK(MPI_COMM_WORLD,myid...)
DO iter=1, N
    if (myid .gt. 0) then
       call MPI_RECV(buf(1, 1),num,MPI_REAL,myid-1,...)
    endif
    DO i=1, MAX
       DO j=1, MAX
          A(i,j)=B(i,j)*C(i,j)+buf(i,j)
       END DO
    END DO
    if (myid .lt. numprocs-1) then
       call MPI_SEND(A(1, 1),num,MPI_REAL,myid+1,...)
    endif
END DO
call MPI_FINALIZE(rc)
```

- **Obtaining Sequential Computation Time for Each Process:** The sequential computation time for each MPI process is measured through executing each process separately on a node of the target platform with deterministic replay techniques. For now, we just assume that we obtain the accurate computation time for each MPI process which can be filled into the traces generated in step 1. Figure 10(b) shows obtained sequential computation time for process 0 of the program in Figure 11.

- **Using a Trace-Driven Simulator to Convolute Communication and Computation Performance:** Finally, a trace driven simulator, called SIM-MPI, is used to convolute communication and computation performance. As shown in Figure 10(c), the simulator reads trace files generated in step 1, the sequential computation time obtained in step 2, and network parameters of target platforms, to predict the communication performance of each communication operation and convolute it with sequential computation time to predict the execution time of the whole parallel application on the target platform. Our SIM-MPI is similar to DIMEMAS [9], but with a more accurate communication model, called LogGPO, which is an extension of LogGP model (Alexandrov, et al., 1997). It can model the overlap between computation and communication more accurately than existing communications models. Our simulator is a trace-driven simulator which should be fed with communication event trace before predicting the performance of parallel programs. Event trace is a time sequenced stream of event records. To get the communication event trace in parallel program based MPI policy, MPI communication library should be instrumented. We write our own MPI wrapper library with the MPI profile interface. The operational flow of our simulator is shown in Figure 12. We enumerate all the processes in a loop. When a process *i* is current process, we simulation a MPI routine of it, by calling a corresponding function defined in protocol level such as *MPI_Send*, *MPI_Waitall* and *MPI_Finalize*.

- **Definition and Obtaining Sequential Computation Time:** Our approach is based on data-replay techniques to acquire sequential computation time. Our approach of replay-based requires two platforms. One is the host platform, which is used to collect the message logs of applications like traditional data-replay techniques. The other is one single node of the target platform on which we want to predict performance. For homogeneous HPC systems, just one node of the target platform is sufficient for our approach. More nodes of the target platform can be used to replay different processes in parallel. If the target platform is heterogeneous, at least one node of each architecture type is needed. The main steps of our approach to acquiring sequential computation time of applications include:

  ○ **Building Message-Log Database:** Record all necessary information as in the data-replay tools when executing the application on the host platform and store this information to a message-log database. This step is only done once and the message-log database can be reused in the future prediction.

  ○ **Replaying Each Process Separately:** Replay each process of the application on the single node separately and collect the elapsed time for each sequential computation unit.

To accurately measure the effects of resource contention on application performance, we propose the strategy of concurrent replay in PHANTOM. During the replay phase, we replay multiple processes simultaneously according to the number of processes running on one node of the target platform. Thus, the effects of resource contention can be captured during the concurrent execution.

Figure 12. The flow chart of our SIM-MPI

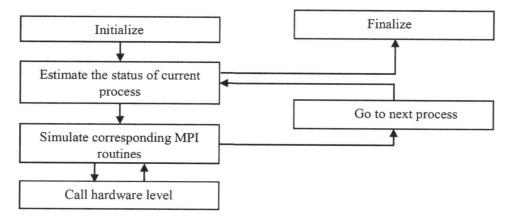

PHANTOM FRAMEWORK

We implement a performance prediction framework for parallel applications based on *representative replay*, called PHANTOM. In fact, *representative replay* can be used in other prediction framework for improving prediction accuracy, such as PERC and macro-level simulation (Snavely, et al., 2002; Susukita, et al., 2008). PHANTOM is an automatic tool chain which requires little manpower for understanding the algorithm and implementation of the parallel application. Figure 13 gives an overview of PHANTOM. PHANTOM consists of three main modules, *CompAna*, *CommAna* and *NetSim*.

Figure 13. Overview of PHANTOM

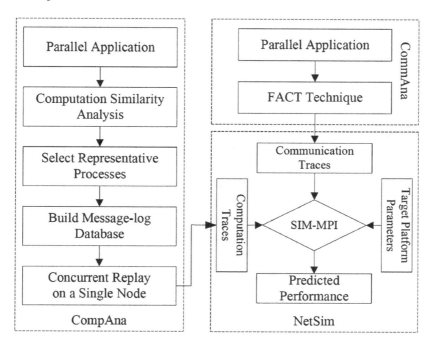

Table 1. Parallel platforms used in the evaluation

System	Explorer	Dawning	DeepComp-F	DeepComp-B
CPU type	Intel E5345	AMD 2350	Intel X7350	Intel E5450
CPU speed	2.33GHz	2.0GHz	2.93 GHz	3.0 GHz
#cores/node	8	8	16	8
#nodes	16	32	16	128
mem/node	8GB	16GB	128GB	32GB
Network	Infiniband	Infiniband	Infiniband	Infiniband
Shard FS	NFS	NFS	StorNext	StorNext
OS	Linux	Linux	Linux	Linux

Table 1 gives a description of parallel platforms used in our evaluation. *Explorer platform* serves as the host platform used to collect message logs of applications. The other three platforms are used to validate the prediction accuracy of our approach.

We evaluate our approach with 6 NPB programs (Bailey, et al., 1995), BT, CG, EP, LU, MG, SP and ASCI Sweep3D (S3) (LLNL, 2009). The version of NPB is 3.3 and input data set is Class C. For Sweep3D, both execution modes are used, strong-scaling and weak-scaling modes. For strong-scaling mode (S3-S), the total problem size of $512\times512\times200$ is used. For weak-scaling mode (S3-W), the problem size is $100\times100\times100$ which is fixed for each process.

We compare the predicted time using PHANTOM with a recent prediction approach proposed by Barnes *et al.* (regression-based model) (Barnes, et al., 2008). This model predicts the execution time T of a given parallel application on p processors by using several instrumented runs of this program on q processors, where $q \in \{2,...,p_0\}, p_0 < p$. Through varying the values of the input variables $(x_1, x_2, ..., x_n)$ on the instrumented runs, this model aims to calculate coefficients $(\beta_0, ..., \beta_n)$ by linear regression fit for $\log_2(T)$.

$$\log_2(T) = \beta_0 + \sum_{i=1}^{n} \beta_i \log_2(x_i) + g(q) + error \qquad (4)$$

In this model $g(q)$ can be either a linear function or a quadratic function for the number of processors, q. Once these coefficients are determined, above equation can be used to predict the application performance on p processors. In this chapter, we use three different processor configurations for training set: $p_0=16$, $p_0=32$, and $p_0=64$. For each program, we predict the performance with two forms of $g(q)$ function given by the authors, and the best results are reported.

In PHANTOM, all the sequential computation time of representative processes is acquired using a single node of the target platform. The network parameters needed by SIM-MPI are measured with micro-benchmarks on the network of the target platform. In this chapter, error is defined as

$$\frac{\left(measured\ time - predicted\ time\right)}{(measured\ time \times 100)}$$

and all the experiments are conducted for 5 times.

We predict the performance for Sweep3D on three target platforms. The real execution time is measured on each target platform to validate our predicted results. All the message logs are collected on Explorer platform. As shown in Figure 14, PHANTOM can get high prediction accuracy on these platforms. Prediction errors on Dawning, DeepComp-F and DeepComp-B platforms are on average 2.67%, 1.30% and 2.34% respectively, with only -6.54% maximum error on Dawning platform for 128 processes. PHANTOM has a better prediction accuracy as well as greater stability across different platforms compared to the regression-based approach. For example, on the DeepComp-B platform, the prediction error for PHANTOM is 4.53% with 1024 processes, while 23.67% for regression-based approach ($p_0 = 32, 64, 128$ used for training). Note that while Dawning platform has lower CPU frequency and peak performance than DeepComp-F platform, it has better application performance before 256 processes. DeepComp-B platform presents the best performance for Sweep3D among three platforms.

Figure 15 demonstrates the prediction results with both PHANTOM and the regression-based approach for seven programs on the Dawning platform. As shown in Figure 15, the agreement between the predicted execution time with PHANTOM and the measured time is remarkably high. The prediction error with PHANTOM is less than 8% on average for all the programs. Note that EP is an embarrassing parallel program, which does not need communications. Its prediction accuracy actually reflects the accuracy of sequential computation time acquired with our approach. For EP, the prediction error is only 0.34% on average. Table 2 also lists the prediction errors with PHANTOM and the regression-based approach (Due to the limitations of the regression-based approach, only the performance of applications with p processes ($p > p_0$) can be predicted.). The prediction accuracy with PHANTOM is much higher than that with the regression-based approach for most programs.

Figure 14. Performance prediction for Sweep3D on Dawning, DeepComp-F and DeepComp-B platforms (M means the real execution time, P means predicted time with PHANTOM, R means predicted time with regression-based approach)

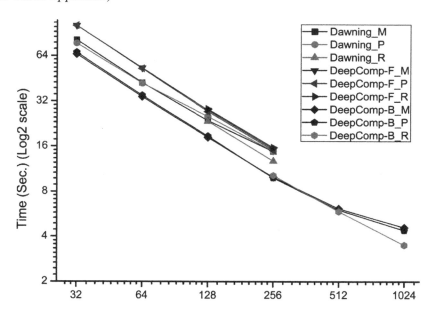

Figure 15. Predicted time with PHANTOM compared with that with regression-based approach on Dawning platform; measured means the real execution time of applications, comm means communication time percentage of total execution time

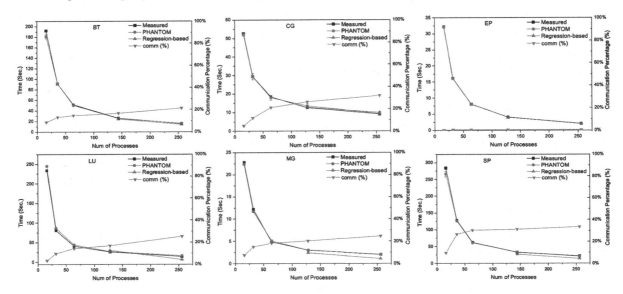

Table 2. Prediction errors (%) with PHANTOM (P.T.) vs. regression-based approach (R.B.) on Dawning platform

Proc. #	Approach	BT	CG	EP	LU	MG	SP	S3-S	S3-W
128	P.T.	2.22	-7.60	-0.34	-3.95	0.97	-2.29	-6.54	-0.15
	R.B.	6.32	-2.22	0.01	-15.02	20.58	17.72	1.30	-4.75
256	P.T.	-3.27	-2.65	-0.27	-14.28	-0.97	5.97	-0.52	-0.27
	R.B.	9.50	-8.95	0.76	53.20	45.32	34.38	13.41	-0.28

CONCLUSION

In this chapter, we have described a novel approach, called FACT, to acquiring communication traces of large parallel message passing applications on small-scale systems. It can preserve the spatial and volume communication attributes while greatly reducing the time and memory overhead of trace collection process. We have implemented FACT and evaluated it with several parallel programs. Experimental results show that FACT is very effective in reducing the resource requirements and collection time. In most cases, we get 1-2 orders of magnitude of improvement. Our approach exploits the technique of program slicing in the compiler. With FACT, we are able to understand the communication patterns of parallel applications. It can be used to assist in tedious and error-prone tasks such as program debugging, testing and maintenance. For predicting performance of parallel applications, we extend existing trace-driven simulation framework by using deterministic replay techniques to measure computation time process by process on prototype of target systems. We further propose a representative replay scheme, which employs similarity of computation pattern in parallel applications to reduce time of prediction significantly. The approach proposed in this chapter is a combination of operating system and performance analysis techniques. We expect this chapter to motivate more interactions between these two fields in the future.

REFERENCES

Aho, A. V., Sethi, R., & Ullman, J. D. (1986). *Compilers: principles, techniques, and tools.* Boston, MA: Addison-Wesley Longman Publishing Co., Inc.

Alexandrov, A., Ionescu, M. F. K., Schauser, E., & Scheiman, C. (1997). LogGP: Incorporating long messages into the logp model for parallel computation. *Journal of Parallel and Distributed Computing, 44*(1), 71–79. doi:10.1006/jpdc.1997.1346

Appel, A. W. (1997). *Modern Compiler Implementation in C: Basic Techniques.* New York: Cambridge University Press. doi:10.1017/CBO9781139174930

Bailey, D., Harris, T., Saphir, W., Wijngaart, R. V. D., Woo, A., & Yarrow, M. (1995). *The NAS Parallel Benchmarks 2.0.* Moffett Field, CA: NAS Systems Division, NASA Ames Research Center.

Bailey, D., Harris, T., Saphir, W., Wijngaart, R. V. D., Woo, A., & Yarrow, M. (1995). *The NAS Parallel Benchmarks 2.0.* Moffett Field, CA: NAS Systems Division, NASA Ames Research Center.

Banning, J. (1979). An efficient way to find side effects of procedure calls and aliases of variables.*Proceedings of ACM SIGACT/SIGPLAN Symposium on Principles of Programming Languages (POPL'79)*, San Antonio, Texas, USA. ACM. doi:10.1145/567752.567756

Barnes, B. J., Rountree, B., Lowenthal, D. K., & Reeves, J., B. Supinski de, & Schulz M. (2008). A regression-based approach to scalability prediction. *Proceedings of International Conference on Supercomputing (ICS'08)*, Island of Kos, Aegean Sea, Greece, USA. ACM.

Chen, H., Chen, W., Huang, J., Robert, B., & Kuhn, H. (2006). MPIPP: an automatic profile-guided parallel process placement toolset for SMP clusters and multi-clusters.*Proceedings of International Conference on Supercomputing (ICS'06).* Cairns, Australia. doi:10.1145/1183401.1183451

Chodnekar, S., Srinivasan, V., Vaidya, A. S., Sivasubramaniam, A., & Das, C. R. (1997). Towards a communication characterization methodology for parallel applications. *Proceedings of High-Performance Computer Architecture HPCA '97,* San Antonio, TX, USA. IEEE. doi:10.1109/HPCA.1997.569693

Choudhury, N., Mehta, Y., Wlmarth, T. L., Bohm, E. J., & Kalé, L. V. (2005). Scaling an optimistic parallel simulation of large-scale interconnection networks.*Proceedings of the 2005 Winter Simulation Conference (WSC'05)*, Huntington Beach. IEEE. doi:10.1109/WSC.2005.1574299

Ferrante, J., Ottenstein, K. J., & Warren, J. D. (1987). The program dependence graph and its use in optimization.*ACM Transactions on Programming Languages and Systems, 9*(3), 319–349. doi:10.1145/24039.24041

Horwitz, S., Reps, T., & Binkley, D. (1990). Interprocedural slicing using dependence graphs. *ACM Transactions on Programming Languages and Systems, 12*(1), 26–60. doi:10.1145/77606.77608

Intel Ltd. Intel trace analyzer & collector (2009). Retrieved from: http://www.intel.com/cd/software/products/asmo-na/eng/244171.htm

Kerbyson, D. J., Alme, H. J., Hoisie, A., Petrini, F., Wasserman, H. J., & Gittings, M. (2001). Predictive performance and scalability modeling of a large-scale application.*Proceedings of International Conference on High Performance Computing, Networking, Storage and Analysis (SC'01)*, Denver, Colorado, USA. IEEE. doi:10.1145/582034.582071

Kim, J., & Lilja, D. J. (1998). Characterization of communication patterns in message-passing parallel scientific application programs. In P.K. Dhabaleswar, & C.B. Stunkel (Ed.), Network-Based Parallel Computing Communication, Architecture, and Applications (pp. 202-216). New York, NY: Springer. doi:doi:10.1007/BFb0052218 doi:10.1007/BFb0052218

Labarta, J., Girona, S., Pillet, V., Cortes, T., & Gregoris, L. (1996). DiP: A parallel program development environment.*Proceedings of International Conference on Euro-Par Parallel Processing (Euro-Par'96)*, Lyon, France. Springer.

LLNL. (2014). ASCI purple benchmark. Retrieved from: https://asc.llnl.gov/computing_resources/purple/archive/benchmarks/

Mohr, B., & Wolf, F. (2003). KOJAK-A tool set for automatic performance analysis of parallel programs. *Proceedings of International Conference on Euro-Par Parallel Processing (Euro-Par'03)*, Klagenfurt, Austria. Springer. doi:10.1007/978-3-540-45209-6_177

Muchnick, S. S. (1997). *Advanced Compiler Design and Implementation*. San Francisco, CA: Morgan Kaufmann Publishers Inc.

Nagel W. E., Arnold A., Weber M., Hoppe H. C., & Solchenbach K. (1996). VAMPIR: Visualization and analysis of MPI resources. *Supercomputer*, 12(1).

Preissl, R., Kockerbauer, T., Schulz, M., Kranzlmuler, D., Supinski, B. R., & Quinlan, D. J. (2008). Detecting patterns in MPI communication traces.*Proceedings of International Conference on Parallel Processing (ICPP'08)*, Portland, OR, USA. IEEE. doi:10.1109/ICPP.2008.71

Preissl, R., Schulz, M., Kranzlmuller, D., Supinski, B. R., & Quinlan, D. J. (2008). Using MPI communication patterns to guide source code transformations. In M. Bubak, G. D. Albada, J. Dongarra, & P. M. A. Sloot (Eds.), *Network-Based Parallel Computing Communication, Architecture, and Applications* (pp. 253–260). New York, NY: Springer. doi:10.1007/978-3-540-69389-5_29

SGI. Open64 compiler and tools. (2008). Retrieved from http://www.open64.net

Shende, S., & Malony, A. D. (2006). TAU: The tau parallel performance system. *International Journal of High Performance Computing Applications*, 20(2), 2006. doi:10.1177/1094342006064482

Snavely, A., Carrington, L., Wolter, N., Labarta, J., Badia, R., & Purkayastha, A. (2002). A framework for application performance modeling and prediction.*Proceedings of International Conference on High Performance Computing, Networking, Storage and Analysis (SC'02)*, Baltimore, USA. IEEE.

Susukita, R., Ando, H., Ando, M., ... (2008). Performance prediction of large-scale parallell system and application using macro-level simulation. *Proceedings of International Conference on High Performance Computing, Networking, Storage and Analysis (SC'08)*, Austin, Texas, USA. IEEE.

Vetter, J. S., & McCracken, M. O. (2001). Statistical scalability analysis of communication operations in distributed applications.*Proceedings of ACM SIGPLAN Symposium on Principles and Practice of Parallel (PPoPP'01)*, Snowbird, Utah, USA. ACM. doi:10.1145/568014.379590

Vetter, J. S., & Mueller, F. (2002). Communication characteristics of large-scale scientific applications for contemporary cluster architectures.*Proceedings of International Parallel and Distributed Processing Symposium (IPDPS'02)*, Florida, USA. IEEE. doi:10.1109/IPDPS.2002.1015504

Weiser, M. (1984). Program slicing. *IEEE Transactions on Software Engineering*, *10*(4), 352–357. doi:10.1109/TSE.1984.5010248

Xue, R., Liu, X., Wu, M., Guo, Z., Chen, W., Zheng, W., & Voelker, G. M. et al. (2009). MPIWiz: subgroup reproducible replay of mpi applications.*Proceedings of ACM SIGPLAN Symposium on Principles and Practice of Parallel (PPoPP'09)*, North Carolina, USA. ACM. doi:10.1145/1594835.1504213

Zhai, J., Hu, J., Tang, X., Ma, X., & Chen, W. (2014). CYPRESS: Combining Static and Dynamic Analysis for Top-Down Communication Trace Compression.*Proceedings of International Conference on High Performance Computing, Networking, Storage and Analysis (SC'14)*, New Orleans, LA, USA. IEEE. doi:10.1109/SC.2014.17

Zhang, J., Zhai, J., Chen, W., & Zheng, W. (2009). Process mapping for mpi collective communications.*Proceedings of International Conference on Euro-Par Parallel Processing (Euro-Par'09)*, Delft, Netherlands. Springer.

KEY TERMS AND DEFINITIONS

FACT: The technique we used to perform fast communication trace collection for large-scale parallel applications on small-scale systems.

HPC: It most generally refers to the practice of aggregating computing power in a way that delivers much higher performance than one could get out of a typical desktop computer or workstation in order to solve large problems in science, engineering, or business.

PHANTOM: A performance prediction framework, which integrates the computation-time acquisition approach with a trace-driven network simulator.

SIM-MPI: A trace-driven simulator which can be used for performance prediction of large scale parallel program based on MPI library.

Section 2
Heterogeneous Clusters

Chapter 6
Multicore and Manycore:
Hybrid Computing Architectures and Applications

Pedro Valero-Lara
University of Manchester, UK

Abel Paz-Gallardo
Research Center for Energy, Environment and Technology, Spain

Erich L Foster
Università della Svizzera Italiana, Italy

Manuel Prieto-Matías
Universidad Complutense de Madrid, Spain

Alfredo Pinelli
City London University, UK

Johan Jansson
Basque Center for Applied Mathematics, Spain

ABSTRACT

This chapter presents an overview of the evolution of computer architecture, giving special attention on those advances which have promoted the current hybrid systems. After that, we focus on the most extended programming strategies applied to hybrid computing. In fact, programming is one of the most important challenges for this kind of systems, as it requires a high knowledge of the hardware to achieve a good performance. Current hybrid systems are basically composed by three components, two processors (multicore and manycore) and an interconnection bus (PCIe), which connects both processors. Each of the components must be managed differently. After presenting the particular features of current hybrid systems, authors focus on introducing some approaches to exploit simultaneously each of the components. Finally, to clarify how to program in these platforms, two cases studies are presented and analyzed in deep. At the end of the chapter, authors outline the main insights behind hybrid computing and introduce upcoming advances in hybrid systems.

INTRODUCTION

"Moore's Law" (Moore, 1965) is probably the most cited prediction in the computing era. It was in 1965, when one of Intel's co-founders, Gordon Moore, realized that, with the advances achieved in the integration technology, it was economically to double the number of transistors per chip every 18

DOI: 10.4018/978-1-5225-0287-6.ch006

months. This prediction will possibly reach a limit someday, as (Krauss, & Starkman, 2004) stated, due to the *Bekenstein bound*, but as (The International Technology Roadmap for Semiconductors, 2013) confirmed, it is expected to hold true for the next few years.

Nothing about processing performance was said by Gordon Moore when he made his prediction. His observation only links integration levels to production cost (Själander, Martonosi, & Kaxiras, 2014). However, a few years later (Dennard, Gaensslen, Rideout, Bassous, & LeBlanc, 1974) from IBM, articulated a set of rules (i.e., Dennard scaling) that link transistor size with performance and power. The key observation they made was that smaller transistors can switch quickly at lower supply voltages, resulting in more power-efficient circuits and keeping the power density constant (Själander, Martonosi, & Kaxiras, 2014). For about four decades, Moore's law coupled with Dennard scaling have prescribed that every technology generation have more transistors that are, not only smaller, but are also much faster and more energy efficient. However, the transistor scale has also brought new challenges. In fact, with the introduction of the 45 nm node, the insulation became too thin, and power leakage has been a huge problem ever since.

Computer architects have been able to increase the performance of processors, even without increasing their area and power. Indeed, during the 80's and early 90's, actual processor performance increased faster than Moore's law and Dennard scaling predicted (Hennesy, & Patterson, 2011). The surplus of transistors was used by computer architects to integrate complex techniques to hide memory access latency and extract instruction level parallelism (ILP). Some relevant examples were out-of-order execution, branch prediction and speculative execution, register renaming, non-blocking caches or memory dependence prediction. Notoriously, all of them were able to improve performance while maintaining the conventional Von Neumann computational model. In other words, these techniques were virtually invisible to software, avoiding the need to rewrite the applications and letting them improve their performance as technology scaled (Hennesy, & Patterson, 2011).

The breakdown of Dennard scaling prompted the switch to multicore and multithreaded architectures, which has been the driving force in computational technology over the last decade. Broadly speaking, the semiconductor industry has abandoned complex cores in favor of integrating more cores on the same chip (Geer, 2005). Further, hardware multithreading has become essential to mask long-latency operations such as main memory accesses (Nemirovsky, & Tullsen, 2013). The assumption of this new paradigm is that as the number of processors/threads on a chip doubles, the performance of a scalable parallel program will also continue to improve. However, there is now a major problem at the software level. In contrast to previous generations, programmers are in charge of exposing the parallelism in their applications and need it to improve performance; this is not a simple task. Despite more than 40 years' experience with parallel computers, we know that parallel programs are usually difficult to design, implement and debug, and their performance do not always scale well with the number of cores/threads. Despite Amdahl law (Amdahl, 1967) introduces several inconveniences to efficiently extract sufficient parallelism from many applications, the Gustafson law (Gustafson, 1988) defends that any application can be reformulated to take advantage of a higher number of processors. However, the reformulation or porting of a particular application (programming) to a new and bigger computer system can become a non-trivial task.

The first general-purpose processor that included multiple processing cores on the same die was released by IBM in 2001, the IBM POWER4 processor (Olukotun, 2007). Since then, multi-core processors have become the norm. In fact, the major way to improve the performance of high-end processors has been to add support for more threads, either by increasing the number of cores per chip, or through hardware multithreading (Vajda, 2011). This new trend is well exemplified by modern GPUs (Lindholm, Nickolls, Oberman, & Montrym, 2008), which rely on fine-grained multithreading coupled with simple processing cores and SIMD (Single Instruction Multiple Data) execution to maximize performance when parallelism is abundant (Garland, & Kirk, 2010).

Parallel computing was not new when multi-core chips were born a decade ago as a new paradigm. In fact, parallelism has always been a means to satisfy our never-ending hunger for ever-faster and ever-cheaper computation (Denning, & Dennis, 2010), and many of the design principles behind current architectures have been used in the past. The very first multiprocessor architecture was the Burroughs B5000, which was designed in the early 60's. This machine, along with its successors, used shared memory multiprocessors in which a crossbar switch connected groups of four processors and memory boxes. Server and mainframe markets in the mid 80's were dominated by computers containing multiple processors sharing a common memory. The early systems were introduced by famous small companies such as Encore and Sequent. The early 1990s brought a dramatic advance in the shared memory bus technology, including faster electrical signaling, wider data paths, pipelined protocols, and multiple paths. Distributed memory systems and massive parallel processors (hereinafter MPPs) used complex networks that allowed higher scalability (Culler, Gupta, & Singh, 1997). An evolution of these types of interconnects can be found today in multicore chips (Sánchez, Michelogiannakis, & Kozyrakis, 2010). The ILLIAC IV, designed by (Barnes, Brown, Kato, Kuck, Slotnick, & Stokes, 1968) during the late 60's and delivered to NASA Ames Research Center in 1971, was one of the first attempts to build a SIMD array processor. Other supercomputers of the era, such as the classic Cray-1 (Russell, 1978), used instead a single vector processor with multiple pipelined functional units.

It is also remarkable the amazing advances in the shared memory bus technology, including faster electrical signaling, wider data paths, pipelined protocols, and multiple paths (Lee, 2009).

Technology scaling overtook the specialized SIMD and vector processor in favor of MPPs such as the Intel Paragon (Esser, & Knecht, 1993), or the Cray T3E (Scott, 1996), and cluster of workstations (COWs) in the 90's. The appearance of Beowulf clusters, originally developed (Sterling, Becker, Savarese, Dorband, Ranawake, & Packer, 1995) at NASA, provided considerable computational resources using commodity hardware components such as PCs and Ethernet switches. The reduced economic cost of such systems paved the way for the popularization of parallel computing since many university labs and research centers could afford them.

The peripheral processor of the Control Data Corp (CDC 6600) developed in the 1960s and the Hybrid Element Processor system developed in the late 1970s (Smith, 1981) are notable examples of the early use of multithreaded architectures. In such architectures, a single processor has the ability to follow multiple streams of execution without the aid of software context switches that require many thousands of cycles. A multithreaded architecture can access the state of multiple threads, which allows it to quickly switch between threads. Several models of multithreading have been explored and implemented since then (Ungerer, Robic, & Silc, 2003). Prototypes such as Imagine (Kapasi, Dally, Rixner, Owens, & Khailany, 2002), and Merrimac (Dally, Labonte, Das, Hanrahan, Ahn, Gummaraju, Erez, Jayasena, Buck, Knight, & Kapasi, 2003), and SPI Storm (Khailany, Williams, Lin, Long, Rygh, Tovey, & Dally, 2006), exploit block multithreading. This is a coarser-grain strategy in which a thread continues to run until it encounters a long-latency operation, at which point a different thread is selected for execution. These machines explicitly partition programs into blocks of high-latency memory access (load/store) operations and tasks in which memory accesses are restricted to on-chip (local) memory. When a block finishes processing its on-chip data, a different block, which required high-latency memory accesses, has been loaded onto the chip and executed. Overlapping the block's data transfer, for one or more tasks, while another block is executing, hides memory-access latency. The Tera (Alverson, Alverson, Callahan, Koblenz, Porterfield, & Smith, 1990) and (Alverson, Alverson, Callahan, Koblenz, Porterfield, & Smith, 1992), prototype and the Sun Niagara (Kongetira, Aingaran, & Olukotun, 2005), processors used fine-grain multithreading to hide long latency operations at the expense of sacrificing single-threaded performance. These processors are able to switch between threads at finer granularity than block multithreading (even at each clock cycle), achieving impressive performance for workloads in which parallelism is abundant. As mentioned above, this multithreading technique has evolved into the architecture used in modern GPUs today.

About hybrid architectures, despite much progress, multicore designs are also encountering scaling problems, notably the "Dark Silicon" phenomenon (Esmaeilzadeh, Blem, Amant, Sankaralingam, & Burger, 2011). Power and cooling concerns suggest the number of dynamically active transistors on a single die may be greatly constrained in the near future. In other words, even if the number of transistors per chip continues to follow Moore's law, users will not be able to use all of them simultaneously. This problem may lead to scenarios in which only a small percentage of the chip's transistors can be "on" at a time. Hybrid architectures may be an answer to this challenge. In these architectures, some general-purpose cores are augmented by other cores that implement different microarchitectures or even specialized accelerators that are more efficient for a particular computational purpose. Again, the main problem is at the software level side. Programmers need to address the difficult optimization challenge of choosing the right processor for different parts of their applications in order to achieve the best performance or performance-per-watt on those complex hybrid architectures. In fact, hybrid computing already dominates major market segments:

- **Hybrid Platforms in HPC:** Most multi-core processors for high performance computing (HPC) are still homogeneous both in instruction set architecture and performance. They have a Thermal Design Power (TDP) of 100 Watts and integrate 4-16 heavyweight cores. However, many of the most powerful supercomputers today (Top 500 list, 2015), are based on platforms that combine multicore processors with data parallel accelerators. The fastest system, which is currently (June 2015) the Tianhe-2 supercomputer from China, uses Intel's Xeon Phi coprocessors, while the runner-up, the Titan supercomputer from Oak Ridge National Laboratory, uses NVIDIA GPUs.
- **Hybrid Processors in Mobile Platforms:** Hybrid architectures already provide power consumption advantages over homogeneous architectures. This is why they are extensively used today in low power embedded and mobile platforms. In this market segment processors integrate fewer cores and have lower TDP (around 2.5 to 10 Watts) than desktop and high performance processors. However, they are able to achieve competitive performance integrating:
  - Data-parallel (graphics) accelerators with distinct programming and memory models (Branover, Foley, & Steinman, 2012) and (Gronqvist, & Lokhmotov, 2014), and
  - Many fixed-function accelerator blocks.

Asymmetric "Big LITTLE" architectures that combine different types of cores are also popular (Jeff, 2012). Since energy efficiency is of vital importance to have future Exascale system, some research projects (Mont-Blanc, 2014), have envisioned the use of this kind of low-power hybrid processor on future high performance computing systems.

Figure 1. Intel-based (5520/5500 chipset) hybrid server
Intel Corporation (2009).

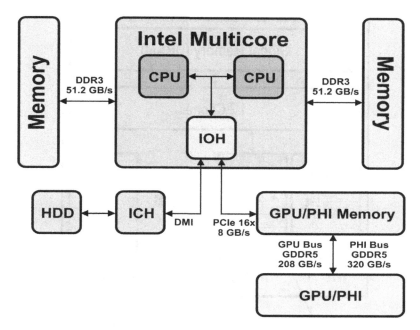

Figure 1 graphically illustrates an example of the possible organization of an Intel-based hybrid server. As mentioned above, this is also the building block of hybrid supercomputers. The hardware accelerator (or accelerators in multi-accelerator configurations) is attached directly via a fast PCI express link to the I/O HUB (IOH), which is already integrated on the processor die. Future system may integrate a single address space, but till now, the accelerators and the processor have independent memory spaces. Accelerators have a great deal of internal memory bandwidth but exchanging data between both spaces is a high latency operation that can cause huge bottlenecks. This forces programmers to design new algorithms that minimize memory transfers between the GPU and the host. When these transfers cannot be omitted, some code transformations can allow the overlapping of computation with memory transfers to hide such overheads.

Figure 2 shows an abstract block diagram of NVIDIA's (Kepler) GPUs (Nvidia Corporation, 2014). The GPU is organized into several multiprocessors, which in turn are composed of various simple processors (cores) that operate in SIMD fashion. The multiprocessors have fine-grained multithreading capabilities, which mean that they support hundreds of threads in-fly. Every multiprocessor switches to a different set of threads every clock cycle, which helps to maximize computational resources and hide the long latency memory accesses to a share GPU main memory, usually called "global memory". In addition, within a multiprocessor, there are a large set of registers and on-chip shared caches to speed up memory access.

More recently, Intel has introduced the Intel Xeon Phi Accelerator. This is a new family of processors based on the Intel MIC Architecture (Jeffers, & Reinders, 2013) that incorporates earlier work on the Larrabee architecture (Seiler, Carmean, Sprangle, Forsyth, Abrash, Dubey, Junkins, Lake, Sugerman, Cavin, Espasa, Grochowski, Juan, & Hanrahan, 2008). The Corner is a PCIe vector co-processor which integrates up to 61 in-order dual issue x86 cores, which trace some history to the original Pentium core,

Figure 2. NVIDIA Kepler GK110 architecture
Nvidia Corporation (2014).

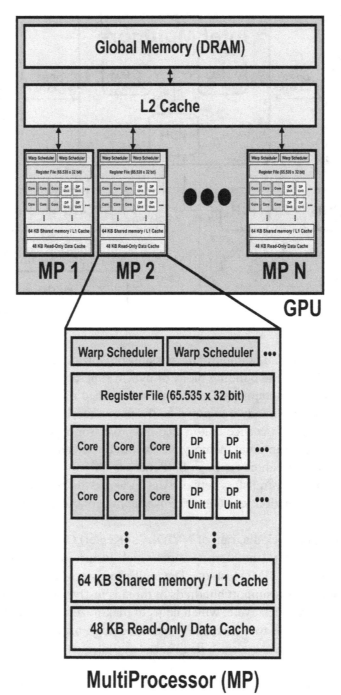

like the Larrabee's predecessor. Among other enhancements, the Corner's cores are augmented with 64-bit support, 4 hardware threads per core (resulting in more than 200 hardware threads available on a single device) and 512-bit SIMD instructions (Gardner, 2014). Each core has a 512KB L2 cache locally but has also access to all other L2 caches in the system through a high-speed bidirectional ring (Jeffers, & Reinders, 2013). Unlike previous GPUs, L2 cache that is kept fully coherent by a global-distributed tag directory.

Obviously the changes in hardware have important consequences in the way in which applications are implemented (Sutter, 2005) and (Moreland, 2012). After covering the evolution in computer architecture, in the next sections we introduce the programming models and approaches to efficiently exploit both architectures. Then, two cases studies will be presented to show where each model best fits. Finally, the chapter outlines the main insights behind hybrid computing and concludes with some interesting advances in these architectures that are expected to be seen in the near future.

PROGRAMMING

Granularity

The concept of granularity regards the level of distribution of the elements on threads/cores. It is also known as thread/core mapping. Due to some architectonic features such as, class of parallel computer in Flynn's taxonomy (Hennessy, & Patterson, 2011), number of cores, memory hierarchy, etc., a particular level of granularity must be used.

We here explain two basic and widely extended levels of granularity in this kind of systems: coarse and fine-grained. The coarse-grained level distributes a set of elements of a particular data structure over one single thread/core, being an appropriate data distribution for those computer architectures composed by a relative low number of cores (dozens) and big cache memories (low-latency oriented architectures). Otherwise, the fine-grained approach distributes one data element over one single thread/core. This last data distribution is more convenient for throughput-oriented (high latency) architectures, in which we find a high number of cores (hundreds and even thousands) with small cache memories and simple memory hierarchies.

To clarify, we introduce a simple problem, vector addition, to explain the differences among both granularities in more detail. Let u and v be vectors, then vector addition is defined in the following way:

$$u = \begin{bmatrix} u_1 \\ u_2 \\ u_3 \\ . \\ u_{n-1} \\ u_n \end{bmatrix}, v = \begin{bmatrix} v_1 \\ v_2 \\ v_3 \\ . \\ v_{n-1} \\ v_n \end{bmatrix}, u+v = \begin{bmatrix} u_1 + v_1 \\ u_2 + v_2 \\ u_3 + v_3 \\ . \\ u_{n-1} + v_{n-1} \\ u_n + v_n \end{bmatrix} \tag{1}$$

The coarse-grain approach distributes a set of elements of both vectors to each of the threads/cores, e.g. $u_k, \ldots, u_{k+m-1}$ and $v_k, \ldots, v_{k+m-1}$ to the kth thread/core (where m might be defined as m=n/number of cores). On the other-hand, the fine-grain approach distributes each element to a single thread, e.g. u_k and v_k are distributed to thread k. In this case our processor must be able to execute as many threads as there are components of the vectors, i.e. n for the case described above.

Memory Management

As previously introduced, multicore architectures include big cache memories composed of several levels, while GPUs exploit a simpler and smaller in-chip memory. It forces us to manage and control both types of memory in different ways. Next, we explain some known approaches, which help us to adapt our codes to each type of memory.

The fist approach is the so-called Array of Structures (AoS) approach, while the second is the Structure of Arrays (SoA) approach (Bernaschi, Fatica, Melchiona, Succi, & Kaxiras, 2010; Januszewski, & Kostur, 2014). To better explain the different approaches, we present several pseudo-codes based on the style of *C* programming language. The AoS approach stores the attributes of each element for a particular data structure in nearby memory positions. This approach can be efficiently managed in cache memories of multicore processors and using a coarse-grained data distribution. The pseudo-code shown in Listing 1 demonstrates how to implement this approach.

Unlike the AoS approach, in which the attributes a, b and c, relating to one of the structure elements, are not stored in consecutive memory locations, the SoA approach does store each attribute of the structure elements in consecutive memory locations. This approach is more efficient for throughput-

Listing 1. Array of Structures (AoS) approach

```
1. struct AoS{
2.     int a;
3.     double b;
4.     int c[4];
5. };
6. main(){
7.     int i, j;
8.     struct AoS test = new AoS[n];
9.     for(i = 0; i < n;  i++){
10.        test[i]→a;
11.        test[i]→b;
12.        for(j = 0; j < 4; j++){
13.        test[i]→c[j];
14.        }
15.     }
16. }
```

Listing 2. Structure of Arrays (SoA) approach

```
1.  struct SoA{
2.      int a[n];
3.      double b[n];
4.      int c[n][4];
5.      };
6.  main(){
7.      int i, j;
8.      struct SoA test = new SoA[1];
9.      for(i = 0; i < n; i++){
10.         test→a[i];
11.         test→b[i];
12.         for(j = 0; j < 4; j++){
13.         test→c[i][j];
14.         }
15.     }
16. }
```

oriented processors by using a fine-grained granularity. It allows us to access memory in a coalesced way, consecutive threads access consecutive memory locations (as in the fine-grained approach for the case study vector addition introduced in the previous subsection). The implementation of this approach can be seen in Listing 2.

Finally, we present another approach, which is a combination of the two previous approaches and is known as a Structure of Arrays of Structures (SoAoS) (Shet, Siddharth, Sorathiya, Deshpande, Sher-lekar, Kaul, & Ansumali, 2013). This allows one to take advantage of current multicore processors which have vector support. Vector units are composed of a number of arithmetic units which allow one to execute the same arithmetic operation over a set of different data, simultaneously. Thus, to take advantage of this, one should use an SoAoS approach, which can be implemented using the pseudo code shown in Listing 3.

In particular, m should be set as the number of vector units available per core.

To clarify, we show in Figure 3 some examples of memory mappings, one over each of the approaches previously presented, AoS, SoA and SoAoS:

Programming Environment

Today, the most extensive way to program hybrid, multicore and GPU, platforms is the combination of the gcc/g++ (multicore) compiler with nvcc (GPU) compiler, the native NVIDIA compiler based on the C programming language. However, it is important to keep in mind that there exist other programming environments able to deal with hybrid systems (PGI Compilers & Tools, 2015; OpenACC, 2015).

In the two compiler approach two codes, one with the extension .c/.cpp and one with the extension .cu, are necessary. While the gcc/g++ (.c/.cpp) code manages the multicore resources, the nvcc (.cu) code manages the communication among both processors and GPU resources. Both codes are linked by

Listing 3. Structure of Arrays of Structures (SoAoS) approach

```
1. struct SoAoS{
2.     int a[m];
3.     double b[m];
4.     int c[m][4];
5. };
6. main(){
7.     int i, j, k;
8.     struct SoAoS test = new SoAoS[ n/m ];
9.     for(i = 0; i < n/m; i++){
10.        for(j = 0; j < m j++){
11.            test[i]→a[j];
12.            test[i]→b[j];
13.            for (k = 0; k < 4; k++){
14.            test[i]→c[j][k];
15.            }
16.        }
17.    }
18. }
```

using the extern "C" clause. This extern "C" clause allows for the CUDA code, compiled with nvcc, to be linked by C functions using C compatible header files, which are built by gcc/g++. To better understand the process to link CUDA codes with C/C++ codes, we present a simple example in Listings 4 and 5.

Obviously, these codes have to be compiled and linked. This is performed via the commands in Listing 6.

As gcc/g++ does not recognize GPU code, it is ignored and linked. This process is very useful for hybrid builds, and allows us to combine both codes. The CPU linker is always the last one ran. When gcc/g++ is used for linking, the user must explicitly include the "-*lcudart*" flag.

Figure 3. Memory mapping for each of the approaches, AoS, SoA, SoAoS

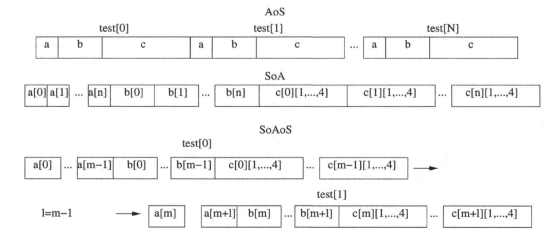

Listing 4. Host code

```
1. C++ (multicore) code "main.cpp"
2. extern "C" void kernel(int *p);
3. int main(){
4.     int i, *p_host;
5.     p_host = (int*) malloc(sizeof(int)*N);
6.     for(i = 0; i < N; i++)
7.       p_host[i] = rand();
8.     kernel(p_host);
9. }
```

Listing 5. Device (GPU) code

```
1. CUDA (GPU) code "kernel.cu"
2. __global__ void kernel_GPU(int *p){
3.     int position;
4.     position = threadIdx.x + blockDim.x * blockIdx.x;
5.     p[position] += 100;
6. }
7. extern "C" void kernel(int *p){
8.     int *p_device;
9.     cudaMalloc((void**)&p_device, sizeof(int)*N);
10.    cudaMemcpy(p_device, p_host, sizeof(int)*N, cudaMemcpyHostToDevice);
11.    kernel_GPU<<<N/BlockSize,BlockSize>>>(p_device);
12.    cudaMemcpy(p_host, p_device, sizeof(int)*N, cudaMemcpyDeviceToHost);
13. }
```

Listing 6. Commands for compiling a hybrid code

```
1. nvcc -c kernel.cu
2. g++ kernel.o main.cpp -lcudart -o run
```

Overlapping

As can be seen in Figure 1, there are important differences, in terms of bandwidth, between the various connections. From Figure 1 we see a significant bottleneck, when dealing with multicore + GPU systems, at the connection between CPU and GPU, which are connected via a PCIe 16x bus. This bus provides a transfer rate of 8GB/s in each direction and is significantly slower than the other connections, such as multicore-Memory (51.2GB/s) or GPU-GPU memory (208GB/s). As a consequence, the main and most important bottleneck when dealing with hybrid multicore + GPU systems is found in the multicore-GPU communication.

Listing 7. Overlapping multicore-GPU memory transfers with GPU computing

```
1. void main(){
2.     cudaStream_t stream[2];
3.     for(int i=0; i<2; i++)
4.       cudaStreamCreate(&stream[i]);
5.     cudaMemcpyAsync(in_gpu1,in_cpu1,size,cudaMemcpyHostToDevice,stream[0]);
6.     Kernel_1<<<N/BlockSize,BlockSize,0,stream[0]>>>(in_gpu1,out_gpu1);
7.     cudaMemcpyAsync(out_cpu1,out_gpu1,size,cudaMemcpyDeviceToHost,stream[0]);
8.     cudaMemcpyAsync(in_gpu2,in_cpu2,size,cudaMemcpyHostToDevice,stream[1]);
9.     Kernel_2<<<N/BlockSize,BlockSize,0,stream[1]>>>(in_gpu2,out_gpu2);
10.    cudaMemcpyAsync(out_cpu2,out_gpu2,size,cudaMemcpyDeviceToHost,stream[1]);
11. }
```

Currently, hybrid multicore-GPU systems are composed by three independent components, as can be seen in Figure 1. These consist of the following independent components: multicore processors, GPUs, and PCIe buses. All of which can be exploited simultaneously.

Depending on the problem being computed, the communication overhead might be insignificant, with respect to total runtime, and so in some cases it may be more relevant, in terms of acceleration, to overlap multicore and GPU computation instead of overlapping communication. Next, we present some approaches to overlap and exploit these independent components.

One of the most common approaches consists of overlapping GPU computation with multicore-GPU memory transfers. To clarify, we show an example (pseudo-code) in in Listing 7 in which this approach is carried out.

This approach makes use of a special data-type called a "stream". Each couple of kernel and memory transfer calls includes its own "stream" as a parameter. To compute asynchronism memory transfers, the call **cudaMemcpyAsync** must be used. This strategy is beneficial in cases where we have more than one kernel. However, it does not take advantages of multicore processor.

Another approach consists of overlapping multicore-GPU memory transfers with multicore computing. This can be implemented by following the scheme in Listing 8.

Listing 8. Overlapping multicore-GPU memory transfers with multicore computing.

```
1. void main(){
2.     cudaStream_t stream[1];
3.     cudaStreamCreate(&stream[1]);
4.     cudaMemcpyAsync(in_cpu1,in_gpu1,size,cudaMemcpyDeviceToHost,stream[0]);
5.     Multicore_Function(in_cpu_2,out_cpu_2);
6. }
```

Listing 9. Overlapping multicore and multicore computing

```
1. void main(){
2.     cudaMemcpy(in_gpu1,in_cpu1,size,cudaMemcpyHostToDevice);
3.     Kernel_1<<<N/BlockSize,BlockSize>>>(in_gpu1,out_gpu1);
4.     Multicore_Function(in_cpu_2,out_cpu_2);
5.     cudaThreadSynchronize();
6.     cudaMemcpy(out_cpu1,out_gpu1,size,cudaMemcpyDeviceToHost);
7. }
```

Finally, another approach with which we can overlap multicore and GPU computing is shown in Listing 9.

For an effective overlapping, the **cudaThreadSynchronize()** must be located at the end of the overlapping multicore-GPU region. Also, all the previous strategies can be combined each other (Valero-Lara, & Pelayo, 2011), (Valero-Lara & Pelayo, 2013), and (Valero-Lara & Pelayo, 2015).

Example

Finally, we analyze, as case study, one widely known numerical problem, scalar tridiagonal systems. This can help us to understand those features to be highlighted in each of architectures. First, let's introduce briefly some numerical details of the problem. Given a tridiagonal linear $Au=y$ system, in which the A coefficients matrix:

$$A = \begin{bmatrix} b_1 & c_1 & & & & \\ a_2 & b_2 & c_2 & & & \\ & a_3 & b_3 & c_3 & & \\ & & \cdot & \cdot & \cdot & \\ & & & a_{n-1} & b_{n-1} & c_{n-1} \\ & & & & a_n & b_n \end{bmatrix}, u = \begin{bmatrix} u_1 \\ u_2 \\ u_3 \\ \cdot \\ u_{n-1} \\ u_n \end{bmatrix}, y = \begin{bmatrix} y_1 \\ y_2 \\ y_3 \\ \cdot \\ y_{n-1} \\ y_n \end{bmatrix} \qquad (2)$$

where y is given and u is unknown.

Next, we present several algorithms, which can deal with tridiagonal problems, and the features of each approach. Finally, we discuss the advantages or disadvantages of porting them on multicore and GPU.

The optimum implementation is the so-called Thomas algorithm (*TA*) (Conte, & de Boor, 1976). The structure of such systems allows us to solve it quite efficiently via the Thomas Algorithm, i.e. in $O(n)$ operations instead of $O(n^3)$ operations. *TA* consists of two stages, commonly denoted as forward elimination and backward substitution.

The forward stage eliminates the lower diagonal as follows:

$$c_1' = \frac{c_1}{b_1} \ , \ c_i' = \frac{c_i}{b_i - c_{i-1}' a_i} \text{ for } i = 2, 3, ..., n-1 \tag{3}$$

$$y_1' = \frac{y_1}{y_1} \ , \ y_i' = \frac{y_i - y_{i-1}' a_i}{b_i - c_{i-1}' a_i} \text{ for } i = 2, 3, ..., n-1 \tag{4}$$

and then the backward stage recursively solves each row in reverse order:

$$u_n = y_n' \ , \ u_i = y_i' - c_i' u_{i+1} \text{ for } i = n-1, n-2, n-3, ..., 1 \tag{5}$$

Overall, the complexity of *TA* is optimal: $8n$ operations in $2n$-1 steps. Unfortunately, this algorithm is purely sequential. When dealing with multiple tridiagonal systems via *TA* every system must be computed in a single thread. It supposes, for a *nxn* system, that this approach requires a high computational cost per system, $8n$ operations, and a high memory space, $5n$ memory elements. This approach presents several drawbacks with respect to implementation on GPUs. To achieve enough threads which can exploit the large number of cores available in current GPUs, we would need a high number of independent systems. The memory required per system/thread and the memory layout of each system makes it difficult to carry out efficient memory exploitation (coalesced accesses to memory). Large processes can degrade the performance on GPUs systems and favor the divergence among threads. On the other hand, this approach can be efficiently implemented over current multicore systems by following a coarse grain scheme where several independent systems are assigned to one single core. It also presents an effective cache memory usage.

Cyclic Reduction (*CR*) (Zhang, Cohen, & Owens, 2010) is a parallel alternative to *TA*. It also consists of two phases (reduction and substitution). In each intermediate step of the reduction phase, all even-indexed *(i)* equations $a_i x_{i-1} + b_i x_i + c_i x_{i+1} = d_i$ are reduced. The values of a_i, b_i, c_i and d_i are updated in each step according to:

$$a_i' = -a_{i-1} k_1 \ , \ b_i' = b_i - c_{i-1} k_1 - a_{i+1} k_2 \tag{6}$$

$$c_i' = -c_{i+1} k_2 \ , \ b_i' = b_i - c_{i-1} k_1 - a_{i+1} k_2 \tag{7}$$

$$k_1 = \frac{a_i}{b_{i-1}} \ , \ k_2 = \frac{c_i}{b_{i+1}} \tag{8}$$

After $\log_2 n$ steps, the system is reduced to a single equation which is solved directly. All odd-indexed unknowns x_i are then solved in the substitution phase by introducing the already computed u_{i-1} and u_{i+1} values:

$$u_i = \frac{y_i' - a_i' x_{i-1} - c_i' x_{i+1}}{b_i'} \qquad (9)$$

Overall, the *CR* algorithm needs $17n$ operations and $2\log_2 n - 1$ step. Figure 4 shows its access pattern. Despite being considerably more computationally expensive in terms of number of operation, this algorithm presents some relevant features to be efficiently implemented on GPUs. Unlike the *TA* algorithm, the most remarkable feature is allowing it to be intrinsically parallel. A *nxn* tridiagonal system can be implemented using $n/2$ threads, at least in the first/last step in the reduction/substitution phase, being this algorithm susceptible to be implemented via a fine-grained fashion, and reducing considerably the computational cost and memory requirements per thread. However, this algorithm presents an irregular memory access pattern, which is susceptible to generate bank conflicts. Also the number of independent elements decreases/increases for reduction/substitution, which makes it difficult to implement. It forces some threads launched at the beginning to be idle depending on the level of the process. Additionally, synchronization points are mandatory to guarantee the absence of race conditions, which will degrade performance. In contrast, we can take advantage of shared memory, as all input elements have to be read several times along the process. Otherwise, this approach is not so convenient for multicore systems, as low-latency oriented platforms are not amenable to fine-grained parallelism. This approach, apart from presenting a higher computational cost, does not efficiently exploit the hierarchy of memory via a fine-grained distribution. A better exploitation of memory would be achievable via a coarse-grained mapping, in which a set of tridiagonal systems are distributed on a single core, instead of distributing a set of elements per core and iterating over systems. However, for a coarse-grained distribution the *TA* algorithm requires a lower number of operations, such that it continues to be the best choice for multicore systems.

Parallel Cyclic Reduction (*PCR*) (Zhang, Cohen, & Owens, 2010), is a variant of *CR*, which only has the substitution phase. For convenience, we consider cases where $n = 2^s$, which involve $s = \log_2 n$ steps. Similarly, to *CR* a, b, c and y are updated as follows, for $j = 1, 2, ..., s$ and $k = 2^{j-1}$:

$$a_i' = \alpha_i a_i \; , \; b_i' = b_i - \alpha_i c_{i-k} + \beta_i a_{i+k} \qquad (10)$$

$$c_i' = \beta_i c_{i+1}, \; b_i' = b_i - \alpha_i c_{i-k} + \beta_i a_{i+k} \qquad (11)$$

$$\alpha_i = \frac{-a_i}{b_{i-1}}, \; \beta_i = \frac{-c_i}{b_i} \qquad (12)$$

Figure 4. Access pattern of the CR algorithm

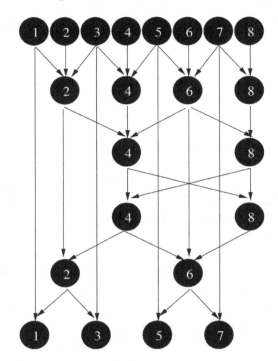

Finally, the solution is:

$$u_i = \frac{y_i'}{b_i} \tag{13}$$

Essentially, at each reduction stage, the current system is transformed into two smaller systems and after $\log_2 n$ steps the original system is reduced to n independent equations. Overall, the operation count of *PCR* is $12n \log_2 n$ and Figure 5 sketches the corresponding access pattern.

We should highlight, that apart from their computational complexity, these algorithms differ in their data access and synchronization patterns, which also have a strong influence on their actual performance. For instance, in the *CR* algorithm synchronizations are introduced at the end of each step and its corresponding memory access pattern may cause bank conflicts. *PCR* needs less steps and its memory access pattern is more regular, which is more convenient for GPU-based systems. A lower number of steps minimizes the overhead for synchronizations. Also a regular pattern of access to memory is more appropriate for shared memory exploitation.

Other hybrid combinations, which exploit the characteristics of the above algorithms have been explored, (Zhang, Cohen, & Owens, 2010), (Sakharnykh, 2010), (Davidson, Zhang, & Owens, 2011), and (Kim, Wu, Chang, Hwu, 2011). One of these hybrid schemes is *CR–PCR*, which reduces the system to a certain size using the forward reduction phase of *CR* and then solves the reduced (intermediate) system with the *PCR* algorithm. Finally, it substitutes the solved unknowns back into the original system using the backward substitution phase of *CR*. The following Figure 6 illustrates the access pattern of the *CR–PCR* combination.

Figure 5. Access pattern of the PCR algorithm

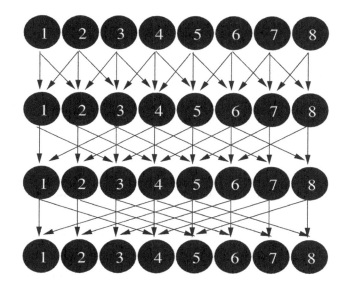

Figure 6. Access pattern of the hybrid CR-PCR algorithm

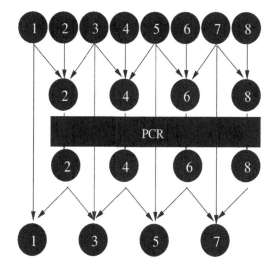

In the next section, we study deeply the performance and viability of each approach.

CASE STUDIES

In this section, we present some case studies to demonstrate the use of the various approaches discuss in the previous section. To that end, we will apply these approaches to two common problems, the 3D Poisson problem, and finally Fluid Structure Interaction via the Lattice Boltzmann Method.

Three Dimensional Poisson Problem

The *Poisson problem* is chosen, because the operator involved is very common in many systems. The Poisson problem represents the most time consuming part of larger simulation codes which tackle a variety of physical situations. Our proposed parallel implementation (i.e., the classical cyclic reduction algorithm) to tackle large linear systems which arise from the discretized form of the elliptic problem, schedules the computing on both the GPU and the multicore processors in a cooperative way.

Block Tridiagonal Algorithm

In this subsection, we briefly summarize a classical direct method for the discrete solution of separable elliptic equations based on a block cyclic reduction algorithm (Swarztrauber, 1974). This method is commonly used when tackling the solution of a linear system of equations arising from the second order centered finite difference discretization of 2D separable elliptic equations. From the standpoint of computational complexity (speed and storage), for a mxn grid, its operation count is proportional to $mn \log_2 n$, and the storage requirements are minimal, since the solution is returned in the storage occupied by the right hand side of the equation (i.e., $m \times n$ locations are required).

Consider the 2D separable elliptic equation having $u(x,y)$ as unknown field (*Poisson* equation is a particular case of what follows):

$$\frac{\partial}{\partial x}\left(a(x)\frac{\partial u}{\partial x}\right) + b(x)\frac{\partial u}{\partial x} + c(x)u + \frac{\partial}{\partial y}\left(d(y)\frac{\partial u}{\partial y}\right) + e(y)\frac{\partial u}{\partial y} + f(y)u = g(x,y) \tag{14}$$

If we discretize (14) with given *Dirichlet* or *Neumann* boundary conditions assigned on the edges of a square, using the usual five-point scheme with the discrete variables ordered in a lexicographic fashion, we obtain a linear system of mxn equations (having m nodes in the x direction and n in y one): $\vec{Au} = \vec{g}$, where A is a block tridiagonal matrix.

$$A = \begin{bmatrix} B_1 & C_1 & & & & \\ A_2 & B_2 & C_2 & & & \\ & A_3 & B_3 & C_3 & & \\ & & \cdot & \cdot & \cdot & \\ & & & A_{n-1} & B_{n-1} & C_{n-1} \\ & & & & A_n & B_n \end{bmatrix} \tag{15}$$

and the vector $\vec{u}$ and $\vec{g}$ are consistently split as a set of sub-vectors $\vec{u}_j$ and $\vec{g}_j$, $j = 1,...,n$, of length m each (i.e., the solution along the jth domain row):

$$u = \left[\vec{u}_1, \vec{u}_2, ..., \vec{u}_n\right]^T \tag{16}$$

$$g = \left[\vec{g}_1, \vec{g}_2, ..., \vec{g}_n \right]^T \tag{17}$$

There is no restriction on m; however, cyclic reduction algorithms require, with large values of k for optimal performances. The blocks A_i, B_i and C_i are $m \times m$ square matrices. In particular, the *BLKTRI* algorithm requires them to be of the form:

$$A_i = a_i I \tag{18}$$

$$B_i = B + b_i I \tag{19}$$

$$C_i = c_i I \tag{20}$$

where a_i, b_i and c_i are scalars. Having used a standard five point stencil for the discretization of (14), the matrix B has a tridiagonal structure. The solution is obtained using an extended cyclic reduction algorithm, which consists of the following phases, more details are found in (Swarztrauber, 1974):

1. **Recursive Reduction:** A sequence of linear systems is generated starting from the original complete system by decoupling odd and even equations. At each step, or level r, about half the unknown vector $\vec{u}_i$ are reduced by eliminating essentially half the remaining unknown vectors until a single unknown vector $\vec{u}_2^k$ remains.

2. **Back-Substitution:** The solution vectors $\vec{u}_i$ are determined by first solving the final system generated in the above phase $\vec{u}_2^k$. Then the linear systems are solved in reverse order, determining more solution vectors, by substituting the previously computed solutions.

3. **Preprocessing:** This phase consists of computing the roots of certain matrix polynomials. This set of intermediate results only depends on the entries of A (not on the right hand side (RHS) of the equation).

Overall, during the reduction phase the following equations are solved (Swarztrauber, 1974):

$$q_i^{(r+1)} = \left(B_i^r \right)^{-1} B_{i+2^{r-1}}^{r-1} B_{i-2^{r-1}}^{r-1} p_i^r \tag{21}$$

$$p_i^{(r+1)} = \alpha_i^r \left[B_{i-2^{r-1}}^{r-1} \right]^{-1} q_{i-2^r}^{(r)} + \gamma_i^r \left[B_{i+2^{r-1}}^{r-1} \right]^{-1} q_{i+2^r}^{(r)} - p_i^r \tag{22}$$

where g is split into two different terms, q and p. B stores the roots calculated in the preprocessing phase. This procedure is required to stabilize the method (Swarztrauber, 1974). α and γ have the following form:

$$\alpha_i^{(r)} = \prod_{j=i+2^{r-1}}^{i} a_j \tag{23}$$

$$\gamma_i^{(r)} = \prod_{j=1}^{i+2^{r-1}} c_j \tag{24}$$

Conversely, in the last phase the following equations are solved, for

$$r = k, k-1,...,0$$

and

$$i = 2^r, 3 \times 2^r, 5 \times 2^r, ..., 2^{k-r} \times 2^r \sqrt{2} :$$

$$u_i = \left(B_i^r\right)^{-1} B_{i-2^{r-1}}^{r-1} B_{i+2^{r-1}}^{r-1} \left[p_i^{(r)} - \alpha_i^r \left(B_{i-2^{r-1}}^{r-1}\right)^{-1} u_{i-2^r} - \gamma_i^r \left(B_{i+2^{r-1}}^{r-1}\right)^{-1} u_{i+2^r} \right] \tag{25}$$

This method is implemented in a *FORTRAN* package library (FISHPACK, 2015), *BLKTRI* routine, which is widely used and well known within the computational fluid dynamics community.

To obtain the aforementioned terms the solution of a set of scalar tridiagonal systems of equations must be faced. The solution of these systems represents the most expensive stage of the algorithm. Nevertheless, other basic mathematical operations such as vector sums or scalar-vector multiplication introduce a non-negligible cost.

The above Figure 7 schematically shows the potential for parallelism of the problem following the sequence of the algorithm. In this Figure, we have highlighted three different stages: two with a high level of intrinsic parallelism and one with a lower potential. The two highly parallel ranges correspond to the first and last steps of the reduction and substitution phase, respectively. The red area refers to low parallelism corresponding to the last steps of the reduction phase and the first steps of the substitution phases.

Parallel Block Cyclic Reduction

As mentioned above, a key element of the *BLKTRI* algorithm is how to solve a set of scalar tridiagonal systems. The original *BLKTRI* implementation in the fishpack package makes use of the Thomas algorithm (*TA*). Unlike *TA* algorithm, there are other approaches, introduced in the previous section, which are amenable to parallelism.

The reduction and back-substitution phases are the core of the *BLKTRI* algorithm. In this section, we focus on describing how to map these phases onto GPUs. The mapping to multicore systems requires fewer transformations to the original *BLKTRI* code. In this case, the most effective scheme consists in using a coarse-grain strategy for distributing the independent tridiagonal problems which arise at the

Figure 7. Parallel potential for a generic 2D BLKTRI problem

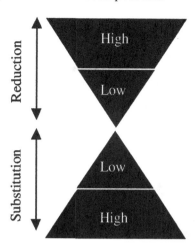

different steps of the algorithm across the different cores. This way, these tridiagonal systems are solved sequentially on each core using the optimal *TA* algorithm. This distribution is well balanced and data locality is optimized, mapping a subset of continuous systems onto each core. The original *FISHPACK BLKTRI* routine can be easily parallelized with this approach, annotating some of its loops with OpenMP pragmas.

Otherwise, for our mapping on GPUs, we have identified four main kernels, which are graphically illustrated, along with their dependencies, in Figure 8. All data needs to be uploaded to the GPU memory before launching the q kernel and finally, the solution u is transferred back to the CPU memory. For convenience, we have denoted $\alpha_i^r \left[B_{i-2^{r-1}}^r - 1 \right]^{-1} q_{i-2^r}^{(r)}$ as α and $\gamma_i^r \left[B_{i+2^{r-1}}^r - 1 \right]^{-1} q_{i+2^r}^{(r)}$ as γ. The p kernel consists of the addition of three vectors. The core of the computation is performed in the remaining three kernels, which share a similar pattern sketched in the *Generic Tridiagonal Kernel*. Essentially, these three kernels solve an independent set of tridiagonal systems but differ in their pre- and post-processing calculations.

Figure 9., at the end of this paragraph, shows with more detail the mapping of the generic kernel on the GPU. At the top of this Figure, we see a coarse-grain scheme similar to the multicore counterpart. In this coarse distribution a set of tridiagonal systems are mapped onto a CUDA block so that each CUDA thread fully solves a system using the *TA* algorithm. Unfortunately, this approach, which is relatively easy to implement, does not exploit efficiently the memory hierarchy of the GPU since the memory footprint of each CUDA thread becomes too large. However, other fine-grain alternatives based on *PCR* are more amenable to be efficiently exploited over GPU architectures. In this case, as we can see at the bottom of the Figure 6, each tridiagonal system is distributed across the threads of a CUDA block so that the shared memory of the GPU can be used more effectively (both the matrix coefficients and the right hand side of each tridiagonal system are hold on the shared memory of the GPU).

Figure 8. Main kernels of the reduction and substitution phases of the BLKTRI algorithm

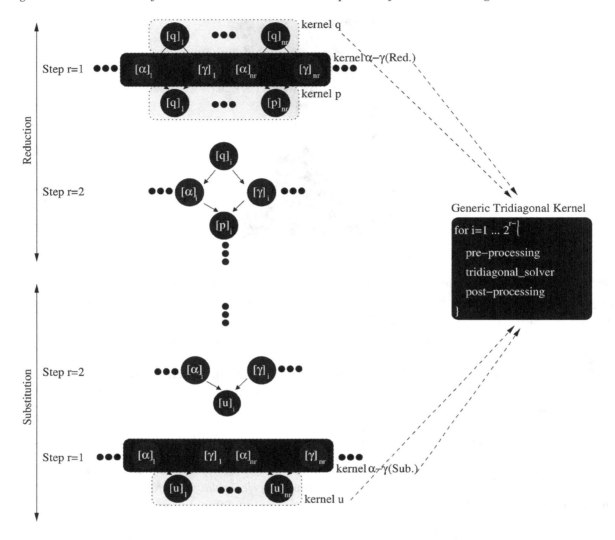

Table 1. Main features of the platforms used

Platform	2 x Intel Xeon E5520 (2.26 GHz)	4 x NVIDIA Kepler K20c
Cores	8	2496
On-Chip Memory	L1 32KB (per core)	SM 16/48 KB (per MP)
	L2 512 KB (unified)	L1 48/16 KB (per MP)
	L3 20 MB (unified)	L2 768 KB (unified)
Memory	64 GB DDR3	5GB GDDR5
Bandwidth	51.2 GB/s	208 GB/s
Compiler	The Portland Group (PGI) Fortran	The Portland Group (PGI) Fortran
Flags	-fast -Mipa = fast, inline -mp -Mcuda	-fast -Mipa = fast, inline -mp -Mcuda
SO	Fedora Linux 16	Fedora Linux 16

Figure 9. Coarse (top) and fine (bottom) distributions of the generic kernel

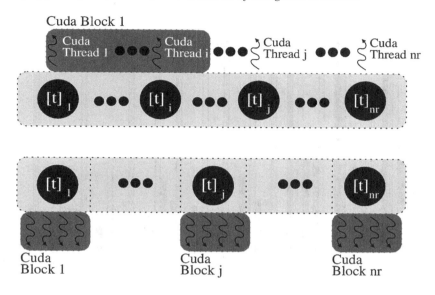

Figure 10. Execution time of the reduction phase

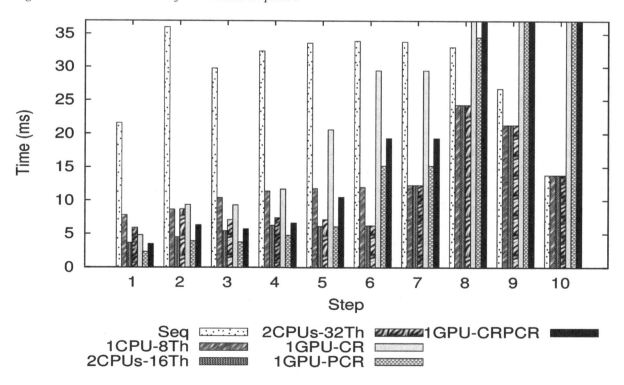

Figure 11. Execution time of the substitution phase

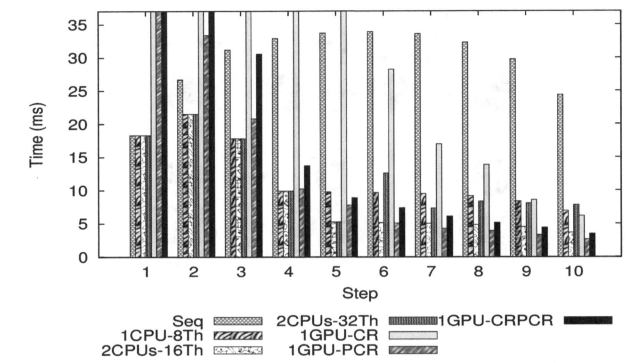

Parallel BLKTRI Performance

In this subsection, a performance analysis is carried out comparing the sequential implementation of *BLKTRI* included in *FISHPACK*, and the different parallel approaches aforementioned which exploit whether current multicore or GPU architectures previously presented. All the results are given in terms of speedup and execution time. For a complete overview of the platforms considered, see Table 1.

Figures 10 and 11 (strong scaling) compares the different approaches using as a simplified test a single 1024x1024 2D problem. Each step of the algorithm has a different level of parallelism but, the computational load of all of them is similar since as the level of parallelism reduces, the number of iterations of the generic tridiagonal kernel increases. The parallel implementations outperform the sequential *BLKTRI* routine in most cases. Only for the steps with reduced parallelism, the GPU version becomes ineffective. This is the expected behavior since in these cases the number of CUDA blocks is very small, i.e. just one CUDA block in the last (first) step of the reduction (substitution) phase.

Figures 12, 13 show the speedup at each step of the extended block cyclic reduction algorithm over the sequential counterpart. As mentioned above, the coarse thread distribution based on the TA algorithm does not perform well on GPUs, but on multicore, this coarse approach does provide satisfactory speedups across all steps despite this is a small problem, achieving best performance when running 16 threads on 2 CPUs and 16 cores. On GPUs, *PCR* provides satisfactory speedups on the first (last) steps of the reduction (substitution) phases and is able to outperform *CR* and the hybrid *CR–PCR* algorithms across all steps.

Figure 12. Speedup for the reduction phase

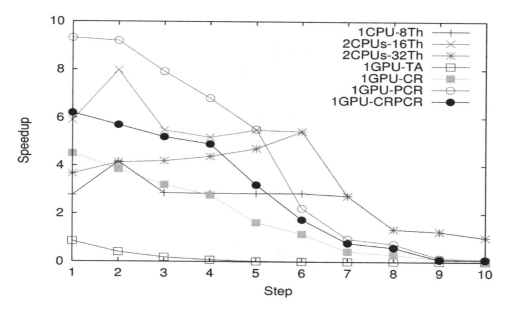

Figure 13. Speed for the substitution phase

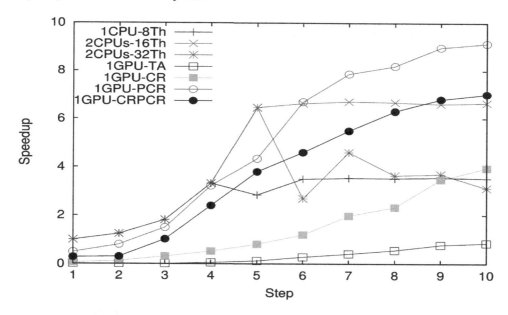

According to these results, the optimal approach appears to be a hybrid combination of *PCR* on the GPU and *TA* (16 threads) on multicore for those steps with lower parallelism. Nevertheless, this combination requires additional CPU–GPU data transfers that may degrade the actual performance, among the different regions executed whether in CPU or in GPU (Figure 14). Figures 15 and 16 show the overall speedups on Kepler for different problem sizes taking into account these data transfer overheads. We

Figure 14. CPU-GPU communication for one 2D BLKTRI problem

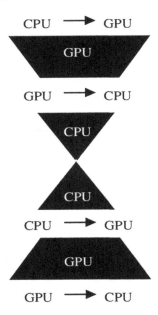

have fixed 5 different computing platforms and increased the size of the problem to carry out a weak scaling study. The hybrid approach is able to outperform the homogeneous multicore counterpart in all cases. A fully homogeneous GPU implementation (not shown in Figures 15 or 16) does not provide satisfactory results due to the low level of parallelism.

Figure 15. Overall time increasing the size of the problem

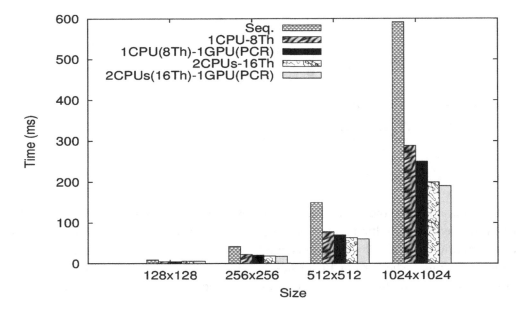

Figure 16. Overall speedup increasing the size of the problem

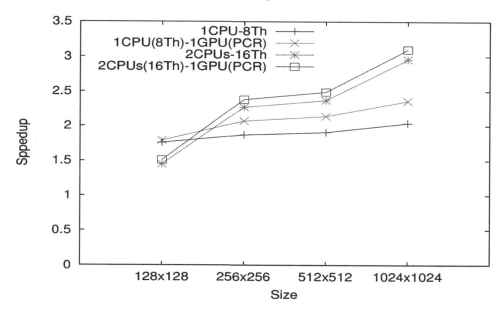

Three Dimensional Elliptic Systems

Next, we briefly explain the numerical development followed to solve a classical 3D *Poisson* equation:

$$\frac{\partial^2_u}{\partial^2 x} + \frac{\partial^2_u}{\partial^2 y} + \frac{\partial^2_u}{\partial^2 z} = f\left(x, y, z\right) \tag{26}$$

defined on a *Cartesian* domain Ω with prescribed conditions on its boundary $\partial\,\Omega$.

Discretizing the domain using a Cartesian mesh uniform along each direction, for each *(i,j,k)* interior node we obtain:

$$\wp^2_x\left(i, j, k\right) + \wp^2_y\left(i, j, k\right) + \wp^2_z\left(i, j, k\right) = f_{i,j,k} \tag{27}$$

where

$$\wp^2_x\left(i, j, k\right) = \left(u_{i-1,j,k} - 2u_{i,j,k} + u_{i+1,j,k}\right) / \Delta^2_y \tag{28}$$

$$\wp^2_y\left(i, j, k\right) = \left(u_{i,j-1,k} - 2u_{i,j,k} + u_{i,j+1,k}\right) / \Delta^2_y \tag{29}$$

Figure 17. The Fourier based decoupling algorithm

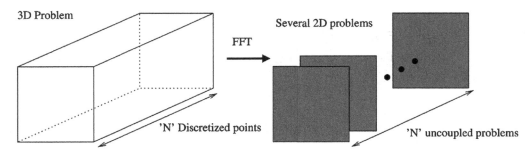

$$\wp_z^2\left(i,j,k\right) = \left(u_{i,j,k-1} - 2u_{i,j,k} + u_{i,j,k+1}\right) / \Delta_z^2 \tag{30}$$

are the finite difference centered approximations to the second derivatives along each direction. The boundary conditions which we will consider are either of *Dirichlet* or *Neumann* type in the y and z directions, while we use a periodic boundary condition in the x-direction. The periodic condition applied in one of the directions allows us to uncouple the 3D problem into a set of several independent 2D problems (Fig. 17) using a discrete *Fourier* transform. We will briefly explain how the decoupling process takes place; Let *N* be the number of equidistant nodes in the *x*-direction which cover the interval *(0,2π)* . We expand the unknown function *u(x,y,z)* and *f(x,y,z)* in *Fourier* series as:

$$u_{n,j,k} = \frac{1}{N}\sum_{l=1}^{N} u'_{l,j,k} e^{-i\alpha(n-1)} \text{ with } \alpha = \frac{2\pi\left(l-1\right)}{N} \tag{31}$$

where $u'_{l,j,k}$ is the *l*[th] *Fourier* coefficient of the expansion. Next, the expansion is used in *equation 27*, obtaining the relationship:

$$\frac{1}{N}\sum_{l=1}^{N} e^{-i\alpha(n-1)}\left\{\frac{u'_{l,j,k}}{\Delta x^2}\left(e^{-i\alpha} - 2 + e^{i\alpha} + \wp_y^2 u'_{l,j,k} + \wp_z^2 u'_{l,j,k}\right)\right\} = \frac{1}{N}\sum_{l=1}^{N} F'_{l,j,k} e^{-i\alpha n} \tag{32}$$

Eq. (31) is equivalent to the set of *N* equations (l = 1 . . . N):

$$\frac{u'_{l,j,k}\left(2\cos\left(\alpha\right)-2\right)}{\Delta_x^2} + \frac{u'_{l,j+1,k} - 2u'_{l,j,k} + u'_{l,j-1,k}}{\Delta_y^2} + \frac{u'_{l,j,k+1} - 2u'_{l,j,k} + u'_{l,j-1,k-1}}{\Delta_z^2} = F'_{l,j,k} \tag{33}$$

Having used the identity $e^{i\alpha} + e^{-i\alpha} = 2\cos\left(\alpha\right)$. In short (33) reads as:

$$\frac{u'_{l,j+1,k} + u'_{l,j-1,k}}{\Delta_y^2} + \frac{u'_{l,j,k+1} + u'_{l,j,k-1}}{\Delta_z^2} + \beta_l u'_{l,j,k} = F'_{l,j,k}, l=1,...,N \tag{34}$$

with

$$\beta_l \, / \, 2 = \cos\big(\alpha\big) - 1 \, / \, \Delta x^2 - 1 \, / \, \Delta y^2 - 1 \, / \, \Delta z^2 \, .$$

Thus, by considering the *Fourier* transform (direct *FFT*) of *F* one obtains a set of *N*, 2D independent problems where the unknowns are the Fourier coefficients $u'_{l,j,k}, l = 1,..,N$. Each independent problem concerns the solution of a linear system of equations which coefficient matrix is block tridiagonal. Of course, each one of these linear systems can now be solved in a distributed fashion, in parallel. Once the solution is obtained in *Fourier* space a backward *FFT* can be used to recast the solution in physical space. Figure 17 provides an algorithmically sketch of the method.

To deal with each decoupled 2D problem, we have chosen a direct method based on a block cyclic reduction algorithm. As shown above, the whole method provides for a blend of coarse and fine-grain parallelism that can be exploited when mapped on hybrid platforms.

Parallel Three Dimensional Elliptic Systems

In this section, we present the proposed approaches to solve in parallel a Three Dimensional Elliptic Systems problem on hybrid platforms. The *FFT* method can be computed in parallel on both multicore and GPUs platforms. This is a well-known problem and there are several libraries that provide satisfactory results (FFT OpenMP. 2015), (3D FFT, 2015), and (cuFFT, 2015). We have focused instead on solving the set of independent 2D problems in parallel, which is the main contribution of this work. In the 2D case, the homogeneous GPU implementation does not provide satisfactory results and the hybrid counterpart is able to achieve the best performance. We want to know if this is still valid for the 3D problem.

Unlike the 2D case (Figure 7), the 3D case (Figure 18) needs to be solved as a set of independent 2D problems; hence, the level of parallelism increases by the size of the 2D problem.

Figure 18. Parallel potential for a generic 3D (set of independent 2D BLKTRI problems) problem

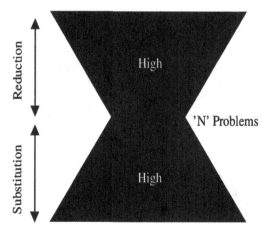

The mapping of a 3D problem onto our target computing platform is similar to their 2D counterparts. For the multicore approach, we follow a coarse-grain approach, mapping a set of 2D problems to each core, which are then solved sequentially using the TA algorithm. On the other hand, for the GPU approach we follow a fine-grain approach based on the PCR algorithm, which is essentially the same as in the 2D problem. The major difference is the number of CUDA blocks at each step, which is N times higher in 3D. A hybrid combination of the multicore and GPU implementation is also possible, as in the 2D case. The data transfer overheads are potentially much lower than in the 2D case, since it is possible to perform them asynchronously. As shown graphically in Figure 19, this allows the overlapping of data transfers with useful computation on the GPUs or CPUs, and indirectly, for GPUs with CPUs computation.

3D Poisson Problem Performance

Figures 20 and 21 (time), and 22 and 23 (speedup) compares (strong scaling) the homogeneous multicore and homogeneous GPU implementations for the Poisson problem discretized using a 512^3 grid. Unlike the 2D case, the speedup figures are less dependent on the step of the algorithm due to the higher level of parallelism. In fact, in all the steps the speedup figures are close to the highest speedup attainable in the 2D case. Another important consequence is that the GPU version always outperforms the multicore counterpart.

These results question the potential benefits that the hybrid strategy could achieve since it seems that the homogeneous GPU implementation is able to exploit all the available parallelism. Figures 24 (time) and 25 (speedup) compares (weak scaling) the homogeneous and hybrid approaches. First, we should highlight that in the homogeneous GPU implementation data transfers incur a very small overhead (lower than 2% of the execution time). This is the expected behavior since the arithmetic intensity of the 3D problem is very high. In spite of this, the hybrid approach is able to outperform the homogeneous counterpart since it benefits from actual GPU-CPU overlap. As shown, these gains grow with the S factor. Overall, the extra benefit of the hybrid implementation can reach up to 15% in terms of execution time over the homogeneous GPU counterpart.

Figure 19. Hybrid approach for computing several 2D BLKTRI problems

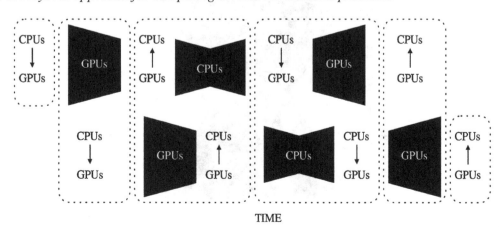

Figure 20. Execution time of the reduction phase

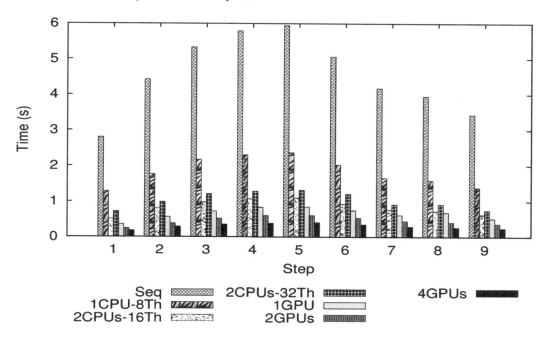

Figure 21. Execution time of the substitution phase

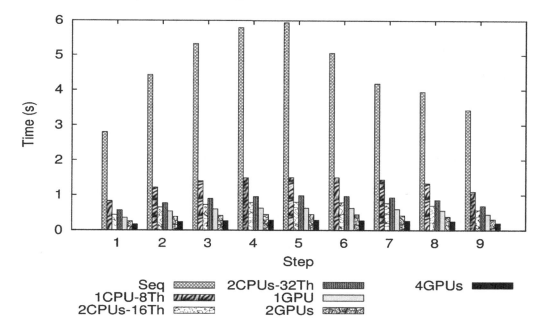

Figure 22. Speedup for the reduction phase

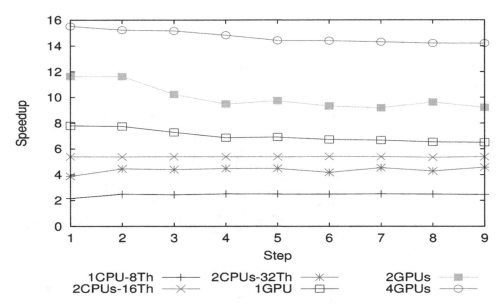

Figure 23. Speedup for the substitution phase

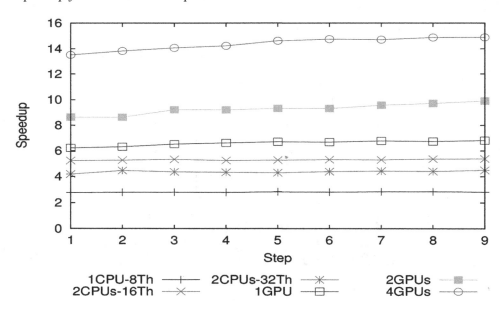

Figure 24. Overall time increasing the size of the problem

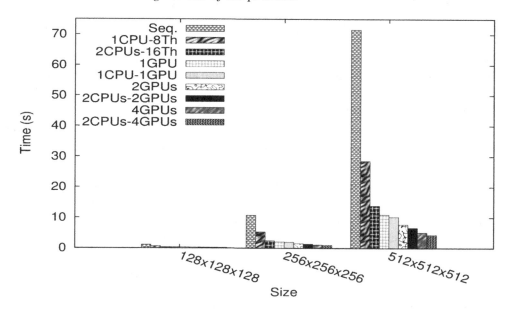

Figure 25. Overall speedup increasing the size of the problem

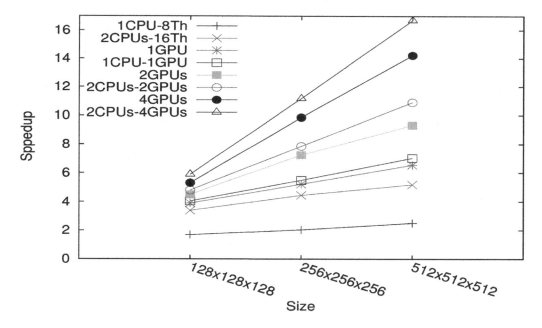

Fluid-Solid Interaction Using Lattice-Boltzmann and Immersed Boundary Coupled Simulations

In this subsection, we present the other case study where we attempt to tackle the problem of the interaction of solids with an incompressible fluid flow via a numerical approach based on the Lattice-Boltzmann (LBM) and Immersed Boundary (IB) methods. This is a very optimum and novel method to solve this problem and is a growing research topic in Computational Fluid Dynamics. We explain in detail the parallelization of the whole method on both GPUs and a hybrid GPU-multicore platform and describe different optimizations, focusing on memory management and multicore-GPU communication. Our performance evaluation consists of a series of numerical experiments that simulate situations of industrial and research interest. Based on these tests, we have shown that the baseline LBM implementation achieves satisfactory results on GPUs. Unfortunately, when coupling LBM and IB methods on GPUs, the overheads of IB degrade the overall performance. The main objective of this work consists of minimizing the overhead caused by the simulation of solid-fluid interaction on multicore-GPU hybrid platforms. In particular, it is proposed a multicore-GPU hybrid scheduler which distributes either to GPU or multicore the different parts of the whole solver depending on their parallel features.

Lattice-Boltzmann and Immersed Boundary Method

The LBM combined with an IB technique is highly attractive when dealing bodies for two main reasons: the shape of the boundary, tracked by a set of *Lagrangian* nodes is a sufficient information to impose the boundary values; and the force of the fluid on the immersed boundary is readily available and thus easily incorporated in the set of equations that govern the dynamics of the immersed object. In addition, it is also particularly well suited for massively parallelized simulations, as the time advancement is explicit and the computational stencil is formed by few local neighbors of each computational node (support). The fluid is discretized on the regular *Cartesian* mesh while the shape of the solids is discretized in a Lagrange fashion by a set of points which obviously do not necessarily coincide with mesh points.

The LBM has been extensively used in the past decades, see (Succi, 2001) for a complete overview, and now is regarded as a powerful and efficient alternative to classical *Navier Stokes* solvers. In what follows, we briefly recall the basic formulation of the method. The LBM is based on an equation that governs the evolution of a discrete distribution function $f_i(x, t)$ describing the probability of finding a particle at Lattice site x at time t with speed $v = e_i$. In this work, we consider the *BGK* formulation that relies upon a unique relaxation time τ toward the equilibrium distribution $f_i^{(eq)}$:

$$f_i\left(x + e_i \Delta t, t + \Delta t\right) - f_i\left(x, t\right) = -\Delta t / \tau \left(f_i\left(x, t\right) - f_i^{(eq)}\left(x, t\right)\right) + \Delta t F_i \qquad (35)$$

The particles can move only along the links of a regular Lattice defined by the discrete speeds ($e_0 = c(0,0)$; $e_i = c(\pm 1, 0)$, $c(0, \pm 1)$, $i = 1, ..., 4$; $e_i = c(\pm 1, \pm 1)$, $c(\pm 1, \pm 1)$, $i = 5, ..., 8$ with $c = \Delta x / \Delta t$) so that the synchronous particle displacements $\Delta x_i = e_i \Delta t$ never take the fluid particles away from the Lattice. For the present study, the standard two-dimensional 9-speed Lattice D2Q9 is

Figure 26. Standard D2Q9 LBM

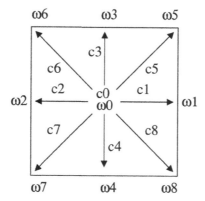

used (Figure 26), but all the techniques that will be presented can be extended in a straightforward manner to three dimensional lattices. The equilibrium function $f^{(eq)}(x,t)$ can be obtained by Taylor series expansion of the Maxwell-Boltzmann equilibrium distribution:

$$f_i^{(eq)} = \rho \omega_i \left[1 + \frac{e_i \cdot u}{c_s^2} + \frac{(e_i \cdot u)^2}{2c_s^4} - \frac{u^2}{2c_s^2} \right] \tag{36}$$

In equation 36, c_s is the speed of sound ($c_s = 1/3$) and the weight coefficients ω_i are $\omega_0 = 4/9$, $\omega_i = 1/9$, $i = 1,...,4$ and $\omega_i = 1/36$, $i = 5,...,8$ according to the current normalization (Figure 23). The macroscopic velocity u in Equation 36 must satisfy a Mach number requirement $|u| / c_s \approx M \square 1$. This stands as the equivalent of the *CFL* number for classical *Navier Stokes* solvers. Finally, in Equation 35, F_i represents the contribution of external volume forces at lattice level that in our case include the effect of the immersed boundary. Given any external volume force, the contribution on the lattice is computed according to the formulation proposed (Guo, Zheng, & Shi, 2002) as:

$$F_i = \left(1 - \frac{1}{2\tau} \right) \omega_i \left[\frac{e_i - u}{c_s^2} + \frac{e_i \cdot u}{c_s^4} e_i \right] \cdot f^{(ib)} \tag{37}$$

The multi-scale *Chapman Enskog* expansion of *equation 35*, neglecting terms of $O(M^2)$ and using Equation 37, returns the *Navier-Stokes* equations with body forces and the kinematic viscosity related to lattice scaling as $v = c_s^2 (\tau - 1/2) \Delta t$.

Without the contribution of the external volume forces stemming from the immersed boundary treatment, Equation 35 is typically advanced in time in two stages, the collision and the streaming ones. Given $f_i(x,t)$ compute:

$$\rho = \sum f_i(x,t) \text{ and } \rho u = \sum e_i f_i(x,t) \tag{38}$$

Collision stage:

$$f'_i(x, t + \Delta t) = f_i(x,t) - \frac{\Delta t}{\tau}\left(f_i(x,t) - f_i^{(eq)}(x,t)\right) \tag{39}$$

Streaming stage:

$$f_i(x + e_i\Delta t, t + \Delta t) = f'_i(x, t + \Delta t) \tag{40}$$

Depending on the ordering of the two stages two different strategies arise. The classical approach is known as the push method and performs collision before streaming. We have adopted instead for pull method (Wellein, Zeiser, Hager, & Donath, 2006), which performs the steps in the opposite order. This can lead to an important performance enhancement on fine grained parallel machines.

We end this section by briefly explaining the IB method that we use both to enforce boundary values and to recover the fluid force exerted on immersed objects within the framework of the LBM algorithm (Pinelli, Naqavi, Piomelli, & Favier, 2010). In the present IB approach as in several others, the fluid is discretized on a regular Cartesian lattice while the immersed objects are discretized and tracked in a *Lagrangian* fashion by a set of markers distributed along their boundaries. The general set up of the present LBM-IB method can be recast in the following algorithmic sketch.

Given $f_i(x,t)$ compute:

$$\rho = \sum f_i(x,t), \text{ and } \rho u = \sum e_i f_i(x,t) + \frac{\Delta t}{2} f^{ib} \tag{41}$$

Collision stage:

$$f''_i(x, t + \Delta t) = f_i(x,t) - \frac{\Delta t}{\tau}\left(f_i(x,t) - f_i^{(eq)}(x,t)\right) \tag{42}$$

Streaming stage:

$$f'_i(x + e_i\Delta t, t + \Delta t) = f''_i(x, t + \Delta t) \tag{43}$$

Compute:

$$\rho' = \sum f'_i(x + e_i\Delta t, t + \Delta t) \text{ and } \rho u = \sum e_i f_i(x,t) + \frac{\Delta t}{2} f^{ib} \tag{44}$$

Interpolate on Lagrangian markers (volume force):

$$U'\left(X_k, t + \Delta t\right) = I\left(u'\right), \text{ and } f^{(ib)}\left(x, t\right) = \frac{1}{\Delta t} S\left(U_d\left(X_k, t + \Delta t\right) - U'\left(X_k, t + \Delta t\right)\right) \tag{45}$$

Repeat Collision with body forces (see *equation 37*) and Streaming:

$$f_i'\left(x, t + \Delta t\right) = f_i\left(x, t\right) - \frac{\Delta t}{\tau}\left(f_i\left(x, t\right) - f_i^{(eq)}\left(x, t\right)\right) + \Delta t F_i, \text{ and}$$
$$f_i\left(x + e_i \Delta t, t + \Delta t\right) = f_i'\left(x, t + \Delta t\right) \tag{46}$$

As outlined above, the basic idea consists in performing each time step twice. The first one, performed without body forces, allows to predict the velocity values at the immersed boundary markers and the force distribution that restores the desired velocity boundary values at their locations. The second one applies the regularized set of singular forces and repeats the procedure advancing (using Equation 37) to determine the final values of the distribution function at the next time step. The key aspects of the algorithm and of its efficient implementation depend on the way the interpolation I and the S operators (termed as spread from now on) are applied. Here, following the work introduced (Pinelli, Naqavi, Piomelli, & Favier, 2010), we perform both operations (interpolation and spread) through a convolution with a compact support mollifier meant to mimic the action of a *Dirac*'s delta. Combining the two operators we can write in a compact form:

$$f^{(ib)}\left(x, t\right) = \frac{1}{\Delta t} \int_\gamma \left[U_d\left(s, t + \Delta t\right) - \int_\Omega u'\left(y\right)\delta'\left(y - s\right)dy\right]\delta'\left(x - s\right)ds \tag{47}$$

where δ' is the mollifier, γ is the immersed boundary, Ω is the computational domain, and U_d is the desired value on the boundary at the next time step. The discrete equivalent of 47 is simply obtained by any standard composite quadrature rule applied on the union of the supports associated to each Lagrangian marker. As an example, the quadrature needed to obtain the force distribution on the lattice nodes is given by:

$$f_l^{(ib)}\left(x_i, y_j\right) = \sum_{n=1}^{N_e} F_l^{(ib)}\left(X_n\right)\delta'\left(x_i - X_n, y_j - Y_n\right)\epsilon_n \tag{48}$$

where the superscript l refers to the lth component of the immersed boundary force, (x_i, y_j) are the lattice nodes (*Cartesian* points) falling within the union of all the supports, N_e is the number of *Lagrangian* markers and ϵ_n is a value to be determined to enforce consistency between interpolation and the convolution. More details about the method and in particular about the determination of the n values can be found in the work (Pinelli, Naqavi, Piomelli, & Favier, 2010).

Figure 27. An immersed curve discretized with Lagrangian points (●); three consecutive points are considered with the respective supports.

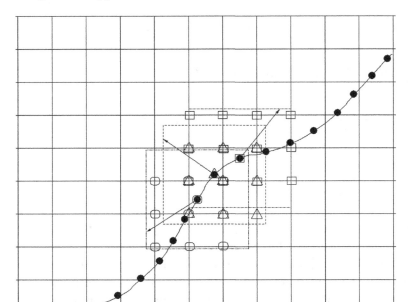

In what follows we will give more details on the construction of the support cages surrounding each *Lagrangian* marker since it plays a key role in the parallel implementation of the IB algorithm. Figure 27 illustrates an example of the portion of the lattice units that falls within the union of all supports. As already mentioned, the embedded boundary curve is discretized into a number of markers X_I, $I = 1, ..., N_e$. Around each marker X_I we define a rectangular cage Ω_I with the following properties:

1. It must contain at least three nodes of the underlying Eulerian lattice for each direction;
2. The number of nodes of the lattice contained in the cage must be minimized.

The modified kernel, obtained as a *Cartesian* product of the one dimensional function (Pinelli, Naqavi, Piomelli, & Favier, 2010):

$$\delta'(r) = \begin{cases} \frac{1}{6}\left(5 - 3|r| - \sqrt{-3\left(1 - |r|^2 + 1\right)}\right) & 0.5 \square |r| \square 1.5 \\ \frac{1}{3}\left(1 + \sqrt{-3r^2 + 1}\right) & 0.5 |r| \square 0.5 \\ 0 & otherwise \end{cases} \tag{49}$$

will be identically zero outside the square Ω_I. We take the edges of the square to measure slightly more than three lattice spacings Δ (i.e., the edge size is $3" + \epsilon = 3 + \epsilon$ in the actual LBM normalization). With such choice, at least three nodes of the lattice in each direction fall within the cage. Moreover, a value of $\epsilon \square 1$ ensures that the mollifier evaluated at all the nine (in two dimensions) lattice nodes takes on a non-zero value. The interpolation stage is performed locally on each nine points support: the values of velocity at the nodes within the support cage centered about each *Lagrangian* marker deliver approximate values (i.e., second order) of velocity at the marker location. The force spreading step requires information from all the markers, typically spaced $\Delta=1$ apart along the immersed boundary. The collected values are then distributed on the union of the supports meaning that each support may receive information from supports centered about neighboring markers, as in *equation 48*. The outlined method has been validated for several test cases including moving rigid immersed objects and flexible ones (Favier, Revell, & Pinelli, 2014).

Lattice-Boltzmann and Immersed Boundary Method on Hybrid CPU+GPU Platforms

Parallelism is abundant in the LBM update and can be exploited in different ways. On our GPU implementation, the lattice nodes are distributed across GPU cores using a fine-grained distribution.

As shown in Figure 28, we used a 1D Grid of 1D CUDA Block. Each CUDA-thread performs the LBM update of a single lattice node. Another important issue is how to implement a single LBM update. We have opted to use the pull scheme introduced in the work (Rinaldi, Dari, Vénere, & Clausse, 2012). In this case, the body of the loop performs the streaming operation before collision, i.e. the distribution functions are gathered (pulled) from the neighbors before computing the collision. Listing 10 shows the implementation considered to compute LBM over GPU.

Next, it is presented the strategy that we have adopted for the efficient parallelization of the IB algorithm. The computations related with the *Lagrangian* markers (support) distributed on the solid/s surface can be parallelized efficiently on, CPU and GPU, (Valero-Lara, 2014). To compute the IB method and the Body Force contribution, it is necessary to store the information of the coordinates, velocities and forces of all the *Lagrangian* points and their supports. In order to facilitate memory bandwidth exploitation

Figure 28. Fine-grained distributions of the lattice nodes

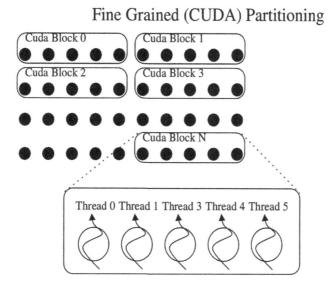

Listing 10. Pseudo-code for LBM-pull approach

```
1. Pull (f₁, f₂, ω, cₓ, c_y)
2. x, y, x_stream, y_stream   x and y are the coordinates for a particular lattice
node
3. local_ux, local_uy, local_ρ, localf_l9], f (eq), cu
4. for i = 1 → 9 do
5.     xs_tream = x - cx_l i]
6.     ys_tream = y - cy_l j]
7.     localf_l i] = f₁[X_stream][y_stream][i]
8. end for
9. for i = 1 → 9 do
10.     local_ρ += localf_l i]
11.     localu_x + = cx_l i]xlocalf_l i]
12.     localu_y + = cy_l i]xlocalf_l i]
13. end for
14. localu_x = localu_x / localρ_15. localuy = localuy / localρ
16. for i = 1 → 9 do
```

$$17. \quad cu = \left(c_x\left[i\right]\cdot local_{ux} + c_y\left[i\right]\cdot local_{uy}\right)$$

$$18. \quad f^{(eq)} = \omega\left[i\right]\cdot\rho\cdot\left(1 + 3\cdot\left(cu\right) + \left(cu\right)^2 - 1.5\times\left(\left(local_{ux}\right)^2 + \left(local_{uy}\right)^2\right)\right)$$

$$19. \quad f_2\left[x\right]\left[y\right]\left[i\right] = local_f\left[i\right]\cdot\left(1 - \frac{1}{\tau}\right) + f^{(eq)}\cdot\frac{1}{\tau}$$

```
20. end for
```

and the parallel distribution of the workload, memory structures based on the style of C programming language have been used. Two different memory management approaches are proposed depending on the use of multicore or GPU, since both architecture show different memory features and hierarchy.

The multicore approach stores the information of a particular Lagrangian point and its support in nearby memory locations, which benefits the exploitation of coarse grain parallelisms. In contrast, in order to achieve a coalescing access to global memory, the GPU approach distributes the information of all Lagrangian points in a set of one-dimensional arrays. In this way, continuous threads access to continuous memory locations.

Several approaches to implement the IB method are proposed. The degree of parallelism of the IB method is given by the number of *Lagrangian* points. The multicore approach carries out a coarse-grain parallelism by mapping a set of continuous *Lagrangian* points on each core which are solved sequentially. This distribution is well balanced and the use of the memory is optimized by using the memory structures previously described. The set of *Lagrangian* points can be easily parallelized with this approach, annotating some of its loops with OpenMP pragmas. On the GPU, the implementation consists of using 2 basic kernels to avoid the data dependences among both. The first one, denoted as Immersed Forces (IF) kernel, assembles the velocity field on the supports, undertakes the interpolation at the *Lagrangian* markers and determines the *Eulerian* volume force field on each node of the union of

Figure 29. CUDA block-thread distribution for the Immersed Boundary method

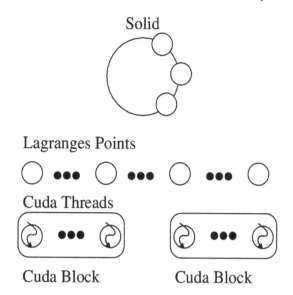

the supports. The second kernel, denoted as Body Forces (BF) kernel, computes the lattice forces and repeats the LBM time update only on the union of the supports including the IB forces contribution. Both kernels use the same CUDA block-thread distribution (Figure 29). Next, we show two sketches, one per each kernel, IF and BF:

In the first kernel (IF), and after the spreading step, the forces are stored in the global memory by using atomic functions. These atomic functions are performed to prevent race conditions. Particularly, we have used these operations to avoid incoherent executions, since the supports of different Lagrangian points can share the same *Eulerian* points (Figure 27). After the execution of the IB related computations (IF kernel), the lattice forces, need to be determined (BC kernel). Before tackling this next stage it is necessary to introduce a synchronization point that guarantees that all the IB forces have been

Listing 11. Pseudocode for IF kernel

```
1. IF (solid s, Uₓ, U_y)
2. velₓ,vel_y,forceₓ,force_y
3. for i = 1 → numSupport do
4.      velₓ += intelpol(Uₓ[s.Xsupp[i]],s)
5.      vel_y += intelpol(U_y[s.Ysupp[i]],s)
6. end for
```

7. $force_x = computeForce\left(vel_x, s\right)$ 8. $force_y = computeForce\left(vel_y, s\right)$

```
9. for i = 1 → numSupport do
10.      AddAtom(s.Xforce[i],spread(forceₓ,s))
11.      AddAtom(s.Yforce[i],spread(force_y,s))
12. end for
```

Listing 12. Pseudocode for BF kernel

```
1. BF (solid s, ω, cx, cy,
```

2. $F_{body}\left(BodyForce\right), x, y, vel_x, vel_y, cu_x, cu_y$

```
3. for i = 1 → numSupport do
```

4. $\quad x = s \cdot Xsupport\left[i\right]$ 5. $\quad x = s \cdot Ysupport\left[i\right]$ 6. $\quad vel_x = s \cdot VelXsupport\left[i\right]$ 7. $vel_x = s \cdot VelYsupport\left[i\right]$

```
8.      for j = 1 → 9 do
```

9. $\quad cu_x = c_x\left[j\right] - vel_x$ 10. $\quad cu_y = c_y\left[j\right] - vel_y$ 11.

$F_{body} = \left(1 - 0.5 \cdot \dfrac{1}{\tau}\right) \cdot \omega\left[j\right] \cdot \left(3 \cdot \left(cu_x \cdot s.XForceSupp\left[i\right] + cu_y \cdot s.XForceSupp\left[i\right]\right)\right)$ 12.

$AddAtom\left(f^{n+1}\left[x\right]\left[y\right]\left[j\right], F_{body}\right)$

```
13.      end for
14. end formulation
```

actually computed on all the points within the union of the supports. Nonetheless, the global memory access required to determine the system of lattice forces is larger than in the previous stage: 9 velocities for each lattice node in the support. Also in this case to inhibit race conditions it has been necessary to resort to atomic functions.

Our first parallel implementation of the LBM-IB method performs all the major steps on the GPU. The host CPU is used exclusively for a pre-processing stage that sets up the initial configuration and uploads those initial data to the GPU memory and a monitoring stage that downloads the information of each lattice node (i.e., velocity components and density) back to the CPU memory when required. As shown in Figure 30, this implementation consists of three CUDA kernels denoted as LBM, IF and BF respectively, that are launched consecutively for every time step. The first kernel implements the LBM method while the other two perform the IB correction. The overhead of the preprocessing stage performed on the CPU is negligible and the data transfer of the monitoring stage is mostly overlapped with the execution of the LBM kernel.

Although this approach achieves satisfactory results, its speedups are substantially lower than those achieved by pure LBM solvers. The obvious reason behind this behavior is the ratio between the characteristic volume fraction and the fluid field, which is very small. Therefore, the amount of data parallelism in the LBM kernel is substantially higher than in the other two kernels. In fact, for the target problems investigated, millions of threads compute the LBM kernel, while the IF and BF kernels only need thousands of them. But in addition, those kernels also require atomic functions due to the

Figure 30. Homogeneous GPU pipeline for our LBM-IB method

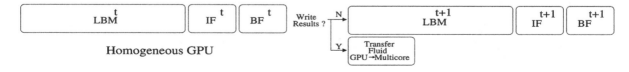

Figure 31. Hybrid multicore+GPU pipeline for our LBM-IB method

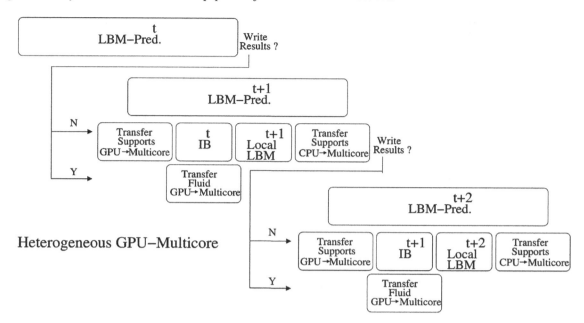

intrinsic characteristics of the IB method and those operations degrade performance. As an alternative to mitigate those problems, we have explored a hybrid implementation graphically illustrated in Figure 31. The LBM kernel is computed on the GPU as in the previous approach but the whole IB method and an additional local correction to LBM on the supports of the Lagrangian points is performed on the CPU in a coordinated way. This way, we are able to overlap the prediction of the fluid field for the "*t +* *1*" iteration with the correction of the IB method on the previous iteration "*t*" at the expense of a local LBM computation of the "*t + 1*" iteration on the CPU and additional transfers of the supports between the GPU and the CPU at every simulation step.

LBM-IB Performance

The performance of the developed LBM-IB solver has been evaluated, considering a number of tests executed on a CPU-GPU (i.e., Xeon-Kepler) system. More details about the specific architectures that have been used for performance evaluation are given in the platforms Table 1 shown in the previous case study. All the simulations have been performed using double precision and as a performance metric we have used the conventional *MFLUPS* metric (millions of fluid lattice updates per second) used in most LBM studies.

The first tests shown by Figure 32 focus exclusively on the IB method using a synthetic simulation without considering the LBM method and analyze its acceleration on both multicore and GPU. Even for a moderate number of Lagrangian nodes, we achieve substantial speedups over the sequential implementation on both platforms. Despite the overheads mentioned above, our GPU implementation is able to outperform the multicore counterpart (8 cores) from 2500 Lagrangian markers.

Figure 32. Speedups of the IB method on multicore and GPU increasing number of Lagrangian nodes

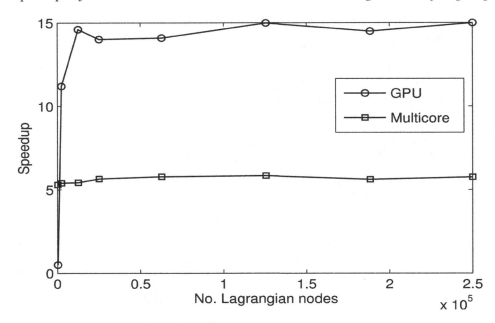

The performance of the whole LBM-IB solver is analyzed in Figures 33 and 34. We have investigated two realistic scenarios with characteristics volume fractions of 0.5% and 1% respectively (i.e. the amount of embedded *Lagrangian* markers over the amount of *Eulerian* lattice nodes). Obviously, the number of *Lagrangian* nodes also grows with the number of lattice nodes. The performance of the homogeneous GPU implementation of the LBM-IB method drops substantially over the pure LBM implementation. The slowdown is around 15% for a solid volume fraction of 0.5%, growing to 25% for the 1% case. In contrast, for these fractions our hybrid approach is able to hide the overheads of the IB method, reaching similar performance to the pure LBM implementation.

Figure 33. Performance of our homogeneous GPU solver in terms of MFLUPS for LBM-IB simulations

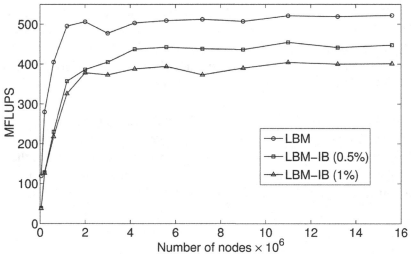

Figure 34. Performance of our hybrid multicore-GPU solver in terms of MFLUPS for LBM-IB simulations

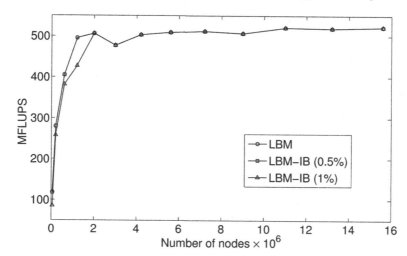

CONCLUSION

This chapter has introduced the main features about current hybrid multicore-GPU platforms, and some of the most extended approaches for an efficient exploitation of both processors, even simultaneously. Finally, two cases studies based on recent works (Valero-Lara, 2014), (Valero-Lara, Pinelli, Favier, & Prieto-Matías, 2012), (Valero-Lara, Pinelli, & Prieto-Matías, 2014a), and (Valero-Lara, Pinelli, Favier, & Prieto-Matías, 2014b) are described, where the approaches presented previously are adapted to the particular features of those problems implemented.

One of the case studies consists of the efficient solution of block tridiagonal linear systems, which is of crucial importance, since it is the major bottleneck of several large scale simulation codes dealing with time-dependent elliptic partial differential equations. We have analyzed the performance of different parallel implementation that exploit homogeneous multicore and GPU systems, as well as hybrid multicore-GPU platforms. On multicore, a coarse grain approach based on the Thomas algorithm is the best option for solving the intermediate scalar tridiagonal systems that arise on both 2D and 3D problems. In contracts, on GPUs, it is much better a fine grain alternative based on using the PCR algorithm. The hybrid approach that combines both implementations is the best option on 2D problems. For 3D problems, we have shown that this is also the best choice despite the 3D problem has both higher arithmetic intensity and higher parallelism than the 2D case. Indeed, the homogeneous GPUs implementation outperforms the multicore counterpart even for medium size. However, the hybrid approach benefits from multicores-GPUs overlapping and is able to achieve an additional 15% performance gain.

In the other case study, we present the design and analysis of a hybrid implementation for a coupled Lattice-Boltzmann and Immersed Boundary method that simulates the contribution of solid behavior within an incompressible fluid. This implementation matches the performance of state-of-the-art pure LBM solvers by mapping the LBM maps on GPUs, while IB is performed on multicore without overheads thanks to overlapping execution.

We attempt to prove that both architectures, multicore and GPU, can be efficiently exploited, even simultaneously. In particular, we have intentionally chosen two cases studies, which exhibit a unbalancing in terms of computational load. This means that some important factors such as, parallel power limit, memory requirements, communication, number of memory accesses, memory access pattern, among others, vary along their executions. This kind of problems are amenable to be adapted on hybrid system by mapping those parts which present a higher parallel power on GPU (manycore), while other sections which are not amenable to be computed by a high number of threads are mapped on multicore. However, those applications with a uniform computational load can also be efficiently ported on hybrid system by distributing sections of the problem on both processors (Valero-Lara, Igual, Prieto-Matías, Pinelli, & Favier, 2015). Depending of the particular features of the problem to be implemented, one of the aforementioned approaches (Section 3) can be used.

The following years will be very interesting from the high performance computing point of view, because of the new hardware products that are coming from NVIDIA and Intel. The performance achieved by Knight Corner chips is usually outperformed by NVIDIA's counterparts (Nvidia Corporation, 2013). However, in 2014 Intel announced the Knights Landing processor (Smith, 2014), that should significantly improve MIC performance. The Landing is based on a different out-of-order Silvermont x86-core (used also by Atom processors) that implements the AVX-512 SIMD instructions. Up to 72 cores will be integrated on the same chip and the double precision floating point performance expected to exceed 3 TFLOPs. Memory performance will also improve significantly thanks to the introduction of Micron's through-silicon vias (TSV)-based stacked DRAM. The Landing main memory can scale up to 16 GB of RAM while offering up to 500GB/sec of memory bandwidth, which is nearly 50% more than Knights Corner's GDDR5. From a systems perspective, the major change is that the Landing will be also available as a standalone processor (Smith, 2014). Intel is expected to release the successor of the Knights Landing in the first quarter of 2018, with the codename Knights Hill. This release will include all the improvements of the Knights Landing plus other expectations like four-way hyper-threading and a higher number of cores per processor (Gardner, 2014).

On the other hand, NVIDIA will continue its hardware release pace with the Maxwell (desktop models starting from 2015), Pascal and Volta generations. Pascal and Volta will be an important change if NVIDIA achieves what they promise with the appearance of NVLink, that in a nutshell, is NVIDIA's effort to supplant PCI-Express with a faster interconnect bus. The main intention of the NVLink is to allow compute workloads to better scale across multiple GPUs, achieving about 20 gigatransfers per second (8 lanes rated for about 20 Gbps) compared to the 8 GT/s for PCIe 3.0 (NVIDIA Corporation, 2014). PCIe 4.0 in turn will eventually bring higher bandwidth yet than PCIe 3.0 (although is not expected as higher as NVIDIA one), so this bus-healthy-war that is coming has many things to say in the months to come.

REFERENCES

Alverson, G., Alverson, R., Callahan, D., Koblenz, B., Porterfield, A., & Smith, B. (1990). The tera computer system.*Proceedings of the Fourth international Conference on Supercomputing* (pp 1-6) doi:10.1145/77726.255132

Alverson, G., Alverson, R., Callahan, D., Koblenz, B., Porterfield, A., & Smith, B. (1992). Exploiting heterogeneos parallelism on a multithreading multiproccesor.*Processing of the Sixth International Conference on Supercomputing* (pp. 188-197). doi:10.1145/143369.143408

Amdahl, M. G. (1967). Validity of the single processor approach to achieving large scale computing capabilities. In *Proceedings of the Spring Joint Computer Conference* (pp. 483-485). ACM Press. doi:10.1145/1465482.1465560

Barnes, G. H., Brown, R. M., Kato, M., Kuck, D. J., Slotnick, D. L., & Stokes, R. A. (1968). The ILLIAC IV Computer. *IEEE Transactions on Computers, C-17*(8), 746–757. doi:10.1109/TC.1968.229158

Bernaschi, M., Fatica, M., Melchiona, S., Succi, S., & Kaxiras, E. (2010). A flexible high- performance lattice boltzmann gpu code for the simulations of fluid flows in complex geometries. *Concurrency Computa.: Pract. Exper., 22*(1), 1–14. doi:10.1002/cpe.1466

Branover, A., Foley, D., & Steinman, M. (2012). AMD fusion APU: Llano. *IEEE Micro, 32*(2), 28–37. doi:10.1109/MM.2012.2

Conte, S. D., & de Boor, C. (1976). *Elementary Numerical Analysis*. New York: McGraw-Hill.

cuFFT. (n. d.). Retrieved from http://developer.nvidia.com/cuda/cufft

Culler, D. E., Gupta, A., & Singh, J. P. (1997). *Parallel Computer Architecture: A Hardware/Software Approach*. San Francisco, CA, USA: Morgan Kaufmann Publishers Inc.

Dally, W. J., Labonte, F., Das, A., Hanrahan, P., Ahn, J., Gummaraju, J., & Kapasi, U. J. et al. (2003). Supercomputing with streams.*Proceedings of the ACM/IEEE Conference on Supercomputing* (pp. 35).

Davidson, A. A., Zhang, Y., & Owens, J. D. (2011). An Auto-tuned Method for Solving Large Tridiagonal Systems on the GPU.*Proceedings of the 25th IEEE International Symposium on Parallel and Distributed Processing* (pp. 956-965). doi:10.1109/IPDPS.2011.92

Dennard, R. H., Gaensslen, F. H., Rideout, V. L., Bassous, E., & LeBlanc, A. R. (1974). Design of ion-implanted mosfet's with very small physical dimensions. *IEEE Journal of Solid-State Circuits, 9*(5), 256–268. doi:10.1109/JSSC.1974.1050511

Denning, J. P., & Dennis, B. J. (2010). The resurgence of parallelism. *Communications of the ACM, 53*(6), 30–32. doi:10.1145/1743546.1743560

Esmaeilzadeh, H., Blem, E., St. Amant, R., Sankaralingam, K., & Burger, D. (2011). Dark silicon and the end of multicore scaling.*Proceedings of the 38th Annual International Symposium on Computer Architecture* (pp 365-376). ACM press. doi:10.1145/2000064.2000108

Esser, R., & Knecht, R. (1993). Intel paragon xp/s - architecture and software environment. In *Proceedings of Supercomputer* (pp. 121–141). Springer Berlin Heidelberg. doi:10.1007/978-3-642-78348-7_13

Favier, J., Revell, A., & Pinelli, A. (2014). A Lattice Boltzmann–Immersed Boundary method to simulate the fluid interaction with moving and slender flexible object. *Journal of Computational Physics, 261*(0), 145–161. doi:10.1016/j.jcp.2013.12.052

3D. FFT. (n. d.). Retrieved from http://charm.cs.uiuc.edu/cs498lvk/projects/kunzman/index.htm

FFT OpenMP. (n. d.). Retrieved from http://people.sc.fsu.edu/~jburkardt/c_src/fft_openmp/fft_openmp.html

FISHPACK. (n. d.). Netlib. Retrieved from http://www.netlib.org/fishpack/

Gardner, E. (2014). *What public disclosures has Intel made about Knights Landing?* Intel Corporation.

Garland, M., & Kirk, D. B. (2010). Understanding throughput-oriented architectures. *Communications of the ACM*, *53*(11), 58–66. doi:10.1145/1839676.1839694

Geer, D. (2005). Industry trends: Chip makers turn to multicore processors. *Computer*, *38*(5), 11–13. doi:10.1109/MC.2005.160

Gronqvist, J., & Lokhmotov, A. (2014). Optimising OpenCL kernels for the ARM Mali tm-t600 GPUs. In W. Engel (Ed.), *GPU Pro 5: Advanced Rendering Techniques*. CRC Press. doi:10.1201/b16721-25

Guo, Z., Zheng, C., & Shi, B. (2002). An extrapolation method for boundary conditions in lattice Boltzmann method. *Physics of Fluids*, *14*(6), 2007–2010. doi:10.1063/1.1471914

Gustafson, J. L. (1988). Reevaluating Amdahl's Law. *Communications of the ACM*,31(5), 532-533.

Hennessy, J. L., & Patterson, D. A. (2011). Computer Architecture: A Quantitative Approach (5th ed.). San Francisco, CA, USA: Morgan Kaufmann Publishers Inc.

Intel Corporation. (2009). Intel 5520 chipset and Intel 5500 chipset-datasheet.

Januszewski, M., & Kostur, M. (2014). Sailfish: A flexible multi-GPU implementation of the lattice Boltzmann method. *Computer Physics Communications*, *185*(9), 2350–2368. doi:10.1016/j.cpc.2014.04.018

Jeff, B. (2012). Big.LITTLE system architecture from ARM: saving power through heterogeneous multiprocessing and task context migration. In P. Groeneveld, D. Sciuto, & S. Hassoun (Eds.), *DAC* (pp. 1143–1146). ACM. doi:10.1145/2228360.2228569

Jeffers, J., & Reinders, J. (2013). *Intel Xeon Phi Coprocessor High Performance Programming*. San Francisco, CA, USA: Morgan Kaufmann Publishers Inc.

Jeffers, J., & Reinders, J. (2013). *Intel Xeon Phi Coprocessor High Performance Programming*. San Francisco, CA: Morgan Kaufmann Publishers Inc.

Kapasi, U., Dally, W. J., Rixner, S., Owens, J. D., & Khailany, B. (2002). The imagine stream processor. *Proceedings of the 2002 IEEE International Conference on Computer Design: VLSI in Computers and Processors* (pp. 282-288). IEEE Computer Society. doi:doi:10.1109/ICCD.2002.1106783 doi:10.1109/ICCD.2002.1106783

Khailany, B. K., Williams, T., Lin, J., Long, E. P., Rygh, M., Tovey, D. W., & Dally, W. J. (2008). A programmable 512 GOPS stream processor for signal, image, and video processing. *IEEE Journal of Solid-State Circuits*, *43*(1), 202–213. doi:10.1109/JSSC.2007.909331

Kim, H.-S., Wu, S., Chang, L.-W., & Hwu, W.-W. (2011). A Scalable Tridiagonal Solver for GPUs. *Proceedings of the 40nd International Conference on Parallel Processing* (pp. 444-453).

Kongetira, P., Aingaran, K., & Olukotun, K. (2005). Niagara: A 32-way multithreaded SPARC processor. *IEEE Micro*, *25*(2), 21–29. doi:10.1109/MM.2005.35

Krauss, L. M., & Starkman, G. D. (2004). Universal Limits of Computation.

Lee, M. C. (2009). A Divide-and-Conquer Strategy and PVM Computation Environment for the Matrix Multiplication.*Proceedings of the 9th International Conference on Algorithms and Architectures for Parallel Processing* (pp. 535-544). doi:10.1007/978-3-642-03095-6_51

Lindholm, E., Nickolls, J., Oberman, S., & Montrym, J. (2008). NVIDIA tesla: A unified graphics and computing architecture. *Micro, IEEE*, *28*(2), 39–55. doi:10.1109/MM.2008.31

Mont-Blanc Project, from http://www.montblanc-project.eu/

Moore, G. E. (1965). Cramming more components onto integrated circuits. *Electronics*, *38*(8), 56–59.

Moreland, K. D. (2012). Oh, $#*@! Exascale! The Effect of Emerging Architectures on Scientific Discovery. High Performance Computing, Networking. *Storage and Analysis*, *224*(231), 10–16.

Nemirovsky, M., & Tullsen, M. D. (2013). *Multithreading Architecture. Synthesis Lectures on Computer Architecture*. Morgan and Claypool Publishers.

NVIDIA Corporation. (2004). NVIDIA NVLink High-Speed Interconnect: Application Performance.

NVIDIA Corporation. (2013). Just the facts.

NVIDIA Corporation. (2014). NVIDIA Next Generation CUDA Compute Architecture: Kepler GK110/210 (Whitepaper version 1.1).

Olukotun, K. (2007). *Chip Multiprocessor Architecture: Techniques to Improve Throughput and Latency. Synthesis Lectures on Computer Architecture*. Morgan and Claypool Publishers.

OpenACC, from http://www.openacc-standard.org/

PGI Compilers & Tools, (n. d.) Retrieved from http://www.pgroup.com/

Pinelli, A., Naqavi, I., Piomelli, U., & Favier, J. (2010). Immersed-Boundary methods for general finite- differences and finite-volume Navier-Stokes solvers. *Journal of Computational Physics*, *229*(24), 9073–9909. doi:10.1016/j.jcp.2010.08.021

Rinaldi, P. R., Dari, E. A., Vénere, M. J., & Clausse, A. (2012). A Lattice-Boltzmann solver for 3D fluid simulation on GPU. *Simulation Modelling Practice and Theory*, *25*, 163–171. doi:10.1016/j.simpat.2012.03.004

Russell, R. M. (1978). The cray-1 computer system. *Communications of the ACM*, *21*(1), 63–72. doi:10.1145/359327.359336

Sakharnykh, N. (2010). Tridiagonal solvers on the GPU and applications to fluid simulation.*Proceedings of the NVIDIA GPU Technology Conference*.

Sánchez, D., Michelogiannakis, G., & Kozyrakis, C. (2010). An analysis of on-chip interconnection networks for large-scale chip multiprocessors. *ACM Transactions on Architecture and Code Optimization*, *7*(1), 1–4. doi:10.1145/1736065.1736069

Scott, S. L. (1996). Synchronization and communication in the T3E multiprocessor. *SIGPLAN Not.*, *31*(9), 26–36. doi:10.1145/248209.237144

Seiler, L., Carmean, D., Sprangle, E., Forsyth, T., Abrash, M., Dubey, P., & Hanrahan, P. et al. (2008). Larrabee: A many-core x86 architecture for visual computing.*Proceedings of the 35th International Conference and Exhibition on Computer Graphics and Interactive Techniques* (Vol. 18, pp. 1-15), New York, NY: ACM Press. doi:10.1145/1399504.1360617

Shet, A. G., Siddharth, K., Sorathiya, S. H., Deshpande, A. M., Sher-lekar, S. D., Kaul, B., & Ansumali, S. (2013). On Vectorization for Lattice Based Simulations. *International Journal of Modern Physics C*, 24(12).

Själander, M., Martonosi, M., & Kaxiras, S. (2014). *Power-Efficient Architectures: Recent Advances. Synthesis Lectures on Computer Architecture*. Morgan and Claypool Publishers.

Smith, B. J. (1982). Architecture and applications of the HEP multiprocessor computer system.*Proceedings of the International Society for Optical Engineering* (Vol. 298, pp 241-248).

Smith R. (2014). Intel's Knights Landing Xeon Phi coprocessor.

Sterling, T., Becker, D. J., Savarese, D., Dorband, J. E., Ranawake, U. A., & Packer, C. V. (1995). Beowulf: A parallel workstation for scientific computation.*Proceedings of the 24th International Conference on Parallel Processing* (pp. 11-14). CRC Press.

Succi, S. (2001). *The lattice Boltzmann equation: for fluid dynamics and beyond*. New York: Oxford university press.

Sutter, H. (2005). The free lunch is over: A fundamental turn toward concurrency in software. *Dr. Dobb's journal*, 30(3), 202-210.

Swarztrauber, P. N. (1974). A direct Method for the Discrete Solution of Separable Elliptic Equations. *SIAM Journal on Numerical Analysis*, *11*(6), 1136–1150. doi:10.1137/0711086

The International Technology Roadmap for Semiconductors. (2013). *Technical report*. ITRS.

TOP500 List. (n. d.). Retrieved from http://www.top500.org/

Ungerer, T., Robic, B., & Silc, J. (2003). A survey of processors with explicit multithreading. *ACM Computing Surveys*, *35*(1), 29–63. doi:10.1145/641865.641867

Vajda, A. (2011). *Programming Many-Core Chips*. Springer. doi:10.1007/978-1-4419-9739-5

Valero-Lara, P. (2014). Accelerating solid-fluid interaction based on the immersed boundary method on multicore and GPU architectures. *The Journal of Supercomputing*, *70*(2), 799–815. doi:10.1007/s11227-014-1262-2

Valero-Lara P., Igual F. D., Prieto-Matías M., Pinelli A., & Favier J. (2015). Accelerating fluid–solid simulations (Lattice-Boltzmann & Immersed-Boundary) on heterogeneous architectures. *Journal of Computational Science*. Doi:10.1016/j.jocs.2015.07.002.

Valero-Lara, P., & Pelayo, F. L. (2011). Towards a More Efficient Use of GPUs.*Proceedings of International Conference on Computational Science and Its Applications Workshops* (pp. 3-9).

Valero-Lara, P., & Pelayo, F. L. (2013). Analysis in performance and new model for multiple kernels executions on many-core architectures. *Proceedings of the IEEE 12th International Conference on Cognitive Informatics and Cognitive Computing* (pp. 189-194). doi:doi:10.1109/ICCI-CC.2013.6622243 doi:10.1109/ICCI-CC.2013.6622243

Valero-Lara, P., & Pelayo, F. L. (2015). Full-Overlapped Concurrent Kernels.*Proceedings of the 28th International Conference on Architecture of Computing Systems* (pp. 1-8).

Valero-Lara, P., Pinelli, A., Favier, J., & Prieto-Matías, M. (2012). Block Tridiagonal Solvers on Heterogeneous Architectures.*Proceedings of 10th IEEE International Symposium on Parallel and Distributed Processing with Applications Workshop* (pp. 609-616).

Valero-Lara, P., Pinelli, A., & Prieto-Matías, M. (2014a). Fast finite difference Poisson solvers on heterogeneous architectures. *Computer Physics Communications*, *185*(4), 1265–1272. doi:10.1016/j.cpc.2013.12.026

Valero-Lara, P., Pinelli, A., & Prieto-Matías, M. (2014b). Accelerating Solid-fluid Interaction using Lattice-boltzmann and Immersed Boundary Coupled Simulations on Heterogeneous Platforms.*Proceedings of the International Conference on Computational Science* (pp. 50-61). doi:10.1016/j.procs.2014.05.005

Wellein, G., Zeiser, T., Hager, G., & Donath, S. (2006, September). On the single processor performance of simple lattice Boltzmann kernels. *Computers & Fluids*, *35*(8-9), 910–919. doi:10.1016/j.compfluid.2005.02.008

Zhang, Y., Cohen, J., & Owens, J. D. (2010). Fast tridiagonal solvers on the GPU. *Proceedings of the 20th ACM SIGPLAN Symposium on Principles and Practice of Parallel Programming* (pp. 127-136).

KEY TERMS AND DEFINITIONS

Elliptic: In Mathematics, Elliptic equation is a general partial differential equation of second order. In computer science, this kind of equations cover a large number of applications, such as computational fluid dynamics, image processing and mathematical finance.

Eulerian: In Computational Fluid Dynamics, the Eulerian vision of the flow is a way of seeing the fluid, focusing on specific locations in the space through which the fluid goes through.

Hybrid: It refers to those systems where more than one kind of processors, typically CPUs and GPUs co-exist. These systems attempt to improve the performance by adding different computer architectures for specialized processing capabilities.

Lagrangian: In Computational Fluid Dynamics, the Lagrangian specification is a way of seeing the fluid by following an individual element of the fluid as it moves through space and time.

Manycore: A computer architecture composed of a large number of cores and small cache memories. It is also known as throughput-oriented processors.

Multicore: It is a single computational component composed by two or more independent processing units (cores). Each of the units integrates its own arithmetic-logic and control units. All cores can access an integrated shared memory. It is also known as low-latency-oriented processors.

Navier-Stokes: In Computational Fluid Dynamics, they refer to computational frameworks based on Navier-Stokes method, which describe the motion of viscous fluid substances. These models can deal with a large number of problems that affect to fluid flow. Biology, aeronautic, weather prediction, are just a few examples of its application areas.

SIMD: Single Instruction Multiple Data, in Flynn's taxonomy, refers to one particular kind of processors, which are composed of multiple processing elements that commonly share the same control unit, and can perform the same operation on different data simultaneously.

Thread: In computer science, a thread is known as a sequence of instructions. On a parallel processor, such as multicore or manycore, multiple threads can be executed simultaneously.

Chapter 7
CPU–GPU Computing:
Overview, Optimization, and Applications

Xiongwei Fei
Hunan City University, China

Wangdong Yang
Hunan University, China

Kenli Li
Hunan University, China

Keqin Li
State University of New York, USA

ABSTRACT

Heterogeneous and hybrid computing has been heavily studied in the field of parallel and distributed computing in recent years. It can work on a single computer, or in a group of computers connected by a high-speed network. The former is the topic of this chapter. Its key points are how to cooperatively use devices that are different in performance and architecture to satisfy various computing requirements, and how to make the whole program achieve the best performance possible when executed. CPUs and GPUs have fundamentally different design philosophies, but combining their characteristics could avail better performance in many applications. However, it is still a challenge to optimize them. This chapter focuses on the main optimization strategies including "partitioning and load-balancing", "data access", "communication", and "synchronization and asynchronization". Furthermore, two applications will be introduced as examples of using these strategies.

INTRODUCTION

As processor speeds steadily increase, high energy consumption and heat dissipation become harder to mitigate. At the same time, design engineers must devise processors with multiple cores to satisfy the demand for high performance. Central Processing Units (CPUs) and Graphics Processing Units (GPUs) have evolved to support more cores than ever, but the development of the two processor types follows different philosophies. CPU development focuses on low latency by using sophisticated control, while GPU development aims for high performance by using a greater number of simple cores. GPUs often serve as coprocessors with CPUs. In many supercomputers, such as Tianhe and Titan, CPUs and GPUs cooperate together to produce powerful computing. For example, each computing node of the Tianhe-1A has two Intel® Xeon® X5670 CPUs and one Nvidia Tesla™ M2050 GPU. In personal computers, the typical combination of the CPU and GPU provides low price and high performance.

DOI: 10.4018/978-1-5225-0287-6.ch007

The popularity of such heterogeneous systems necessitates adaptation of applications to optimize their performance. Three types of adaptation are necessary. First, because of the multiple cores, the applications must be adapted for parallel processing to maximize use of available resources. Second, effort should be made to combine the properties of the CPU and the GPU to partition and map tasks. Third, focus on specific techniques to enhance performance as much as possible. In this chapter, four techniques are introduced:

- Workload balancing and distribution between the CPU and the GPU.
- Efficient use of hierarchical memories, such as hiding data access latency, coalescing data access, efficient shared memory, virtual addressing between GPU and CPU, etc.
- Reduction of communication overhead, such as by zero copy or streaming data transmission.
- Asynchronization such as concurrent copying and execution, sub-task pipeline, and so on.

This chapter discusses CPU and GPU heterogeneous hardware and hybrid OpenMP and CUDA software. They are two sides of a coin, so this chapter discusses the architecture of the CPU and the GPU, and the mixing method of OpenMP and CUDA. Performance measurement techniques are described to evaluate the performance of applications running on such heterogeneous computers. Specifically, the metrics of execution time, bandwidth, occupancy, and speedup will be provided. Furthermore, two synthesized examples –parallel Sparse Matrix-Vector multiplication (SpMV) and Advanced Encryption Standard (AES) –are provided to demonstrate the use of some of these techniques on heterogeneous computers and to provide some inspiration for development of hybrid parallel applications. High-performance applications for heterogeneous computing environments can be achieved with a thorough understanding of the essential properties of the hardware and the application and the use of specific optimization techniques.

The remainder of this chapter is organized as follows: the next section briefly discusses the advances of heterogeneous and hybrid computing models. Then, section "HETEROGENEOUS AND HYBRID COMPUTING MODELS" describes in more details the heterogeneous and hybrid computing models, including GPU and CPU hardware architectures, and CUDA and OpenMP platforms. After that, section "OPTIMIZATION STRATEGIES" provides some optimization strategies, such as partitioning and load-balancing, data access optimization, reducing communication in heterogamous and hybrid environments; performance evaluation is also provided in this section. Section "APPLICATIONS" offers two typical applications of heterogeneous and hybrid computing models. One of these applications involves hybrid parallel matrix computing, and the other involves hybrid parallel encrypting /decrypting. Finally, the chapter concludes.

BACKGROUND

Heterogeneous and hybrid computing refers to the use of various cores and resources cooperating to accomplish a common computing task. In common usage, "heterogeneous computing" denotes that the hardware has a mixed architecture; whereas, "hybrid computing" means that the software is split into various parts and mapped to the hardware.

Heterogeneous hardware architecture has developed to address four issues or limitations of traditional homogeneous computing:

- **Energy Limitation:** Traditional homogeneous computers rely on one type of computing resource: the CPU. To enhance processing speed, high-frequency computing cores or multiple, integrated, relatively low-frequency cores are used. Because the CPU has complicated logic and control parts, it consumes a great deal of energy. If the CPU has many cores or its frequency reaches a certain level, the energy demand becomes unaffordable--especially for computers with thousands of such cores. This led to the development of coprocessors, mainly GPUs, to off-load some computation and reduce the energy demand.

- **High Temperature Limitation:** To meet the large energy demand in traditional homogeneous computers, heat becomes a significant problem. Higher frequency cores consume more energy and produce more heat. The heat must be dissipated quickly to avoid loss of function, damage to the system or burn out. Heterogeneous computers with low frequency and high energy efficiency coprocessors eliminate this problem.

- **Cost Limitation:** The goal of homogeneous cores is low latency of computing. Thus, complicated control and logic processes are used, such as branching, instruction pipelines, out-of-sequence execution, etc. Although this can produce high performance for complicated applications, it is not always appropriate for applications which demand high throughput. Heterogeneous computing uses many low frequency and simple cores is to obtain high throughput. The complicated parts of homogeneous computers cost more than the simple parts of heterogeneous computers. From the perspective of cost to performance, a heterogeneous computer is more marketable than a homogeneous computer.

- **Manufacturing Process Limitation:** To improve the performance of homogeneous computers, more advanced manufacturing processes are used to integrate more cores or raise the frequency of cores; but, manufacturing process enhancement is difficult to sustain. This limitation in homogeneous computers hinders higher performance; but can be overcome by moving to heterogeneous computers with more but relatively simple computing cores. Heterogeneous computers need relatively simple and mature manufacturing processes and can support low-cost and large scale production.

The production of heterogeneous computers is now mainstream, for the reasons listed above. This verified by the current ranking of supercomputers on the market. Whether in Top 500 (TOP500.org, 2015) or Green 500 (CompuGreen, 2015), heterogeneous computers dominate.

Heterogeneous computers generally adopt the CPU as the master and the GPU as the slave processor. Each has different properties and should take on computing tasks matching their abilities to obtain the biggest benefit. The CPU is good at complexity control and lowering the latency of computing while the GPU is good at high throughput. Thus, hybrid computing will best utilize the assets of both resources in collaboration. In other words, various aspects of each task should be assigned to the CPU and GPU based on their properties to achieve the effect of "one plus one is larger than two." Specifically, the parts of a task that need low latency should be assigned to the CPU; those with high throughput needs to the GPU. This is a basic principle, but not the only one. Another consideration is the need to keep the workload between the CPU and the GPU balanced. If the workload loses balance, one of the processors must wait for the other. This wastes time and resources. Workload distribution to achieve balance can be a difficult issue, as it is dependent on the specific hardware and the application.

Recently, much research focuses on the use of multiple kernels concurrently executing on a single GPU to improve performance. Kernels can be scheduled by various methods. The main methods include "merged kernels", "concurrent kernels", and "dynamic kernels". Valero-Lara and Pelayo (2013) analyzed and compared two methods of concurrent execution (concurrent kernels and merged kernels) and found that increasing computation implies a decrease in performance. Valero-Lara and Pelayo (2015) investigated three methods (concurrent kernels, merged kernels, and dynamic parallelism) to execute multiple kernels and found that "concurrent kernels" is a more efficient method. They further reduced the bottleneck of communication by overlapping data transference and kernel execution. When multiple jobs concurrently run on the GPU, memory accesses continue to be the bottleneck to improving performance. Valero and Pelayo (2011) merged multiple independent tasks and ran them simultaneously on the GPU and evaluated the effects of different amounts of memory accesses in several scenarios. With the memory accesses increasing and possible memory conflicts occurring, the performance decreases. Guevara et al. (2009) developed a scheduler, *cusub*, to determine when to merge multiple kernels on the GPU. When the memory or computing resources required by tasks exceed the available amount, the scheduler will not merge the kernels but will dispatch them serially. They also found too much data transferring will decrease the performance of a merged kernel. Gregg et al. (2012) presented a software kernel scheduler, *KernelMerge*, that "hijacks" the OpenCL runtime and can concurrently execute two OpenCL kernels on a single GPU device. The scheduler is able to work in two scheduling algorithms-- round-robin and static percentage--the latter of which approximates the optimal performance of the two kernels.

Another research advance involves task scheduling on heterogeneous systems. For a single heterogeneous node, Jiménez et al. (2009) improved the scheduling algorithms, which are based on First Free algorithm and the past performance history of applications, to allow multiple applications to fully utilize all available resources of the CPU and the GPU, so that their performance is improved by 30% ~ 40%. For heterogeneous clusters, Zhang and Wu (2013) aimed to balance and maximize workload and proposed a greedy heuristic task scheduling involving the weights of the processors.

HETEROGENEOUS AND HYBRID COMPUTING MODELS

This section discusses in some details the heterogeneous and hybrid computing models from three aspects. First, it introduces the GPU architecture and Compute Unified Device Architecture. Second, it presents the CPU multi-Core architecture and Open Multi-Processing. Third, it discusses the CPU-GPU master-slave computing.

GPU Architecture

A Graphics Processing Unit (GPU) is used primarily to process graphics or as a coprocessor with a Central Processing Unit (CPU). Because of its powerful computing ability, users expect that it can process general data for more applications. Fortunately, this has been achieved since 2006 when the GPU evolved to the General Purpose GPU (GPGPU) under the support of certain frameworks, such as the Compute Unified Device Architecture (CUDA) offered by Nvidia. The GPU has many simple and cheap cores and can yield high throughput. These cores are organized as an array of parallel processors known as Streaming Multiprocessors (SMs) that can work in the Single Instruction Multiple Thread (SIMT) fashion (Sanders & Kandrot, 2010).

Figure 1 shows the architecture of a GPU. The GPU has memory, control, and an Arithmetic Logic Unit (ALU) as well as the CPU. The GPU consists of an array of Streaming Multiprocessors (SMs), each of which is capable of supporting thousands of co-resident and concurrent threads. Current GPUs have about 2 ~ 13 SMs, such as the Nvidia K20, which has 13 SMs and the Nvidia GT 640M, which has 2 SMs. Each SM comprises a set of processors, shown as the SPs (Streaming Processors) in Figure 1. Currently, each SM usually has 192 cores, such as the Nvidia K20, GT 640M, etc. The total number of cores can be calculated by multiplying the number of SMs by the number of SPs. For example, K20 has $13 \times 192 = 2496$ cores while GT 640M has $2 \times 192 = 384$ cores. At each clock cycle, a multiprocessor executes the same instruction on a group of threads called a warp. The warp size of current GPUs is 32.

Figure 1 illustrates only global memory and Per Block Shared Memory (PBSM). In fact, the GPU has six different memories that are discussed later. The global memory can share data between SMs, but the PBSM is shared only by threads in the same block that owns the PBSM.

Figure 1. GPU architecture

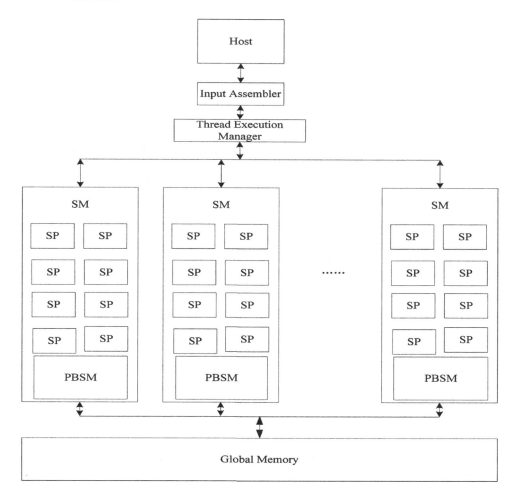

Figure 2. GPU data transfer

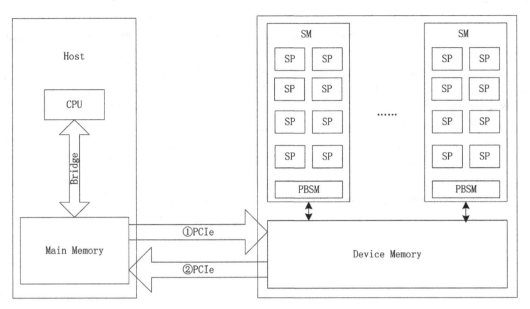

The GPU has lightweight thread execution managers that can quickly issue, schedule, and manage massive threads with low overhead. Because many active warps reside in a GPU, if the warp has enough resources, threads will be issued and scheduled quickly; whereas, warps that lack resources will wait until the execution conditions are satisfied.

The CPU is in charge of loading GPU kernel codes and transferring data. The process of transferring data is shown in Figure 2. First, the CPU allocates memory space in the GPU by calling the *cudaMalloc* function for storing data that is needed in later computation by the kernel. Then CPU transfers data from main memory to device memory using the Peripheral Component Interface Express (PCIe) bus. This is done by the CPU calling the *cudaMemcpy* function. After that, the GPU accesses these data and executes the kernel. When the computation of the kernel is completed, the results can be returned to main memory by calling *cudaMemcpy* again. These processes are shown as the arrows in Figure 2.

The GPU possesses six types of memory: registers, local memory, shared memory, constant memory, texture memory, and global memory.

Registers are private to a thread when they are assigned to it until the thread is finished. Their speed is the fastest but their amount is very limited. For example, on the K20 GPU, the maximum number of registers per thread is 63 and the maximum number of registers per multiprocessor is 65535.

Local memory also belongs privately to a thread. Usually a local array will be stored in local memory. Another scenario is that too many registers have been used. In this scenario, the excessive requirement for registers cannot be satisfied; but the problem can be solved by storing some data in local memory. If the thread is finished, the local memory allocated to it will be released.

Shared memory is also a limited resource. Shared memory is slower than registers, but is capable of sharing data within a block. For instance, the K20 possesses 48 KB of shared memory per multiprocessor. Shared memory cannot be replaced by other memory when encountering excessive requirements. This is to say that although there are enough blocks, the active blocks will be affected by the shared memory afforded. For example, on the K20 for a given kernel, if each block needs 4 KB of shared memory, an SM can reside simultaneously in a maximum of 12 blocks. But if each block needs 12 KB of shared memory, an SM can simultaneously reside in only 4 blocks at most, even if there are more blocks.

Constant and texture memory are both read-only. This means that they must be initialized at allocation. Another consideration is whether they have caches. If a kernel has space locally, it will lead to more cache hits and therefore improved performance; otherwise, it will result in more cache misses and poor efficiency.

Global memory has the largest space but is slowest compared to the other memories in the GPU. It can be used to load and store data for all the threads of the whole grid. The CPU transfers data between host memory and global memory at kernel start and finish phases, respectively. Global memory can be used to share data between different blocks, even between blocks in different SMs.

Figure 3 shows the layout of GPU memories. Registers are located in SMs on-chip. Local memory dynamically resides in global memory when threads privately possess them. Shared memory is logically allocated to a block and also exists on-chip. Constant memory and texture memory are located on-chip, but global memory exists off-chip.

Figure 3. GPU memory layout

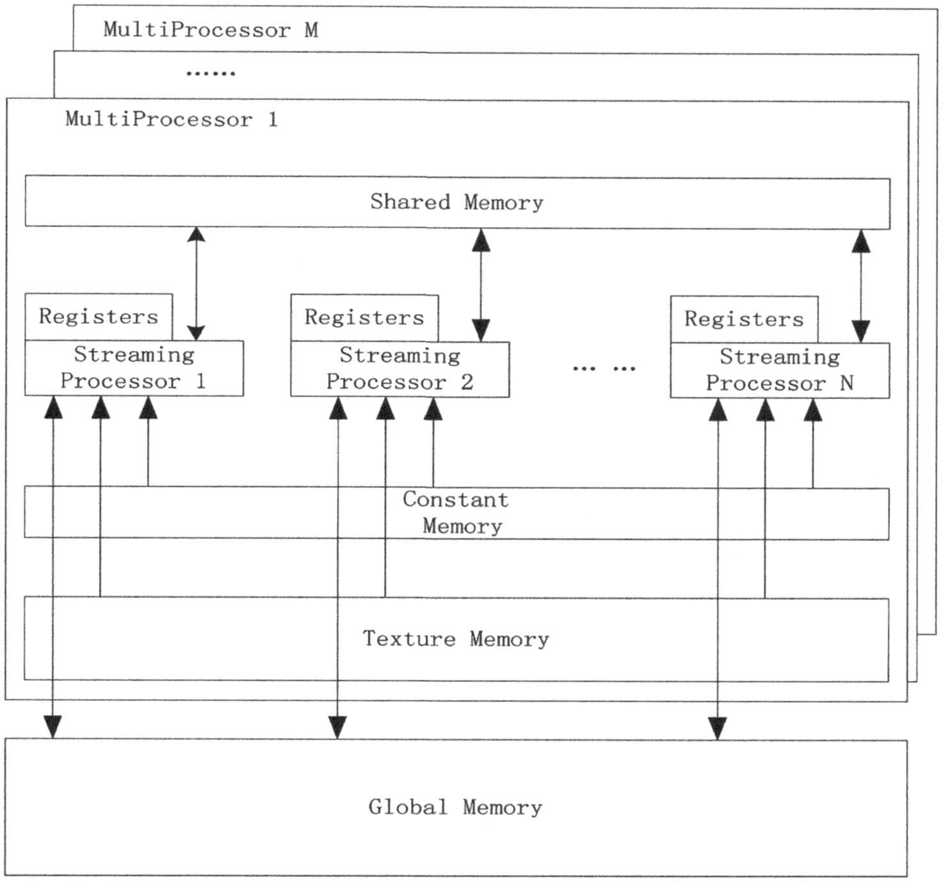

Compute Unified Device Architecture

Compute Unified Device Architecture (CUDA) provides the environment for programming GPUs to support general computing. CUDA reduces the programming effort by offering some libraries and encapsulating Application Programming Interfaces (APIs). Currently, CUDA releases include C/C++ and FORTRAN versions. These APIs need to be embedded into traditional C/C++ or FORTRAN programs. A key point is that the thread organization needs to be assigned, where these threads will be run in parallel in the Single Instruction Multiple Data (SIMD) manner. Therefore, programmers need to code the work of a thread and all the threads will be executed on SMs in parallel.

CUDA provides four important elements: CUDA C/FORTRAN and the corresponding Compiler, CUDA library, CUDA runtime, and CUDA driver, as shown in Figure 4. In fact, CUDA C/FORTRAN is a variant of C/FORTRAN, but adds four main properties. These properties are: how to define which parts of a program run on the GPU or the CPU; how to use different GPU memories; how to define a kernel, block, and grid to execute parallel computing; and how to state variables. CUDA libraries include many useful mathematical applications, such as cuFFT (CUDA Fast Fourier Transform library). CUDA runtime is a Just-in-time (JIT) compiler through which Parallel Thread Execution (PTX) intermediate codes are dynamically compiled to hardware codes compatible with the specific platform. CUDA driver is the bridge between the API and the GPU. A CUDA program is executed in two parts--host and device--corresponding to the CPU and the GPU, respectively.

Figure 4. CUDA software stack

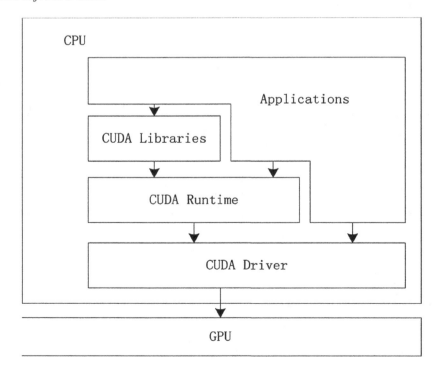

Figure 5. Thread organization

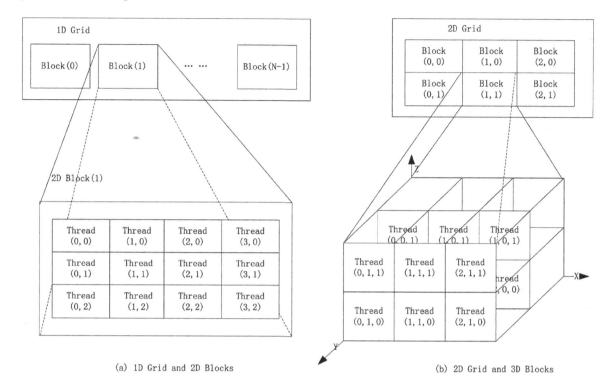

(a) 1D Grid and 2D Blocks   (b) 2D Grid and 3D Blocks

The host organizes and sends the tasks to the device, and the device runs the computing tasks in parallel. When the host encounters a task to be performed in parallel on the device, it invokes a kernel function; then, the kernel function will be executed on the device in parallel. A kernel function will be in the form of *__global__ void kernel<<<dmGrid, dmBlock>> (Parameter list)*, where *dmGrid* and *dmBlock* define the organization of blocks and threads respectively and can be one, two, or three dimensions.

For example, Figure 5(a) illustrates a 1D grid and one of its 2D blocks. The 1D of the grid is defined by *dim3 dmGrid(N)*, where *Block(i), i=0...N-1*, represents the index of blocks. The 2D blocks are defined by *dim dmBlock(4,3)*, where *thread(i, j), i =0, ..., 3, j =0, 1, 2*, denotes the index of threads residing in a block.

For another example, Figure 5(b) demonstrates a 2D grid and one of its 3D blocks. The 2D of the grid is defined by *dim3 dmGrid(3, 2)*, where *Block(i, j), i=0, 1,2, j =0, 1*, represents the index of blocks. The 3D blocks are defined by *dim dmBlock(3, 2, 2)*, where *Thread(i, j, k), i =0, 1, 2, j =0, 1, k=0, 1* denotes the index of threads residing in a block.

Threads in the same block can commonly use shared memory exclusively allocated to that block. Each thread in a block can use its registers individually. To fully utilize resources, CUDA needs to optimally organize the threads by using something such as shared memory to relieve the overhead of accesses.

CPU Multi-Core Architecture

Current CPUs have multiple cores but fewer than GPUs. This is because CPU cores have more complicated control and logic parts in order to lower latency and improve the performance of a single thread. Multiple cores mean a CPU can execute multi-threads in parallel. These threads work in SIMD fashion. If they do not have data dependence, they will run in parallel without communication or synchronization; otherwise, some of them must wait for data from others. Obviously, the latter will consume more time and reduce performance.

Generally, each core has its own independent space, including registers and Level 1 cache, for storing data exclusively. Communication between threads can be achieved by sharing Level 2 caches, which has larger space for storing more data. The architecture of Level 1 and Level 2 caches can be seen in Figure 6. When data needed by cores do not exist in the Level 1 cache, a stall occurs. This stall ends once the data have been loaded from the Level 2 to the Level 1 cache. If the Level 2 cache does not have the data, it will resort to the Level 3 cache, if it exists. In Figure 6, there is no Level 3 cache, so Level 2 will resort to main memory, shown as Dynamic Random Access Memory (DRAM).

Because closer memories have smaller space but shorter latency, the CPU adopts multi-level memories to reduce latency as much as possible. However, statistically, the CPU still spends almost 99% of its time waiting for data transferred from multi-level memories (Tatourian, 2013).

Open Multi-Processing

Open Multi-Processing (OpenMP) is an API that can be used to explicitly direct multi-threaded and shared memory parallel programs (Chandra, 2001). It consists of three main components: compiler directives, runtime library routines, and environment variables. OpenMP makes it easy to use multiple cores in a processor in parallel.

Figure 6. CPU architecture

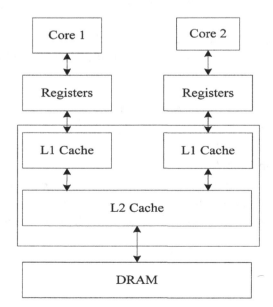

A multi-threaded program can be produced by inserting compiler directives into existing source code in C/C++ or FORTRAN. A compiler that supports OpenMP then generates code that spawns threads as indicated by the directives and/or the values of the environment variables. These threads can execute simultaneously on multi-core CPUs and communicate conveniently by shared memory.

CPU-GPU Master-Slave Computing

As described above, the CPU and GPU can work in master-slave mode, with the CPU as master and the GPU as slave, to undertake a common task by splitting it. Part of the task can be assigned and executed on the CPU in parallel using OpenMP. The rest of the task can be assigned and be executed on the GPU in parallel with support from the CPU. The support mainly includes kernel invoking and data transfers between main memory and device memories. Therefore, this master-slave computing can fully use the hardware resources of both the CPU the GPU, and in terms of software, it combines CPU parallelism offered by OpenMP and GPU parallelism provided by CUDA.

Details of master-slave computing are shown in Figure 7. The CPU side of the figure shows four threads running simultaneously, while the GPU side runs a kernel function in parallel. One of threads on the GPU side is marked as a service thread, and the other threads are marked as work threads. The service thread is used to transfer data and call the kernel function that will run in parallel on the GPU. The service thread first copies data from main memory to device memory, and then calls the kernel function. After the kernel has finished, the service thread is in charge of copying data back to main memory. The work threads are also used to execute some parts of the task at this time.

As shown in Figure 7, the kernel function is simultaneously performed by the threads organized as a 2D grid with 1D blocks. There are eight threads in a block and six blocks in the grid. In other words, there are $6 \times 8 = 48$ threads executing on the GPU simultaneously. All-in-all, there are four threads on the CPU side and 48 threads in the GPU side running simultaneously. Thus, in this hybrid programming model, the CPU and the GPU can cooperate to perform a task and make full use of the respective resources.

Figure 7. Cooperative computing model

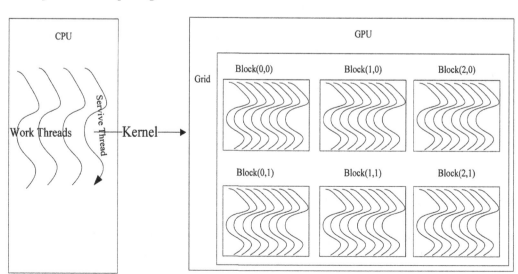

OPTIMIZATION STRATEGIES

This section lists some of the optimization strategies that can be employed in heterogeneous and hybrid computing models. It also discusses how to evaluate the performance of parallel applications.

Partitioning and Load-Balancing

Number and Size of GPU Blocks

Mapping a data-parallel problem onto a set of GPGPU cores is done by CUDA. First, the programmer needs to set the number and sizes of the grid and blocks. Second, the dataset must be partitioned into many blocks according to the grid characteristics of CUDA. Then, the blocks are assigned to GPGPU core groups and will be executed by CUDA. Therefore, the parallel computation efficiency of GPGPU core groups depends on the number and the size of the data blocks allocated to them.

To determine the number of blocks per grid (or grid size), the primary consideration is to keep the entire GPU as busy as possible. Basically, the number of blocks in a grid should be more than the number of SMs so that every SM executes at least one block. Furthermore, there should be multiple active blocks per SM so that the blocks can keep the hardware busy because of no waiting for __syncthreads () , which acts as a barrier at which all threads in the block must wait before being allowed to proceed. This recommendation is subject to resource availability; therefore, it should be determined by the number of threads per block or block size. The number of blocks a kernel launches should be tens of thousands according to the scale of future devices.

In order to maintain high occupancy of the SMs, every SM should be assigned as many active warps as possible. However, the number of active warps per SM is implicitly determined by the execution parameters along with resource constraints, such as registers and shared memory. Thus, choosing execution parameters is a matter of striking the balance between occupancy and resource utilization.

The number and the size of data blocks are determined by the size of the dataset and resource constraints of the GPU; but occupancy is not determined by block size alone, because it is important to remember that multiple concurrent blocks can reside on an SM. In particular, a larger block size does not imply a higher occupancy. Larger block size could reduce the number of blocks allocated onto SMs, and the number of active warps per SM could reduce accordingly. Furthermore, due to resource constraints, fewer blocks can be assigned onto an SM because of blocks that are too large. Thus, there are many factors involved in selecting block size, so some experimentation is inevitably required. However, a few rules of thumb should be followed (NVIDIA, 2015a):

- Threads per block should be a multiple of the warp size to avoid wasting computation on under-populated warps and to maximize the throughput of global memory.
- A minimum of 64 threads per block should be used only if there are multiple concurrent blocks per multiprocessor.
- Between 128 and 256 threads per block are better choices and a good initial range for experimentation with different block sizes.
- Use several (3 to 4) smaller thread blocks rather than one large thread block per multiprocessor if latency affects performance. This is particularly beneficial to kernels that frequently call __syncthreads() function.

Note that if a thread block allocates more registers than are available on an SM, the kernel function will fail to launch, because too much shared memory is required or too many threads are requested.

Partitioning CPU-GPU Tasks

The GPU does not have process control capability as a device in CUDA, which is controlled by the CPU. Data is transported from host memory to global memory of the GPU. Then the CPU invokes the calculation process of the GPU by calling a kernel function (Yang, Li, Mo, & Li, 2015).

The tasks partition model is illustrated in Figure 8, where D_1, D_2, D_3, D_4, ..., D_{i1}, D_{i2}, D_{i3}, D_{i4} are subtasks that are stored in the host memory, and $Thread_1$, $Thread_2$, $Thread_3$, $Thread_4$, ..., $Thread_{i1}$, $Thread_{i2}$, $Thread_{i3}$, $Thread_{i4}$ are multiple threads that are assigned to cores of CPUs (Yang et al., 2015).

To partition a computing task: divide the task into multiple sub-tasks, then assign the sub-tasks to threads of the CPUs to perform. In the processing, two groups of threads are created in parallel sections of OpenMP, where a group of threads is dedicated to controlling the GPUs, while the other threads undertake the computing workload by utilizing the remaining CPU cores.

Data partitioning algorithms, including those that have already been proposed for hybrid platforms, rely on performance models of processors. In Fatica (2009), constants representing the sustained performance of the application on the CPU/GPU were used to partition data. The constants were found prior to partitioning. In Yang et al. (2010), a similar Constant Performance Model (CPM) was proposed, but it was built adaptively, using the history of performance measurements. The fundamental assumption of the data partitioning algorithms based on CPMs is that the absolute speed of the CPU/GPU does not depend on the size of a computing task. However, it becomes less accurate when some parts of the task fit into different levels of memories or when the CPU/GPU switches between different codes.

Figure 8. A task partitioning model for heterogeneous platforms

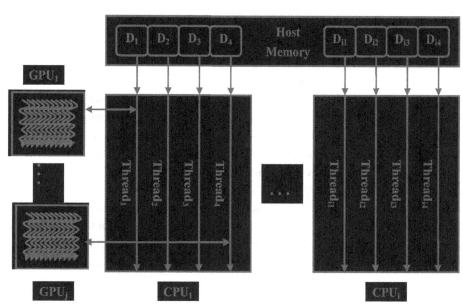

Load-Balancing on SMs

Load balancing in the thread grid of CUDA is achieved by constructing a shared data object that stores all tasks created before and under execution. A processing unit can acquire a new task from the shared data object when it has finished its work. The workload will be balanced between processing units as long as the tasks are sufficiently fine-grained (Cederman & Tsigas, 2008). But the scheduling unit in the GPU is a warp with 32 threads. All threads of a warp run at the same time on an SM, so the running time of a warp is the runtime of the thread with the longest running time. Assume that a block contains at most T threads for the thread grid on the GPU, and the T threads are scheduled to run on an SM by half-warp on a device with compute capability of 1.2 or higher. Executing other warps when one warp is paused or stalled is the only way to hide latency and keep the hardware busy because thread instructions are executed sequentially in CUDA, so more warps are needed to run on an SM.

Load Balancing between CPU and GPU

To achieve the maximum performance of a system with hybrid multicore CPUs and GPUs, it is essential to balance workloads between the CPUs and the GPUs, taking into account the heterogeneity of the processors. However, load balancing on this type of platform is complicated by several factors, such as resource contention, limited local memory on GPUs and ever-increasing gaps of performance and communication speed between GPUs and the PCIe bus (Zhong, Rychkov, & Lastovetsky, 2012).

The load balancing algorithms used in heterogeneous computing systems can be classified as static or dynamic. Static algorithms require some *a priori* information about parallel applications and the platform (for example, those based on data partitioning), and they have been used in Fatica (2009), Yang et al., (2010), Luk et al. (2009), and Ogata et al. (2008). The information can be gathered either at compile-time or at runtime. Dynamic algorithms balance the load by moving fine-grained tasks between processors during the calculation, such as task scheduling and work stealing. Dynamic algorithms do not require *a priori* information about execution, but may incur significant communication overhead due to data migration (Song, Tomov, & Dongarra, 2012).

For a large task to be computed in parallel on GPUs and CPUs, it should be partitioned into multiple sub-tasks that will be computed on CPUs and/or GPUs, respectively. The task is partitioned into K sub-tasks $A_1, A_2 \ldots A_K$, according to the ratio of computing power of the processors.

A computing task must first be divided into multiple sub-tasks, so that these sub-tasks are assigned to the multicores of the CPUs to perform. To balance the load, the computing scale of a sub-task should match the computing power of the processor. Next, in the process of execution, two groups of threads are created in the parallel sections of OpenMP, where a group of threads are dedicated to controlling the GPUs, while other threads undertake the workload of the CPU by utilizing its remaining cores (Yang et al., 2015). But the communication cost of the PCIe bus should be considered for task partitioning between CPUs and GPUs (Fatica, 2009).

A GPU is suitable for the calculation of a dataset with a large volume of regular data because it has both high data bandwidth and a large thread bundle. But the frequency of a GPU is lower than that of a CPU. The differences in data access and computing power of the CPU and GPU should be considered when a task is partitioned. For example, a sparse matrix is partitioned into some blocks to be performed. Sparse Matrix-Vector multiplication (SpMV) on CPUs and GPUs is shown in Figure 9 according to load balancing.

Figure 9. Load balancing partitioning between CPUs and GPUs

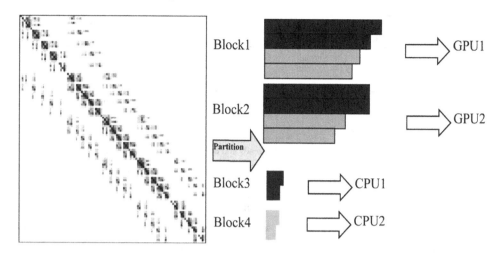

Multi-Level Memory System and Data Access

Host Memory and Device Memory

The peak theoretical bandwidth between device memory and a GPU is much higher (288 GB/s on the NVIDIA Tesla K20c, for example) than the peak theoretical bandwidth between host memory and device memory (8 GB/s on the PCIe ×16). Hence, it is important to minimize data transfers between host and device for the best performance of the overall application; otherwise, running a kernel on a GPU could possibly not demonstrate any speedup compared to running the application on a host CPU.

Intermediate data structures should be created in device memory, operated by the device, and destroyed without ever being mapped by the host or copied to host memory. Additionally, batching many small transfers into one larger transfer provides significantly better performance than executing separate transfers because of the overhead associated with every transfer.

Page-locked or pinned memory transfers attain the highest bandwidth between host and device. Pinned memory is allocated using *cudaHostAlloc()* function in the runtime API. The *bandwidthTest. cu* program in the NVIDIA GPU Computing SDK shows how to use these functions as well as how to measure memory transfer performance (NVIDIA, 2015b).

Device Memory Spaces

CUDA devices use several memory spaces that have different characteristics that reflect their distinct usages in CUDA applications. These memory spaces include global, local, shared, texture, and registers, as shown in Table 1.

Among these different memory spaces, global memory is the most plentiful. Global, local, and texture memory have the greatest access latency, followed by constant memory, shared memory, and the register file.

Table 1. Salient features of device memory

Memory	Location	Size	Hit Latency	Program Scope	Description
Register	On-chip	65536 per block	None	Thread	Dynamically partitioned among the threads running on it.
Shared	On-chip	48 KB per block	≈ register latency	Block	Local scratchpad that can be shared among threads in a thread block. Organized into 16 banks. Does not appear to have error detection. If instructions issued in the same cycle access different locations in the same bank, a bank conflict stall occurs. It is possible to organize both threads and data such that bank conflicts seldom or never occur.
Constant	On-chip	64 KB total	≈ register latency	Global	8 KB cache per SM, with data originally residing in global memory. The 64 KB limit is set by the programming model. Often used for lookup tables. The cache is single ported, so simultaneous requests within an SM must be to the same address or delays will occur.
Texture	On-chip	Up to global	> 100 cycles	Global	16 KB cache per two SMs, with data originally residing in global memory. Capitalizes on 2D locality. Can perform hardware interpolation and have configurable returned-value behavior at the edges of textures, both of which are useful in certain applications, such as video encoders.
Local	Off-chip	Up to global	Same as global	Block	Space for register spilling, etc.
Global	Off-chip	1 GB ~ 12 GB	200 ~ 300 cycles	Global	Large DRAM. All data reside here at the beginning of execution. Directly addressable from a kernel using pointers. Backing store for constant and texture memories. Used more efficiently when multiple threads simultaneously access contiguous elements of memory, enabling the hardware to coalesce memory accesses to the same DRAM page.

Hidden Data Access Latency

Often GPU applications expend significant time in data transfers between the host and the device. Because PCIe has lower available bandwidth than DRAM and the device overhead is associated with each transfer, an efficient implementation should minimize data transfers (Che, Sheaffer, & Skadron, 2011).

Data transfers between host and device using the *cudaMemcpy( )* function are blocked transfers; that is, control is returned to the host thread only after the data transfers are complete. The *cudaMemcpyAsync( )* function is a non-blocking variant of *cudaMemcpy( )* in which control is returned immediately to the host thread. In contrast with *cudaMemcpy( )*, the asynchronous transfer version requires pinned host memory, and contains an additional argument −stream ID. A stream is simply a sequence of operations performed on a device in sequence. Operations in different streams can be interleaved and in some cases overlapped. This is a property that can be used to hide data transfers between the host and the device (NVIDIA, 2013b).

Figure 10 compares sequential versus concurrent copying and kernel execution. The execution process of a sequential stream is shown in the top of the figure; concurrent processing of four asynchronous streams is illustrated in the bottom of the figure. Asynchronous transfers enable overlap data transfers and computation in two different ways. It is possible to overlap host computation, asynchronous data transfers, and device computation on all CUDA-enabled devices.

Figure 10. Sequential vs. concurrent copying and kernel execution

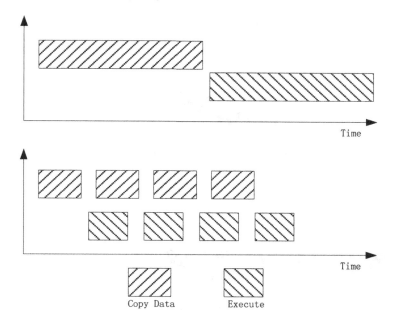

Data Access Coalescing

The SMs of a GPU schedule and execute threads in groups of warps. Global memory of the GPU accesses within a half-warp can be coalesced into the minimum number of memory transactions. An important performance optimization for a GPU is the coalescing of global memory accesses generated by SMs (supported on NVIDIA hardware since the GT200 generation). Figure 11 shows a simple example: if the k-th thread accesses the k-th word in a segment, a single 64-byte transaction is required. Different scenarios and requirements for memory coalescing are documented in detail in the NVIDIA technical guide (NVIDIA, 2015b).

Figure 11 gives an example of memory coalescing. If threads access contiguous data elements, multiple thread accesses can be coalesced. Each element is as long as 4 bytes in this example. Global memory loads and stores generated by threads of a warp (or a half warp for devices with compute capability 1.x) are coalesced into as few as one transaction when certain access requirements are met, so the single most important consideration for performance in programming on the CUDA architecture is the coalescing of global memory accesses.

Figure 11. Memory coalescing

Threads

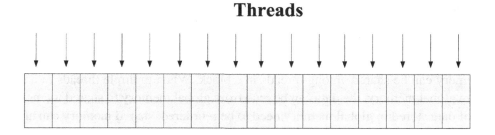

Figure 12. Access patterns of a warp for 128-byte L1 cache

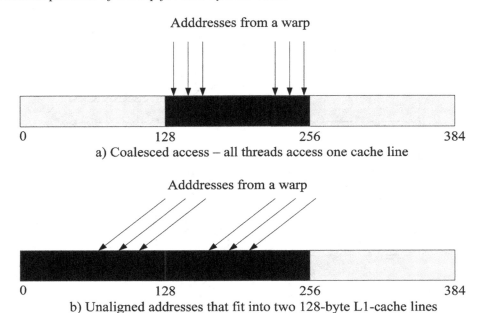

a) Coalesced access – all threads access one cache line

b) Unaligned addresses that fit into two 128-byte L1-cache lines

The concurrent accesses of the threads of a warp will coalesce into a number of transactions equal to the number of cache lines necessary to serve all of the threads of the warp for devices with compute capability 2.x or higher. By default, all accesses are cached through L1 cache, which has 128-byte lines. For a scattered access pattern, sometimes it can be useful to cache only in L2 cache with shorter 32-byte lines to reduce fetches. If every thread of a warp accesses the adjacent 4-byte word, that is a single 128-byte L1 cache line, a single coalesced transaction will serve this memory access. Such a pattern is shown in Figure 12.a. If sequential threads in a warp access memory sequentially but not aligned with a cache line, two128-byte L1 cache lines will be requested as shown in Figure 12.b.

Shared Memory and Memory Banks

Some equally-sized memory modules (called banks) that can be accessed simultaneously are separated from shared memory to achieve high memory bandwidth for concurrent accesses. Therefore, any memory load or store of n addresses that spans n distinct memory banks can be served simultaneously, yielding an effective bandwidth that is n times as high as the bandwidth of a single bank. Each bank has a bandwidth of 32 bits per clock cycle and the successive 32-bit words belong to the successive bank. So the bandwidth of shared memory is 32 bits per bank per clock cycle (NVIDIA, 2015a).

A shared memory request for a warp is split into one request for the first half and one request for the second half, because warp size is 32 and the number of banks is 16 for devices with compute capability of 1.x. If only one memory location per bank is accessed by 16 (a half of a warp) threads, no bank conflict will occur.

Shared memory can be shared among threads in a block. When multiple threads in a block use the same data from global memory, the data can be read from global memory to shared memory only once. Furthermore, if data stored in global memory need to be reordered, shared memory can also be used to avoid uncoalesced memory accesses by loading and storing the data in a coalesced pattern from global memory and then reordering it in shared memory. There is no penalty for non-sequential or unaligned accesses for a warp in shared memory because the access latency of shared memory is far lower than that of global memory.

The use of shared memory is illustrated via a simple example (Listing 1) of matrix multiplication $C = A \times B$ in the case A has the dimension of $M \times w$, B has the dimension of $w \times N$, and C has the dimension of $M \times N$. A natural decomposition of the problem is to use a block and tiles with size of $w \times w$ threads. Therefore, in terms of $w \times w$ tiles, A is a column matrix, B is a row matrix, and C is their outer product, as shown in Figure 13. A grid of $N/w \times M/w$ blocks is launched and each thread block calculates the elements of a different tile in C from a single tile of A and a single tile of B (NVIDIA, 2015a). Figure 13 shows Block-Column Matrix (A) multiplied by Block-Row Matrix (B) with the resulting Product Matrix (C).

Unified Virtual Addressing between CPUs and GPUs

Devices with compute capability of 2.x support a special addressing mode called Unified Virtual Addressing (UVA) on 64-bit Linux, MacOS, and Windows XP and on Windows Vista/7/8 systems when using TCC driver mode. Host memory and device memories of all installed and supported devices share a single virtual address space with UVA (NVIDIA, 2015b). UVA is also a necessary precondition for enabling peer-to-peer (P2P) transfers of data directly across the PCIe bus for supported GPUs in supported configurations, bypassing host memory.

Figure 13. Matrix multiplication

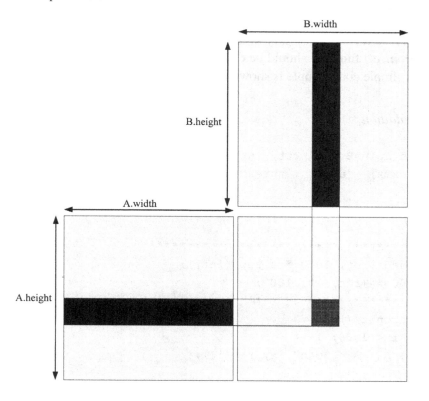

Listing 1. Matrix multiplication

```
__global__ void sharedABMultiply(float *a, float* b, float *c, int N)
{
  // TILE_W is 16 for devices of compute capability 1.x or 32 for devices of
  compute capability 2.x.
  __shared__ float aTile[TILE_W][TILE_W], bTile[TILE_W][TILE_W];
  int row = blockIdx.y * blockDim.y + threadIdx.y; int col = blockIdx.x *
  blockDim.x + threadIdx.x;
  float sum = 0.0f;
  aTile[threadIdx.y][threadIdx.x] = a[row*TILE_W+threadIdx.x];
  bTile[threadIdx.y][threadIdx.x] = b[threadIdx.y*N+col];
  __syncthreads();
  for (int i = 0; i < TILE_W; i++)
    sum += aTile[threadIdx.y][i]* bTile[i][threadIdx.x];
  c[row*N+col] = sum;
}
```

Prior to UVA, an application needed two pointers for the data used in the GPU; one referencing device memory while the other referenced host memory. Furthermore, the data in device memories and host memory must be copied to each other as hard-coded information in the program. But the physical memory space to which a pointer points can be determined simply by inspecting the value of the pointer obtained by the *cudaPointerGetAttributes()* function.

Pinned host memory allocated with *cudaMallocManaged()* function will have identical host and device pointers under UVA, so it is not necessary to call *cudaHostAlloc()* function for such an allocation. But *cudaDeviceSynchronize()* function should be called to avoid access conflicts after the kernel function has been called. A simple code sample is shown in Listing 2.

Listing 2. Matrix addition

```
__global__ void AplusB(int *ret, int a, int b)
{  ret[threadIdx.x] = a + b + threadIdx.x; }
int main()
{
int *ret;
//************************************************
cudaMallocManaged(&ret, 1000 * sizeof(int));
AplusB<<<1, 1000>>>(ret, 10, 100);
//************************************************
cudaDeviceSynchronize();
for(int i = 0; i < 1000; i++)
    printf("%d: A + B = %d\n", i, ret[i]);
cudaFree(ret);
return 0;
}
```

Communication

Zero Copy

"Zero Copy" is a feature added to version 2.2 of the CUDA Toolkit that enables GPU threads to access host memory directly. It requires mapped pinned (non-pageable) memory for this purpose. Mapped pinned memory always gains performance for integrated GPUs (i.e., GPUs with the integrated field of the CUDA device property structure setting to 1), because it avoids superfluous copies when integrated GPU and CPU memory are physically the same (Tatourian, 2013).

For discrete GPUs, mapped pinned memory is advantageous only in certain cases. Mapped pinned memory should be read or written only once because its data is not cached in the GPUs, and the global loads and stores should be coalesced. Zero copy can be used in place of streams because kernel-originated data transfers automatically overlap kernel execution without the overhead of setting up and determining the optimal number of streams (NVIDIA, 2015a).

Streaming Data Transfer

A stream is a sequence of commands that execute on the GPU in order. On one hand, different streams may execute their commands out of order with each other or concurrently. On the other hand, this behavior is not guaranteed and therefore should not be relied upon for correctness (e.g. inter-kernel communication is undefined).

Assigning a task to the GPU includes three steps: data transfers, computing, and memory accesses on the GPU. For a stream, these steps are processed sequentially, but different steps of different streams can be overlapped to hide transfer time. So an asynchronous computing mode can be built using multiple asynchronous streams to improve the throughput of the GPU.

A stream is defined by creating a stream object and specifying its ID as a parameter of a sequence of kernel launches. However, data transfers from host to device memory that are allocated to different streams cannot overlap. The following code sample (Listing 3) creates two streams and allocates an array *hostPtr* of float in page-locked memory, where *hostPtr* consists of two segments of storage space for the two streams.

Each of these streams is defined by the following code sample (Listing 4) as a sequence of one memory copy from host to device, one kernel launch, and one memory copy from device to host. A *cudaDeviceSynchronize()* function should be called after all streams have been executed.

Listing 3. Stream creation and memory allocation

```
cudaStream_t cuStream[2];
for (int i = 0; i < 2; ++i)
  cudaStreamCreate(&cuStream[i]);
float* hostPtr;
cudaMallocHost(&hostPtr, 2 * size);
```

Listing 4. Data transfers and kernel launch

```
for (int i = 0; i < 2; ++i)
{
cudaMemcpyAsync(inputDevPtr + i * size, hostPtr + i * size, size, cudaMemcpy-
HostToDevice, cuStream[i]);
MyKernel<<<100, 512, 0, cuStream[i]>>> (outputDevPtr + i * size, inputDevPtr +
i * size, size);
cudaMemcpyAsync(hostPtr + i * size, outputDevPtr + i * size, size, cudaMemcpy-
DeviceToHost, cuStream[i]);
}
cudaDeviceSynchronize();
```

Synchronization and Asynchronization

Synchronization of Threads in the Same Warp

Once a block is assigned to an SM, it is further divided into warps in the GPU implementation. In fact, warps are not a part of the CUDA specification; but, the knowledge of warps can be helpful in understanding and optimizing the performance of CUDA applications on particular generations of CUDA devices.

An SM should be assigned at least two warps. There are some long-latency operations such as global memory accesses, and a warp is not selected for execution when an instruction executed by the threads in this warp must wait for the results of a previously initiated long-latency operation. If there are multiple warps assigned to an SM, another resident warp can execute the other operations and be no longer waiting for the results. A priority mechanism is used to select which warp to execute if more than one warp is ready for execution. This mechanism of filling the latency of expensive operations with work from other threads is often referred to as latency hiding (NVIDIA, 2015a).

If enough warps are ready, the hardware will probably find a warp to execute at any point in time, so as to make full use of the execution hardware in spite of these long-latency operations. Due to thread scheduling using hardware, the selection of ready warps for execution does not introduce any idle time into the execution timeline, so this is referred to as zero-overhead thread scheduling (NVIDIA, 2015a). The long waiting time of warp instructions is hidden by executing instructions from other warps. In GPUs, there is not as large a chip area for cache memory and branch prediction mechanisms as in CPUs, resulting in a poor ability to tolerate long-latency operations. As a result, GPUs can dedicate most of their chip area to floating-point execution resources (NVIDIA, 2015a).

Synchronization of Threads in the Same Block

The execution time of a thread block depends on the thread with the longest executing time, because all threads in a block must have completed a phase of their execution of the kernel before any thread moves to the next phase. In order to achieve thread synchronization, threads in the same block can coordinate their activities using a barrier synchronization function (i.e., __syncthreads ()) in CUDA. The thread

Listing 5. Overlapping computation and data transfer

```
cudaMemcpyAsync(a_d, a_h, size, cudaMemcpyHostToDevice, 0);
kernel<<<grid, block>>>(a_d);
cpuFunction();
```

that executes the function call will be held at the calling location until every thread in the block reaches that location.

Execution constraints on threads in a block are also imposed when the synchronize mechanism is used. All these threads should execute in almost the same time to avoid excessively long waiting. This constraint can be satisfied by assigning execution resources to all threads in a block as a unit in CUDA runtime systems. That is, all other threads in the same block are also assigned to the same amount of resources when a thread is assigned to certain execution resources. Every thread in the same block should be assigned the same amount of computing tasks to prevent excessive waiting time during barrier synchronization and to ensure that all threads in a block spend an approximate amount of time.

Asynchronization of Data Transmission and Computing on GPUs

The asynchronous mechanism of CUDA enables overlapped CPU computation and GPU computation. On all CUDA-enabled devices, it is possible to overlap host computation, asynchronous data transfers, and device computation. When the host transfers data to the GPU, it does not wait for the end of transmission and immediately begins call computing function of CPU. For example, Listing 5 demonstrates that host executes computation in the routine *cpuFunction()* while the data *a_h* is transferred to device and then a kernel is executed on the device (NVIDIA, 2015b). The host function *cpuFunction()* can overlap its execution and GPU computation because both the memory copying and the kernel execution return control to the host immediately.

Asynchronous transfers also enable overlap data transfers and computation for multiple streams. The last argument in the *cudaMemcpyAsync()* function is stream ID, and in this case it uses the default stream, i.e., stream 0. For the same stream, a kernel will not begin to execute until the memory copying completes; therefore, no explicit synchronization is needed. So in Listing 1, the memory copying and the kernel execution run sequentially.

It is possible to overlap kernel execution on the device and data transfers between the host and device for devices capable of concurrently copying and computing. The *deviceOverlap* field of *cudaDeviceProp* structure (or listed in the output of the *deviceQuery* SDK sample) indicates whether a device has such capability. The overlap once again requires pinned host memory on a device that has this capability (NVIDIA, 2015b). Additionally, data transfers and kernel execution must use different and non-default streams that have non-zero stream IDs. Non-default streams are required for this overlap because memory setting, memory copying, and kernel execution functions that use the default stream begin only after all the preceding calls have completed in any streams and no new operation commences until they are finished. Listing 6 illustrates the basic technique.

Listing 6. Concurrent copying and execution

```
cudaStreamCreate(&cuStream1);
cudaStreamCreate(&cuStream2);
cudaMemcpyAsync(a_d, a_h, size, cudaMemcpyHostToDevice, cuStream1);
kernel<<<grid, block, 0, cuStream2>>>(otherData_d);
```

Listing 7. Staged concurrent copying and execution

```
size = N*sizeof(float)/nStreams;
for(i=0; i<nStreams; i++)
{
offset = i*N/nStreams;
cudaMemcpyAsync(a_d+offset, a_h+offset, size, dir, cuStream[i]);
kernel<<<N/(nThreads*nStreams), nThreads, 0, cuStream[i]>>>(a_d+offset);
}
```

In Listing 6, two streams are created and used in the data transfer and kernel execution respectively, as specified in the last arguments of the *cudaMemcpyAsync* and the kernel's execution configuration, respectively (NVIDIA, 2015b). Kernel execution of *cuStream2* overlaps asynchronous data transfer of *cuStream1*.

Listing 7 demonstrates how to launch multiple kernels to operate on different chunks of the data, if the data can be broken into chunks transferred in multiple stages, where *nStreams* expresses the number of streams. Listing 7 produces results equivalent to Listing 5.

Data transfers and kernel execution can be processed simultaneously and asynchronously on current GPUs. One asynchronous data transfer and kernel execution can be performed on GPUs with a single copy engine. GPUs with two copy engines can simultaneously perform one asynchronous data transfer from host to device and from device to host. The *asyncEngineCount* field of the *cudaDeviceProp* structure indicates the number of copy engines on GPUs (NVIDIA, 2015b). The timeline of execution of Listings 1 and 3 is shown in Figure 10, where *nStreams* is equal to 4.

In this example, it is assumed that the data transfer and the kernel execution are comparable in time. In such a case, if the execution time (*tE*) exceeds the transfer time (*tT*), a rough estimation of the overall time is *tE* + *tT/nStreams* for the staged version versus *tE* + *tT* for the sequential version. If the transfer time exceeds the execution time, a rough estimation of the overall time is *tT* + *tE/nStreams* (NVIDIA, 2015b).

Pipelined Model Based on CPU and GPU

The pipelined computing model is illustrated in Figure 14. First, a large task is input to CPU. Second, the large task is partitioned into some sub-tasks (C_1, C_2 ... C_k). Third, the sub-tasks (C_1, C_2 ... C_k) are executed in the GPU. They are transported into the GPU by streams, and the computed results are also obtained by the streams. Fourth, these results are merged in the CPU. Finally, the results of the large task are output.

Figure 14. Pipelined CPU-GPU computing model

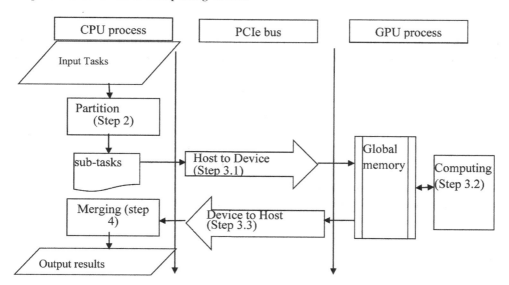

To improve computational efficiency, the process is split into three sub-steps that put data into the GPU (step 3.1), executing computation on the GPU (step 3.2), and getting results from the GPU (step 3.3). For a stream, these steps are processed sequentially; nevertheless, different steps of different streams can be overlapped to form an implicit pipeline. So steps 3.1, 3.2, and 3.3 can be executed concurrently to compose a pipeline, in which, steps 3.1 and 3.3 are asynchronous transfer processes based on the stream model, while step 3.2 is processed in the GPU.

Performance Evaluation

When attempting to optimize codes on CPU-GPU heterogeneous platforms, it is beneficial to know how to measure performance accurately and to understand the roles different metrics play in performance measurement.

Measurement of Execution Time

CPU timers can be used to measure the executing time of programs that are executed on CPU-GPU heterogeneous platforms. When CPU timers are used, it is critical to remember that many CUDA API functions are asynchronous. That is, they return control back to the calling CPU thread before completing their work. All kernel launches are asynchronous. The memory copying functions with the *"Async"* suffix on their names are also asynchronous (NVIDIA, 2015b). Therefore, it is necessary to synchronize the CPU threads and the GPU threads by calling *cudaDeviceSynchronize()* before starting and stopping the CPU timer immediately to accurately measure the elapsed time for a particular call or a sequence of CUDA calls.

The CUDA event API provides functions that create and destroy events, record events (via timestamp), and convert timestamp differences into a floating-point value in milliseconds (NVIDIA, 2015b).

Bandwidth

Bandwidth is one of the most important factors in performance and it is the rate of how fast data can be transferred. With the rapid increase in the number of cores on a GPU, data transmission has been a bottleneck of GPU computing because of the restriction of the bandwidth of PCIe. So many optimization strategies have been proposed to fully utilize the bandwidth.

There are many methods that calculate theoretical and effective bandwidth for measuring performance accurately. Effective bandwidth is calculated by knowing how much data is accessed by a program and by timing the program activities. Due to bad design or implementation issues, effective bandwidth in practice is generally lower than theoretical bandwidth. Increasing effective bandwidth should be the primary goal of subsequent optimization efforts, if effective bandwidth is much lower than theoretical bandwidth. Theoretical bandwidth can be calculated using hardware specifications available in the product literature.

Occupancy

Improving the utilization rate of hardware is the key to improve computing performance. Although thread instructions are executed sequentially in CUDA, when one warp is paused or stalled, other warps can be executed to hide latency and keep the hardware busy. To show the utilization rate of hardware, define a metric of occupancy that is the ratio of the number of active threads per SM to the maximum number of possible active threads (NVIDIA, 2015a).

Occupancy is related to the number of active warps on an SM; therefore, it is important in determining how effectively the hardware keeps busy. How to improve the occupancy is an important goal of optimizing CUDA programs. Occupancy is related to the number and the size of blocks, and the configurations of hardware, such as the number of registers.

Higher occupancy generally can produce higher performance, but does not always equate to higher performance because there is a point above which additional occupancy does not improve performance. However, low occupancy always results in performance degradation because it will interfere with hiding memory latency (NVIDIA, 2015a). One of several factors that determine occupancy is register availability. The number of thread blocks that can reside on an SM is reduced if each thread block processes too much data and uses too many registers so that the occupancy of the SM will be decreased.

Speedup

Speedup is a metric used to express relative performance improvement. The notion of speedup was established by Amdahl's law, which particularly focuses on the context of parallel processing. However, speedup can be used more generally to show the effect of any performance enhancement. Speedup is defined by Equation 1 (Hennessy & Patterson, 2011):

$$S = \frac{T_{old}}{T_{new}} \tag{1}$$

where S is the resultant speedup, T_{old} is the old execution time, i.e., the execution time on CPU-only or GPU-only, and T_{new} is the new execution time, i.e., the execution time on CPU-GPU heterogeneous platforms.

APPLICATIONS

This section provides two applications to show how to use some of the optimization strategies listed in the previous section in heterogeneous and hybrid environments. One of the applications presents the hybrid parallel matrix computing, and the other presents the hybrid parallel encryption and decryption.

Hybrid Parallel Matrix Computing

Sparse Matrix-Vector Multiplication

Sparse Matrix Vector multiplication (SpMV) is an important issue in scientific computing and engineering applications that is very suitable for computing in parallel. The implementation and optimization of SpMV on GPU are research hotspots.

Due to some irregularities of sparse matrix, the effect is not satisfactory at a single compression format. The hybrid storage format can expand the range of adaptation of the compression algorithm. However, for the imbalances of non-zero elements that are divided into compression storage format, the parallel computing power of a GPU cannot be utilized fully. Parallel computing power of a CPU is also rising with the increase in the number of cores. In GPU computing processes, the CPU controls the process instead of being involved in calculation, so it does not produce any computational efficiency.

For the hybrid storage format of sparse matrix, the data can be distributed to the CPU and GPU and then computed at the same time. The CPU-GPU heterogeneous computing model can take full advantage of computing resources of both the CPU and GPU to improve processing performance. With analysis of the characteristics of the CPU and the GPU, some optimization strategies of sparse matrix partitioning and the distribution of the threads can improve computing performance of SpMV in the heterogeneous computing environment (Yang et al., 2015).

GPUs and Multicore CPUs Hybrid Parallel Programming

With the rapid development of multicore technology, the number of cores in a CPU has been increased. CPUs with 4 cores, 6 cores, 8 cores, and more occur in general computers and provide the powerful ability of parallel processing. A heterogeneous computing environment can be built up in GPUs and multicore CPUs.

A GPU does not have process control capability and functions as a device in CUDA that is controlled by a CPU. The data are transported from host memory to global memory of the GPU. Then the CPU invokes the calculation process of the GPU by calling kernel functions.

OpenMP provides a simple and easy-to-use parallel computing model for multi-threading on multicore CPUs. A heterogeneous programming model can be established by combining OpenMP and CUDA in a CPU-GPU heterogeneous computing environment. OpenMP dedicates a thread to control the GPU, while the other threads are used to share the workload that the remaining CPU cores should process. The CPU-GPU heterogeneous parallel computing model is shown in Figure 1.

The CPU-GPU hybrid parallel computing model is illustrated in Figure 8, where D_1, D_2, D_3, D_4, ..., D_{i1}, D_{i2}, D_{i3}, D_{i4} are submatrices that are stored in host memory, and $Thread_1$, $Thread_2$, $Thread_3$, $Thread_4$, ..., $Thread_{i1}$, $Thread_{i2}$, $Thread_{i3}$, $Thread_{i4}$ are multi-threads that are assigned to cores of CPUs (Yang et al., 2015).

Parallel Implementation of SpMV on CPU/GPU

The data processed by a GPU must be transported from host memory to global memory of the GPU by the PCIe bus. Global memory has greater access latency than shared memory, which is shared by a thread block. A multicore CPU can reduce the delay of access memory by using a multi-level cache mechanism, but the use and distribution of the caches is controlled by the processor management of operating system.

A GPU with higher data bandwidth and a larger thread bundle than a CPU is more suitable for the calculation of a dataset that has large volumes, uniform distribution, and better independence. But the frequency of a GPU is lower than a CPU and floating-point calculation of a GPU is also lower than a CPU. Partitioning the dataset into a GPU and a CPU should consider the differences of data accesses and computing features of both the CPU and the GPU.

HYB is a hybrid format of ELLPACK format (ELL) and coordinate format (COO) for sparse matrix. With a few non-zero values, some rows are extracted to be stored as COO, resulting in few zero-padded values in ELL. A sparse matrix can be divided into two parts. One is a data matrix with the same number of rows as the original matrix and another is a dataset of COO. The matrix that is stored as ELL is more suitable for transferring to a thread grid on a GPU. With more loose distribution and the lack of balance, the dataset of COO does not fit a GPU, but fits multicore CPU use.

The details of some parallel implementations of SpMV on CPU/GPU can be seen in Li et al. (2015), Yang et al. (2015), and Yang et al. (2014).

Hybrid Parallel Encryption/Decryption

Advanced Encryption Standard

The Advanced Encryption Standard (AES), i.e. Rijndael algorithm (FIPS, 2009), was chosen as the encryption standard by NIST for its properties of strong security and high performance. Naturally, it is being used by many companies and organizations. Based on the bit-size of its keys, AES implementations can be classed as three variants, i.e., AES-128, AES-192, and AES-256. A longer key means more computation and stronger security in encrypting and decrypting.

AES is a symmetric and block cipher. In fact, the plaintext is encrypted and decrypted in the same work process as groups of 16 bytes. More specifically, each AES block is repeatedly encrypted or decrypted in several rounds using the same key, as shown in Figure 15. Because of the similarity of encrypting and decrypting, only encrypting is described here.

Figure 15. Advanced encryption standard process

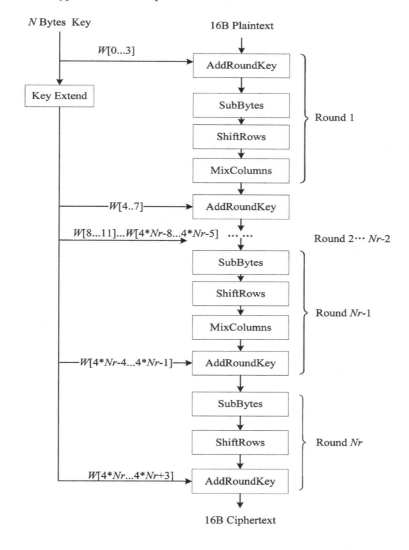

The number of rounds (*Nr*) is decided by the size of key (*N* bytes). AES-128 needs a key as long as 16 bytes and involves 10 rounds of encrypting. AES-192 needs a key as long as 24 bytes and involves 12 rounds encrypting. AES-256 needs a key as long as 32 bytes and involves 14 rounds of encrypting. For a certain AES, there are *Nr* rounds and every round needs a different key. This means the key should be extended to *Nr+1* words, because the initial round also needs a key of 4 words. For instance, encrypting with AES-128, the number of rounds is 10, so the key should be extended to $4 \times 11 = 44$ words. The first 4 words are used by the initial round, and then the successive words are used by Rounds 1 to 10 as groups of 4 words as shown in Figure 15.

Each round is divided into several smaller steps, some of which often implement with the aid of tables as described in the referenced implementation (FIPS, 2009). These steps are *SubBytes*, *ShiftRows*, *MixColumns*, and *AddRoundKey* and are executed in order. As shown in Figure 15, there are two special rounds. One is the initial round, which has only one *AddRoundKey* step. The other is the last round, which omits a *MixColumns* step.

Each of these steps has a special purpose and its details can be found in FIPS (2009). *SubBytes* are performed through substituting bytes in a block with other bytes that can be pre-computed in a table of multiplication coefficients. *ShiftRows* can be achieved by byte rotations along the lines of the logical AES state block. *MixColumns* are operated by columns in a block with the sum of a constant polynomial. *AddRoundKey* adds the extended key of the round to the state.

Parallel AES

AES encrypts plaintext as groups, which are independent. If adopting Electronic Code Book (ECB) or CTR (Counter) Mode as described in Lipmaa et al. (2000), AES can be fully parallelized.

The first paper that adopts CUDA to parallelize AES on a GPU and reported about 20 times speedup for OpenSSL (Open Secure Socket Layer) data is Manavski (2007). Li et al. (2012) parallelized AES by CUDA on NVIDIA Tesla C2050 and obtained the maximum throughput of around 60 Gbps. Maistri et al. (2011) also obtained good performance with an excellent price/performance ratio. Also, some further analysis and optimization for parallel AES on a GPU can be found in Bos et al. (2009), Shao et al. (2010), Liu et al. (2009), and Nhat-Phuong et al. (2013).

Parallelizing AES on a CPU has been thoroughly researched in recent years. This is because there are still some computers not equipped GPUs or equipped with old GPUs yet do not support general computing. For instance, Navalgund et al. (2013) used OpenMP to implement a parallel AES and achieved attractive performance improvement. Duta et al. (2013) parallelized AES by making use of CUDA, OpenMP, and OpenCL respectively, and found that their performances are ranked as CUDA, OpenCL, and OpenMP. Additionally, POUSA et al. (2012) implemented three parallel AES algorithms by OpenMP, MPI, and CUDA respectively and CUDA also shows the best performance. Ortega et al. (2011) parallelized AES on a multicore CPU using OpenMP and on GPUs using CUDA respectively, and observed that the latter is superior to the former.

Based on the research, parallelizing AES by CUDA or OpenMP has made much progress and continues with the development of new technologies.

Hybrid Parallel AES and Optimization

Hybrid parallel AES splits the plaintext to be encrypted into two parts corresponding to the computing power of the GPU and the CPU. To improve the performance of a GPU parallel part, some optimization methods are recommended, as listed here:

- **Storing Extended Key in Shared Memory:** The key extending needs to be executed only once and has data dependency, so it will be executed serially in the CPU. The extended keys will be used in encryption for every group. For all threads in a block, they use the same extended key to encrypt different plaintext groups. For AES-128, all the extended keys are as long as 4 x (10 + 1) = 176 bytes. For current general GPUs, the shared memory that can be allocated to a block is as large as 48 KB. Therefore, the shared memory is large enough to store the extended keys. Because shared memory has less access latency, for the threads in a block, they can read the extended keys from global memory once and then use them multiple times in the encryption. This will reduce the access time and improve performance.

- **Adopting Lookup Tables and Storing Them in Shared Memory:** The process of MixColumns involves the finite field multiplications. This is an intensive computing process in encrypting with AES. Fortunately, this process can be accelerated by using four fixed tables, each of which has a length of 1 KB. Thus, the shared memory has enough space to store them. When executing MixColumns, looking up the data stored in tables instead of multiplication will significantly reduce the amount of computing, to improve the performance of AES.

- **Employing Suitable Block Size:** Block size is decided by the resources of the GPU, such as registers and shared memory, and some limitations of hardware. A block size that is too large means that fewer blocks can be placed on the GPU and will result in performance degradation. However, too small a block size means that each block does not have enough threads. Moreover, the number of blocks will easily reach the permitted maximum number of blocks. For example, on GPUs with computing capacity of 3.0, the maximum blocks per multiprocessor are 16. If the block size is 32, the number of blocks placed on one multiprocessor of a GPU at a time is 16. This means that 32 x 16 = 512 threads will reside on one multiprocessor. If the block size is 64, the number of blocks placed on one multiprocessor of the GPU at a time is 16. This means that 64 x 16 = 1024 threads will reside on one multiprocessor. But too large a block size probably results in a smaller number of blocks. For example, if registers per thread are 40 and the total available registers on an SM are 65535, for block size 576, there are 2 blocks at most, i.e., 2 x 576 = 1152 threads, residing on one multiprocessor, whereas for block size 512, there are 3 blocks at most, i.e., 3 x 512 = 1536 threads, residing on one multiprocessor.

CONCLUSION

This chapter describes the cooperative use of CPU and GPU resources on heterogeneous systems to improve the performance of applications as much as possible. CPUs and GPUs can work in a master-slave manner. The CPUs derive multiple threads using OpenMP, one of which is used to trigger the invocation of kernels and the others of which are used to perform some parts of a task. The GPUs organize many threads under the support of CUDA to perform the other parts of the task.

The applications must be adapted for parallel processing to maximize use of available resources. This can be achieved by four main optimizing strategies. The first one is keep workload balancing and distribution between the CPUs and the GPUs. The second one is efficient use of hierarchical memories, such as hiding data access latency, coalescing data access, efficient shared memory, virtual addressing between GPU and CPU, etc. The third one is reduction of communication overhead, such as by zero copy or streaming data transmission. The fourth one is asynchronization such as concurrent copying and execution, sub-task pipeline, and so on. These strategies can be adopted in many applications, but need to be employed carefully and creatively for better performance. In order to evaluate the performance of a parallel application, the metrics of execution time, bandwidth, occupancy, and speedup are provided also.

Two synthesized examples – parallel Sparse Matrix-Vector multiplication (SpMV) and Advanced Encryption Standard (AES) – are provided to demonstrate the use of some of these techniques on heterogeneous computers and to provide some inspiration for development of hybrid parallel applications. High-performance applications for heterogeneous computing environments can be achieved with a thorough understanding of the essential properties of the hardware and the application and the use of specific optimization techniques.

REFERENCES

Bos, J. W., Osvik, D. A., & Stefan, D. (2009). *Fast Implementations of AES on Various Platforms.* IACR Cryptology ePrint ArchiveR.

Cederman, D., & Tsigas, P. (2008, June). On dynamic load balancing on graphics processors. *Proceedings of the 23rd ACM SIGGRAPH/EUROGRAPHICS symposium on Graphics hardware* (pp. 57-64). Aire-la-Ville, Switzerland: Eurographics Association.

Chandra, R., Dagum, L., Kohr, D., Maydan, D., McDonald, J., & Menon, R. (2001). *Parallel programming in OpenMP.* San Francisco, CA: Morgan Kaufmann.

Che, S., Sheaffer, J. W., & Skadron, K. (2011, November). Dymaxion: optimizing memory access patterns for heterogeneous systems. *Proceedings of the 2011 International Conference for High Performance Computing, Networking, Storage, and Analysis.* ACM. doi:10.1145/2063384.2063401

CompuGreen. (2015, June). *Green500 list.* Retrieved from http://green500.org/news/green500-list-june-2015

Daemen, J., & Rijmen, V. (1999). *AES proposal: Rijndael.* Retrieved from http://www.science.upm.ro/~apetrescu/OLD/public_html/Tehnologia%20Informatiei/Securitatea%20informatiei/Laborator/AES/rijndael%20doc%20V2.pdf

Duta, C. L., Michiu, G., Stoica, S., & Gheorghe, L. (2013, May). Accelerating encryption algorithms using parallelism. *Proceedings of the 2013 19th International Conference on Control Systems and Computer Science* (pp. 549-554). IEEE. doi:10.1109/CSCS.2013.92

Fatica, M. (2009, March). Accelerating Linpack with CUDA on heterogenous clusters. *Proceedings of the 2nd Workshop on General Purpose Processing on Graphics Processing Units* (pp. 46-51). ACM. doi:10.1145/1513895.1513901

FIPS. P. (2001, November). *Specification for the Advanced Encryption Standard.* Retrieved from http://csrc.nist.gov/publications/fips/fips197/fips-197.pdf

Gregg, C., Dorn, J., Hazelwood, K., & Skadron, K. (2012, June). Fine-grained resource sharing for concurrent GPGPU kernels. *Paper Presented at the 4th USENIX conference on Hot Topics in Parallelism*, Berkeley, CA, USA.

Guevara, M., Gregg, C., Hazelwood, K., & Skadron, K. (2009, September). Enabling task parallelism in the CUDA scheduler. *Proceedings of the First Workshop on Programming Models for Emerging Architectures* (pp. 69-76). IEEE.

Hennessy, J. L., & Patterson, D. A. (2011). *Computer architecture: a quantitative approach.* Waltham, MA: Elsevier.

Tran, N.-P., Lee, M., Hong, S., & Lee, S.-J. (2013). High throughput parallelization of AES-CTR algorithm. *IEICE Transactions on Information and Systems, 96*(8), 1685–1695.

Iwai, K., Kurokawa, T., & Nisikawa, N. (2010, November). AES encryption implementation on CUDA GPU and its analysis.*Proceedings of the 2010 First International Conference on Networking and Computing* (pp. 209-214). IEEE. doi:10.1109/IC-NC.2010.49

Jiménez, V. J., Vilanova, L., Gelado, I., Gil, M., Fursin, G., & Navarro, N. (2009). Predictive runtime code scheduling for heterogeneous architectures. In *High Performance Embedded Architectures and Compilers* (pp. 19–33). Springer Berlin Heidelberg. doi:10.1007/978-3-540-92990-1_4

Li, K., Yang, W., & Li, K. (2015). Performance analysis and optimization for SpMV on GPU using probabilistic modeling. *IEEE Transactions on Parallel and Distributed Systems, 26*(1), 196–205. doi:10.1109/TPDS.2014.2308221

Li, Q., Zhong, C., Zhao, K., Mei, X., & Chu, X. (2012, June). Implementation and analysis of AES encryption on GPU.*Proceedings of the 2012 IEEE 14th International Conference on High Performance Computing and Communication & the 2012 IEEE 9th International Conference on Embedded Software and Systems* (pp. 843-848). IEEE. doi:10.1109/HPCC.2012.119

Lipmaa, H., Wagner, D., & Rogaway, P. (2000). Comments to NIST concerning AES modes of operation: CTR-mode encryption. *Paper presented at the2000 Symmetric Key Block Cipher Modes of Operation Workshop*, Baltimore, MD.

Liu, G., An, H., Han, W., Xu, G., Yao, P., Xu, M., & Wang, Y. et al. (2009, December). A program behavior study of block cryptography algorithms on GPGPU.*Proceedings of the 2009 Fourth International Conference on Frontier of Computer Science and Technology* (pp. 33-39). IEEE. doi:10.1109/FCST.2009.13

Luk, C. K., Hong, S., & Kim, H. (2009, December). Qilin: exploiting parallelism on heterogeneous multiprocessors with adaptive mapping.*Proceedings of the 42nd Annual IEEE/ACM International Symposium on Microarchitecture* (pp. 45-55). IEEE. doi:10.1145/1669112.1669121

Maistri, P., Masson, F., & Leveugle, R. (2011, September). Implementation of the Advanced Encryption Standard on GPUs with the NVIDIA CUDA framework.*Proceedings of the 2011 IEEE Symposium on Industrial Electronics and Applications* (pp. 213-217). IEEE. doi:10.1109/ISIEA.2011.6108701

Manavski, S. (2007, November). CUDA compatible GPU as an efficient hardware accelerator for AES cryptography.*Proceedings of the 2007 IEEE International Conference on Signal Processing and Communications* (pp. 65-68). IEEE. doi:10.1109/ICSPC.2007.4728256

Nagendra, M., & Sekhar, M. C. (2014). Performance Improvement of Advanced Encryption Algorithm using Parallel Computation. *International Journal of Software Engineering and Its Applications, 8*(2), 287–296.

Navalgund, S. S., Desai, A., Ankalgi, K., & Yamanur, H. (2013). Parallelization of AES Algorithm Using OpenMP. *Lecture Notes on Information Theory, 1*(4), 144–147. doi:10.12720/lnit.1.4.144-147

NVIDIA. (2015a). *CUDA C best practices guide*. Retrieved from http://docs.nvidia.com/cuda/cuda-c-best-practices-guide/index.html

NVIDIA. (2015b). *CUDA C programming guide*. Retrieved from http://docs.nvidia.com/cuda/cuda-c-programming-guide/index.html

Ogata, Y., Endo, T., Maruyama, N., & Matsuoka, S. (2008, April). An efficient, model-based CPU-GPU heterogeneous FFT library.*Proceedings of the 22nd IEEE International Symposium on Parallel and Distributed Processing* (pp. 1-10). IEEE.

Ortega, J., Trefftz, H., & Trefftz, C. (2011, May). Parallelizing AES on multicores and GPUs.*Proceedings of the 2011 IEEE International Conference on Electro/Information Technology* (pp. 15-17). IEEE.

Pousa, A., Sanz, V., & De Giusti, A. (2012). Performance Analysis of a Symmetric Cryptographic Algorithm on Multicore Architectures.*Proceedings of the 2012 Computer Science & Technology Series-XVII Argentine Congress of Computer Science-Selected Papers* (pp. 57-66). La Plata, Argentina: Edulp.

Sanders, J., & Kandrot, E. (2010). *CUDA by example: an introduction to general-purpose GPU programming*. Addison-Wesley Professional.

Shao, F., Chang, Z., & Zhang, Y. (2010, February). AES encryption algorithm based on the high performance computing of GPU.*Proceedings of the 2010 Second International Conference on Communication Software and Networks* (pp. 588-590). IEEE. doi:10.1109/ICCSN.2010.124

Song, F., Tomov, S., & Dongarra, J. (2012, June). Enabling and scaling matrix computations on heterogeneous multi-core and multi-GPU systems.*Proceedings of the 26th ACM international conference on Supercomputing* (pp. 365-376). ACM. doi:10.1145/2304576.2304625

Tatourian, A. (2013). *NVIDIA GPU architecture & CUDA programming environment*. Retrieved from http://tatourian.com/2013/09/03/nvidia-gpu-architecture-cuda-programming-environment/

TOP500.org. (2015, June). *Top500 list*. Retrieved from http://www.top500.org/list/2015/06/

Valero, P., & Pelayo, F. L. (2011, June). Towards a more efficient use of GPUs.*Proceedings of the 2011 International Conference on Computational Science and Its Applications* (pp. 3-9). IEEE. doi:10.1109/ICCSA.2011.55

Valero-Lara, P., & Pelayo, F. L. (2013, July). Analysis in performance and new model for multiple kernels executions on many-core architectures.*Proceedings of the 12th IEEE International Conference on Cognitive Informatics & Cognitive Computing* (pp. 189-194). IEEE. doi:10.1109/ICCI-CC.2013.6622243

Valero-Lara, P., & Pelayo, F. L. (2015, March). Full-Overlapped Concurrent Kernels.*Proceedings of the 28th International Conference on Architecture of Computing Systems* (pp. 1-8). VDE.

Yang, C., Wang, F., Du, Y., Chen, J., Liu, J., Yi, H., & Lu, K. (2010, September). Adaptive optimization for petascale heterogeneous CPU/GPU computing.*Proceedings of the 2010 IEEE International Conference on Cluster Computing* (pp. 19-28). IEEE. doi:10.1109/CLUSTER.2010.12

Yang, W., Li, K., Liu, Y., Shi, L., & Wan, L. (2014). Optimization of quasi-diagonal matrix–vector multiplication on GPU. *International Journal of High Performance Computing Applications*, 28(2), 183–195. doi:10.1177/1094342013501126

Yang, W., Li, K., Mo, Z., & Li, K. (2015). Performance Optimization Using Partitioned SpMV on GPUs and Multicore CPUs. *IEEE Transactions on Computers, 64*(9), 2623–2636. doi:10.1109/TC.2014.2366731

Zhang, K., & Wu, B. (2013, May). Task Scheduling Greedy Heuristics for GPU Heterogeneous Cluster Involving the Weights of the Processor. *Proceedings of the 27th IEEE International Parallel and Distributed Processing Symposium Workshops & PhD Forum* (pp. 1817-1827). IEEE. doi:10.1109/IPDPSW.2013.38

Zhong, Z., Rychkov, V., & Lastovetsky, A. (2012, September). Data partitioning on heterogeneous multicore and multi-GPU systems using functional performance models of data-parallel applications. *proceedings of the 2012 IEEE International Conference on Cluster Computing* (pp. 191-199). IEEE. doi:10.1109/CLUSTER.2012.34

KEY TERMS AND DEFINITIONS

Barrier: A barrier is used to allow synchronization of threads. When threads encounter a barrier, they must wait until all the threads reach it, and then continue with the next operation.

Dynamic Random Access Memory (DRAM): A widely used memory type, which uses capacitors to store data, and must refresh data periodically. DRAM can write and read data to and from its story units randomly, respectively. Wherever elements are, DRAM can access them almost at the same speed.

Kernel: The same program which is executed by all threads on a Nvidia GPU in parallel.

Latency: The time elapsed to finish a task; i.e., from the task starts to the task ends.

Parallel Thread Execution (PTX): A pseudo-assembly language for supporting parallel deal on many cores of NVIDIA's GPUs. The *nvcc* compiler translates code written in CUDA into PTX first, and then the PTX is translated into a binary code by the graphics driver. The binary code can then run on the processing cores.

Peripheral Component Interface Express (PCIe): A high-speed serial computer expansion bus standard designed to replace the older PCI, PCI-X, and AGP bus standards.

Single Instruction Multiple Thread (SIMT): A parallel execution model in which multiple threads execute concurrently by the same instruction.

Single Instruction Multiple Data (SIMD): Refers to the ability of the same instruction to operate on multiple data elements. SIMD was defined in the Flynn's taxonomy in 1966.

Thread: An independent and single order control flow. A thread has its own call stack for methods being invoked, their arguments and local variables. Each application has at least one running thread when it is started.

Warp: A group of threads which is issued and scheduled as a basic unit on Nvidia GPUs. Currently, the size of a warp is 32, so 32 threads is issued and scheduled at the same time by an SM.

Chapter 8
Task–Based Crowd Simulation for Heterogeneous Architectures

Hugo Perez
Barcelona Supercomputing Center, Spain

Isaac Rudomin
Barcelona Supercomputing Center, Spain

Benjamin Hernandez
Oak Ridge National Laboratory, USA

Eduard Ayguade
Barcelona Supercomputing Center, Spain

ABSTRACT

Industry trends in the coming years imply the availability of cluster computing with hundreds to thousands of cores per chip, as well as the use of accelerators. Programming presents a challenge due to this heterogeneous architecture; thus, using novel programming models that facilitate this process is necessary. In this chapter, the case of simulation and visualization of crowds is presented. The authors analyze and compare the use of two programming models: OmpSs and CUDA. OmpSs allows to take advantage of all the resources available per node by combining the CPU and GPU while automatically taking care of memory management, scheduling, communications and synchronization. Experimental results obtained from Fermi, Kepler and Maxwell GPU architectures are presented, and the different modes used for visualizing the results are described, as well.

INTRODUCTION

Nowadays there are 502 cities with over one million inhabitants, 74 with more than 5 million and 29 megacities with populations above 10 million; in total, there are around 3.9 billion human beings living in urban areas. As a result, it is important to develop computer models that describe the behavior of populations. Crowd simulations allow safe application of the scientific method and may aid in the analysis of certain subsets of the crowd phenomena, such as disease propagation, building evacuation during emergencies, traffic modeling or social evolution. Prediction before, during and after daily crowd events may reduce risks and associated logistic costs. Crowd simulation is usually expressed at macroscopic and microscopic levels (Pelechano, 2008). Macroscopic modeling describes global interactions

DOI: 10.4018/978-1-5225-0287-6.ch008

with the environment and the crowd itself. On the other hand, microscopic level exposes the interactions between individuals within a group; each agent should be processed individually to simulate a crowd. We are interested in modeling crowds at the microscopic level using Agent-Based Models (ABM). An ABM simulates the actions and interactions of autonomous agents; it promotes the progressive assembly of agents into groups resulting in global-scale behaviors (Bonabeau, 2002). In particular, this research focuses on real-time large-scale crowd simulation and in-situ visualization for heterogeneous architectures, considering the requirements that exascale computing will demand.

Real-time performance is crucial for applications such as risk mitigation or disaster control and offers the next advantages:

- Results are available immediately, minimizing time-to-solution.
- Simulation can be restarted almost instantaneously when unexpected outcomes are obtained, saving time and resources.
- Enables simulation steering allowing users to interact with the simulation through parameters.

In-situ visualization consists of visualizing results on the same cluster where simulation is running (Ahrens, J, 2010). This conveys two advantages for this research: relevant results are stored before simulation finishes, and data movement from processors through different memory hierarchies and storage is reduced or avoided.

Crowd simulation and visualization at megacity scale requires significant computational power and memory resources commonly available on High-Performance Computing platforms (HPC). According to Top500[1] Supercomputer Sites list, the use of heterogeneous architectures combining multi-core processors and accelerators is becoming a common practice. Examples to accelerators include Intel Xeon Phi and the NVIDIA Tesla GPU. In our purposes, the GPU has two advantages: accelerates computation, and efficient rendering for in-situ visualization.

Current HPC clusters have hundreds of thousands and even millions of processors. The community is in a transitioning stage between the petascale and the exascale era. Industry trends indicate that exascale clusters will have thousands of millions of cores (Moreland, 2013). The technical challenges for crowd simulation and visualization are intertwined with challenges from other areas including communication, programming models, and hardware architecture.

The rest of the chapter is organized as follows. The following section introduces the programming models, behavior models and current platforms commonly used in crowd simulation. The algorithm, implementation and results obtained from our case study are discussed in the Crowd Simulation section. After that, different crowd visualizations are described in the Visualization section. Finally, the chapter concludes.

BACKGROUND

Programming Models

A long time ago (2005), while still in Mexico, Our group (led by Dr. Rudomin) started to explore moving our crowd simulation from the CPU to the GPU. This because even then, simulation performance was significantly increased in comparison with desktop CPUs, allowing for simulation of larger crowds with high performance at a fraction of the cost of grid or cluster based alternatives. Another advantage was that massive crowds could be visualized in real time as agent data is already located on the GPU hardware. We were the first to do this, but it started a trend that has become common (Richmond, 2009) (Lysenko, 2008). By 2012 we required even larger crowds. By now GPU computing was part of heterogeneous supercomputing clusters such as Minotauro, the cluster at Barcelona Supercomputing Center, and we started studying how to use this kind of hardware for our problem. This trend is even more evident today with Titan at Oakridge, as well as the plans for future hardware by Department of Energy (DOE) in USA.

We use ABM for crowd simulation handling each agent individually and applying general behavior rules in a single-rule-multiple-agents fashion, which suits the GPU's Single Instruction Multiple Data (SIMD) model. Before CUDA and OpenCL programming models, and while precursor GPGPU languages such as Brook and Sh were in active development, GPUs were already being used for general purpose computing (GPGPU). Pioneers in this regard are Rudomin, Millan and Hernandez (Rudomin, 2005) that through XML scripting defined Finite State Machines to determine the behavior of agents implemented in fragment shaders. This was possible even when neither the GPU hardware architecture nor the programming language was oriented to this type of tasks.

The emergence of CUDA in 2007, and OpenCL in 2008, and new GPU unified hardware architecture, has allowed developers to take advantage of the GPU resources using C-like language syntax. Today, there is a vast variety of projects that use the computing power of the GPU for the simulation and visualization of crowds (Rudomin, 2013). Despite the widespread use of CUDA and OpenCL, they have the following drawbacks: they require explicit device selection; data transfers between host and devices; and, flow control through queues and events. In addition, there is no implicit way to use the CPU and GPU resources concurrently and effectively; Therefore, programmers need to use OpenMP + CUDA/OpenCL to control each resource within a node or a cluster explicitly by using MPI.

The need for combining these programming models makes evident the programming complexity of heterogeneous HPC systems. In an effort to reduce such complexity, we use OpenMP Superscalar - OmpSs (Duran, 2011), a programming model developed by the Barcelona Supercomputing Center (BSC). It uses a set of directives and library routines that can be embedded in high-level programming language code to develop concurrent applications. OmpSs' main goal is to provide a productive environment for application development in modern HPC systems. OmpSs is built on top of the Mercurium (Balart, 2004) a source-to-source compiler, which emits calls to the Nanos++ (Nanos++, 2015) runtime system. Nanos++ uses the information provided by user annotations to build a task dependency graph dynamically at runtime, which is used to schedule tasks in a data-flow way.

An alternative programming model targeted to reduce the programming complexity of heterogeneous systems is OpenACC. Launched in 2010, OpenACC is a collection of compiler directives used to specify loops and regions of code whose execution is offloaded to an accelerator in standard C, C++ or FORTRAN. The advantage offered over OmpSs is the automatic generation of CUDA kernels; however, it still has limited functionality. There is work in progress to implement similar characteristics in OmpSs (Ozen, 2014). OmpSs and OpenACC developers are part of the OpenMP Standard Group; they influence the design of OpenMP. Therefore, it is possible in future, to integrate the best features of both technologies into OpenMP 4.x.

Behavior Models

There is a large body of work in the simulation of crowds, below we present a brief description of the main behaviors models.

- **Boids (Reynolds, 1987):** Reynolds proposed the first known solution for large groups of entities with emergent behavior being an extension of particle systems. It is based on three basic rules: separation, alignment, and cohesion. These rules maintain together, in a direction and free of collisions a group of boids or bird-like objects. .
- **Social Forces (Helbing, 1995):** These methods operate on crowds composed of basic pedestrians obeying physics-based laws. The agents' behavior is based on forces, called social forces. These forces, applied to a pedestrian, can be attractive acting as their destination, or repulsive such as obstacles or strangers. However, it is also possible to introduce other social interactions just as the presence of friends or storefronts, which are modeled through attractive forces that fade over time. It is then possible to give the pedestrians some more decision-making abilities.
- **Predictive/Velocity-Based Models (Paris, 2007):** In these methods, agents calculate the set of velocities that lead to a collision with an obstacle; to move on routes without collision, agents choose velocities outside this domain. This concept is expanded by Van den Berg (Van den Berg 2008), (Van den Berg, 2011), introducing the notions of Velocity Obstacles (VO) and Reciprocal Velocity Obstacles (RVO) and the notion of Optimal Reciprocal Collision Avoidance (ORCA).
- **Synthetic Vision (Ondřej, 2010; Moussaïd, 2011):** In the everyday exercise of controlling their locomotion, human beings rely on the visual information obtained from the perception of the environment to achieve collision-free navigation. Cognitive science allows extracting relatively succinct information from perception to reach a safe locomotion, e.g., using the distance of obstructions in candidate lines of sight, pedestrians apply simple heuristics to adapt their walking speeds and directions. These models predict individual trajectories and collective patterns of motion in good quantitative agreement with a large variety of empirical and experimental data.

A deep study of this topic is beyond the scope of this chapter, thus we recommend our previous work (Rudomin, 2013). This article describes advanced methods for simulating, generating, animating and rendering crowds such as encoding neighbor information on world maps, i.e., in the environment rather than the agents and thereby reduces the problem of determining neighbor contributions to O(n). They discuss local collision avoidance methods that use truncated Voronoi diagrams followed by a ray marching technique over a radius of vision to sense the viewing area in the direction of the agent.

In the same paper (Rudomin, 2013), we, based on scatter and gather operations, describe the development of two data-parallel techniques for proximity queries that are suitable for simulating thousands of agents in real time with accurate collision avoidance. They first perform proximity queries in the graphics hardware, followed by some method of collision avoidance (Reynolds, Helbing, RVO, Synthetic Vision or any other heuristics).

The scatter-based method follows the idea that an agent should be able to find its closest neighbors with only one texture fetch. To accomplish this, each agent paints in a world map an area where it is visible. Each pixel in the environment map holds a list with the IDs of neighbor agents. A Layered frame buffer (LFB) is used to generate the nearest neighbor lists and render the environment map for the scatter-based technique. Contrary to the scatter-based technique, in the gather-based technique each agent only writes its ID in the corresponding cell in the world map. To find their neighbors, every agent scans over an area within the world map. In this way, each agent generates its neighbor list. This eliminates the need to create an LFB.

We have noted that scatter-based techniques sometimes have race conditions when two neighboring queries must write to the same memory location. This is solved by using atomic operations, but it also serializes the execution. Gather-based techniques do not have this issue making them faster; as a consequence, a simplified gather-based method is chosen in this research.

Current Platforms

Simulations of hundreds or thousands of agents are currently standard, but simulations with hundreds of thousands or millions of agents are still an issue to be solved. The complexity, fidelity and size of simulation and visualization systems are proportional to the processing capacity. Therefore, the manufacture of increasingly powerful computers raises the requirements and characteristics of these systems, and that is why they are in constant evolution.

In addition, crowd simulation and visualization is a very active research field which has led to the development of commercial platforms used mostly for the simulation of massive events, film scenes, video games, among other purposes. They are designed to run on a single workstation, so the size of the simulation (the number of agents) and its complexity is limited by the memory and processing capacity. Some examples of such systems are:

- **Legion (Still, 2000):** Uses speed, density and space utilization maps to qualitatively and quantitatively analyze the use of space over time. Legion oversimplifies the behavioral representation of individuals by using four parameters and one decision rule based on least effort to simulate individual behaviors.
- **Massive (Thompson, 2006):** Originally developed for its use in The Lord Of The Rings film trilogy. Subsequently it was adopted as a standard tool for film and TV productions around the world. It provides crowd-related visual effects and autonomous character animation.
- **Golaem Studios (Golaem, 2015):** Develops character animation software for VFX artists, animation and game studios that need to populate backgrounds and mid-grounds for films, TV series, commercials and games.

The development of a scalable system is necessary to overcome memory and processing limitations. Below there is a description of projects, some designed to run on clusters, others are research oriented or provide open source modules and libraries.

- **TRANSIMS (Transportation Analysis SIMulation System) (Nagel, 2001):** An activity and agent-based model that virtually creates an entire region and simulates the second-by-second movement of all travelers and vehicles. It has a visualization module called TransimsVIS and a GUI TRANSIMS RTE, it is developed by the Transportation Research and Analysis Computer Center (TRACC) in USA.

- **FLAME (Flexible Large-Scale Agent Modelling Environment) (Kiran, 2010):** A framework to develop agent-based simulations which automatically produces parallelizable code to execute on different parallel hardware architectures. FLAME-GPU was developed as extension of FLAME. FLAME-GPU is designed to be executed in a workstation and is used to accelerate the simulation using the Graphic Processing Unit. Both are developed by the Sheffield University.
- **Pandora (Rubio-Campillo, 2014):** An open-source framework designed to provide a simulation environment for social scientists. It includes a C++ and Python environment that splits the workload of a simulation across computer nodes using MPI, and also uses multiple cores relying on OpenMP. It is developed by the Barcelona Supercomputing Center.

These projects are designed to run on CPU clusters and do not take advantage of accelerators. Current research on crowd simulation has shown excellent results can be obtained on a single workstation with GPUs. For this reason, FLAME and Pandora frameworks are starting to take advantage of them. However, the use of accelerators in HPC is relatively new (Hernandez, 2014) and the simulation and visualization of crowds on GPU clusters need to be explored further.

Crowd simulation and visualization have also been implemented on cloud computing facilities using techniques such as MapReduce and tools like Hadoop (Yu, 2015). The number of simulated agents is lower than HPC based crowd simulations due to restrictions on computing power and communication latency. Nevertheless, it offers advantages such as resource elasticity and decentralized computation. In the future, mixed implementations combining HPC and cloud computing facilities should be considered to ensure system availability.

CROWD SIMULATION

In this section, we describe the implementation of a crowd simulation using two programming models CUDA and OmpSs and present a preliminary comparison between them.

Algorithm Overview

Several behaviors can be observed within a crowd, one of them is wandering behavior where agents move randomly in a space avoiding collisions against obstacles or other agents. We have chosen this behavior for its simplicity as it allows them to introduce with ease the reader to crowd simulation using task-based parallelism in OmpSs.

A naïve implementation of wandering behavior has O (N2) complexity, i.e., each agent position must be compared with all the remaining positions to detect collisions. Current techniques reduce the complexity of the algorithm using geometrical or hierarchical approaches (Rudomin, 2013; Kappadia, 2014). In this case, the complexity of the algorithm is reduced by partitioning the navigable space into a grid that cut down the search space. Additional reduction of the search space is done by defining a search radius for each agent, thus complexity decreases to:

O (N/t * r)

where N is the number of agents, t is the number of tiles in the grid, and r is the search radius.

The algorithm uses three vectors:

1.   The Agents vector stores position in the x-y axis, speed and direction.
2.   The Ids vector contains a unique agent identifier and the tile to which the agent belongs.
3.   The vector World stores the navigation space grid, where zero value is used for free cells, and a cell with the value of an agent id means it is occupied.

It is important to emphasize that crowd simulations at microscopic level, interactions between the agents are local, i.e., an agent just perceives and avoids nearby obstacles, in contrast to n-body gravitational problems, where all interactions between all entities need to be considered.

The basic sequential algorithm is decomposed into three primary tasks as shown in the next steps:

Step 1: Navigation space is discretized using a grid (Figure 1).
Step 2: Initialize the agents' information (position, direction, and speed) randomly according to the navigation space size.
Step 3: Update position for each agent:
-   Calculate collision avoidance within a given radius. Evaluation starts in the agent's motion direction and switches every 45 degrees covering a total of eight directions counterclockwise (Figure 2).
-   The agent is moved in the direction in which there are unoccupied cells or fewer agents within this radius.

Figure 1. Navigation space discretization

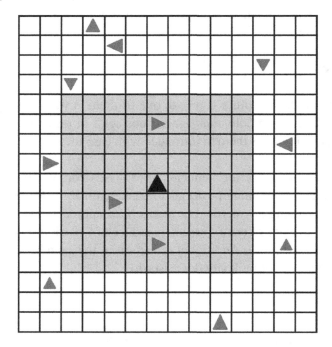

Figure 2. Search radius

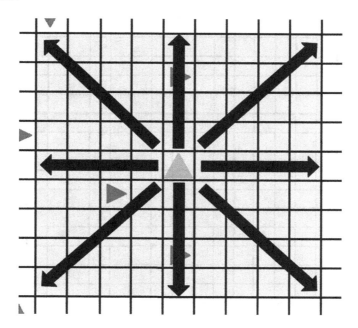

Processing these tasks in parallel requires tiling and stencil computations. First, the navigation space (from now it will be called the World) and agents information is divided into tiles. Then, the tasks performed in each tile can be executed in parallel by either a CPU or GPU (Figure 3). Once the world is divided into tiles, stencil computations are performed. In this case, calculation of the agent's new position requires the information of its surrounding cells. While agents inside each zone have all the necessary information, agents that are on the borders do not have such information. Therefore is necessary to exchange it with neighboring tiles. To keep to a minimum, the exchange of data between tiles, only the information of occupied cells is transferred. When an agent crosses a border and moves from one tile to another, the agent's information is sent to the new tile.

The following steps show the new tasks taking into account these observations:

Step 1: Divide the navigation space into tiles.
  ◦ Each tile will be computed by a CPU or GPU.
  ◦ Each CPU or GPU store their corresponding tile of the world.
Step 2: Set-up the communication topology between tiles.
Step 3: Exchange the occupied cells in the borders (stencils) data between tiles.
Step 4: Update position for each agent in parallel:
  ◦ Calculate collision avoidance within a given radius. Evaluation starts in the agent's motion direction and switches every 45 degrees covering a total of eight directions counterclockwise.
  ◦ The agent is moved in the direction in which there are unoccupied cells or fewer agents within this radius.
Step 5: Exchange agents' information that crossed a border and moved to another tile

Figure 3. Dividing the domain in tiles

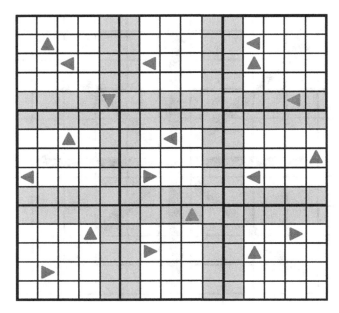

Implementation

CPU Version

We present the CPU version of the parallel algorithm shown earlier. As a starting point, the CPU sequential version of the algorithm was used. Translating the sequential algorithm into one based on tasks consisted in encapsulating the main steps into functions, turn these functions to tasks and define data dependencies between tasks (Listing 1). Data dependencies definition is important so the Nanos runtime system can use data locality for automatic scheduling. Also, OmpSs allows us to parallelize a sequential code incrementally and preliminary test it on each new task.

Notice OmpSs annotations are similar to those in OpenMP. The directive *in* is used to specify read-only input data for a task. *Out* directive indicates write-only output data. *Inout* directive apply for read and write data access. Synchronization points are defined by *taskwait* for all threads or by *taskwait on* for a given set of threads when computing specific variables. The runtime system uses these directives to generate a task dependency graph.

Listing 1. OmpSs syntax to define a task

```
#pragma omp task [ in(...)] [ out(...)] [ inout (...)]
{ function or code block }
#pragma omp taskwait [on (...)]
```

Listing 2. Conversion to a task of updatePosition function

```
//Task definition
#pragma omp task inout(
([agents_total_buffer]agents)[0;count_agents_total],
([agents_total_buffer]ids)[0;count_agents_total],
[world_cells_block]world)
void updatePosition(
 float4 *agents,
 float4 *ids,
 int *world,
 ...) { ... }
//Task execution
bool runSimulation()
{ ...
 for (int i = 0 ; i < num_tiles ; i ++)
    updatePosition(agents[i], ids[i], world[i], ...);
 ...
#pragma omp taskwait
 ...
}
```

Listing 2 illustrates the OmpSs-CPU code where a task updates the position of the agents. This task will read and update some variables; thus, *inout* directive is used. From Listing 2, the agent's vector is read and updated with the new agent position; the ids vector is read to query the agent id and the current tile it belongs to. Then, the ids vector is updated with the new tile according to the new agent position. Finally, the world vector is updated to mark the grid cells as free or busy according to the agents' movement. All the tiles are executed in parallel inside the *for loop*.

Another OmpSs feature is its ability to maintain memory consistency only for a particular region of data, e.g., the agents' vector can have 100 elements (agents_total_buffer = 100), but may operate just on the first 10 (count_agents_total = 10), then OmpSs guarantees memory consistency over these 10 elements. This makes memory management more efficient.

Profiling and analysis of the previous code were done using Extrae (Extrae, 2015) and Paraver (Paraver, 2015), respectively; the next traces were generated using these tools. OmpSs allows us to do a flexible use of resources; we can define the number of CPUs to use in each execution, through a runtime variable. Figure 4 shows an example trace of the simulation using eight threads. Notice from Listing 2 only the updatePosition function was converted into a task. With only one task, it is easier to understand this trace. On the other hand, Figure 5 shows the execution of the simulation using twelve threads; in this case, all the functions were already converted into tasks and were scheduled automatically by the runtime system.

Figure 4. Simulation executed with eight threads and only one task

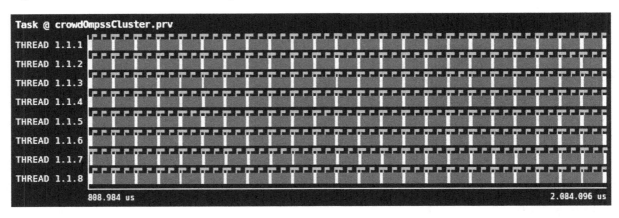

Figure 5. Simulation executed with twelve threads and all functions converted into tasks

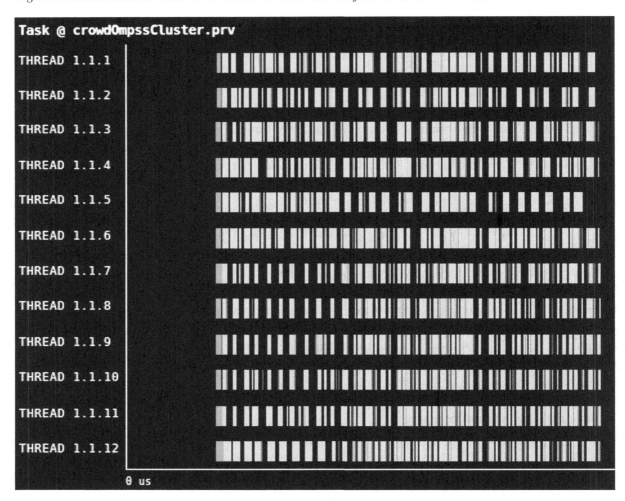

CUDA First Version

The first version of the simulation using CUDA (CUDA1GPU-V1) implements the basic wandering algorithm described earlier with no domain decomposition and only uses one GPU. All data is transferred from main memory to the GPU memory at the beginning and at the end of the execution. This version is used as a reference to analyze whether additional steps that involve dividing the domain can reduce the simulation performance. Preliminary results showed a speedup of 83x when compared to the sequential version of the algorithm.

CUDA Second Version

The CUDA1GPU-V1 code was updated, so domain decomposition of the simulation was possible. This new code (CUDA1GPU-V2) supports larger problems even if data does not fit in GPU memory. In this case, a simulation step consists in transferring a subset of the data from CPU to GPU, and then the GPU computes new positions and transfers the results back to CPU which sends a new data subset to the GPU to be computed. These steps are repeated until all the data is processed. A speedup similar to the CUDA1GPU-V1 code is achieved by using CUDA streams to process kernels in parallel and overlap communication with computation.

The additional steps performed by CUDA 1GPU-V2 code when compared to the CUDA 1GPU-V1 code are:

- Create a data structure to manage the data in the GPU.
- Allocate special host memory (pinned memory) to handle more than one CUDA stream.
- Split the data between the GPUs.
- Create streams to control the flow of operations.
- Select the GPU in each operation.
- Synchronize operations.

OmpSs GPU Version

CUDA 1GPU-V2 code is taken as a basis for the development of the OmpSs-GPU code. Listing 3 shows the OmpSs syntax that translates a function to a task, which in turn will be executed by an accelerator.

In particular, the *target* directive indicates the device and programming model used to execute such task; the *ndrange* directive is used to configure the number of dimensions (work_dim), the global size of each dimension (gwork_size) and the number of work-items for each workgroup (lwork_size).

Listing 3. OmpSs syntax to execute tasks on a heterogeneous computer

```
#pragma omp target device ({ smp | cuda | opencl })      \
          [ndrange(work_dim, gwork_size, lworksize)]\
            [ implements (function_name)]\
            { copy_deps | [ copy_in (array_spec, ...)] [ copy_out (...)] [
copy_inout (...)] }
#pragma omp taskwait [on (...)] [noflush]
```

Directive *implements* allows to define multiple task implementations of the same function, for example, one in the CPU and one in the GPU, the runtime decides which is better during execution and can even execute both in parallel.

Directive *copy_deps* ensures there is a valid and consistent copy of the data in the device. Therefore, the programmer does not need to do explicit memory allocations for the device or data transfers between the host and devices.

A synchronization point is defined by using *taskwait*, and all data is copied from the device to the CPU memory. Similarly, *taskwait on*, synchronize the execution and transfers specific variables. With *no flush* directive synchronization occurs but data is not transferred to CPU memory.

An overall view of the OmpSs-GPU code is illustrated in Listing 4. In this case *target* directive indicates the *updatePosition* task will be executed by the GPU using the CUDA 1GPU-V2 kernel. OmpSs will take care of the memory management according to directive *copy_deps*. There is an explicit definition of data dependency for variables agents, ids and world, which are the input and output variables of the task. Task execution is done just by calling *updatePosition* as it was done for the OmpSs-CPU code.

Listing 4. Converting updatePosition function into a task to be executed as a CUDA kernel

```
// Kernel definition as a task
#pragma omp target device (cuda)
ndrange(2, (int) sqrt(count_agents_total), (int)sqrt(count_agents_total), 8,
8) copy_deps
#pragma omp task inout(
([agents_total_buffer] agents) [0; count_agents_total],
([agents_total_buffer] ids) [0: count_agents_total],
[world_cells_block] world)
extern "C" global void updatePosition(
 float4 *agents,
 float4 *ids,
 int *world,
...);
// Kernel execution
bool runSimulation ()
{
 ...
 for (int i = 0 ; i < num_tiles; i ++)
 { ...
     updatePosition(agents[i], ids[i], world[i], ...);
  ...
 }
#pragma omp taskwait
 ...
}
```

Figure 6. Thread 1.1.2 and 1.1.3 are CPU threads in charge of one GPU each one. Thread 1.1.13 and 1.1.14 are GPU threads. CPU Threads and GPU threads are executing tasks in parallel.

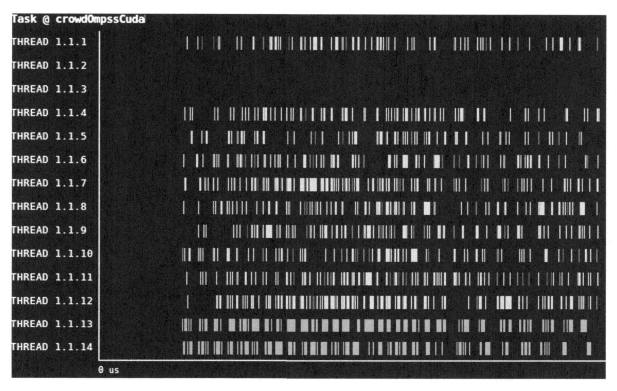

Using OmpSs with multiple GPU offers the next advantages:

- It is not necessary to select the device for each operation.
- There is no need to allocate special memory in the host (pinned memory) or the device.
- It is not necessary to transfer data between host and devices as OmpSs maintains memory coherence efficiently and reduces transfers using data regions.
- Programmers do not need to declare streams as OmpSs implements them by default.
- All available devices are used by default, therefore, the application scale through all the devices.
- OmpSs does all these operations automatically.

Figure 6 shows a trace illustrating how OmpSs manage the hardware resources. In this case, full node allocation is done using twelve CPU threads where Thread 1.1.2 and 1.1.3 are used to control the GPUs. As mentioned earlier, memory management, scheduling, communications and synchronization are done automatically.

On the other hand, CUDA profiling was done using Nvidia nvvp tool. Figure 7 shows communication and computation overlapping. Ten CUDA streams were created by OmpSs, two for communications and eight for kernel execution. However, it is possible to define the number of streams to use with a runtime variable. In particular, "Stream seven" manages communication Host to Device, "stream nine" manages communication Device to Host, and streams from 12 to 19 do the computation. We decided to use eight streams in each GPU for computation to match with the number of tiles.

207

Figure 7. Communication and computation overlapping

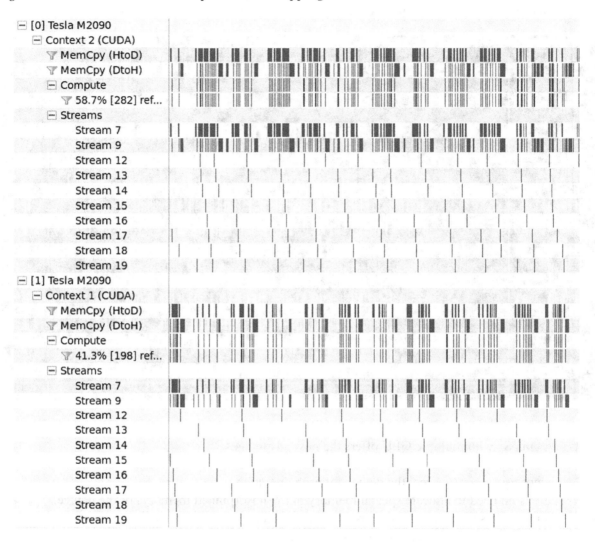

We mentioned earlier there are different runtime variables to control how OmpSs allocates resources, these variables are:

- NX_SMP_WORKERS sets the number of CPU cores used for computation. All available CPU cores are used by default.
- NX_GPUS sets the number of GPUs used for computation. All available GPUs are used by default.
- NX_GPUPREFETCH sets the number of CUDA streams used for computation. One CUDA stream is used by default.
- NX_GPUOVERLAP overlaps communication with computation when active. Active by default.
- NX_GPU_CONCURRENT_EXEC executes kernels concurrently when active. Active by default.

Results

We performed a test that consisted of simulating 67 millions of agents, which is the maximum number of agents that can be processed by CUDA1GPU-V1 code, in a world discretized in 27852x27852 cells and decomposed in 16 tiles.

The test was performed on two different platforms. The first platform was a node from the BSC's Minotauro Cluster. Each node has two processors Intel Xeon E5649 6-Core at 2.53 GHz running Linux operating system with 24 GB of RAM memory and 12MB of cache memory. They also have 2 NVIDIA Fermi M2090 cards with 512 CUDA Cores and 6GB of GDDR5 Memory. We use CUDA 5.0, Mercurium compiler version 1.99.9 and Nanos runtime system version 0.9a. The speedup is calculated with respect to the sequential version performance.

Table 1 shows the speedup and characteristics of each version and Figure 8 shows speedup for all versions in a graph.

The second platform was a workstation with an Intel Core i7-4820K CPU 4-cores at 3.70 GHz (hyper threading is disabled), running Linux operating system with 16 GB of RAM memory and 10MB of cache memory. It includes a GeForce Kepler GTX TITAN Black with 2880 CUDA cores and 6 GB of GDDR5 memory, and a GeForce Maxwell GTX 980 with 2048 CUDA cores, and 4 GB of GDDR5 memory. We use CUDA version 6.5, Mercurium 1.99.9, Nanos runtime system version 0.9a. The speedup is calculated with respect to the sequential version performance.

Table 2 shows the speedup and characteristics of each version, and Figure 9 shows speedup for all versions in a graph.

The workstation has a PCI Express 3.0 (16 GB/s) interface, and each node of Minotauro Cluster has a PCI Express 2.0 (8GB/s) interface.

Figure 8. This graph shows the speedup for Platform 1

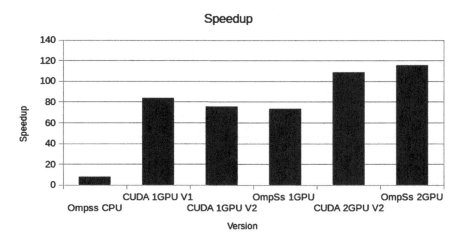

Table 1. Shows speedup values for Platform 1

Code	Speedup	Domain Divided	Comments
OmpSs-CPU	7.67	Yes	Using 12 CPU threads.
CUDA1GPU -V1	83.57	No	Using one GPU. This version transfers all the data just once and all iterations are done in the GPU. Domain decomposition is not performed.
CUDA1GPU- V2	75.57	Yes	Using one GPU. Domain decomposition is done. Thus, it shows additional tasks affecting the speedup. However, this version can use more than one GPU.
OmpSs-1GPU	73.31	Yes	Using one GPU. Speedup difference between this version and CUDA1GPU-V2 suggests there's some overhead involved in creating OmpSs' tasks, although this is negligible considering the benefits of using OmpSs.
CUDA2GPU-V2	108.62	Yes	Using two GPUs. Performance is better than the performance of the same version using one GPU, as expected.
OmpSs-2GPU	115.5	Yes	Using two GPUs. Due to advanced scheduling and memory management, OmpSs can deliver better performance than the CUDA2GPU-V2 code.

Table 2. Shows speedup values for Platform 2

Code	Speedup	Domain Divided	Comments
OmpSs-CPU	3.41	Yes	Using four CPU Threads.
CUDA1GPU-V1 - TB	103.19	No	Using GPU Titan Black. This version transfers all the data just once and all iterations are done in the GPU. Domain decomposition is not performed.
CUDA1GPU-V1 - 980	102.46	No	Using GPU GTX 980. This version gets similar results such as version CUDA1GPU-V1 – TB.
CUDA1GPU-V2 - TB	142.64	Yes	Using GPU Titan Black. Faster bandwidth and overlapping communications with computation allowed the fastest performance.
CUDA1GPU-V2 - 980	135.34	Yes	Using GPU GTX 980. Since GTX 980 has less computer power than GTX Titan Black is comprehensible that get slightly less speedup.
OmpSs-1GPU - TB	131.67	Yes	Using GPU Titan Black. The difference in speedup compared to CUDA1GPU-V2 - TB code suggest there is some overhead involved in creating OmpSs tasks. However, it may be negligible considering the benefits of using OmpSs.
OmpSs-1GPU - 980	118.77	Yes	Using GPU GTX 980. This version gets similar results such as version OmpSs-1GPU – TB.
CUDA2GPU-V2	96.67	Yes	Using two GPUs. Depending on the size of the problem, a better speedup can be achieved with one or both GPUs.
OmpSs-2GPU	122.78	Yes	Using two GPUs. Due to advanced techniques of scheduling and memory management, OmpSs can even get better performance than the CUDA 2GPU-V2 code.

VISUALIZATION

Computational solutions produce a vast amount of data that require further processing to offer insights about the results. Such information usually is simplified before analysis; however, simplifications may hide relevant details. On the other hand, visualization, which transforms these findings into graphical and color representations, can enhance human cognition improving analysis. In addition, in-situ

Figure 9. This graph shows the speedup for Platform 2

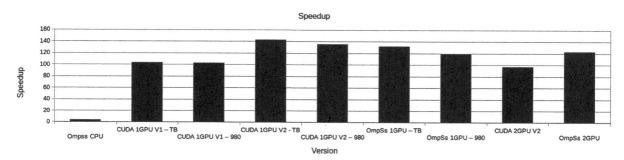

Figure 10. Crowd engine modules

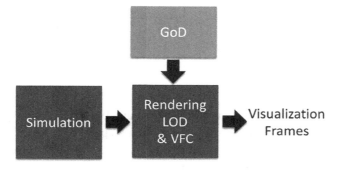

visualization reduces I/O operations (Ma, 2009), (Yu, 2010) by avoiding full data transfer of results. It also reduces time, allowing the researcher to inspect partial simulation results and perform simulation adaptations as required.

Before adopting OmpSs, we developed a configurable crowd engine (Figure 10) composed of two main modules: generation of diversity (GoD) and rendering. Details on GoD module can be found in (Ruiz, 2013) and details of optimizations and rendering of crowds can be found in (Hernández, 2011). The different engine configurations are described next.

Streaming

Accessing simulation results for visualization in any computer is one of the system's goals. It is desirable to enable researchers to access their results for visualization and analysis remotely, and such access may occur during or after simulation. A second goal is to couple the crowd engine to existing Pandora framework without significant modifications in any of the platforms. However, interactive crowd visualization can be affected by bandwidth, latency and image transport technology. BSC's Minotauro cluster has a fast network connection to BSC's LAN and default visualization delivery system uses VirtualGL. This allows rendering crowds at interactive rates. Nevertheless, external connections to Minotauro are restricted resulting in a visualization frame rate drop to 1-2 fps (frames per second).

To achieve these goals, *streaming configuration* transmits simulation data (agents' positions) instead of rendered frames from a remote resource to the end user's workstation or visualization server (Figure

Figure 11. Streaming mode allows to visualize simulations or results being calculated or stored in remote resources

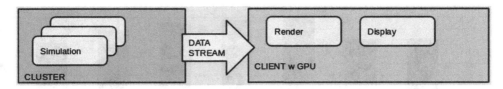

Figure 12. In-Situ, simulation and visualization occur in the cluster

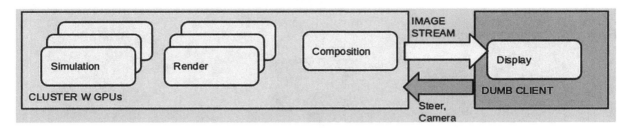

11). The current streaming algorithm does not implement any buffering technique. However, the crowd engine interpolates the received agents' positions between steps to avoid artifacts due to possible data loss. This configuration is suitable when the bandwidth is lower than the required one for transferring images. However, the size of the simulation is limited by the number of agents the workstation can render.

In-Situ

The crowd engine was modified to support MPI communications and off-screen rendering (Figure 12). MPI communications enable the engine to assign simulation/rendering work to each participating node, share simulation results between nodes, and transmit partial renderings for the final composition. Off-screen rendering enables each node to capture a visualization frame with color and depth information encoded in an RGBA array where the depth component is stored in the alpha channel. Then this information is downloaded to RAM and transferred to the master node.

Once the master node receives the color plus depth images from each node, it generates the final composite. This image is generated based on sort last depth compositing algorithm (Molnar, 1994) implemented in OpenGL Shading Language GLSL. Finally, the composite image can be sent to the client through VirtualGL.

The *In-Situ configuration* is suitable for larger problems and does not require additional rendering resources; however, the end user needs to be connected internally to Minotauro cluster.

Web

A particular requirement of the *Streaming configuration* is the use of a high-end system for visualization. On the other hand, *In-situ configuration* requires an internal connection between the user and Minotauro cluster. We have designed the *Web configuration* to fill the gap between streaming and in-situ. This option allows researchers to access visualization results on any device and away from the desktop.

Figure 13. The Web system architecture allows to display visualization results in web browsers

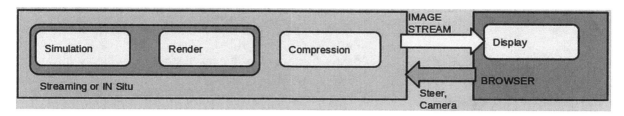

Inspired by cloud gaming technology, this configuration captures the results from visualization and streams them out to a web browser (Figure 13). It follows the client/server architecture: the server executes the simulation, visualization and streaming, and the client displays the visualization frames and captures user interaction events that are sent back to the server.

RESULTS

We have designed two experiments to test the *Streaming configuration* performance. The first test consisted in streaming data of a wandering behavior previously simulated in Pandora Framework from a remote resource to a test system. The simulation size was 4096 agents and the test system contains a Nvidia TITAN GPU. For this case, a consistent frame rate of 60 fps was achieved.

The second test consisted of running a simulation of wandering behavior in Minotauro cluster and streamed out results every step to the test system. The simulation size was 4096 agents as in the first case. The system was also able to render 4096 characters at 60 fps.

In-situ configuration was tested in the Minotauro cluster using five nodes, the simulation was decomposed into four tiles, then four nodes simulated and rendered 4096 characters and the remainder performed image composition (Figure 14). Figure 15 shows a close-up view of the simulation. In this case, we obtained frame rates between 15 to 20 fps for a simulation size of 16K characters; notice Minotauro's node uses a Tesla M2090 GPU.

We have designed two experiments to verify the functionality of the *Web configuration*. In the first experiment, we ran the system different web browsers to detect potential compatibility issues (Figure 16). The results showed that Chrome, Firefox, and Opera browsers were able to display the visualization successfully. A simple inspection of the interaction did not show any lag between user commands and simulation response.

In the second experiment, two clients were connected to the testing system. The first client was Windows 7 system, and the second client was an Android-based mobile device. The same visualization was displayed successfully on both devices; however, the lag between user commands and simulation response was noticeable.

Figure 14. Far distance view

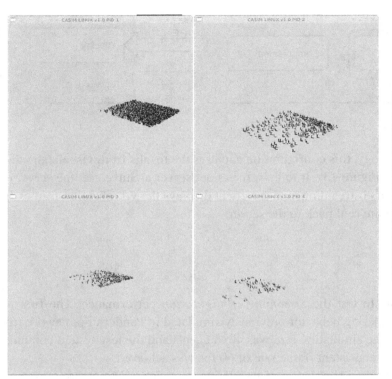

Figure 15. Close-up view

Figure 16. Web configuration results: left: OpenGL/glut window; right: visualization is displayed in Chrome browser.

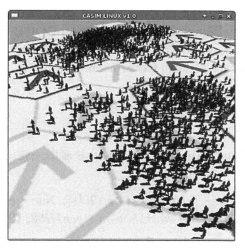
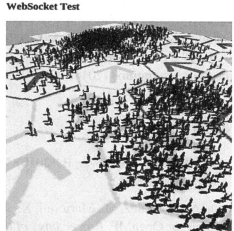

CONCLUSION

This chapter presented an algorithm for real-time crowd simulation using a task-based approach implemented using OmpSs and CUDA. OmpSs allows parallelizing the algorithm incrementally, and performing partial tests of each function being converted into a task. OmpSs takes care of memory management, scheduling, communications and synchronization automatically. The main changes were the subdivision of the domain, and the exchange of information between tiles. Although these techniques incur extra processing, they have allowed taking advantage of the CPU and GPU processors. The time required for creating tasks is negligible considering the benefits of using OmpSs. Due to the advanced techniques of scheduling and memory management, OmpSs can even get a better speedup than relying on CUDA only.

Programming with CUDA requires explicit operations like device selection, data transfers between host and devices, flow control through queues and events, among others. This kind of operations makes programming difficult and prone to errors. On the other hand, OmpSs facilitates the use of all available GPUs in one node, makes flexible use of resources and exploits their full capacity, and scales the system to multiple CPUs or GPUs without modifying the program.

Regarding the visualization, we have designed a configurable crowd engine that supports three configurations: streaming, in-situ, and web. The S*treaming configuration* supports crowd visualization in machines connected outside the BSC's LAN; while the *Web configuration* allows us to display simulations on any device, and *In-situ configuration* allows using the GPU resources for simulation and visualization.

Streaming and Web configuration offer flexibility and may reduce infrastructure costs when advanced visualization systems such as the CAVE or Tiled Display Walls are remotely available. It also avoids the difficulty of coupling already existing simulation tools. The *Web configuration* can be used to take advantage of sensors available on mobile devices to improve user interaction. Finally, *In-situ configuration* offers a testbed to analyze further scalability behavior of interactive simulations that use the GPU for computation and rendering.

ACKNOWLEDGMENT

This research was partially supported by: CONACyT doctoral fellowship 285730, CONACyT SNI 54067, BSC-CNS Severo Ochoa program (SEV-2011-00067), CUDA Center of Excellence at BSC, Oak Ridge Leadership Computing Facility at the Oak Ridge National Laboratory, under DOE Contract No. DE-AC05-00OR22725, the Spanish Ministry of Economy and Competitivity under contract TIN2012-34557, and the SGR programme (2014-SGR-1051) of the Catalan Government.

REFERENCES

Ahrens, J., Rogers, D., & Springmeyer, B. (2010). Visualization and data analysis at the exascale (Technical Report LLNL-TR-474731).

Balart, J., Duran, A., Gonzàlez, M., Martorell, X., Ayguadé, E., & Labarta, J. (2004). Nanos mercurium: a research compiler for OpenMP. *Proceedings of the European Workshop on OpenMP* 8, 103-109.

Barcelona Supercomputing Center. (2015, June 15). *Extrae*. Retrieved from http://www.bsc.es/computer-sciences/extrae

Barcelona Supercomputing Center. (2015, June 15). *Nanos++*. Retrieved from https://pm.bsc.es/projects/nanox

Barcelona Supercomputing Center. (2015, June 15). *Paraver*. Retrieved from http://www.bsc.es/computer-sciences/performance-tools/paraver

Bonabeau, E. (2002). Agent-based modeling: Methods and techniques for simulating human systems. Proceedings of the National Academy of Sciences of the United States of America, 99(Suppl. 3), 7280–7287. PubMed PMID:12011407

Crowd Studios. (2015, June 15). *Golaem*. Retrieved from http://www.golaem.com

Duran, A., Ayguadé, E., Badia, R. M., Labarta, J., Martinell, L., Martorell, X., & Planas, J. (2011). OmpSs: A proposal for programming heterogeneous multi-core architectures. Parallel Processing Letters, 21(2), 173–193.

Helbing, D., & Molnar, P. (1995). Social force model for pedestrian dynamics. Physical Review E: Statistical Physics, Plasmas, Fluids, and Related Interdisciplinary Topics, 51(5), 42–82. PubMed PMID:9963139

Hernández, B., & Rudomin, I. (2011). A rendering pipeline for real-time crowds. GPU Pro, 2, 369–383.

Hernandez, B., Pérez, H., Rudomin, I., Ruiz, S., de Gyves, O., & Toledo, L. (2014). Simulating and Visualizing Real-Time Crowds on GPU Clusters. Computación y Sistemas, 18(4), 651–664.

Kappadia, M., Pelechano, N., Guy, S., Allbeck, J., & Chrysanthou, Y. (2014). Simulating heterogeneous crowds with interactive behaviors. *Eurographics 2014 - Tutorials*.

Kiran, M., Richmond, P., Holcombe, M., Chin, L. S., Worth, D., & Greenough, C. (2010). FLAME: simulating large populations of agents on parallel hardware architectures. *In Proceedings of the 9th International Conference on Autonomous Agents and Multiagent Systems*, 1(1), 1633-1636.

Lysenko, M., & D'Souza, R. M. (2008). A framework for megascale agent based model simulations on graphics processing units. Journal of Artificial Societies and Social Simulation, 11(4), 10.

Ma, K. L. (2009). In situ visualization at extreme scale: Challenges and opportunities. IEEE Computer Graphics and Applications, 29(6), 14–19. PubMed PMID:24806775

Molnar, S., Cox, M., Ellsworth, D., & Fuchs, H. (1994). A sorting classification of parallel rendering. IEEE Computer Graphics and Applications, 14(4), 23–32.

Moreland, K.D. (2013). Oh %24%23*%40! Exascale! The Effect of Emerging Architectures on Scientific Discovery. In *High Performance Computing, Networking, Storage and Analysis (SCC)* (pp. 224 – 231).

Moussaïd, M., Helbing, D., & Theraulaz, G. (2011). How simple rules determine pedestrian behavior and crowd disasters. Proceedings of the National Academy of Sciences of the United States of America, 108(17), 6884–6888. PubMed PMID:21502518

Nagel, K., & Rickert, M. (2001). Parallel implementation of the TRANSIMS micro-simulation. Parallel Computing, 27(12), 1611–1639.

Ondřej, J., Pettré, J., Olivier, A. H., & Donikian, S. (2010). A synthetic-vision based steering approach for crowd simulation. ACM Transactions on Graphics, 29(4), 123.

Ozen, G., Ayguadé, E., & Labarta, J. (2014). On the roles of the programmer, the compiler and the runtime system when programming accelerators in OpenMP. In Using and Improving OpenMP for Devices (pp. 215–229).

Paris, S., Pettré, J., & Donikian, S. (2007). Pedestrian reactive navigation for crowd simulation: A predictive approach. Computer Graphics Forum, 26(3), 665–674.

Pelechano, N., Allbeck, J. M., & Badler, N. I. (2008). Virtual crowds: Methods, simulation, and control. Synthesis Lectures on Computer Graphics and Animation, 3(1), 1–176.

Reynolds, C. W. (1987). Flocks, herds and schools: A distributed behavioral model. Computer Graphics, 21(4), 25–34.

Richmond, P., Coakley, S., & Romano, D. M. (2009, May). A high performance agent based modelling framework on graphics card hardware with CUDA. *Proceedings of the 8th International Conference on Autonomous Agents and Multiagent Systems* (Vol. 2, pp. 1125-1126).

Rivas, J. I. R., Gyves, O. D., Rudomín, I., & Pelechano, N. (2014). Coupling Camera-tracked Humans with a Simulated Virtual Crowd. *Proceedings of GRAPP Conference 2014* (pp. 312-321).

Rubio-Campillo, X. (2014). Pandora: A Versatile Agent-Based Modelling Platform for Social Simulation. *Proceedings of the SIMUL 2014: The Sixth International Conference on Advances in System Simulation* (pp. 29-34).

Rudomin, I., Hernández, B., deGyves, O., Toledo, L., Rivalcoba, I., & Ruiz, S. (2013). GPU generation of large varied animated crowds. Computación y Sistemas, 17(3), 365–380.

Rudomín, I., Millán, E., & Hernández, B. (2005). Fragment shaders for agent animation using finite state machines. Simulation Modelling Practice and Theory, 13(8), 741–751.

Ruiz, S., Hernández, B., Alvarado, A., & Rudomín, I. (2013). Reducing memory requirements for diverse animated crowds. Proceedings of Motion on Games (pp. 77-86).

Still, G. K. (2000). Crowd dynamics [Doctoral dissertation]. University of Warwick.

Thompson, K. M. (2006). Scale, Spectacle and Movement: Massive Software and Digital Special Effects in The Lord of the Rings. Cap, 16, 283–299.

Van Den Berg, J., Guy, S. J., Lin, M., & Manocha, D. (2011). Reciprocal n-body collision avoidance. In Robotics Research (pp. 3-19).

Van den Berg, J., Patil, S., Sewall, J., Manocha, D., & Lin, M. (2008). Interactive navigation of multiple agents in crowded environments. *Proceedings of the 2008 symposium on Interactive 3D graphics and games* (pp. 139-147).

Yu, H., Wang, C., Grout, R. W., Chen, J. H., & Ma, K. L. (2010). In situ visualization for large-scale combustion simulations. IEEE Computer Graphics and Applications, 3, 45–57. PubMed PMID:20650717

Yu, T., Dou, M., & Zhu, M. (2015). A data parallel approach to modelling and simulation of large crowd. Cluster Computing, 18(3), 1307-1316.

KEY TERMS AND DEFINITIONS

Generation of Diversity (GoD): A module of the crowd engine that generates and animates 3D characters semi-automatically.

In-Situ Visualization: A technique to couple simulation and visualization while the simulation is still running, executing both on the same machine avoiding transfers of data.

Level of Detail (LoD): An optimization technique commonly used in Computer Graphics, which represents geometric objects with different details according to a given metric (i.e., distance between the object and the viewer is usually used to render with more or less details such object).

Programming Models: An abstraction of the underlying hardware architecture which allows programmers to achieving better productivity, performance and portability by letting them focus on the development of algorithms.

Task-based Parallelism: A technique to design algorithms in terms of tasks instead of the specifics of threads and hardware resources like CPU cores. Implemented as a programming model creates a task dependency graph at runtime, which is used to schedule tasks in a data-flow way. It can take advantage of data locality, distribute tasks among hardware resources (even heterogeneous hardware) while maintaining load balancing, and scaling automatically if there are more available computing resources.

ENDNOTE

[1]   http://top500.org

Section 3
Reliability and Fault Tolerance

Chapter 9
Fault Tolerance Techniques for Distributed, Parallel Applications

Camille Coti
Université Paris 13, France

ABSTRACT

This chapter gives an overview of techniques used to tolerate failures in high-performance distributed applications. We describe basic replication techniques, automatic rollback recovery and application-based fault tolerance. We present the challenges raised specifically by distributed, high performance computing and the performance overhead the fault tolerance mechanisms are likely to cost. Last, we give an example of a fault-tolerant algorithm that exploits specific properties of a recent algorithm.

INTRODUCTION

Current systems used for high performance computing feature growing numbers of components. Even with the most reliable components that can be produced by the industry, the larger the system is, the higher the failure probability is (Reed, Lu, & Mendes, 2006).

If failures are independent from each other, the law of total probability can be applied to compute the Mean Time Between Failures (MTBF) of a system. In this case, the mean time between failures is equal to the average time between failures. If the system is made of N components, each of which having a MTBF denoted $MTBF_i$ for component i, the global $MTBF$ of the system can be given by Equation 1:

$$MTBF_{total} = \left(\sum_{i=0}^{n-1} \frac{1}{MTBF_i} \right)^{-1}$$

(1)

DOI: 10.4018/978-1-5225-0287-6.ch009

Figure 1. Mean time between failures for systems that use components that have different individual MTBFs

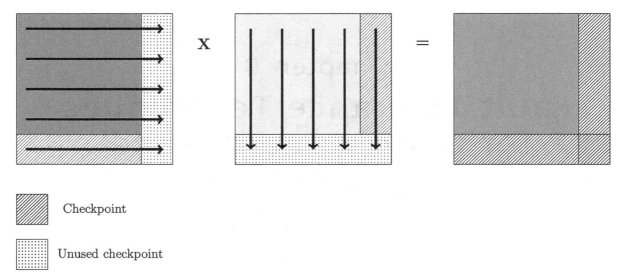

▨ Checkpoint

▨ Unused checkpoint

By using Equation 1, one can compute the MTBF of a system with respect to its size for various individual MTBFs. Some of them are represented by Figure 1. We can see that, the MTBF being a hyperbolic function of the size of the system, it drops to only a few hours for large systems even with very reliable components. For instance, a system made components with an individual MTBF of 100,000 hours (which is very reliable) will have a global MTBF of 10 hours if it is made of 10,000 components, and only one hour if it is made of 100,000 components. As a comparison, in the 10 fastest machines of the June 2015 Top 500 list[1], all the machines feature more than 100,000 cores and 5 machines feature more than 500,000 cores.

As a consequence, failures are unexceptional events at large-scale and must be handled when they occur during a computation.

Originally, the default behavior of distributed run-time environment such as MPI (Message Passing Interface Forum (2004)) consisted in terminating the surviving processes and ending the application. Therefore, a computation that runs for longer than the MTBF of the system is unlikely to complete and all the computation is lost.

This observation motivates the need for systems that can handle and tolerate failures and make completion possible in spite of the volatile nature of the resources they are running on. On the other hand, in the context of high performance computing, the overhead induced by the fault-tolerance mechanisms must be as small as possible in order to maintain this performance goal.

Fault tolerance can be handled at two levels. It can be implemented in the distributed middleware that supports the execution of a distributed environment, making it transparent for the application. This is called *system-level* fault tolerance. Fault tolerance can also be implemented by the application itself. In this case the application support system must provide mechanisms to implement fault tolerance, but the way the computation survives beyond failures is actually implemented by the application itself. This is called *application-level* fault tolerance.

This chapter presents a set of techniques used by distributed systems for high performance computing to tolerate failures. Hardware techniques such as Triple Modular Redundancy (TMR) (Lyons & Vanderkulk, 1962) or lockstep (Klecka, Bruckert, & Jardine, 2002) are used to improve the reliability of hardware systems. From a different point of view, data centers also need to tolerate failures to ensure high availability. Some placement strategies are designed to improve the node availability (Ford, Labelle, Popovici, Stokely, Truong, Barroso, Grimes & Quinlan, 2010). These strategies are the responsibility of the resource management system, which is the component that decides which resources will be used by applications. Fault tolerance is also a critical issue in the interconnection network used by data centers. Specific topologies and routing algorithms are designed specifically to be robust and maintain acceptable service level (Walraed-Sullivan, Vahdat, & Marzullo, 2013). In this chapter, we focus on the fault-tolerance aspects of distributed applications.

Section "Replication" presents software replication. Section "Rollback Recovery" presents system-based, checkpoint-based rollback recovery techniques. Application-level fault tolerance, also called user-level failure mitigation, is presented in section "Application-based Fault Tolerance". An example of a fault-tolerant application is presented in section "Example: an MPI-3-based, Fault-Tolerant QR Factorization".

REPLICATION

The most direct form of fault tolerance consists replicating resources. If a node fails, another one can be used as a backup. However, implementing replication in practice is not that straightforward and choices must be made depending on the expected semantics.

An overview of replication techniques is given in Guerraoui and Schiper (1997). The authors give a survey of replication techniques for servers, including group communication primitives and consensus required to implement replicated services. In this section, we present and compare the architecture of the frameworks used for replication: primary-backup replication (section "Primary-Backup Replication") and active replication (section "Active Replication").

Semantics and Criteria

The idea behind replication consists in using several resources, called *replicas*, all of which keep a copy of the state of the process. If a resource fails, a replica is used as a backup and no data is lost.

In Guerraoui and Schiper (1997), the authors define a correctness criterion called *linearizability*, stating that it "gives clients the illusion of non-replicated servers". in other words, the other processes interact with a replicated process without knowing how many instances are actually being executed and holding replicated data.

In the following, we consider that processes are *clients* and *servers*, the client interacting with its server by sending a request *req* and receiving an acknowledgement *ack* when the server is done. When the replicated server enforces linearizability, the client sends a *req* and receives an *ack* regardless of the number of replicas being used.

Figure 2. Primary-backup replication: a request between a client and a server made of one primary replica and two backup replicas

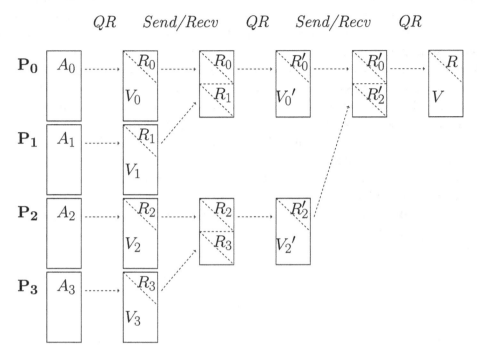

Another criterion is *determinism*. An operation is deterministic if its outcome depends only on the initial state and the sequence of operations that have been performed. If a process can be impacted by an external event such as the failure of another process it is communicating with, this process is non-deterministic.

Primary-Backup Replication

Primary-backup replication is a technique that involves two categories of replicated servers: a *primary* replica and several backup *replicas*. A client contacts the primary replica, which replicates the request on the backup replica. Once *all* the backup replicas have sent their acknowledgement to the primary replica, the latter sends its acknowledgement to the client. This mechanism is depicted in Figure 2.

In other words, with primary-backup replication, the server itself is in charge with replication. The servers only see the primary replica, and the replication protocol is implemented between the primary replica and the backup replicas.

If a backup replica fails, the client does not see it. If the primary server fails, the client sees the failure and contacts a backup replica that becomes the primary server in place of the failed one.

During failure-free executions or if only backup replicas fail, *linearizability* is enforced by the fact that the client contacts one server and gets one response. If the primary replica fails, linearizability is ensured by a failure detection mechanism and the selection of a new primary replica.

In a situation where the primary replica fails, a specific action must be taken to select a new one and re-emit its request. Therefore, this technique is not *deterministic*.

Figure 3. Active replication: a request between a client and a server made of tree replicas

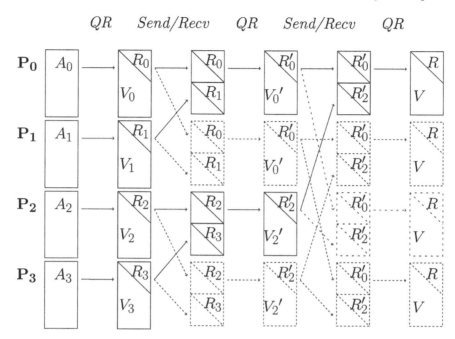

Active Replication

On the other hand, *active replication* requires that the client itself performs the replication among replicated processes. The client sends its request to all the available replicas, in a multicast fashion. All the replicas send their acknowledgement: therefore, once the client has received one acknowledgement, it can consider that one server is done; once the has received all the acknowledgements, it can consider that all of them are done. In other words, with active replication the redundancy is enforced by the client itself. This mechanism is depicted in Figure 3.

The communication between the client and the replicas is a *multicast* communication. To be correct, this multicast primitive must be robust and preserve the order and atomicity of the operations. Considering such a multicast communication primitive, failures are transparent for the client. As a consequence, requests do no need to be re-emitted and therefore this technique ensures *determinism*. Also, thanks to the properties offered by this multicast communication primitive, the client performs only one communication to send its request and *linearizability* is preserved.

Resilience and Overhead

Replication implements pure redundancy between processes of a distributed system. It is the most basic and direct form of fault tolerance: if a process fails, another process is ready to take its place immediately.

However, it has a strong overhead: if one wants to tolerate N failures of a given process, there must exist $N+1$ instances of this process. Overall, if one wants to tolerate N failures in a system, there must exist $N+1$ instances of each process. As a consequence, the part of the processes that are taking part of the computation is divided by the redundancy ratio.

Moreover, both techniques have an overhead on failure-free executions. Primary-backup replication (section "Primary-backup replication") requires the client to perform a multicast communication primitive, which is more expensive than a unicast communication. Active replication (section "Active Replication") requires the client to perform a multicast communication primitive, which is more expensive than a unicast communication. However, it does not necessarily wait for all of the replicas' answer, but it can proceed as soon as it has received one reply.

ROLLBACK RECOVERY

In this section, we are describing a set of techniques used for fault tolerance by *rollback recovery*. They rely on application checkpointing for restart (described in section "Checkpointing a distributed system"). However, we will see that checkpointing a distributed application is not straightforward. This section presents two categories of rollback recovery protocols: coordinated checkpointing and non-coordinated checkpointing.

This section also presents implementations of these protocols and the corresponding architectures that support the protocols. Some examples of implementations are presented here, but most widely-used distributed programming environments such as OpenMPI (Hursey, Mattox, & Lumsdaine, 2009), MPICH-V (Bouteiller, Herault, Krawezik, Lemarinier & Cappello, 2006), Charm++ (Zheng, Shi, & Kalé, 2004) or LAM/MPI (Sankaran, Squyres, Barrett, Sahay, Lumsdaine, Duell, Hargrove & Roman, 2005). A longer survey on the theoretical aspects of these protocols can be found in Elnozahy, Alvisi, Wang, and Johnson (1996) and Elnozahy, Alvisi, Wang and Johnson (2002).

Checkpointing a Distributed System

Recovering the state of a crashed process in a distributed system by rolling it back in a previous state is not trivial. In this section, we are presenting the reason why it is not as easy as for a sequential process.

Checkpointing a Process

Checkpointing a process consists in taking a *snapshot* of the state of this process. This snapshot can be stored in a file and be read later to restart the process from this state. The state of a running process is made of the contents of its virtual memory and the registers it is using, the program counter and the status of open file descriptors. Libraries exist for this both at system-level and user-level, among which BLCR (Roman, Duell, & Hargrove, 2003), Condor's Checkpoint Mechanism (Litzkow, Tannenbaum, Basney & Livny, 1997) or Libckpt (Plank, Beck, Kingsley & Li, 1995).

Distributed Application Model

A distributed application is made of a set of *processes* and *communication channels* that are used to communicate between processes. Communication channels are a state made of the messages that are in the queues associated with them or in transit on these channels. As a consequence, the *state of a distributed system* is made of the set of states of this processes and its communication channels.

When a process is rolled back to a previous state, it might need to receive some messages it has already received and send some messages it has already sent. For instance, this situation is depicted in Figure 4. If the process restarts from the snapshot, it will wait to send and receive messages: if they are not replayed, such messages are called *orphan messages*. A process waiting for a message that will not be re-emitted can also be called an *orphan process*. Both orphans can be found in the literature.

A state that does not have orphan messages is called a *consistent state*. The whole purpose of rollback recovery-based fault tolerance mechanisms is to recover a consistent state after failures.

Rollback Recovery of a Distributed System

If each process takes a snapshot of its state and saves it independently from the other processes, there may be some orphan messages when this process restarts from this state later. One possibility consists in triggering a rollback on the remote process this process needs to communicate with. Therefore, the remote process will re-emit its communication and the message will not be an orphan

one anymore. However, dependencies between processes might lead to triggering rollbacks in chain, creating what is called a *domino effect*. If this domino effect is unbound, the application will roll back to its initial state: in this case, the fault tolerance mechanism will appear to be useless.

When a process or several of them rollback to a previous state, the resulting state of the system form what is called the *recovery line*.

Figure 4. A process sends and receive messages through its execution, possibly between a checkpoint and a crash

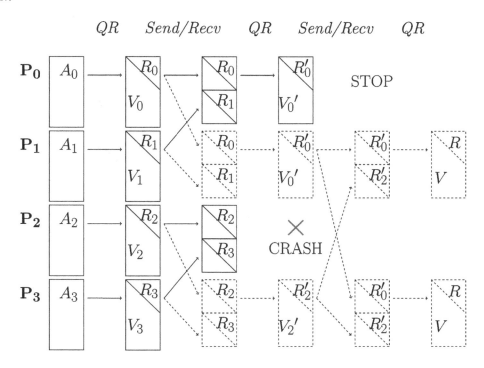

Stable Components that Support the Fault Tolerance Protocols

In general, fault tolerance protocols introduce architectures relying on additional components that support the fault tolerance mechanisms. These components are considered as *stable*. This stability can be explained by several factors. They can be located on machines that are particularly reliable and monitored with specific care. They can also be implemented in a fault-tolerant way, for instance by using replication. There is also a statistical explanation for this. In a large-scale system, failures are likely to occur on any process of the system, as presented in the introduction of this chapter. However, the additional components are executed on a small set of machines. Therefore, they are unlikely to be hit by a failure, compared to the failure likelihood of any process of the application.

Coordinated Checkpointing

Coordinated checkpointing is a set of techniques that perform a *global checkpoint* of all the processes of the system. It relies on the notion of *coherent cut*, which is a cut of the system which is not crossed by any message (see Figure 5) and form a consistent state (see section "Distributed Application Model"). In the global state saved by the global snapshot, no process will in the future wait for a reception that was sent before the snapshot of the sender was taken, and no process will in the future send a message that was received by its destination before the snapshot was taken.

Figure 5. Coherent cut between 5 processes that communicate using message passing (red dashed line)

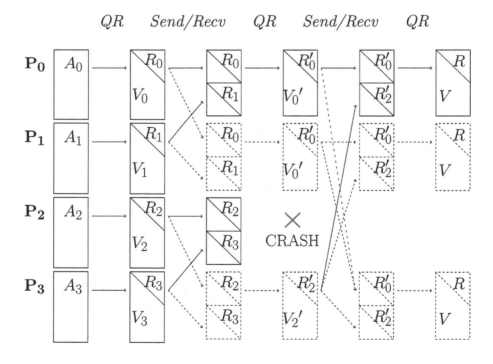

As a consequence, a global snapshot taken by a coherent cut is a coherent state from which the system can restart. *Coordinated* checkpointing protocols define how this coherent cut is made. Most of them rely on the Chandy-Lamport algorithm (Chandy & Lamport, 1985) to build a *distributed snapshot*. This idea is to form a global snapshot made of the snapshots of all the processes of the system.

Taking a distributed snapshot using the Chandy-Lamport algorithm uses a *checkpoint wave*. A process initiates the wave and a *marker* circulates between all the processes to propagate it. How communication channels are dealt with depends on the implementation of this protocol. There exist two options for this implementation: *blocking* or *non-blocking*.

As their name suggests, *blocking* protocols block the execution during the checkpoint wave (Coti, Herault, Lemarinier, Pilard, Rezmerita, Rodriguez & Cappello, 2006; Buntinas, Coti, Herault, Lemarinier, Pilard, Rezmerita, Rodriguez & Cappello, 2008). Once a process receives a marker, it pauses its execution, forwards the marker to all the other processes and takes a snapshot. Processes resume their execution only once they have received a marker from each of the other processes of the application. Since we assume that communication channels have the FIFO property, no message can overtake the marker; therefore, there can be no message crossing the checkpoint wave, and the distributed snapshot forms a coherent cut.

On the opposite, *non-blocking* protocols do not stop their execution during the checkpoint wave. Instead of that, they log the messages exchanged during the wave (Bouteiller, Lemarinier, Krawezik & Cappello, 2003; Lemarinier, Bouteiller, Herault, Krawezik, & Cappello, 2004). The messages received after the reception of the first marker and before the reception of the last marker are stored with the checkpoint.

Failure recovery is quite straightforward. When a process fails, all the other processes are killed and restart from the last completed checkpoint wave. If a failure occurs during a checkpoint wave, they restart from the previous one, which is the latest one that was completed.

The architecture of the infrastructure required to implement a coordinated checkpointing protocol is described in Figure 6. The architecture is quite simple. A *checkpoint server* is used to store all the checkpoints of the computing processes. A *checkpoint scheduler* process initiates the checkpoint wave and collects markers from all the processes to determine that the wave is completed. A specific process (for MPI applications, the *mpiexec* process) is in charge with monitoring the computing processes, sending a signal to kill them all in case of a failure and restarting all the processes.

An improvement for this protocol was introduced in Lemarinier, Bouteiller, Herault, Krawezik and Cappello (2004). Restarting an application requires to rollback all the computing processes, which stresses the checkpoint server when *all* the computing processes download their latest snapshot from it. To reduce the congestion, processes keep a local copy of their snapshot. When all the processes need to rollback, the surviving one's restart from the local copy of their latest snapshot and only the process that replaces the dead one downloads it from the checkpoint server.

Non-Coordinated Checkpointing

Unlike with coordinated checkpointing protocols, in non-coordinated checkpointing protocols processes take snapshots independently from each other. The goal for the protocols is to avoid the domino effect described in section "Rollback Recovery of a Distributed System" and reach a consistent state again.

Figure 6. Architecture of a distributed system-level fault-tolerance support based on coordinated check-pointing: MPICH-Vcl

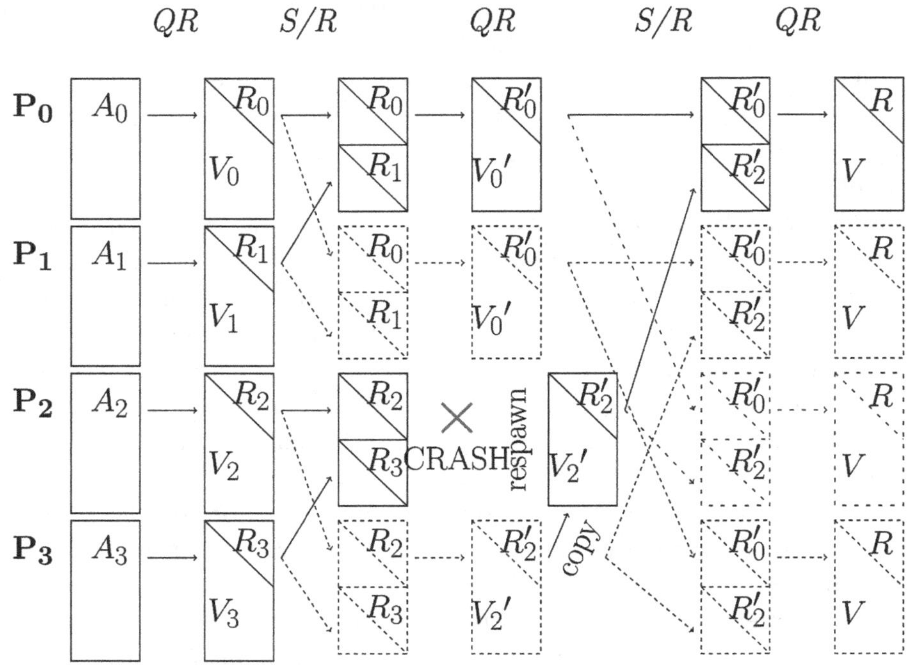

Message Logging Protocols

The state of a *deterministic* process depends, by definition, on its initial state and the sequence of events that happen to it. For a given initial state, a deterministic process always reaches the same

final state. In particular, it is made of a sequence of non-deterministic events (interactions with the rest of the world) and the execution of deterministic events between them. If these non-deterministic events are replayed in the same order between executions, then for any given initial state, the final state is always the same. This principle is called the *piecewise deterministic assumption* (PWD).

Message-logging protocols rely on the PWD. In the distributed system we are considering here, non-deterministic events are message receptions. As a consequence, if a failed process is restarted and the messages are replayed, this process will be able to reach the same state as before the failure. It requires restarting only the failed processes upon failures, and during failure-free executions, processes store their snapshot independently from each other. Hence, message-logging protocols are *non-coordinated* checkpointing protocols.

As stated in the introduction of this section, non-coordinated checkpointing protocols store the messages sent between the processes in order to replay them when a process fails and needs to be restarted. Message-logging protocols can be classified in three categories (Alvisi & Marzullo):

- Optimistic message logging,
- Pessimistic message logging,
- Causal message logging.

Figure 7. Pessimistic message logging   *Figure 8. Optimistic message logging*

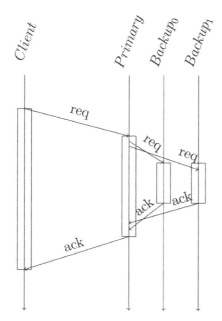
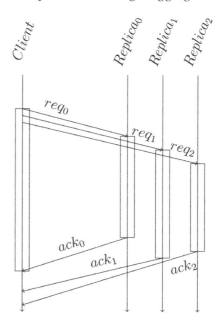

Optimistic message logging protocols make the assumption that when two processes communicate with one another, no process will crash before the message is securely stored. Pessimistic message logging protocols do not make this assumption and store the message prior to delivering it (see Figure 7 and Figure 8). As a consequence, pessimistic introduces come latency while waiting for the message to be stored before actually sending the message to its destination. Causal message logging protocols try to combine both approaches.

Messages can be saved by their sender or their receiver. In this chapter, we describe sender-based message logging protocols, but receiver-based protocols are close.

Channel Memory

A straightforward way of saving the state of communication channels consists in using *channel memory*. Each channel is equipped with an additional component that stores the data going through it. In practice, this channel memory is a software component. When a process sends a message to another process, it sends the message to the channel memory that stores it and forwards it to its destination. This mechanism is depicted by Figure 9. Since the message is stored before it is delivered to its destination, it is a *pessimistic message logging* protocol.

Figure 9. Channel memory between two MPI processes

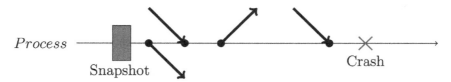

Figure 10. Architecture of a distributed system-level fault-tolerance support based on channel memory and rollback recovery: MPICH-V1

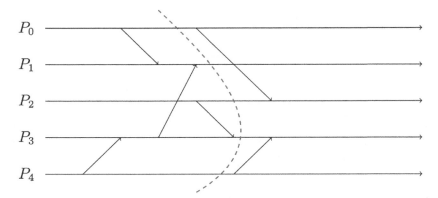

This idea was implemented in the fault-tolerant MPI library MPICH-V1 (Bosilca, Bouteiller, Cappello, Djilali, Fedak, Germain, Herault, Lemarinier, Lodygensky, Magniette, Neri & Selikhov, 2002). The MPICH-V project aims at providing system-level, transparent fault tolerance. Because the fault tolerance mechanisms considered are transparent, any MPI application can run without being modified. The robustness and recovery mechanisms are implemented in the middleware that supports the parallel, distributed execution.

MPICH-V is also a framework for implementing, evaluating and comparing fault-tolerance protocols. The architecture of MPICH-V1 is depicted on Figure 10. A set of processes are used as communication channels, another set of processes is used to store checkpoints and a process called the dispatcher orchestrates process checkpointing and implements a failure detector.

Sender-Based Message Logging

Messages can be stored by either the sender or the receiver. In the case of *sender-based message logging*, the sender is in charge with saving it. Messages are stored on a reliable storage system and then sent to the destination. Therefore, when the message is received by the destination, it has been saved securely before (before or "quite at the same time" depending on whether the protocol is optimistic or pessimistic).

As a consequence, any message that impacts another process can be replayed. If the destination process fails, the messages it has received before the failure can be replayed.

In practice, the sender process only stores the messages in memory and the receiver stores the causality information of a message on the remote storage system (Bouteiller, Lemarinier, Krawezik & Cappello, 2003). The *causality information* of a message is a set of logical clock values (Lamport, 1978) that define the causal ordering of messages. In this case, the reception of a message is made of two steps: 1) the message is received by the communication daemon and the process sends its causality information to the remote storage system 2) when this storage is acknowledged, the message is delivered to the process.

When a process is checkpointed, the messages is kept in memory are saved with the checkpoints. When a process fails and needs messages to be replayed, it gets the sequence of events and asks the messages themselves to their sender. It reduces the time to save the messages, but increases memory usage on the processes.

This protocol was implemented in the MPICH-V framework in MPICH-V2 (Bouteiller, Cappello, Herault, Krawezik, Lemarinier & Magniette, 2003). The additional component used to store the causality information of the reception events is called an *event logger*. The complete protocol for sending and receiving a message is depicted on Figure 11.

Causal Message Logging

Causal message logging aims at combining the safety of pessimistic message logging with the low latency overhead of optimistic message logging. In a similar way as with sender-based protocols, the messages are kept by their sender in memory. The causality information is added in piggyback of the message sent. As a consequence, if a process crashes, the information required to recover to a coherent state is still somewhere in the system. When a process sends a message, it adds the previously received causality information with the new one and puts the concatenated information in the piggyback of the message.

The causality information of the messages can be stored on a reliable storage system, called and *event logger* (Bouteiller, Herault, Krawezik, Lemarinier & Cappello, 2006). The architecture that supports such protocols are represented in Figure 12. In a similar way as with optimistic protocols, the sending process does not wait for any acknowledgement from the storage system to proceed with the communication. The difference here is that the causality information is still added in piggyback of the message until the event logger acknowledges storage. The impact of the event logger was evaluated in (Bouteiller, Collin, Herault, Lemarinier & Cappello, 2005). The event logger reduces the size of the piggyback of each message and therefore, the overhead on the bandwidth.

Communication-Induced Checkpointing

Communication-induced checkpointing (CIC) does not log any message at all and yet, processes take snapshots without any synchronization mechanism similar to the ones used for coordinated checkpointing. The basic idea is to avoid *domino effect* by triggering a chain of rollbacks (Hélary, Mostefaoui & Raynal, 1999).

Figure 11. Sender-based message logging with an event logger

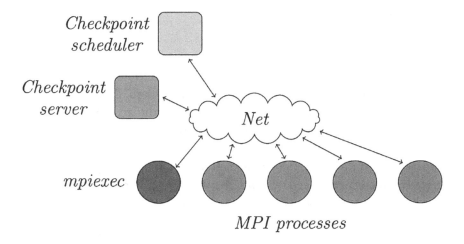

Figure 12. Architecture of a distributed system-level fault-tolerance support based on causal message-logging: MPICH-Vcausal

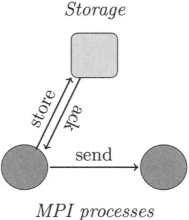

CIC uses two kinds of checkpoints: *local checkpoints* and *forced checkpoints*. Local checkpoints are taken by processes independently from each other. Forced checkpoints are taken to make sure that the recovery line is progressing, based on inter-process dependencies (*i.e.* communications). In other words, they bound the chain of rollbacks: a process that rolls back can trigger a checkpoint on a remote process to avoid orphan messages, until a snapshot is available and this process can be rolled back.

Forced checkpoints can be decided based on two categories of techniques: *model-based* and *index-based* protocols. It was proved that the two techniques are equivalent (Hélary, Mostéfaoui & Raynal, 1997), but in practice the number of forced checkpoints is generally lower with index-based checkpointing (Alvisi, Rao, Husain, De Mel & Elnozahy, 1999).

Messages are not logged but the checkpointing protocol still needs some data to be passed between processes. Instead, protocol information is sent in the piggyback of the messages. Generally, this data represents the identifiers of the processes that are in causal dependency, *i.e.* between which messages have been exchanged. Based on the analysis of these causal dependencies, the checkpointing protocol can decide when to force a checkpoint or not.

Performance Considerations

Several practical evaluations and comparisons of these protocols have been made. Coordinated checkpointing protocols have been compared for instance in Coti, Herault, Lemarinier, Pilard, Rezmerita, Rodriguez, and Cappello (2006) and in Buntinas, Coti, Herault, Lemarinier, Pilard, Rezmerita, Rodriguez, and Cappello (2008). In the same framework, a comparison between coordinated and non-coordinated (channel memory, causal and pessimistic message-logging) was presented in Lemarinier, Bouteiller, Herault, Krawezik, and Cappello (2004) and Bouteiller, Herault, Krawezik, Lemarinier, and Cappello (2006).

Overall, message-logging introduces an overhead on the communications. In the case of causal message logging, this overhead can be reduced by using an event logger to reduce the size of the information carried in the piggyback of the messages (Bouteiller, Collin, Herault, Lemarinier, & Cappello, 2005). Channel memory introduces a bottleneck on the storage processes in the case of communication-intensive applications. This issue can be handled by using several storage processes. However, this solution introduces a large number of reliable components, which makes the fault tolerance support expensive.

Coordinated checkpointing protocols give better performance during fault-free executions. However, when a single process fails, all the processes of the system need to rollback, hence losing a lot of computation time.

APPLICATION-BASED FAULT TOLERANCE

Unlike automatic approaches presented in the previous sections (section "Replication" and section "Rollback Recovery"), Application-Based Fault Tolerance requires the application itself to implement the behavior that must be followed upon failures, in particular how the application can proceed and survive failures. This approach is also called user-level failure mitigation: the user himself/herself is in charge with defining how the application must behave upon failures in order to tolerate them and proceed with the computation in spite of failures.

This approach has many advantages on the performance point of view, in particular because it allows to implement application-specific algorithms. For instance, instead of checkpointing all the memory space of a process, a programmer can choose to save only the data that is necessary to recover the state of the computation, without any temporary data for instance. Hence, the goal for application-based fault tolerance is to have a lower overhead than the automatic approaches.

However, on the other hand, it requires some action from the application programmer, who needs to take failures into account and implement the actions that must be taken upon failures, whereas the automatic approaches do not require any modification in the code.

This section presents the possibilities that can be provided by the middleware to implement ABFT (section "Fault tolerant Middleware"), an approach based on user-level checkpointing (section "Diskless Checkpointing") and last, some fault-tolerant algorithms for linear algebra (section "Fault Tolerant Linear Algebra").

Fault Tolerant Middleware

To implement fault tolerance inside the distributed application, the middleware that supports its execution on distributed resources (see section "Introduction") needs to provide some features:

- It must be able to survive the failure and keep providing the same level of service to the other processes;
- It must provide specific features to implement the fault tolerance strategy chosen by the programmer.

Semantics for Fault Tolerance

The basic issue for fault tolerance is: which semantics does the application need to follow in case of a failure? In Fagg and Dongarra (2000) and Fagg, Gabriel, Bosilca, Angskun, Chen, Pjesivac-Grbovic, London, and Dongarra (2004), the authors defined a set of four behaviors. In the case of MPI, processes that communicate together are grouped in *communicators*. The default, global communicator *MPI_COMM_WORLD* contains all the processes of the application. Processes are numbered in communicators using unique integers, called their *rank*. If an application containsprocesses, the ranks of the ranks are in the interval.

The semantics of this *MPI_COMM_WORLD* communicator in case of a failure are the following ones:

- **ABORT:** This semantics is the default one of non-fault-tolerant MPI implementations. When a process fails, the whole application is terminated.
- **REBUILD:** In this semantics, the dead process is replaced by a new one.
- **BLANK:** The failed process is not replaced, there is a "hole" in the communicator instead: a blank process, as stated in Fagg, Gabriel, Bosilca, Angskun, Chen, Pjesivac-Grbovic, London and Dongarra (2004, June) and in Fagg, Gabriel, Chen, Angskun, Bosilca, Pjesivac-Grbovic and Dongarra (2005). The MPI 1 standard (Message Passing Interface Forum (2004)) defines that blank processes must behave as *MPI_PROC_NULL*: processes that try to communicate with it do not get any error message.
- **SHRINK:** The communicator is reduced to fill the gaps and maintain consecutive rank numbers without any hole. Therefore, the surviving processes are renumbered.

Resilient Middleware

To be able to support an application that can survive a failure, the run-time environment used by this application must be able to survive it in the first place. Therefore, it needs to be resilient: it needs to be able to keep providing the same level of service to the other processes, meaning that no process must be disconnected and the communication properties in terms of performance must remain close to the original one. It also needs to be able to detect failures (Aguilera, Chen, & Toueg, 1997) and notify the communication library and the remaining processes.

The middleware itself must rely on a robust communication topology. Initially, the *ring topology* was used for this purpose (Butler, Gropp & Lusk, 2001). If a process fails, the ring is re-knit. However, it cannot tolerate simultaneous failures: two failures disconnect the ring. Moreover, a ring topology does not implement scalable communications.

Trees provide interesting communication capabilities in terms of scalability; however, they are not resilient: a single non-leaf node failure disconnects part of the processes. In order to avoid this problem while keeping the interesting scalability properties of the trees, *k-ary sibling trees* are (k-ary) trees in which the nodes of each level are connected by a ring (Angskun, Fagg, Bosilca, Pješivac-Grbović, & Dongarra, 2010).

Binomial graphs are another interesting topology to build a robust while high-performance communication infrastructure [ABD07]. The idea is that each process of rank is connected to its neighbors of rank, with starting at 0 and such that if denotes the number of processes. In other words, each process sees its neighbors in a binomial tree in the forward direction and another binomial tree in the backward direction. Therefore, it is a reasonable trade-off between resilience and communication performance. Moreover, it can be built in a robust way and rebuilt after failures (Bosilca, Coti, Herault, Lemarinier & Dongarra, 2009).

Diskless Checkpointing

We have seen in section "Rollback recovery" that system-level checkpointing uses additional components to store checkpoints. Moreover, in this approach, a checkpoint is a complete image of the state of a process, including the whole memory space of this process (see section "Rollback recovery", subsection "Checkpointing a process"). It is an automatic approach that does not require any intervention from the programmer. However, it might be possible to restart a process with not all of this memory space: for instance, an iterative matrix computation might be able to recover from a failure during a step by using the state of the computation at the end of the previous step.

In the approach presented in Plank, Li, and Puening (1998), the authors use two kinds of processes in an application: some of them are used to perform the parallel computation, while the other ones are used to store the checkpoints.

Fault Tolerant Linear Algebra

This approach can be extended to store not just the whole state of the process, but algorithm-specific pieces of data.

Figure 13 depicts how a matrix can be mapped on a 2-D process grids of 16 processes. An extra line and an extra column can be added to this process grid to store additional data such as a checksum: each line and each column have an extra process (Figure 14). The processes store the checksum of the processes of line; The processes store the checksum of the processes of column.

If a checksum process fails, its state can be recovered from the bottom-right process that holds two checksums: one for the line checksums and one for the column checksums.

In practice, this checksum can be implemented using an *exclusive or* operation over the data of the processes. If a process fails, its state can be recovered from the data held in by the processes of the same line including the checksum process by doing an exclusive or. It can also be recovered in the same way using the processes of the same column.

Figure 13. 2D-Grid process mapping on a matrix   *Figure 14. Line and column checkpointing*

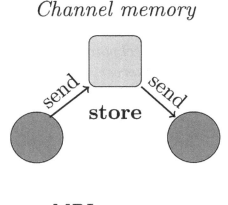

We can notice that this algorithm can tolerate multiple failures in most cases. If two processes fail on a given line, their state cannot be recovered using their line checksum. However, it can be recovered using their column checksum. One situation that cannot be recovered is when several failed process form a square on the process mesh: in this case, the processes cannot recover from their line checksum because it includes multiple failed processes, but they cannot recover from their column checksum either for the same reason.

Bosilca, Delmas, Dongarra and Langou (2009) gives another example of a parallel matrix-matrix multiplication that can tolerate failures. In this algorithm, only one dimension is used to store checkpoints (Figure 13). The previous approach presented in Figure 14 involve collective communications between the processes of each line and the processes of each column. The approach presented here involves local computations only.

If we denote the two matrices to be multiplied and an additional line and an additional column can be added to the matrices with checksum matrices and as follows in Equation (2):

$$A = \begin{pmatrix} A & AC_R \\ C_C^T A & C_C^T A C_R \end{pmatrix}; B = \begin{pmatrix} B & BC_R \\ C_C^T B & C_C^T B C_R \end{pmatrix} \tag{2}$$

When these two matrices are (partly) multiplied, the resulting matrix is given in Equation (3):

$$\begin{pmatrix} A \\ C_C^T & A \end{pmatrix} \begin{pmatrix} B & BC_R \end{pmatrix} = \begin{pmatrix} AB & ABC_R \\ C_C^T AB & C_C^T ABC_R \end{pmatrix} \tag{3}$$

This result includes the result of the multiplication. This operation is depicted by Figure 15.

Figure 15. Fault tolerant matrix-matrix multiplication with checkpoint matrices

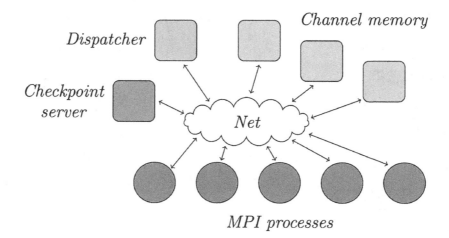

In a similar way Plank, Kim, and Dongarra (1995) gives algorithms to store the necessary data to be able to restore failed processes in QR, LU and Cholesky factorization and an iterative equation solved (Preconditioned Conjugate Gradient). These operations work by *step*, and for each step: on each step, part of the matrix can be saved for checkpoint.

EXAMPLE: AN MPI-3-BASED, FAULT-TOLERANT QR FACTORIZATION

Communication-avoiding algorithms were introduced in Demmel, Grigori, Hoemmen, and Langou (2008). The idea is to minimize the number of inter-process communications, should it involve additional computations. These algorithms perform well on current architectures, ranging from multicore architectures (Donfack, Grigori & Gupta, 2010) to aggregations of clusters (Agullo, Coti, Dongarra, Herault & Langou, 2010), because of the speed difference between computations and data movements.

As seen in the previous sections, tolerating failures requires some form of *redundancy*, such as checkpoints or checksums stored in additional processes (Bosilca, Delmas, Dongarra & Langou, 2009).

In this section, we propose to exploit the redundant computations made by communication-avoiding algorithms for fault-tolerance purpose. In this section, we illustrate this idea with a communication-avoiding algorithm for tall and skinny matrices (TSQR). This algorithm can be used to compute the QR factorization of matrices with a lot of rows and few columns, or as a panel factorization for QR factorization (Hadri, Ltaief, Agullo & Dongarra, 2009; Coti, 2015).

Computing the R with TSQR

The TSQR relies on successive steps that consist of local QR factorizations, involving *no inter-process communications*, and one inter-process communication. Initially, the matrix is decomposed in submatrices, each process holding one submatrix. On the first step, each process performs a QR factorization on its local submatrix. Then odd-numbered processes send the resulting $\tilde{R}$ to the previous even-numbered process: rank 1 sends to rank 0, rank 3 sends to rank 2, and so on and so forth. The algorithm itself is given by Algorithm 1.

Even-numbered processes concatenate the two $\tilde{R}$ matrices by creating a new matrix whose upper half is the $\tilde{R}$ it has computed and whose bottom half is the $\tilde{R}$ it has received. Then the odd-numbered process is done with its participation to the computation of the *R*. If the *Q* matrix is computed, it will work again when the moment comes, after the computation of the *R* is done.

Even-numbered processes perform a local QR factorization of the resulting matrix, and produce another $\tilde{R}$. A similar communication and concatenation step is performed between processes of rank $r \pm 2^{step}$, if denotes the rank of each process. An illustration of this communication, recombination, and local computation process on four processes is depicted by Figure 16.

At each step, half of the participating processes send their $\tilde{R}$ and are done. The other half receive an $\tilde{R}$, concatenate it with their own $\tilde{R}$ and perform a local QR factorization. This communication-computation progression forms a binary reduction tree (Langou, 2010),

We can see on this example that once it has sent its $\tilde{R}$, each process becomes idle. Eventually, process 0 is the only working process that remains. Half of the processes are idle after the first step, one quarter are idle after the second step, and so on until only one process is working at the end.

Algorithm 1. TSQR

```
1.  Data: Submatrix A
2.  Q, R = QR(A);
3.  step = 0 ;
4.  while (! done()) do {
5.      if (isSender(step)) then {
6.          /* I am a sender */
7.          b = myBuddy(step) ;
8.          send(R, b) ;
9.          return;
10.     } else {
11.         /* I am a receiver */
12.         b = myBuddy(step) ;
13.         recv(R', b) ;
14.         A = concatenate(R, R');
15.         Q, R = QR(A);
16.         step++ ;
17.     }
18. }
19. /* The root of the tree reaches this point and owns the final R
20. */
21. return R;
```

Figure 16. Computing the R of a matrix using a TSQR factorization on 4 processes

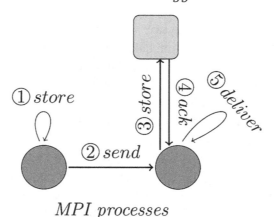

Redundant TSQR

We have seen in section "Computing the R with TSQR" that:

1. Only one process eventually gets the resulting $\tilde{R}$, and
2. At each step, half of the working processes get idle.

The idea behind *Redundant TSQR* is to use these spare processes to produce copies of the intermediate $\tilde{R}$ factors, in order to tolerate process failures during the intermediate steps.

Semantics

With *Redundant TSQR*, at the end of the computation, all the processes get the final R matrix. If some processes crash during the computation but enough processes survive (see section "Redundant TSQR", subsection "Robustness"), the surviving processes have the final R factor.

Algorithm

The basic idea is that when two processes communicate with each other, instead of having one sender and one receiver that assembles the two $\tilde{R}$ matrices, the processes *exchange* their matrices. Both of them assemble the two matrices and both of them proceed with the local QR factorization. This algorithm is given by Algorithm 2.

Algorithm 2. Redundant TSQR

```
1. Data: Submatrix A
2. Q, R = QR(A);
3. step = 0 ;
4. while(! done()) do {
5.     b = myBuddy(step) ;
6.     f = sendrecv(R, R', b) ;
7.     if (FAIL == f) then {
8.         return;
9.     }
10.     A = concatenate(R, R');
11.     Q, R = QR(A);
12.     step++ ;
13. }
14. /* All the surviving processes reach this point and own the final R
15. */
16. return R
```

Figure 17. Computing the R of a matrix using a TSQR factorization on 4 processes with redundant factors

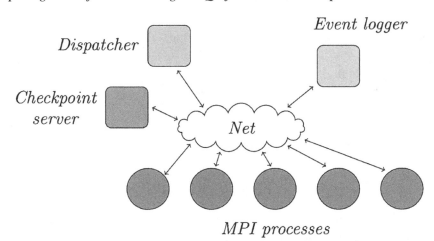

This algorithm is represented on four processes in Figure 17. Plain lines represent the regular TSQR pattern. During the first communication stage, the redundancies are represented by dashed lines: P_1 and P_3 exchange data with P_0 and P_2 respectively, and therefore obtain the same intermediate matrices. Then same data exchange is performed during the following step, resulting in a first level of redundancy (obtained from the $P_0 \leftrightarrow P_2$ exchange), represented by loosely dashed lines, and a secondary level of redundancy (obtained from the $P_1 \leftrightarrow P_3$ exchange), represented by dashed lines.

Robustness

We can see that at each step, the data exchange creates one extra copy of each intermediate matrix. As a consequence, the redundancy rate doubles at each step of the algorithm. Therefore, if s denotes the step number, the number of existing copies in the system is 2^s. Hence, this algorithm can tolerate 2^s-1 process failures.

We can see that the number of failures that this algorithm can tolerate increases as the computation progresses. This fact is a direct consequence from the fact that the number of redundant copies of the data is multiplied by 2 at each step. For instance, the computation can proceed if no more than 1 process have failed by the end of step 1, no more than 3 processes have failed by the end of step 2, etc. In the meantime, the number of failures in the system increase with time: the longer a computation lasts, the more processes will fail (Reed, Lu, & Mendes, 2006). Therefore, the robustness of this algorithm increases with time, which is consistent with the need for robustness.

Behavior upon Failures

When a process fails, the other processes proceed with the execution. Processes that require data from the failed process end their execution, and those that require data from ended processes end theirs as well (see line 7 of Algorithm 2)

Figure 18. Redundant TSQR on 4 processes with one process failure

P_{00}	P_{01}	P_{02}	P_{03}
P_{10}	P_{11}	P_{12}	P_{13}
P_{20}	P_{21}	P_{22}	P_{23}
P_{30}	P_{31}	P_{32}	P_{33}

For instance, Figure 18 represents the execution of Redundant TSQR on four processes. Process P_2 crashes at the end of the first step. The data it contained is also held by process P_3, therefore the execution can proceed. However, process P_0 needs data prom the failed process at the following step. Therefore, process P_0 ends its execution. At the end of the computation, the final result R has been computed by processes P_1 and P_3 and therefore, the final result is available in spite of the failure.

Replace TSQR

Semantics

The semantics of *Replace TSQR* is similar to the one with *Redundant TSQR*: at the end of the computation, all the processes get the final R matrix. If some processes crash during the computation but enough processes survive (see section "Replace TSQR", subsection "Robustness"), the surviving processes have the final R factor.

Algorithm

The fault-free execution of the *Replace TSQR* algorithm is exactly the same as with *Redundant TSQR* (see section "Redundant TSQR", subsection "Algorithm"). The data held by processes along the reduction tree of the initial TSQR algorithm is replicated on spare processes that would normally stop their execution.

The difference comes when a failure occurs. In this case, the process that needs to communicate with another process gets an error when it tries to communicate with it. Then, it finds a *replica* of the process it is trying to communicate with (line 8 of Algorithm 3) and exchanges its matrix with it. If no replica can be found alive, it means that too many processes have failed and no extra copy of this submatrix exists. Then the process exits. The algorithm is described by Algorithm 3.

Algorithm 3. Replace TSQR

```
1.  Data: Submatrix A
2.  Q, R = QR(A);
3.  step = 0;
4.  while (! done()) do {
5.      b = myBuddy(step) ;
6.      f = sendrecv(R, R', b) ;
7.      while(FAIL == f) { do
8.          b = findReplica(b) ;
9.          if(None == b) { then
10.             return;
11.         }
12.         f = sendrecv(R, R', b) ;
13.         A = concatenate(R, R');
14.         Q, R = QR(A);
15.     step++ ;
16. }
17. /* All the surviving processes reach this point and own the final R
18. */
19. return R;
```

Robustness

We have seen in subsection "Algorithm" that this algorithm can keep progressing as long as there exists at least one copy of each submatrix. We have seen this in section "Redundant TSQR", subsection "Robustness", that at each step s, the number of existing copies in the system is 2^s. Hence, this algorithm can tolerate 2^s-1 process failures, just like the *Redundant TSQR* algorithm.

The difference between the *Redundant TSQR* and the *Replace TSQR* is that with the former, the processes that need to communicate with a failed process exit, whereas with the latter, they try to find a replica. Therefore, if the root of the tree does not die, it holds the final result R at the end of the computation.

Behavior upon Failures

If a process fails, the processes that try to communicate with it fail to do so and try to find a replica to communicate with.

For instance, Figure 19 represents the execution of Redundant TSQR on four processes. Process P_2 crashes at the end of the first step. The data it contained is also held by process P_3, therefore the execution can proceed. However, process P_0 needs data from the failed process at the following step. As a consequence, P_0 fails to communicate with P_2 and finds out that P_3 holds the same data as P_2. Then P_0 exchanges data with P_3.

Figure 19. Replace TSQR on 4 processes with one process failure

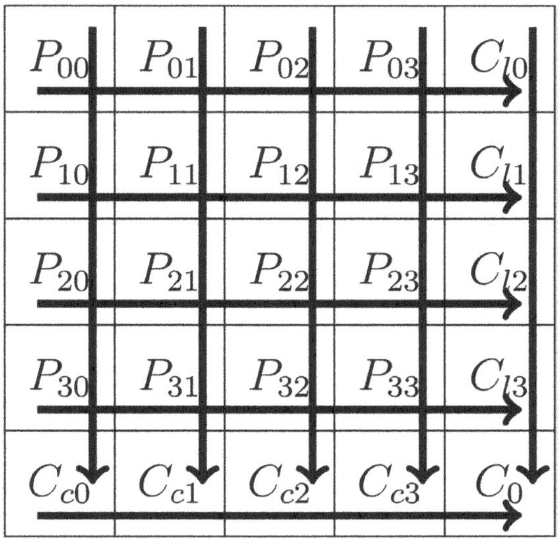

Self-Healing TSQR

The previous algorithms described here, Redundant TSQR and Replace TSQR, proceed with the execution without the dead processes. Here we are describing an algorithm that replaces the dead process with a new one.

Semantics

With *Self-Healing TSQR*, at the end of the computation, all the processes get the final R matrix. If some processes crash during the computation but enough processes survive at each step (see further subsection "Robustness"), the final number of processes is the same as the initial number and all the processes have the final R factor.

Algorithm

This algorithm follows the same basic idea as *Redundant TSQR* (see section "Redundant TSQR") in a sense that at each step of the computation, all the processes send or receive their $\tilde{R}$ matrices and compute the R of the resulting matrix. As a consequence, the data required by the computation (the inter-

Algorithm 4. Self-healing TSQR: initialization

```
1. Data: Submatrix A
2. step = 0 ;
3. R = shtsqr(A, step) ;
4. return R;
```

Algorithm 5. Self-healing TSQR: process restart

```
1.  /* Gets my data from a process that holds the same as me. */
2.  t = mytwin() ;
3.  R, step = recv(t) ;
4.  /* Proceed with the computation
5.  R = shtsqr(R, step) ;
6.  * At the end of the computation, this process holds the final R.*/
7.  return R;
```

Algorithm 6. Self-healing TSQR: computation

```
1.  Function shtsqr(A, step):
2.      Q, R = QR(A);
3.      while(! done()) { do
4.          b = myBuddy(step) ;
5.          f = sendrecv(R, R', b) ;
6.          if(FAIL == f) { then
7.            spawnNew(b) ;
8.          }
9.          A = concatenate(R, R');
10.         Q, R = QR(A);
11.           step++ ;
12.     }
13.     /* All the processes reach this point and own the final R
14.     */
15.     return R;
```

mediate submatrices) are *replicated*. This part is described by Algorithm 4 with the initialization described by Algorithm 5.

In this algorithm, the failed processes are replaced by newly spawned ones. We have seen that the data contained by the failed process has been replicated by the redundant computations. Consequently, a failed process can be recovered completely and a newly spawned process can replace it (see Algorithm 6).

The fault-free execution of this algorithm is similar with the execution represented by Figure 17.

Robustness

We have seen in section "Redundant TSQR" that at each step s, the data necessary for each process from the original algorithm is replicated 2^s times on other processes. As a consequence, this algorithm can tolerate 2^s-1 process failures *at each step*.

Similarly, with *Redundant TSQR*, the robustness of the algorithm increases as the need for robustness increases (see section "Redundant TSQR", subsection "Robustness"). The big difference with Redundant TSQR in terms of robustness is that Self-Healing TSQR replaces the failed processes. Therefore, this

Figure 20. Self-healing TSQR on 4 processes with one process failure

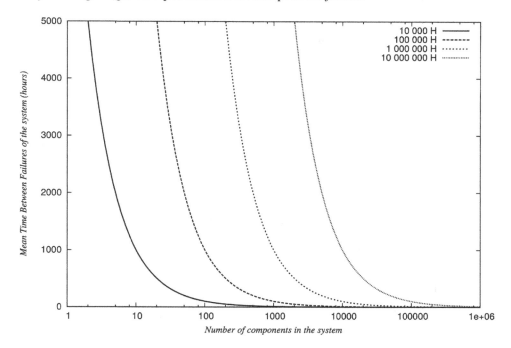

redundancy rate gives the number of failed processes that can be accepted *at each step*. For instance, 1 process can fail at step 1; it will be respawned and 3 additional processes can fail at step 2. As a consequence, the total number of failures this algorithm can tolerate is $\sum_{k=1}^{\log_2(p)} \left(2^k - 1\right)$. Besides, at each step s it can tolerate 2^s-1 process failures.

Behavior upon Failures

When a process fails, the process that was supposed to communicate with it detects the failure and spawns a new process. The new process obtains the redundant data from one of the processes that hold the same data as the failed process. Then the computation continues normally. We can see this mechanism on an example with 4 processes in Figure 20.

CONCLUSION

This chapter presented an overview of fault tolerance techniques for distributed systems. It demonstrated why tolerating failures is an important question in large-scale systems, and why it is not a trivial issue. The chapter described both automatic and non-automatic, application-based approaches. Automatic approaches discussed here are replication and rollback recovery. The details of both coordinated and non-coordinated checkpointing algorithms for rollback recovery are also provided with some examples of supporting architectures to implement them. Non-automatic approaches presented here include diskless checkpointing and algorithm-based fault tolerance. Last, the chapter presented an example of algorithm-based fault tolerant algorithm with the computing of the R factor of a QR factorization. Three fault-tolerant algorithms are presented, and for each one of them we presented the semantics of the fault tolerance, robustness and behavior (recovery) upon failures.

REFERENCES

Aguilera, M. K., Chen, W., & Toueg, S. (1997). Heartbeat: A timeout-free failure detector for quiescent reliable communication. In Distributed Algorithms (pp. 126-140). Springer Berlin Heidelberg.

Agullo, E., Coti, C., Dongarra, J., Herault, T., & Langou, J. (2010, April). QR factorization of tall and skinny matrices in a grid computing environment.*Proceedings of the IEEE International Symposium on Parallel & Distributed Processing (IPDPS)*,(pp. 1-11). IEEE. doi:10.1109/IPDPS.2010.5470475

Alvisi, L., & Marzullo, K. (1995, May). Message logging: Pessimistic, optimistic, and causal.*Proceedings of the 15th International Conference on Distributed Computing Systems* (pp. 229-236). IEEE. doi:10.1109/ICDCS.1995.500024

Alvisi, L., Rao, S., Husain, S. A., De Mel, A., & Elnozahy, E. (1999, June). An analysis of communication-induced checkpointing.*Proceedings of the Twenty-Ninth Annual International Symposium on Fault-Tolerant Computing, Digest of Papers*. (pp. 242-249). IEEE. doi:10.1109/FTCS.1999.781058

Angskun, T., Bosilca, G., & Dongarra, J. (2007). Binomial graph: A scalable and fault-tolerant logical network topology. In *Parallel and Distributed Processing and Applications* (pp. 471–482). Springer Berlin Heidelberg. doi:10.1007/978-3-540-74742-0_43

Angskun, T., Fagg, G., Bosilca, G., Pješivac-Grbović, J., & Dongarra, J. (2010). Self-healing network for scalable fault-tolerant runtime environments. *Future Generation Computer Systems, 26*(3), 479–485. doi:10.1016/j.future.2009.04.001

Bosilca, G., Bouteiller, A., Cappello, F., Djilali, S., Fedak, G., Germain, C., Selikhov, A. (2002, November). MPICH-V: Toward a scalable fault tolerant MPI for volatile nodes. *Proceedings of Supercomputing, ACM/IEEE 2002 Conference* (pp. 29-29). IEEE.

Bosilca, G., Coti, C., Herault, T., Lemarinier, P., & Dongarra, J. (2009). *Constructing Resilant Communication Infrastructure for Runtime Environments* (pp. 441–451). PARCO.

Bosilca, G., Delmas, R., Dongarra, J., & Langou, J. (2009). Algorithm-based fault tolerance applied to high performance computing. *Journal of Parallel and Distributed Computing, 69*(4), 410–416. doi:10.1016/j.jpdc.2008.12.002

Bouteiller, A., Cappello, F., Herault, T., Krawezik, G., Lemarinier, P., & Magniette, F. (2003, November). MPICH-V2: a fault tolerant MPI for volatile nodes based on pessimistic sender based message logging.*Proceedings of the 2003 ACM/IEEE conference on Supercomputing* (p. 25). ACM. doi:10.1145/1048935.1050176

Bouteiller, A., Collin, B., Herault, T., Lemarinier, P., & Cappello, F. (2005, April). Impact of event logger on causal message logging protocols for fault tolerant mpi.*Proceedings of the 19th IEEE International Conference on Parallel and Distributed Processing Symposium* (pp. 97-97). IEEE. doi:10.1109/IPDPS.2005.249

Bouteiller, A., Herault, T., Krawezik, G., Lemarinier, P., & Cappello, F. (2006). MPICH-V project: A multiprotocol automatic fault-tolerant MPI. *International Journal of High Performance Computing Applications*, *20*(3), 319–333. doi:10.1177/1094342006067469

Bouteiller, A., Lemarinier, P., Krawezik, G., & Cappello, K. (2003, December). Coordinated checkpoint versus message log for fault tolerant MPI.*Proceedings of the 2003 IEEE International Conference on Cluster Computing* (pp. 242-250). IEEE. doi:10.1109/CLUSTR.2003.1253321

Buntinas, D., Coti, C., Herault, T., Lemarinier, P., Pilard, L., Rezmerita, A., & Cappello, F. et al. (2008). Blocking vs. non-blocking coordinated checkpointing for large-scale fault tolerant MPI protocols. *Future Generation Computer Systems*, *24*(1), 73–84. doi:10.1016/j.future.2007.02.002

Butler, R., Gropp, W., & Lusk, E. (2001). Components and interfaces of a process management system for parallel programs. *Parallel Computing*, *27*(11), 1417–1429. doi:10.1016/S0167-8191(01)00097-7

Chandy, K. M., & Lamport, L. (1985). Distributed snapshots: Determining global states of distributed systems. *ACM Transactions on Computer Systems*, *3*(1), 63–75. doi:10.1145/214451.214456

Coti, C. (2015). Exploiting Redundant Computation in Communication-Avoiding Algorithms for Algorithm-Based Fault Tolerance. *arXiv preprint arXiv:1511.00212*.

Coti, C., Herault, T., Lemarinier, P., Pilard, L., Rezmerita, A., Rodriguez, E., & Cappello, F. (2006, November). Blocking vs. non-blocking coordinated checkpointing for large-scale fault tolerant MPI.*Proceedings of the 2006 ACM/IEEE conference on Supercomputing* (p. 127). ACM. doi:10.1145/1188455.1188587

Demmel, J., Grigori, L., Hoemmen, M., & Langou, J. (2008). Communication-avoiding parallel and sequential QR factorizations. *CoRR abs/0806.2159*.

Donfack, S., Grigori, L., & Gupta, A. K. (2010, April). Adapting communication-avoiding LU and QR factorizations to multicore architectures.*Proceedings of the International Symposium on Parallel & Distributed Processing (IPDPS)* (pp. 1-10). IEEE. doi:10.1109/IPDPS.2010.5470348

Elnozahy, E. N., Alvisi, L., Wang, Y. M., & Johnson, D. B. (1996). A Survey of Rollback-Recovery Protocols in Message-Passing Systems (Technical Report CMU-CS-96-181). Carnegie Mellon Univ.

Elnozahy, E. N., Alvisi, L., Wang, Y. M., & Johnson, D. B. (2002). A survey of rollback-recovery protocols in message-passing systems. *ACM Computing Surveys*, *34*(3), 375–408. doi:10.1145/568522.568525

Fagg, G. E., & Dongarra, J. J. (2000). FT-MPI: Fault tolerant MPI, supporting dynamic applications in a dynamic world. In Recent advances in parallel virtual machine and message passing interface (pp. 346-353). Springer Berlin Heidelberg.

Fagg, G. E., Gabriel, E., Bosilca, G., Angskun, T., Chen, Z., Pjesivac-Grbovic, J., & Dongarra, J. J. et al. (2004, June). Extending the MPI specification for process fault tolerance on high performance computing systems.*Proceedings of the International Supercomputer Conference (ICS)* (pp. 97-104).

Fagg, G. E., Gabriel, E., Chen, Z., Angskun, T., Bosilca, G., Pjesivac-Grbovic, J., & Dongarra, J. J. (2005). Process fault tolerance: Semantics, design and applications for high performance computing. *International Journal of High Performance Computing Applications, 19*(4), 465–477. doi:10.1177/1094342005056137

Ford, D., Labelle, F., Popovici, F. I., Stokely, M., Truong, V. A., Barroso, L., & Quinlan, S. et al. (2010, October). *Availability in Globally Distributed Storage Systems* (pp. 61–74). OSDI.

Guerraoui, R., & Schiper, A. (1997). Software-based replication for fault tolerance. *Computer, 30*(4), 68–74. doi:10.1109/2.585156

Hadri, B., Ltaief, H., Agullo, E., & Dongarra, J. (2009, September). Tall and Skinny QR Matrix Factorization Using Tile Algorithms on Multicore Architectures. *LAPACK Working Note, 222*, ICL.

Hélary, J. M., Mostéfaoui, A., & Raynal, M. (1997). *Virtual precedence in asynchronous systems: Concept and applications*. Springer Berlin Heidelberg.

Hélary, J. M., Mostefaoui, A., & Raynal, M. (1999). Communication-induced determination of consistent snapshots. *IEEE Transactions on Parallel and Distributed Systems, 10*(9), 865–877. doi:10.1109/71.798312

Hursey, J., Mattox, T. I., & Lumsdaine, A. (2009, June). Interconnect agnostic checkpoint/restart in Open MPI. *Proceedings of the 18th ACM international symposium on High performance distributed computing* (pp. 49-58). ACM. doi:10.1145/1551609.1551619

Klecka, J. S., Bruckert, W. F., & Jardine, R. L. (2002). *U.S. Patent No. 6,393,582*. Washington, DC: U.S. Patent and Trademark Office.

Lamport, L. (1978). Time, clocks, and the ordering of events in a distributed system. *Communications of the ACM, 21*(7), 558–565. doi:10.1145/359545.359563

Langou, J. (2010). Computing the R of the QR factorization of tall and skinny matrices using MPI_Reduce. *arXiv preprint arXiv:1002.4250*.

Lemarinier, P., Bouteiller, A., Herault, T., Krawezik, G., & Cappello, F. (2004, September). Improved message logging versus improved coordinated checkpointing for fault tolerant MPI. *Proceedings of the 2004 IEEE International Conference on Cluster Computing*, (pp. 115-124). IEEE. doi:10.1109/CLUSTR.2004.1392609

Litzkow, M., Tannenbaum, T., Basney, J., & Livny, M. (1997). *Checkpoint and migration of UNIX processes in the Condor distributed processing system*. Computer Sciences Department, University of Wisconsin.

Lyons, R. E., & Vanderkulk, W. (1962). The use of triple-modular redundancy to improve computer reliability. *IBM Journal of Research and Development, 6*(2), 200–209. doi:10.1147/rd.62.0200

Message Passing Interface Forum (2004). MPI: A message-passing interface standard *(Technical Report UT-CS-94-230)*. Department of Computer Science, University of Tennessee.

Plank, J. S., Beck, M., Kingsley, G., & Li, K. (1995, January). Libckpt: transparent checkpointing under Unix. *Proceedings of the USENIX 1995 Technical Conference Proceedings* (pp. 18-18). USENIX Association.

Plank, J. S., Kim, Y., & Dongarra, J. J. (1995, June). Algorithm-based diskless checkpointing for fault tolerant matrix operations. In *Proceedings of the Twenty-Fifth International Symposium on Fault-Tolerant Computing, (FTCS-25). Digest of Papers.*,(pp. 351-360). IEEE. doi:10.1109/FTCS.1995.466964

Plank, J. S., Li, K., & Puening, M. (1998). Diskless checkpointing. *IEEE Transactions on Parallel and Distributed Systems*, 9(10), 972–986. doi:10.1109/71.730527

Reed, D. A., Lu, C.-D., & Mendes, C. L. (2006). Reliability challenges in large systems. *Future Generation Computer Systems*, 22(3), 293–302. doi:10.1016/j.future.2004.11.015

Roman, E., Duell, J., & Hargrove, P. (2003). *The design and implementation of Berkeley Lab's Linux Checkpoint/Restart. Technical Report publication LBNL-54941.* Berkeley Lab.

Sankaran, S., Squyres, J. M., Barrett, B., Sahay, V., Lumsdaine, A., Duell, J., & Roman, E. et al. (2005). The LAM/MPI checkpoint/restart framework: System-initiated checkpointing. *International Journal of High Performance Computing Applications*, 19(4), 479–493. doi:10.1177/1094342005056139

Walraed-Sullivan, M., Vahdat, A., & Marzullo, K. (2013, December). Aspen trees: balancing data center fault tolerance, scalability and cost.*Proceedings of the ninth ACM conference on Emerging networking experiments and technologies* (pp. 85-96). ACM. doi:10.1145/2535372.2535383

Zheng, G., Shi, L., & Kalé, L. V. (2004, September). FTC-Charm++: an in-memory checkpoint-based fault tolerant runtime for Charm++ and MPI.*Proceedings of the 2004 IEEE International Conference on Cluster Computing* (pp. 93-103). IEEE. doi:10.1109/CLUSTR.2004.1392606

KEY TERMS AND DEFINITIONS

Checkpoint: Snapshot and checkpoint are often used as synonyms. A checkpoint is often seen as the point of the execution of a process when its state is stored in a snapshot.

Distributed System: A distributed system is a set of autonomous resources that cooperate together to perform a given task in a coherent way.

Error, Failure, Fault: An *error* is a part of a system which is wrong; a *failure* is the consequence of an error and it refers to the inability to perform the required task; a *fault* is an incorrect behavior.

Fault Tolerance: A system that can resume its execution or proceed with it in spite of faults is said to be *fault-tolerant.*

Replication: A (software or hardware) component of a system is *replicated* when several instances of it coexist. These instances are called *replica.*

Robustness: When a system is able to keep working in spite of failures, it is said to be robust. In general, robustness is considered to characterize this ability to keep working without any change or adaptation from the initial configuration of the system.

Self-Healing: A system that can not only survive failures, but also modify itself to get back to a state it could have reached if this failure had not happened, is said to be *self-healing.*

Snapshot: A snapshot is an image of a process. The execution of this process can be resumed from this snapshot; therefore, the snapshot must contain enough information to represent the state of this process. A snapshot can contain the state of a single process or the state of a whole distributed system: in this case, it can be called a *distributed snapshot*.

ENDNOTE

[1]   http://www.top500.org/

Chapter 10
A Theoretic Representation of the Effects of Targeted Failures in HPC Systems

A. Don Clark
West Virginia University, USA

ABSTRACT

High performance computing (HPC) systems are becoming the norm for daily use and care must be made to ensure that these systems are resilient. Recent contributions on resiliency have been from quantitative and qualitative perspectives where general system failures are considered. However, there are limited contributions dealing with the specific classes of failures that are directly related to cyber-attacks. In this chapter, the author uses the concepts of transition processes and limiting distributions to perform a generic theoretical investigation of the effects of targeted failures by relating the actions of the cyber-enemy (CE) to different risk levels in an HPC system. Special cases of constant attack strategies are considered where exact solutions are obtained. Additionally, a stopped process is introduced to model the effects of system termination. The results of this representation can be directly applied throughout the HPC community for monitoring and mitigating cyber-attacks.

INTRODUCTION

High performance computing (HPC) systems use supercomputers and computer clusters to perform complex processing and computational applications. In the scientific domain, HPC systems have been used to solve sophisticated computational problems in technical areas such as meteorology, fluid dynamics, and big data analytics. For military operations, these systems are currently being used for command, control, communications, computers, intelligence, surveillance, and reconnaissance (C4ISR). Because data parallelism has enhanced the performance of HPC systems by several orders of magnitude (Nyland, Prins, Goldberg, & Mills, 2000; Ravichandran, Pantel, & Hovy, 2004), HPC systems will interest business of all sizes due to the increasing demands of processing power and speed. Although HPC systems have demonstrated computational prowess, in terms of solving complex problems efficiently, the reliability

DOI: 10.4018/978-1-5225-0287-6.ch010

of these systems is expected to decrease as more and more systems are moving towards the design of petascale and exascale class systems (Shroeder & Gibson, 2007; Chen & Dongarra, 2009). Furthermore, researchers have noted that when undesirable failure rates occur, troubleshooting HPC systems is difficult because they are massive in both component count and complexity (Robinson & Stearly, 2011). These factors also make HPC systems vulnerable to cyber-attacks. Therefore, care must be made to ensure that these systems are resilient.

In terms of HPC systems, resilience is defined as the ability of a system to continue operation despite the presence of faults associated with it (DeBardeleben *et al.*, 2009). With this in mind, researchers have focused their attention on developing quantitative and qualitative methods for reliability and resilience detection and analysis. Work in these areas include system failures, application failures, and fault tolerance (Daly, Pritchett, & Michalak, 2008; Jones, Daly, & DeBarteleben, 2008; Raicu, Foster, & Zhao, 2008), where the primary goal is to continue running within some performance threshold when one or more system failures occur. Although research in this area help to provide various classes of processes to handle certain general families of failures, these failures do not directly consider *targeted failures* – when deliberate attacks affect overall system performance. In these cases, continuing to run the system when failures occur could be detrimental because the cyber-enemy (CE) could learn about the system and submit subsequent attacks that manipulate and cause serious damage resulting in system shut-down. Furthermore, these attacks are not necessarily related to the system failure rate, which has an inverse relationship to the mean time between failures. In other words, attacks can happen when either the failure rate is both low, representing a more reliable system, or when the failure rate has increased. Additionally, flexibility, in stopping the system, needs to be accounted for to consider times when technicians and engineers stop the system when anomalies occur. Therefore, care must be made to account for the effects of targeted failures by considering when actions of the cyber-enemy (CE) while considering the failure rate of the system.

The author addresses these concerns by conducting a theoretical investigation of the effects of targeted failures in HPC systems by modeling the relationship between the failure risk levels and the actions of the cyber-enemy (CE). From the general abstract formulation, cases of continuous and constant-level cyber-attacks are considered, where closed-form dynamical solutions are obtained. Next, for the case of two-level constant attacks, extreme conditions related to the system failure rate are considered that include the most reliable and least reliable systems. Then, a theoretic formulation is proposed that models the effects of system termination in terms of a stopped process. The investigations posed in this chapter provide scientists, engineers, and technicians a universal understanding of the overall dynamics to design effective strategies for mitigation. Furthermore, the mathematical model posed provides technicians of HPC systems, such as systems administrators (SAs), the macro understanding prior to troubleshooting these systems on a micro, or component, level.

This chapter is organized in the following manner. The next section provides a summary of the background and literature review. This is followed by a section that describes the theoretical description of the model, which is based on the work of Faissol and Gallagher (Faissol & Gallagher, 2014). It is here where dynamical representations are posed for one and two-level constant attack strategies. Next, the description of system termination is also proposed in the third section. And, lastly, the conclusions along with the future directions of this work are presented in the final two sections.

Related Work

Understanding the effects of resilience in distributed systems first began with Von Neumann who analytically studied physical redundancy usage to construct highly reliable systems (Von Neumann, 1956). In his model, Neumann noted that a redundancy of 20,000 was needed in order to get a reliable system where the mean time between failures (MTBF) would equal 100 years. Three decades later, Gray revolutionized this concept by first noticing that Tandem systems have migrated to modular construction, which was not considered in Von Neumann's model (Gray, 1986). Adding this factor reduced the redundancy factor from 20,000 to 2 when this was considered. From his statistical analysis, Gray noted that failure causes can be categorized into software-related (50%), hardware-related (30%), environment-related (5%), and operator-related (10-15%). Gray later revisited his analysis on later versions of Tandem systems (Gray, 1990) and noted that faults are predominately software-related (60%). His conclusion here was that, because hardware has increasingly become more reliable, software-related faults are more dominant. Gray's analysis spawned researchers to understand various causes of failures in different systems such as telephone networks (Kuhn, 1997; Enriquez, Brown, & Patterson, 2002), networks of workstations (Thakur & Iyer, 1996; Kalyanakrishnam, Kalbarczyk, & Iyer, 1999; Xu, Kalbarczyk, & Iyer, 1999), enterprise-class server environments (Sullivan & Chillarege, 1992; Lee & Iyer, 1995; Murphy & Gent; 1995), and network and internet systems (Mahajan, Wetherall, & Anderson, 2002; Oppenheimer, Ganapathi, & Patterson, 2003). In each of these cases, the conclusions drawn, regarding the primary cause of failures, depended on the data presented as well as types of systems analyzed. For example, the results in the works Kuhn (Kuhn, 1997) and Enriquez *et al.* (Enriquez *et al.*, 2002) agree that human behavior accounted for approximately 50% of failures when examining telephone network data. However, the works of Thakur and Iyer (Thakur & Iyer, 1996) and Kalyanakrishnam *et al.* (Kalyanakrishnam *et al.*, 1999) draw similar conclusions that, when looking at failures in workstation networks, most failures were software-related. These results conflicted with the work of Xu *et al.* (Xu *et al.*, 1999), who conducted a similar study where operators were allowed to note the failure causes. As a result, the authors found that planned maintenance as well as installation and configuration of software caused the largest number of outages whereas system software and planned maintenance caused the largest amount of total downtime.

Explorations on this topic have also been extended to understand the failures in large scale parallel systems. Motivated by the work of Sahoo *et al.*, who researched failures in large AIX clusters (Sahoo, Sivasubramaniam, Squillante, & Zhang, 2004), Liang *et al.* examined failures in IBM's BlueGene/L (BG/L) architecture where failure logs were analyzed over a period of 84 days (Liang *et al.*, 2005). The authors concluded that the majority of failures in this architecture are due to network, memory, and midplane switches. Later, Schroeder and Gibson conducted an extensive study by examining failure behavior in 22 HPC systems, including a total of 4,750 machines and over 24,000 processors (Schroeder & Gibson, 2005; Schroeder & Gibson, 2007). Here, the authors note the root causes of failures are due to hardware, software, network, environment, and human operators.

Investigating failures in distributed systems also evolved from solely understanding the primary causes of failures to further examining *how* and *why* failures happen. The works of Tang *et al.* studied these effects by researching error logs on a VAX cluster system and, using a semi-Markov failure model, showed the correlation of failure distributions between different machines (Tang, Iyer, & Subramani, 1990; Tang & Iyer, 1991). Tang's later work investigated the impact of correlated failures in a multi-computer environment (Tang & Iyer, 1992). Xu *et al.* studied error logs from a heterogeneous system of approximately 500 personal computer (PC) servers (Xu *et al.*, 1999). From that work, the authors showed that failures on a PC occur in bursts because rebooting systems do not completely absolve the problem. They also note indicators of error propagation across the network – linking the correlation between different node failures. With respect to the BG/L architecture, Liang *et al.* performed a three-step filtering algorithm followed by temporal filtering to categorize failure events while coalescing failure logs of similar errors from different locations (Liang *et al.*, 2005). After preprocessing the data, the authors observed that there is an inverse relationship between the number of failure records per time unit (i.e. *rate process*) and the time between failures (i.e. *increment process*). Schroeder and Gibson's data analysis (Schroeder & Gibson, 2005) showed that inter-arrival times of failures at individual nodes can be characterized by a gamma or Weibull distribution. They also showed that repair times can be characterized by a lognormal distribution. Their later work on petascale systems (Schroeder & Gibson, 2007) showed an inverse relationship between expected growth in failure rates and the mean time to interrupt (MTTI). The authors also characterized the relationship between the checkpoint overhead, MTTI, and the time between checkpoints.

Research into the effects of *targeted failures* in distributed systems has been mainly done in the context of malicious objects in computer networks. By drawing the analogies between disease spread and computer virus propagation, scientists have been working to adopt an equivalent epidemic models to describe virus attacks (Yuan & Chen, 2008). Particularly, recent investigative efforts have been made to examine the dominant effects of viruses and worms and the impact of antivirus measures (Data & Wang, 2005; Mishra & Jha, 2007). Motivated by the works of Kermack and McKendrick (1927, 1932, 1933), Newman *et al.* developed mathematical models to describe the effects of vaccination in email networks (Newman, Forrest, & Balthrop, 2002). Additional epidemic models, such as susceptible-infectious-susceptible (SIS) (Kim, Radhakrishnan, & Jang, 2006) and susceptible-exposed-infectious-recovered-susceptible (SEIRS) models (Mishra & Jha, 2010; Mishra & Prajapati, 2014), were produced to understand how malicious attacks spread in a computer network. Furthermore, models to describe the transmission of malicious objects depending on certain network parameters were also made with the focus being worm and infection dynamics (Chen & Jamil, 2006; Zou, Gong, & Towsley, 2003). Later, Mishra and Pandey modeled the propagation of worms in a computer network via a susceptible-exposed-infectious-susceptible with vaccination (SEIS – V) framework (Mishra & Pandey, 2013). Here, the authors derived an explicit equation for the reproduction number of the infected nodes while evaluation of an efficient virus software was performed. Extensions of the propagation modeling of worms has recently been extended to investigate the behavior propagation of different network topologies such as peer-to-peer (P2P) topologies (Chen, 2013; Chen, Zhang, & Wu, 2013), Facebook and email networks (Fan & Yeung, 2013), and mobile network topologies (Wang, 2013).

In the context of *targeted failures* in HPC systems, game theoretic approaches have been used. Motivated by the works of Moscibroda *et al.* (Moscibroda, Schmid, & Wattenhofer, 2006), and Koutsoupias and Papadimitriou (Koutsoupias & Papadimitriou, 2009), Faissol and Gallagher's approach explored this concept by modeling these types of failures as a simple two-player zero-sum discrete stochastic game (Faissol & Gallagher, 2014). Here, they numerically examined the impact of these types of failures via looking at the *price of anarchy* and *price of malice*, respectively. Here, the *price of anarchy (POM)* is defined as the impact of malicious users on the system whereas the *price of anarchy (POA)* is given as the impact of selfish users (Moscibroda *et al.*, 2006). From these definitions, the authors were able to characterize the system's ability of detection, the relative cost of attacks and repairs, the game length, and background system characteristics.

Figure 1. Abstraction of Faissol and Gallagher's arrangement that compares the payoff actions of the cyber-enemy (CE) $x\left(t\right)$ *to the associated risk levels* $x_1,\ldots,x_N$ *in a HPC system*

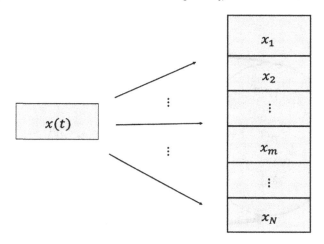

ANALYTICAL DEVELOPMENT

Faissol and Gallagher's theoretical investigation (Faissol & Gallagher, 2014), illustrated in Figure 1, can be viewed as a comparison between the payoff actions of the cyber enemy (CE) to a countable large number of enrolled risk levels of a HPC system. Therefore, this arrangement can be viewed as a Markovian process where each state has an associated risk level. The overall goal is to find the likelihood such that

$$W\left(x,t\right) = P\left\{x\left(t\right) = x\right\},\tag{1}$$

where *W(x,t)* is the probability density function, *x(t)* is the payoff action associated with the cyber-enemy (CE), and *x* is the resulting payoff action associated with the HPC risk level. The model formulation for *W(x,t)* is done by first assuming that for each risk level there exists a transition probability $p^m(x,t\mid\psi,s)$ such that

$$p^m\left(x,t\mid\psi,s\right) = P\{x\left(t\right) = x \in x_m \mid x\left(s\right) = \psi \in x_m\},\tag{2}$$

where $s < t$. Consequently, Equation (2) can be expressed as a Taylor series approximation with respect to the time delay $t - s > 0$ as

$$p^m\left(x,t\mid\psi,s\right) = \delta\left(x - \psi\right) + p_t^m\left(x,t\mid\psi,s\right)\left(t - s\right) + O\left(|t - s|\right),\tag{3}$$

where $p_t^m\left(x,t\mid\psi,s\right)$ is defined as

$$p_t^m\left(x,t\mid\psi,t\right) = \lim_{dt\to 0,dt>0}\left\{\left\{p^m\left(x,t + dt\mid\psi,t\right) - \delta\left(x - \psi\right)\right\}/dt\right\}\tag{4}$$

Figure 2. Illustration of the proposed Markovian process. The development of the mathematical transitions between risk levels in a HPC system takes into account the transition between the tempered distributions p^m and W^m, for each state x_m while considering the overall collection of states.

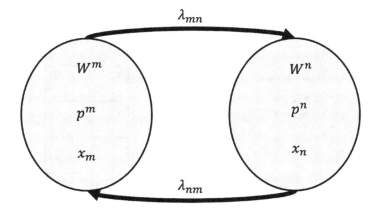

Next the inherent assumption is made that $p^m\left(x,t \mid \psi,s\right)$ and $p_t^m\left(x,s \mid \psi,s\right)$ are tempered distributions associated with each state. Hence, the changes in these distributions are described by defining the transition rate as follows

$$\lambda_{mn} = \lim_{dt \to 0}\left\{P\left\{x\left(t+dt\right) \in x_n \mid x\left(t\right) \in x_m\right\}\right\} / dt\,. \tag{5}$$

Next, $W^m\left(x,t\right)$ is introduced as the conditional probability density expressed as

$$W^m\left(x,t\right) = P\left\{x\left(t\right)=x \mid x \in x_m\right\}.. \tag{6}$$

Using the Chapman-Kolmogorov relationship (Cinlar, 2013), substituting Equation (3), and allowing $dt \to 0$ achieves the following expression for $W^m\left(x,t\right)$ (Desilles, 1998):

$$\frac{\partial W^m}{\partial t} = p_t^m\left(x,t \mid \rho,t\right),W^m\left(\rho,t\right)+\sum_{m \neq n}\left(\lambda_{mn}W^n - \lambda_{nm}W^m\right), \tag{7}$$

where the first term is defined as

$$p_t^m\left(x,t \mid \rho,t\right),W^m\left(\rho,t\right)=\int_{x_1}^{x_N}p_t^m(x,t \mid \rho,t)W^m\left(\rho,t\right)d\rho\,, \tag{8}$$

for all of the possible intermediate states within the risk level domain *L*. From the conditional probability function, defined by Equation (6), the joint probability for each state is given by

$$W^m\left(x,t\right)\mu_m\left(t\right)=P\left\{x\left(t\right)=x\cap x\in x_m\right\},\tag{9}$$

where $\mu_m\left(t\right)=P\left\{x=x_m\right\}$. The likelihood expression in (9) relates the actions of the CE $x\left(t\right)$ to an associated failure risk level x_m; however, it is imperative to consider all of the possible risk levels. This is done via the joint probability density function $W\left(x,t\right)$ given by

$$W\left(x,t\right)=\sum_m W^m\left(x,t\right)P\left\{x\in x_m\right\}=\sum_m W^m\left(x,t\right)\mu_m\left(t\right),\tag{10}$$

where μ_m satisfies the following system of ordinary differential equations (Van Kampen, 2007):

$$\frac{d\mu_m}{dt}=\sum_{m\neq n}\left(\lambda_{mn}\left(t\right)\mu_n\left(t\right)-\lambda_{nm}\left(t\right)\mu_m\left(t\right)\right).\tag{11}$$

Next, the supposition is made that approaching the different risk levels are equally likely and therefore $\mu_m=\mu_n=\mu$. Hence, from Equation (11), the Markov process reduces to a Poisson process where

$$\lambda_{mn}=\lambda_{nm}=\lambda\tag{12}$$

The model also builds on the assumption that the transition between risk levels depends on the payoff actions of the cyber-enemy (CE), which can be abstractly modeled via the differential equation

$$\frac{dx_m}{dt}=f_m\left(x,t\right),\tag{13}$$

where x_m is the payoff action associated with the particular risk level. Employing Equation (12), it can be noted that $p_t^m\left(x,s\mid\psi,s\right)$ can be expressed as

$$p_t^m\left(x,t\mid\psi,t\right)=-\delta\left(x-\psi\right)f_m\left(\psi,t\right).\tag{14}$$

Therefore, combining Equations (7), (12), and (14) achieves the following master equation:

$$\frac{\partial W^m}{\partial t}=-\nabla\cdot\left(f_m W^m\right)+\lambda\sum_{n\neq m}\left(W^n\left(x,t\right)-W^m\left(x,t\right)\right).\tag{15}$$

Equation (17) states that the probabilistic transition of targeted failure levels in a HPC system has both *intra* and *inter* dependence. What this means is that the probabilistic failure transitions within the targeted risk level is dependent on both the information within the state (i.e. risk level) as well as other states within the system. Furthermore, it is important to note that, in order for existence and uniqueness to hold, a sufficient condition is that the behavior be Lipschitz continuous within the determination of each state. Next, the assumption that the initial probability distribution is defined as

$$W(x,0) = N(\mu,\sigma), \tag{16}$$

with respect to the mean and variance.

Exploring the Case of Consistent Attacks

Faissol and Gallagher's work considered the case where the CE consistently achieves different failure risk levels by continuously attacking the system at a constant rate a. Here, the attack rate is assumed undetectable by the systems administrator (SA) and the cyber-enemy is continually causing threats to the system. For this case, the kinematic Equation (13) can be described as

$$\frac{dx_m}{dt} = a, \tag{17}$$

where $a > 0$ and m is representative of the designated risk level. Because in this case, the attacker does not change their strategy, $x_m = x$. Therefore, from the master Equation (15), the probabilistic transitions between levels can be expressed in terms of the advection equation

$$\frac{\partial W}{\partial t} + a\frac{\partial W}{\partial x} = 0. \tag{18}$$

Considering the initial condition, given by Equation (16), the following solution is achieved:

$$W(x,t) = W_0(x - at), \tag{19}$$

where $W_0 = W(x,0)$. This analytical result, which also agrees with the work in (Faisol & Gallagher, 2014), states that the transitions between failure risk levels directly depends on the attack rate that the CE chooses to infiltrate the system. Thus, until the SA is notified of a problem, the CE can continue to attack reaching increasingly vulnerable levels and doing more damage.

This case can also be modified for cases where the consistent attacks are varied such that

$$\frac{dx}{dt} = f(x,t), \tag{20}$$

where $f(x,t)$ is the consistent payoff action that determines all of the risk levels and f is multi-valued such that $f(x,t) = f(x_1,\ldots,x_k,t)$. Therefore, Equation (15) reduces to

$$\frac{\partial W}{\partial t} + \nabla \cdot \left(fW \right) = 0 \,. \tag{21}$$

Additionally, if f is single-valued, the following exact solution for $W\left(x,t\right)$ can be achieved:

$$W\left(x,t\right) = W\left(x_0,0\right) \cdot e^{-F\left(x,t\right)} \,, \tag{22}$$

where

$$F\left(x,t\right) = \int_0^t \frac{\partial f\left(x,\eta\right)}{\partial x} d\eta \tag{23}$$

which is computed from the characteristic equation described in Equation (20).

Exploring the Case of Constant Two-Level Attacks

Next, the investigation is extended to the case where the CE changes their attack strategy from one risk level to the next. Here, the case of two-leveled attacks is considered, which can be described via the following kinematic equations:

$$\frac{dx_m}{dt} = a$$

$$\frac{dx_n}{dt} = b \,, \tag{24}$$

where $b \neq a$ and $b > 0$. Hence, employing Equation (15) and taking the spatial Fourier transform of the result yields the following coupled system of equations:

$$\frac{d\hat{W}^m}{dt} = -j\omega a \hat{W}^m + \lambda\left(\hat{W}^n\left(\omega,t\right) - \hat{W}^m\left(\omega,t\right) \right)$$

$$\frac{d\hat{W}^n}{dt} = -j\omega b \hat{W}^n + \lambda\left(\hat{W}^m\left(\omega,t\right) - \hat{W}^n\left(\omega,t\right) \right), \tag{25}$$

where $\hat{W}^m$ and $\hat{W}^n$ represent the Fourier transform of the conditional probabilities as defined by Equation (6), which take into account the attackers ability to achieve risk levels m and n. The coupled system can be solved by making the following assumption:

$$\hat{W}^{m,n}\left(\omega,t\right) = A_{m,n}\left(\omega\right)e^{ct}, \tag{26}$$

where c represents the speed of the disturbance. For nontrivial solutions to exist, it is required that

$$c_{1,2} = -\frac{j\omega\left(a+b\right)}{2} - \lambda \pm \sqrt{\lambda^2 - \omega^2\left(\frac{b-a}{2}\right)^2}, , \tag{27}$$

where $j = \sqrt{-1}$. From Equation (27), the general solution for $\hat{W}\left(\omega,t\right)$ can be described as

$$\hat{W}\left(\omega,t\right) = A_1\left(\omega\right)\left[\frac{1+©}{2}\right]e^{c_1 t} + A_2\left(\omega\right)\left[\frac{1-©}{2}\right]e^{c_2 t}, \tag{28}$$

where Ω is defined as

$$\Omega = \frac{1}{\lambda}\left[\sqrt{\lambda^2 - \omega^2\left(\frac{a-b}{2}\right)^2} + \frac{j\omega\left(a-b\right)}{2}\right] \tag{29}$$

and the general constants can be determined by applying the appropriate initial conditions. Equation (28) indicates that the probabilistic disturbance of failure levels, caused by the CE, depends on three factors: the attack rates within each risk level, the rate of transmission between each risk level as well as the frequency. This relationship can also be seen by examining the eigenvalues in Equation (27).

Next, care is considered to investigate the initial behavioral dynamics where the general assumption is made that the conditional probabilities are not identically distributed such that $W^m\left(x,0\right) \neq W^n\left(x,0\right)$. Making the additional assumption that these conditional probabilities are also normally distributed achieves the following initial conditions:

$$\hat{W}\left(\omega,0\right) = \hat{W}_0\left(\omega\right) = N\left(\mu,\sigma\right),$$

$$\left.\frac{d\hat{W}}{dt}\right|_{t=0} = G\left(\omega\right) = \frac{-j\omega}{2}\left(aN\left(\mu_1,\sigma_1\right) + bN\left(\mu_2,\sigma_2\right)\right), \tag{30}$$

where $\mu \neq \mu_1 \neq \mu_2$ and $\sigma \neq \sigma_1 \neq \sigma_2$. Employing the initial conditions, given by Equation (30), yields the following solution for $\hat{W}\left(\omega,t\right)$:

$$\hat{W}\left(\omega,t\right) = e^{\eta t}\hat{H}\left(\omega,t\right), \tag{31}$$

where $\eta = -\lambda - j\omega\left(a+b\right)/2$,

Table 1. Description of parameters $A(\omega), B(\omega), \phi_1$ and ϕ_2

Parameter	Mathematical Description
ϕ_1	$\sqrt{\lambda^2 - \omega^2 \left(\dfrac{b-a}{2}\right)^2}$
ϕ_2	$\sqrt{\omega^2 \left(\dfrac{b-a}{2}\right)^2 - \lambda^2}$
$A(\omega)$	$\dfrac{\left(G(\omega) - c_1 \hat{W}_0(\omega)\right)}{\phi_1}$
$B(\omega)$	$\dfrac{\left(G(\omega) - c_1 \hat{W}_0(\omega)\right)}{\phi_2}$

$$\hat{H}(\omega,t) = \begin{cases} \hat{W}_0(\omega)e^{\phi_1 t} + A(\omega)\sinh(\phi_1 t), & \phi_1^2 > 0 \\ \hat{W}_0(\omega)e^{j\phi_2 t} + B(\omega)\sin(\phi_2 t), & \phi_1^2 < 0 \end{cases}, \tag{32}$$

and the parameters $A(\omega), B(\omega), \phi_1$, and ϕ_2 are described in Table 1. It is noted that the formulation of the solution, given by Equations (31) and (32), can be customized for simpler cases. For example, if the assumption is considered that the initial conditional probabilities are identically distributed such that $W^m(x,0) = W^n(x,0)$, the solution would take the form of $\hat{W}(\omega,t)$ with $G(\omega)$ given as

$$G(\omega) = \frac{-j\omega(a+b)}{2} N(\bar{\mu}, \bar{\sigma}), \tag{33}$$

where $\bar{\mu} = \mu_1 = \mu_2$ and $\bar{\sigma} = \sigma_1 = \sigma_2$.

The transition between failure risk levels in an HPC system is also determined by the predicted elapsed time between failure risk levels – otherwise known as the mean time between failures (MTBF). In this scenario, the MTBF is important because as the cyber-enemy moves within failure risk levels, there are time lapses between them. Thus, the transition rate λ is also known as the failure rate, which is mathematically described as (Wolstenholme, 1999)

$$\lambda = \frac{1}{MTTF}, \tag{34}$$

Table 2. An example of system mean time between failures (MTBF), in hours, for some large scale installations

Year	Cores	MTBF (Hours)	Failure Rate	System	Location
2002	8192	6.5	0.154	ASCI Q	LANL
2002	8192	40	0.025	ASCI White	LANL
2004	3016	9.7	0.103	Lemieux	PSC
2004	15000	1.2	0.833	Google	Google
2006	131072	147.8	0.007	BlueGene/L	LANL
2007	6656	351	0.003	Seaborg	NERSC

Kogge et al., 2008.

where MTTF is the mean time to failure (MTTF). The mean time between failures (MTBF) can also be used and using this estimate is both intuitive and conservative (Finkelstein, 2008; United States Department of Defense, 1998). Furthermore, although the failure rate is time-dependent, for complex large scale systems, such as HPC systems, a constant estimation can be used (United States Department of Defense, 1998). Table 2 is an example of MTBF measurements for some large scale installations over a five-year period. Here, it can be seen that the MTBF varies from one system to the next so care must be taken to account for these variations. Typically, failure rate determines how reliable the system is: the lower the failure rate, the more reliable the system. However, in the case of targeted failures, the failure rate can also be indicative of the lack of detection of the CE's behavior or impact on a system. For example, if the failure rate is low, this typically means that the system is pretty reliable. However,

It could also mean that the CE is operating "under the radar" and is potentially infiltrating the system prior to notification of either system, risk level, or component failure. Conversely, if the failure rate is large, this means that the result of the enemy's behavior is detectable in the sense of them causing failures in the system. Therefore, the following analysis considers the effects of the cyber-enemy when $\lambda \to 0$ and when $\lambda \to \infty$. Doing so practically enables scientists, engineers, and technicians to design robust measures for better resilience and security because these additional behaviors would be properly accounted for. When $\lambda \to 0$, it can be shown that the dynamic response, given by Equations (31) and (32), reduces to

$$\hat{W}\left(\omega, t\right) = \left(\hat{W}_0 + \bar{B}\left(\omega\right)\right)e^{-j\omega at} - \bar{B}\left(\omega\right)e^{-j\omega bt}, \tag{35}$$

where the second constant is described as

$$\bar{B}\left(\omega\right) = \frac{G\left(\omega\right) + j\omega a \hat{W}_0}{j\omega\left(b - a\right)} \tag{36}$$

under the conditions that $b \neq a$. Consequently, when $\lambda \to \infty$, the dynamic response reduces to

$$\hat{W}\left(\omega, t\right) = \hat{W}_0 e^{-\frac{j\omega}{2}(a+b)t}, \tag{37}$$

which, after taking the inverse Fourier transform, produces the following solution

$$W\left(x, t\right) = W_0\left(x - \left[\frac{a+b}{2}\right]t\right), \tag{38}$$

Containing the initial distribution given by equation (16). These responses, described by equations (35) – (38), illustrate the different kinds of attack dynamics associated with the extreme detection levels of the attacker, which also depend on the affected risk levels. As the CE's attacks become more difficult to detect, the conjecture can be made that this behavior depends on the dominance of the attack rate with each risk level. Consequently, as the payoff actions of the CE becomes easily detected, the transition between the two levels directly depends on the average of the attack rates in both risk levels – bearing slight resemblance in behavior represented in Equation (19). For both limiting cases, it is important to note that the response, as $b \to a$, the dynamic response approaches the behavior of the constant attack case.

MODELING THE EFFECTS OF SYSTEM TERMINATION

Equation (15) poses a dynamical representation of the impact of failure levels in HPC systems caused by the cyber-enemy (CE). However, care must also be accounted for cases of system shut-down that depends on the payoff actions of the CE. This is done by introducing a *stopped process*, which is described as follows (Gardiner, 1985; Shreve, 2004; Cinlar, 2013):

$$\xi^\tau\left(t\right) = \begin{cases} x\left(t\right), t < \tau \\ x\left(\tau\right), t \geq \tau \end{cases}, \tag{39}$$

where $x\left(t\right)$ represents the payoff actions of the CE, $x\left(\tau\right)$ is the resulting payoff value at the terminated process at the stopping time $t = \tau$ described as

$$\tau = \inf\left\{t : x\left(t\right) \in D\right\}, \tag{40}$$

where D is a closed subdomain representative of the behavior *immediately prior* to the interruption of the process. With a stopped process, prior to time $t = \tau$, the behavior agrees with the attack behavior. However, once the stopped time is reached, it is frozen at the specified value of $\xi^\tau\left(\tau\right)$. If the process stops and a value of $x\left(\tau\right)$ is not reached, then the interpretation is that $\tau = \infty$ (Shreve, 2004). In the context of HPC systems, the stopped process considers the specific action when the technician, such as a systems administrator (SA), either terminates the process either temporarily or permanently. Here, the action can either be automatically (where the SA would preset a threshold level for termination) or manually (when the SA would suddenly stop the system after noticing suspicious behavior).

To model this behavior, it is best to work with the *backwards representation* of Equation (7) to evaluate the first passage of time between states m and n. To do this, an intermediary state k is defined such that the conditional probability is defined as

$$W^{m,k}\left(x,t\mid z,s\right) = P\left\{x\left(t\right) = x \in x_k \mid x\left(s\right) = z \in x_m\right\}. \tag{41}$$

Next, Equation (41) can be expressed in terms of the following generic Taylor series expansion:

$$W^{m,k}\left(x,t\mid z,s+\Delta s\right) = W^{m,k}\left(x,t\mid z,s\right) + \Delta s\, \partial_s W^{m,k}\left(x,t\mid z,s\right) + o\left(\Delta s\right), \tag{42}$$

where ∂_s represents the partial derivative with respect to s. It is important to note that this explicit representation can be expanded as follows (Gardiner, 1985; Rosenthal, 2006):

$$W^{m,k}\left(x,s\mid z,s+\Delta s\right) = \delta\left(m-k\right)\delta\left(x-z\right) - \delta\left(m-k\right)p_s^k\left(x,s\mid z,s\right)\Delta s -$$
$$\Delta s\sum_{m\neq k}\delta\left(x-z\right)\lambda_{mk} + \delta\left(m-n\right)\Delta s\sum_{m\neq k}\delta\left(x-z\right)\lambda_{km} + o\left(\Delta s\right) \tag{43}$$

Similarly, the conditional probability between states k and n is defined such that the following *forward expansion* is computed for $W^{k,n}\left(x,t+\text{''}\,t\mid z,t\right)$:

$$W^{k,n}\left(x,t+\Delta t\mid z,t\right) = \delta\left(n-k\right)\delta\left(x-z\right) + \delta\left(n-k\right)p_t^n\left(x,t\mid z,t\right)\Delta t +$$
$$\Delta t\sum_{n\neq k}\delta\left(x-z\right)\lambda_{kn} - \delta\left(n-k\right)\Delta t\sum_{n\neq k}\delta\left(x-z\right)\lambda_{nk} + o\left(\Delta t\right) \tag{44}$$

Next, the following Chapman-Kolmogorov relationship

$$W^{m,n}\left(x,t\mid y,s\right) = \sum_{k\in S}\left\{\int_{x_1}^{x_N}W^{m,k}\left(x,t\mid z,s+\Delta s\right)W^{k,n}\left(z,s+\Delta s\mid y,s\right)dz\right\} \tag{45}$$

is applied where S represents the collection of intermediate risk levels. Combining the results of Equations (42), (44), and (45) yield the following representation between states m and n:

$$\partial_s W^{m,n}\left(x,t\mid y,s\right) = -W^{m,n}\left(x,t\mid \rho,s\right), p_s^n\left(\rho,s\mid y,s\right) -$$
$$\lambda\left\{\sum_{k\neq n}\left[W^{m,k}\left(x,t\mid y,s\right) - W^{m,n}\left(x,t\mid y,s\right)\right]\right\} \tag{46}$$

Also, the transition rate is constant to take into consideration the fact that these transitions are representative of a Poisson process.

With a stopped process, it is important to consider the behavior immediately prior to the stopping time. This is done by considering the stopped process hits the boundary D in the interval $t \in [0, t)$. Therefore, the goal is to find the likelihood such that

$$\pi(y, t) = P\{\xi^\tau(t) \in D \mid \xi^\tau(0) = y\}, \tag{47}$$

where $\pi(y, t)$ is the conditional probability density function and y is the resulting payoff action associated with the HPC risk level prior to termination. In defining $\pi(y, t)$, the initial condition $\xi^\tau(0) = y$ accounts for the final attack behavior prior to shut down. Next, associating the payoff actions of the CE with system interruption is done by letting that $f(\xi^\tau(t), t) \in C^2[0, t)$ be a twice continuous and differential function. For the case where $s < t$, it is assumed that the process has the initial condition that $\xi^\tau_m(s) = y \in S_m$. Let β^n be the conditional expectation given by

$$\beta^n(y, t, s) = E[g(y, t, s)] = \sum_m \left[\int_{x_1}^{x_N} g(y, t, s) W^{m,n}(x, t \mid y, s) \mu_m(t) dy \right], \tag{48}$$

where $g(y,t,s)$ is expressed as

$$g(y, t, s) = g\left(\xi^\tau_m(s) = y, t\right). \tag{49}$$

Taking into account the evolution of $\beta^n(y, t, s)$ with respect to s achieves the following result:

$$\partial_s \beta^n(y, t, s) = E[\partial_s g(y, t, s)] - \beta^n(\rho, t, s), p_s^n(\rho, s \mid y, s) - \\ \lambda \left\{ \sum_{k \neq n} [\beta^k(y, t, s) - \beta^n(y, t, s)] \right\}. \tag{50}$$

Considering the case where the behavior prior to termination is consistent, it can be assumed that the process is time invariant yielding the following relationship:

$$\beta^n(y, t, s) = \beta^n(y, t - s, 0) = \beta^n(y, u), \tag{51}$$

where *u=t - s*. Therefore, Equation (50) becomes

$$\partial_{u'}\beta^n(y,u) = -E\left[\partial_u g(y,u)\right] + \beta^n(\rho,u), p_u^n(\rho,u \mid y,u) + \\ \lambda\left\{\sum_{k\neq n}\left[\beta^k(y,u) - \beta^n(y,u)\right]\right\}$$ (52)

where *g(y, u)* is defined as

$$g(y,u) = g\left(\xi_m^\tau(0) = y, u\right).$$ (53)

Next, an approximation to (53) is introduced by considering the following sequence (Desilles, 1998)

$$g_{l,\varepsilon}(y,u) = 1_{\{\xi_m^\tau(0)=y\}} e^{-l\hat{Q}_\varepsilon(t)},$$ (54)

where, $l \in Z^* = \{0\} \cup Z^+$, $\hat{Q}_\varepsilon(t)$ is defined as

$$\hat{Q}_\varepsilon(t) = \int_0^t \hat{q}_\varepsilon\left(\left\{\xi_m^{(1-\varepsilon)\tau}(0) = y\right\}, u\right) du,$$ (55)

and $\hat{q}_\varepsilon\left(\left\{\xi_m^{\tau_\varepsilon}(0) = y\right\}, u\right) \in C^2[0,t]$ is a twice continuous and differential function such that

$$\begin{cases} \hat{q}_\varepsilon\left(\left\{\xi_m^{(1-\varepsilon)\tau}(0) = y\right\}, u\right) > 0, & d(y,D) < \varepsilon \\ 0, & d(y,D) \geq \varepsilon \end{cases}.$$ (56)

In Equation (56), the term *d(y, D)* represents the Euclidean distance between the final payoff action *y* and the termination boundary *D* for $\varepsilon \in [0,1)$. Equations (55) and (56) basically state that the probabilistic behavior of the stopped process depends on the condition that $t \in [(1-\varepsilon)\tau, \tau]$. Furthermore, it is important to note that $g_{l,\varepsilon}$ is a simple random variable that satisfies the following propositions (Rosenthal, 2006):

Proposition 1: For every random variable $X \geq 0$, there exists a sequence $\{X_l\}$ of positive, simple random variables with $X_l \uparrow X$ (i.e. X_l increases to X).

Proposition 2: If $X \geq 0$ and $\{X_l\}$ is a sequence of positive, simple random variables with $X_l \uparrow X$, then $E(X_l) \uparrow E(X)$.

Additionally, the Monotonic Convergence Theorem (MCT) (Rosenthal, 2006) is also satisfied. Next, noting the approximate expectation as

$$\beta_{l,\varepsilon}^n\left(y,u\right)=E\left[g_{l,\varepsilon}\left(y,u\right)\right] \tag{57}$$

the following relationship is achieved

$$E\left[\partial_u g_{l,\varepsilon}\left(y,u\right)\right]=-l\hat{q}_\varepsilon\left(y\right)\beta_{l,\varepsilon}^n\left(y,u\right). \tag{58}$$

Noting the behavior as $l\to\infty$ and $\varepsilon\to 0$ while taking into account the limiting behavior of $g_{l,\varepsilon}\left(y,u\right)$ yields the following result (Desilles, 1998)

$$\partial_s\pi^n\left(y,u\right)=\pi^n\left(\rho,u\right),p_s^n\left(\rho,u\mid y,u\right)+\lambda\left\{\sum_{k\neq n}\left[\pi^k\left(y,u\right)-\pi^n\left(y,u\right)\right]\right\}, \tag{59}$$

where $\pi^n\left(y,u\right)$ is defined as

$$\pi^n\left(y,u\right)=P\left\{\xi^\tau\left(u\right)\in D\mid\xi^\tau\left(0\right)=y\in S_n\right\}. \tag{60}$$

From Equation (60), the total probability is calculated as

$$\pi\left(y,u\right)=\sum_n\left\{\pi^n\left(y,u\right)\cdot P\left(\xi^\tau\left(0\right)=y\in S_n\right)\right\}. \tag{61}$$

This formulation of the stopped condition, described by Equations (59) and (61), describe the conditional likelihood of the first passage of the boundary D associated with the stopping time. This condition in addition to the dynamic behavior, described by Equation (15), models the complete behavior by considering the probabilistic transitions of cyber-attacks for the cases of system operation and termination. Understanding the effects of these attacks from a system termination point of view is equally important because it provides technical protectors of HPC systems a complete picture of these attacks as well as learn the impact of these attacks at termination.

CONCLUSION

This chapter provides a universal representation illustrating the effects of *intentional* or *targeted* failures in HPC systems. Here, a mathematical representation is presented that illustrates the probabilistic impact of cyber-attacks in HPC systems from a system's perspective that relates the general actions of the CE to various failure risk levels in terms of tempered probability distributions. Next, further analysis is explored where the special cases of constant and two-level strategies are considered. For the case of consistent constant attacks, the trivial results agree with Faissol and Gallagher's results that there exists a direct relationship between the transition between failure levels and the cyber-enemy's (CE's) attack rate. For the special case of two-level attack strategies, it is demonstrated that, with regards to *intentional failures*, the transition between two different risk levels depends on three factors: the attack rates between risk levels, the frequency of the targeted response, and the transition rate between the risk levels. Using this fact, exact solutions are obtained that incorporates these three factors together where further analysis is conducted in order to observe the limiting behavior of the response in terms of system reliability. The idea here is that cyber-attacks happen regardless of reliability – just because the failure rate of a system is low is not indicative that there are no cyber-attacks. Therefore, care must also be made to understand this limiting behavior. Finally, the concept of a stopped process is introduced to account for system termination.

This work is an advancement of previous approaches on this topic because it provides a universal and flexible approach to understanding the systemic effects of targeted failures. The game theoretic representation, posed by Faissol and Gallagher, is limited because the authors do not take into account the complete understanding of the impact of the actions of the CE and the relationship between systems reliability. Using game theory to model these effects appear attractive due to the compact nature of the system dynamics and termination when a certain threshold is reached; however, two major limitations are overlooked when using this approach. If the constraints in the game are not properly defined – either the constraints are too limiting or too free – the actions of the CE would not be completely realized, which can affect the overall analysis and behavior detection. At the same time, if the dynamics of the game are not completely understood, there is a greater risk that the cyber-activity would not be completely captured. Finally, there is a risk of continuing to run the system in hopes of obtaining an optimum solution because the CE can learn about the system while doing severe damage. Another major advancement in this work is modeling these effects as continuous time Markovian processes. HPC systems perform approximately a billion operations per second given a clock speed of one nanosecond (Landau, n.d.). Therefore, it can be concluded that cyber-attacks perform similarly and this must also be considered when investigating intentional failures. Furthermore, obtaining a discrete Markov process can be done via finite discretization. Finally, instead of relying on the constraints to be reached for termination, incorporating the effects of system termination using the definition of a *stopped process* provides much more flexibility to the technician where they have the option to either automatically or manually terminate the process. A practical application here is that the technician might want to stop the process when certain anomalies occur to perform detailed investigation and troubleshooting analysis.

PRACTICAL SCENARIOS

Practical situations where this work directly applies are in the Distributed Denial of Service arena where reflection and amplification attacks can be used to invade the system. An example of this is Domain Name Server (DNS) amplification where the CE exploits susceptibilities in DNS servers turning small queries into larger ones. Here, initial queries are made with forged internet protocol (IP) addresses to the victim's open DNS resolver to get a response. Once the network communication has been established, the attacker sends larger attacks to flood the system. It is important to note these type of attacks is a family of attacks where other network protocols like Simple Network Management Protocol (SNMP), and Network Transfer Protocol (NTP) can also be used.

What makes these types of attacks particularly dangerous is that the initial communication can be disguised as legitimate traffic. Additionally, attacks like DNS amplification have a 70:1 amplification factor (Blagov, n.d.). What this means is that an attacker who controls a single machine with 1 Gigabits per second (Gbps) could effectively direct 70 Gbps of traffic toward the victim's server. Furthermore, in NTP reflection attacks, the response ratio is anywhere from 20:1 to 200:1 or higher (Blagov, n.d.). Currently, common techniques for mitigating and preventing these types of attacks include tightening server security, traffic filtering, or overprovisioning. However, these methods do not pinpoint or eliminate attack sources. Furthermore, if traffic filtering is too extreme, communication between these systems can be interrupted and can hinder legitimate user access. Therefore, understanding the effects of targeted attacks can create a system that offers on demand provisioning to handle variations of these types of attacks.

FUTURE RESEARCH DIRECTIONS

Although the work presented here is promising, there are several avenues of future development that need to be explored. Currently, work is being done to implement the proposed model while considering parallelization strategies for real-time monitoring and analysis. Next, development is currently underway to perform experimental simulation in the context of a HPC environment. Doing so will make the representation presented more robust and practical by preparing it for actual system responses. Furthermore, there is a need to investigate these effects on a node level. Doing so affords scientists, engineers, and technicians the ability to understand these effects microscopically while drawing the connection to the overall systems response. Together, these aspects provide a universal framework for understanding this emerging and practical phenomenon.

REFERENCES

Blagov, M. (n.d.). *DDoS Attack Glossary.* Retrieved November 13, 2015, from www.incapsula.com

Cambell, S., & Mellander, J. (2011). Experiences with Intrusion Detection in High Performance Computing. In *Proceedings of the Cray User Group (CUG)*. Fairbanks, AK.

Chandler, C. F., Leangsuksun, C., & DeBardeleben, N. (2009). Towards Resilient High Performance Applications Through Real Time Reliability Metric Generation and Autonomous Failure Correction. In *Proceedings of the 2009 Workshop on Resiliency in High Performance (Resilience '09)*. Munich, Germany. doi:10.1145/1552526.1552527

Chen, T., Zhang, X., & Wu, Y. (2014). FPM: Four-Factors Propagation Model for Passive P2P Worms. *Future Generation Computer Systems*, *36*, 133–141. doi:10.1016/j.future.2013.06.025

Chen, T. M., & Jamil, N. (2006). Effectiveness of Quarantine in Worm Epidemic, In *Proceedings of the IEEE International Conference on Communications*.

Chen, T. M., Zhang, X.-, Li, H.-, Wang, D., & Wu, Y. (2013). Propagation Modeling of Active P2P Worms Based On Ternary Matrix. *Journal of Network and Computer Applications*, *36*(5), 1387–1394. doi:10.1016/j.jnca.2013.02.032

Chen, Z., & Dongarra, J. (2009). Algorithm-based Fault Tolerance for Fail-Stop Failures. *IEEE Transactions on Parallel and Distributed Systems*, *9*(12).

Cinlar, E. (2013). *Introduction to Stochastic Processes*. Dover.

Daly, J. (2006). A Higher Order Estimate of the Optimum Checkpoint Interval for Restart Dumps. *Future Generation Computer Systems*, 22(3), 303–312. doi:10.1016/j.future.2004.11.016

Daly, J., Pritchett, L., & Michalak, S. (2008). Application MTTFE vs. Platform MTBF: A Fresh Perspective on System Reliability and Application Throughput for Computations at Scale. In *Proceedings of the IEEE Symposium on Cluster Computing and the Grid*. Lyon, France. doi:10.1109/CCGRID.2008.103

Data, S., & Wang, H. (2005). The Effectiveness of Vaccinations on the Spread of Email-Borne Computer Viruses. In *Proceedings of the IEEE Canadian Conference on Electrical and Computer Engineering*. Saskatoon, Canada. doi:10.1109/CCECE.2005.1556914

DeBarteleben, N., Laros, J., Daly, J., Scott, S., Engelmann, C., & Harrod, W. (2009). *High-End Computing Resilience: Analysis of Issues facing the HEC Community and Path Forward for Research and Development. (Whitepaper)*. Oak Ridge, TN: Oak Ridge National Laboratory.

Desilles, G. (1998). *Differential Kolmogorov Equations for Transiting Processes*. (Masters thesis). Massachusetts Institute of Technology, Boston, MA.

Englemann, C., Vallee, G., Naughton, T., & Scott, S. (2009). Proactive Fault Tolerance Using Preemptive Migration. In *Proceedings of 17th Euromicro International Conference on Parallel, Distributed, and Network-Based Processing*.

Enriquez, P., Brown, A., & Patterson, D. A. (2002). Lessons from the PSTN for Dependable Computing. In *Proceedings of the Workshop on Self-Healing, Adaptive and Self-Managed Systems*.

Faissol, G., & Gallagher, B. (2014). *The Price of Anarchy and Malice: A Game Theoretic Study of Targeted Failures in HPC Systems. (Technical report)*. Livermore, CA: Lawrence Livermore National Laboratory.

Fan, W., & Yeung, K. (2013). Virus Propagation Modeling in Facebook. In *The Influence of Technology on Social Network Analysis and Mining*. Springer. doi:10.1007/978-3-7091-1346-2_8

Gardiner, C. W. (1985). *Handbook of Stochastic Methods for Physics, Chemistry, and the Natural Sciences*. Springer-Verlag. doi:10.1007/978-3-662-02452-2

Gray, J. (1986). Why do computers stop and what can be done about it? In *Proceedings of the 5th Symposium on Reliability in Distributed Software and Database Systems*. Los Alamitos, CA.

Gray, J. (1990). A Census of Tandem System Availability between 1985 and 1990. *IEEE Transactions on Reliability*, 39(4), 409–418. doi:10.1109/24.58719

Iyer, R. K., Rossetti, D. J., & Hsueh, M. C. (1986). Measurement and Modeling of Computer Reliability as Affected by System Activity. *ACM Transactions on Computer Systems*, 4(3), 214–237. doi:10.1145/6420.6422

Jones, W., Daly, J., & DeBarteleben, N. (2008). Application Resilience: Making Progress In Spite of Failures. In *Proceedings of the IEEE Symposium on Cluster Computing and the Grid*. Lyon, France. doi:10.1109/CCGRID.2008.99

Kalyanakrishnam, M., Kalbarczyk, Z., & Iyer, R. (1999). Failure Data Analysis of a LAN of Windows NT based computers. In *Proceedings of the 18th IEEE Symposium on Reliable Distributed Systems*. doi:10.1109/RELDIS.1999.805094

Kermack, W., & McKendrick, A. (1927). Contributions to the Mathematical Theory of Epidemics I. In *Proceedings of the Royal Society of London, Series A*.

Kermack, W., & McKendrick, A. (1932). Contributions to the Mathematical Theory of Epidemics II: The Problem of Endemicity. In *Proceedings of the Royal Society of London, Series A*.

Kermack, W., & McKendrick, A. (1933). Contributions to the mathematical theory of epidemics III: Further studies of the problem of endemicity. In *Proceedings of the Royal Society of London, Series A*.

Kim, J., Radhakrishnan, S., & Jang, J. (2006). Cost Optimization in SIS Model of Worm Infection. ETRI Journal, 28(5).

Kogge, P., Bergman, K., Borkar, S., Campbell, D., Carlson, W., Dally, W., . . . Yelick, K. (2008). ExaScale Computing Study: Technology Challenges in Achieving Exascale Systems. (Technical report). Defense Advanced Research Projects Agency Information Processing Techniques Office. Washington, DC: DARPA IPTO.

Koutsoupias, E., & Papadimitriou, C. (2009). Worst-Case Equilibria. *Computer Science Review*, *3*(2), 65–69. doi:10.1016/j.cosrev.2009.04.003

Kuhn, D. R. (1997). Sources of failure in the public switched telephone network. *IEEE Computer, 30*(4).

Landau, R. H. (n.d). *A beginner's guide to high performance computing*. Retrieved June 9, 2015, from http://www.shodor.org/petascale/resources/search/view/2594/

Lee, I., & Iyer, R. (1995). Software Dependability in the Tandem GUARDIAN System. *IEEE Transactions on Software Engineering*, *21*(5).

Lee, J., Chapin, S., & Taylor, S. (2003). Reliable Heterogeneous Applications. *IEEE Transactions on Reliability*, *52*(3), 330–339. doi:10.1109/TR.2003.819502

Liang, Y., Zhang, Y., Sivasubramaniam, A., Sahoo, R., Moreira, J., & Gupta, M. (2005). Filtering Failure Logs for a BlueGene/L Prototype. In *Proceedings of the International Conference on Dependable Systems and Networks (DSN '05)*. Yokohama, Japan.

Mahajan, R., Wetherall, D., & Anderson, T. (2002). *Understanding BGP Misconfiguration*. In *Proceedings of SIGCOMM*. Pittsburgh, PA.

Mishra, B., & Prajapati. (2014). A Mathematical Model on Attack by Malicious Objects Leading to Cyber War. *International Journal of Nonlinear Science, 17*(2).

Mishra, B., & Jha, N. (2007). Fixed Period of Temporary Immunity after run of Anti-Malicious Software on Computer Nodes. *Applied Mathematics and Computation*, *190*(2), 1207–1212. doi:10.1016/j.amc.2007.02.004

Mishra, B., & Jha, N. (2010). SEIRS Model for the Transmission of Malicious Objects in Computer Network. *Applied Mathematical Modelling*, *34*(3), 710–715. doi:10.1016/j.apm.2009.06.011

Mishra, B., & Pandey, S. (2013). Dynamic Model of Worm Propagation in Computer Network. *Applied Mathematical Modelling, 38*(7).

Moscibroda, T., Schmid, S., & Wattenhofer, R. (2006). When selfish meets evil: Byzantine players in a virus inoculation game. In *Proceedings of the 25th Annual ACM Symposium on Principles of Distributed Computing*. doi:10.1145/1146381.1146391

Murphy, B., & Gent, T. (1995). Measuring System and Software Reliability Using an Automated Data Collection Process. *Quality and Reliability Engineering International, 11*(5), 341–353. doi:10.1002/qre.4680110505

Nagarajan, A. B., & Mueller, F. (2007). Proactive Fault Tolerance for HPC with Xen Virtualization. In *Proceedings of the 21st Annual International Conference on Supercomputing*. doi:10.1145/1274971.1274978

Newman, M. E., Forrest, S., & Balthrop, J. (2002). Email Networks and the Spread of Computer Viruses. *Physical Review E: Statistical, Nonlinear, and Soft Matter Physics, 66*(3), 035101. doi:10.1103/PhysRevE.66.035101

Nyland, L. S., Prins, J. F., Goldberg, A., & Mills, P. H. (2000). A Design Methodology for Data-Parallel Applications. *IEEE Transactions on Software Engineering, 26*(4), 293–314. doi:10.1109/32.844491

Oppenheimer, D., Ganapathi, A., & Patterson, D. A. (2003). Why do Internet Services Fail, and What Can Be Done About It? In *Proceedings of the 4th Usenix Symposium on Internet Technologies and Systems*. Seattle, WA.

Raicu, I., Foster, I., & Zhao, Y. (2008). Many-Task Computing: Bridging the Gap Between High Throughput Computing and High Performance Computing. In *Proceedings of the Workshop on Many-Task Computing on Clouds, Grids, and Supercomputers (MTAGS)*. Austin, TX.

Ravichandran, D., Pantel, P., & Hovy, E. (2004). The Terascale Challenge. In *Proceedings of the KDD Workshop on Mining for and from the Semantic Web*.

Robinson, D., & Stearly, J. (2011). *Resilience of High Performance Computing Systems. (Technical report)*. Albuquerque, NM: Sandia National Laboratories.

Rosenthal, J. S. (2006). *A First Look at Rigorous Probability Theory*. World Scientific Publishing. doi:10.1142/6300

Sahoo, R. K., Sivasubramaniam, A., Squillante, M. S., & Zhang, Y. (2004). Failure Data Analysis of a Large-Scale Heterogeneous Server Environment. In *Proceedings of the International Conference on Dependable Systems and Networks (DSN)*. Florence, Italy. doi:10.1109/DSN.2004.1311948

Schroeder, B., & Gibson, G. (2005). *A Large-Scale Study of Failures in High Performance Computing Systems. (Technical report)*. Pittsburgh, PA: Carnegie Mellon University.

Schroeder, B., & Gibson, G. (2007). Understanding Failures in Petascale Computers. *Journal of Physics: Conference Series 78*, No. 1. IOP Publishing.

Shreve, S. E. (2004). *Stochastic Calculus for Finance II: Continuous-Time Models*. Springer. doi:10.1007/978-1-4757-4296-1

Sullivan, M. S., & Chillarege, R. (1992). A Comparison of Software Defects in Database Management Systems and Operating Systems. In *Proceedings of the 22nd International Symposium on Fault-Tolerant Computing*. Boston, MA. doi:10.1109/FTCS.1992.243586

Tang, D., & Iyer, R. (1991). Impact of Correlated Failures on Dependability in a VAX Cluster System. In *Proceedings of the IFIP Working Conference on Dependable Computing for Critical Applications*.

Tang, D., & Iyer, R. (1992). Analysis and Modeling of Correlated Failures in Multicomputer Systems. *IEEE Transactions on Computers*, *41*(5), 567–577. doi:10.1109/12.142683

Tang, D., Iyer, R., & Subramani, S. (1990). Failure Analysis and Modeling of a VAX Cluster System. In *Proceedings of the International Symposium on Fault-Tolerant Computing*.

Thakur, A., & Iyer, R. (1996). Analyze NOW: An Environment for Collection and Analysis of Failures in a Network of Workstations. *IEEE Transactions on Reliability*, *46*(4).

United States Department of Defense. (1998). *Military Handbook: Electronic Reliability Design Handbook*. Washington, D.C.: Author.

Van Kampen, N. G. (Ed.). (2007). *Stochastic Processes in Physics and Chemistry*. Elsevier.

Wang, P., González, M. C., Menezes, R., & Barabási, A.-L. (2013). Understanding the Spread of Malicious Mobile-Phone Programs and their Damage Potential. *International Journal of Information Security*, *12*(5), 383–392. doi:10.1007/s10207-013-0203-z

Wolstenholme, L. (1999). *Reliability Modeling: A Statistical Approach*. Chapman & Hall/CRC Press.

Xu, J., Kalbarczyk, Z., & Iyer, R. (1999). Networked Windows NT System Field Failure Data Analysis. In *Proceedings of the IEEE Pacific Rim International Symposium on Dependable Computing*. Hong Kong, China.

Yuan, H., & Chen, G. (2008). Network Virus-Epidemic Model with the Point-to-Group Information Propagation. *Applied Mathematics and Computation*, *206*(1), 357–367. doi:10.1016/j.amc.2008.09.025

Zou, C. C., Gong, W., & Towsley, D. (2003). Worm Propagation Modeling and Analysis Under Dynamic Quarantine Defense. In *Proceedings of the ACM CCS Workshop on Rapid Malcode*. doi:10.1145/948187.948197

KEY TERMS AND DEFINITIONS

Consistent Attack: A continuous attack strategy that is employed by the cyber-enemy (CE) in achieving failure risk levels in a HPC system. These attacks can be constant or variable.

Cyber-Enemy (CE): A person (or group of people) whose intent is to interrupt or cause harm to the HPC system.

Failure Rate: A universal factor, usually a constant, which is used to determine how well a system is reliable.

Failure Risk Level: A level that indicates the amount of harm (or damage) to the HPC system.

Leveled-Attack: An attack strategy that is used by the cyber-enemy (CE) to achieve (or operate) in one failure risk level that is suddenly changed to operate at another risk level.

Mean Time Between Failures (MTBF): The predicted elapsed time between failures of a HPC system. This calculation assumes that the HPC system will be immediately repaired.

Mean Time To Failure (MTTF): The predicted elapsed time between failures of a HPC system. Contrary to MTBF, this calculation assumes that the HPC system will not be immediately repaired (i.e. infinite repair time).

System Administrator (SA): A person (or group of people) whose intent is to monitor and protect the HPC system.

Targeted-Failures: Failures that are directly caused by the cyber-enemy (CE).

Chapter 11
Analyzing the Robustness of HPC Applications Using a Fine–Grained Soft Error Fault Injection Tool

Qiang Guan
Los Alamos National Laboratory, USA

Song Fu
University of North Texas, USA

Nathan DeBardeleben
Los Alamos National Lab, USA

Claude H. Davis IV
Clemson University, USA

Sean Blanchard
Los Alamos National Lab, USA

William M. Jones
Coastal Carolina University, USA

ABSTRACT

As the high performance computing (HPC) community continues to push towards exascale computing, HPC applications of today are only affected by soft errors to a small degree but we expect that this will become a more serious issue as HPC systems grow. We propose F-SEFI, a Fine-grained Soft Error Fault Injector, as a tool for profiling software robustness against soft errors. We utilize soft error injection to mimic the impact of errors on logic circuit behavior. Leveraging the open source virtual machine hypervisor QEMU, F-SEFI enables users to modify emulated machine instructions to introduce soft errors. F-SEFI can control what application, which sub-function, when and how to inject soft errors with different granularities, without interference to other applications that share the same environment. We demonstrate use cases of F-SEFI on several benchmark applications with different characteristics to show how data corruption can propagate to incorrect results. The findings from the fault injection campaign can be used for designing robust software and power-efficient hardware.

DOI: 10.4018/978-1-5225-0287-6.ch011

INTRODUCTION

If you cannot measure it, you cannot improve it. – Lord Kelvin

Exascale supercomputers are likely to encounter failures at higher rates than current high performance computing systems. Next generation machines are expected to consist of a much larger component count than current petascale machines. In addition to the increase in components, it is expected that each individual component will be built on smaller feature sizes, which may prove to be more vulnerable than current parts. This vulnerability may be aggravated by near-threshold voltage designs meant to dramatically decrease power consumption in the data center (Kaul et al., 2012). Due to high error rates it is estimated that exascale systems may waste as much as 60% (DeBardeleben et al., 2009) of their computation cycles and power due to the overhead of reliability assurance. These high error rates pose a serious threat to the prospect of exascale systems.

Soft errors fall into three categories (Snir et al., 2014): DCE (Detected and Corrected Error), DUE (Detected but Uncorrectable Error) and SE (Silent Error). Most DRAM in supercomputers is protected by Chipkill (Jian, Duwe, Sartori, Sridharan, & Kumar, 2013; Sridharan, Stearley, DeBardeleben, Blanchard, & Gurumurthi, 2013; Walker & Betz, 2013), which makes DUE events rare and SE events even more rare. SRAM in cache layers, however, is generally protected by SECDED (Single Error Correction and Double Errors Detection) or parity and is therefore more vulnerable to SE events. In addition, logic circuits have varying levels of internal protection and we expect these error rates to be on the rise as well.

Silent errors pose a serious issue when they lead to Silent Data Corruption (SDC) in user applications. If undetected by the application, a single SDC can corrupt data causing applications to output incorrect results malfunction or hang. Unfortunately, detecting and correcting SDC events at the application layer is challenging. It requires expert knowledge of the algorithm involved to determine where an application might be most vulnerable and how it will behave if an SDC should occur. Even with such knowledge it is difficult to test any mitigation techniques an application author might attempt since SDC events occur rarely and in most cases randomly.

In order to facilitate the testing of application resilience methods, detection and correction mechanisms require the study of hardware faults that may affect the execution of any instruction of the target application. However, a brute-force way that explores billions of instructions of an application or benchmark may result in trillions of vulnerable sites and requires a prohibitively large number of experiments to cover all possible cases. In order to perform the fault injection efficiently and effectively, at least three aspects need to be clarified.

- **Where to Inject:** The fault injector should allow users to define the location of the errors to be injected, e.g., application, function, line-of-code, even variable and register.
- **When to Inject:** The fault injector should grant the ability to users to fully control the injection at runtime to investigate the susceptibility of application under different stages.
- **How to Inject:** The fault injector should provide different fault models to users with different interests.

Therefore, we present a fine-grained soft error fault injector named F-SEFI, which is built on the previous work (DeBardeleben, Blanchard, Guan, Zhang, & Fu, 2011; Guan, Fu, DeBardeleben, & Blanchard, 2014; Guan, DeBardeleben, Blanchard, & Fu, 2014). F-SEFI allows for the targeted injection of soft errors into instructions belonging to the application of interest and that application's individual subroutines. F-SEFI leverages the QEMU (Bellard, 2005) virtual machine (VM) and its hypervisor (Song et al., 2008; Henderson et al., 2013). QEMU uses Tiny Code Generation (TCG) to reference and translate binary instruction sets between the guest and host architectures before the instructions are delivered to the host system for execution. F-SEFI provides the ability to emulate soft errors and corrupt data at runtime by intercepting instructions and replacing them with contaminated versions during the TCG translation. With the addition of a binary symbol table, F-SEFI supports a tunable fine-grained injection strategy where soft errors can be injected into chosen instructions in specified functions of an application. In addition, F-SEFI allows multiple fault models to mimic the upsets in hardware (e.g., probabilistic model, single bit fault model and multiple-bits fault model). Overall, F-SEFI manages the fault injections and the user decides where, when, and how to inject faults.

We implemented a prototype F-SEFI testbed and conducted the fault injection campaigns on different applications from numerical computation algorithms to image processing parallel programs. The experimental results show that injected faults are leading the execution into incorrect states. Some faults are amplified after the propagation to other components and result in a significant deviation from the fault-free execution. Studies using F-SEFI provide sufficient instruction level soft error samples with different fault models and can assist the programmers to understand the susceptibility of applications under the presence of errors and faults. Furthermore, this can help the design of resilient strategies to mitigate the impact of SDC.

The rest of the chapter is organized as follows. In Section BACKGROUND we discuss related work in this field and in Section F-SEFI DESIGN we use this to motivate why we felt the need to design our own tool. In FAULT MODEL Section we discuss our fault model and then in Section FAULT INJECTION MECHANISMS we describe the specifics of the design of F-SEFI. Five application benchmarks are studied in CASE STUDY and we show how fault injections are amplified and results in unexpected outputs in these applications. Finally, we discuss some of the implications of our tool, draw some conclusions and discuss the future work.

BACKGROUND

Studying the behavior of applications in the face of soft errors has been growing in popularity in recent years. Several efforts have been made to develop techniques for injecting faults into a running application or system to test the susceptibility of applications and system hardware components. General approaches range from instruction-level injection to memory corruption and include techniques such as source code modification, debugger injection, binary modification, or virtual machine injection. In this section we focus on topics most closely related to the approach used by F-SEFI.

Dynamic Binary Instrumentation-Based Fault Injection

One category of recent research focuses on injecting soft errors into an application binary dynamically. Thomas et al. (Thomas & Pattabiraman, 2013) propose LLFI, a programming level fault injection tool using the LLVM (Lattner & Adve, 2004) Just-In-Time Compiler (JITC) to al-low injections to intermediate code based on data categories (pointer data and control data). FULFI (Kontrollable Utah LLVM Fault Injector) (Sharma, Haran, Rakamari´c, & Gopalakrishnan, 2013) is another instruction level fault injector based on LLVM, which is able to inject random single bit errors at instruction level. FULFI is capable of choosing static or dynamic fault injection mode. However, the performance of LLVM-based fault injectors is restricted by the compiler specification (only GCC is supported), the heuristic study of the source codes and by the support of the instrumented Intermediate Representation (IR) of the machine code. LLVM-based approaches have historically had problems with parallel programs and large scientific codes written in FORTRAN. For our work, these problems are a limitation.

GOOFI (Aidemark, Vinter, Folkesson, & Karlsson, 2001) (Generic Object-Oriented Fault Injection) is a pre-runtime software implemented fault injection. GOOFI injects faults into the program and data areas of the target application before it starts to execute. The fault-injected functions replace the functions of a target program and compiles with single or multi-bit faults. Recompilation of source code for different test scenarios reduces the controllability and it is impossible to emulate a permanent fault in memory, cache or registers.

Li et al. (Li, Vetter, & Yu, 2012) designed BIFIT to investigate an application's vulnerability to soft errors by injecting faults at arbitrarily chosen execution points and data structures. BIFIT is closely integrated with PIN (Luk et al., 2005), a binary instrumentation tool. BIFIT relies on application knowledge by profiling the application to generate a memory reference table of all data objects. This approach becomes less practical when the application uses a random seed to dynamically initialize the input data set. Additionally, many scientific applications load their input data from disk and, as such, studying their behavior needs to be done over a representative sample of input data sets. Finally, due to the limitations of PIN, BIFIT is constrained to specific (although popular) hardware architectures.

Virtualization-Based Fault Injection

Virtualization provides an infrastructure-independent environment for injecting hardware errors with minimal modification to the system or application. In addition, virtualization can be used to evaluate a variety of hardware and explore new architectures.

Levy et al. (Levy, Dosanjh, Bridges, & Ferreira, 2013) propose a virtualization-based framework that injects errors into a guest's physical address and evaluates fault tolerance technologies for HPC systems (e.g. Palacios (Lange et al., 2010)). Their Virtual Hardware Fault Injector (VMFI) is only able to inject crash failures and IDE disk failures.

Winter et al. (Winter, Tretter, Sattler, & Suri, 2013) designed a software-implemented fault injector (SWIFI) based on the Xen Virtual Machine Monitor. Using Xen Hypercalls, Xen SWIFI can inject faults into the code, memory and registers of Para-Virtualization (PV) and Full-Virtualization (FV) virtual machines. PV intrudes into the original system via modifications to kernel device drivers. Because the injection targets registers (i.e., EIP, ESP, EFL and EAX) that Xen SWIFI does not directly control, it is not possible to be certain that an injection affects the application of interest. SWIFI and the Palacios VMFI are both useful for studying whole systems but for our work we are focused on studying application responses to data corruption in an effort to quantifiably improve its resilience.

CriticalFault (Xu & Li, 2012) and Relyzer (Sastry Hari, Adve, Naeimi, & Ramachandran, 2013) are based on Simics, a commercial simulator. With static pruning and dynamic profiling of the application, instructions are categorized into several classes, i.e., control, data store and address. This process reduces the number of potential fault injection sites by pruning the injection space. Depending on the test scenario, soft errors are injected into different categories, which produce different faulty outputs, e.g., crash or SDC. However, CriticalFault and Relyzer cannot always establish the correlations between the instruction level fault injection and the faulty behaviors, because tracing back from instructions to high-level languages is difficult. Therefore, only coarse-grained injection is available. This makes it challenging to improve the resilience of the original program based on insights learned from the fault injection studies.

GemFI (Parasyris, Tziantzoulis, Antonopoulos, & Bellas, 2014), proposed by Parasyris et al, is a fault injection tool based on the full system simulator Gem5 (Binkert et al., 2011). GemFI can emulate the faults in register files within a process to emulate the behaviors of a micro-component of process under the presence of soft errors. GemFI provides a solution from architectural level to inject the faults and study the propagation of faults, but by bringing in extra cycles in the application, the control of injection is operated inside of the source code to activate the corresponding injection functionality. These extra cycles are also vulnerable to the faults.

Wanner et al. (Wanner, ELmalaki, Lai, Gupta, & Srivastava, 2013) designed VarEMU, an emulation testbed built on top of QEMU. Injection is controlled by a guest OS system call. In order to inject faults, users have to import a library to interface with system calls and insert fault injection codes into the applications that run in the guest OS. The user space controls cannot guarantee that injections are applied to the specific user space application. If another user space application is running the same type of instructions and sharing the CPU with the injector targeted application, the consequence of fault injection is unpredictable and uncontrollable.

F-SEFI DESIGN

In the previous section we discussed background in the fault injection field. While these are interesting in their own ways, no one tool currently combines all of the features we desired in a tool meant to study the behavior of applications in the presence of faults. The key features of F-SEFI are summarized as follows:

Non-Intrusive

In designing F-SEFI we were keenly focused on providing fault injection with as little impact on the operating environment as possible. Our approach is non-intrusive in that it requires no modifications to the application source code, compilers, middleware and operating systems. It does not require custom hardware and runs entirely in user space so it can be run on production supercomputers alongside scientific applications. These constraints are pragmatic at a production DOE facility and also exclude any possibility of side effects due to intrusive changes, vital in science that requires verification and validation (V&V). Additionally, our approach allows other applications to run alongside the application under fault injection. In particular, this facilitates studies in resilient libraries and helper applications.

Infrastructure Independency

F-SEFI is designed as a module of the QEMU hypervisor and, therefore, benefits from virtualization. Since the hyper-visor supports a wide range of platforms, so does our fault injection capability. This enables us to explore hardware that we might not physically have as well as explore new hardware approaches. For instance, we can implement triple-modular redundancy (TMR) in certain instructions and generate errors probabilistically to evaluate classes of applications that might be resilient on such hardware. In addition, since all guest OSs are isolated, multiple target guest OSs from different architectures can work at the same time without any interference. Faults can then be contained and we can run multiple applications in different guest OSs and inject faults into them concurrently. Similarly, since F-SEFI can target a specific application, we can inject into multiple applications running within the same guest OS. This can help reduce the effects of the virtualization overhead by studying multiple applications (or input sets) concurrently.

Application Knowledge

F-SEFI performs binary injection dynamically without augmentation to source code. Moreover, it adapts to the dynamicity of data objects, covering all static and dynamic data. This is especially useful for applications that operate on random or file-loaded data or whose fault characteristics vary when given different input datasets. F-SEFI does not require the memory access information of the data objects at runtime. All the injections target the instructions, covering the opcodes, addresses, and data in registers copied from memory.

Tunable Injection Granularity

F-SEFI supports tunable injection granularity, allowing it to inject faults semantically. Faults can target the entire application or focus in on specific functions. Furthermore, the faults can be configured to infect specific operands and specific bit ranges. Particularly with function-level injection, F-SEFI can provide a gprof-like (Graham, Kessler, & Mckusick, 1982) vulnerability profile, which is useful to programmers analyzing coverage vulnerability. While fine-grained tunability operates on the symbol table extracted from an unstripped binary, F-SEFI can still do fault injections into random locations in the application if the symbol table is not available.

Injection Efficiency

F-SEFI can be configured to inject faults only in specific micro-operations and "get out of the way" for others. As such, it can be configured to only cause SDCs by flipping bits in mathematical operations. Or, it can be used to explore control corruptions (such as looping and jumps) or crashes (accessing protected memory, etc.). This generality allows a user of F-SEFI to focus their attention on studying the effects of specific SDC scenarios.

FAULT MODEL

In this paper we consider soft errors that occur in the function units (e.g., ALU and FPU) of the processor. In order to produce SDCs, we corrupt the micro-operations executed in the ALU (e.g., XOR) and FPU (e.g., FADD and FMUL) unit(s) by tainting values in the registers during instruction execution. Fault characteristics can be configured in several ways to comprehensively study how an application responds.

Soft errors can be injected into any machine instruction. In this paper we study corrupted FADD, FMUL, and XOR instructions. Since QEMU does guest-to-host instruction translation, we merely modify this process to perform the type of corruption we want to study and finely control the injection from the virtual machine hypervisor.

Figure 1. The overall system infrastructure of F-SEFI

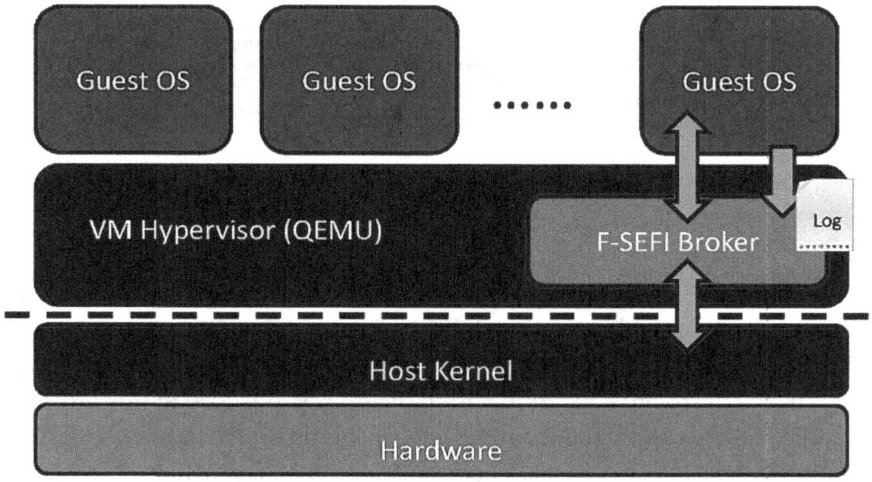

F-SEFI offers both random (for coarse-grained) and targeted (for fine-grained) fault injections. Initial development of the tool demonstrated the coarse-grained injection by randomly choosing instructions to corrupt in an application (DeBardeleben et al., 2011). This technique provides limited resilience evaluation at the application level. F-SEFI now also has the ability to do targeted fault injection into specific instructions and functions of an application. This allows a finer-grained study of the vulnerabilities of an application.

Any number of bits can be corrupted in an instruction using F-SEFI. This allows for the study of how applications would behave without different forms of error protection as well as faults that cause silent data corruption.

While injecting faults to instructions, F-SEFI can deterministically flip any bit of the input or output register(s). It can also be configured to apply a probability function to determine which bits are more vulnerable than others. For example, one can target the exponent, mantissa, or sign bit(s) of a floating point value.

FAULT INJECTION MECHANISMS

F-SEFI leverages extensive open source work on the QEMU processor emulator and virtualizer by interfacing with the hypervisor as a plug-in module. After the QEMU hypervisor starts a virtual machine image, the F-SEFI broker is loaded dynamically. As instructions are issued by applications running within a guest OS, F-SEFI intercepts these and potentially corrupts them before sending them on to the host kernel. This interaction is depicted in Figure 1.

F-SEFI runs entirely in user space and can be run as a "black box" on the command-line. This launches the tool, performs the fault injections, tracks how the application responds, and logs all the results back to the host file system. This is particularly useful for batch mode analysis to do campaign studies of the vulnerability of applications. F-SEFI consists of five major steps: profiler, configurator, probe, injector, and tracker as shown in Figure 2. These are explained in more detail in the next few sections.

Figure 2. The five major steps of F-SEF

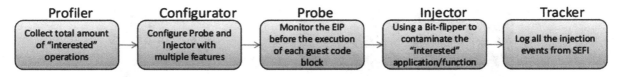

Step 1: Profiler.

As with most dynamic fault injectors, F-SEFI profiles the application to gather information about it before injecting faults. As described in Section 4, F-SEFI can target specific instructions for corruption. It is in this profiling stage that F-SEFI gathers information about how many occurrences of each instruction, there are as well as their relative location within the binary. It is also in this profiling stage that the function symbol table (FST) is extracted from the unstripped binary. This allows F-SEFI to understand where the application's functions start/end. Then the Execution Instruction Pointer (EIP) is observed through QEMU to trace where the application is at runtime. Table 1 shows the relevant information for a sample symbol table used in a later case study.

Step 2: Configurator.

The configuration contains all the specifics related to the faults that will be injected. This includes what application is to be studied, functions to target, the injection granularity, and the instructions to alter. Additionally, probabilities of alteration can be assigned to specific bit regions where injections are desired.

The configuration contains all the specifics related to the faults that will be injected. This includes what application is to be studied, functions to target, the injection granularity, and the instructions to alter. Additionally, probabilities of alteration can be assigned to specific bit regions where injections are desired.

Step 3: Probe.

Once profiled and configured, the application under analysis is run within the guest OS. The F-SEFI probe component then dynamically observes the guest instruction stream before it is sent to the host

Table 1. A subset of the function symbol table (FST) for the K-means clustering algorithm studied in Section 6.4; this is extracted during the Profiling stage and used to trace where the application is at runtime for targeted fault injections.

Function Name	Offset	Size
Find_nearest_point	x08048130	136
Clusters	x080489a0	143
Kmeans_clustering	x080491f0	661
Main	x08048a70	1713

hardware for execution. This instruction stream is snooped at a block-level where blocks of instructions in QEMU are organized to reduce over-head. The probe monitors the Execution Instruction Pointer (EIP) and if it enters the memory region belonging to the target application the probe then switches to instruction-level monitoring. At this more fine-grained level the probe begins checking micro-operations of each instruction that passes to the host. If the underlying instruction satisfies the conditions defined in the configuration phase, then the probe phase activates the injector.

Step 4: Injector.

QEMU has translation functions for how to translate each instruction on guest architecture into an instruction (or series of instructions) on host architecture. The injector phase of F-SEFI substitutes the original function with a modified one. The new corrupted version is controlled by the configuration to conditionally flip bits in the registers used during the calculation. This translation is entirely transparent to the QEMU hypervisor and allows F-SEFI to closely emulate faulty hardware without the associated overheads and limitations of hardware fault injection.

Step 5: Tracker.

F-SEFI maintains very detailed logs of what happens during the monitoring of an application as well as carefully tracking fault injections. When it decides to inject a fault it reports information about what instruction was being executed and the state of the registers before and after injection and the information is saved in a database. This way it is possible to analyze post-mortem the way in which the application behaved when faults occurred.

CASE STUDY

In this section we demonstrate F-SEFI injecting faults into five benchmark applications: Fast Fourier Transform (FFT), Bit Matrix Multiplication, Algorithm-Based Fault Tolerant Matrix Multiplication, K-Means Clustering and Speckle Reducing Anisotropic Diffusion (SRAD). These experiments were conducted using the QEMU virtual machine hypervisor with 30,000 trials for each benchmark. The guest kernel used was Linux version 2.6.0 running on Ubuntu 9.04. The host specifications are unimportant as all that is required is that QEMU can run on it in user space.

Table 2 gives specifics about the benchmarks we studied including the functions targeted for fault injection. Each benchmark was profiled as explained in Section 5.1 to deter-mine the number of floating point addition (FADD), floating point multiplication (FMUL), and exclusive-or (XOR) operations. These results are shown in Figure 3 and are the basis for the instructions that are targeted in the following

Fast Fourier Transform (FFT)

The Fast Fourier Transform (FFT) is a classic algorithm used in a wide range of scientific and engineering applications. Here we present results from fault injection experiments on 1- and 2-D FFTs using the extended split-radix FFT (Takahashi, 2001) algorithm.

Table 2. Benchmarks and target functions for fine-grained fault injection

Benchmarks	Target Functions for Injection
FFT: Fast Fourier Transform using Radix-2,3,4 and 8 FFT routine.	**FFT4b:** Radix 4 routine
	FFT8b: Radix 8 routine
BMM: Bit Matrix Multiply Algorithm from CPU suite Benchmark.	**Maketable:** construct the lookup tables
	Bmm_update: apply 64bits matrix multiply based on lookup tables
ABFT-MM: Algorithm-based Fault Tolerant Matrix Multiplication.	**Innerproduct:** vector dot-product
Kmeans: Kmeans Clustering Algorithm from Rodinia Suite Benchmark.	**Kmeans_clustering:** update the cluster center coordinate
	Find_nearest_point: update membership
SRAD: Speckle Reducing Anisotropic Diffusion from Rodinia Suite Benchmark.	**Main.omp.fn:** OpenMP parallel block

Figure 3. Instruction profiles for the benchmarks studied; each benchmark is reported as a whole application (coarse-grained) and one or two functions that were targeted (fine-grained), while both FFT, K-Means and ABFT-MM have a large number of FADD and FMUL instructions, the BMM benchmark is almost entirely XOR.

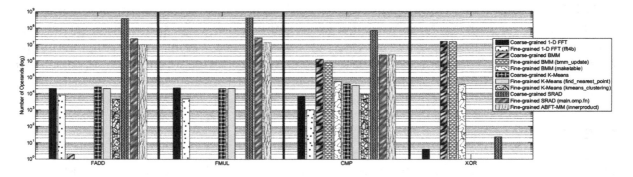

1-D FFT

After profiling the benchmark we chose to target the fft4b function. This function comprises a large percentage of the FADD and FMUL instructions. F-SEFI was configured to inject one and two single-bit errors into the benchmark into randomly selected FADD and FMUL instructions in the fft4b routine. Selected results from these four experiments are shown in Figure 4-7 and are presented in magnitude and phase. In each of the figures the thick blue line represents the correct output, without faults injected. The thinner red line shows what happens when F-SEFI injects faults into the specified regions. The whole process is shown in Figure 8

In Figure 4-7 we can see the differences in the high frequency area. This can be explained by signal processing theory because a transient and sharp peak or trough occurring at a certain time will strengthen the power of the high frequency components. Therefore, the variation in FFT outputs implies a significant spike/trough in the input time series due to data corruption by F-SEFI. It is interesting to see that in double faults injected in both FADD and FMUL experiments we can see two overlapping waves.

Figure 4. a) 1-D FFT magnitude output with and without a single FADD fault; b) 1-D FFT phase output with and without a single FADD fault

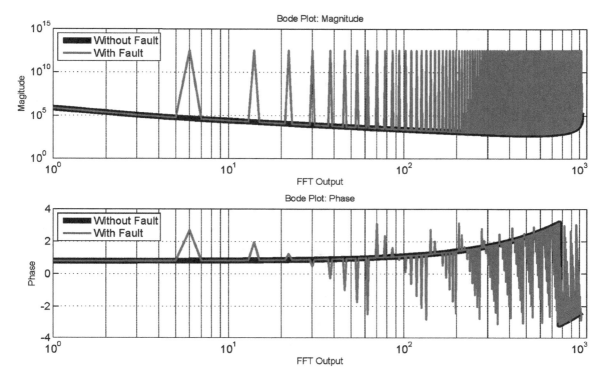

Figure 5. a).1-D FFT magnitude output with and without a double FADD fault; b).1-D FFT phase output with and without a double FADD fault

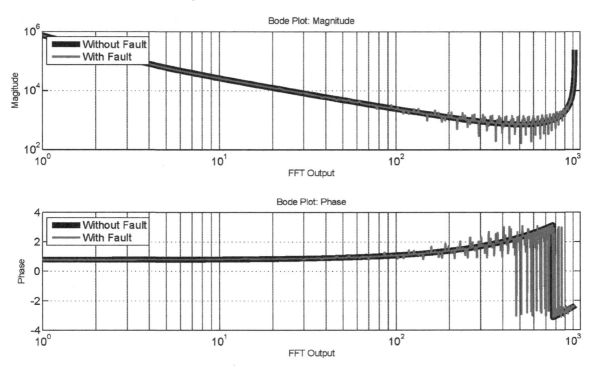

Figure 6. a).1-D FFT magnitude output with and without a single FMUL fault; b).1-D FFT phase output with and without a single FMUL fault

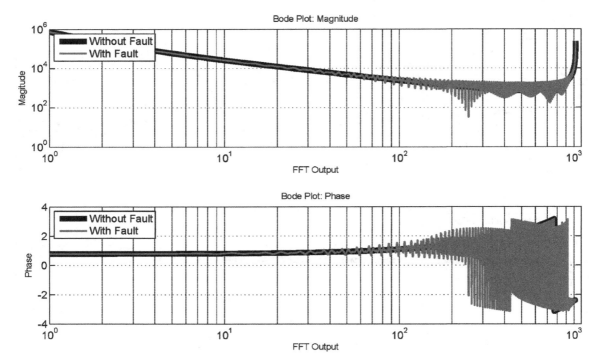

Figure 7. a).1-D FFT magnitude output with and without a double FMUL fault; b).1-D FFT phase output with and without a double FMUL fault

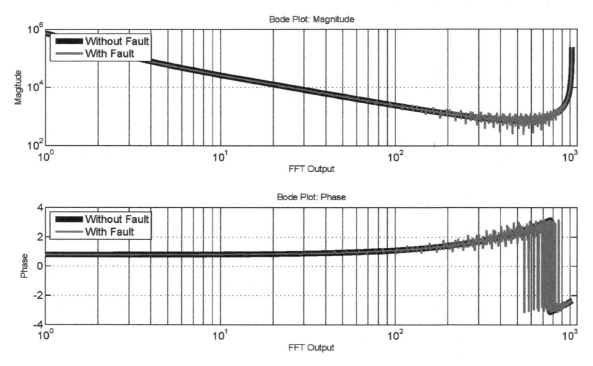

Figure 8. 1-D FFT algorithm with soft errors injected by F-SEFI

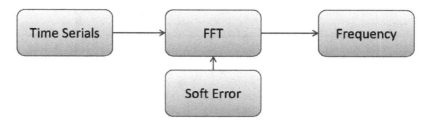

For the FMUL faults shown in Figure 6 and 7 and the double FADD faults, shown in Figure 5, the difference of the magnitude output is less significant compared with that of the single FADD faults. However, for the phase output, faults are distinguishable. In order to quantify the output difference introduced by F-SEFI, we use the forward error to compare the faulty 1-D FFT outputs with the original 1-D FFT outputs. The forward error is calculated as.

$$forward\ error = \frac{\|F - O\|_n}{\|O\|_n} \tag{1}$$

where F and O are the faulty and original output vectors, respectively, and $\|F - O\|_n$ is the L_n norm of the difference between the two output vectors O_n and L_n is the norm of the output vector of the original FFT. They are further calculated as:

$$\|F - O\|_n = \left(\sum_{i-1}^{n} |F_i - O_i|^n \right)^{\frac{1}{n}}$$
$$\|O\|_n = \left(\sum_{i-1}^{n} |O_i|^n \right)^{1/n} \tag{2}$$

L_2 error is also called the relative root mean square (RMS) and, therefore, we use the relative RMS to quantify the impact of the injected soft errors on the application execution. The FFT problem size was varied and the above four fault injection experiments were performed. The results are shown in Figure 9. While it is visually obvious from Figures 4-7 that all of the faults we injected cause output differences, from the RMS calculations we can see that the FADD faults caused the most noticeable output variations. Furthermore, we can see that as the problem size increases, the FADD faults caused more significant difference.

2-D FFT

We also tested a 2-D FFT for fault injection using F-SEFI. In the 2-D FFT an image is transformed by FFT into the frequency domain. Then, an Inverse FFT (IFFT) algorithm is performed which converts it back to the original image. The whole process is shown in Figure 10. For easy visualization of the data corruption output we chose to use an 8x8 spiral gray image. This original image is shown in the left-most picture in Figure 11.

Figure 9. The relative mean square root (RMS) of 1-D FFT outputs with different problem sizes showing that for the faults we injected into FMUL instructions the output varied only slightly

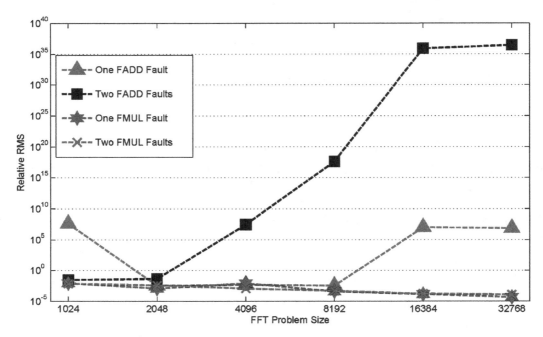

Figure 10. 2-D FFT algorithm with soft errors injected by F-SEFI

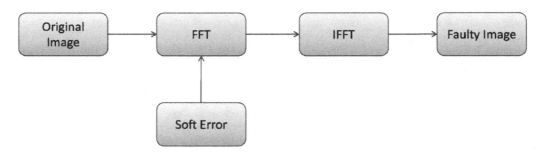

Figure 11. 8x8 spiral images with FADD and FMUL fault injections

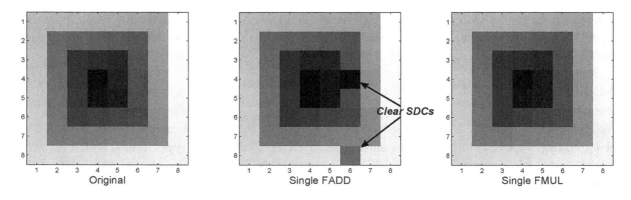

We chose to inject into the fft4b function during the FFT portion of the algorithm. This corrupts the original image in its conversion to the frequency domain. Then, the inverse FFT correctly converts the corrupted image back and we are able to visualize the output. For this experiment, single FADD and FMUL faults were injected, separately, to see how the image would be affected.

The FADD fault appears in the center picture in Figure 11. We can see that the (x,y) locations $(6,4)$ and $(6,8)$ were affected by a single fault injection and exhibit data corruption. On the contrary, the FMUL fault shown to the right in 11 ure 8 affects the image to a lesser extent. The difference of the image cannot be distinguished visually but careful analysis shows each pixel is on average 3% different from the original image. This difference may not be visually apparent but for an application using this result it could be catastrophic.

Bit Matrix Multiply (BMM)

Bit-matrix multiplication is similar to a numerical matrix multiplication, where numerical multiplications are replaced by AND bit-wise operations and numerical additions are replaced by XOR bit-wise operations. This algorithm is used in various fields including symmetric-key cryptography (Yang, Li, Sun, & Yang, 2008) and bioinformatics (Akutsu, Miyano, & Kuhara, 2000; Koyuturk, Szpankowski, & Grama, 2004). BMM can be generally defined as:

$$Y^{(m)} = \sum_{n=0}^{N-1} B^{(m \cdot n)} A^{(n)} \tag{3}$$

where $A^{(n)} \left(n = 0, 1, \ldots, N-1 \right)$ is an N-dimensional input vector, $Y^{(m)} \left(m = 0, 1, \ldots, M-1 \right)$ is the M-dimensional output vector, and $B^{(m \cdot n)}$ is an $N \times M$ matrix.

Here we present fault injection results from the BMM benchmark in the VersaBench benchmark suite (Rabbah & Agarwal, 2004). This benchmark uses a randomly generated input matrix of 2^{17} 64-bit elements. Each multiplication result is compressed to a 9-bit signature code as shown in Figure 12 and a 512-entry vector is used to statistically accumulate the frequency of code occurrences. This vector is used as a checksum for validation.

The BMM loop is repeated for 8 iterations and performs a total of $2^{17} \times 8 = 1,048,576$ 64-bit "multiply" operations (implemented as XOR as explained above). As shown in the profiling results in Figure 3, there are only XOR instructions in the BMM algorithm. Two core functions; bmm_update and maketable contain 93% and 0.24% of the XOR operations, respectively. We inject one and two single-bit faults into the XOR instruction used in the functions bmm_update and maketable and compare the output checksum vector with that from a fault-free BMM run.

From Figure 13, we observe that for our fault injections the total number of corrupted outputs was very small (between 200 and 300 corrupted outputs out of approximately one million). Moreover, we found that for the bmm_update function, when we injected two single-bit errors the number of corrupted outputs increased on average by 26%. For the maketable function we saw that two single-bit errors increased the number of corrupted outputs by an average of 47%. Whether this is significant enough to matter for this algorithm is difficult to tell without examining the results in the context of the parent application that uses this algorithm.

Figure 12. The Bit Matrix Multiply algorithm compresses the 64-bits of output to a 9-bit signature code used to checksum the result.

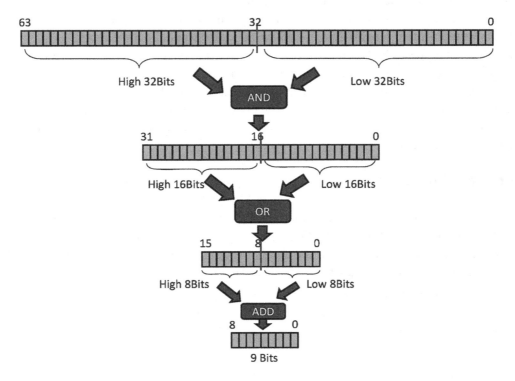

Figure 13. The Bit Matrix Multiply algorithm compresses the 64-bits of output to a 9-bit signature code used to checksum the result.

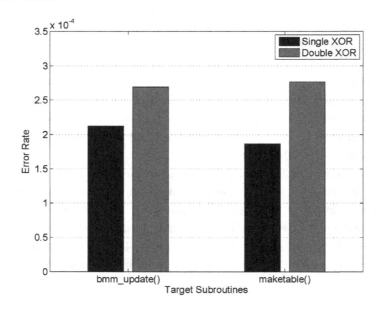

ABFT Matrix Multiplication

Algorithm-based Fault Tolerant matrix multiplication (ABFT-MM) is a checksum-based dense integer or fixed-point matrix multiplication strategy proposed by Abraham in (Huang & Abraham, 1984; Jou & Abraham, 1986). In this strategy, when calculating the matrix product, $C = A \times B$, checksumed matrices A' and B' are created by adding an additional row to A and column to B that represent the sum of each column and row of A and B respectively. After checksuming A and B, a fully checksumed matrix C' is produced by simply performing traditional matrix multiplication, $C' = A' + B'$, where C' has both an additional row and column containing the row and column checksums of C. One benefit of this strategy is that the nature of checksum relationships of A' and B' is preserved through C' via the operation of matrix multiplication, without any modification to the normal algorithm. Details are shown in Figure 14.

After multiplication, C''s row and column checksums can then be directly computed from the contents of C' and compared against the existing row and column checksums in C', i.e. the last row and column of C', respectively, to both detect and correct errors in C'. Using this simple variation of Abraham's more generic ABFT MM strategy, one cell error in C' can easily be detected and corrected. Abraham's strategy can be used to provide an arbitrary degree of error detection and correction by simply adding additional row and column checksums; however, the space and time overheads of doing so rapidly become prohibitive, especially in application domains of interest to the US DOE complex.

Here, we present the results of studying a double precision floating-point implementation of ABFT MM in the presence of injected faults using the F-SEFI fault injector. In this benchmark, we targeted the fault injection on the traditional triply nested FOR LOOP structure of the dense matrix multiply. Specifically, we used F-SEFI to corrupt a single randomly chosen bit in the output of a randomly chosen FMUL operation in the algorithm's inner-product calculation. Our benchmark included 30,000 trials divided into 3 different categories. Given that we were interested in studying the efficacy of a floating-

Figure 14. In ABFT MM, input matrices A and B are checksumed to produce A' and B' prior to standard dense matrix multiplication. After multiplying $A' \times AB'$, fully checksumed matrix C' is produced and is used for error detection and correction.

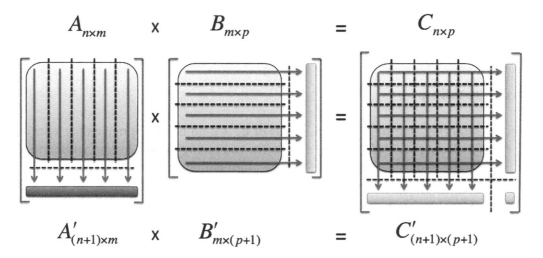

Table 3. Results fROm 30K trials of ABFT-MM in F-SEFI fault injection study

Severity	MLoB	MUoB	Exp.
Benign	18.67%	1.84%	1.85%
Correctable	6.59%	98.16%	98.15%
Silent Corruption	10.98%	0.00%	0.00%
Uncorrectable	3.76%	0.00%	0.00%

point implementation of ABFT MM, we targeted three separate bit-field ranges of the corrupted FMUL output by either having the error injected into the lower-order bits of the mantissa (M_{LOB}), or the upper-order bits of the mantissa (M_{UOB}), or the exponent (*Exp*).

After each execution, a pre-computed "golden" answer for C' was compared to the result of the ABFT MM after error detection and correction to determine whether the algorithm had successfully detected and corrected any errors in C'. The results of the 30,000 trials are summarized in Table 3. Injected errors were either:

1. Benign, in which case the computed was bit-wise identical to the pre-computed golden C',
2. Correctable, in which case the ABFT MM algorithm successfully detected and corrected the error in C',
3. Silent, in the sense that the algorithm did not detect the presence of an error but the computed C' bit-wise differed from the pre-computed golden C', or finally,
4. Uncorrectable in the sense that the algorithm detected the presence of one or more errors, but could not satisfactorily correct them.

We can see that all errors injected into either the exponent or the upper-order bits of the mantissa were either correctable or benign; however, in the case of errors injected into the lower-order bits of the mantissa, 10.98% of the trials resulted in silent data corruption and 3.76% resulted in detectable but uncorrectable errors. The benign errors, as well as the SDC and uncorrectable errors are a result of floating-point round-off error. This result is somewhat expected, given that the original algorithm was designed to work with integers and fixed point data types. The important result here is that F-SEFI proved to be an excellent vehicle to quickly test the performance of the ABFT MM strategy when directly implemented on double precision floating point numbers. By making use of F-SEFI, we will be able to comprehensively test any further refinements to this implementation.

K-Means Clustering

The K-Means Clustering algorithm (and variations of it) is used in a wide range of scientific and engineering fields including computer vision, astronomy, and biology when dealing with large data sets. K-Means inputs include dimensional particles to be clustered into clusters. The clusters' centers and cluster membership (which cluster each particle belongs to) vector is produced as output.

There are two key functions in the K-Means algorithm: kmeans_clustering and find_nearest_point. At the beginning of each iteration, the kmeans_clustering function updates the center of each cluster by calculating the centroid based on the distances between particles. For the newly generated cluster centers,

Table 4. K-means clustering centroids with and without fault injection showing the impact of corrupting data in the centroid calculations and clustering calculations for individual particle

# of Particles	2-D Coordinates of Cluster Centers			
	Cluster Index	Center w/o Faults	Center w/ Faults (Kmeans_clustering)	Center w/ Faults (find_nearest_point)
300	1	(194.92, 66.32)	(194.04, 67.07)	(195.88, 66.29)
	2	(126.39, 189.90)	(68.26, 202.14)	(126.39, 189.90)
	3	(44.53, 200.69)	(52.38, 4.2E+19)	(44.53, 200.69)
	4	(66.45, 68.25)	(66.35, 76.43)	(67.34, 68.25)
	5	(210.85, 181.85)	(195.63, 185.41)	(210.85, 181.85)

the find_nearest_point function updates the membership of each particle by searching for the nearest clustering center. These two functions can be represented with following formulas (Hastie, Tibshirani, & Friedman, 2001).

kmeans_clustering:

$$m_k = \frac{\sum_{i:C(i)=k} x_i}{N_k}, k = 1, \dots, K \qquad (4)$$

find_nearest_point:

$$C(i) = \arg\min \left\| x_i - m_k \right\|^2, i = 1, \dots, N \qquad (5)$$

where $x_i, \dots, x_N$ are particles, $C(i)$ denotes cluster membership of the ith particle. m_k is the mean vector of the kth cluster and N^k is the number of the particles in k^{th} cluster.

As shown in Figure 3, the find_nearest_point function contains 82.13% of the FADD micro-operations and 100% of the FMUL micro-operations. The kmeans_clustering function has no FMUL micro-operations and has the remaining 17.87% FADD ones. We chose to inject faults into the FADD instruction in these two functions.

Results from these experiments appear in Table 4 and are shown visually in Figure 15-16. This experiment uses a small data distributed 2-D data points for clustering and we chose to find five clusters.

By injecting a fault into the kmeans_clustering function the centroid for cluster 3 was sent far from the other data points. This causes the data points to effectively cluster into only four groups as shown in Figure 15 (cluster 3 centroid is not shown for clarity).

When a fault was injected into the find_nearest_point function a single particle becomes mislabeled. This is shown in Figure 16 and this causes the particle to be grouped with cluster 4 instead of cluster 1. This also augments the centroids for those clusters as can be seen in Table 4. This makes sense as the find_nearest_point function compares distances between a particle and the cluster centroids. The

Figure 15. K-means clustering without (left) and with (right) one single-bit FADD fault injected into the kmeans_clustering function; the uniformly distributed data clusters into only four clusters when one centroid is relocated far away.

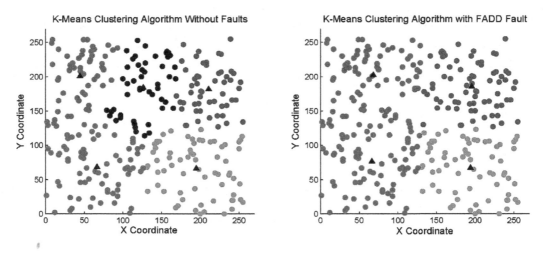

Figure 16. K-means clustering without (left) and with (right) one single-bit FADD fault injected into the find_nearest_point function; a single particle is affected and gets mislabeled. This also causes the centroids for clusters to change slightly.

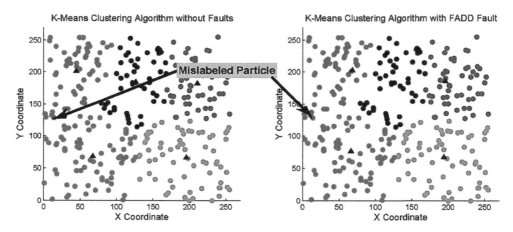

particle is assigned to the cluster that is closest and corrupting this calculation makes it incorrectly assign a single particle to the wrong cluster. Therefore, faults contained to this function will only affect a single particle while faults that affect the kmeans_clustering function cause much larger differences.

To demonstrate this, we performed FADD injections into the kmeans_clustering function while scaling up the number of particles. These results are shown in Figure 17. It can be seen that for our uniformly distributed dataset causing one of the cluster centroids to be removed has an effect on approximately 28% of the data points being clustered incorrectly. Also the centroids for each cluster then are wrong.

Figure 17. The number of mislabeled particles in the K-means clustering algorithm under fault injection as a function of the total number of particles; an FADD fault injected into kmeans_clustering causes about 28% of the particles to be mislabeled.

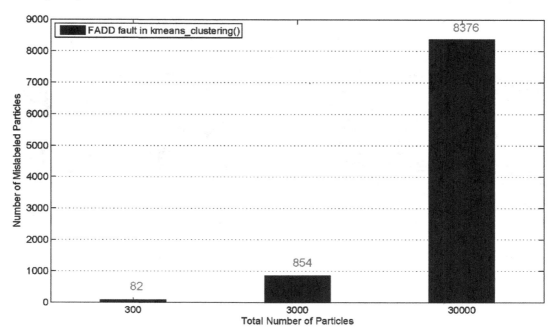

Speckle Reducing Anisotropic Diffusion

FSEFI can be used for testing the resilience of medical image processing algorithms. We applied FSEFI to the Speckle Reducing Anisotropic Diffusion (SRAD) algorithm. SRAD is a diffusion method for ultrasonic, astronomic and radar imaging applications. SRAD utilizes a set of partial differential equation (PDEs). Normally it is widely used for removing locally correlated noise, which are called speckles, without erasing any important image features. SRAD is used as the initial stage of Heart Wall Application, which is a heart movement-tracking program based on a sequence of ultrasound images. The input image for SRAD is a vague and coarse heart ultrasonic image (456x502 grayscale) as shown in Figure 18. Figure 19 displays the output image after processed being by the SRAD algorithm. The image looks smoother. However, if injected with the FADD fault, the output image is corrupted. There still exist some speckles that will affect the consequential analysis (Heart Wall) and degrade precision and resolution. Figure 20 shows that FADD fault that injected into SRAD algorithm fails the smoothing process to the speckled ultrasonic image.

In order to quantify the de-noise effect of the SRAD algorithm, we introduce Signal-to-Noise Ratio (SNR) (Murphy & Davidson, 2012) to noise of the surrounding background from which the signal should be distinguished. Usually we use decibel (dB) as the unit to quantify SNR. Images with lower SNRs have worse image quality compared to images with higher SNRs. We make use of routines of PyAs-

Figure 18. Original ultrasonic heart image with speckles

Figure 19. Speckles reduced ultrasonic heart image with SRAD algorithm

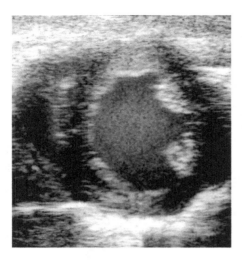

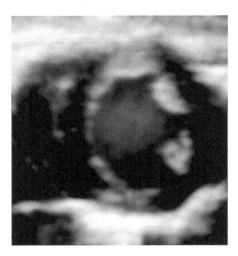

Figure 20. SRAD algorithm processed ultrasonic heart image with FADD fault injected in the smoothing processing

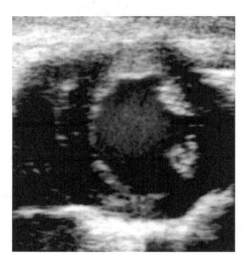

tronomy ((Czesla, Schroter, Schneider, Huber, & Pfeifer, n.d.), a collection of Python routines providing a serial of astronomy related data describe image quality. SNR is the ratio of a signal to the processing algorithms. An image is divided into regions with a fixed size. The SNR is calculated by assuming that the resulting chi-square value is properly distributed according to the chi-square distribution. The SNRs for three images, raw vague image, fault-free SRAD processed image and FADD fault injected SRAD processed image, are shown in Table 5.

Table 5. The estimate of SNR (Signal-of-Noise Ratio) of three images shown in Figures 18-20; the raw image is obviously poor and grainy-looking with SNR less than 12 dB. SRAD smoothing algorithm increase the quality of images by removing the sparkles with SNR around 50 dB, FADD injected in the SRAD algorithm reduce the effect of the noise removal by 66% which makes the image look still quite coarse and grainy.

Images	Estimate of the SNR (DB)
Raw Image	11.5556
SRAD Output Image	49.92474
FADD Fault Injected SRAD Output Image	17.74177

DISCUSSION

Overhead

Fault injection techniques are notoriously slow. Vendors use a combination of Register-Transfer Level (RTL) simulations and hardware fault injection to study chip behavior. Both of these approaches are obviously limited. RTL simulations require proprietary information about hardware designs and hardware approaches require specialized hardware. By contrast, our approach trades this for flexibility, working inside of a freely available virtual machine and running in user space.

F-SEFI adds an overhead of about 30% on top of the QEMU virtualization overhead in average. An example running BFS (Breadth First Search) algorithm shows the slowdown by injecting faults using F-SEFI in Figure 21. In contrast to other virtualization fault injection techniques that add about 200% overhead, our approach seems favorable. The QEMU overhead can be substantial due to the processor emulation and in our experiences might add as much as a 200x slowdown over running an application natively. This performance impact is still generally faster than RTL-based approaches.

However, it is important to realize that studying applications for their vulnerabilities is an offline exercise. Furthermore, processor emulation provides us a lot of capabilities to study interesting new hardware approaches and how they affect reliability. Finally, if applications have a small enough memory footprint they can be run concurrently inside the same guest OS and F-SEFI can perform fault injection experiments in parallel and without interaction between the processes.

Characterizing Fault Propagations

It is often difficult for a software designer to understand how an error might propagate through their application and what it might affect. F-SEFI provides a means for studying that propagation, which we demonstrated with the K-Means Clustering algorithm. For that algorithm, we saw that the kmeans_clustering function is particularly vital to protect as it has an impact on all of the centroids and about 28% of the particles were mislabeled when a fault occurred. In contrast, the find_nearest_point function only affects the classification of a single particle and some of the related centroids.

Figure 21. The execution time of running BFS (Breadth First Search) algorithm from Rodinia Benchmark; edge list generation step possesses most of the execution time. We can clearly observe that with FSEFI the execution time for edge list generation and graph construction slowdown by about 30%. But the mean search time has limited impact from attaching F-SEFI to the execution.

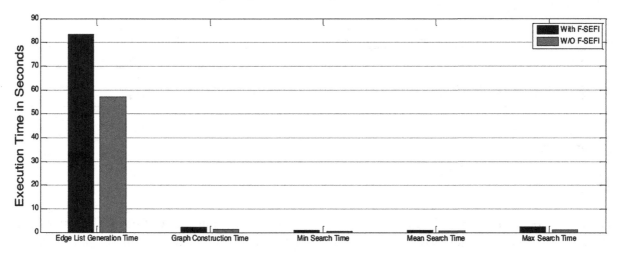

Based on analysis like this, the functions of an application can be divided into several vulnerability zones that characterize the impact of soft errors. These vulnerability zones can then be translated into a vulnerability map that quantifies with ranked scores how data corruption affects individual portions of an application. This is valuable information for a programmer to decide where to focus their attention to provide resilience techniques.

Effective SDC Studies

Faults can cause application crashes, data corruption, hangs, and also have no impact (are benign). Many applications can tolerate crashes much more than data corruption where getting the wrong answer can have drastic impacts on what actions are taken within a code or the scientific integrity of a result. As such, in our work we have particularly focused on the "getting the right answer" portion of the problem. While it is possible to study crashes using F-SEFI through corrupting moves, jumps, and conditional instructions we have not focused on that at this time.

One of the benefits of our approach is that since F-SEFI can target faults with extreme precision, we can study just how data corruption at specific points of an application affects the results. Also, because of our focus on causing data corruption rather than crashes it makes large-scale studies more practical. Many similar approaches require an extremely large number of fault injections to cause data corruption. While these approaches are valuable for studying data corruption probabilities in a code, they make it difficult to study the questions we are focused on with F-SEFI – how do corruptions at specific locations in an application cause it to behave? Our approach makes studying this question more effective and practical.

Figure 22. FADD faults (2000 in total) are injected into the different bits of a double precision floating-point.

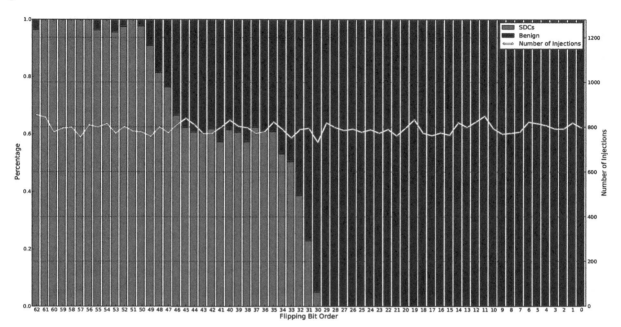

Correlation between SDCs and the Injected Order of Bit

We injected 2000 faults into FADD micro-operations of the k-means algorithm to statistically study the vulnerability of targeted bits of a double floating-point register used for FADD micro-operation. Bits are partitioned into sign, exponent and mantissa. The number of faults to select for injections is calculated using the functions proposed in (Leveugle, Calvez, Maistri, & Vanhauwaert, 2009). The two main functions find_nearest_point and kmeans_clustering are randomly chosen to inject the fault. Figure 22 shows that injections on different bits result in different outcomes to the clustering results. Sign bit and exponent bits are more vulnerable than the mantissa bits. Most of the mantissa bits have little impacts to the execution of the application when contaminated by a soft error.

FUTURE RESEARCH DIRECTIONS

In future work we intend to extend F-SEFI to enable the injection of faults into distributed parallel applications to satisfy the requirements of resilience analysis on exascale HPC applications. This is especially important when a single error in a parallel program propagates and causes a cascading effect, not only within the local process, but also to all other processes.

CONCLUSION

For a number of reasons there is call to be concerned about rates of silent data corruption in applications on next generation machines. Many of the applications that are run on leadership-class supercomputers are intolerant of data corruption and these applications are often used for science where knowing you have the right answer is extremely important. As the HPC community goes through this transition period towards exascale there is an opportunity to redesign applications so that they are made more resilient to these types of errors. However, knowing where to focus the attention has historically been difficult. Studies on the presence and impact of silent data corruption have been lacking due to the silent nature of the errors. They are difficult to reproduce and identify and are largely environmentally dependent. We have presented F-SEFI, which makes that effort easier by allowing an application programmer the ability to survey where an application is vulnerable and where it is more resilient.

F-SEFI leverages a robust and actively developed open source processor emulator, QEMU, to emulate faults as close to hardware as possible to do in software. By intercepting instructions in the translation of architectural instruction sets, F-SEFI is capable of injecting soft errors that cause incorrect execution results. F-SEFI can control when and how to inject the errors into which function in what application with different granularities. We demonstrated the use of F-SEFI on a variety of benchmark applications and have shown how data corruption can alter results. The tool is capable of doing large, campaign studies of fault injections into applications and provides access to a rich set of fault models. The tool can be useful in studying new approaches to resilience both at the hardware and software level and actually quantifying the benefits of them.

REFERENCES

Aidemark, J., Vinter, J., Folkesson, P., & Karlsson, J. (2001). Goofi: generic object-oriented fault injection tool.*Proceedings of International conference on dependable systems and networks (DSN).*IEEE. doi:10.1109/DSN.2001.941394

Akutsu, T., Miyano, S., & Kuhara, S. (2000). Algorithms for identifying boolean networks and related biological networks based on matrix multiplication and fingerprint function.*Proceedings of ACM international conference on computational molecular biology*. ACM. doi:10.1145/332306.332317

Bellard, F. (2005). Qemu, a fast and portable dynamic translator.*Proceedings of usenix annual technical conference*. ACM.

Binkert, N., Beckmann, B., Black, G., Reinhardt, S. K., Saidi, A., Basu, A., & Wood, D. A. (2011, August). The gem5 simulator. *SIGARCH Comput. Archit. News*, *39*(2), 1–7. doi:10.1145/2024716.2024718

Che, S., Boyer, M., Meng, J., Tarjan, D., Sheaffer, J. W., Lee, S.-H., & Skadron, K. (2009). Rodinia: A benchmark suite for heterogeneous computing.*Proceedings of IEEE international symposium on workload characterization (IISWC)*. IEEE. doi:10.1109/IISWC.2009.5306797

Czesla, S., Schroter, S., Schneider, C. P., Huber, K. F., & Pfeifer, F. (2015) *Pyastronomy*. from http://www.hs.uni-hamburg.de/DE/Ins/Per/Czesla/PyA/PyA/index.html

DeBardeleben, N., Blanchard, S., Guan, Q., Zhang, Z., & Fu, S. (2011). *Experimental framework for injecting logic errors in a virtual machine to profile applications for soft error resilience. Proceedings of Euro-par workshops*. ACM.

DeBardeleben, N., Laros, J., Daly, J. T., Scott, S. L., Engelmann, C., & Harrod, B. (2009). *High-end computing resilience: Analysis of issues facing the HEC community and path-forward for research and development (Whitepaper)*. DOE.

Graham, S. L., Kessler, P. B., & Mckusick, M. K. (1982). Gprof: A call graph execution profiler.*Proceedings of symposium on compiler construction*. ACM.

Guan, Q., DeBardeleben, N., Blanchard, S., & Fu, S. (2014). Towards exploring the soft error susceptibility of heapsort algorithms.*Proceedings of the 44th annual IEEE/IFIP international conference on dependable systems and networks (DSN)*. IEEE.

Guan, Q., Fu, S., DeBardeleben, N., & Blanchard, S. (2014). F-SEFI: A fine-grained soft error fault injection tool for profiling application vulnerability.*Proceedings of IEEE 28th international symposium on parallel distributed processing (IPDPS).*IEEE. doi:10.1109/IPDPS.2014.128

Hastie, T., Tibshirani, R., & Friedman, J. (2001). *The elements of statistical learning*. New York, NY, USA: Springer New York Inc. doi:10.1007/978-0-387-21606-5

Henderson, A., Prakash, A., Yan, L. K., Hu, X., Wang, X., Zhou, R., & Yin, H. (2013). make it work, make it right, make it fast, building a platform-neutral whole-system dynamic binary analysis platform. *Proceedings of the international symposium on software testing and analysis (ISSTA)*. ACM.

Huang, K.-H., & Abraham, J. (1984). Algorithm-based fault tolerance for matrix operations. *IEEE Transactions on Computers*, *C-33*(6), 518–528.

Jian, X., Duwe, H., Sartori, J., Sridharan, V., & Kumar, R. (2013). Low-power, low-storage-overhead chipkill correct via multi line error correction.*Proceedings of the international conference on high performance computing, networking, storage and analysis* (pp. 24:1–24:12). New York, NY, USA: ACM. doi:10.1145/2503210.2503243

Jou, J.-Y., & Abraham, J. (1986, May). Fault-tolerant matrix arithmetic and signal processing on highly concurrent computing structures.*Proceedings of the IEEE*, *74*(5), 732–741. doi:10.1109/PROC.1986.13535

Kaul, H., Anders, M., Hsu, S., Agarwal, A., Krishnamurthy, R., & Borkar, S. (2012). Near-threshold voltage (ntv) design: opportunities and challenges. *Proceedings of the 49th annual design automation conference*. ACM.

Koyuturk, M., Szpankowski, W., & Grama, A. (2004). Biclustering gene-feature matrices for statistically significant dense patterns.*Proceedings of IEEE computational systems bioinformatics conference*. IEEE. doi:10.1109/CSB.2004.1332467

Lange, J., Pedretti, K., Hudson, T., Dinda, P., Cui, Z., Xia, L., & Brightwell, R. (2010). Palacios and kitten: New high performance operating systems for scalable virtualized and native supercomputing. *Proceedings of IEEE international symposium on parallel distributed processing (IPDPS)*. IEEE. doi:10.1109/IPDPS.2010.5470482

Lattner, C., & Adve, V. (2004). Llvm: a compilation framework for lifelong program analysis transformation. *Proceedings of International symposium on generation and optimization (CGO)*. ACM. doi:10.1109/CGO.2004.1281665

Leveugle, R., Calvez, A., Maistri, P., & Vanhauwaert, P. (2009). Statistical fault injection: Quantified error and confidence. *Proceedings of design, automation test in Europe conference exhibition* (pp. 502-506). IEEE

Levy, S., Dosanjh, M. G. F., Bridges, P. G., & Ferreira, K. B. (2013). Using unreliable virtual hardware to inject errors in extreme-scale systems. *Proceedings of the 3rd workshop on fault tolerance for HPC at extreme scale*. IEEE. doi:10.1145/2465813.2465820

Li, D., Vetter, J., & Yu, W. (2012). Classifying soft error vulnerabilities in extreme-scale scientific applications using a binary instrumentation tool. *Proceedings of IEEE/ACM international conference on high performance computing, networking, storage and analysis (SC)*. IEEE. doi:10.1109/SC.2012.29

Luk, C.-K., Cohn, R., Muth, R., Patil, H., & Klauser, A., Lowney, Hazelwood, K. (2005). Pin: building customized program analysis tools with dynamic instrumentation. *Proceedings of acm conference on programming language design and implementation (PLDI)*. *ACM.* doi:doi:10.1145/1065010.1065034 doi:10.1145/1065010.1065034

Murphy, D. B., & Davidson, M. W. (2012). *Fundamentals of light microscopy and electronic imaging*. John Wiley and Sons, Inc. doi:10.1002/9781118382905

Parasyris, K., Tziantzoulis, G., Antonopoulos, C. D., & Bellas, N. (2014). Gemfi: A fault injection tool for studying the behavior of applications on unreliable substrates. *Proceedings of IEEE 28th international symposium on parallel distributed processing (IPDPS)*. IEEE. doi:10.1109/DSN.2014.96

Rabbah, R., & Agarwal, A. (2004). Versatility and versabench: A new metric and a benchmark suite for flexible architectures. *Proceedings of international conference on architectural support for programming language and operating systems (ASPLOS), the wild and crazy idea session.* ACM.

Sastry Hari, S., Adve, S., Naeimi, H., & Ramachandran, P. (2013). *Relyzer: Application resiliency analyzer for transient faults. Proceedings of Micro*. IEEE.

Sharma, V. C., Haran, A., Rakamari'c, Z., & Gopalakrishnan, G. (2013). Towards formal approaches to system resilience. *Proceedings of the 19th IEEE pacific rim international symposium on dependable computing (PRDC)*. IEEE.

Snir, M., Wisniewski, R. W., Abraham, J. A., Adve, S. V., Bagchi, S., Balaji, P., & Hensbergen, E. V. (2014). Addressing failures in exascale computing. *International Journal of High Performance Computing Applications*, *28*(2), 129–173. doi:10.1177/1094342014522573

Song, D., Brumley, D., Yin, H., Caballero, J., Jager, I., Kang, M., & Gxena, P. (2008). BitBlaze: A new approach to computer security via binary analysis. *Proceedings of international conference on information systems security (ICISS)*. Springer Berlin Heidelberg. doi:doi:10.1007/978-3-540-89862-7_1 doi:10.1007/978-3-540-89862-7_1

Sridharan, V., Stearley, J., DeBardeleben, N., Blanchard, S., & Gurumurthi, S. (2013). Feng shui of supercomupter positional effects in dram and sram faults.*Proceedings of International conference for high performance computing, networking, storage and analysis (SC)*. IEEE. doi:10.1145/2503210.2503257

Takahashi, D. (2001). An extended split-radix fft algorithm. *Signal Processing Letters, IEEE, 8*(5), 145–147. doi:10.1109/97.917698

Thomas, A., & Pattabiraman, K. (2013). Error detector placement for soft computation.*Proceedings of IEEE/IFIP International Conference on Dependable Systems and Networks (DSN)*. IEEE.

van Dam, H. J. J., Vishnu, A., & de Jong, W. A. (2013). A case for soft error detection and correction in computational chemistry. *Journal of Chemical Theory and Computation, 9*(9), 3995–4005. doi:10.1021/ct400489c PMID:26592395

Walker, R. C., & Betz, R. M. (2013). An investigation of the effects of error correcting code on gpu-accelerated molecular dynamics simulations. *Proceedings of the conference on extreme science and engineering discovery environment: Gateway to discovery* (pp. 8:1–8:3). New York, NY, USA: ACM. doi:doi:10.1145/2484762.2484774 doi:10.1145/2484762.2484774

Wanner, L., El Malaki, S., Lai, L., Gupta, P., & Srivastava, M. (2013). Varemu: An emulation testbed for variability-aware software. *Proceedings of the international conference on hardware/software co-design and system synthesis*. IEEE.

Winter, S., Tretter, M., Sattler, B., & Suri, N. (2013). simfi: From single to simultaneous software fault injections.*Proceedings of International conference on dependable systems and networks (DSN)*. IEEE. doi:10.1109/DSN.2013.6575310

Xu, X., & Li, M.-L. (2012). Understanding soft error propagation using efficient vulnerability-driven fault injection.*Proceeding of IEEE/IFIP international conference on dependable systems and networks (DSN).*IEEE.

Yang, Y., Li, C.-T., Sun, X., & Yang, H. (2008). Removable visible image watermarking algorithm in the discrete cosine transform domain. *Journal of Electronic Imaging, 17*(3).

KEY TERMS AND DEFINITIONS

Error: A deviation from the normal and correct operation of system.

Failure: Occurs when the system fails to deliver its required functionalities.

Fault Injection: A technique to generate fake signal to emulate the fault occurring on the hardware.

Fault Tolerance: To keep application running correctly in the face of failure of hardware.

Fault: A defect within the system at runtime.

QEMU: A generic and open source machine emulator and virtualizer.

Vulnerability: The capability of the software application dealing with the occurrence of the faults on the hardware.

Chapter 12
Verification of Super–Peer Model for Query Processing in Peer–to–Peer Networks

J. Pourqasem
University of Guilan, Iran

S.A. Edalatpanah
Ayandegan Institute of Higher Education, Iran

ABSTRACT

Equal peers in peer-to-peer (P2P) networks are the drawbacks of system in term of bandwidth, scalability and efficiency. The super-peer model is based on heterogeneity and different characteristics of peers in P2P networks. The P2P networks and large- scale distributed systems based on P2P networks use the super-peer model to design the query processing mechanism. This chapter first reviews the query processing methods in P2P networks, in which the authors classify theses query processing approaches in Unstructured and Structured mechanisms. Furthermore, the query processing techniques in distributed systems based on P2P networks are discussed. Afterward, authors concentrate on super-peer model to process the query of peers in P2P networks. Authors present the query processing methods in P2P-based distributed systems using the super node. Finally, the chapter provides some examples of each of the presented query processing techniques, and then illustrates the properties of each of them in terms of scalability and performance issues.

INTRODUCTION

P2P networks are distributed systems in which resources are shared by direct exchange between autonomous nodes. The shared resources contain documents, storage capacity, bandwidth, and CPU cycles. Each peer links to a small subset of other peers, so logical overlay networks are formed on top of the physical one (usually the Internet). Existing P2P systems have already had advantages of scalability, load balancing, self-organization, adaptation and fault tolerance (Xiao, Zhuang, & Liu, 2005; Hawa, As-Sayid-Ahmad, & Khalaf, 2013; Torkestani, 2012). In pure P2P systems, all peers play equal roles and

DOI: 10.4018/978-1-5225-0287-6.ch012

take same responsibilities regardless of their capabilities. Moreover, in query flooding process, any peer could be a query sender and the query receiver (Navimpour & Milani, 2015). However, as the size of P2P network grows, weak peers will seriously limit the scalability of P2P systems and become bottlenecks.

The peers in P2P networks usually have different characteristics with respect to their capabilities, e.g. available bandwidth, storage space or processing power (Nejdl et al., 2003; Cholvi, Felber, & Biersack, 2004). A discussion about the different capabilities of peers lead to an efficient network topology in P2P networks (Yang & Garcia-Molina, 2002). There is a small subset of peers with high capacity, called super-peers that takes over specific responsibilities for peer aggregation, query routing, query processing and possibly mediation (Cao, Li, & Liu, 2008). In this topology, the symmetry of pure P2P systems is broken by assigning additional responsibilities to super nodes (Garbacki, Epema, & van Steen, 2007). Consequently, super-peers make the decentralized networks more efficient by exploiting heterogeneity of peers and distributing load to machines that can handle the burden.

The super-peer network comprises the two-layer architecture (Awan, Ferreira, Jagannathan, & Grama, 2005). In the low layer, the super-peer is a node that acts as a centralized server to a subset of connected clients. When the clients need resource/file, submit queries to their super-peer and receive results from it (Yang & Garcia-m, 2003; Tan, Lü, & Lin, 2012). In the higher-layer, the super-peers are connected to each other and form the overlay network. The super-peers route messages over this overlay network, and submit and answer queries on behalf of their clients (Mastroianni, Talia, & Verta, 2005b). The super-peers are equal in terms of search, and all the client peers are equal in terms of download. Consequently, the client peers with low capacity are shielded from massive query traffic, which improves the scalability of the system. The peers use resources of network more efficiently because the super-peers provide the efficient and reliable query processing function.

The authors of (Garbacki et al., 2010; Keller & Martin-Flatin, 2006; Loser, Naumann, Siberski, Nejdl, & Thaden, 2004; Yu & Li, 2008; Yang & Garcia-m, 2003; Jelasity, Montresor, Babaoglu, 2009; Xiao et al., 2005) have proposed the super-peer networks. The authors of (Kirk, 2015; Yang & Garcia-m, 2003) addressed the principles and guidance of designing a super-peer overlay network. The authors of (Kaller & Martin-Flatin, 2006; Yu & Li, 2008; Jelasity et al., 2009) used network proximity for building a super-peer overlay, in which the client peers are connected to super-peers based on their distances. These studies considered decreasing the communication latency between nodes by exploring the network proximity. However, these studies have not discussed the efficiency a super-peer overlay by using the high capacity nodes. Super-peer selection has to make a trade-off between latency and efficiency features. The authors of (Garbacki et al., 2010; Loser et al., 2004; Nejdl et al., 2003) investigated the semantic similarity of peers in building process of a super-peer overlay. In selection process based on semantic similarity, the client peers that share the same interest are connected to the same super-peers. Furthermore, there are several design issues with the super-peer networks such as what should be the number of clients that a super peer serves? What should be the topology among super peers (Yang & Garcia-m, 2003)?

Every client peer in a super-peer network is connected to a fixed, very small number (usually one) of super-peers randomly and statically. The static assignment cannot adapt to the changes in the network structure or to the peer characteristics and capabilities. Moreover, single super-peer makes load balancing among the super-peers difficult and becomes a performance and scalability bottlenecks. The super-peer network suffers from super node crashing, in which restoring the system structure back to a consistent situation requires a considerable effort. Moreover, the super-peer systems are more vulnerable to attacks, as there is usually a single super-peer in the network (Yang & Garcia-m, 2003; Mahdy, Deogun & Wang,

2007). As a super-peer network is a combination of centralized and decentralized/distributed systems, it has the efficiency of a centralized search with the autonomy, load balancing and robustness to attacks provided by distributed search (Yang &Garcia-m, 2003).

This chapter provides the main idea, advantages and disadvantages of the various query-processing techniques. The remainder of this chapter is organized as follows: in the following section, the query processing of P2P networks and distributed systems based on P2P networks is introduced. Then, query processing in super-peer networks is presented. After that, the authors discuss the query processing of P2P-based distributed systems using the super-peer model. Finally, the chapter concludes.

QUERY PROCESSING IN P2P NETWORKS

In P2P systems, users submit queries to other peers and receive results (such as actual data, or pointers to data) in return. The queries can also take an appropriate format with respect to the type of shared resources. For example, the queries in a file-sharing system may be unique identifiers, or keywords with regular presentations. The nodes, which connect together, are called neighbors. Messages in P2P systems are routed along the neighboring path only. The length of the path traveled by a message is known as its hop count (Yang & Garcia-m, 2003).

When a user submits a query to all of its neighbors, local node becomes a query source. There are other routing protocols that send the query to a selected subset of neighbors (Crespo & Garcia-Molina, 2002; Yang &Garcia-Molina, 2002). When a node receives a query, it will process the query in its local collection of resources. If a result is found, it will return a single response message back to the query source. Furthermore, the node may also forward the query to its neighbors. In the baseline of Gnutella search, a Time to Live (TTL) is given to query messages, which specifies how many hops the message may take and it limits the search scale. Once a node receives a query, it decreases the TTL. Until the TTL is greater than zero, the node forwards the query to all its neighbors. Naturally, in P2P systems, the responding node does not know the location of the query source or requesting node. Consequently, the response message will be forwarded back along the same path the query message traversed. Otherwise, the responder can open a temporary connection to the source node and transfer results directly. The first method uses more aggregate bandwidth than the second one, but it provides anonymity for the query source (Yang & Garcia-Molina 2003).

The P2P systems can be divided into two categories based on the structure of nodes in network and its control strategy: Unstructured and Structured mechanisms. Next sections discuss the query processing in both categories.

Unstructured Mechanisms for Query Processing

In unstructured P2P systems, there are no specific constraints for the placement of resources, which are randomly spread across peers in the network (Shojafar et al., 2015). These systems use flooding or random walk approach to forward a query among a large number of peers (Qiao & Bustamante, 2006). In this environment each peer is randomly connected to a fixed number of peers and there is no information about the location of resources (Shamshirband, Petkovic, Javidnia, & Gani, 2015; Khan, Kiah, Ali, Madani, & Shamshirband, 2014; Trunfio et al., 2007).

Figure 1. Query processing in Napster

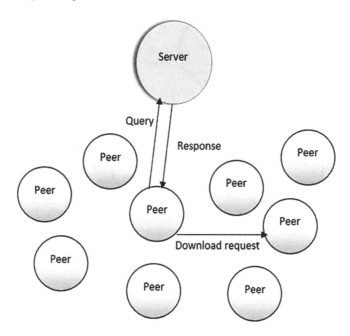

Napster is the first P2P system, which was introduced in 1999. It contained a central server that stored the index of all files shared by the peers in the network. For locating process, a user sends a query to the central server using the name of the file and receives the IP address of a peer containing the file. As illustrated in Figure 1, the communications between the requesting peer and the file owner's peer is direct (Navimipour & Milani, 2014). However, the central index server is used in Napster is not easy to scale and was a single point of failure. Although Napster is generally considered as the first unstructured P2P system, the existence of a central index distinguishes it considerably from today's unstructured P2P systems (Trunfio et al., 2007).

Gnutella is one of the most popular unstructured P2P systems that emerged after Napster. Any active node in Gnutella bootstraps the network. The search for a file was fulfilled via the basic flooding approach. Its overlay maintains messages that contain ping, pong and bye. The pings are used to discover peers on the network; the pongs are replies to pings and contain information about the amount of responding peer's data and other peers it knows about. The bye messages are optional messages that inform about the upcoming closing of a connection. For processing the query, Gnutella employs a simple flooding strategy, where a query is propagated to all neighbors within a certain number of hops. To limit the query-related traffic, maximum number of hops or TTL parameter is considered (Qiao & Bustamante, 2006). Figure 2 shows the query processing in Gnutella (Navimipour & Milani, 2014). The query sender floods the query message to its neighbors for some files. Each neighbor peer that receives the query, checks whether itself holds the matching file. If there is not result locally, the peer forwards a copy of query to its neighbors. Otherwise, the peer returns a response message to the peer that has received query from it. This response message is forwarded continuously to reach the query sender. Finally, the requested peer contacts the peer owning the file for downloading (Jin & Chan, 2010).

Figure 2. Query processing in Gnutella

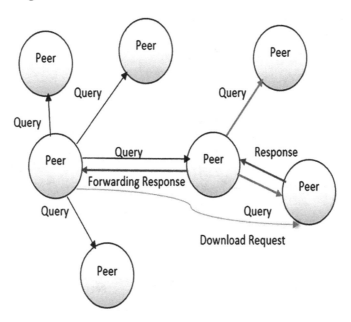

This searching method was never stable, due to peers frequently disconnect. When the network grows large enough, it gets saturated and often causes high delays. As a result, queries often drop and searches make unsatisfactory results, as only minor portion of peers are searched (Meshkova, Riihijarvi, Petrova, & Mähönen, 2008). The new production of the Gnutella attempted to improve query efficiency and reduce the overhead of controlling the traffic through a two-level hierarchy. The core of this approach consists of high capacity super-peers that connect to other super-peers and leaf-peers, which will be discussed in the related section.

Structured Mechanisms for Query Processing

The structured P2P systems provide a distributed indexing service, which is based on hashing function, and is known as Distributed Hash Table (DHT). Peers and files are usually mapped through the same hash function to a key space. The indices of peers and files are structured according to their keys, which facilitates locating the files. Most structured P2P systems support certainly exact match queries in O (log N) hops, where N is the size of the key space. Still, they do not directly support keyword searches, which constitute the core of queries in real P2P systems (Trunfio et al., 2007).

DHT-based systems can find a network location for a value in key space. The systems based on DHT are fully decentralized, scalable, and provide a certain fault tolerance and load balancing features. However, the main drawback of such systems is failure to support complex queries (Meshkova et al., 2008). In this approach, if a user wants to publish a certain file in the network, the name of the file is hashed to generate a unique file ID: the key. Then, the search function is called to estimate the pair (key, value); in DHT method (file ID, file location), the pair will be stored. When an appropriate node is discovered, this pair is propagated in DHT overlay. In DHT-based discovery system, requests are routed towards the appropriate node ID and the file location is returned. Lastly, the user can download the needed file (Meshkova et al., 2008).

Chord is the original structured P2P system as is depicted in Figure 3 (Stoica, Morris, Karger, Kaashoek, & Balakrishnan, 2001). The Chord maps the both peers and files through the same hash function to an m-bit key space. The peers in Chord are structured in one-dimensional circle according to their keys, and packets are always forwarded to one direction via the ring until they arrive to the destination node (Trunfio et al., 2007). The (key, value) pairs are located at the first node whose ID is equal to or greater than the value of the key (Meshkova et al., 2008). To process the query request, each node only needs to know its successor. However, to speed up the query process, the nodes store O (log N) elements in its routing table. In the routing table, a node maintains one entry to the one-quarter node, one entry to the one-eighth node and so on. Therefore, the nodes have a neighborhood and know them better than far away nodes in the ring. The search process emulates the binary search, thus requires O (log N) steps and messages. For example, in Figure 3, a user sends a query (file ID=50) to a node (ID=8). This node sends query to its neighbor node (ID=42). Because the node's ID is not equal to or greater to the value of the file's ID, it sends query to a neighbor node (ID=51). The joining or leaving of a peer does not have a global effect, but affects at most log N peers. Every time a peer joins the network, it takes responsibility of certain file keys previously assigned to its successor. Once a peer leaves the network, all of its allocated file keys become the responsibility of its predecessor. In general, each peer is in charge for an equal number of keys; therefore, load balancing is achieved (Trunfio et al., 2007). However, Chord cannot support range queries and multi-attribute-based lookups and suffers from search latency.

Figure 3. The structure of Chord

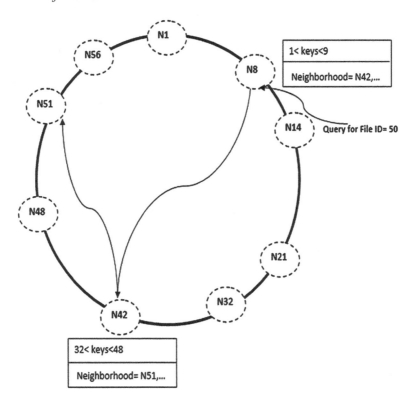

Content Addressable Network (CAN) is another structured P2P system, in which routing strategy is performed in a virtual d-dimensional coordinate space on a d-torus (Ratnasamy, Francis, Handley, Karp, & Shenker, 2001). Each node is assigned a unique region in the coordinate space. The coordinates of this region identify the node and are utilized in the routing strategy. The CAN exploits greedy routing strategy where a message is routed to the neighbor of the current node that is situated closer to the required location. Thus, for the effective routing, a node requires to know only the coordinates of its neighbors and their corresponding IP addresses. The (key, value) pairs are assigned uniformly on the d-torus using a hash function on resources, and each node hosts the pairs that are allocated to its zone (Meshkova et al., 2008). First peer in CAN keeps track of the entire d-torus. When a new peer is added, d-torus is divided into two equal volume regions and is assigned to the peers. Consequently, regions are divided or combined as the peers join or leave the network. A resource is located by forwarding a query message to the region that is responsible for keys specified in the query (Bandara & Jayasumana, 2013). The fundamental operations of the CAN are insertion, lookup and deletion. This mechanism attempts to limit the number of neighbors of each peer, regardless of the size of the network or the key space (Ratnasamy et al., 2001). An extension of CAN utilizes more than one hash function on the same space to obtain multiple coordinates for the same key in order to reduce lookup latency and support reliability and fault tolerance in case of unpredictable departures of the peers (Ratnasamy et al., 2001). The CAN is greatly scalable, robust, and fault-tolerant and self-organized (Meshkova et al., 2008), however it does not support range queries completely; moreover, it does not provide any additional mechanism to increase data availability, and the data are missed when some nodes are crashed.

A multi-attribute addressable network (MAAN) mechanism was presented in (Cai, Frank, Chen, & Szekely, 2004), which supports multi-attribute range queries by extending the Chord (Ratnasamy et al., 2001). MAAN uses the locality preserving hashing and a recursive multidimensional query processing mechanism. For numerical attributes, MAAN uses locality-preserving hashing functions to assign each attribute value an identifier in the m-bit space, and then maps it to Chord. In addition, it distributes resources to all nodes equally and achieves good load balancing. MAAN supports multi-attribute queries by making multiple DHTs for each attribute and range queries by using the hashing functions; however, the attribute schema of resources has to be fixed and known in advance. (Navimipour, Rahmani, Navin, & Hosseinzadeh, 2014). Furthermore, once the range of queries is very large, flooding method can be more efficient than routing it to nodes one by one, as MAAN does (Cai et al., 2004). Moreover, as DHT is created once and is updated at discrete intervals, the dynamic-attribute queries are not supported.

Summary of Query Processing in P2P networks

This section described the two mechanisms of query processing in P2P network: Structured and Unstructured mechanisms. The query processing approaches in P2P networks have scalability, load balancing and fault tolerance features. There is not any central server to answer the query in this network. The unstructured mechanisms forward the received query to neighbor peers using methods such as flooding. The unstructured approaches are not stable and generate high traffic in network. This approach suffers from delay in large-scale environments, queries often drop, and searches make unsatisfactory results. The structured mechanisms use the distributed indexes and hash function. Peers and resources are structured in a key space. The structured methods provide scalability and load balancing features well, but cannot support range and complex queries. In this approach, when some nodes crash, the data is missed. Table 1 provides the properties of query processing methods in P2P networks.

Table 1. The properties of query processing methods in P2P networks

Technique	Main Idea	Advantages	Disadvantages
Napster	• It has a client/server structure. • A central server indexes the resources (files) of all peers.	• It is simple and efficient query processing method. • It has low latency.	• It has low scalability. • It suffers from bottlenecks and single point of failure.
Gnutella	• It has a decentralized topology. • Query messages are forwarded to all the peers.	• It has fault tolerance and load balancing features. • It removes the bottlenecks and single point of failure.	• This method is not stable and generates high network traffic. • It has high delay and makes unsatisfactory results in large scale.
Chord	• It uses distributed indexing, and hashes the peers and files to m-bit key space. • Peers are structured in one-dimensional circle.	This method has the scalability and load balancing features.	• It does not support range and multi-attribute queries. • It suffers from search latency.
CAN	• It has a d-dimensional coordinate space on a d-torus. • Peers are assigned a unique region. • It uses greedy routing strategy.	This method is fault-tolerant, self-organized, and scalable.	• It cannot support the range queries. • Its data availability is low.
MAAN	It uses locality preserving hashing and a recursive multidimensional query processing.	• It supports multi-attribute range queries. • It makes load balancing.	• This method does not support dynamic-attribute queries. • The attribute schema of resources has to be fixed and known in advance.

QUERY PROCESSING IN P2P-BASED DISTRIBUTED SYSTEMS

One key issue in distributed systems is processing the query and discovering the requested resources. As the scale of distributed systems become larger, discovering methods face multiple problems such as bottlenecks and single points of failure. To find the requested resource efficiently, the decentralized approaches can be utilized. The distributed systems have adopted the P2P networks in order to avoid the above problems. The query processing approaches based on P2P networks are more scalable and fault tolerant than centralized or hierarchical methods.

The Grid is an important distributed system based on P2P networks. Grid is a vast collection of heterogeneous resources as a single and unified resource to solve large scale computing and data intensive problems for advanced science and engineering (Balasangameshwara & Raju, 2012; Erdil, 2012; Iamnitchi & Foster, 2004; Sathya, & Babu, 2010; Kocak & Lacks, 2012; Pourqasem, Karimi, & Edalatpanah, 2014). A large-scale and complex Grid application could include hundreds or thousands of geographically distributed resources. With the growth of application requirements, and system's size, the Girds should have the adaptation ability to provide performance, fault tolerance and scalability features (Deng, Wang, & Ciura, 2009). The Grids have adopted P2P networks to decentralize system functionality and to provide the load balancing, fault tolerance and scalability features (Javanmardi, Shojafar, Shariatmadari, Abawajy & Singhal, 2014). Figure 4 shows the query processing approach based on P2P networks (Caminero, Robles-Gómez, Ros, Hernández, & Tobarra, 2013). In this approach, the Virtual Organizations (VOs) of Grid are the peers of P2P networks. When a user of peer 1 needs a resource, submits query to local broker. If the requested resource is found locally, then it will be assigned to user's application. Otherwise, the broker of peer 1 forwards the query to the broker of peer 2. The VOs communicate with each other and send query to neighbor VOs/peers based on P2P network's protocol. If there is result in peer 2, it is returned along the same path back to the peer 1.

Figure 4. Query processing method in P2P-based grid

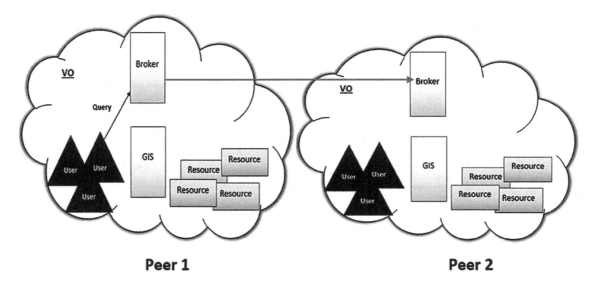

Iamnitchi and Foster

Iamnitchi and Foster presented a fully decentralized method for resource discovery in Grid environments (Iamnitchi & Foster, 2004). This resource discovery solution consists of four components: membership protocol, overlay construction, preprocessing, and request processing. The membership protocol defines how a new node joins the network and how new node learns about each other. The overlay construction function chooses the set of collaborators from the local membership list. In practice, this set may be restricted by factors such as available bandwidth, message-processing load, security or administrative policies and topology specifications. The preprocessing component indicates the off-line processing used to enhance search performance before executing the requests. For example, a preprocessing technique is spreading resource descriptions, which advertises descriptions of the local resources to other nodes in the network. The request-processing task has a local and a remote component. The local component searches a request in the local information, and the remote component implements the request-forwarding rule. Every participant in a VO publishes information on one or more local servers, which called node or peer. A node may publish information about one or multiple resources. Users generally send their requests to a local node. Then, it responds with a resource whose description matches the requirements; otherwise, the local node forwards the request to other nodes. Intermediary nodes forward a request until its TTL is expired or the requested resource is found (Iamnitchi & Foster, 2004). This mechanism supports attribute-based search and there is no central control. However, it does not scale well because the flooding algorithm produces large volume of query messages. Furthermore, the search results are not deterministic and this approach cannot guarantee to find the desired resource even if it exists (Iamnitchi & Foster, 2004).

Torkestani

Torkestani proposed a decentralized learning automata-based resource discovery algorithm for large-scale unstructured P2P Grids (Torkestani, 2012). This algorithm decreases the negative impacts of flooding problem on the network performance, and supports the multi-attribute range queries. In this mechanism, each peer can use a learning automaton. The queries are forwarded through the shortest path (the path with the minimum hop count) toward the peers of Grid, which more likely has the requested resources. In this method, each peer selects randomly a communication link by the automaton to route the resource provider. If the selected route at each step is shorter than the average length of the routes selected so far, then the algorithm prizes the selected route; otherwise, it is penalized. Therefore, as the proposed the algorithm proceeds, it converges to the route with the minimum expected length. This algorithm supports the high dynamicity of the scalable P2P Grid systems where the peers frequently and unpredictably join, leave, and rejoin the system.

ACO

Ant Colony Optimization (ACO) is a query processing mechanism for large-scale P2P Grid systems (Deng et al., 2009). Each peer in this system is configured as a nest. When users need a resource, they send a query to the nest. Then, the nest issues one ant or several ants to locate the resources with regard to the user requirement. At first, the ants walk randomly from nest to nest to discover the resources. If one ant finds the required resources, it will return the same path back to original nest and updates the routing information on the path with the collected information. The initial TTL of the ant is adjusted as the default value. The other ants of that nest, which are searching for the same resources, will travel in the network according to the routing information. Then, the ants most likely select the shortest path to travel in the system. This approach avoids a large-scale flat flooding by sending packets along the routes that are frequently traveled. Furthermore, the searching efficiency can be improved by utilizing multiple ants in parallel. The ants in ACO mechanism can carry a large amount of information in their memory when it is required. As the multiple requirements of the user are maintained in ant's memory, this method supports multi-attribute range query (Deng et al., 2009).

Brunner et al.

An approach was presented to reduce the lookup costs of the resource discovery services in the Grids (Brunner, Caminero, Rana, Freitag, & Navarro, 2012). This technique uses the data summarization based on Cobweb clustering algorithm (Fisher, 1987) to generate summaries of resource properties. This method supports the scalability of P2P-based content networks, because this way reduces the amount of data transferred between domain's brokers in the discovery process. The summaries are generated in three different steps; namely, pruning, leafing, and filtering. To reduce the network latency, the brokers filter and select the results from search results below a threshold based on a Round Trip Time (RTT) parameter. The brokers in each domain act as peers and propagate the summaries of the local resources to other domains. When users want to execute a job, they contact their local broker. If the requested resource is not found in local domain, the broker searches among the summaries that other domains have forwarded to it. The broker finds the domain that more likely has the resources matching the query and yields the lowest RTT. Finally, the query is sent to the chosen domain to answer it.

Caminero et al.

The prior technique has a drawback, in which all the domains in the system have access to summaries of all other domains. Another approach (Caminero et al., 2013) tackled this limitation by using the Routing Indices (RIs) (Crespo & Garcia-Molina, 2002) and a new version of it, called Hop Count Routing Index (HRI) to construct summaries and route queries to neighbor peers. The HRI (Crespo & Garcia-Molina, 2002) consider the number of hops that is needed to reach a datum. To adapt the summaries to be used within RIs, n-level summarization is presented. In n-level summarization technique, the precision of the j-level summary of a domain becomes higher than i-level summary if i < j. This method filters the attribute–value pairs whose probabilities are below a threshold value. This approach uses the goodness function (Crespo & Garcia-Molina, 2002) based on HRI table to decide which of the neighbors more likely have the resources matching some set of requirements. This function is computed for each neighbor domain using the summaries stored in the local HRI, and represents the probability of each neighbor domain of having a resource with the needed requirements.

Summary of Query Processing in P2P-Based Distributed Systems

This section presented the query processing in P2P-based Grid systems. Traditionally, the Grid systems have centralized or hierarchical structure and suffer from bottlenecks and single points of failure. Adopting the P2P networks and Grid systems can increase the scalability, load balancing and fault tolerance of Grid systems. However, decentralized approaches usually use flooding algorithm for processing the query, which generate high traffic on the network. Moreover, some techniques such as Routing Indices, summarization and learning automaton can improve the performance of query processing. Table 2 illustrates some examples of query processing techniques in P2P-based distributed systems.

QUERY PROCESSING IN SUPER-PEER NETWORKS

The super-peer networks act as a pure P2P network; however, every node is a super-peer, which is connected to a set of clients. The clients are usually connected to a single super-peer. Figure 5 illustrates the architecture of a super-peer network (Yang & Garcia-m, 2003). In a super-peer network, there are connections between client peers and super-peers, which can be seen as peer clustering. A cluster in this context is simply the set of peers that are joined to the same super-peer (Garbacki et al., 2007). The cluster size is number of nodes in the cluster including the super-peer itself. The peers (nodes) in different clusters communicate via their super-peers. In clustering method, cluster heads (super nodes, super-peers, or ultra-peers) are selected dynamically between the nodes in the network. In order to select a super-peer, the nodes in the cluster exchange an array of parameters, e.g., processing power, throughput, or number of neighbors to choose the most powerful nodes for the cluster's super-peer. The super-peer role can pass from node to node while the network is working (Mahdy, Deogun & Wang, 2007).

There is usually two-phase search process in super-peer model. First, the search is conducted among the cluster heads, which maintain the index of a group of ordinary or client nodes. This index includes sufficient information to answer all queries. For example, if the shared resources are files and queries are keyword searches based on file title, then the super-peer may keep lists containing the titles of files. When the super-peer in a local cluster locates the requested resource, it forwards the query to the re-

Table 2. Some example of query processing techniques in p2p-based distributed systems

Technique	Main Idea	Advantage	Disadvantage
Iamnitchi & Foster	• It is a decentralized method for query processing in Grid system. • It comprises four components: membership protocol, overlay construction, preprocessing, and request processing. • Each VO in the Grid publishes information on peer.	• There is no a central control in the network. • This technique provides load balancing and fault tolerance features. • This technique supports attribute-based query	• The scalability of this technique is low. • The search results are not deterministic. • Discovery of resource is not guaranteed.
Torkestani	• It offers a decentralized query processing for large-scale P2P Grids. • It is based on learning automata. • The queries are forwarded through the shortest path.	• This approach avoids flooding algorithm. • It improves the query processing performance. • It supports the multi-attribute range queries. • Scalability of the system is high.	There is delay in query processing until convergence.
ACO	• It provides a query processing mechanism for large-scale P2P Grid systems. • Peers in the system form a nest. • This technique updates the routing information on the path by ant's information.	• It avoids flooding algorithm. • This method supports multi-attribute range query.	• Each ant carries a large amount of information in memory. • There is overhead for updating the routing information.
Brunner et al.	• It is a resource discovery method in Grids that reduces the lookup costs. • It uses a summarization technique based on Cobweb conceptual clustering tree. • It uses Round Trip Time parameter to filter and select the results from the query processing.	• This method decreases the latency in query processing. • It increases the scalability of the system. • The amount of transferred information in system is reduced.	• The summary information of a domain is forwarded to other domains. • This technique suffers from overhead of keeping the summary information up-to-date.

spective client node that hosts the requested resource in second phase. It is also possible the super-peer does not send the query to the client node, and directly forwards the answer to the requesting node on behalf of the client peer (Meshkova et al. 2008). Consequently, once a super-peer receives a query from the neighbor super-peers, it will process the query on behalf of its clients, instead of forwarding the query to its clients. If the super-peer finds any results, it will return a response message containing the address of each client whose collection produced a result (Yang & Garcia-m, 2003). If not, the local super-peer submits the query to its neighbors. The neighbor super-peers process the query and generate the response message, if results are found. The local super-peers also forward any response messages from neighbor super-peers back to the clients (Yang & Garcia-m, 2003). As super-peers shield clients from all query processing and traffic, the peers with low capacity can be made into clients. Hence, as mentioned before, the super-peer networks exploit the heterogeneity of peers to organize the network topology (Yang & Garcia-m, 2003).

When a client joins a cluster, it sends metadata with respect to its collection to the super-peer of the cluster, and the super-peer will add this metadata to its index. If a client leaves the network, its super-peer will remove its metadata from the index. Moreover, a super-peer receives every updates of client's data (e.g., insertion, deletion or modification of an item) and changes its index. The super-peer model

Figure 5. A super-peer network

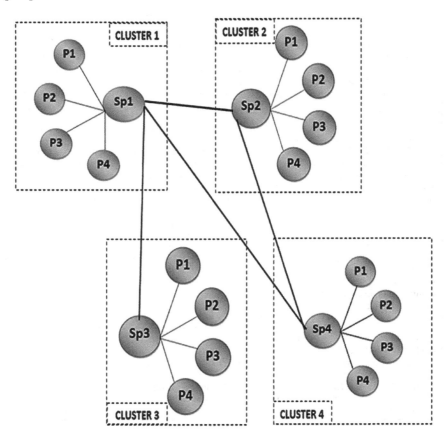

increases scalability of the system; however, the maintenance overhead of this overlay is high. When peers join or leave the system they make high overhead related to the maintenance of the indexes. Moreover, the information on the super peers is regularly updated by the client node's changes. If a super-peer fails, the associated indexes on it disappear, and its connected peers must join another super-peer (Yang & Garcia-m, 2003). In addition, failure of several super nodes could significantly degrade the network performance. Consequently, the super-peer system suffers from the lack of effective self-recovery mechanism (Yang, Zhan, & Shen, 2004).

Listing 1 illustrates the query processing in super-peer networks (Mastroianni, Talia, & Verta, 2005a). A number of techniques are adopted to decrease the load of process (Mastroianni et al., 2005b; Mastroianni et al., 2005a).

1. The number of hops in search process is limited by a TTL parameter; the TTL is decremented when the query is forwarded between two super-peers.
2. Each query message contains a field used to annotate the nodes that query traverses along its path. A super-peer does not forward a query to a neighbor super-peer that has already received it.
3. Each super-peer maintains a cache where it annotates the IDs of the last received query messages.

Listing 1. Query processing algorithm executed in the super-peer network

```
Step 1: v = max number of neighbors
Step 2: q.list: list of hosts traversed by the query q
Step 3: q.sender: neighbor super-peer from which q has been received
Step 4: q.id: query identifier
Step 5: q.ttl: current value of ttl
Step 6: for each incoming query q:
Step 7: if <q.id is in the cache> then queryInCache: =true;
Step 8: else <put q.id in the cache>
Step 9: q.ttl -= 1;
Step 10: if ((q.ttl>0) and not queryInCache) {
Step 11: select at most v best neighbours
Step 12: for each selected neighbour n:
Step 13: if <n is not in q.list> {
<Add this super-peer to q.list>
Step 14: forward a copy of q to n
}
}
<Ask the local information service for resources matching q>
Step 15: if <there are such resources> {
Step 16: send to q.sender a response message containing the IDs of the nodes
owning the requested resources;
Step 17: send notifications to the hosts owning the resources;
}
```

A super-peer discards the queries that it has already received. Whenever a super-peer receives a query, it finds several resources that satisfy the query constraints. Then, it constructs and forwards only one response message containing the IDs of those nodes which handle the found resources. Techniques (2) and (3) are used to avoid the formation of cycles in the query path. Technique (2) can prevent cycles only in particular cases (i.e. when a forwarded query is delivered to the same super-peer subsequently), whereas technique (iii) can remove cycles in all the other cases (e.g., when two copies of a query which are sent by super-peer A to super-peers B and C, are subsequently delivered to the remote super-peer D).

Gnutella2

As we mentioned before, the Gnutella does not scale well in very large scales and suffers from drawback produced by flooding. Low scalability of the original Gnutella was the motivation for developing of the second version of this system in 2002. In Gnutella2, there are two types of nodes: leaves (peers) and hubs (super-peer or cluster heads) (Meshkova et al., 2008). Each normal peer has one or two connections to hubs. The hubs index the resources of hundreds of peers by means of a query routing table based on hashes of keywords describing the resources. When a peer needs a resource, it sends a request to a hub. If the hub can find the result, the peer downloads the file directly from the peer that hosts the resource.

If not, the request is forwarded by the current hub to neighbor hubs. The address of hubs is taken from the hub's routing table. If the requested item is found or all the known hubs are searched or a predefined search limit is reached, the search stops. This approach significantly reduces the network traffic and makes the system much more scalable than the original Gnutella. However, the complexity of Gnutella2 is high and requires additional network maintenance. Furthermore, the system is vulnerable to DoS and other malicious attacks on the hubs (Meshkova et al., 2008).

FastTrack

FastTrack network employs super-peer clustering architecture at two-level hierarchy to achieve the necessary scalability in P2P networks (Meshkova et al., 2008). The peers are connected to the super-peers. The super-peers index the information of resources that the peers provide, and answer the query on behalf of the peers. The search method among the super-peers is conducted via flooding (Sakaryan, Wulff, & Unger, 2004). The super-peers are elected dynamically based on parameters such as high bandwidth, low latency, and plenty of computational and memory resources (Liang, Kumar, & Ross, 2004). In addition, the peers can choose the super-peers depending on other factors such as the workload of the super-peer and the locality considerations. Each super node normally connects to 40–50 of other super nodes and supports about 50–160 ordinary nodes. The ordinary nodes provide information about a given file to a super-peer. The information includes the single filename, the file size, the file descriptors and the content hash that is used to identify the file in an HTTP download request. The super-peers as central servers provide registration and log onto the clients, which in principle can be a single point of failure in the system.

KaZaA

KaZaA was introduced in March 2001 and it implemented the super-peer model in its design. Many millions of people used the KaZaA program to share files without any server (Navimipour et al., 2014). KaZaA consists of two types of nodes, super nodes (i.e., super-peers) and leaf nodes (i.e., peers). An overlay network is formed among the super nodes that each of them connects to a set of leaf nodes. Each super-peer indexes the files that the nodes own and answers the query on behalf of the peers. Therefore, the query is handled amongst the super-peers likely via flooding. The super-peers are selected dynamically based on high bandwidth, low latency, and plenty of computational and memory resources. When a node needs a file, it issues a request to its super node. Then, the super node initiates a query process in the overlay network to locate the requested resource (Chen, Zhang, Chen, & Shi, 2008). Figure 6 illustrates the query process in KaZaA (Jin & Chan, 2010). A peer sends the query message to the closest super peer. The super peer either returns a response message containing the peer's address matching the query, or forwards the query to the neighbor super peers. Finally, if the query result is found, the requested peer will download the file from the peer owning the file.

KaZaA is more scalable than Napster and Gnutella for its two-level architecture. However, KaZaA cannot support complex queries since the queries are routed in spite of their contents. At the time the work was conducted, there were approximately three million nodes in KaZaA network, of which roughly 30,000 were super nodes. Therefore, the super nodes in KaZaA network are very sparsely connected, and each super node is connected to about 0.1% of other super nodes. The typical lifetime of a super-peer is around 2.5 hours. The major disadvantage of KaZaA is the large amount of false files that users can encounter during their searches. The properties of super-peer based query processing techniques are presented in Table 3.

Figure 6. Query processing in KaZaA

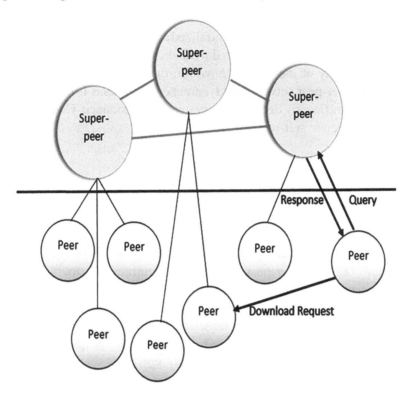

Table 3. The properties of super-peer based query-processing approaches

Technique	Main Idea	Advantage	Disadvantage
Gnutella2	• Gnutella2 has two types of peers: leaves and hubs. • Leaves connect to hubs. • Each super-peer indexes the information of the resources in the cluster by Query Routing Table. • The address of super-peers is taken from the Routing Table in each super-peer.	• The traffic in this technique is low. • It is more scalable than Gnutella.	• It is more complex than Gnutella. • It has maintenance overhead. • The super-peer is vulnerable to DoS and other malicious attacks.
FastTrack	• It is a super-peer clustering architecture. • It has two level architecture. • Each super-peer indexes the resource information and processes the query. • Super-peer selection is based on high capability such as high bandwidth and plenty of computational resources. • Super-peers are the central server for the ordinary peers.	This technique increase the scalability and efficiency of P2P networks.	• Super-peers forward queries to neighbors based on flooding algorithm. • Super-peers represent the single points of failure in the system.
KaZaA	• KaZaA is a sharing program. • There is no servers in its design. • Super-peers form an overlay network at higher level. • Super-peers are responsible for query processing and resource indexing.	KaZaA is more scalable than Napster and Gnutella.	• Super-peers use the flooding algorithm. • It does not support complex query. • Super-peers are sparsely connected. • There is a large number of false files.

Summary of Query Processing in Super-Peer Networks

The super-peer model makes a balance between centralized and distributed architecture for query processing in P2P networks. The super-peers are selected dynamically based on high capabilities. The super-peer model increases scalability of the system; however, there is single-point of failure problem. The maintenance overhead of super-peer networks in dynamic environments is high. Furthermore, failure of several super-peers could significantly decrease the network performance. Consequently, the super-peer networks cannot support effective self-recovery mechanism.

QUERY PROCESSING IN P2P-BASED DISTRIBUTED SYSTEMS USING SUPER NODE

Super-peer networks have been proposed to achieve a balance between the inherent efficiency of centralized searches, autonomy, load balancing and fault tolerance features offered by distributed searches (Yang & Garcia-Molina, 2003). A super-peer node acts as a centralized resource for a number of regular peers, while the super-peers connect to each other to form a network that exploits the P2P mechanisms at a higher level. The super-peer model allows for a very efficient implementation of information service and it is naturally appropriate for designing the large-scale and distributed systems.

A Grid can be viewed as a network composed of small-scale, proprietary Grids, called Virtual Organizations (VOs). Within each VO, one or more nodes, e.g. those that have the highest capabilities, can act as super-peers, while other nodes can use super-peers to access the Grid system. Whenever a VO wants to join the Grid, the corresponding super-peer must know the address of at least another super-peer and explores the topology of the system to constitute its neighbor set. As is illustrated in Figure 7 (Mastroianni et al, 2005b), the Grid has been configured by exploiting the super-peer model. In this configuration, the super-peers exploit the information services that are provided by the Grid infrastructure. The super- peers in each VO are responsible for answering all queries that are sent by client peers and neighbor super-peers. There is no requirement for all VOs to utilize the same Grid middleware, but all the super- peers must be able to communicate with each other using a P2P overlay network (Mastroianni et al., 2005b).

In this model, once a peer joins the VO or cluster, it must send information on its resources to its super-peer. Then, super-peer will index this information and maintain it. When a peer leaves the cluster or VO, the cluster's super-peer removes the resource information about that peer from the index. Furthermore, the super-peers receive updated information when the peer's resource information is changed. The query messages of Grid nodes are forwarded to the local super-peer. The local super-peer searches the local domain to find result for that request. If there is result, the super-peer sends a response message containing the ID or address of node that owns the requesting resources. If not, the super-peer forwards a copy of the query to neighbor super-peers by flooding or selection strategy. When there are resources in neighbor domain that matching the requirement, a response message is generated and is returned along the same path back to the requesting node (Mastroianni et al., 2005a).

Figure 7. The Grid configuration based on super-peer model

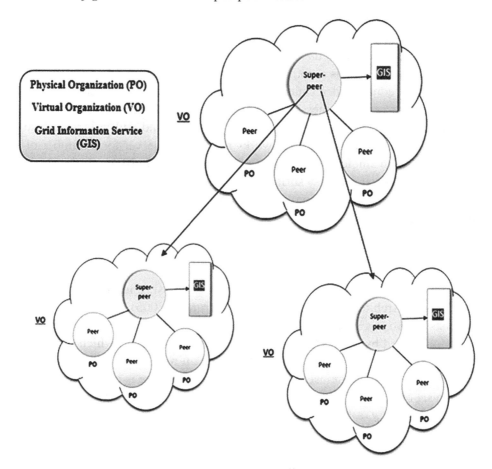

Mastroianni et al.

Mastroianni et al. implemented the super-peer model for designing a P2P-based Grid information service (Mastroianni et al., 2005b). In this environment, each super-peer exploits the centralized/hierarchical information service provided by the Grid infrastructure of the local VO. A super-peer realizes two main tasks: it is responsible for the communications with the other VOs, and it holds metadata about all the resources belonging to nodes of the local VO. The set of nodes belonging to a VO (i.e. the super-peer and the client nodes) is also represented to as a cluster. This model uses contact nodes to connect the super-peers. A contact node is a node in Grid system that plays the role of an intermediary node. There are one or more contact nodes available in each VO. Each time a VO wants to connect to the Grid, the corresponding super-peer contacts a subset of contact nodes and registers at those. Therefore, the selected contact nodes randomly choose a number of previously registered super-peers and link their addresses to the requesting super-peer to establish a neighbor set. Each super-peer communicates with contact nodes either periodically or every time it detects a neighbor super-peer disconnection. The query process mechanism is defined as follows. A node in Grid system forwards the query messages to the local super-peer. The local super-peer examines the local information service for the requested resources.

The super-peer returns a response message containing the ID of the node whose resources matching the request. Moreover, the super-peer forwards a copy of the query to a selected number of neighbor super-peers. Every time a matched resource is found in a remote VO, a response message is generated and is forwarded along the same path back to the requesting node. Then the remote super-peer to the node that handles the requested resource sends a notification message. The set of neighbor super-peers that are selected at forwarding procedure are determined through an experiential approach. Each super-peer keeps statistics on the amount of response messages received from all the known super-peers (Mastroianni et al., 2005b). This approach provides autonomy, load balancing and fault tolerance features in query processing. However, since a super-peer node works as a central server for a number of client peers, this mechanism suffers from single point of failure in each cluster. Furthermore, when the number of requests is increased, the super-peers may suffer from bottleneck, which may limit the scalability of this system. Lastly, as the resource information is updated periodically, this super-peer mechanism cannot support dynamic-attribute queries.

Talia and Trunfio

Talia and Trunfio presented a P2P architecture for query processing in Grids, which was compliant with Open Grid Service Architecture (OGSA) (Talia & Trunfio, 2005). As illustrated in Figure 8, the architecture consists of two layers. The lower layer is a hierarchy of Index Services (IS), which publish resource information owned by each VO; the upper layer is a P2P Layer, which contains two types of Grid Services: Peer Services (PS), which are used to perform resource lookup, and Contact Services (CS), which allow PS to organize themselves in a P2P network. There is one PS for each VO. Each PS is connected with a set of neighbor PSs with which it exchanges query and response messages in a P2P method. To process the query, a PS invokes the top level Index Service of the corresponding VO. A query response is sent back along the same path that query is forwarded. When a PS wants to join the P2P network, it must know the address of at least one PS. The CSs store the addresses of known PSs and a PS may communicate one or more well-known CS to obtain the address of registered PSs (Ebadi & Mohammad Khanli, 2011).

HPRDG

HPRDG (Hypercube P2P-based Resource Discovery in Grid) is another technique that uses the super-peer models to process queries in hypercube-P2P based Grid (Ali & Ahmed, 2012). HPRDG consists of two layers: an intra- overlay Circle Hypercube Service Node (CHyperSN), and a Hypercube Root Node (HyperRN) overlay. Each CHyperSN is a set of Hypercube Service Nodes (HyperSNs) connected using ring topology. HyperSNs are structured by Service Nodes (SNs) connected using hypercube topology. The SNs are nodes, which have high capabilities compared with other nodes within the organization; i.e., nodes, which have high availability, high CPU speed and high bandwidth connection. The SNs are selected based on the mentioned metrics. The SNs act as super nodes in the network and take responsibilities such as maintaining a continuous range r_a of attribute values and processing query among a set of clients (i.e., ordinary nodes in an organization). Each HyperSN is responsible for maintaining resource information within the organization belonging to a specific attribute (e.g. CPU load, Memory load). Consequently, the number of HyperSN at each organization is equal to number of existing attributes in organization. Each SN of HyperSN overlay is in charge for sub-range of attribute's range Value.

Figure 8. The two-layer architecture for query processing in Grid

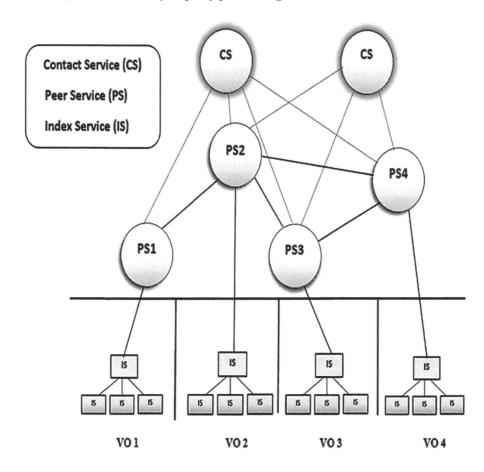

The HyperRN is a set of Root Nodes, which are the registration servers of each organization (Cholvi et al., 2004). In addition, the Root Nodes are gateways between the groups for forwarding query between organizations. To preserve the path locality, the RN of each organization connects with other RNs in other organizations based on distance metric. The HyperRN routes query message among different organizations. This technique provides the load balancing between SNs within the organization even if the distribution of resources is highly-skewed. HPRDG is suitable for distributed resource sharing systems in large scale with heterogeneous resources and different sharing policies. Moreover, this technique can support range and multi attribute queries (Navimipour et al., 2014); however, it suffers from a single point of failure in each SN.

Puppin et al.

Puppin et al. presented a Grid Information Service (GIS) based on P2P networks and Routing Indices (RI) technique (Puppin et al., 2005). As illustrated in Figure 9, the system consists of two main entities: Agent and Aggregator. The agent is responsible for publishing information about the resources of the nodes belonging to a super-peer. The aggregator indexes data from agent, answers queries and forwards them to the other super-peers in each super node. It also maintains an index about the resource information stored in neighbor super-peers. This mechanism is based on Globus Toolkit and complies with the OGSA standard. The information system is made as a network of super-peers, which aggregates the information about resources within VO. This method used the Routing Indices (RIs) to improve the performance of query routing, and to avoid high traffic in network. The RI represents the availability of resources of a specific type in the neighbor super-peers. This method employed a version of RI, called Hop-Count Routing Index (HRI), which considers the number of hops needed to reach a result (Puppin et al., 2005). Each node submits the query to its cluster's super-peer, which will pass it to other super-peers, if needed (Puppin et al., 2005). The system has problems such as false-positive error and single point of failure in each cluster. However, this approach can be built as a redundant network, where super-peers are replicated within each cluster. Furthermore, the regular updates may limit the dynamic-attribute queries in highly dynamic networks, but the range and multi-attribute queries are supported.

Summary of Query Processing in P2P-Based Distributed Systems Using Super Node

This section presented the Grid systems, and used the super-peer model to configure the Grid infrastructure. The Grid was comprised of several VOs or clusters, in which each super node with high capability is a central server for client peers. The scalability of these systems is high and they have a good performance. However, they suffer from single point of failure and bottleneck, and cannot support dynamic-attribute queries in highly dynamic environments. Table 4 lists the properties of query process techniques in P2P-based distributed systems using super node.

Figure 9. The overview of Grid Information Service based on super-peer model

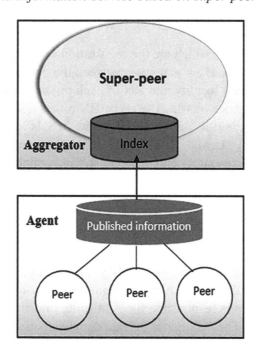

Table 4. The properties of query processing techniques in P2P-based distributed systems using super node

Technique	Main Idea	Advantage	Disadvantage
Mastroianni et al.	• It uses super-peer model to design a P2P-based Grid information service. • The information services are centralized or hierarchical. • Neighbor selection is based on statistic approach.	This technique provides load balancing, fault tolerance and autonomy features.	• Each super-peer in a cluster is a single point of failure in the system. • There are bottlenecks in high traffic of query messages. • This technique cannot support the dynamic-attribute queries.
Talia and Trunfio	• It is a two-layer architecture for query processing query in Grids. • It is compliant with OGSA standard. • It utilizes the hierarchical information service in lower layer. • The second layer is P2P layer.	This technique provides scalability and load balancing features.	• This approach forwards queries using the flooding algorithm and generates high traffic in network. • There is single point of failure problem in the system.
HPRDG	• It is a query processing technique in hypercube-P2P based Grids. • It contains two layers: Circle Hypercube Service Node and Hypercube Root Node.	• This technique preserves path locality and provide load balancing. • It supports range and multi- attribute queries. • This technique is highly scalable.	This technique suffers from single point of failure.
Puppin et al.	• It is a Grid Information Service based on P2P network. • It uses the Routing Indices for routing the queries. • It is based on Globus toolkit and complaint with OGSA standards.	• This technique is scalable and avoids flooding approach. • It supports range and multi-attribute queries.	• It suffers from false-positive errors and single points of failure in each cluster. • There are limitations for providing the dynamic-attribute queries in highly dynamic networks.

CONCLUSION

The super-peer models utilize the heterogeneity of the peers and increase the scalability and performance in P2P networks. In super-peer models, a node with high capability takes the responsibility for processing the query. The other peers send requests to super-peer and are shielded from processing load in the network. This chapter presented the super-peer model which is widely employed in P2P networks and distributed systems such as Grid. The chapter also discussed the query processing approaches in P2P networks, super-peer models and distributed systems based on P2P and Super-peer networks. Furthermore, it provided in detail the major developments and performance issues of each approach. Examples and properties of the available techniques are also presented.

REFERENCES

Ali, H., & Ahmed, M. (2012, October). HPRDG: A scalable framework hypercube-P2P-based for resource discovery in computational Grid. *Proceedings of the 2012 22nd International Conference on Computer Theory and Applications (ICCTA)* (pp. 2-8). IEEE.

Awan, A., Ferreira, R. A., Jagannathan, S., & Grama, A. (2005). Unstructured Peer-to-Peer Networks for Sharing Processor Cycles. *Parallel Computing*, *32*(2), 115–135. doi:10.1016/j.parco.2005.09.002

Balasangameshwara, J., & Raju, N. (2012). A hybrid policy for fault tolerant load balancing in grid computing environments. *Network and Computer Applications*, *35*(1), 412–422. doi:10.1016/j.jnca.2011.09.005

Bandara, H. D., & Jayasumana, A. P. (2013). Distributed, multi-user, multi-application, and multi-sensor data fusion over named data networks. *Computer Networks*, *57*(16), 3235–3248. doi:10.1016/j.comnet.2013.07.033

Brunner, R., Caminero, A. C., Rana, O. F., Freitag, F., & Navarro, L. (2012). Network-aware summarisation for resource discovery in P2P-content networks. *Future Generation Computer Systems*, *28*(3), 563–572. doi:10.1016/j.future.2011.03.004

Cai, M., Frank, M., Chen, J., & Szekely, P. (2004). MAAN: A multi-attribute addressable network for grid information services. *Journal of Grid Computing*, *2*(1), 3–14. doi:10.1007/s10723-004-1184-y

Caminero, A. C., Robles-Gómez, A., Ros, S., Hernández, R., & Tobarra, L. (2013). P2P-based resource discovery in dynamic grids allowing multi-attribute and range queries. *Parallel Computing*, *39*(10), 615–637. doi:10.1016/j.parco.2013.08.003

Cao, Z., Li, K., & Liu, Y. (2008). A Multi-Level Super Peer Based P2P Architecture. *In proceeding of the International Conference on Information Networking* (ICOIN), Busan. IEEE.

Chen, S., Zhang, Z., Chen, S., & Shi, B. (2008). Efficient file search in non-DHT P2P networks. *Computer Communications*, *31*(2), 304–317. doi:10.1016/j.comcom.2007.08.011

Cholvi, V., Felber, P., & Biersack, E. (2004). Efficient search in unstructured peer-to-peer networks. *Euroapen Transection on Telecomunications*, *15*(6), 535–548. doi:10.1002/ett.1017

Crespo, A., & Garcia-Molina, H. (2002). Routing indices for peer-to-peer systems. *Proceeding of the International Conference on Distributed Computing SystemsICDCS,* Vienna, Austria. IEEE. doi:10.1109/ICDCS.2002.1022239

Deng, Y., Wang, F., & Ciura, A. (2009). Ant colony optimization in spired resource discovery in P2P Grid systems. *The Journal of Supercomputing*, *49*(1), 4–21. doi:10.1007/s11227-008-0214-0

Ebadi, S., & Mohammad Khanli, L. (2011). A new distributed and hierarchical mechanism for service discovery in a grid environment. *Future Generation Computer Systems*, *19*(5), 836–842. doi:10.1016/j.future.2010.11.011

Erdil, D. C. (2012). Simulating peer-to-peer cloud resource scheduling. *Peer-to-Peer Networking and Applications*, *5*(3), 219–230. doi:10.1007/s12083-011-0112-8

Fisher, D. H. (1987). Knowledge acquisition via incremental conceptual clustering. *Machine Learning*, *2*(2), 139–172. doi:10.1007/BF00114265

Garbacki, P., Epema, D. H. J., & Steen, M. (2010). The design and evaluation of a self-organizing super-peer network. *Computers. IEEE Transactions.*, *59*(3), 317–331.

Garbacki, P., Epema, D. H. J., & van Steen, M. (2007). Optimizing peer relationships in a super-peer network. *Proceeding of27th International Conference on Distributed Computing Systems ICDCS '07*, Toronto: IEEE. doi:doi:10.1109/ICDCS.2007.126 doi:10.1109/ICDCS.2007.126

Hawa, M., As-Sayid-Ahmad, L., & Khalaf, L. (2013). On enhancing reputation management using peer-to-peer interaction history. *Peer-to-Peer Networking and Applications, 6*(1), 101–113. doi:10.1007/s12083-012-0142-x

Iamnitchi, A., & Foster, I. (2004). A peer-to-peer approach to resource location in grid environments. In J. Nabrzyski, J. M. Schopf, & J. Węglarz (Eds.), *Grid Resource Management* (pp. 413–429). Springer, US. doi:10.1007/978-1-4615-0509-9_25

Javanmardi, S., Shojafar, M., Shariatmadari, S., Abawajy, J. H., & Singhal, M. (2014). PGSW-OS: A novel approach for resource management in a semantic web operating system based on a P2P grid architecture. *The Journal of Supercomputing, 69*(2), 955–975. doi:10.1007/s11227-014-1221-y

Jelasity, M., Montresor, A., & Babaoglu, O. (2009). T-Man: Gossip-based fast overlay topology construction. *Computer Network Elsevier, 53*(13), 2321–2339. doi:10.1016/j.comnet.2009.03.013

Jin, X., & Chan, S.-H. G. (2010). Unstructured peer-to-peer network architectures. In X. Shen, H. Yu, J. Buford, & M. Akon (Eds.), *Handbook of Peer-to-Peer Networking* (pp. 117–142). Springer. doi:10.1007/978-0-387-09751-0_5

Keller, A., & Martin-Flatin, J.-P. (2006). *Self-Managed Networks, Systems, and Services*. Springer. doi:10.1007/11767886

Khan, A. N., Kiah, M. M., Ali, M., Madani, S. A., & Shamshirband, S. (2014). BSS: Block-based sharing scheme for secure data storage services in mobile cloud environment. *The Journal of Supercomputing, 70*(2), 946–976. doi:10.1007/s11227-014-1269-8

Kirk, P. (n. d). *RFC-Gnutella 0.6*. Retrieved from http://rfc-gnutella.sourceforge.net/index.html

Kocak, T., & Lacks, D. (2012). Design and analysis of a distributed grid resource discovery Protocol. *Cluster Computing, 15*(1), 37–52. doi:10.1007/s10586-010-0147-2

Liang, J., Kumar, R., & Ross, K. (2004). The KaZaa overlay: A measurement study. *Proceedings of the 19th IEEE Annual Computer Communications Workshop*, Bonita Springs, Florida, USA.

Loser, A., Naumann, F., Siberski, W., Nejdl, W., & Thaden, U. (2004). Semantic Overlay Clusters within Super-Peer Networks. In K. Aberer et al (Ed.), *Databases, Information Systems, and Peer-to-Peer Computing: proceeding of the First International Workshop, DBISP2P (LNCS)* (Vol. 2944, pp. 33-47). Berlin Heidelberg, Germany: Springer.

Lua, E. K., Zhou, X., Crowcroft, J., & Mieghem, P. V. (2008). Scalable multicasting with network-aware geometric overlay. *Computer Communication Elsevier, 31*(3), 464–488. doi:10.1016/j.comcom.2007.08.046

Mahdy, A. M., Deogun, J. S., & Wang, J. (2007). A Dynamic Approach for the Selection of Super Peers in Ad Hoc Networks. *proceeding of the Sixth International Conference on Networking (ICN)*. Martinique: IEEE. doi:10.1109/ICN.2007.1

Mastroianni, C., Talia, D., & Verta, O. (2005a). Advances in Grid Computing. In P. M. A. Sloot et al (Ed.), *A Super-Peer Model for Building Resource Discovery Services in Grids: Design and Simulation Analysis:Proceeding of the 2005 European Grid Conference,* Amsterdam, LCNS (*Vol. 3470*, pp. 132-143). Springer Berlin Heidelberg.

Mastroianni, C., Talia, D., & Verta, O. (2005b). A super-peer model for resource discovery services in large-scale Grids. *Future Generation Computer Systems, 21*(8), 1235–1248. doi:10.1016/j.future.2005.06.001

Meshkova, E., Riihijarvi, J., Petrova, M., & Mähönen, P. (2008). A survey on resource discovery mechanisms, peer-to-peer and service discovery framework. *Computer Networks, 52*(11), 2097–2128. doi:10.1016/j.comnet.2008.03.006

Navimipour, N. J., Rahmani, A. M., Navin, A. H., & Hosseinzadeh, M. (2014). Resource discovery mechanisms in grid systems: A survey. *Journal of Network and Computer Applications, 41*, 389–410. doi:10.1016/j.jnca.2013.09.013

Navimpour, N. J., & Milani, F. S. (2014). A comprehensive study of the resource discovery techniques in peer-to-peer networks. *Peer–to-Peer Networking and Applications, 8*(3), 474–492. doi:10.1007/s12083-014-0271-5

Nejdl, W., Wolpers, W., Siberski, W., Schmitz, C. H., Schlosser, M., Brunkhorst, I., & Loser, A. (2003). Super-peer-based routing strategies for RDF-based peer-to-peer networks. *Web Semantics: Science, Services, and Agents on the World Wide Web, 1*(2), 177–186. doi:10.1016/j.websem.2003.11.004

Pourqasem, J., Karimi, S., & Edalatpanah, S. A. (2014). Comparison of Cloud and Grid Computing. *American Jornal of Software Engineering, 2*(1), 8–12.

Puppin, D., Moncelli, S., Baraglia, R., & Tonellotto, N. (2005). A grid information service based on peer-to-peer. *Proceedings of the 11th international Euro-Par conference on parallel processing* (ISTI CNR), Lisbon, Portugal. Springer Berlin Heidelberg. doi:doi:10.1007/11549468_52 doi:10.1007/11549468_52

Qiao, Y., & Bustamante, F. E. (2006). Structured and unstructured overlays under the microscope: a measurement-based view of two P2P systems that people use. *Proceedings of the annualconference on USENIX' 06 annual technical conference*. Berkeley, CA, USA: ACM.

Ratnasamy, S., Francis, P., Handley, M., Karp, R., & Shenker, S. (2001). A scalable content-addressable network. Proceedings of the 2001 conference on applications, technologies, architectures, and protocols for computer communications (SIGCOMM). San Diego, California: ACM. doi:doi:10.1145/383059.383072 doi:10.1145/383059.383072

Sakaryan, G., Wulff, M., & Unger, H. (2004). Search methods in P2P networks: a Survey. In T. Böhme et al (Ed.), Innovative Internet Community Systems. Proceedings of I2CS-Innovative Internet Community Systems, Guadalajara, Mexico. Springer Berlin Heidelberg.

Sathya, S. S., & Babu, K. S. (2010). Survey of fault tolerant techniques for grid. *Computer Science Review, 4*(2), 101–120. doi:10.1016/j.cosrev.2010.02.001

Shamshirband, S., Petkovic, D., Javidnia, H., & Gani, A. (2015). Sensor Data Fusion by Support Vector Regression Methodology—A Comparative Study. *Sensors Journal, IEEE, 15*(2), 850–854. doi:10.1109/JSEN.2014.2356501

Shojafar, M., Abawajy, J. H., Delkhah, Z., Ahmadi, A., Pooranian, Z., & Abraham, A. (2015). An efficient and distributed file search in unstructured peer-to-peer networks. *Peer-to-Peer Networking and Applications, 8*(1), 120–136. doi:10.1007/s12083-013-0236-0

Stoica, I., Morris, R., Karger, D., Kaashoek, M. F., & Balakrishnan, H. (2001). Chord: A scalable peer-to-peer lookup service for internet applications. *Computer Communication Review, 31*(4), 149–160. doi:10.1145/964723.383071

Talia, D., & Trunfio, P. (2005). Peer-to-Peer protocols and Grid services for resource discovery on Grids. *Advances in Parallel Computing, 14*, 83–103. doi:10.1016/S0927-5452(05)80007-3

Tan, Y. H., Lü, K., & Lin, Y. P. (2012). Organisation and management of shared documents in super-peer networks based semantic hierarchical cluster trees. *Peer-to-Peer Networking and Applications, 5*(3), 292–308. doi:10.1007/s12083-012-0123-0

Torkestani, J. A. (2012). A distributed resource discovery algorithm for P2P grids. *Journal of Network and Computer Applications, 35*(6), 28–36.

Trunfio, P., Talia, D., Papadakis, H., Fragopoulou, P., Mordacchini, M., Pennanen, M., & Haridi, S. et al. (2007). Peer-to-Peer resource discovery in Grids: Models and systems. *Future Generation Computer Systems, 23*(7), 864–878. doi:10.1016/j.future.2006.12.003

Xiao, L., Zhuang, Z., & Liu, Y. (2005). Dynamic layer management in super-peer architectures. *IEEE Transactions on Parallel and Distributed Systems, 16*(11), 1078–1091.

Yang, B., & Garcia-m, H. (2003). Designing a super-peer network.*Proceedings of the 2003 19th international conference on the data engineering (ICDE)*.IEEE.

Yang, B., & Garcia-Molina, H. (2002). Improving search in peer-to-peer systems.*Proceedings of the 22nd International Conference on Distributed Computing Systems (ICDSC)*, Vienna, Austria. IEEE. doi:10.1109/ICDCS.2002.1022237

Yang, F., Zhan, S. H., & Shen, F. (2004). Maintaining and self-recovering global state in a super-peer overlay for service discovery. In M. Li & X. Sun & Q. Deng & J. Ni (Eds.), *Grid and Cooperative Computing: proceeding of Second International Workshop (GCC)*. Springer Berlin Heidelberg. doi:doi:10.1007/978-3-540-30208-7_120 doi:10.1007/978-3-540-30208-7_120

Yu, J., & Li, M. (2008). CBT: A proximity-aware peer clustering system in large scale Bit Torrent-like Peer-to-Peer networks. *Computer Communications, 31*(3), 591–602. doi:10.1016/j.comcom.2007.08.020

KEY TERMS AND DEFINITIONS

Cluster: A topology among client nodes and super nodes in super-peer model that allows them to communicate.

Grid: A distributed system for integrating and sharing heterogeneous resources in a large scale. It provides a corporation infrastructure usually for scientific communities.

Information Service: A data structure that indexes and stores information about the available resources in form of a database.

P2P Networks: A technology for sharing files and resources in large-scale environments without any centralized servers. It is an overlay network comprised of dynamics nodes.

Query Processing: Discovering the requested resource/file to download or run as an application.

Super-Peer Model: A structure consists of super nodes and client nodes. The super node is a central server for several clients and is more powerful than the clients are. The super-peers form a P2P network at higher layer.

Virtual Organization: A logical entity in Grid systems that consists of physical organizations. Each virtual organization can be seen as a peer in P2P Grid systems.

Section 4
Mobile, Cloud, and Internet of Things

Chapter 13
High Performance Computing on Mobile Devices

Atta ur Rehman Khan
King Saud University, Saudi Arabia

Abdul Nasir Khan
COMSATS Institute of Information Technology, Pakistan

ABSTRACT

Mobile devices are gaining high popularity due to support for a wide range of applications. However, the mobile devices are resource constrained and many applications require high resources. To cater to this issue, the researchers envision usage of mobile cloud computing technology which offers high performance computing, execution of resource intensive applications, and energy efficiency. This chapter highlights importance of mobile devices, high performance applications, and the computing challenges of mobile devices. It also provides a brief introduction to mobile cloud computing technology, its architecture, types of mobile applications, computation offloading process, effective offloading challenges, and high performance computing application on mobile devises that are enabled by mobile cloud computing technology.

INTRODUCTION

In the past few years, smartphones have emerged as a new computing platform that provides a wide range of applications, multifunctional sensors, and powerful operating systems. The smartphones support for complex applications from various domains, such as education, entertainment, business, and healthcare, has contributed much to its popularity.

It is expected that the number of smartphone shipments will increase each year with a record growth of about 16%-18% reaching a total of 2.6 billion units by 2016 (Canalys, 2015; IBM, 2010). According to the International Data Corporation (IDC), by 2015 (in USA) the number of mobile device Internet users will surpass the number who uses personal computers, making smartphone a primary computing platform for mobile users (IDC, 2013).

DOI: 10.4018/978-1-5225-0287-6.ch013

The advancing features and complexity of smartphone applications demand an ever increasing computational power and energy (IBM, 2010). To cater to these demands, manufacturers release new models of smartphones with enhanced features on a regular basis. However, due to size constraint of the smartphones, the advances in hardware are unable to cater to users/applications computational power and energy demands. Consequently, many applications are considered resource intensive for the smartphones due to their limited processing power, memory, storage, and battery life.

To make the smartphones more energy efficient and computationally capable, major software level changes are needed, because hardware level changes alone may not enable smartphones to achieve true unlimited computational power. Considering this, researchers envision the usage of cloud computing technology for mobile device (A. Khan, Mat Kiah, Ali, Shamshirband, & Khan, 2015).

This chapter provides a brief introduction to cloud and mobile cloud computing technology, mobile cloud architecture, types of mobile applications, computation offloading process, types of offloading, mobile cloud application models, offloading challenges, and high performance computing applications on mobile devises that are enabled by mobile cloud computing technology.

CLOUD COMPUTING

Cloud computing is a coalesce of many computing fields and is widely used in multiple domains (A. R. Khan, Othman, Madani, & Khan, 2014). By using cloud computing, small businesses can expand their IT resources based on service demands and avail equal opportunities of growth to compete with other businesses within the market. Cloud Computing has gained much popularity in the recent years due to features, such as virtually unlimited resources, low capital cost, ease of adoption, flexible resource provisioning, and high scalability (A. R. Khan, Othman, Xia, & Khan, 2015).

The cloud platform has three main layers, namely IaaS (Infrastructure as a Service), PaaS (Platform as a Service), and SaaS (Software as a Service). In most cases, the cloud layers are more of a pyramid structure where IaaS has enormous resources, PaaS runs a smaller number of software development frameworks and tools, and SaaS runs a number of applications that use the underlying resources and functionality (Hassan, 2011). Figure 1 shows the execution support and example services of each layer.

Figure 1. Layers of cloud platform

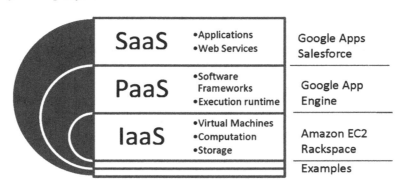

Infrastructure-as-a-Service

In IaaS layer, the computer infrastructure is provided as a service. IaaS provides guaranteed processing power, storage and bandwidth. The computation power and storage is provided in form of VM image executing on virtualized server(s) that can achieve guaranteed quality-of-service, irrespective of Operating System (OS) used. Some of the well-known IaaS platforms include Amazon Elastic Compute Cloud (EC2) (Amazon, 2015) and Rackspace (Rackspace, 2015). In EC2, users can create a particular Virtual Machine (VM) with specific hardware resource requirements and deploy the required OS and applications on top of the VM. The users can also upload their own VM image with pre-installed OS and applications. IaaS services are usually billed on usage basis (also known as utility computing), where users pay only for what they use (computation, storage and bandwidth).

Platform-as-a-Service

PaaS layer provides a virtualized platform that consists of one of more servers, operating systems and software frameworks. The PaaS platform can be utilized in form of assigned physical server (s) with pre-installed software frameworks or a VM Image that contains user required software frameworks and execution runtime (Mustafa, Nazir, Hayat, Khan, & Madani). PaaS based platforms are usually used for development, management and hosting of applications. PaaS differs from IaaS in a way that PaaS provides execution platform, software stacks, and services with focus on a particular set of applications, while IaaS lacks those software stacks. The renowned examples of PaaS include Google App Engine (Google, 2015a) and Microsoft Azure (Microsoft, 2015). PaaS based services are usually charged on usage basis.

Software-as-a-Service

SaaS layer provides remote access of applications over the Internet. The applications are deployed in the cloud and users can access those applications without installing them locally. SaaS based applications can be accessed through web browsers or locally installed thin client applications. Moreover, the cloud resources are used in form of web services that allow users to access applications without purchasing them. Hence, the users can subscribe for usage of applications on fixed leased period basis or usage basis. Google Apps (Google, 2015c) and Salesforce (Salesforce, 2015) are renowned examples of SaaS.

MOBILE CLOUD COMPUTING

The usage of cloud computing for mobile devices gives birth to a new domain called *mobile cloud computing*, which is defined as:

An integration of cloud computing technology with mobile devices to make the mobile devices resourcefull in terms of computational power, memory, storage, energy, and context-awareness. (A. R. Khan et al., 2014)

The primary objective of mobile cloud computing is to provide enhanced user experience to mobile users in terms of computational time, battery time, communications, services, and mobile device resource enhancement. Mobile cloud computing makes the mobile devices resourceful and energy efficient by enabling them to offload resource-intensive computational tasks to the resource-rich cloud. Consequently, the tasks use cloud computational cycles, which ultimately enhances the applications performance, reduces energy consumption, and executes applications that are unable to execute due to insufficient smartphone resources. For mobile cloud computing, the selection of a cloud service depends upon the operation of applications. Therefore, to overcome smartphones resource constraints, any of the aforementioned cloud service layers can be utilized (A. N. Khan, Mat Kiah, Khan, Madani, & Khan, 2013).

Mobile Cloud Architecture

The term *mobile cloud* is generally referred to in two perspectives, namely infrastructure-based and ad-hoc. In *infrastructure-based* architecture, the cloud hardware infrastructure remains stationary and provides services to the mobile users. On the other hand, in *ad-hoc* architecture, multiple mobile devices form a group that acts as a cloud and offer services to other mobile devices However, the offered cloud service may be virtual (group based) or real, where requests are sent to the real cloud (A. R. Khan, M. Othman, F. Xia, et al., 2015). Figure 2 shows that basic architecture of mobile cloud.

Figure 2. Mobile cloud architecture

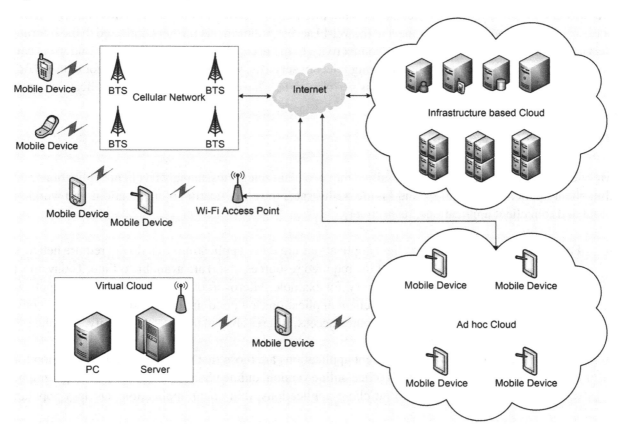

Figure 3. Classification of mobile applications

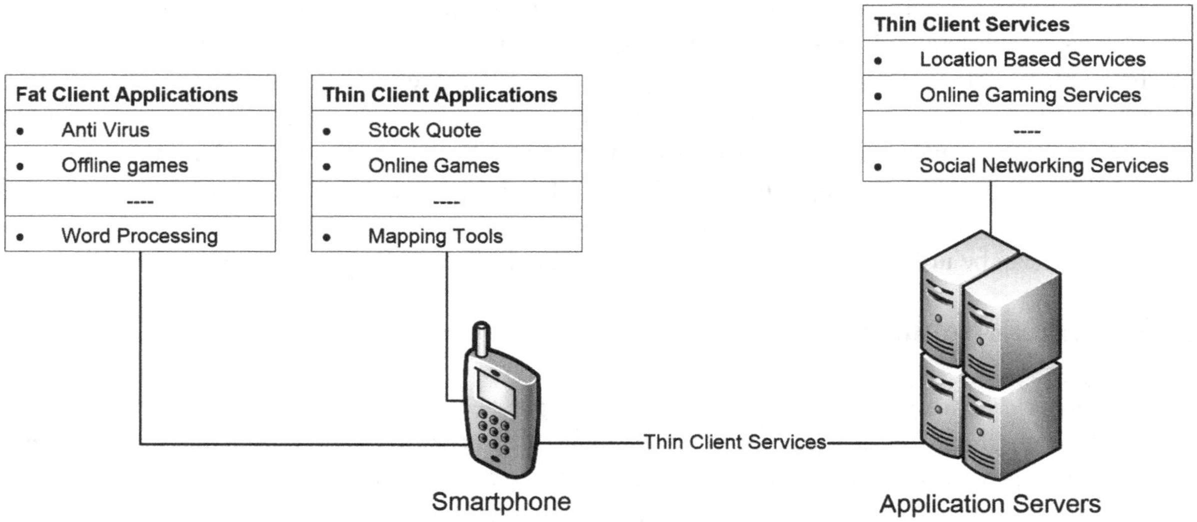

In the current mobile cloud architecture, mobile devices can access cloud services in two ways, i.e., through mobile network (telecom network) or through access points. In the mobile network (telecom network) case, the mobile devices connect to a network through a Base Station (BS). The telecom networks are further connected to the Internet and provide Internet connectivity to the users. Alternatively, in the access point case, mobile users connect to the Wi-Fi access points that is further connected to the Internet Service Provider (ISP) to offer Internet connectivity to the users. Therefore, the mobile cloud users can access cloud based services without utilizing telecom services, which may charge them for data traffic.

Before we discuss, how the offloading is performed, let's have a look at the mobile application types, which are discussed as follows:

Types of Mobile Applications

Mobile applications can be broadly classified into two main categories, namely fat client applications and thin client applications. Figure 3 and Figure 4 illustrates the classification of applications and working of fat and thin client applications, respectively.

- **Fat Client Applications:** Fat client applications are those applications that do not require network connection for operation as most of the required resources (data) are available offline. Today, most of the applications fall into this category, for example, Microsoft office package, antivirus applications, and high graphics games. Fat client applications are good in terms of the availability, compatibility, security, and hardware resource access, whereas bad in terms of portability, complexity, and resource consumption.
- **Thin Client Applications:** Thin client applications are those that require network connection for their operation, such as Microsoft office online version, online photo editing tools, and high graphics online games. Compared to fat client applications, thin client applications are less popular.

Figure 4. Working of mobile applications

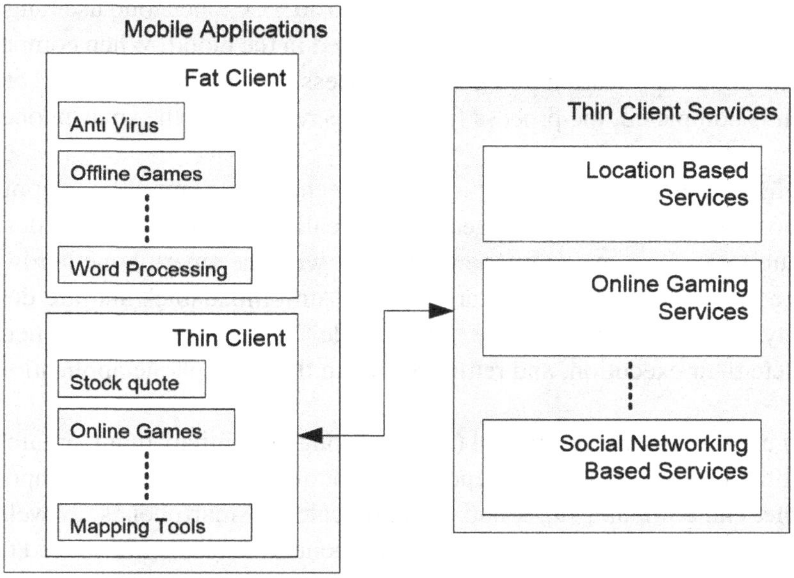

Thin client applications are good in terms of portability, complexity and resource consumption, however, they are useless without the network connectivity, suffer from high latency, and have limited access to local hardware resources.

Mobile cloud computing can be used for both type of applications. However, as the Internet connectivity and provision of local virtual/ad-hoc cloud is not always feasible, fat client applications are preferred for mobile devices. Hence, it is expected that the mobile cloud enabled applications may execute with cloud support in the presence of required resources (Internet and Cloud), and execute locally vice versa.

Computation Offloading

To utilize mobile cloud resources, the computational tasks migrate from a smartphone to the cloud. This is achieved via a procedure named *computation offloading* (A. R. Khan, Othman, Khan, Abid, & Madani, 2015). There are many techniques that can be used to perform computation offloading, which are discussed as follows:

- **Process Migration:** In this technique, a smartphone application migrates a process to the cloud, where it completes its execution and returns the result to the smartphone application. The process migration can be preemptive (offloading before the execution) or non-preemptive (offloading in mid execution). The preemptive process migration is easy and has low administrative overhead compared to the non-preemptive approach.

CloneCloud (Chun, Ihm, Maniatis, & Naik, 2010) is one of such models that uses process migration to utilize cloud resources for the smartphone applications. To do so, CloneCloud uses augmented execution technique in which a clone of the smartphone is maintained in the cloud. When computation offloading is required, the smartphone application transfers the process state to the cloud and continues execution. Once the execution is completed, the process final state is returned to the smartphone.

- **Component Migration:** In component migration technique, a smartphone application is divided (or pre-composed) into multiple manageable parts called components, each designated for a particular task/sub-task. As some components interact with the smartphone hardware (sensors) and User Interface (UI), such components are marked "un-offloadable" and are designated for local execution only. On the other hand, the "offloadable" (independent) components migrate to the cloud, complete their execution, and return results to the smartphone application.

For instance, in elastic applications model (Zhang, Jeong, Kunjithapatham, & Gibbs, 2010) a single application is partitioned into multiple independent functional units, called components or weblets. A component/weblet can compute, store, and communicate on smartphones, as well as, in the cloud. Hence, when computation offloading is required, a component/weblet is transferred to the cloud where it completes its execution and returns back to the smartphone.

- **Application Migration:** In application migration technique, the whole application migrates to the cloud along with the data, performs the required computations in the cloud, and returns the result to the smartphone. In this technique, a copy of the application may be pre-deployed in the cloud or may migrate on the runtime. It is noteworthy that runtime application migration may incur higher delays and the offloading might not be useful (in terms of performance) for the first time.

This type of offloading technique in demonstrated in (Ahmed et al., 2015), where the researchers offload applications to the cloud to achieve offloading benefits. Application migration technique is usually helpful in scenarios where the smartphone resources are not sufficient for local execution of the applications.

- **Virtual Machine Migration:** In this technique, a smartphone based Virtual Machine (VM) that contains the application and data is migrated to the cloud. The VM is re-launched in the cloud, where it performs the required computations and migrates back to the smartphone along with the updated data. For example, the model presented in (Satyanarayanan, Bahl, Caceres, & Davies, 2009) uses a VM migration concept that runs on trusted and resource-rich computer(s) or cloud. In this technique, the VM execution is suspended on a mobile device, and the processor, disk, and memory states are saved. The VM along its states information is transferred to the cloud where it completes the execution and returns back to the mobile device.

Please note that it is not always necessary to migrate a component/application/VM from a smartphone to the cloud and vice versa. Depending on the working of an application model, it may require runtime migration, one-time migration, or pre-deployment of a component/application/smartphone clone in the cloud. For more details on mobile cloud application development models, the readers are encouraged to study (A. R. Khan et al., 2014).

EFFECTIVE COMPUTATION OFFLOADING AND ITS CHALLENGES

Computation offloading is not always favorable for performance enhancement, energy efficiency, and application execution. Figure 5 presents the decision workflow to determine if offloading would be beneficial. The workflow starts with the execution of an application followed by checking the user's offloading permission. If offloading is enabled, then the application checks the connectivity to the cloud resources and notes the available/assigned resources. The next step involves deciding whether the offloading is favorable, depending on the users' desired objective(s). If it is favorable, then the computation offloading is performed. Otherwise, the application performs all computations locally.

Figure 5. Computation offloading process

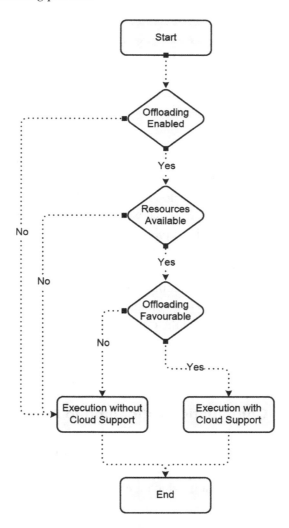

Figure 6. N-Queens problem solving with and without mobile cloud computing support

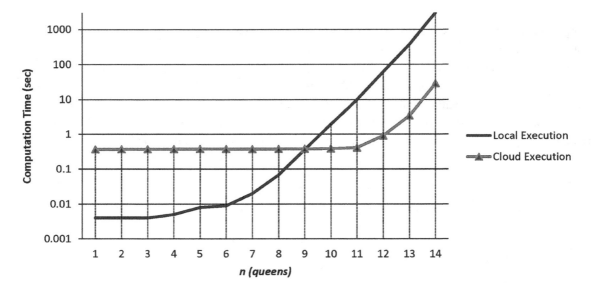

When to Offload?

As discussed in the previous section, computation offloading is not always beneficial. Cases may where local execution is favorable compared to the cloud based execution. In such cases, local execution of a task takes less time compared to cloud based execution due to higher offloading delays (low communication speed, large data size) or overloaded cloud resources. To prove this, we developed an Android application (N-Queens Problem (Alfeld, 2015)) that was capable of offloading computations to Google App Engine F1 instance (Google, 2015b). The application was executed on Sony Xperia S (GSMArena, 2015). In this experiment, we varied the number of queens from 1 to 14 and checked the computational time on the smartphone with and without mobile cloud computing support (see Figure 6). It is evident that when $n < 9$, local execution is favorable compared to the cloud based execution. It is because the time required for local computations is very low compared to the time required for cloud based execution (offloading time + cloud execution time). On the other hand, when $n > 9$ then cloud based execution is favored. This offloading decision is effected by multiple parameters, for instance, available smartphone resources, computation offloading technique, communication technology (Wi-Fi, Cellular), data size, and available cloud resources (A. R. Khan, M. Othman, A. N. Khan, et al., 2015).

Challenges in Effective Computation Offloading to Achieve High Performance

To achieve effective computation offloading, mobile cloud computing faces multiple challenges, namely objectives counter effects, application partitioning, computational time estimation, offloading time estimation, and resource utilization prediction, which are discussed as follows:

- **Objectives Counter Effects:** As mentioned earlier, mobile cloud computing offers multiple benefits, namely performance enhancement, energy efficiency, and execution support. However, these objectives are interlinked and achieving one may affect the others (A. R. Khan, M. Othman, F.

Xia, et al., 2015). For example, one may achieve execution support using mobile cloud computing, but it may overconsume the mobile device energy in terms of communications. Likewise, for other applications, energy efficiency may be achieved using mobile cloud computing but it may affect the performance (overall computation time) of the task. In (A. R. Khan, M. Othman, A. N. Khan, et al., 2015), researchers demonstrate that different applications may not achieve all benefits of mobile cloud computing, and their level of achievement may vary from application to application.

- **Application Partitioning:** Usually, most of the mobile applications are designed to perform multiple tasks of variable computational intensity. For instance, a photo editing application may perform face detection, face features recognition, count number of faces/people, and apply different filters. For effective computation offloading, it is very important to partition the application and offload only the resource-intensive components. However, the identification of resource-intensive components is not an easy task. It is because there is no hard rule to measure the complexity of a component. For example, an application component may be resource intensive for an old model smartphone, but not for a new model smartphone with upgraded resources.

- **Computational Time Estimation:** Calculating the computational time is a challenge because it varies on the basis of the nature of the task (instructions type/size/complexity), and available mobile device/cloud resources. It is difficult to assume a fixed computational time for a particular task on a mobile device because the mobile devices vary in terms of architecture (32/64 bit, instruction set, number of cores) and computational load (of executing applications). Similarly, the computational time of a task may vary in the cloud based on the assigned/available resources.

- **Offloading Time Estimation:** The communication time for offloading a particular task and getting the computed result is also unpredictable. It is because the communication time varies on the basis of adopted technology (Wi-Fi, cellular), mobility of the device, task data size, cloud location, and available bandwidth. Hence, to make effective computation offloading decisions in order to achieve high performance computing on mobile devices, the devices must be aware of the computational as well as the communication time.

- **Resource Utilization Prediction:** For effective computation offloading decisions, the prediction of resource utilization on mobile devices and cloud is very important. For example, consider a scenario in which only 10% of the smartphone resources are utilized. At this point, a major portion of the smartphone resources are free due to which a decision is made that smartphone based execution is favorable. However, as the task begins to execute, the user starts more applications and overloads the smartphone resources. Consequently, the task does not complete in the required time. Similar scenario can occur at the cloud end, and the favorable offloading decisions can soon turn unfavorable due to changing environment.

HIGH PERFORMANCE COMPUTING APPLICATIONS ON MOBILE DEVICES ENABLED BY MOBILE CLOUD COMPUTING TECHNOLOGY

The traditional mobile applications are designed to execute entirely on the mobile devices or with limited support of online services. Therefore, such applications support only data storage and application-specific cloud services, such as DropBox (DropBox, 2015), Siri (Apple, 2015b), and iCloud (Apple, 2015a). Mobile devices can benefit from mobile cloud computing technology in multiple perspectives.

As mobile cloud computing is a comparatively new domain, it has not been adopted for application development in real essence. Researchers are still exploring its potential applications, some of which are listed, but not limited to:

- **Mathematical Tools:** Complex computational operations, such as multiplication of very large matrices and finding very large prime numbers require significant amount of resources. Unfortunately, this demand cannot be fulfilled by many mobile devices. As a result, many applications are considered resource intensive or unsuitable for mobile devices. As a proof of concept, many researchers (Khan, Othman, Khan, et al., 2015; Satyanarayanan et al., 2009; Ma, Lam, & Wang, 2011) have used mobile cloud computing to develop mathematical tools (Gnumeric, 2012) and solve mathematical problems, such as N-Queens problem (Alfeld, 2015). These researchers have proved that mobile devices can achieve significant performance with the help of mobile cloud computing.

- **Image Processing:** As image processing largely depends on mathematical operations, specialized image processing tasks, such as rendering a highly detailed 3D model from a source file may overload the mobile devices or may take hours to process the task. In fact, professional designers use heavy duty (powerful) workstations for such tasks. To prove that mobile cloud computing can be beneficial for image processing, some researchers have implemented image processing tasks, namely face detection, face recognition, and 3D rendering in (Khan, Othman, Khan, et al., 2015; Zhang et al., 2010; March et al., 2011; Giurgiu, Riva, Juric, Krivulev, & Alonso, 2009), and Cuckoo (Kemp, Palmer, Kielmann, & Bal, 2012).

- **File Indexing and Searching:** Nowadays, many mobile devices are equipped with over 100 gigabytes of storage capacity, which is further increasing with the passage of time. With such capacity, a mobile device can store millions (and even billions) of files locally which are not easy to index or search. In such scenarios, a mobile device may take a few minutes to search the required file(s). Similarly, if a mobile device contains a very large file and is instructed to search a particular text throughout the file, the mobile device may fail to process the request due to low memory or may take a few minutes to process the task. Such problems are addressed using mobile cloud computing technology in (Khan, Othman, Khan, et al., 2015; Chun et al., 2010).

- **Games:** Mobile cloud computing is also beneficial in terms of game experience enhancement. However, as games require resource-intensive computations and quick response time, mobile cloud computing might not be of much help for all types of games. As a proof of concept, the researchers in (Cuervo et al., 2010) implemented chess game on mobile device and used mobile cloud computing to reduce the AI computational (move making) time.

- **Security:** Similar to other technologies, security is one of the main concerns of mobile devices. The increasing threat from malwares and viruses has increased the need for reliable antivirus applications on mobile devices. However, antivirus applications are resource intensive and consume considerable amount of the smartphone's energy. To facilitate in this regard, mobile cloud computing has proved beneficial by offloading resource-intensive scanning task to the cloud. In (Chun et al., 2010), the researchers keeps a copy of the smartphone files in the cloud and performs the required scans without exhausting smartphone's resources.

FUTURE RESEARCH DIRECTIONS

Researchers have tried to address a maximum number of mobile cloud computing issues, but some are still left unaddressed. Below are four research directions that can be used as a starting point for future research in this domain:

- Data privacy is one of the primary issues in adopting cloud computing services. Therefore, a study is required to investigate how the users will react to mobile cloud computing services; as some application development models require sharing/ copy of a data in the cloud.
- There is still a lot of room for research on the security, energy efficiency, and context-awareness aspects of the mobile cloud application development models.
- At present, there is no simulator for mobile cloud environment. Efforts are required to develop a simulator that is capable of simulating a mobile cloud environment.
- Efforts are required to develop new pricing models for the mobile cloud computing services through merger of application providers, cloud service providers, and telecom service providers.

CONCLUSION

This chapter stressed on the importance of mobile devices, the ever increasing demands of the mobile applications, and their future growth. It presented mobile cloud computing as a potential solution to high performance computing on mobile devices and provided a brief introduction to cloud and mobile cloud computing technology. The chapter presented mobile cloud architecture, classification of mobile applications, computation offloading process, offloading techniques, a few mobile cloud application models, and challenges in effective computation offloading. Moreover, the chapter presented some potential high performance computing applications that are enabled by mobile cloud computing technology and are developed as a proof of concept. Lastly, it highlights some future research directions for the interested readers to explore further.

REFERENCES

Ahmed, E., Akhunzada, A., Whaiduzzaman, M., Gani, A., Ab Hamid, S. H., & Buyya, R. (2015). Network-centric performance analysis of runtime application migration in mobile cloud computing. *Simulation Modelling Practice and Theory*, *50*, 42–56.

Alfeld, P. (2015). N-queens problem. Retrieved from http://www.math.utah.edu/~alfeld/queens/queens.html

Amazon. (2015). Amazon Elastic Compute Cloud (EC2). Retrieved from http://www.amazon.com/ec2/

Apple. (2015a). iCloud. Retrieved from http://www.apple.com/icloud/

Apple. (2015b). Siri. Retrieved from http://www.apple.com/ios/siri/

Canalys. (2013). Mobile device market to reach 2.6 billion units by 2016. Retrieved from http://www.canalys.com/newsroom/mobile-device-market-reach-26-billion-units-2016

Chun, B.-G., Ihm, S., Maniatis, P., & Naik, M. (2010). Clonecloud: boosting mobile device applications through cloud clone execution. *arXiv preprint arXiv:1009.3088.*

Cuervo, E., Balasubramanian, A., Cho, D.-k., Wolman, A., Saroiu, S., Chandra, R., & Bahl, P. (2010). MAUI: making smartphones last longer with code offload. *Paper presented at theProceedings of the 8th international conference on Mobile systems, applications, and services.* doi:doi:10.1145/1814433.1814441 doi:10.1145/1814433.1814441

DropBox. (2015). Retrieved from www.dropbox.com/android

Giurgiu, I., Riva, O., Juric, D., Krivulev, I., & Alonso, G. (2009). *Calling the cloud: enabling mobile phones as interfaces to cloud applications Middleware 2009* (pp. 83–102). Springer.

Gnumeric. (2012). Gnumeric spreadsheet. Retrieved from http://freecode.com/projects/gnumeric

Google. (2015a). Google App Engine Retrieved from http://appengine.google.com

Google. (2015b). Google App Frontend Instance Class. Retrieved from https://developers.google.com/appengine/docs/adminconsole/performancesettings

Google. (2015c). Google Apps for Business. Retrieved from http://www.google.com/enterprise/apps/business/

GSMArena. (2015). Sony Xperia S. Retrieved from http://www.gsmarena.com/sony_xperia_s-4369.php

Hassan, Q. (2011). Demystifying Cloud Computing. *The Journal of Defense Software Engineering*, 2011, 16-21.

IBM. (2010). Developer Works survey. Retrieved from http://public.dhe.ibm.com/software/dw/survey/2010surveyresults/2010surveresults-pdf.pdf

IDC. (2013). More Smartphones Were Shipped in Q1 2013 Than Feature Phones, An Industry First According to IDC. Retrieved from http://www.idc.com/getdoc.jsp?containerId=prUS24085413

Kemp, R., Palmer, N., Kielmann, T., & Bal, H. (2012). *Cuckoo: a computation offloading framework for smartphones Mobile Computing, Applications, and Services* (pp. 59–79). Springer. doi:10.1007/978-3-642-29336-8_4

Khan, A., Mat Kiah, M. L., Ali, M., Shamshirband, S., & Khan, A. R. (2015). A Cloud-Manager-Based Re-Encryption Scheme for Mobile Users in Cloud Environment: A Hybrid Approach. *Journal of Grid Computing.* doi:10.1007/s10723-015-9352-9

Khan, A. N., Mat Kiah, M., Khan, S. U., Madani, S. A., & Khan, A. R. (2013). A Study of Incremental Cryptography for Security Schemes in Mobile Cloud Computing Environments. *Paper presented at theIEEE Symposium on Wireless Technology and Applications (ISWTA).* doi:doi:10.1109/ISWTA.2013.6688818 doi:10.1109/ISWTA.2013.6688818

Khan, A. R., Othman, M., Khan, A. N., Abid, S. A., & Madani, S. A. (2015). MobiByte: An Application Development Model for Mobile Cloud Computing. *Journal of Grid Computing*, 13(4), 6005-628. doi:10.1007/s10723-015-9335-x

Khan, A. R., Othman, M., Madani, S. A., & Khan, S. U. (2014). A Survey of Mobile Cloud Computing Application Models. *IEEE Communications Surveys and Tutorials*, *16*(1), 393–413. doi:10.1109/SURV.2013.062613.00160

Khan, A. R., Othman, M., Xia, F., & Khan, A. N. (2015). Context-Aware Mobile Cloud Computing and Its Challenges. *IEEE Cloud Computing*, *2*(3), 42–49. doi:10.1109/MCC.2015.62

Ma, R. K., Lam, K. T., & Wang, C.-L. (2011). eXCloud: Transparent runtime support for scaling mobile applications in cloud. *Paper presented at the 2011 International Conference on Cloud and Service Computing (CSC).*

March, V., Gu, Y., Leonardi, E., Goh, G., Kirchberg, M., & Lee, B. S. (2011). μCloud: Towards a new paradigm of rich mobile applications. *Procedia Computer Science*, *5*, 618–624. doi:10.1016/j.procs.2011.07.080

Microsoft. (2015). Microsoft Azure. Retrieved from http://www.windowsazure.com

Mustafa, S., Nazir, B., Hayat, A., Khan, A. R., & Madani, S. A. Resource management in cloud computing: Taxonomy, prospects, and challenges. *Computers & Electrical Engineering.* doi:10.1016/j.compeleceng.2015.07.021

Rackspace. (2015). Rackspace Cloud. Retrieved from http://www.rackspace.com/

Salesforce. (2015). Salesforce Cloud Computing. Retrieved from http://www.salesforce.com/cloudcomputing/

Satyanarayanan, M., Bahl, P., Caceres, R., & Davies, N. (2009). The case for vm-based cloudlets in mobile computing. *Pervasive Computing*, *8*(4), 14–23. doi:10.1109/MPRV.2009.82

Zhang, X., Jeong, S., Kunjithapatham, A., & Gibbs, S. (2010). *Towards an elastic application model for augmenting computing capabilities of mobile platforms In Mobile wireless middleware, operating systems, and applications* (pp. 161–174). Springer. doi:10.1007/978-3-642-17758-3_12

KEY TERMS AND DEFINITIONS

Computation Offloading: Migrating computational tasks from one device to another (smartphone to cloud and vice versa).

Favorable Offloading: The offloading that is beneficiary in some aspect, such as performance enhancement, energy efficiency, and execution support.

Local Execution: Execution on mobile device.

Mobile Cloud Computing: An integration of cloud computing technology with mobile devices to make mobile devices resource-full in terms of computational power, memory, storage, energy, and context-awareness.

Offloadable Components: Independent components (parts) of application which do not disturb the execution of application upon offloading to the cloud.

Offloading: Moving from one place to another.

Unoffloadable Components: Components which depend on the local hardware for execution, and may disturb application execution upon offloading to the cloud.

Chapter 14
Big Data Analytics in Mobile and Cloud Computing Environments

Muhammad Habib ur Rehman
University of Malaya, Malaysia

Atta ur Rehman Khan
King Saud University, Saudi Arabia

Aisha Batool
Iqra University, Pakistan

ABSTRACT

Multiple properties of big mobile data, namely volume, velocity, variety, and veracity make the big data analytics process a challenging task. It is desired that mobile devices initially process big data before sending it to big data systems to reduce the data complexity. However, the mobile devices have recourse constraints, and the challenge of processing big mobile data on mobile devices requires further exploration. This chapter presents a thorough discussion about mobile computing systems and their implication for big data analytics. It presents big data analytics with different perspectives involving descriptive, predictive, and prescriptive analytical methods. Moreover, the chapter presents a detailed literature review on mobile and cloud based big data analytics systems, and highlights the future application areas and open research issues that are relevant to big data analytics in mobile cloud environments. Lastly, the chapter provides some recommendations regarding big data processing, quality improvement, and complexity optimization.

INTRODUCTION

Research in micro and nanotechnologies has led to the development of small, handheld, mobile, and wearable devices with adequate computational power (Rehman, Liew, Wah, Shuja, & Daghighi, 2015). It is believed that the integration of network and communications technology, such as IPv6, Internet of Things (IoT), and high-speed networks, together with the advancement in mobile devices, and cloud

DOI: 10.4018/978-1-5225-0287-6.ch014

computing technologies will revolutionize the whole digital lifestyle and play a vital role in the evolution of new technologies (Rehman et al., 2015). However, it is an undeniable fact that these technologies will generate a massive amount of data in mobile environments; a challenge that demands timely consideration.

Big data is defined as the amount of data that cannot be stored or processed on conventional Database Management Systems (DBMS) (Hashem et al., 2015). Similarly, the "big data analytics", is defined as the process of executing data analysis methods over large-scale data (streams) to discover maximum actionable knowledge patterns. Big data systems collect a massive amount of multi-format (structured, semi-structured, and unstructured) data from heterogeneous data sources, which makes the big data analytics process a challenging task compared to the conventional data analytics. The popularity of big data is motivating the researchers to develop big data analytics tools and new systems. A variety of data analysis methods and systems are proposed in the literature to effectively analyze the big data and uncover the actionable knowledge patterns (Gaber, Gomes, & Stahl, 2014; Jayaraman, Perera, Georgakopoulos, & Zaslavsky, 2014; Kreps, Narkhede, & Rao, 2011; Palankar, Iamnitchi, Ripeanu, & Garfinkel, 2008). The resultant knowledge patterns are handy for preserving user privacy and provisioning personalized services in user-centric big data environments.

Mobile computing systems are replacing wired computing infrastructures by providing adequate computational power through new computing technologies. In addition, wireless connectivity with Internet, on-board sensors, and the availability of rechargeable power sources has popularized these systems. This popularity is witnessed by the fact that the sales of smartphones and tablet PCs outnumber the sales of desktop computers (Rehman et al., 2015). The addition of wearable devices, unmanned aerial vehicles, and smart cars to mobile computing ecosystem are a few examples that show continuous evolution in mobile computing field. Although, the mobile devices/systems facilitate in provisioning computational power, they are unable to handle the massive amount of big data stream that is generated by the on-board sensory and non-sensory equipment.

Cloud computing technologies ensure provision of on-demand and highly virtualized computing resources. The cloud provides computing, networking, and storage services with the highest level of elasticity to meet the subscribers' demands (Armbrust et al., 2010). The cloud services are orchestrated as Software-as-a-Service (SaaS), Platform-as-a-Service (PaaS), and Infrastructure-as-a-Service (IaaS). SaaS allows deploying cloud-based web applications that are accessible via web browsers. The main advantages of SaaS are the scalability and application access from any Internet connected web browser based computing system. SaaS also ensures to save the applications from data loss in case of unusual termination. PaaS provides tools and cloud services for development and deployment of applications in the cloud environment. Next, IaaS ensures provision of cloud computing resources for commercial users who need infrastructure (CPU cycles, networks, and massive storage) to reduce on-premises management load of computational resources. The cloud computing infrastructures are public (owned and managed by cloud service providers), private (solely operated for a single user/organization), and hybrid (combination of private and public clouds).

This chapter articulates the Six Vs of big data and data processing workflow, and discusses the emergence of big mobile data and their respective sources in mobile environments. It also discusses the prevalence of mobile and cloud computing technologies and presents a thorough literature review of mobile and cloud based big data analytics systems. Lastly, it highlights application areas and open research issues for future research directions.

SIX Vs AND BIG DATA PROCESSING WORKFLOW

Initially, any dataset or data stream with three properties, namely volume, velocity, and value were known as big data sets, and were comparatively easy to handle. However, the addition of three more properties (i.e., variability, veracity, and variety) has increased the big data complexity (Rehman & Batool, 2015). The six Vs (volume, velocity, value, variability, veracity, and variety) of big data are defined as follows:

1. **Volume:** The volume is the most important property of big data. It defines the overall size of big data, which varies from a few GBs (in case of mobile computing systems) to hundreds of Petabytes and even Exabytes (in case of large scale cloud computing systems and data centers) (Gani, Siddiqa, Shamshirband, & Hanum, 2015).
2. **Velocity:** The speed of the incoming data stream presents the velocity of big data, which can vary from a few transactions to millions of social media posts per second. This property restricts big data systems to perform online analysis of incoming data in streaming data environments to make sure that whole data could be considered for processing at least one time. However, this property has minor impact on analytics platform that are used to perform batch analysis of historical big data.
3. **Value:** This property shows the relevance and perceived utility of big data for future utilization. The value property determines the quality of data analytics methods with the help of multiple factors. For example, the statistics produced by data mining and machine learning algorithms, the amount of data processed by big data systems, and the bearable latency in a big data analytics system from data capturing to visualization are a few factors to determine value property.
4. **Variability:** This property represents the variation in the heterogeneous data sources and multi-format representation of the collected data streams. The variability significantly increases complexity in big data by introducing high-dimensional, multi-format, and unstructured data streams. Hence, the number of data features (dimensions) increases along the increase in the number of data sources and data types. In addition, the data capturing in textual and multimedia format significantly impacts the variability of big data, and increases complexity of big data analytics systems in terms of data and computational power.
5. **Veracity:** It presents the authenticity and trustworthiness of big data in systems. This parameter is important because authentic and trustworthy data needs less computational power for preprocessing as compared to fake and unreliable data sources. Efforts must be made to consider veracity property at the time of system and application design to improve big data analytics.
6. **Variability:** The variability in big data determines the data quality and facilitates to reduce complexity. This property shows the inconsistencies in big data, which are handled using anomaly and outlier detection methods. The variability could be reduced if it is handled at the time of data capturing, or as soon as the capturing is performed.

The workflow of big data processing and analysis is based upon six stages (see Figure 1). Firstly, the data streams are collected from heterogeneous data sources in multiple formats, and data fusion is performed to generate complex data sets. After data acquisition, big data systems provide indexing methods for efficient storage in large scale data centers (Gani et al., 2015). The data retrieval is performed using query processing methods over indexing tables, and the required data is retrieved from the storage systems. Prior to analysis, the data is preprocessed by removing noise, duplicate data, and outliers. In

Figure 1. Big data processing and analysis workflow

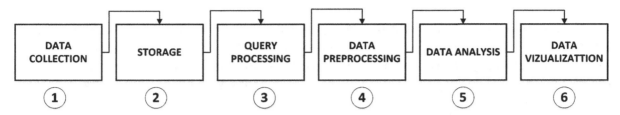

addition, feature extraction methods are applied to retrieve most useful data points from massive data streams. Further, the predictive, descriptive, and prescriptive analytics algorithms are used for data analysis. These algorithms include the implementation of statistical data mining and machine learning techniques. Finally, the results of the data analysis are visualized using big data visualization tools.

MOBILE COMPUTING SYSTEMS AND BIG DATA

Mobile computing systems vary in multiple aspects, such as computational power, energy resources, communication interfaces, sensory configurations, and user interfaces (Rehman et al., 2015). These systems include smartphones, wearable devices, IoT, smart vehicles, Satellite-enabled Remote Systems (SRS), and smart moving objects (SMOs) etc., (see Table 1). The form factor represents the physical size of these systems, which vary from tiny-sized and small scale devices to large-scale rail systems and very large scale satellite systems. Likewise, the computational power also varies in these systems, for instance, small wearable devices are equipped with CPUs having a few hundred MHz of clock speed, whereas large systems have multicore CPUs and GPUs for high computational power. Mobile computing systems also provide different communication interfaces, namely Bluetooth, Wi-Fi, GSM, and satellite communication channels. A huge variety in sensory and non-sensory data sources also increases the heterogeneity of mobile computing systems.

The amount of data generated by sensors (accelerometer, camera, and microphone) of a single smartphone is large enough to hinder the on-board computational resources. The aggregation of such mobile data from millions of users in a big data system creates a voluminous amount of big data streams. The speed of data streams is very fast and complies with the velocity property of the big data. As the collected data maps different data sources, it increases heterogeneity and conform the variety property. The veracity and variability properties are manageable in big mobile data by applying privacy preservation mechanism and removing inconsistencies from collected data streams. This data is also useful for many application areas including customer churn predictions, mobility analysis, activity prediction, and smart cities, etc. Some commonly used data sources of big mobile data are presented in Table 2.

In mobile environment, the data collection is performed using different sensory modalities and placements (Rehman et al., 2015). For instance, the accelerometer embedded in smartphones and wearable activity trackers generate different coordinates. Although, both the devices could be used for same activity recognition, but a few algorithms are designed to consider different modalities and placements for accurate predictions. Similarly, the user behavior during same activities may produce different sensory readings which make the analysis process more difficult. For instance, the driving behavior in busy roads is different as compared to slippery or racing tracks. These data analysis related challenges can be easily

Table 1. Mobile computing systems

Mobile Computing Systems	Form Factor	CPU	RAM	Battery Power	Communication Channels	Sensors	User Interfaces	Example System
Smartphones	Small	Low, Medium	Low, Medium	Low	Wi-Fi, GSM, Bluetooth, Wi-Fi Direct, Bluetooth Low Energy (BLE)	Accelerometer, Camera, GPS Receiver, Proximity	Touch screens, On-screen keyboards	Apple IPhone S6, Samsung, Galaxy S6
Wearable Devices	Tiny, Small	Low, Medium	Low, Medium	Low	Wi-Fi, GSM, BlueTooth, Wi-Fi Direct, BLE	Customized sensors	Touch screens, On-screen keyboards	Jawbone activity tracker, Oculus Rift, Google glass
IoTs	Tiny, Small, Medium, Large	Low, Medium, Large	Low, Medium	Low, Medium	Wi-Fi, GSM, BlueTooth, Wi-Fi Direct, BLE	Customized Sensors	Touch screens, On-screen Keyboards, M2M	Philips Hue, MyFox Security, Awair, Denon
Tablet PCs	Small, Medium	Medium, Large	Medium	Medium	Wi-Fi, GSM, BlueTooth, Wi-Fi Direct, BLE	Accelerometer, Camera, GPS Receiver, Proximity	Touch screens, On-screen Keyboards	MS Windows Surface, Ipad Mini, Nokia N1
Laptops	Medium	Medium, Large	Medium	Medium	Wi-Fi, Ethernet, BlueTooth	Accelerometer, Camera, Gyroscopes	Touch screens, Off-screen Keyboards	Apple MacPro, Dell Inspiron, Asus Aspire
Smart Vehicles	Large, Very large	Medium, Large	Medium	Medium	Wi-Fi, GSM, Wi-Fi Direct	Customized Sensors	Touch screens, Off-screen Keyboards	Fortwo Car, Google's Smart Car
SMOs	Tiny, Small, Medium, Large, Very large	Small, Medium, Large	Small, Medium	Small, Medium	Wi-Fi, GSM, BlueTooth, Wi-Fi Direct, BLE	Customized Sensors	Touch screens, Off-screen Keyboards, M2M	Multi-purpose robotics
SRS	Large, Very large	Large	Large	Large	Satellite Channels	Customized Sensors	M2M	Smart Railways, NASA's Earth Observatories

Table 2. Data sources of big mobile data

Data Source Type	Configuration	Data Type
Sensors	Pedometers	Numeric/Integer
	Blood Glucose Monitor	Numeric/Integer
	Accelerometer	Numeric/Floating point
	Temperature	Numeric/Floating point
	Humidity Monitor	Numeric/Integer
	Air pressure Monitor	Numeric/Floating point
	GPS Location	Numeric/Floating point
	Compass	Text
User-interaction	On-screen Keyboard	Text/Numeric
	Microphone	Audio
	Camera	Images/Video
Device Resident Data	Web Browser Logs	Text
	Application Specific Logs	Text
	Bluetooth Scans	Text
	Wi-Fi Scans	Text
	Contact List	Text
	Call Logs	Text
	SMS data	Text

handled by big data analytics systems to produce overall approximate patterns. For example, instead of analyzing singular data points, the big data systems designed for smart city applications, aggregate information from multiple users and produce results for further utilization (Kitchin, 2014).

The data collection and processing architecture of big mobile data systems is presented in Figure 2. The mobile devices (smartphones, wearable gadgets, and on-body sensors) in user-vicinity generate user-related data points. These devices communicate with other devices and the Internet, using different communication channels like Wi-Fi, GSM, and Bluetooth. Other mobile computing systems, such as smart vehicles and wireless IoTs generate data using on-board sensors and transmit to cloud data stores via Internet. The virtual IoTs are based on the virtual sensors instead of physical sensors, and represent software abstractions of the existing physical sensors (Zhang et al., 2013). Similarly, the sensor clouds deployed in large scale field observatories (e.g. smart agricultural farms, or smart retail store) produce data and transmit to central cloud data stores (Perera, Zaslavsky, Christen, & Georgakopoulos, 2014). The data processing and analysis is performed in central services clouds which provide unlimited compute, network, and storage services. However, the increased bandwidth and handling of massive amount of raw data streams are the bottlenecks in real-time big data analytics (Figure 2).

Figure 2. Big mobile data collection and processing architecture

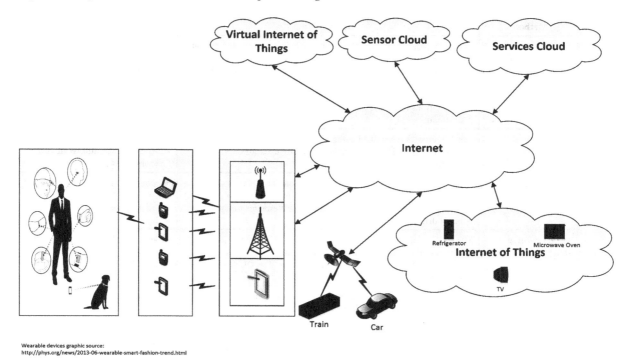

Wearable devices graphic source:
http://phys.org/news/2013-06-wearable-smart-fashion-trend.html

BIG DATA ANALYTICS

Big data analytics is performed in batch mode (on historical data), near-real time, real-time, or on continuous data streams (Assunção, Calheiros, Bianchi, Netto, & Buyya, 2015). The key methods for big data analytics include machine learning methods, data mining algorithms, and statistical analysis techniques (see Table 3). These methods are classified into three groups, namely predictive analytics, descriptive analytics, and prescriptive analytics.

Descriptive Analytics

Online analyses of raw data streams are performed using descriptive statistics. It is the simplest form of big data analytics in which the summary statistics of the analyzed data is presented (LaValle, Lesser, Shockley, Hopkins, & Kruschwitz, 2013). It may involve simple counting the occurrences of specific events, or the application of basic statistical methods like mean, median, mode, standard deviation, and variance to the data stream events. The results of descriptive statistics are directly used for immediate actions, and facilitate in preprocessing methods for predictive and prescriptive analytics. A few examples of big data streams that are analyzed using descriptive analytics methods include counting the number of followers in the social media data streams, calculating average commuters/travelers in large scale urban transport infrastructures, and calculating the differentiating behavior of people in a specific population.

Table 3. Data analysis methods for big data

Type	Methods	Description	Example Methods
Machine Learning	Supervised Learning (SL)	The SL algorithms predict the events from learning models that are trained using labeled data points. The SL models are trained using labelled data points and tested with leave-one-out, cross validation, and 5-fold validation methods. The SL models are widely used for data classification and clustering. However, the SL algorithms have the limitations to handle concept drift (detecting changes) in the data streams.	• Neural Networks (Rojas, 2013) • Decision Trees (Barros, Basgalupp, De Carvalho, & Freitas, 2012) • Bayesian Networks (S. H. Chen & Pollino, 2012)
Machine Learning	Unsupervised Learning (UL)	The UL models are trained using unlabeled data points to predict the future events. The UL models are mainly used for data clustering.	• k-means (Jain, 2010) • DB-SCAN (Amini, Wah, & Saboohi, 2014)
Machine Learning	Semi-Supervised Learning (SSL)	The SSL models are initially developed from labeled data points and continuously updated on the feedback from positively predicted events. The adaptive behavior of SSL models enables to handle concept drift.	• Generative models (Xu, Zhang, Yu, & Long, 2012) • Graph-based • Heuristic-based
Machine Learning	Deep Learning (DL)	The DL models are hierarchical representation of supervised and unsupervised learning models. The DL models are best suitable for large-scale high-dimensional data streams. The DL models are good choice when analyzing big data.	• Deep belief Networks (DBNs) (X.-W. Chen & Lin, 2014) • Convolutional Neural Networks (CNNs)
Data Mining	Classification	The classifiers are built with or without learning models and are used to predict the object class of nominal data points.	• Linear Discriminant Analysis (LDA), • Boosting Methods
Data Mining	Association Rule Mining (ARM)	The ARM algorithms works in two steps. First, the frequent itemsets are outlined by setting a minimum support and then the association between rules is established by giving a minimum confidence threshold.	• Apriori (Rehman, Liew, & Wah, 2014a) • FP-Growth • AClose
Data Mining	Regression Analysis (RA)	The RA methods are based on statistical theories and are used to establish relationship between given data points.	• Linear RA (Draper & Smith, 2014) • Non-linear RA
Statistical Methods	Descriptive Statistics	The descriptive statistical methods are used to produce summary statistics using basic statistical operations over whole input data.	• Mean • Median • Standard Deviation
Statistical Methods	Inferential Statistics	The inferential statistical methods help to infer the behavior of whole population by analyzing representative sample data points.	• T-test • Analysis of Variance

Predictive Analytics

Generating learning models from big data streams, and forecasting the future behavior of knowledge patterns from new data is performed using predictive analytics methods (LaValle et al., 2013). The predictive analytics is a six step iterative process (see Figure 3). First of all, the data scientists understand the data to develop the analysis questions. In the second step, the data is prepared by applying preprocessing methods for data reduction, outlier removals, and dimensionality reduction from millions-features data sets to small and manageable datasets. In the third step, the prediction models are developed using statistical and machine learning model generation methods. In the fourth step, the working and performance of predictive models is evaluated using test data. In the fifth step, the model is deployed in real-world big data applications to predict the future data streams. Finally, in the sixth step, the real-time performance monitoring of the models is performed. This execution cycle keeps on repeating itself unless the predictive models produce optimal results.

Figure 3. The six steps of predictive analytics

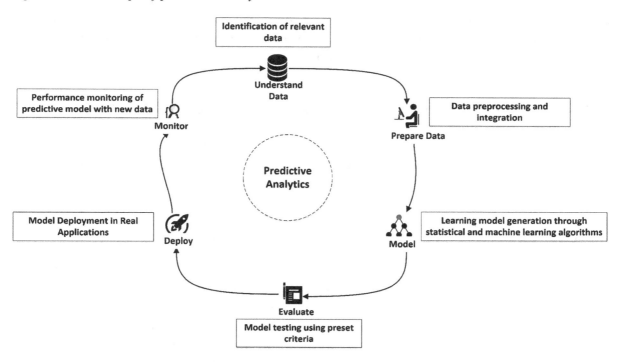

Development of accurate predictive models is not feasible with any dataset, but the data scientists strive to achieve maximum accuracy (Waller & Fawcett, 2013). Some commonly used predictive modeling methods are based on supervised, unsupervised, semi-supervised, and deep learning/theories that are proposed for classification, clustering, statistical analysis, and frequent pattern mining (see Table 3). Although predictive analytics facilitate to forecast new patterns, but the usefulness of the patterns could not be outlined during analytics (Figure 3).

Prescriptive Analytics

Big data systems collect a huge amount of data that may be helpful to forecast new knowledge patterns for useful actionable insights (LaValle et al., 2013). The prescriptive analytics methods facilitate to enhance the predictive models and provide additional features for performing the cause and effect relationships. These methods are developed with a different approach. First of all, the research question (analytics goal) is developed, followed by data collection and analysis. The learning models are generated and deployed after testing with the collected data. Once tested, the model is executed with new data streams and the performance is monitored. If the new predictions do not match the research question and data scientists could not find the required reasons, then the predictive model is regenerated and updated with new data. This iterative process continues unless the learning models produce the desired outcomes. The prescriptive analytics prove to be more effective than descriptive and predictive analytics, and is considered one of the best alternate models for big data analytics. The main problem with this model is that the relevance of research questions may significantly impact the obtained knowledge patterns. Moreover, it requires large amount of data for training the learning models as compared to predictive analytics.

Big data analytics methods are promising tools for harnessing the maximum value from big data systems. However, the impact of other Vs should be considered before devising any big data analysis strategy. In the next section, we present mobile and cloud based data processing systems which facilitate big data analytics in mobile and cloud environments.

BIG DATA ANALYTICS IN MOBILE AND CLOUD COMPUTING SYSTEMS

High performance computing infrastructures, such as grids, clusters, and clouds offer different configurations for big data analytics tools in multiple scenarios (Jackson, Vijayakumar, Quadir, & Bharathi, 2015). In case of cloud infrastructures, the data processing is performed using highly virtualized service-oriented architectures to utilize large-scale unlimited cloud resources (Hassan, Riad, & Hassan, 2012). Cluster computing infrastructures support Hadoop based technologies for large-scale parallel data processing. Similarly, in-memory and in-database analytics tools are deployed with grid computing infrastructure (Garlasu et al., 2013). However, the scope of this chapter is limited to only mobile and cloud computing technologies.

There are two approaches for big data analytics in mobile and cloud computing systems. First is the aggregation of raw data streams in central cloud systems through mobile crowd sensing and participatory sensing systems. This approach provides optimized performance, but it incurs redundant and irrelevant data collection that violates the principles of value and veracity in big data systems. In addition, this approach is affected by privacy related issues (Sanaei, Abolfazli, Gani, & Buyya, 2014). In the second approach, data preprocessing in mobile environments and transmission of only relevant and reduced data streams help to overcome the previously mentioned issues. However, the increased data processing overhead in the mobile environments raises demand for the empowerment of resource-constrained mobile systems with cloud computing technologies. The renowned methods for big data analytics in mobile and cloud computing systems are discussed as follows:

Big Data Analytics in Mobile Environments

The mobile computing systems, with adequate computational and battery power, facilitate on-board big data analytics (Rehman et al., 2014a). A variety of data analytics platforms are proposed to facilitate in this regard (see Table 4). However, the configurations and designs of these systems vary due to different nature of mobile systems (Rehman et al., 2015). For instance, the customized on-board analytics systems are designed for FPGA based mobile systems and provide fast execution support. However, customization for new analytics solutions is required, which is possible through hardware level design modifications (Rehman et al., 2015). On the other hand, the CPU based analytics platforms provide better execution and programming support, but they demand continuous optimizations at the software level (Khan, Othman, Madani, & Khan, 2014). The mobile-based analytics systems work in complex environments, and need to tackle issues of fast mobility while moving in different communication areas. These systems are required to be adaptive with on-board resource dynamics, and allow energy-efficient process execution for maximum data processing in mobile environments (Rehman, Liew, & Wah, 2014b). Another feature of mobile based analytics platforms is the collaborative data processing to harness Mobile Distributed Analytics (MDA) (Jayaraman et al., 2014; Rehman et al., 2014b), which enhances the computational

Table 4. Mobile based big data analytics tools

Tools	Summary
OMM (Haghighi et al., 2013)	Open Mobile Miner (OMM) offers a generic data analytics toolkit for large data stream mining. OMM adopts execution behavior after the input and output data rates. In addition, it provides a library of generic and lightweight data mining algorithms to fully utilize on-board available resources.
Mobile Weka (Liu, Chen, Tang, & Yue, 2012)	Mobile Weka provides a mobile implementation of the WEKA, which is a widely adopted library of data mining algorithms (Hall et al., 2009). Mobile Weka provides a bundle of classification, clustering, and association rule mining algorithms. However, it does not consider the on-board resource dynamics.
PDM (Gaber et al., 2014)	The pocket data mining framework is based on agent-oriented data mining architectures to execute data mining tasks collaboratively on multiple mobile devices. The agent modules support the execution of data mining tasks, resource discoveries and communication between peer devices.
CAROMM (Sherchan et al., 2012)	CAROMM is the extended version of OMM which enables context aware computing in mobile environments. The contextual information is captured in mobile environments, but the situations are inferred in remote cloud environments. CAROMM fully executes data analytics methods in mobile devices.
MARS (Gomes, Krishnaswamy, Gaber, Sousa, & Menasalvas, 2012)	Mobile Activity Recognition System (MARS) classifies the online data stream for physical activity detection. The system is based on adaptive data mining algorithms that are used to detect changes and handle variety (concept drift) in the incoming data streams. The MARS collects on-board accelerometer data from smartphones and applies SL models for classification to recognize users ambulatory activities like walking, jogging, and running etc.
Star (Abdallah, Gaber, Srinivasan, & Krishnaswamy, 2015)	The Star is also an adaptive and online mobile activity recognition system, but its classification methods are executed using unsupervised learning models. The Star uses clustering based classification, where each cluster determines the type of activity. The Star handles concept drift and is capable to perform online activity recognition.

power in mobile environments (Gaber et al., 2014). However, the peer network formation and the scheduling of analytics tasks in MDA platforms are key challenges. Table 4 presents these mobile-based big data analytics platforms.

Cloud-Based Big Data Analytics

The cloud computing technologies offer unlimited computational resources to augment mobile computing systems (Khan, Othman, Khan, Abid, & Madani, 2015). Conventionally, the mobile systems are only used for data collection and transient storage platforms, and offload the collected data in cloud environments whenever these systems are connected to the Internet (Khan, Othman, Khan, et al., 2015). To handle the massive collection of raw data stream, cloud services are orchestrated to efficiently utilize cloud resources. Cloud based big data analytics platforms are useful for large-scale enterprises, where the analytics results are integrated with existing service-oriented architectures and business intelligence solutions (Talia, 2013). Table 5 presents some of the cloud based big data analytics platforms.

High Performance Big Data Analytics in Mobile-Cloud Environments

The uninterrupted and massive data streams generated by mobile systems can hamper the on-board resources due to limitation at the computational and energy resources (Khan, Othman, Madani, et al., 2014). To facilitate in this regard, Mobile Cloud Computing (MCC) offers a potential solution of high performance computing on mobile devices. To do so, the analytics tasks can be partially or fully executed on mobile devices with cloud support to gain high performance and reduce the tasks' computational

Table 5. Cloud based big data analytics tools and services

Vendor	Tools	Summary
Apache	Kafka (Kreps et al., 2011)	Kafka is based on the notion of publish/subscribe, and is one of the early cloud based data stream processing systems. The platform provides transparent and elastic stream processing system that is based on a single cluster working as the backbone of big data system. The execution strategy is based on Ingest and Queuing approach for pipelining the data streams.
	Storm (Marz, 2014)	Storm extends the Kafka by providing support for large-scale distributed systems (based on multiple clusters). It extends the Kafka's ingest/queuing model and pipelines the data streams for real-time processing. The processing model supports data management with NoSQL databases.
	Spark (Zaharia, Chowdhury, Franklin, Shenker, & Stoica, 2010)	Spark is used as an alternative tool of Kafka and Storm. It is based on Hadoop architecture and has three modules for real-time data stream processing. These modules include Apache Spark Cluster Computing, Apache Spark Streaming, and Apache Spark SQL. The first two parts constitute the Stream Processor Workload Management Framework (SPWMF) for real-time big data processing.
Amazon	S3 (Palankar et al., 2008)	Amazon provides Simple Storage Services (S3) for big data management. It allows storing and retrieving any amount of big data from Amazon data centers. The S3 is known to be the simplest, yet more powerful, cloud based data management solution.
	Kinesis (Varia & Mathew, 2013)	Kenesis provides support for real-time and complex event data processing. It provides elasticity, scalability, conventional data warehousing, and map-reduce programming models for parallel processing.
	DynamoDB (Sivasubramanian, 2012)	DynamoDB is a NoSQL service by Amazon for big data management. It offers fast data access and seamless scalability in Amazon EC2 environments. The provision of DynamoDB services reduces the operational burdens of database management tasks, such as configuring, backup, and data replication in distributed systems.
	Elastic Map Reduce (EMR) (Varia & Mathew, 2013)	EMR facilitates to harness map/reduce programming model over Amazon EC2 cloud infrastructures. The EMR is an enhancement of Hadoop and it is the part of Amazon EMR cluster. The Amazon EMR cluster integrates EC2, S3, and DynamoDB.
Google	BigQuery (Sato, 2012)	Google offers BigQuery as a cloud-based big data management tool that supports super-fast SQL-like query execution using WebUI and command-line interfaces. In addition, allows variety of programming languages (Java, Python, PHP etc.) to invoke BigQuery REST API calls.
	Cloud SQL (Krishnan & Gonzalez, 2015)	Cloud SQL provides MySQL services in cloud environments, and offers data replication and high availability. In addition, it supports multiple programming languages and synchronous/ asynchronous data replication.
	Cloud Data Store (Chandra, Griesemer, & Redstone, 2007)	DataStore is a NoSQL implementation in cloud environments. The service ensures schema-less management of big data and replicates data across Google's large data centers using Paxos algorithm.
	FlumeJava (Chambers et al., 2010)	FlumeJava provides parallel data pipeline to manage big data streams. The parallel pipelines could be deployed with a single application or it could be integrated with multiple big data applications simultaneously.
	MillWheel (Akidau et al., 2013)	MillWheel supports low-latency data processing applications. The system provides graph-based data processing and maintains persistency of process execution to ensure fault-tolerance.
Microsoft	Azure	Microsoft Azure is the cloud computing platform that offers embarrassingly parallel and highly virtualized compute, network, and storage services. It supports predictive analytics services and big data management using NoSQL and SQL data stores.
	HDInsight (Sarkar, 2014)	HDInsight is the Hadoop-based service which uses Microsoft Azure. The platform is easily configurable with Windows and Linux OS. In addition, it provides programming support for multiple languages.

time. But, unfortunately, the mobile cloud computing field is still new compared to the cloud computing field, and there is not much work done in this regard. There are numerous frameworks/application development models for mobile cloud computing, but there is not a single specialized big data mobile-cloud application development model.

To facilitate in this regard, we identify MobiByte (Rehman et al., 2015) as a potential mobile cloud application development model that can be used for high performance big data analytics on mobile devices. However, further research is required to substantiate the performance gain with the adoption of MobiByte. It is because the mobile-cloud based big data solutions can be very complex due to fast mobility, on-board resource dynamics, service discovery, and virtual machine migration issues (Khan, Othman, Khan, et al., 2015). The decision of static and dynamic computational offloading (execution of tasks/data processing in remote cloud environment) is also very challenging in MCC environments. Moreover, the application partitioning for classification between lightweight and heavy-weight (resource hungry) tasks is also challenging for designing an effective big data analytics solution in MCC environment (Ahmed, Khan, Yaqoob, Gani, & Salim, 2013).

APPLICATION AREAS AND OPEN RESEARCH ISSUES

Mobile devices and mobile computing systems facilitate to collect massive personal data streams. The effective analysis and utilization of these data streams is useful for big data analytics systems in mobile social networks, smart cities, big personal data mining systems, mobile health, and mobile crowd sensing etc. (Kitchin, 2014). Big data analytics systems that analyze big mobile data can provide data-driven solutions by analyzing the uncovered patterns (Perera et al., 2014), for example, the mobile trajectories are useful for optimal traffic route prediction in smart cities. Similarly, frequent spatiotemporal locations are useful for location-based social networking and personalized recommendations in big data systems (Rehman & Batool, 2015). The analysis of user-behaviors and ambulatory activities (walking, jogging, running etc.,) are also useful for developing big data-based mobile commerce, and smart city applications (Rehman & Batool, 2015). The effective analysis of personal data by keeping the users' privacy intact is useful for developing collective intelligence based big data systems. For example, the big data applications that monitor the emotions and social interactions of mobile users can help in effective advertising and socialization; in big metropolitan cities (Perera et al., 2014). To summarize, there are countless possibilities which can be harnessed by applying big data analytics methods on big mobile data.

However, there are many open research issues which are relevant to big mobile data analytics in mobile and cloud computing environments. A few of the most important challenges are discussed as follows:

Data Collection, Fusion, and Quality

On-board sensing elements of mobile devices can produce different results with different orientations, sensor calibrations, and placements (Rehman et al., 2015). Therefore, the unobtrusive data collection from mobile devices is the key challenge that is needed to be harnessed by data collection modules. The fusion of significant contributing data points to produce useful data streams is another challenge (Shoaib, Bosch, Incel, Scholten, & Havinga, 2014). The application designer needs to thoroughly investigate the key contributing data sources and devise an effective data fusion strategy to generate a crispy and more useful data stream (Shoaib et al., 2014). The interpretation of data quality to meet the analytics goal is another challenge. The analytics systems should be designed to investigate the quality of data at run time, and should be able to produce noise-free and inconsistent data. Effective handling of data collection, fusion, and quality relevant issues facilitate to produce more relevant data, and significantly improve big data in terms of value, variety, variability, and veracity. In addition, these techniques could help to reduce the overall volume of data by removing inconsistent, unimportant, and redundant data.

Context Aware Computing in MCC Environments

Fast mobility and resource dynamics of MCC environments highlight the importance of context-aware execution of big data analytics processes (Khan, Othman, Xia, & Khan, 2015). Context-aware features maximize the performance by considering different contextual parameters, such as locations, user-behaviors, available resources (computations, energy), and execution modes (Rehman et al., 2014b). The periodic analysis of contextual information to infer the best execution mode can help to enhance the performance in MCC environments (Khan, Othman, Xia, et al., 2015). For example, the big data analytics processes are best suited for mobile environment where maximum on-board resources are available. On the contrary, if local resources are limited, then the analytics processes can be offloaded to the cloud. Hence, context-aware computing in MCC environments facilitates to switch between different executions modes and perform the analytics accordingly.

User Privacy and Information Security

The collection of personal data streams in mobile environments has raised serious concerns due to sharing of users' personal information without their consent (Feinleib, 2014). The database marketing companies who indirectly collect personal data from mobile users through unverified applications make millions of dollars each year by selling users' personal information. Hence, the big data analytics systems should be designed in such a way that end-to-end user privacy could be maintained (Khan, Othman, Ali, Khan, & Madani, 2014). In addition, the applications should be designed to provide complete user control over their personal data, and extra measures like secure key sharing, encryption/decryption features should be incorporated in big data analytics systems (Daghighi, Kiah, Shamshirband, & Rehman, 2015). Lastly, raw data streams should be instantly discarded after extracting summary statistics and uncovering useful knowledge patterns.

Analytics-as-a-Service

As cloud computing technologies offer flexible service models, new services could be orchestrated for the provision of big data mining and analysis algorithms (Talia, 2013). The services repository may provide customizable learning models, data mining algorithms, machine learning methods, statistical procedures and other analytical tools for data cleaning, data reduction, data compression/decompression, dimensionality reduction etc., (Delen & Demirkan, 2013). Moreover, the provision of data analytics tools as cloud services may decrease big data application development time, because service repositories are managed by cloud service providers in a uniform format.

CONCLUSION

Big data analytics and mobile cloud computing are two emerging research areas. Big data systems aggregate massive raw data streams in large-scale storage data centers for lateral processing. This data collection needs extra computational and storage resources and increases the complexity in big data systems. Consequently, the overall data analytics process becomes more laborious and complex. Mobile computing systems facilitate to reduce big data complexity by providing data reduction and data filtration algorithms in mobile environments. These systems augmented with massively parallel cloud computing infrastructures to harnesses maximum computational and storage resources for mobile systems. However, new methods are required to produce high quality and consistent data to comply with variability, veracity, and velocity issues of big data. In addition, the improvements in context-acquisition and inference models are much needed to smoothly execute analytics procedures in mobile-cloud environments. Moreover, the user privacy and secure information propagation methods are required to exchange personal data between mobile and cloud computing systems. Furthermore, the service models of MCC systems could be orchestrated to ease the configuration and deployment of big data analytical tools. Similarly, the issues of dynamic computation offloading, service discovery, and scheduling of execution tasks in MCC environments require attention. Lastly, some new methods are required to classify the lightweight and resource-hungry tasks, partition the applications, and optimize the execution strategies accordingly.

REFERENCES

Abdallah, Z. S., Gaber, M. M., Srinivasan, B., & Krishnaswamy, S. (2015). Adaptive mobile activity recognition system with evolving data streams. *Neurocomputing*, *150*, 304–317. doi:10.1016/j.neucom.2014.09.074

Ahmed, E., Khan, S., Yaqoob, I., Gani, A., & Salim, F. (2013). Multi-objective optimization model for seamless application execution in mobile cloud computing. *Paper presented at the 2013 5th International Conference on Information & Communication Technologies (ICICT)*. doi:doi:10.1109/ICICT.2013.6732790 doi:10.1109/ICICT.2013.6732790

Akidau, T., Balikov, A., Bekiroğlu, K., Chernyak, S., Haberman, J., Lax, R., & Whittle, S. et al. (2013). MillWheel: Fault-tolerant stream processing at internet scale. *Proceedings of the VLDB Endowment*, *6*(11), 1033–1044. doi:10.14778/2536222.2536229

Amini, A., Wah, T. Y., & Saboohi, H. (2014). On density-based data streams clustering algorithms: A survey. *Journal of Computer Science and Technology*, *29*(1), 116–141. doi:10.1007/s11390-014-1416-y

Armbrust, M., Fox, A., Griffith, R., Joseph, A. D., Katz, R., Konwinski, A., & Stoica, I. et al. (2010). A view of cloud computing. *Communications of the ACM*, *53*(4), 50–58. doi:10.1145/1721654.1721672

Assunção, M. D., Calheiros, R. N., Bianchi, S., Netto, M. A., & Buyya, R. (2015). Big Data computing and clouds: Trends and future directions. *Journal of Parallel and Distributed Computing*, *79*, 3–15. doi:10.1016/j.jpdc.2014.08.003

Barros, R. C., Basgalupp, M. P., De Carvalho, A. C., & Freitas, A. (2012). A survey of evolutionary algorithms for decision-tree induction. *Systems, Man, and Cybernetics, Part C: Applications and Reviews. IEEE Transactions on, 42*(3), 291–312.

Chambers, C., Raniwala, A., Perry, F., Adams, S., Henry, R. R., Bradshaw, R., & Weizenbaum, N. (2010). FlumeJava: easy, efficient data-parallel pipelines. *Paper presented at the ACM Sigplan Notices.*

Chandra, T. D., Griesemer, R., & Redstone, J. (2007). Paxos made live: an engineering perspective. *Paper presented at theProceedings of the twenty-sixth annual ACM symposium on Principles of distributed computing.* doi:doi:10.1145/1281100.1281103 doi:10.1145/1281100.1281103

Chen, S. H., & Pollino, C. A. (2012). Good practice in Bayesian network modelling. *Environmental Modelling & Software, 37*, 134–145. doi:10.1016/j.envsoft.2012.03.012

Chen, X.-W., & Lin, X. (2014). Big data deep learning: Challenges and perspectives. *Access, 2*, 514–525. doi:10.1109/ACCESS.2014.2325029

Daghighi, B., Kiah, M. L. M., Shamshirband, S., & Rehman, M. H. (2015). Toward secure group communication in wireless mobile environments: Issues, solutions, and challenges. *Journal of Network and Computer Applications, 50*, 1–14. doi:10.1016/j.jnca.2014.11.001

Delen, D., & Demirkan, H. (2013). Data, information and analytics as services. *Decision Support Systems, 55*(1), 359–363. doi:10.1016/j.dss.2012.05.044

Draper, N. R., & Smith, H. (2014). *Applied regression analysis.* John Wiley & Sons.

Feinleib, D. (2014). The Intersection of Big Data, Mobile, and Cloud Computing. In Big Data Bootcamp (pp. 85-101). Springer.

Gaber, M. M., Gomes, J. B., & Stahl, F. (2014). *Pocket data mining* (Vol. 2). Springer. doi:10.1007/978-3-319-02711-1

Gani, A., Siddiqa, A., Shamshirband, S., & Hanum, F. (2015). A survey on indexing techniques for big data: Taxonomy and performance evaluation. *Knowledge and Information Systems, 46*(2), 241-284.

Garlasu, D., Sandulescu, V., Halcu, I., Neculoiu, G., Grigoriu, O., Marinescu, M., & Marinescu, V. (2013). A big data implementation based on Grid computing. *Paper presented at the 2013 11th Roedunet International Conference (RoEduNet).* doi:doi:10.1109/RoEduNet.2013.6511732 doi:10.1109/RoEduNet.2013.6511732

Gomes, J. B., Krishnaswamy, S., Gaber, M. M., Sousa, P. A., & Menasalvas, E. (2012). Mars: a personalised mobile activity recognition system. *Paper presented at the 2012 IEEE 13th International Conference on Mobile Data Management (MDM).* doi:doi:10.1109/MDM.2012.33 doi:10.1109/MDM.2012.33

Hassan, Q.F., Riad, A.M., & Hassan, A.E. (2012). Understanding Cloud Computing. In H. Yang, & X. Liu (Eds.), *Software Reuse in the Emerging Cloud Computing Era* (pp. 204-227). Hershey, PA, USA: IGI Global.

Haghighi, P. D., Krishnaswamy, S., Zaslavsky, A., Gaber, M. M., Sinha, A., & Gillick, B. (2013). Open mobile miner: A toolkit for building situation-aware data mining applications. *Journal of Organizational Computing and Electronic Commerce*, *23*(3), 224–248. doi:10.1080/10919392.2013.807713

Hall, M., Frank, E., Holmes, G., Pfahringer, B., Reutemann, P., & Witten, I. H. (2009). The WEKA data mining software: an update. *ACM SIGKDD explorations newsletter*, *11*(1), 10-18.

Hashem, I. A. T., Yaqoob, I., Anuar, N. B., Mokhtar, S., Gani, A., & Khan, S. U. (2015). The rise of "big data" on cloud computing: Review and open research issues. *Information Systems*, *47*, 98–115. doi:10.1016/j.is.2014.07.006

Jackson, J. C., Vijayakumar, V., Quadir, M. A., & Bharathi, C. (2015). Survey on Programming Models and Environments for Cluster, Cloud, and Grid Computing that Defends Big Data. *Procedia Computer Science*, *50*, 517–523.

Jain, A. K. (2010). Data clustering: 50 years beyond K-means. *Pattern Recognition Letters*, *31*(8), 651–666. doi:10.1016/j.patrec.2009.09.011

Jayaraman, P. P., Perera, C., Georgakopoulos, D., & Zaslavsky, A. (2014). MOSDEN: A scalable mobile collaborative platform for opportunistic sensing applications. arXiv preprint arXiv:1405.5867.

Khan, A. R., Othman, M., Ali, M., Khan, A. N., & Madani, S. A. (2014). Pirax: Framework for application piracy control in mobile cloud environment. *The Journal of Supercomputing*, *68*(2), 753–776. doi:10.1007/s11227-013-1061-1

Khan, A. R., Othman, M., Khan, A. N., Abid, S. A., & Madani, S. A. (2015). MobiByte: An Application Development Model for Mobile Cloud Computing. *Journal of Grid Computing*, 13(4), 605-628.

Khan, A. R., Othman, M., Madani, S. A., & Khan, S. U. (2014). A survey of mobile cloud computing application models. *IEEE Communications Surveys and Tutorials*, *16*(1), 393–413. doi:10.1109/SURV.2013.062613.00160

Khan, A. R., Othman, M., Xia, F., & Khan, A. N. (2015). Context-Aware Mobile Cloud Computing and Its Challenges. *Cloud Computing, IEEE*, *2*(3), 42–49. doi:10.1109/MCC.2015.62

Kitchin, R. (2014). The real-time city? Big data and smart urbanism. *GeoJournal*, *79*(1), 1–14. doi:10.1007/s10708-013-9516-8

Kreps, J., Narkhede, N., & Rao, J. (2011). Kafka: A distributed messaging system for log processing. *Paper presented at theProceedings of the NetDB*.

Krishnan, S., & Gonzalez, J. U. (2015). Building Your Next Big Thing with Google Cloud Platform: A Guide for Developers and Enterprise Architects.

LaValle, S., Lesser, E., Shockley, R., Hopkins, M. S., & Kruschwitz, N. (2013). Big data, analytics and the path from insights to value. *MIT sloan management review, 21*.

Liu, P., Chen, Y., Tang, W., & Yue, Q. (2012). *Mobile weka as data mining tool on android Advances in Electrical Engineering and Automation* (pp. 75–80). Springer. doi:10.1007/978-3-642-27951-5_11

Marz, N. (2014). *History of Apache Storm and lessons learned*. Thoughts from the Red Planet.

Palankar, M. R., Iamnitchi, A., Ripeanu, M., & Garfinkel, S. (2008). Amazon S3 for science grids: a viable solution? *Paper presented at theProceedings of the 2008 international workshop on Data-aware distributed computing*. doi:doi:10.1145/1383519.1383526 doi:10.1145/1383519.1383526

Perera, C., Zaslavsky, A., Christen, P., & Georgakopoulos, D. (2014). Sensing as a service model for smart cities supported by internet of things. *Transactions on Emerging Telecommunications Technologies, 25*(1), 81–93. doi:10.1002/ett.2704

Rehman, M. H., & Batool, A. (2015). The Concept of Pattern based Data Sharing in Big Data Environments. *International Journal of Database Theory and Application, 8*(4), 11–18. doi:10.14257/ijdta.2015.8.4.02

Rehman, M. H., Liew, C. S., & Wah, T. Y. (2014a). Frequent pattern mining in mobile devices: A feasibility study. *Paper presented at the 2014 International Conference on Information Technology and Multimedia (ICIMU)*. doi:doi:10.1109/ICIMU.2014.7066658 doi:10.1109/ICIMU.2014.7066658

Rehman, M. H., Liew, C. S., & Wah, T. Y. (2014b). UniMiner: Towards a unified framework for data mining. *Paper presented at the 2014 Fourth World Congress on Information and Communication Technologies (WICT)*.

Rehman, M. H., Liew, C. S., Wah, T. Y., Shuja, J., & Daghighi, B. (2015). Mining Personal Data Using Smartphones and Wearable Devices: A Survey. *Sensors (Basel, Switzerland), 15*(2), 4430–4469. doi:10.3390/s150204430 PMID:25688592

Rojas, R. (2013). *Neural networks: a systematic introduction*. Springer Science & Business Media.

Sanaei, Z., Abolfazli, S., Gani, A., & Buyya, R. (2014). Heterogeneity in mobile cloud computing: Taxonomy and open challenges. *IEEE Communications Surveys and Tutorials, 16*(1), 369–392. doi:10.1109/SURV.2013.050113.00090

Sarkar, D. (2014). *Introducing hdinsight Pro Microsoft HDInsight* (pp. 1–12). Springer. doi:10.1007/978-1-4302-6056-1_1

Sato, K. (2012). An inside look at google bigquery (White paper). Retrieved from https://cloud.google.com/files/BigQueryTechnicalWP.pdf

Sherchan, W., Jayaraman, P. P., Krishnaswamy, S., Zaslavsky, A., Loke, S., & Sinha, A. (2012). Using on-the-move mining for mobile crowdsensing. *Paper presented at the 2012 IEEE 13th International Conference on Mobile Data Management (MDM)*. doi:doi:10.1109/MDM.2012.58 doi:10.1109/MDM.2012.58

Shoaib, M., Bosch, S., Incel, O. D., Scholten, H., & Havinga, P. J. (2014). Fusion of smartphone motion sensors for physical activity recognition. *Sensors (Basel, Switzerland), 14*(6), 10146–10176. doi:10.3390/s140610146 PMID:24919015

Sivasubramanian, S. (2012). Amazon dynamoDB: a seamlessly scalable non-relational database service. *Paper presented at the2012 ACM SIGMOD International Conference on Management of Data*. doi:doi:10.1145/2213836.2213945 doi:10.1145/2213836.2213945

Talia, D. (2013). Toward Cloud-based Big-data Analytics. *IEEE Computer Science*, 2013, 98-101.

Varia, J., & Mathew, S. (2013). Overview of amazon web services. *Jan-2014.*

Waller, M. A., & Fawcett, S. E. (2013). Data science, predictive analytics, and big data: A revolution that will transform supply chain design and management. *Journal of Business Logistics*, *34*(2), 77–84. doi:10.1111/jbl.12010

Xu, T., Zhang, Z., Yu, P. S., & Long, B. (2012). Generative models for evolutionary clustering. *ACM Transactions on Knowledge Discovery from Data*, *6*(2), 7. doi:10.1145/2297456.2297459

Zaharia, M., Chowdhury, M., Franklin, M. J., Shenker, S., & Stoica, I. (2010). Spark: cluster computing with working sets. *Paper presented at theProceedings of the 2nd USENIX conference on Hot topics in cloud computing.*

Zhang, J., Li, Z., Sandoval, O., Xin, N., Ren, Y., Martin, R., & Cao, J. (2013). Supporting Personizable Virtual Internet of Things. *Paper presented at the Ubiquitous Intelligence and Computing, 2013 IEEE 10th International Conference on and 10th International Conference on Autonomic and Trusted Computing (UIC/ATC).* doi:doi:10.1109/UIC-ATC.2013.48 doi:10.1109/UIC-ATC.2013.48

KEY TERMS AND DEFINITIONS

Big Data: The amount of data which hampers the computational resources in underlying computing systems is called big data. Big data varies in terms of 6Vs (volume, velocity, veracity, variety, variability, and value) and has different granularities for different computing systems.

Big Mobile Data: The big data produced by on-board sensory and non-sensory data sources in mobile computing systems.

High Performance Computing (HPC): The HPC is the aggregation of computing resources (CPU and Memory) from multiple computing systems to provide maximum computational power for commodity hardware (Desktop PCs, Laptops, Resource-constrained mobile devices). The HPC systems include clouds, grids, data centers, and other massively parallel computing infrastructures.

IoTs: The internetwork of electronic devices and systems called 'things' is called IoTs. The 'things' are autonomous, sensible, actuate-able, addressable, and can be accessed via Internet or intranet.

Mobile Cloud Computing: The augmentation of mobile devices/systems with unlimited computational power provided by ad-hoc and/or infrastructures-based cloud architectures.

Satellite-Based Remote Systems: The mobile systems that could communicate with and controlled by satellite systems. Some examples of these systems include unmanned aerial vehicles, smart trains, and NASA's earth observatory.

Smart Moving Objects: The autonomous mobile systems with on-board sensory and adequate computational power. These systems include domestic robotics and drones amongst many others.

Virtual IoTs: The internetwork of virtual 'things' that are created using software abstractions of one or more physical sensors and/or on-board applications.

Chapter 15
Wireless Enabling Technologies for the Internet of Things

Mahmoud Elkhodr
University of Western Sydney, Australia

Seyed Shahrestani
University of Western Sydney, Australia

Hon Cheung
University of Western Sydney, Australia

ABSTRACT

This Chapter provides several comparable studies of some of the major evolving and enabling wireless technologies in the Internet of Things (IoT). Particularly, it focuses on the ZigBee, 6lowpan, Bluetooth Low Energy, LTE, and the different versions of Wi-Fi protocols including the IEEE 802.11ah. The studies, reported in this chapter, evaluate the capabilities and behaviors of these technologies in terms of various metrics including the data range and rate, network size, RF Channels and Bandwidth, Antenna design considerations, Power Consumption, and their Ecosystem. It is concluded that the requirements of each IoT application play a significant role in the selection of a suitable wireless technology.

INTRODUCTION

The Internet of Things (IoT) was about a vision in which all physical objects are tagged and uniquely identified using RFID transponders or readers (Neil, 2000). Nowadays, research into the IoT has extended this vision to the connectivity of things to anything, anyone, anywhere and at any time. The IoT has grown into multiple dimensions, which encompass various networks of applications, computers, devices, sensors, actuators, smart devices as well as physical and virtual objects (Elkhodr, Shahrestani, & Cheung, 2013). Communication, collaboration and sharing of information between the various facets of the IoT are a keystone for the triumph of the IoT. In the IoT, things are interconnected together using various wireless, wired or mobile communication technologies such as ZigBee, Bluetooth, 4G, Wi-Fi, and other evolving communications technologies. The nature of the IoT communications is no longer restricted to

DOI: 10.4018/978-1-5225-0287-6.ch015

human users but also extends to things-to-things communications. This paradigm of things-to-things and things-to-human communications is a major shift from an essentially computer-based network model to a fully distributed network of connected devices.

The IoT has now more potential to provide a real-world intelligent platform for the collaboration of distributed smart objects via local-area wireless and wired networks, and/or via wide-area heterogeneous network interconnections such as the Internet (Elkhodr et al., 2013). This growth can be attributed to many technological advances. Particularly, it is due to the advance of mobile and wireless communications networks, such as 4G, Wi-Fi and 802.11ah, and their wide-range or low-power wireless capabilities. The rapid development and pervasive evolution of wireless technologies have the potential to grow to accommodate the billions of things envisioned in the IoT. Traditionally, network end-users of the Internet are computers and mobile devices. In the IoT, network users will expand to include humans, things, machines, and a combination or group of them. Thus, the IoT will connect devices that we carry or wear, and devices which we interact with at homes, work, and recreational places; creating an entirely new category of connected devices. The IoT creates a proliferation of devices that until recently very few people would have considered it beneficial to connect to the Internet. Reinventing not only the way we connect to the Internet but the way objects around us are used in everyday activities. Ultimately, wireless technologies and their infrastructures will grow to meet the high demand for connectivity created by the vast amounts of IoT devices joining the Internet. The increase in connectivity demands creates new challenges in terms of communication requirements, device hardware characteristics, software, and resilience capabilities.

Nonetheless, an interesting aspect of the adoption of wireless technologies in the IoT is the incorporation of multiple long range and short range wireless technologies into the designs of IoT applications. In eHealth, for example, applications such as body area networks may develop into an autonomous world of small wireless and networked mobile devices attached to their users. They mostly connect to the Internet using a mobile phone as a gateway or via a wireless access point. Wireless technologies in the IoT need to handle a large degree of ad-hoc growth in device connectivity, structure, organization, and significant change in contextual use, including mobility as well. Many devices will constantly be connected to the energy grid such as smart appliances in the smart home application example. On the other hand, many other IoT devices suffer from limited energy resources as they are powered by small batteries or rely on energy harvesting techniques throughout their lifetime (Vecchio, Giaffreda, & Marcelloni, 2014). Examples of these devices are wireless sensors and those deployed in remote locations. Hence, finding an answer to "Which wireless technology best fits the IoT" is subjective to the application requirements and device capabilities. However, it is established that the need to accommodate the requirements for minimum energy and computation, slim and lightweight solutions in various IoT communication scenarios and applications is essential for the proliferation of the IoT (Vermesan & Friess, 2013). Indeed, most of the future growth in wireless IoT connectivity will stem from these requirements. For the real growth to occur, interactions on the IoT between various industry segments are also needed. To achieve this, interoperability of communications between classic and low-power wireless technologies is fundamental to the success of the IoT.

This Chapter investigates and compares some of the evolving and enabling wireless technologies in the IoT. It provides a brief review of the IEEE 802.15.4 technologies, Bluetooth Low Energy, and Wi-Fi in the section "IoT Wireless enabling protocols". Then the Chapter moves to provide several comparative studies between low-power wireless technologies, particularly, ZigBee, 6Lowpan, and 802.11ah, and the other variants of Wi-Fi technology (802.11a/b/g/n/ac), and LTE in the section "A comparative study of IoT enabling technologies". The comparative studies examine various parameters of these wireless technologies such as their data rates and ranges, network sizes, transmission powers, security, and significantly their ecosystem and suitability of adoption in the IoT. The Chapter concludes by providing some practicals observations from the literature.

Connectivity of Things: The Last Few Meters

The first issue to consider in the IoT is how things will join the Internet. There are two ways for a typical computing device to connect to the Internet:

1. Independently using a mobile broadband connection to an Internet Service Provider (ISP). Two popular examples are a laptop equipped with a mobile broadband modem and a mobile device that connects to the Internet via 3G or 4G that has an inbuilt modem; and
2. Via a local-area wireless or wired network that is connected to a base station or a router. Examples are local area networks (LANs) that connect computers and devices within the same geographical area. Each device on the network is regarded as a node with one of them designated as a gateway. A gateway is a device which shares an Internet connection with other nodes and acts as a router.

In the IoT, an IoT device can connect to the Internet directly, that is it uses the IP suite to exchange data with other devices or servers over the Internet. Alternatively, an IoT device on a local network can use a non-IP protocol to communicate with others devices in a local network setup. Non-IP devices can connect to the Internet via an Internet gateway. Therefore, this gateway has the capability of communicating with non-IP devices in the local network on one hand, and with IP devices on the Internet on the other hand. The gateway is responsible for communicating with the local devices e.g. a sensor, and for the processing of the data it receives. Processing of data may include restructuring and formatting using the TCP/IP stack to enable the communication of these data over the Internet. For example, consider the smart home IoT application example. A wireless sensor can form a local network with another device referred to as a controller. The sensor is responsible for sending some sensory information to the controller. The controller can relay this sensory information to a cloud, mobile device, database or any server on the Internet. Therefore, the controller uses TCP/IP for Internet connectivity. However, the communication between the sensor and the controller is not necessarily based on TCP/IP.

The benefit of connecting IoT devices using IP technology to the Internet enables flexibility. It allows the modification or addition of functionalities to a device without changing the communication requirements. However, the implementation of the TCP/IP stack often requires a fair amount of processing power and energy. The TCP/IP stack is considered to be complex and demanding, implying more development time and more expensive hardware. For these reasons, IP technology might not be suited for devices which have low energy, low communication, and computation capabilities. As a result, many IoT devices, such as the sensor in the smart home example stated above, elect to use simpler protocols.

IoT Wireless Enabling Protocols

The IoT covers a broad range of applications and devices. The 802.11 protocol with its 802.11a/b/g/n/ac variants, popularly known as Wi-Fi, is among the first obvious technology candidates for the IoT. Today, almost every house, workplace, cafe and university has a Wi-Fi network. Wi-Fi has become the de-facto term when referring to connecting to the Internet via a wireless access point. The widespread adoption of Wi-Fi definitely makes it a first technology choice for many IoT applications. However, in some IoT applications, the choice of technology is limited to the device's hardware capabilities, low-power consumption requirement, and the overall cost. Many IoT devices require the use of a low-cost and low-power wireless technology when connecting to the Internet. Traditionally, energy consumption has always been a limiting factor in many wireless sensor network applications. This limiting factor will continue as an important challenge facing the development of many applications in the IoT. In fact, for the growth of the IoT, low-power consumption is an essential requirement that needs to be met.

In addition to low-power consumption, there are other associated requirements that need to be considered as well. For instance, the cost of technology, security, simplicity (easy to use and manage), wireless data rates and ranges, among others, are important requirements that need attention. Many evolving wireless technologies such as ZigBee and Bluetooth are competing to provide the IoT with a low-power wireless connectivity solution. Other wireless technologies such as the IEEE 802.11ah and 6Lowpan protocols are emerging as well. They offer similar low-power wireless connectivity solutions for the IoT. Consequently, there could be many choices of low-power wireless protocols in many IoT applications. Consider, for example, a car-parking system application based on the IoT. A typical IoT-based car-parking system combines many components together. It combines a variety of devices, multiple networking protocols, several sources of data, and various wireless and generations of technologies. Many of the devices involved in the communications are lightweight devices such as sensors which operate on battery. They would require a low-power wireless technology to function effectively.

Essentially, low-power wireless technologies contribute to improving not only the way an IoT device connects to the Internet but the efficiency of the overall IoT application as well. A network consisting of low-cost and lightweight IoT devices can be used to monitor relevant operating and contextual parameters. These devices are also capabale of making useful decisions (based on the occurrence of specific events) while simultaneously communicating with a number of other IoT devices. In general, an heterogeneous setup allows an IoT system to perform many automated tasks by combining the various data gathered from these IoT devices. Recall the smart home IoT application example. In this application, IoT devices such as wireless sensors can report the ambiance temperatures in various locations in a house to an IoT central device, referred to as the controller, which in turns can make a decision on varying the output of the air-conditioning system. Adding more IoT devices to the IoT system will increase the intelligence of the system as well. For instance, if some other sensors are providing information on whether the house is occupied or not (whether the people occupying the house are out or no), then the controller will be able to make a better decision on when the heating system should be turned on or off. In this smart home example, the IoT devices are in the form of simple sensor devices which have a small bandwidth and low-power requirement. Hence, the need for low-power wireless technologies in this and many other similar applications in the IoT.

Bluetooth Low Energy

Bluetooth Low Energy (BLE), also known as Bluetooth Smart and Bluetooth version 4 is an enhancement to the classic Bluetooth protocol (Bluetooth SIG, 2001). BLE is leading a revolution in the areas of wearable technologies, entertainment devices, wireless sensor networks and notably, the Internet of Things. The design of the BLE protocol, which puts the device to sleep when it is not needed, allows low-power consumption by a BLE device (Mackensen, Lai, & Wendt, 2012). It allows a device, communicating through BLE and running on a coin-cell battery, to last for more than a year. The BLE protocol operates in the unlicensed 2.4 GHz Industrial, Scientific, and Medical (ISM) band. It uses the Time Division Multiple Access (TDMA) and Frequency-Division Multiple-Access (FDMA) access technologies (Bluetooth SIG, 2012). To counteract interference and fading, BLE uses a frequency hopping scheme that hops between 40 frequencies separated by 2 MHz. Three of these channels are advertising channels, and the rest are data channels (Ahmed, 2013). TDMA scheme provides different time-slots to different data streams in a repetitive cyclic order. The scheme assigns a specific time slot for each device; which allows a device to send and receive data on a particular frequency at a time. The FDMA scheme is based on the concept of allocating a frequency band or channel to each device. To reduce interference with other 2.4 GHz based wireless technologies, Bluetooth supports adaptive frequency hopping (AFH). AFH determines the available frequency by detecting the frequencies of other devices in the spectrum. This technology provides an efficient transmission scheme within the allocated frequency spectrum and therefore increases the performance of Bluetooth even in the presence of other technologies.

Bluetooth is a packet-based protocol. It implements a master-slave communication architecture. A master is a Bluetooth enabled device which has the capability of communicating with a maximum of seven other Bluetooth-enabled devices, referred to as slaves, at a time. In Bluetooth terms, a master is a device which initiates a connection. By agreements, Bluetooth devices can switch roles from a master to slave and vice versa as well (Bluetooth SIG, 2001). BLE allows devices to communicate with each other when they come in a permitted range, normally up to 100 meters depending on the power classification of the device (more power, longer range). The BLE protocol is designed to have an over the air data rate of 1 Mbps and throughput of around 0.27 Mbps (Bluetooth SIG, 2012). However, in practical implementations, the data rate and throughput are much lower (Gomez, Oller, & Paradells, 2012). The low-power consumption feature of BLE is achieved by putting a BLE device to sleep for a longer period of time. The device will only wake up for a shorter amount of time when it is sending or receiving data. However, the fact that BLE is only sending a small amount of data at a time with efficient energy consumption makes it a favorable technology choice for several light IoT applications. On the contrary, BLE can be judged as impractical to use in many other IoT applications which might require the use of a more capable technology in terms of range and bandwidth.

The throughput, range, data rate, and power consumption parameters of BLE are affected by some other parameters such as the connection parameters. Two important aspects of BLE are the physical channels and events. The physical channel specifies the frequency at which data is sent. In terms of events, an event is the time unit in which data is sent between BLE devices. There are two types of events: advertising events and connection events. Advertising events are used to send advertising packets; while connection events are used to send the actual data. Figure 1 shows an example of two connection events and one advertising event. In these events, the slave and master devices are exchanging some packets. The packets of each of the events are sent on a different frequency given that BLE uses a frequency hopping technique. Other important aspects which relate to the BLE are the connection interval and slave latency. A connection interval is a period of time that occurs between two consecutive connection events (Bluetooth SIG, 2012). The slave latency is a parameter that results in power saving by allowing the slave device to skip a number of connection events if it does not have data to send (Ahmed, 2013). Slave latency specifies the maximum number of connection events that can be skipped (Texas Instruments, 2013).

Figure 1. Bluetooth connection and advertising events

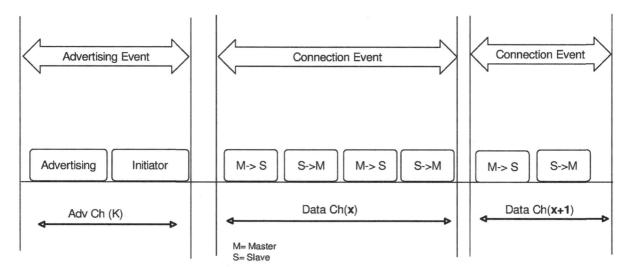

The low-power consumption feature of the BLE protocol enables connectivity, monitoring and sharing of information for many devices, such as home appliances, and wearable devices with a minimal consumption of energy. Significantly, the BLE protocol creates opportunities for a number of IoT applications. It is a strong candidate to be used as a communication protocol in several IoT devices which are limited by their low-power and low-cost characteristics. Examples of these IoT applications and devices range from health monitor devices in e-health, devices in retails applications and in home automation systems ("Bluetooth Smart Technology: Powering the Internet of Things," 2015), and smart appliances in smart grid applications. Additionally, the widespread adoption of smartphones and the advancement made by BLE in terms of energy consumption enable the introduction of many wearables and fitness devices which integrate with smartphones. In addition, BLE has a good potential for becoming an essential technology for the "last 100 meters in low-power and low-cost small devices" of the IoT ("Bluetooth Smart Technology: Powering the Internet of Things," 2015). Using a smartphone or another similar device as a temporary or mobile gateway is increasingly getting popular in numerous IoT applications. Thus, BLE plays a significant role in providing the communication medium needed between this gateway and the IoT devices. There are also some applications where the same IoT device (e.g. a sensor) is used for both mobile and fixed-location applications.

ZigBee

The IEEE 802.15.4 is a protocol designed for low-rate wireless personal area networks (LR-WPANs). It defines the physical and media access control layers (Hackmann, 2006). The IEEE 802.15.4 is the basis for ZigBee (ZigBee Alliance, 2006), WirelessHART (Chen, Nixon, & Mok, 2010), and 6LoWPAN (Kushalnagar, Montenegro, & Schumacher, 2007). The IEEE 802.15.4 operates in the unlicensed 2.4 GHz band which overlaps with other wireless technologies (Wi-Fi, and Bluetooth) sharing the same band. ZigBee is an extension to the 802.15.4 standard. ZigBee is built on top of the 802.15.4's radio layer. It specifies the application, network. and security layers, as described in (ZigBee Alliance, 2014). Often, the terms 802.15.4 and ZigBee are used interchangeably. However, this may not be correct as ZigBee devices are not necessarily compatible with some implementations of the 802.15.4 standard. ZigBee's data rate is considered low when compared with Bluetooth and Wi-Fi. For instance, ZigBee has a data rate that ranges from 20 to 250 kbps (Baker, 2005). On the other hand, Bluetooth has a maximum speed of 3 Mbps and a practical data transfer rate of 2.1 Mbps, whereas Wi-Fi has a data rate that ranges over 54 Mbps. The battery lifetime of Bluetooth classic device is a few days, while that of Wi-Fi is a few hours. In BLE, a battery can last for over a year. However, the battery in a ZigBee device may last for five years before having to be recharged or replaced. Although ZigBee does not have the capability of a high data rate and it is not adequate for real-time applications, it is, per se, serves best in applications where both Wi-Fi and Bluetooth are less suitable.

ZigBee IP is an improvement to the classic ZigBee. ZigBee IP has a layered architecture that makes it suitable to work with other 802.15.4 implementations. The design of ZigBee IP accommodates an IPv6 protocol stack. This stack is developed specifically to operate on low-power and low-cost devices. Moreover, ZigBee IP incorporates technologies, such as 6LoWPAN, that optimize routing and meshing in wireless sensor networks. It supports the requirements of ZigBee Smart Energy version 2.0 as well. This combination of technologies offers a solution that enables the extension of IEEE 802.15.4 based networks to IP-based networks. In terms of the network size, ZigBee IP network is considered to be highly scalable. ZigBee IP protocol does not enforce any limitation on the network size. Theoretically, the size of the network is limited by the hardware specifications of the ZigBee devices such as the available memory and the amount of data exchanged. A typical IEEE 802.15.4 network supports a large number of ZigBee devices. Several ZigBee IP networks can coexist in the same physical area. They can be designed to interconnect at the coordinator level which allows a network to increase the number of connected devices further. The main advantage of ZigBee IP compared to other 802.15.4 technologies is its architecture. ZigBee IP provides a scalable architecture that supports an-end-to end networking based on IPv6. Therefore, many applications in the IoT benefit from this architecture.

ZigBee Network Topology

A typical ZigBee network consists of different types of devices which are the ZigBee coordinator, ZigBee routers and ZigBee end devices (Yang, 2009). Each ZigBee device on the network has a specific functionality that is defined by its operational role. The ZigBee coordinator is responsible for controlling the ZigBee network as it coordinates the messages between the ZigBee routers and ZigBee end devices (Yang, 2009). The ZigBee router acts as a message relay that performs like a bridge for ZigBee networks. The ZigBee end devices are standalone devices that participate in the ZigBee network (Yang, 2009). Figure 2 shows an example of a ZigBee network topology in which the information flow is shown. The coordinator may stand for a smart-home control system. The routers are devices such as an air conditioner or a thermostat, while the end devices can be security sensors and light switches (Jain, 2014), (Yang, 2009).

ZigBee supports different network topologies which include star and mesh topologies (Farahani, 2011). The star topology is used when the devices are close to each other and where the use of one coordinator is sufficient. A star topology can also be a part of a larger mesh network with several routers to each of which several end devices can be connected. A mesh network is a network topology that allows the nodes to communicate via an alternative path in case there is any failure in one of the intermediate devices in an existing path e.g. link redundancy (Yang, 2009). ZigBee has two operational modes, i.e., beacon mode and non-beacon mode. In the beacon node, the nodes are aware of when to communicate with one

Figure 2. ZigBee IP network topology example

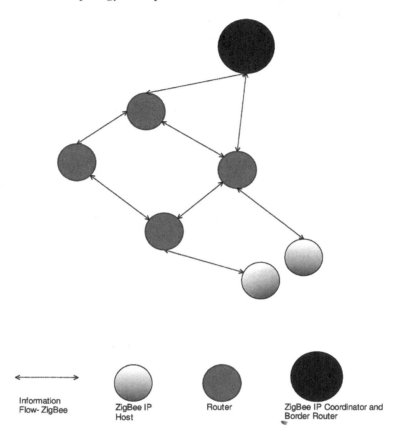

another and the coordinator periodically sends beacons to all devices on the network. Nodes, including the coordinator, may sleep between beacons. The beacons sent by the coordinator check whether there is a message received or not. If there are no messages received, the nodes can go back to sleep mode. On the other hand, the non-beacon mode is characterized by less coordination between the coordinator and the nodes. Since the nodes only communicate when they need to, the coordinator's receiver is always active which enables it to receive messages from other nodes in real-time. Consequently, in the non-beacon mode, the coordinator consumes more energy since it has to be always listening. In contrast, other ZigBee devices on the network save their power since they do not need to stay awake when they are not engaging in any communication. Therefore, they remain in -sleep for a longer period of time. To better understand the differences between the beacon and non-beacon modes, consider the following simple IoT application scenario where the ZigBee network is configured in a non-beacon mode: A wireless switch is used to turn on/off an appliance e.g. a lamp. The switch is battery operated while the ZigBee node at the lamp is connected to the power supply. Therefore, the lamp (the ZigBee coordinator) is always active; while the switch (the ZigBee end device) remains asleep until someone uses the wireless switch to turn on or off the lamp. In this scenario, the switch wakes up and sends a command to the lamp which is always active and listening. The switch then remains active until it receives an acknowledgment from the lamp and then returns to sleep.

ZigBee offers seamless communications across different domains with significant functions for consumers. It allows communication with excellent interoperability among a broad range of smart and innovative business products that enhance everyday life (Elahi & Gschwender, 2009).

The 6Lowpan Protocol

6LoWPAN refers to IPv6 over Low-power Wireless Personal Area Networks. It is a low-power wireless mesh network protocol. By definition, 6LoWPAN is a protocol which enables IPv6 packets to be carried on top of low-power wireless networks, specifically IEEE 802.15.4 networks. The concept is based on the idea that the Internet Protocol should be extended to even the smallest devices, extending the applications of the IP to lightweight devices with limited processing capabilities in the IoT. 6LowPAN uses 802.15.4 in the un-slotted CSMA/CA mode and relies on beacons for link-layer device discovery (Yibo et al., 2011). Similar to ZigBee, the 6LowPAN protocol is developed based on the IEEE standard 802.15.4-2003. It has low processing and low storage costs. 6LowPAN works by fragmenting IPv6 packets and compressing them into UDP/ICMP headers. The 6LoWPAN group defines the header compression and encapsulation techniques that allow IPv6 packets to be communicated across various IEEE 802.15.4 based networks (Caputo, Mainetti, Patrono, & Vilei, 2012). 6LoWPAN is a competitor for ZigBee and BLE protocols. It has applications in smart metering and smart homes as well. 6LoWPAN supports interoperability with other implementations of the 802.15.4 protocol, and with other IP-based devices as well (Lu, Li, & Wu, 2011). Addressing and adaption mechanism are available for devices that communicate across the two different domains of IPv6 and 802.15.4. An example of a 6Lowpan network is provided in Figure 3.

Figure 3. 6Lowpan network example

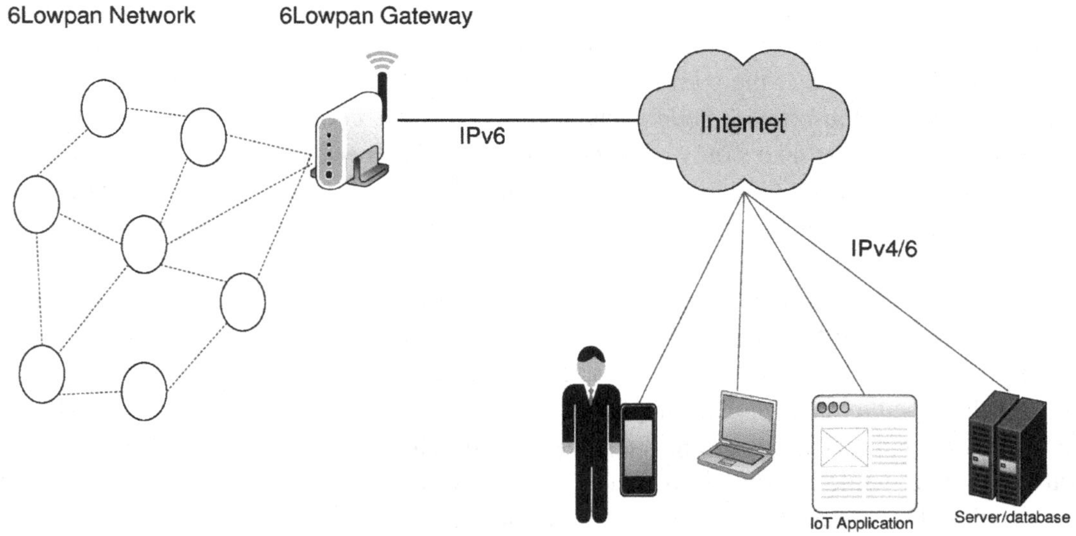

The 802.11 Wireless LAN Protocol

Wireless Local Area Networks (WLANs) is the dominant technology for indoor broadband wireless access. WLAN products have become commodity items used in professional and consumer products alike. Recently, the propagation of WLANs as extensions of wired networks has been increasing dramatically, and thereby, giving devices equipped with wireless interfaces a higher degree of mobility. The two most common WLAN standards are the IEEE 802.11 standard (commonly branded as Wi-Fi) and the European HIPER (High-Performance Radio) LAN (Lemstra, Hayes, & Groenewegen, 2010). The IEEE 802.11 defines two types of configurations, the Infrastructure Basic Service Set (iBSS), and Independent BSS (IBSS). In iBSS, an access point (AP) is the central entity of each coverage area with coordination functionality. Additionally, the AP acts as a bi-directional bridge between the wireless network and the wired infrastructure (i.e., typically Ethernet). Stations (STA) are mostly mobile devices equipped with IEEE 802.11 wireless network interfaces. Communication between the AP and the associated stations occurs over the shared wireless medium that carries the data. A station must associate with an AP in order for it to transmit and receive data to and from the wired infrastructure, and to communicate with other stations on the same WLAN. A Basic Service Set (BSS) is the term used to refer an AP and its associated stations. In large WLANs, multiple BSSs can be joined using a distribution system (DS), thus providing sufficient coverage for a greater number of stations. This setup of having two or more BSSs is referred to as an Extended Service Set (ESS). The DS is the wired backbone connecting APs and allowing the associated stations to access services available on the wired infrastructure. Therefore, Wi-Fi devices can form a star topology with its AP acting as an Internet gateway. The output power of Wi-Fi is higher than other local area network wireless technologies. Full coverage of Internet connectivity is important for Wi-Fi networks so dead spots which may occur are overcome by the use of more than one antenna in the AP.

Wi-Fi operates in the 2.4 and 5 GHz bands. Its operations in the 5 GHz band allow the use of more channels and provide higher data rates. However, the range of 5 GHz radio indoors (e.g. inside buildings) is shorter than 2.4 GHz. The IEEE 802.11b and IEEE 802.11g operate in the 2.4 GHz ISM band. Thus, they encounter interferences from other technologies operating in the same frequency band such as the microwave, cellular and Bluetooth technologies. Interference can be overcome using spectrum technologies like the Direct Sequence Spread Spectrum (DSSS) and orthogonal frequency division (OFDM) methods. The IEEE 802.11 protocol uses the ISM band to achieve good performance with a high or low frequency depending on the environment.

The IEEE 802.11n improves the previous versions of the standard by introducing the multiple input and multiple output methods (MIMO). It operates both in the 2.4 and 5 GHz frequency bands. It supports a data rate ranging from 54 Mbit/s to 600 Mbit/s (Perahia & Stacey, 2013). The IEEE 802.11ac is an improved version of the IEEE 802.11n and it provides high-throughput wireless local area networks (WLANs) in the 5 GHz band with more spatial streams and higher modulation with MIMO yielding data rates up to 433.33 Mbps (Akyildiz, Su, Sankarasubramaniam, & Cayirci, 2002). The IEEE 802.11ac provides a single link throughput of at least 500 Mbps and up to 1 gigabit per second. The IEEE 802.11ac extends the air interface concept defined by the IEEE 802.11n protocol allowing a higher throughput to be achieved. This extension includes a wider RF bandwidth of up to 160 MHz and a higher density modulation up to 256 QAM. It allows more downlink clients, up to 4 clients using multi-user MIMO, and up to eight MIMO spatial streams as well (Akyildiz et al., 2002). The IEEE 802.11ac offers a new range of WLAN use cases. For instance, the mutli-station capability allows the streaming of HD videos simultaneously to multiple clients. The single-link enhancement opens the door to a variety of automated tasks that can be achieved in a rapid and efficient way, such as the rapid synchronization and backup of large files (Bejarano, Knightly, & Park, 2013). Other IEEE 802.11ac usages include a wireless display to HD TVs and monitors, floor automation and large auditorium deployments (De Vegt, 2008). Thus, the IEEE 802.11ac serves as a promising communication technology for many IoT applications, particularly in Multimedia, monitoring and surveillance applications. Also, it is best suited for IoT scenarios that require the real-time exchange of a large amount of data. Examples are Remote Medical Assistance via Wireless Networks (raw surgical camera), Intra-Large-Vehicle Applications (e.g. airplanes, trains), Multi-Media Mesh Backhaul and point to point backhaul as shown in Figure 4. Table 1 highlights the main improvement the IEEE 802.11ac has made to the previous version of the standard, the IEEE 802.11n.

Therefore, the IEEE 802.11ac is a significant improvement in technology and data-carrying capabilities. SU-MIMO (single-user multiple input/multiple output) technology is one of the hallmarks of the older 802.11n standard (Geier, 2014). The IEEE 802.11ac supports multi-user MIMO (MU-MIMO) technology which allows the simultaneous transmission and receiving of multiple separate signals from devices in the same frequency band. As a result, an IEEE 802.11ac router can exchange data at a maximum physical link rate of 1.3Gbps. This can be achieved because the IEEE 802.11ac protocol supports simultaneous operations of up to three streams. In contrast, an IEEE 802.11n router can only support a maximum physical link rate of 150Mbps per stream (Geier, 2014).

Figure 4. The IEEE 802.11ac backhaul capabilities

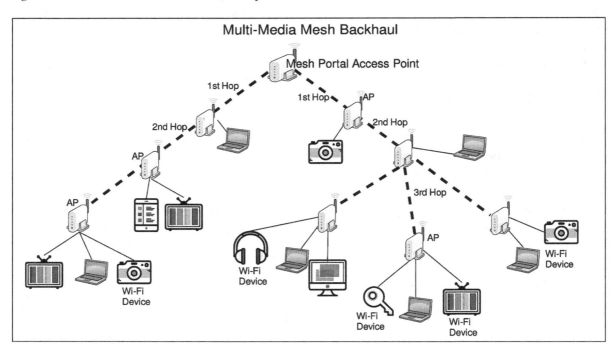

Table 1. Main differences between 802.11n and 802.11ac

	802.11n	**802.11ac**
Frequency band	2.4 and 5 GHz	Only 5 GHz
Spatial Streams	1 to 4(MIMO spatial streams)	1 to 8 (MIMO spatial streams)
Chanel width	20, 40 MHz	20,40,80, [160] MHZ
Mutli-user MIMO	No	Yes
Maximum speed	600 Mbps	3 Gbps +

At the other end of the spectrum, the IEEE 802.11ah standard operates in the unlicensed 900MHz frequency band. A wireless signal operating on the 900MHz band can penetrate walls, but it would deliver a limited bandwidth ranging from 100Kbps to 40Mbps (Adame, Bel, Bellalta, Barcelo, & Oliver, 2014). One common IoT application of this technology would be sensors and actuators in homes or commercial buildings. Thus, IEEE 802.11ah could be positioned as a competitor to Bluetooth and ZigBee protocols in the IoT space.

The IEEE 802.11ah

Wi-Fi, with its 802.11 a/b/g/n/ac variants, might not be suitable to use in some IoT applications where low-power consumption is a vital requirement for the operation of IoT devices. Wi-Fi was originally designed to offer high throughput to a limited number of devices located indoor at a short distance from each other. Therefore, to meet the IoT low-power requirements, the IEEE 802 LAN/MAN Standards Committee (LMSC) formed the IEEE 802.11ah Task Group (TGah) (IEEE, 2015). The task group objective is to extend the applicability area of 802.11 networks. It aims to design an energy efficient protocol allowing thousands of indoor and outdoor devices to work in the same area (Khorov, Lyakhov, Krotov, & Guschin, 2014). The IEEE 802.11ah aims to support a range of throughput options ranging from 150 Kbps up to 40 Mbps over an 8 MHz band (Adame et al., 2014). In term of wireless range, the proposed IEEE 802.11ah protocol supports a wider coverage range when compared to the IEEE 802.11n/ ac protocol. The IEEE 802.11ah supports applications with coverage of up to 1 km in outdoor areas and up to 8191 devices associated with one access point. The IEEE 802.11ah operates in the unlicensed sub-1GHz bands, excluding the TV white-space bands. Sub 1 band provides an extended wireless range when compared to the other bands used by conventional 802.11 Wi-Fi standards which operate in the 2.4 GHz and 5 GHz bands (Qualcomm, 2014). The IEEE 802.11ah relies on the one-hop network topology and employs power saving mechanisms (Adame et al., 2014). Given that the IEEE 802.11ah protocol falls under the overall Wi-Fi umbrella, it is expected that it will be compatible with the existing Wi-Fi infrastructure. The IEEE 802.11ah allows access to more than 8 thousand devices in the range of 1 km within an area with high concentration of small devices such as sensors, and mini controllers. Therefore, the IEEE 802.11ah technology can satisfy the IoT requirements while maintaining an acceptable user experience in parallel with the IEEE 802.11 technologies. One of the interesting functional requirements of the IEEE 802.11ah is to enable coexistence with the IEEE 802.15.4 standard.

The 802.11ah standard includes new PHY and MAC layers grouping devices into traffic induction maps to accommodate small units and machine to machine (M2M) communications (Valerio, 2014). The physical layer allows devices along with the AP to operate over various sub-1GHz ISM bands depending on the regulation of the country (Valerio, 2014). The 900 MHz band is currently used in Europe for GSM 2G cellular facilities. The 900 MHz is used in many devices, and it is suitable for M2M communications specifically in light devices such as wireless sensors. In some countries, the frequency bands vary from 902-928 MHz in the USA, 863-868.6 in Europe, 950.8-957.6 MHz in Japan. Other countries are expected to follow in releasing the spectrum once the 802.11ah standard is finalized.

The 802.11ah Power Saving Mode

The direct advantages of using the sub-1 GHz spectrum, also referred to as Sigsbee, in the IoT is the improvement in the coverage area for IoT devices and applications, in addition to increasing energy efficiency. Nevertheless, Sigsbee plays a significant role in wireless connectivity. It specifically targets wireless sensor networks. Applications can be found in home automation and building automation with intelligent metering instruments (AMI). The IEEE 802.11ah protocol implements energy-saving mechanisms which guarantee that the limited energy resources available for a sensor node are efficiently used. A large number of devices can be accommodated by a single IEEE 802.11ah AP due to the infrequent data exchange in some IoT applications. However, the device' activity needs to be properly distributed over time (Adame et al., 2014).

The IEEE 802.11 standard defines two states for a wireless network interface: awake or sleep. In the awake state, the device's radio is turned on allowing the wireless interface to perform data communications, or just to remain idle (Asha, 2012). In the sleep state, the radio of the device is turned off, and the wireless interface is put to sleep (He, Yuan, Ma, & Li, 2008). This state is specified in the IEEE 802.11 standard as Power Saving Mode (PSM). In PSM, the AP buffers incoming frames destined for mobile stations. It continues doing this until the station wakes up. When the device wakes up, the buffered traffic will be delivered. The station goes back to PSM once the buffered traffic is fully delivered (He et al., 2008). To achieve this, the IEEE 802.11ah standard defines two classes of signalling beacon frames: (a) Delivery Traffic Indication Map (DTIM) which informs which groups of STAs have pending data at the AP, and (b) the Traffic Indication Map (TIM) which specifies which STA in a given STA group has pending data at the AP. Consequently, the PSM, TIM, and Page Segmentation result in a new scheme which improves the overall power efficiency of IEEE 802.11ah devices. For further reading on the new proposed PSM scheme, the reader is referred to (Adame et al., 2013).

On the other hand, the IEEE 802.11af, also called Super Wi-Fi or White-Fi, operates in the unused TV spectrum. 802.11af coverage can extend up to several kilometers as it operates on the frequency bands between 54MHz and 790MHz. It offers a reasonable throughput, estimated at 24Mb/s. It has similar applications as 802.11ah, providing bandwidth for sensors and other devices of the IoT (Mohapatra, Choudhury, & Das, 2014).

A COMPARATIVE STUDY OF IOT ENABLING WIRELESS TECHNOLOGIES

Nowadays, the wireless industry is increasingly adopting the IoT. There is a growing momentum to embrace and design technologies that adhere explicitly to the IoT requirements. This includes the modification of existing technologies e.g. from Bluetooth classic to Bluetooth smart, and from ZigBee to ZigBee IP, as we have seen in the previous sections. Moreover, it also involves the design of new technologies such as the IEEE 802.11ah. These technologies aim at addressing key IoT wireless and devices' requirements, such as low-power consumption, lower computation capabilities, reduced implementation and operational costs, and wider coverage range. The previous section provided a brief review of the IEEE 802.15.4 technologies, Bluetooth Low energy, and the IEEE 802.11ah technology. The IEEE 802.15.4 family of technologies such as the 6Lowpan and ZigBee technologies are currently used in various wireless sensor network applications. These applications are characterized by requirements similar to those encountered in IoT and M2M applications. The Bluetooth Low Energy technology is widely adopted in wearables and consumer products. On the other hand, the IEEE 802.11ah is a new protocol under development. It is designed to operate in the sub-one-gigahertz (900MHz) band. It has an extended range when compared to traditional Wi-Fi, and it is regarded as a competitor for both ZigBee, 6Lowpan, and the other already-established protocols in this sub-one band.

However, all the aforementioned technologies have their positive qualities and obviously have their negatives as well. For instance, the gain in range with the use of the IEEE 802.11ah is lost in bandwidth, whereas with the use of ZigBee the gain in bandwidth is lost in range. Therefore, rather than attempting to nominate the ideal technology for the IoT, this section presents a brief comparison of some of these wireless technologies. The areas of the IoT involve heterogeneous sets of devices which use various communication technologies to share and exchange information. Within the IoT, some IoT applications can be in the form of simple peer-to-peer applications. Other IoT applications can also be based on personal area network setups, involving the use of few devices and users. Other complex applications might involve the use of a variety of heterogeneous devices which communicate using a wide array of technologies, in different setups and topologies. Therefore, a technology that can be deemed suitable for a particular IoT application might not necessarily be suited for adoption in many others. In fact, the ability to connect and coexist amongst various devices operating using several communication technologies is the spirit behind the IoT. Having an ecosystem of coexisted technologies and devices is what enables the IoT vision of extending communications to anything, and anywhere.

Data Rate and Range

The IEEE 802.11ac and LTE advanced have the highest data rate among the wireless technologies in use today. The IEEE 802.11ac specification provides a theoretical maximum data transfer speed of more than 3Gbps. It can provide a transfer speed up to 1.3Gbps as well, and supports up to 8 streams (Siddiqui, Zeadally, & Salah, 2015). On the other hand, LTE Advanced has a1 Gbps fixed speed and a rate of 100 Mbps to mobile users (Stroud, 2015). Figure 5 compares between various wireless technologies in terms of distance coverage in meters, rates, ranges and power consumptions.

In the low-power wireless technology space, Bluetooth Low Energy has the highest data rate of 2.1 Mbps. The ZigBee and 6Lowpan technologies, supported by the IEEE 802.15.4 standard, have a data rate of 250 Kbps in 2.4 GHz frequency band. However, ZigBee's data rate falls to 20 Kbps in the 868 MHz band and to 40 Kbps in the 915 MHz band in some countries (Anitha & Chandrasekar, 2011). On the other hand, the IEEE 802.11.ah has the lowest data rate targeted at 150Kbps with an average of 100 Kbps. In term of the theoretical wireless range, as illustrated in Figure 5, cellular technologies, e.g. LTE, cover a larger area when compared with other Wi-Fi technologies, with IEEE 802.11 variants coming second at an approximate maximum range of a 100 m.

As of the range of low-power wireless technologies, the IEEE 802.11ah rules the chart against 802.15.4 and BLE technologies in terms of range. The 802.11ah coverage range also outperforms that of the other variants of the 802.11 protocol, with a range coverage of approximately 1 km, as shown in Figures 5 and

Figure 5. Comparative study of IoT enabling wireless technologies against power consumption, distance coverage in meters, and data rate

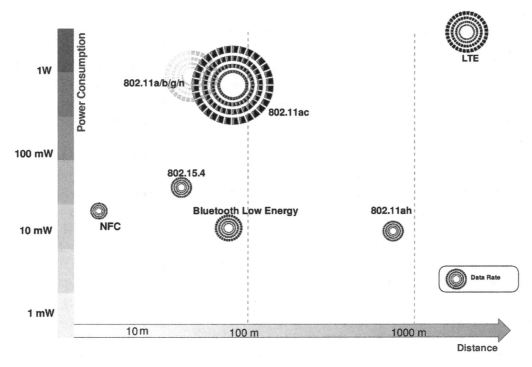

6. On the other hand, it should be noted that the 802.15.4 supports mesh networking. Meshing in mesh networking is a term used to describe when a message is routed through several nodes on a network until it reaches its destination. As such a ZigBee network's range can be easily extended with the use of repeaters in a mesh formation. Data in a ZigBee network "hops" around a mesh of nodes until a route to the host (usually the Internet) is found. Therefore, repeaters and/or a high density of nodes can be used to extend the coverage of a ZigBee network.

Figure 6. IEEE 802.11 a/b/g/n/ac range comparison in meters

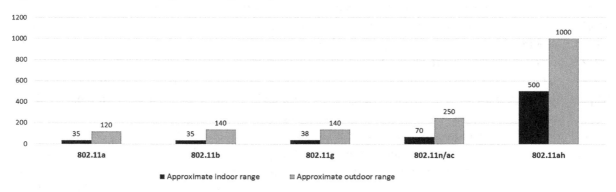

Interestingly, the IEEE 802.11ah is under development with meshing in mind as well. Therefore, the choice of technology in terms of data rate and range come back to the requirements of the IoT applications in hand. Accordingly, if an IoT application requires the use of a larger number of nodes and meshing is an option, ZigBee appears to be a suitable candidate given the data rate edge over its 802.11ah counterpart. On the other hand, in IoT applications that require the deployment of fewer nodes with minimal traffic, 802.11ah is a strong contender to ZigBee. This is due to the reason that 802.11ah has a larger coverage area without relying on any meshing technique, and it is intended to be backward compatible with the variants of 802.11 Wi-Fi technology. However, as we will see in the next subsections, relying on the data rate and range differences only does not provide an efficient measure for the selection of a technology as there are other criteria that should be considered as well.

Network Size

The BLE protocol supports a maximum of 8 nodes per network which include one master device and 7 devices as slaves. ZigBee can have up to 65,000 nodes per network in a star topology (Baker, 2005). Both of these technologies can be extended into more sophisticated networks. For instance, ZigBee can be extended to a cluster tree or mesh network while BLE can be extended to a scatternet network. An interconnected piconet consisting of more than 8 Bluetooth devices is referred to as a scatternet. It is the process of connecting two piconets together. A scatternet can be created when a device belonging to one piconet is elected to be a member of the second piconet as well (McDermott-Wells, 2004).

On the other hand, the baseline IEEE 802.11 standard does not limit the number of devices in the network. However, the limitation can be attributed to the length of some of the fields defined in the management frames of the standard (IEEE 802.11 Working Group, 2010). The Association Identifier (AID) which is a unique value assigned to a station by the AP during an association handshake, is 14 bits long. However, the values other than 1-2007, which are 0 and 2008-16383, are reserved. In particular, AID = 0 is reserved for group addressing traffic (Khorov et al., 2014). Therefore, the AID design limits the number of stations that can be associated with an AP to 2007 (Khorov et al., 2014). Additionally, the Traffic Indication Map (TIM) bitmap enforces the same limit on the number of associated stations as well. The TIM is used for power management mechanisms. It defines the number of buffered frames received from an AP. For these reasons, TGah is extending the range of AID values for 802.11ah's devices from 1-2007 to 0-8191. Also, the IEEE 802.11ah draft standard is increasing the maximal length of the TIM bitmap for 802.11ah's devices from 2008 bits to 8192 bits (Khorov et al., 2014). Therefore, it is quite obvious that ZigBee and the IEEE 802.11ah outperform the classical 802.11a/ac protocol when it comes to the network size requirements. Of course, cellular technologies have an enormous network size. However, cellular connectivity cannot be possible without involving a mobile provider which usually charges a fee per connection. Therefore, while cellular technology can accommodate an enormous network size of devices, the cost involved are dramatically higher than those associated with other technologies such as ZigBee. Table 2 provides a brief comparison between ZigBee, BLE and Wi-Fi in terms of their network size.

Table 2. Network size comparison of ZigBee, BLE and Wi-Fi

Technology	Network Size
ZigBee	Approximately up to 65,000 nodes
Bluetooth	8 nodes per network/piconet
Wi-Fi (802.11a/ac)	2007 associated with an AP
Wi-Fi 802.11ah	Approximately 8000 nodes

RF Channels and Bandwidth

Tables 3 shows some of the main differences between the various wireless technologies. These technologies operate in a broad range of frequencies. For instance, ZigBee operates in the 868/915 MHz, and 2.4 GHz. 6LoWPAN operates in the 900 to 2400 MHz; 802.11a/b/g/n/ac works in the 2.4 and 5 GHz bands. On the other hand, the IEEE 802.11ah is fragmented over various frequency bands based in the country. It is observed that most of these technologies, excluding that of the IEEE 802.11ah, operate in the 2.4 GHz band. In addition to Bluetooth, Wi-Fi, and ZigBee, RFID operates in the 2.45 GHz band (microwave) as well.

Another observation is that the IEEE 802.11ah protocol operates in sub-1GHz band for the purpose of saving power and extending the range of Wi-Fi. However, this shifting of bands for Wi-Fi means 802.11ah's frequency band operations will differ from one country to another. For instance, 802.11ah operates at 868 MHz in Europe, 780 MHz in China, and in a range of other frequencies in other countries. The variability in frequency operations of 802.11ah hampers the unification of Wi-Fi products and adds another level of complexity and fragmentation to the already fragmented IoT. As such, 802.11ah's product makers will have to deal with different sets of regulations and certifications for various regions.

Table 3. Comparative study of various wireless technologies

Wireless Technology	Applications (Example)	Frequency	Range	Data Rate
ZigBee	Home Automation, Industrial Monitoring, Light link.	2.4 GHz	10 to 20 m	250 Kbps
RFID	RFID Tags, Access management, Machine readable documents.	120-150 KHz	10cm-200m	26 Kbps
Bluetooth 4	Bluetooth smart, Fitness tracker, wearable devices.	868/915 2.4GHz	<100m	2.1 Mbps
Cellular e.g. 3G/LTE	Any device with Cellular connectivity capability	Australia: 2100Mhz, 1800MHz, 900Mhz 850MHz	Where signal reach	7.64-100 Mbps up to 1 Gbps fixed in LTE Advanced
802.11 a to ac	Smart Homes	2.4, 3.6, 5, 60 GHz	Up to 100m	Up to 1.3Gbps
NFC	Metro tickets, Mobile payment, Shopping center.	13.56 MHz	< 20 cm	106 to 424 Kbps
6LoWPAN	Smart Homes, Smart Metering	900 to 2400 MHz	10-20 m	200 kbps
Sub-1 GHz 802.11ah	Smart Home Wireless sensor networks, metering automation.	Sub 1 GHz	Up to 1KM	150 Kbps

Table 4. Frequency modulation comparison

Technology	802.11a/n	802.11b	802.11g	802.11ac/ah	ZigBee	Bluetooth
Modulation	OFDM	DSSS	DSSS OFDM	OFDM	BPSK ASK OQPSK	AFH FHSS

In term of modulation, Bluetooth employs frequency hopping (FHSS) with 79 channels and 1 MHz bandwidth; while Wi-Fi uses OFDM modulation in 802.11a/g/n with 14 RF channels and 22 MHz bandwidth, and ZigBee uses direct-sequence spread spectrum (DSSS) with 2 MHz bandwidth and 16 available channels. Refer to Table 4 for a modulation comparison for these technologies. It should be noted that Wi-Fi uses a variety of modulation techniques including BPSK, CCK, OFDM, DSSS, QPSK, and M-QAM.

Antenna Considerations

Designing antennas for wireless devices is becoming an emerging area of research. Typically, larger antennas are required when the devices are operating over a lower frequency band. Therefore, given that a ZigBee 2.4 GHz device can work well with a 6 cm antenna, a sub-GHz device will require under comparable circumstances a larger antenna (Araiza Leon, 2015). For instance, when standardizing 802.11ac, one of the selling point of .11ac technology in addition to its data rate speed, was the reduced size of antenna requirement given that .11ac operates in the 5 GHz band (Qualcomm, 2012). Therefore, it will be interesting to watch the antenna design TGah will adopt in IEEE 802.11ah. The antenna design of MIMO and other solutions are also evolving. Examples are those based on Steerable Square Loop antenna design such as the one proposed in (Pal, Mehta, Mirshekar-Syahkal, Deo, & Nakano, 2014).

Transmission Power

As shown in Figure 5 and Table 5, the 802.15.4 based technologies; BLE and 802.11ah, all have a low power consumption characteristic. The transmission power of BLE ranges from 1 to 10 mW (Dementyev, Hodges, Taylor, & Smith, 2013). ZigBee transmission power is very low estimated to be under 1 mW, while, the Wi-Fi standard has a transmission power of approximately 100 mW. On the other hand, the IEEE 802.11ah has a transmission power of less than 10 mW. It is targeted to be under 1mW with the new proposed PSM scheme which aims for better energy efficiency.

In (Olyaei, Pirskanen, Raeesi, Hazmi, & Valkama, 2013), it was found that in terms of energy consumption, and in the case of a small number of nodes in a low traffic scenario, the IEEE 802.15.4 consumed more average energy for the successful transmission of a packet compared with IEEE 802.11ah. However, in congested networks, the energy consumption of the IEEE 802.11ah was found to be relatively higher than that of IEEE 802.15.4. Therefore, the study concludes that, in terms of energy consumption, the IEEE 802.15.4 outperformed the IEEE 802.11ah, especially in a dense network and non-saturated traffic. However, in terms of throughput, the IEEE 802.11ah has a better performance when compared to IEEE 802.15.4. Nevertheless, it should be noted that, at the time of writing, the IEEE 802.11ah standard is still under development. Thus, more simulations and experimental studies are required to determine the performance of IEEE 802.11ah effectively.

Table 5. A comparative study of low power wireless technologies

Technology	Bluetooth Low Energy	ZigBee	6Lowpan	Wi-Fi
Standard	IEEE 802.15.1	IEEE 802.15.4	IEEE 802.15.4	IEEE 802.11ah
Data rate	1 Mbps	250Kbps	250kbps	150Kbps
Theoretical Range	100 m	10 to 20 m	~20 m	Up to 1000 m
Bandwidth	1 MHz	2Mhz	0.3/0.6; 2 MHz	1,2,4,8,16 MHz
Power consumption	0.01 to 0.5 W	~1mW	~1mW	~1mW
Security	128-bit AES with Counter Mode CBC-MAC and application layer user defined	TLS1.2 AES-128-CCM X.509 v3 certificates and ECC-256 cipher suite	AES link layer TSL/SSL on	Application layer security similar to 802.11

The Ecosystem

In term of the ecosystem, The IEEE 802.11ah has the potential to stand out amongst its counterparts. Given that the IEEE 802.11ah falls under the overall Wi-Fi umbrella, it is expected that it will be compatible with the existing Wi-Fi infrastructure, specifically to be compatible with IEEE 802.11a/b/g/n/ac standards. The IEEE 802.11ah has the potential to grow the Wi-Fi market from its existing computing and mobile platforms to the IoT market significantly. However, since the IEEE 802.11ah still in its early stage of development, it is yet to establish itself against already recognized technologies such as BLE and ZigBee. However, as shown in Figure 7, the IEEE 802.11ah implements the full TCP/IP stack when compared to 6Lowpan and ZigBee.

Nevertheless, ZigBee has been winning grounds in several IoT consumer based applications including electronics, smart meter infrastructure, and home automation. When meshing can be used, ZigBee's data rate differentiates it against the IEEE 802.11ah. ZigBee's is increasingly being adopted in IoT areas such as automated meter reading, leading to participation in the smart grid push by utility companies. This has become an especially active area for ZigBee. However, implementation of ZigBee remains, in greater parts, within closed ecosystems and applications. For instance, the lack of a native support for ZigBee in

Figure 7. Comparative study of TCP/IP stack with ZigBee, 6Lowpan, and IEEE 802.11ah

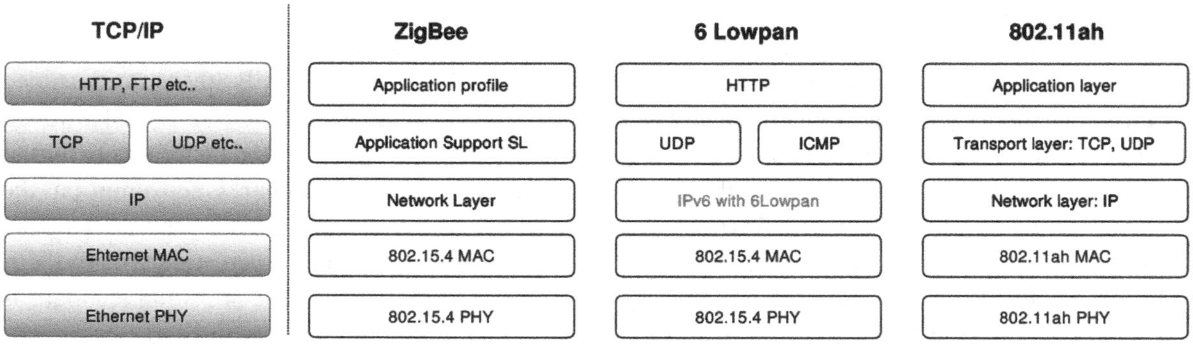

Table 6. Comparative study of ZigBee, BLE and 802.11ah based on various criteria

	Security	Location Detection	Low Cost	Ease of Use	Ecosystem	Low Power	Range	Remote Control	Antenna Size	Networking Size	Frequency Band
802.15.4	✓	✓	✓	✓	✓	✓	✓(✓)	✓	✓	✓	✓
BLE	✓	✗	✓	✓	✓	✓	✗	✓	✓	✗	✓
802.11ah	✓	✓	✓	✓	✓	✓	✓	✓	✓	✓(✓)	✓
Comment			Wi-Fi target: as per ZigBee	Wi-Fi target: as per 802.11	- BLE and 802.11ah have a larger ecosystem. BLE is established in phones, wearables, etc... 802.11ah compatible with 802.11 ZigBee has a closed ecosystem established in some use cases e.g. smart energy	802.11ah target: as per ZigBee	Criteria: 'home'. ZigBee Mesh will improve range. BLE: Room range Wi-Fi: Home range, extendable by mesh		lower frequencies require larger antennas	Criteria: >1000 Nodes per network. ZigBee has an edge of networking size of 65,000 device	802.15.4 and BLE operate on 2.4 GHz; while 802.11ah is fragmented by region

the mobile device domain (smartphones, tablets, laptops, smart watches, gadgets, car multimedia etc.), is a major challenge for early IoT adopters, more specifically, in applications where a mobile device is used as a temporary gateway for IoT devices.

On the other hand, Bluetooth Low Energy is a potential competitor in some IoT areas. It might find applications in medical equipment and in remote control applications. BLE has been dominating the consumer electronics market. Additionally, BLE has been increasingly used to eliminate cabling for peripherals. This brings these peripherals closer to the communication networks and allows the management of these devices. Table 6 compares the ecosystems of ZigBee, BLE, and IEEE 802.11ah.

The criteria considered in the rating of technologies provided in Table 6 and the conclusions that can be drawn from Table 6 include the following:

- The wireless technologies surveyed above have built-in link layer authentication and encryption, which most likely need to be completed with an end-to-end security at the application layer.
- Bluetooth low energy has the potential for less power consumption than IEEE 802.15.4 (less overhead).
- The IEEE 802.15.4 lacks the native support in the important ecosystem of mobile devices.
- The ecosystem with phones, tablets, laptops and phone accessories is driving down the cost of Bluetooth low energy.
- The IEEE 802.15.4 has a data rate advantage over the IEEE 802.11ah. As of coverage, similar to the IEEE 802.11ah, many IEEE 802.15.4 based technologies (e.g. ZigBee) support mesh whereby repeaters can be used to extend the coverage.

- The IEEE 802.11ah can be used in a variety of existing devices which will significantly improve the low-power consumption for these devices.
- 6LoWPAN implementation allows a device to communicate with another device over the Internet without having to go through, for example, a ZigBee-to-IP translation layer/device. At the time of writing, it is not clear as yet if the IEEE 802.11ah is backward compatible with existing IEEE 802.11n/ac infrastructure and if any sort of infrastructure update or upgrade is needed. However, the fact that IEEE 802.11 is widely accepted as the dominant indoor wireless technology including IEEE 802.11 based indoor access points (APs) and stations (Aust, Prasad, & Niemegeers, 2012), makes Wi-Fi's infrastructure compatibility with IEEE 802.11ah is a core aspect for its adoption.
- 6LoWPAN offers interoperability with other wireless IEEE 802.15.4 devices as well as with devices on any other IP network with the use of a simple bridging device. However, bridging between ZigBee and non-ZigBee networks requires a more complex application layer gateway.
- For the IoT scenario that requires the use of thousands of devices, ZigBee has a networking size of 65,000 devices. Similarly, the IEEE 802.11ah can also cater for approximately 8 thousand devices as well. Data rate and the required coverage area play their roles in marking the differences between these two technologies as well.
- The IEEE 802.11ah benefits from the optimal propagation characteristic of sub-1GHz license-exempt frequency bands compared to 2.4 and 5 GHz bands. However, as mentioned before, the IEEE 802.11ah frequency band fragmentation across different countries might be an issue in some IoT applications.

Security

As discussed in the Introduction, the evolution of wireless technologies specifically low-power wireless technologies is driving the growth of the IoT. New devices are increasingly getting connected to the Internet, from connected vehicles to connected homes and cities. This growth in connected devices to the communication networks translates into increased security risks and poses new challenges to security. A device which connects to the Internet, whether it is a constraint or smart device, inherits the security risks of today's computer devices. Almost all security challenges are inherent to the IoT. Hence, some fundamental security requirements in the IoT, such as authorization, authentication, confidentiality, trust, and access control need to be considered. Things should be securely connected to their designated network(s), securely controlled and accessed by authorized entities. Data generated by things need to be collected, analyzed, stored, dispatched and always presented in a secure manner. Notwithstanding, there are security risks associated with things to things communications as well. The heterogeneity of devices and communications in the IoT pose many new security challenges. For instance, the integration of WSNs into the Internet, as part of the IoT, creates new security problems. These security problems are derived from the process of connecting a sensor node with an Internet device. For instance, low-cost and constrained devices that use low-power communication technologies, such as ZigBee or IEEE 802.11ah, need to establish a secure communication channel with more capable devices such as a smartphone. Thus, securing this communication channel requires the use of adequate cryptographic and key management solutions without consuming a lot of bandwidth and energy. This is in addition to the need to employ security protocols which securely connect these devices to the Internet. Add another essential security requirement, such as the need to authorize the devices involved in the communications, and the degree of achieving security for this simple communication scenario increases in complexity.

Table 7. Security features of ZigBee, BLE and Wi-Fi

ZigBee	Bluetooth Low Energy	Wi-Fi
• **Confidentiality:** AES-CTR • **Authentication:** AES-CBC-MAC with 32-, 64-, or 128-bit MAC • **Confidentiality and Authentication:** AES-CCM with 32-, 64-, or 128-bit MAC	• **Security Mode 1:** Is non-secure, with authentication and encryption turned off • **Security Mode 2:** The security manager can implement different security policies and trust levels for different applications. • **Security Mode 3 and 4:** Uses Elliptic Curve Diffie-Hellman (ECDH) public key cryptography for key exchange and link key generation	WPA2: • **Encryption:** Counter Mode with Cipher Block Chaining Message Authentication Code Protocol (CCMP) with 128-bit AES block cipher. • **Data Integrity:** Cryptographic hash function • Support Key Management and reply detection

Significantly, the IoT is vulnerable to the Denial of Service (DoS) attack. Typically, a DoS attack floods a given server with false requests for services. Thus, it prevents legitimate requesters from accessing the server's services (Mirkovic & Reiher, 2004). It attempts to exhaust the computational resources of the server. The IoT vulnerability to the DoS attack is not only limited to things which connect to the Internet directly, but also extended to WSNs. Additionally, the heterogeneous nature and complexity of communications envisioned in the IoT, makes the IoT vulnerable to the distributed denial of service (DDoS) attack. A DDoS attack is a DoS attack made by multiple agents in the network and from various locations (Misra, Krishna, Agarwal, Saxena, & Obaidat, 2011). Therefore, disruptive attacks such as the DoS and DDoS attacks are a serious potential risk to the IoT. Many IoT devices have limited processing capabilities and memory constraints. Therefore, DDoS attacks can easily exhaust their resources. Also, in things- to-things communications, DoS attacks can prove to be difficult to notice before the disruption of the service which could generally be attributed to battery exhaustion (Heer et al., 2011).

In terms of the security features of BLE, ZigBee, 6LowPAN and Wi-Fi, Tables 7 and 8 show the security features supported by these technologies. They show that all the aforementioned technologies support some sort of security. For instance, BLE supports 128-bit AES and ZigBee uses 128-bit keys to implement its security mechanisms. Similarly, 6LowPAN which is based on the IEEE 802.15.4 standard can operate in either secure mode or non-secure mode. The 6lowpan security analysis draft defines two security modes for 6LowPAN: the secure mode and Access Control List. 6LowPAN uses IP at the higher layers. Thus, traditional security protocols which normally are used with Wi-Fi (802.11a/ac) can be used with 6LowPAN. The difference however between Wi-Fi and 6LowPAN is that the later uses a bridge between the end point devices and the router/bridge. This creates a weak intrusion point. For other protocols, depending on the topology of the network, there could be two intrusion points. One at the router or bridge end and one at the gateway end where Internet connectivity is established. The IEEE 802.11ah supports security at the application level. Wi-Fi, in general (IEEE 802.11a/ac), enables unified policy management as the traffic generated from an IoT device can be scanned and secured at the network entry point.

Importantly, 6LowPAN, ZigBee and the rest of low-power wireless protocols have small bandwidth. Thus, adding a security protocol adds to the overhead and reduces the already limited bandwidth available for the communications. For these reasons, the security protocols used by the IEEE 802.15.4 link layer cannot be considered very strong. Thus, technologies based on IEEE 802.15.4 are more vulnerable to intrusions when compared with IEEE 802.11a/ac. Table 8 shows the security suites supported by IEEE 802.15.4. On the other hand, it will be interesting to watch the security mechanism the IEEE 802.11ah is going to adopt once it is finalized.

Table 8. Security suites supported by 802.15.4

Name	Description
AES-CTR	Encryption only, CTR Mode
AES-CBC-MAC-128 AES-CBC-MAC-64 AES-CBC-MAC-32	128 bit MAC 64 bit MAC 32 bit MAC
AES-CCM-128 AES-CCM-64 AES-CCM-32	Encryption with 128 bit MAC Encryption with 64 bit MAC Encryption with 32 bit MAC

Table 9 summarizes the implications to security posed by the use of low-power wireless technologies in the IoT including IEEE 802.11ah, and IEEE 802.15.4 based technologies. It shows that lightweight cryptographic security solutions are needed for the IoT.

Henceforth, devices in the IoT are increasingly becoming wireless, often adopting different wireless technologies and RF interfaces. This diversity of devices and technologies create several security threats. Therefore, it is important to understand the capabilities and security vulnerability of low-power wireless technologies. To overcome these vulnerabilities, existing lightweight security solutions need to be further explored and exploited to determine their applicability in the IoT. On the other hand, IoT applications need to account for security right from their design stage.

To conclude, the choice between Wi-Fi, including IEEE 802.11ah, Bluetooth, and ZigBee comes back to the IoT application requirements. The cost, data rate, range, network size, ecosystem and importantly the level of security required are the requirements that can be used to select a suitable wireless technology in a given IoT application. Additionally, there are other criteria which have not been fully discussed in this Chapter which might impact on the choice of technologies as well. Examples are the QoS and privacy requirements.

Observations

Table 10 provides a summary of some relevant studies from the literature. These studies compared and evaluated some technologies which fall under the low-power wireless technology umbrella.

Table 9. Security requirements and implication in the IoT

Requirements	Security Implications
Low-Power Consumption Low Bandwidth	• Security traffic should be minimal. • Security establishment should continue during the device sleep time. • Security establishment should not exhaust the device battery. Thus, the computational security establishment's cost should be efficient in term of energy consumption.
Several devices might be connected to a single Access Point (AP)	• APs are vulnerable to single point of failure attack. • APs such as an 802.11ah's AP needs to buffer data for sleeping devices. Thus, Security needs to be maintained at all time.
Devices may be mobile	Initial security establishment needs to be maintained during mobility.

Table 10. Case studies

Name of the Study	Findings
Performance Evaluation of IEEE 802.15.4 for Low-Rate Wireless Personal Area Networks. (Lee, 2006)	• IEEE 802.15.4 has better performance in non-beacon mode • The highest raw data rate achieved is 156 kbps
Performance Evaluation of IEEE 802.15.4 Physical Layer Using MatLab/Simulink. (Alnuaimi, Shuaib, & Jawhar, 2006)	Signal Bit Error Rate (BER) and Signal to Noise Ratio (SNR) values are affected by the data rate and number of bits per symbol.
Comparative assessments of IEEE 802.15.4/ZigBee and 6LoWPAN for low-power industrial WSNs in realistic scenarios. (Toscano & Bello, 2012)	• ZigBee network is greatly influenced by the beacon interval • under low workload, the 6LoWPAN performance is more affected by the duty cycle than by the actual workload • On average, 6LoWPAN protocol provided smaller end-to-end delay when compared with ZigBee • A low-power WSN characterized by low workload should keep the beacon intervals as small as possible • ZigBee network can support smaller duty cycles and provide smaller maximum end -to-end delays and update times slightly closer to the theoretical value than 6LowPAN • 6LoWPAN network shows smaller mean end-to-end delays and higher reliability when compared with ZigBee
A Comparative Study of Wireless Protocols: Bluetooth, UWB, ZigBee, and Wi-Fi. (Pothuganti & Chitneni, 2014)	• The required transmission time is proportional to the data payload size and disproportional to the maximum data rate. • The transmission time ZigBee is longer than BLE and Wi-Fi • In terms of data coding efficiency: for large data sizes, Bluetooth, and Wi-Fi have much better efficiency of over 94%, as compared to 76.52% of ZigBee. • In terms of Power consumption, ZigBee consumed slightly less energy when compared with Bluetooth
Performance comparison between Slotted IEEE 802.15.4 and IEEE 802.11ah in IoT based applications. (Olyaei et al., 2013)	• In congested networks: IEEE 802.11ah outperformed 802.15.4 in terms of throughput. • In some scenarios, the IEEE 802.15.4 slightly outperformed the IEEE 802.11ah in terms of energy consumption.

CONCLUSION

In the early days of the Internet which was basically centered on computers, a network of networks was the term used to define the Internet. In the IoT, it seems everything is going to be connected, pants, shoes, shirts, fridges, glasses, washing machines, gardens, dogs, cars, airplanes, cities, you name it. Yet, the term network of networks can still be used to define the IoT. What's new is that connected networks are no longer limited to IP-connected devices/networks in the fashion that we know today. Instead, there are islands of networks using various network technologies. A proliferation of technology protocols has rapidly emerged, with each standard hoping to fill a void or improve on another. This Chapter reviewed and compared some of these enabling technologies particularly, ZigBee, 6lowpan, BLE, and Wi-Fi including the low-power IEEE 802.11ah protocol. It provided comparative studies of these technologies by evaluating their capabilities and behaviours in terms of various metrics including the data range and rate, network size, RF Channels and Bandwidth, antenna design considerations, power consumption, security, and the ecosystem. It is concluded that the choice of a network protocol is greatly influenced by the requirements of the IoT application in hand. Therefore, a technology that might seem right for a particular IoT application might not necessarily be suited for adoption in many others. Ultimately, the challenge remains on how to allow interoperability between these various technologies creating an ecosystem of coexisted devices connecting to the Internet using various wireless protocols, enabling the true IoT vision of extending communications to anything, and anywhere.

REFERENCES

Adame, T., Bel, A., Bellalta, B., Barcelo, J., Gonzalez, J., & Oliver, M. (2013). *Capacity analysis of IEEE 802.11 ah WLANs for M2M communications*. Springer.

Adame, T., Bel, A., Bellalta, B., Barcelo, J., & Oliver, M. (2014). IEEE 802.11 AH: The WiFi approach for M2M communications. *IEEE Wireless Communications*, *21*(6), 144–152. doi:10.1109/MWC.2014.7000982

Ahmed, H. (2013). *Study on the trade off between throughput and power consumption in the design of Bluetooth Low Energy applications*. The University of Tennessee At Chattanooga.

Akyildiz, I. F., Su, W., Sankarasubramaniam, Y., & Cayirci, E. (2002). Wireless sensor networks: A survey. *Computer Networks*, *38*(4), 393–422. doi:10.1016/S1389-1286(01)00302-4

Alnuaimi, M., Shuaib, K., & Jawhar, I. (2006). Performance evaluation of IEEE 802.15. 4 physical layer using MatLab/simulink. *Paper presented at the Innovations in Information Technology*, Dubai, UAE.

Anitha, P., & Chandrasekar, C. (2011). Energy Aware Routing Protocol For Zigbee Networks. *Journal of Computer Applications*, *4*(3), 92–94.

Araiza Leon, J. C. (2015). *Evaluation of IEEE 802.11 ah Technology for Wireless Sensor Network Applications* [Master's thesis]. Tampere University of Technology.

Asha, M. M. (2012). Analysis of PS Protocols Using Markov and Cluster Modelin 802.11 WLANS. *Analysis*, *2*(2), 298–305.

Aust, S., Prasad, R. V., & Niemegeers, I. G. (2012). IEEE 802.11 ah: Advantages in standards and further challenges for sub 1 GHz Wi-Fi. *Paper presented at theIEEE International Conference on Communications (ICC)*, Ottawa, Canada.

Baker, N. (2005). ZigBee and Bluetooth: Strengths and weaknesses for industrial applications. *Computing & Control Engineering Journal*, *16*(2), 20–25. doi:10.1049/cce:20050204

Bejarano, O., Knightly, E. W., & Park, M. (2013). IEEE 802.11 ac: From channelization to multi-user MIMO. *IEEE Communications Magazine*, *51*(10), 84–90. doi:10.1109/MCOM.2013.6619570

Bluetooth SIG. (2001). Bluetooth specification version 1.1. Retrieved from http://www.bluetooth.com

Bluetooth, S. I. G. (2012). Bluetooth Core Version 4.0. Retrieved from https://www.bluetooth.org/Technical/Specifications/adopted.htm

Bluetooth Smart Technology. (2015). Powering the Internet of Things. Retrieved from http://www.bluetooth.com/Pages/Bluetooth-Smart.aspx

Caputo, D., Mainetti, L., Patrono, L., & Vilei, A. (2012). Implementation of the EXI schema on wireless sensor nodes using Contiki. *Paper presented at the2012 Sixth International Conference on Innovative Mobile and Internet Services in Ubiquitous Computing (IMIS)*, Palermo, Italy.

Chen, D., Nixon, M., & Mok, A. (2010). *WirelessHART*. Springer. doi:10.1007/978-1-4419-6047-4

De Vegt, R. (2008). 802.11 ac Usage Models Document. *IEEE 802.11-09/0161r2*.

Dementyev, A., Hodges, S., Taylor, S., & Smith, J. (2013). Power Consumption Analysis of Bluetooth Low Energy, ZigBee and ANT Sensor Nodes in a Cyclic Sleep Scenario. *Microsoft Research*.

Elahi, A., & Gschwender, A. (2009). *ZigBee wireless sensor and control network*. Pearson Education.

Elkhodr, M., Shahrestani, S., & Cheung, H. (2013). The Internet of Things: Vision & Challenges. *Paper presented at the IEEE Tencon*, Sydney, Australia. doi:doi:10.1109/TENCONSpring.2013.6584443 doi:10.1109/TENCONSpring.2013.6584443

Farahani, S. (2011). *ZigBee wireless networks and transceivers*. Newnes.

Geier, E. (2014). What's next for Wi-Fi? A second wave of 802.11ac devices, and then: 802.11ax. *PC World*. Retrieved from http://www.pcworld.com/article/2366929/what-s-next-for-wi-fi-a-second-wave-of-802-11ac-devices-and-then-802-11ax.html

Gomez, C., Oller, J., & Paradells, J. (2012). Overview and evaluation of bluetooth low energy: An emerging low-power wireless technology. *Sensors (Basel, Switzerland)*, *12*(9), 11734–11753.

Hackmann, G. (2006). *802.15 Personal Area Networks*. Department of Computer Science and Engineering, Washington University.

He, Y., Yuan, R., Ma, X., & Li, J. (2008). The IEEE 802.11 power saving mechanism: An experimental study. *Paper presented at theIEEE Wireless Communications and Networking Conference*, Las Vegas, USA. doi:doi:10.1109/WCNC.2008.245 doi:10.1109/WCNC.2008.245

Heer, T., Garcia-Morchon, O., Hummen, R., Keoh, S. L., Kumar, S. S., & Wehrle, K. (2011). Security Challenges in the IP-based Internet of Things. *Wireless Personal Communications*, *61*(3), 527–542. doi:10.1007/s11277-011-0385-5

IEEE 802.11 Working Group. (2010). IEEE Standard for Information Technology–Telecommunications and information exchange between systems–Local and metropolitan area networks–Specific requirements–Part 11: Wireless LAN Medium Access Control (MAC) and Physical Layer (PHY) specifications Amendment 6: Wireless Access in Vehicular Environments. *IEEE Std, 802*, 11.

IEEE802.org. (2015). IEEE P802.11 Sub 1GHz Study Group. Retrieved from http://www.ieee802.org/11/Reports/tgah_update.htm

Jain, R. (2014). Wireless Protocols for Internet of Things: Part II–ZigBee. Retrieved from www.cse.wustl.edu/~jain/cse574-14/j_13zgb.htm

Khorov, E., Lyakhov, A., Krotov, A., & Guschin, A. (2014). A survey on IEEE 802.11 ah: An enabling networking technology for smart cities. *Computer Communications*, *2014*, 53–69.

Lee, J. S. (2006). Performance evaluation of IEEE 802.15. 4 for low-rate wireless personal area networks. *IEEE Transactions on Consumer Electronics*, *52*(3), 742–749. doi:10.1109/TCE.2006.1706465

Lemstra, W., Hayes, V., & Groenewegen, J. (2010). *The innovation journey of Wi-Fi: The road to global success*. Cambridge University Press. doi:10.1017/CBO9780511666995

Lu, C.-W., Li, S.-C., & Wu, Q. (2011). Interconnecting ZigBee and 6LoWPAN wireless sensor networks for smart grid applications. *Paper presented at theFifth International Conference on Sensing Technology (ICST)*, Palmerston North, New Zealand.

Mackensen, E., Lai, M., & Wendt, T. M. (2012). Bluetooth low energy (ble) based wireless sensors. *Paper presented at the IEEE Sensors*, Taipei, Taiwan.

McDermott-Wells, P. (2004). What is bluetooth? *IEEE Potentials*, *23*(5), 33–35. doi:10.1109/MP.2005.1368913

Mirkovic, J., & Reiher, P. (2004). A taxonomy of DDoS attack and DDoS defense mechanisms. *Computer Communication Review*, *34*(2), 39–53. doi:10.1145/997150.997156

Misra, S., Krishna, P. V., Agarwal, H., Saxena, A., & Obaidat, M. S. (2011). A learning automata based solution for preventing distributed denial of service in Internet of things. *Paper presented at the International Conference on Internet of Things (iThings)*, Dalian, China. doi:doi:10.1109/iThings/CP-SCom.2011.84 doi:10.1109/iThings/CPSCom.2011.84

Mohapatra, S. K., Choudhury, R. R., & Das, P. (2014). The Future Directions in Evolving WI-FI: Technologies, Applications, and Services. *International Journal of Next-Generation Networks*, *6*(3), 13–22. doi:10.5121/ijngn.2014.6302

Neil, G. (2000). *When things start to think*. Holt Paperbacks.

Olyaei, B. B., Pirskanen, J., Raeesi, O., Hazmi, A., & Valkama, M. (2013). Performance comparison between slotted IEEE 802.15. 4 and IEEE 802.1 lah in IoT based applications. *Paper presented at the IEEE 9th International Conference on Wireless and Mobile Computing, Networking and Communications (WiMob)*, Lyon, France.

Pal, A., Mehta, A., Mirshekar-Syahkal, D., Deo, P., & Nakano, H. (2014). Dual-Band Low-Profile Capacitively Coupled Beam-Steerable Square-Loop Antenna. *IEEE Transactions on Antennas and Propagation*, *62*(3), 1204–1211. doi:10.1109/TAP.2013.2294866

Perahia, E., & Stacey, R. (2013). *Next Generation Wireless LANs: 802.11 n and 802.11 ac*. Cambridge university press. doi:10.1017/CBO9781139061407

Pothuganti, K., & Chitneni, A. (2014). A Comparative Study of Wireless Protocols: Bluetooth, UWB, ZigBee, and Wi-Fi. In *Advance in Electronic and Electric Engineering* (pp. 2231-1297).

Qualcomm. (2012). IEEE802.11ac: The Next Evolution of Wi-FiTM Standards. Retrieved from www.qualcomm.com/documents/qualcomm-research-ieee80211ac-next-evolution-wi-fi

Qualcomm. (2014). Improving whole home coverage and power efficiency. Retrieved from www.qualcomm.com/invention/research/projects/wi-fi-evolution/80211ah

Siddiqui, F., Zeadally, S., & Salah, K. (2015). Gigabit Wireless Networking with IEEE 802.11 ac: Technical Overview and Challenges. *Journal of Networks*, *10*(3), 164–171. doi:10.4304/jnw.10.3.164-171

Stroud, F. (2015). 802.11ac. *Webpedia*. Retrieved from http://www.webopedia.com/TERM/8/802_11ac.html

Texas Instruments. (2013). Texas Instruments CC2540/41 Bluetooth® Low Energy Software Developer's Guide v1. 4.0. *SWRU271F Version*. Retrieved from http://www.ti.com/lit/ug/swru271f/swru271f.pdf

Toscano, E., & Bello, L. L. (2012). Comparative assessments of IEEE 802.15. 4/ZigBee and 6LoWPAN for low-power industrial WSNs in realistic scenarios. *Paper presented at the9th IEEE International Workshop on Factory Communication Systems (WFCS)*, Lemgo, Germany.

Valerio, P. (2014). *Can Sub-1GHz WiFi Solve The IoT Connectivity Issues?* The New Global Enterprise.

Vecchio, M., Giaffreda, R., & Marcelloni, F. (2014). Adaptive Lossless Entropy Compressors for Tiny IoT Devices. *IEEE Transactions on Wireless Communications*, *13*(2), 1088–1100. doi:10.1109/TWC.2013.121813.130993

Vermesan, O., & Friess, P. (2013). *Internet of things: converging technologies for smart environments and integrated ecosystems*. River Publishers.

Yang, B. (2009). Study on security of wireless sensor network based on ZigBee standard. *Paper presented at theInternational Conference on Computational Intelligence and Security*, Beijing, China doi:doi:10.1109/CIS.2009.208 doi:10.1109/CIS.2009.208

Yibo, C., Hou, K.-m., Zhou, H., Shi, H.-l., Liu, X., Diao, X., . . . De Vaulx, C. (2011). 6LoWPAN stacks: a survey. *Paper presented at the7th International Conference on Wireless Communications, Networking and Mobile Computing (WiCOM)*, Wuhan, China.

ZigBee Alliance. (2006). Zigbee specification. Retrieved from http://www.zigbee.org/zigbee-for-developers/network-specifications/

ZigBee Alliance. (2014). ZigBee architecture and specifications overview. Retrieved from http://www.zigbee.org/zigbee-for-developers/network-specifications/zigbeeip/

KEY TERMS AND DEFINITIONS

6LoWPAN: 6LoWPAN is an acronym of IPv6 over Low power Wireless Personal Area Networks. 6LoWPAN is a low-power wireless mesh network where every node has its own IPv6 address.

Actuators: Actuators are devices responsible for moving or controlling a mechanism or system.

BLE: Bluetooth low energy also known as Bluetooth Smart, Bluetooth LE, Bluetooth 4.0, is a wireless personal area network technology.

IEEE 802.11ah: A wireless networking protocol that is an amendment of the IEEE 802.11-2007 wireless networking standard. It is intended to work with low-power devices.

Internet of Things: The Internet of things is a technology that connects physical objects and not only computer devices to the Internet, making it possible to access data/services remotely and to control a physical object from a remote location.

Location Privacy: The process of using a protecting technique such as location obfuscation for the purpose of protecting the location of a user.

Network Management: Network management refers to the activities and tools that pertain to the operation, administration, maintenance, and provisioning of networked systems.

ZigBee IP: ZigBee IP is a technology that enables Internet connectivity of ZigBee devices using IPv6 protocol.

Chapter 16
Internet of Things Applications:
Current and Future Development

Mahmoud Elkhodr
Western Sydney University, Australia

Seyed Shahrestani
Western Sydney University, Australia

Hon Cheung
University of Western Sydney, Australia

ABSTRACT

The Internet of Things (IoT) brings connectivity to about every objects found in the physical space. It extends connectivity not only to computer and mobile devices but also to everyday objects. From connected fridges, cars and cities, the IoT creates opportunities in numerous domains. This chapter briefly surveys some IoT applications and the impact the IoT could have on societies. It shows how the various application of the IoT enhances the overall quality of life and reduces management and costs in various sectors.

INTRODUCTION

The Internet of Things (IoT) is the future of the Internet. It provides societies, communities, governments, and individuals with the opportunity to connect and obtain services over the Internet wherever they are and whenever they want. The IoT enhances communications on the Internet among not only people, but also things. The IoT introduces a new concept of communications which extends the existent interactions between human and computer's applications to things. Things are objects of the physical world (physical things) or of the information world (virtual things). Things are capable of being identified and integrated into the communication networks. Physical things such as industrial robots, products and electrical equipment, are capable of being sensed, actuated and connected to the Internet. More specifically, a physical thing can be described as a physical object equipped with a device that provides the capability of connecting this physical object to the Internet. The International Telecommunication Union (ITU) defines a device in the IoT as a piece of equipment with the mandatory capabilities of communications,

DOI: 10.4018/978-1-5225-0287-6.ch016

and the optional advanced capabilities of sensing and actuating (ITU, 2005). On the other hand, virtual things are not necessarily physical or tangible objects. They can exist without any association with a physical thing. Examples of virtual things are multimedia contents (Francesco, Li, Raj, & Das, 2012), and web services which are capable of being stored, processed, shared and accessed over the Internet. Notwithstanding this, a virtual thing may be used as a representation of a physical thing as well. For instance, most of today's computer databases and applications use some sort of virtual representation of physical entities i.e. the use of objects or classes in object oriented programing approaches (Rumbaugh, Blaha, Premerlani, Eddy, & Lorensen, 1991). Therefore, communications in the IoT can occur between not only the users and things, but also exclusively between things. This includes "physical things" to "physical things" communications, "virtual things" to "virtual things" communications, and "physical things" to "virtual things" communications. This heterogeneity of communications extends computation and connectivity on the Internet to anything, anyplace and anytime. As a result, the IoT is expected to be seen everywhere and in numerous application domains, such as manufacturing, smart cities, agriculture and breeding, environmental management, smart homes, and in a variety of service sectors among many others.

From a networking perspective, the IoT can be described as a heterogeneous network that combines together several wired and wireless networks, including low-power wireless networks and personal area networks, with an increasingly complex structure (Elkhodr, Shahrestani, & Cheung, 2014). This heterogeneous network connects a mixture of devices together. It encompasses devices which connect to the Internet using various types of wireless and LAN technologies such as Wi-Fi, RFID, ZigBee, Bluetooth, and 3G or 4G technologies among other evolving communication technologies.

The term IoT, while it may sound odd, was first coined in 1999 by the founders of the original MIT Auto-ID Center Kevin Ashton (Ashton, 22 July 2009). Auto-ID refers to any broad class of identification technologies used in the industry to automate, reduce errors, and increase efficiency. These technologies include barcodes, smart cards, sensors, voice recognition, and biometrics. Therefore, the initial vision of the IoT was to tag physical objects, using RFID tags, and to uniquely identify these objects using RFID transponders or readers. RFID technology has enabled users to identify and track objects within a relatively small networked environment e.g. within a warehouse. As Neil Gershenfeld noted as early as 2000, the cost of individual RFID tags had dropped below a one cent, making their adoption within diverse business areas not just technically possible but economically feasible as well (Neil, 2000).

Nowadays, the IoT has grown from RFID tags to a global infrastructure of connected things. The current advance in technologies has extended the vision of the IoT by encompassing other technologies such as sensor networks. The IoT has now more potential to provide an intelligent platform for the collaborations of distributed things via local-area wireless and wired networks, and/or via a wide-area of heterogeneous and interconnected networks such as the Internet. This is inspired by not only the success of RFID technology, but by the advance of wireless communication technologies and their wide range and low-power consumption capabilities.

Consequently, the availability of information coming from non-traditional computer devices in the digital world will, in great parts, lead to improving the quality of life. If the IoT spreads to all sectors of the daily life, then information technology would be taken to a whole new level. Over the next couple of years, it is predicted that the industrial value of the Internet of Things will surpass that of the Internet 30 times over, and to be a market that is worth more than $100 billion dollars (Clendenin, 2010). On the other hand, it is estimated that there will be more than 20 billion devices connected to the Internet by 2020 (Lomas, 2009). The number of connected devices rises to over 50 billion as predicted by Cisco (Evans, 2012).

The IoT will revolute many industries and elevate communications on the Internet. The opportunities offered by the IoT are endless. IoT services provide the user with numerous services and capabilities. The obvious ones are the ability to control and monitor the physical environment remotely over the communication networks. Typical examples are the ability of closing a door or receiving smoke alert notifications remotely over the Internet. However, the revolution in technology actually occurs when things and group of things are connected together. The interconnection of things allows not only things to communicate with each other, but also offers the opportunities of building intelligence and pervasiveness into the IoT. The interconnected network of things, along with backend systems involved in a number of collaboration activities with the users and other things, in tandem with cloud computing systems, Big Data, web services, and Location Based Services, will transform not only communications on the Internet but also societies (Elkhodr, Shahrestani, & Cheung, 2013). The IoT will enable the sharing of information between different domains which leads to improving the overall quality of services (Zorzi, Gluhak, Lange, & Bassi, 2010). For example, the ability of sharing health information between different healthcare professionals such as nurses, doctors, and pharmacists will enhance the quality of healthcare (Parwekar, 2011). Consequently, it is expected that the IoT will penetrate many industries. It is regarded as a new wave of technology that will not only benefit the everyday user, but also offer many organizations promising businesses opportunities.

Henceforth, this chapter surveys some of the most envisioned IoT applications and the impact the IoT could have on various aspects of life. It explores some of the major opportunities offered by the IoT. Given that the possibilities promised by the IoT are enormous and are only limited to our imaginations, the chapter mainly focuses on a few interesting IoT applications rather than attempting to survey all anticipated IoT applications. For instance, one important area in which the IoT is promising to revolute is healthcare. The aim of bringing the IoT to the health sector is to enhance healthcare and medical service delivery; hence, saving more lives. Assisted living, remote health monitoring, smart homes, smart water, automation, industrial manufacturing, and transportation, are some of the other sectors that will be enhanced through the application of the IoT (Atzori, Iera, & Morabito, 2010). Nonetheless, the IoT will be used in many areas for the purpose of enhancing the quality of services, efficiencies and safety. For instance, vehicle-to-vehicle communications and smart roads (Foschini, Taleb, Corradi, & Bottazzi, 2011), that sense and control traffic flow are examples of these applications which contribute towards improving the safety on roads and efficiency of the transport system, specifically in congested cities.

In the rest of this chapter, the Section "IoT in Healthcare" describes the many areas of healthcare that benefit from the adoption of the IoT technologies. The section "Smart Home" transitions the reader from the typical smart home scenario to a new vision of IoT smart home systems. Other interesting IoT applications such as smart water, smart cars, smart lighting and structural health monitoring systems are discussed under the Section "Smart Cities: A holistic Vision". The chapter then concludes by highlighting some of the main challenges facing the realization of the IoT.

IoT DEVELOPMENT IN HEALTHCARE

Healthcare is an important aspect of the society. The healthcare services and communication technology industry have the potential for growth in specialized e-health services such as electronic health (e-health), remote monitoring systems, home and community care among many others. The IoT offers numerous opportunities which improve the healthcare services and operations. The IoT promotes a wider approach to healthcare by addressing the health needs of a population as a whole instead of individuals, and by stimulating practices that reduce the effects of diseases, disability and accidental injuries. Additionally, combining healthcare applications with other areas of the IoT stimulates sustainability in healthcare (Boulos & Al-Shorbaji, 2014). It is established in the healthcare community that prevention of diseases is as equally important as providing medical treatments (Fries, Koop, Sokolov, Beadle, & Wright, 1998). Consequently, the IoT creates the opportunity of maintaining sustainable environments for a healthier lifestyle. Other contribution the IoT provides is in reducing the implications of climate change on the health and well-being of the population (Vermesan et al., 2011). It is essential for the future sustainability of healthcare to enable healthcare providers and services to integrate sustainability principles within their organizations such as, energy and water efficiency, and environmental compliances among many others. Also, it is critical to foster environments that protect and promote the health of communities. Hence, the IoT plays a significant role towards the realization of a sustainable environment, which in turn contributes to a better approach to healthcare.

In terms of IoT applications in healthcare, monitoring of medications and the delivery of drugs are amongst the various envisioned application in this domain (Laranjo, Macedo, & Santos, 2012). The use of IoT aims at making the field of medicine more efficient than it has been in the past. People are able to receive and share information about illnesses and treatments more efficiently. The IoT allows individuals to acquire medical or treatment information in real-time and help in the early detection and prevention of diseases (Zhao, Wang, & Nakahira, 2011). Thus, it helps individuals to escape contacting a given disease, or to treat diseases as early as possible. The backend system responsible for operating the IoT health application(s) will be able to maintain important health records of patients. In e-health, this information is termed as Electronic Health Records (EHR) (Kalra & Ingram, 2006). Therefore, combining the IoT with EHRs systems will improve access and retrieval of healthcare related information, the availability and sharing of EHRs between different healthcare organizations.

The IoT in healthcare is expected to improve remote health monitoring systems as well. Remote health monitoring technology provides solutions for monitoring patients at home. These systems aim to deliver higher quality of care and reduce the cost on patients and governments without affecting the quality of the healthcare services provided (Elkhodr, Shahrestani, & Cheung, 2011b). The use of a remote monitoring system allows biomedical signals of a patient to be measured ubiquitously during his or her daily activities. Such a system allows the collection of medical data and signals related to patients' bodies, such as their heart rates, remotely via the Internet. There are also benefits associated with improving the quality of care and services, such as reliability, accessibility, frequency, accuracy and availability (Elkhodr, Shahrestani, & Cheung, 2011a).

An IoT based remote monitoring system is capable of detecting any changes in the person's body conditions, and monitoring their vital medical signs. The availability of the collected data by this system on the Internet, and the ability to access this data in real-time by various other systems and entities such as healthcare providers and medical centers, open the door to numerous opportunities. For instance, an alert system can be designed based on analyzing the EHRs received by the remote monitoring systems (Baig & Gholamhosseini, 2013). In the case of a medical emergency, the system can be configured to alert the healthcare professionals, emergency services, relatives and others concerned parties. Also, the system can provide insight into the health condition of a monitored person so the necessary help can be provided as early as possible, and thus, saving patients' lives.

Additionally, the IoT services can help in the monitoring, early detection, prevention and treatment of several illnesses (Pang et al., 2015). This includes diabetes, heart disease, cancer, seizures, and pulmonary diseases, among others. Such diseases usually require constant monitoring of body actions, so the person needs to be under a constant watch. Traditionally, the medical practitioners and healthcare professionals are responsible for the constant monitoring of patients. However, patients' monitoring is costly and not as effective as it ought to be (Lara et al., 2012). For instance, the doctor is not capable of constantly watching over one patient with an undivided attention.

An example of how the IoT can improve patients' monitoring is the integration of Body Sensor Networks (BSN) with others IoT health systems (Savola, Abie, & Sihvonen, 2012). As an example, a BSN system can monitor the patient's body functions using a biodegradable chip or by using some wearables wireless Biosensor devices (Ozkul & Sevin, 2014). This chip or Biosensor device will be capable of monitoring the vital signs of the patient. They detect any anomaly in the bodily functions of the patient and report such problems to the IoT system. The IoT system can then makes the necessary action such as alerting a healthcare professional. Also, it allows healthcare professionals to make better diagnosis of diseases and communicate effectively with patients. In case of emergencies, the healthcare professional, or depending on how the system is designed, can alert an ambulance team for assistance.

Therefore, IoT health monitoring systems can be seen as an environment of surrounding intelligence which aims to provide a platform for remote monitoring and assistance to patients or the elderly in their homes or on the move (Elkhodr et al., 2011a). Monitoring patients in the early stages of their diseases can increase their chances of survival. It will also help healthcare providers to react before a serious medical condition such as, a heart attack or diabetic emergency occurs. The use of remote monitoring systems could also help reducing medical errors since electronic health records (EHRs) are digitally available via the IoT (Scurlock & D'Ambrosio, 2015). The digital availability of EHRs makes its retrieval and access more accurate and organized. This will not only help in reducing medical errors, but also provide speedy access to data, while maintaining access control privileges as well.

IoT applications in healthcare also extend to personal area networks (PANs) (Neuhaeuser & D'Angelo, 2013). In a PAN, individuals are capable of tracking their bodily functions using various wearable technologies such as a wearable smart sensor, a smart wrist device or a smart watch. As the technology and IoT evolve, wearable technologies in healthcare are evolving as well. Therefore, this evolvement of technologies will result in providing the capabilities which allow individuals to monitor various aspects of their health. Examples of these health aspects are the monitoring of blood pressure, sugar and insulin levels, medicine intakes, heart beats, sleeping patterns, calories intake, exercises levels and others. The capabilities offered by the IoT in this regards are vast. Healthcare professional will be able to access remotely these information and provide treatment if necessary. This enhances the sharing of information and self-administration of health problems in addition to the early detection of diseases.

Consequently, IoT healthcare applications encompass various sensors and monitoring devices. These devices are generally synchronized and interconnected with one another for the purpose of enhancing information sharing (Vermesan & Friess, 2013). Figure 1 is an example of an IoT based healthcare system which provides an array of healthcare services. It shows that an IoT system can be designed to combine together the followings healthcare subsystems:

- **The Healthcare Personal Area Network Application:** This application involves the use of personal devices in closed or local area setups. Examples are wearable technologies that can be used for the self-monitoring and administrating of a person's health.

Figure 1. An example of an IoT based healthcare system

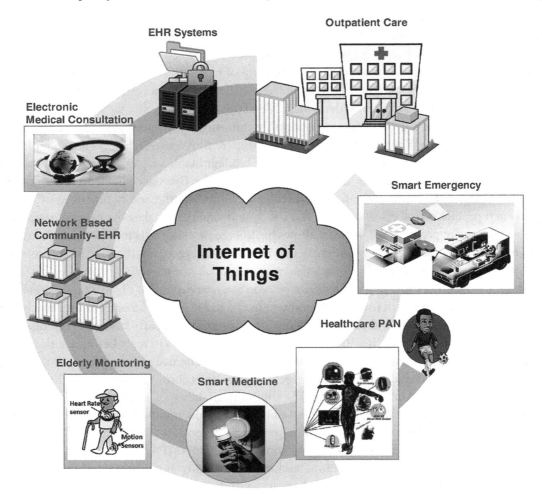

- **Elderly Monitoring:** This application relies on a set of sensor devices which monitor the health condition of an elderly. The system can be used to collect information relating to the physical activities such as dietary and sleep patterns of the elderly as well. Importantly, the system allows healthcare professionals and care takers to monitor the health condition of elderlies in real-time. It implements alert and notification strategies in the case of emergencies such as automatically calling an ambulance when needed.
- **Smart Medicine:** This application involves the administration of medications. It ensures that patients are taking the right medicine, with the correct dose on time as specified by their healthcare professionals. The system can also alert a doctor in case a patient does not take his or her medication as prescribed.
- **Community Based EHR:** This includes outpatient care and electronic medical consultation subsystems that involve the digitation of health care operations. These subsystems collectively enhance eHealth services by reducing medical errors, saving cost and increasing efficiencies.

- **Smart Emergency:** The smart emergency application is centered on collaborations and sharing of information between the various healthcare subsystems. It is an important component in each of the healthcare subsystems described above. Obviously this is due to fact that emergency services, such as calling an ambulance, are required in medical emergencies. However, the smart emergency application operations are not only limited to providing the service of automatically calling an ambulance. They involve other advanced services such as communicating the status of the patient automatically back to the hospital during transport including the required treatment. This process improves emergency services in hospitals as well. It helps with the better allocations and distribution of patients in hospitals in a given geographical area. Thus, ensuring that there is a space to accommodate the transported patient. Moreover, they help in the optimization of the medical resources and services such as X-ray services and CAT scans.

Therefore, the ability of accessing health information instantly and remotely via the Internet enables healthcare professionals to access a new category of information which was unknown to them before. An example of this information includes the factors which might affect the patient's health, such as any daily routine activities. Gaining insight into the life of a patient helps in providing a better treatment approach. Generally, traditional remote monitoring applications lack the interoperation that the IoT can provide. Ambient Assisted Living (AAL) will be possible with the introduction of an IoT based system that works effectively with other IoT devices such as sensors and actuators. For instance, people will know how many times they have taken their medications, and when they need to take them next (Vermesan & Friess, 2013). Patients will be able to obtain pharmaceutical information regarding the type of medicine required instantly and in real-time. This includes information about the right dosage, allergy advice, side effects among others.

Pharmaceuticals

The pharmaceutical industry is directly associated with the healthcare industry. It is concerned with the manufacturing, distribution, storage, and administration of medications prescribed to patients. There are various ways through which the IoT will be of use to the pharmaceutical industry. For instance, the use of sensors or RFID technology on medications during supply and consumption enhances the proper use and safe intake of these drugs. The IoT helps in ensuring that medications are transported and stored in the right conditions (Melo et al., 2011). Also, the IoT improves the administration of medicines.

Accordingly, an IoT health application, through the use of sensors and other forms of devices, ensures that drugs are stored in an ideal environment in terms of temperature, sunlight exposure, among other important environmental factors (Atzori et al., 2010). Furthermore, the use of sensors and RFID technology helps in the identification of counterfeit drugs (Taylor, 2014). RFID technology in that sense can be used to monitor a certain medication right from manufacturing till consumptions as well.

Child Monitoring

Child monitoring is another area of healthcare which the IoT promises to enhance. An IoT based monitoring application, through the use of sensors and other IoT devices, is capable of monitoring the health and conditions of an infant or a child (Hoy, 2015). Therefore, parents or guardians will be able to find out whether their kid is sleeping, breathing well, seated or lying down properly, and whether it is mobile or not (Rost & Balakrishnan, 2006). The IoT technology will provide the capabilities of remotely monitoring the status and health conditions of a child outside their homes as well such as at a childcare center. This technology allows the design of a notification system which extends to parents, guardians, care takers, teachers, childcare workers, healthcare professionals, emergency services and many others. This enhances the current child monitoring systems in use which are, in most cases, limited to providing an alert when a baby makes a noise or cries. Henceforth, the enhancements introduced by the IoT promise to revolute child monitoring in the healthcare industry. The real-time availability of data that can be collected from a child contributes towards the design and development of other innovative IoT health solutions. For example, by using an IoT based child remote monitoring system, the capabilities of monitoring a child's social activities and group interactions go beyond monitoring his or her physical health (Kinnunen et al., 2016). It extends to monitoring the child mental health as well (Sula et al., 2013). The IoT will now offer insights into kids' activities such as the way they interact with their friends, families, teachers and strangers. The advantages of gaining insights into the social and general activities of a child are numerous. They help in the fight against bullying and identifying psychological problems, among other behavioral issues at a very early stage. Additionally, the results obtained from analyzing the collected data can be used to identify malnutrition among kids and, thus, the design and administration of healthier diets. Child abuse, domestic violence and alcohol related problems are among other social issues in which the IoT helps in the early detection and prevention (Pereira & Santos, 2015).

IoT Health Application Requirements

Table 1 is an effort to summarize the general requirements for IoT healthcare systems. It categorizes the requirements based on three application categories: Healthcare providers (e.g. a hospital), Remote monitoring systems, and health Personal Area Networks (e.g. personal fitness). Access point (AP) mobility, traffic type, location, and security are among the requirements defined for each of the aforementioned applications. However, it is noted that these requirements vary depending on the application's design and its requirements. Within the IoT space, several heterogeneous sets of devices may use various communication strategies amongst them to provide services. Thus, the requirements change from a network topology to another and from an application design to another even within the same application domain (e.g. different applications designed for remote monitoring systems). Consequently, Table 1 should be regarded as an attempt to define the requirements of IoT healthcare applications in specific cases rather than standardizing these requirements. The work in (Elkhodr, Shahrestani, & Cheung, 2016) reviews a variety of wireless technologies. These technologies are strong candidates for supporting communications in the IoT. It highlights an assortment of communication technologies such as ZigBee, IEEE 802.11ah and Bluetooth Low Energy. Each of these technologies caters for specific application requirements in the IoT.

SMART HOME

The smart home is another area in which the IoT promises to grow. The IoT enables everyday household objects, electronics and appliances to communicate with one another either locally or via the Internet. Thus, it allows the user to control these household items in various ways (Vermesan & Friess, 2013). The smart home system will be capable of connecting different types of objects in the house, and thus providing the user with the capabilities of not only monitoring but also controlling these objects. This

Table 1. General IoT healthcare systems requirements

	Healthcare Providers	**Remote Monitoring Systems**	**Health PAN**
Environment type	Commercial building e.g. hospital, clinic	Home, Nursing home, Community care	Home, Gym, Casual run
Location	Indoor	Indoor (high), Outdoor (low)	Indoor, Outdoor
Mobility requirement	Very Low (e.g. walking to the toilet, X-ray room)	Low (e.g. casual walk)	Low-medium (e.g. running)
Actors	Examples are: Electrocardiogram, heartrate monitor, blood pressure monitor	Examples are: heartrate monitor, blood pressure monitor, fall detection sensors	Examples are: wearable devices, heartrate monitor, pace detector
Devices Mobility requirement	Fixed (High), Mobile (Low)	Fixed (High), Mobile (Low)	Fixed (High), Mobile (High)
Device to AP Communication	Mainly Unidirectional (e.g. monitoring)	Bidirectional (Send and receive)	Unidirectional, (send)
Traffic type	Real-time and Event-based (emergency)	Real-time or Periodic, event-based	Event-based or Periodic
Coverage needed	Depends on the design: multi-story medical center requires higher density and extended coverage area	Independent home living model can have low coverage (e.g. around the house); Community care center might require extended coverage	Depends on the application design and AP mobility requirements
Reliability requirement	High	High	High
Security Requirement	'Higher than Commercial-grade'	Range from 'Higher than Commercial-grade' to 'Commercial-grade'	'Commercial-grade'

includes the ability of monitoring the objects' statuses and controlling the environment e.g. checking if a light is left on or closing a door remotely etc. This can be achieved by equipping normal household objects with smart sensors and actuator devices (Mainetti, Patrono, & Vilei, 2011). The IoT also improves the security of homes. The smart home system will be able in real-time to identify residents of the house, visitors and strangers. Thus, the system enables the detection of potential security breaches or risks (Schneps-Schneppe, Namiot, Maximenko, & Malov, 2012). Other features of the smart home system are the ability to monitor changes in various areas of the house such as monitoring the water level in a swimming pool, water leakage from pipes, and electricity consumptions. Users are able to know about their energy consumption levels in real-time and are able to make necessary changes. The system can provide recommendations to users which help reducing electricity consumptions during peak hours for example (Mohsenian-Rad, Wong, Jatskevich, Schober, & Leon-Garcia, 2010).

Apart from providing information, monitoring and controlling the general appliances of the house, the IoT will bring connectivity to various unconventional objects. Thus, in addition to smart fridges, smart ovens and other smart appliances, a new category of smart products will emerge which have the capability of connecting to the Internet directly or indirectly via the smart home network. Some of these smart products have already started to emerge or are under development. The followings are examples of these smart products:

- Smart Door and Window Locks (Jaykumar & Blessy, 2014).
- Smart Garage Door Openers.

- Smart Doorbells.
- Networked Cameras and Video Storage & Viewing.
- Smart Lighting Controls (Li, Suna, & Hua, 2012).
- Smart Thermostats.
- Multi-Sensors Detection Devices.
- Smart Blinds and Drapes.
- Smart Wall Outlets, Plugs, and Power Strips.

Most of these devices operate using low-power wireless technologies and connect via the smart home local network to the Internet.

From Traditional Smart Home Systems to the IoT

Most of the existent smart home systems use devices at the lower end of the envisioned capabilities. Typically, these devices are capable of storing data, responding to user commands from smartphones, tablets and computers, and sending alerts over Bluetooth or Wi-Fi. They generally operate in a standalone manner. The IoT brings a new type of home management, integration of devices, surveillance, intelligence and more importantly connectivity to these devices. Intelligence may be contained completely within a device, combined with platform intelligence in the cloud, or reside almost completely within a platform to which the device connects to perform some functions.

Therefore, smart home devices incorporate the capabilities inherent in the IoT and provide enhanced benefits. Smart home devices can be static objects, such as smart plugs or lights that simply report their properties. They can also be sensors that measure the physical conditions of an object or its status, actuators that perform operations (opening doors, turning on or off appliances), or devices that combine both of these services. Therefore, the IoT enables users to manipulate these devices through an interface which could be in the form of a smartphone application, tablet, or computer that remotely operates the device in the home. Significantly, the IoT system will enable these devices to be queried or controlled by other platforms, controllers, or IoT applications that coordinate multiple objects without the interference of the human user. In addition, the data collected from smart home devices can be integrated with external data collected from other IoT systems, e.g. a healthcare system, which create value-added services. Therefore, the user benefits from added intelligence, modeling, and weaving of information which enable the smart home system to make better decisions on behalf of a user, or to provide personalized and optimized services (Chan, Campo, Estève, & Fourniols, 2009).

Therefore, by integrating the smart home system with the IoT, smart home devices will be capable of communicating with each other. They will also be capable of obtaining information from or controlling the physical environment based on the user's preferences. They can use information external to their specific environment to enhance the operation of that device to the user's benefits. Ultimately, homes will evolve to have their own ecosystems. However, the provision of such information will require the sharing of information among the stakeholders (Da Xu, He, & Li, 2014). This raises numerous concerns in terms of security, privacy, management and others (Wilson, Hargreaves, & Hauxwell-Baldwin, 2015). Figure 2 is an example of a smart home system. It shows that the IoT brings connectivity to a number of appliances such as TVs and fridges and to unconventional objects such as light switches, electricity sockets, and gas leak sensors among others.

Figure 2. An IoT smart home example

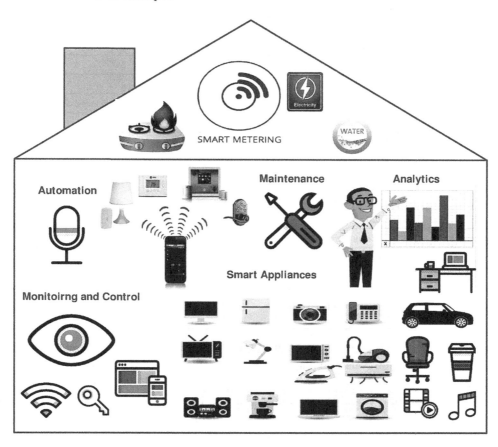

IoT Smart Home Application Requirements

Table 2 summarizes some of the IoT Smart Home Application requirements. As with the application's requirements of the IoT in healthcare discussed in the section "IoT health application requirements", the requirements of the smart home system vary according to the application design and its specific requirements as well. Initially, as shown in Table 2, the application environment of smart home applications is indoor within the home building. Devices are mostly in the form of sensors and actuators in addition to smart appliances and consumer electronics which are generally stationary. Sensors and actuators will be deployed in the home in appropriate locations. A number of these devices are likely to be powered by batteries. The typical coverage of such a network of devices is the entire home, with an estimated maximum number of no more than few hundred devices per household (Basu, Moretti, Gupta, & Marsland, 2013). The payload data being transmitted can be estimated to be very small with no stringent latency or jitter requirements (Qin, Denker, Giannelli, Bellavista, & Venkatasubramanian, 2014). Multimedia real-time devices such as an IP camera will have specific requirements to their sensing device counterparts. Many wireless technologies such as ZigBee, and Wi-Fi can be employed in such IoT space.

Table 2. IoT smart home application general requirement

Category	Comment
Environment type	Home (building)
Location	Indoor
Mobility requirement	Stationary
Actors	Multimedia devices, IP cameras, Sensors, Actuators, Smart Appliances, Smart phones.
Devices Mobility Requirement	Stationary
Device to AP Communication	Bidirectional (Send information; and receive instructions)
Traffic type	Varies from: • Multimedia Real-time traffic - few megabytes every second • Periodic- few 100 bytes every few seconds • Event-based- few 100 bytes per event
Coverage needed	Indoor
Reliability requirement	Medium
Security Requirement	Commercial-grade

SMART CITIES: A HOLISTIC VISION

Over the past few years, the definition of "Smart Cities" has evolved to mean many things to many people. Yet, one thing remains constant: part of being "smart" is utilizing information and communications technology (ICT) and the Internet to address urban challenges (Clarke, 2013). A city-wide network of sensors provides real-time valuable information on the flow of citizens, noise and other forms of environmental pollution, as well as traffic and weather conditions. This enables the local authorities to streamline city operations including better environmental management, cost reduction, and economic improvement, and social and environmental sustainability. A smart city is the result of an incremental process of connecting the various facets and applications of the IoT together. The inter-communication, collaboration and exchange of information amongst the various IoT devices and systems will ultimately lead to the realization of a true vision of a smart city. Thus, connecting e-health systems with smart homes, smart streets, smart parking, smart water, smart bridges and the rest of the various applications envisioned in the IoT, will provide the digital infrastructure necessary for building the smart cities of the future. This digital infrastructure enables people to actively contribute to, and becomes part of the drive for sustainable development, as well as to self-manage their home, environment, natural recourses, and their own health for a better life and sustainable future.

The smart city technology brings together almost all of the other applications of the IoT. These include systems which provide services such as water leakage detection, flood detection, pollution detection, traffic control, smart roads, healthcare applications, smart home, among others.

It is important to note that this technology may not be able to succeed without the implementation of proper policies regarding the disclosure and sharing of information (Vermesan & Friess, 2013). All parties involved need to be willing to share information and for that to happen, suitable management, security and privacy challenges need to be overcome. The rest of this Section discusses the major developments which may contribute to building the IoT smart city.

Smart Water

Perhaps, the IoT cannot interfere with the climate and make the sky rain; but the IoT, through various applications in smart homes and smart cities, can enhance water consumption. Thus, the IoT helps in reducing water wastage by improving the efficiency of water consumption. This is of a great importance particularly in places where drought is an issue (Sanchez et al., 2014). The envisioned developments in water IoT based infrastructure systems are numerous. An IoT based water system can be used to improve water's quality, transportation, consumption (TongKe, 2013), supply and demand, leakage, treatment, pollutions, and storage facilities such as in household tanks or on a larger scale such as in reservoirs (Wu, Chen, & Lei, 2012). For instance, an Australian company is using networked sensors connected to the Cloud to monitor water runoff at construction sites (Pearce, 2009). Libelium ("Open Aquarium - Aquaponics and Fish Tank Monitoring for Arduino," 2014) is another company which uses the IoT to improve water consumption efficiency in aquariums and gardens. It utilizes a platform consisting of wireless sensors which automates the control and maintenance tasks within an aquarium or a garden.

In an aquarium environment, Libelium's platform use sensors which monitor various aspects of water such as temperature, conductivity and pH levels ("Open Aquarium - Aquaponics and Fish Tank Monitoring for Arduino," 2014). Also, the platform utilizes a pump and actuator devices which regulate water temperature, feed the fish and administer medication. The platform simulates day and night cycles by controlling light intensity as well ("Open Aquarium - Aquaponics and Fish Tank Monitoring for Arduino," 2014). The platform sends wirelessly information collected by the sensors and actions triggered by the actuators to a web or mobile interface. This interface enables users to monitor and control their aquarium. In gardening, Libelium uses a platform which monitors plant conditions and facilitate care. On one hand, the platform utilizes a set of sensors which collect environmental and soil related information such as moisture, temperature and humidity. On the other hand, the platform controls water irrigation, lights and oxygen using actuators. These are just few examples that showcase how an IoT water system could form an important integral part of other IoT systems. The integration of water's systems in the IoT leads to improving not only the efficient consumption of water but also the overall management of gardening, crops and aquariums (Duan, 2014).

Moreover, an IoT based water system can be set to remotely determine the status and working condition of a water's device (open or closed, on or off, full or empty, etc.). A pump can be remotely turned on or off to adjust the flow of water through a water transportation system. Pumps, gates and other equipment with moving parts in the water infrastructure can be monitored for vibration and other indications of failure. If a water pump is leaking or about to fail, the user or the relevant parties will be alerted so the necessary action can be taken. Connected smart water filters can report their statuses whether they are clean and functioning properly (Robles et al., 2014). The IoT system can measure water pressure in pipes to find leaks faster in the water transportation system or the presence of certain chemicals in the water supply and maybe even organic contaminants (Muhic & Hodzic, 2014). Another focus for water savings should be landscape irrigation in parks, medians and elsewhere. This is a major use of water in cities (Mylonas & Theodoridis, 2015). Nationwide, it is estimated to be nearly one-third of all residential water use and as much as half of this water is wasted due to runoff, evaporation or wind (Farbotko, Walton, Mankad, & Gardner, 2014). In agriculture, the application of IoT water systems combines weather data with other sensory data such as moisture, heat, type of soil and the relative exposure to sunshine at a particular time of the day for a more efficient use of water (Dlodlo & Kalezhi, 2015).

Water Transportation

The IoT will also be applied in the water management sector through various ways. This will enhance water quality and distribution to various parts of the world. By sensing portable water and movement from one place to another, an IoT WSN based system will be capable of communicating with the cloud or other systems to show information on the quality and movement of waters in cities (Bohli, Skarmeta, Victoria Moreno, Garcia, & Langendorfer, 2015). The Radio Frequency Identification (RFID) application connects with various services providers in the city and various other stakeholders to give information about the reliability and quality of the water being transported within a given community. The idea behind the IoT is to interconnect the available applications with one another via local network setups or the Internet. This enhances the sharing of information which in turn improves the quality of goods and services, and thus quality of human life (Fan & Bifet, 2013). For instance, the IoT capabilities can be extended to other areas associated with the water transport industry as well (Misra, Simmhan, & Warrior, 2015). The IoT system will be capable of not only monitoring the quality of water or detecting water leakages during transport, but also that of the truck itself and the driver. The safety of the driver, including his or her behavior also enhances road safety as the system will be able to report any incidents to the relevant parties. The IoT will be capable of enhancing the performance of the water transport sector, as well as other transport sectors by promoting the sharing of information in real time (Misra et al., 2015).

Water Pollution

The IoT will be capable of detecting pollution in water reservoirs, and natural water systems such as rivers (Kar & Kar, 2015). The system uses a ranges of sensors that detect chemical leakages and analyzes the purity of water (ZHU & PAN, 2015). The sensors communicate with other IoT applications providing valuable information on water quality. For instance, the sensors will be able to detect waste from factories dumped into a river and alert the relevant authorities, and the local communities that could be affected by the presence of these chemicals or waste. The IoT water monitoring system can be used for monitoring and detecting pollution of waters as well e.g. ocean waters (Tiwari, 2011). Thus, the IoT can help maintaining the safety of the marine ecosystem. It does that by detecting and reporting the individual and industrial activities that could be harmful to the marine life (Domingo, 2012).

Water Leakages

Water is an important natural resource. Wasting water is attributed to a number of factors including water leakage either during transport, storage or consumptions (TongKe, 2013). Therefore, the IoT can help conserving this important natural resource by reducing leakages. An IoT water monitoring system utilizes smart water sensors that can detect water leakages in a tank or pipe (Lundqvist, de Fraiture, & Molden, 2008). The sensors can be used to measure the pressure levels in pipes and their variances. The system can be used to detect pipe bursting in real-time (Y. Kim, Suh, Cho, Singh, & Seo, 2015). Thus, it enhances the real time response to such leakages which in turn reduces water wastage. Nonetheless, the system could be used to prevent possible pipe bursts. It does that by monitoring water levels and pressures within water systems; which allow the early detection of faults and accelerate incidents and response management (Chowdhury, Bhuiyan, & Islam, 2013).

Flood Control

IoT devices will be capable of detecting flooding in rivers (Tai, Celesti, Fazio, Villari, & Puliafito, 2015), dams and water reservoirs by measuring the water levels and ensuring that all changes are detected when they occur (Gubbi, Buyya, Marusic, & Palaniswami, 2013). The system alerts the concerned parties regarding the changes in water levels and provides options for responding to such changes. This technology will also be important for the detection of flooding of seas by detecting changes in water levels and any abnormal activities. Floods can be disastrous and their effects are damaging to the economy, including the obvious loss of life and property. The IoT may not be promising a complete solution to flooding, but it contributes by providing a better way of controlling or responding to flooding alerts. Additionally, the IoT can be used to predict and detect the rise in water levels, and to predict tsunami such as the work proposed in (Kawamoto, Nishiyama, Yoshimura, & Yamamoto, 2014). This can be achieved by combining weather data such as rains, wind directions and other information such as water flow on ground. Communicating and combining this information in an IoT system contribute towards the design of a better and effective response system to this natural disaster. Importantly, the ability of predicting flooding in rivers or seas can help in building solutions which prevent flooding, or at least reduce their impact.

IoT Metering

IoT metering systems, including smart grid systems, are an interesting IoT area. IoT metering is concerned with the metering of water, gas, and electricity (Benzi, Anglani, Bassi, & Frosini, 2011) within a smart home environment or on a larger scale e.g. within a city. Typically, metering applications rely heavily on sensor network technologies. For example, in environmental and agricultural monitoring systems, the IoT system uses wireless sensors for the monitoring of water, gas and electricity consumptions (Erol-Kantarci & Mouftah, 2011). IoT metering is mainly concerned with metering the consumption of those resources by providing the user with important usage statistics. This provides the users with important statistical information such as the time when water is mostly consumed, the devices which are consuming electricity the most among others. Additionally, IoT metering applications can be extended to provide advanced analytics functionalities as well (W.-H. E. Liu, 2010). Thus, apart from simply logging the resource consumptions such as time, the device in use and the amount of water, gas or electricity being consumed, the IoT metering system can provide fruitful recommendations. Examples include providing recommendations on how to save energy e.g., by turning a washing machine on during off peak hours only, boiling water using an electrical kettle instead of using a gas stove etc. On a larger scale, smart grid applications are concerned with optimizing the energy sector within a city or even across a country (S. A. Kim, Shin, Choe, Seibert, & Walz, 2012). A smart grid application can combine and make use of the following systems and services:

- Renewable Energy Management, including the management of solar energy and wind farming harvesting services, which help in optimizing energy consumption.
- Reducing overall demand on the grid by shifting usage and energy consumption to off peak time.
- Systems which store energy, using batteries, generated at off-pick time.
- Systems which detect disturbance or failure in the grid: This leads to better management of supply fluctuation by isolating the area under disturbance.

Tables 3 outlines some of the general requirements for IoT metering applications. It shows that IoT metering has applications in indoor and outdoor areas with traffic ranging from continuous, burst to periodic. Metering devices are usually in the form of sensors and small control devices which are most likely stationary and require little to no mobility requirement.

Smart Cars

Industry experts estimate that every car will be connected to a communication network by 2025, and the market for connected vehicle technology will reach $54 billion by 2017 (*Connected Car Forecast: Global Connected Car Market to Grow Threefold Within Five Years*, 2014). Car technology is evolving from a car being controlled by the driver to partially automated cars, and to fully automated self-driven vehicles (Nelson, 2015). Such automated vehicles also referred to as driverless cars are capable of navigating through a city or driving upcountry without any human control. For the realization of a fully automated vehicle, such as a driverless car, truck or bus, a series of complex interactions and technology advancements are needed. Driverless vehicle technology integrates a network of connected devices in the form of sensors, motion detectors and actuators (Chong et al., 2013). It includes internal sensors that determine the vehicle's speed, direction of traffic, location, gas or petrol level, and temperature of the vehicle among other performance metrics (Braun, Neumann, Schmidt, Wichert, & Kuijper, 2014). It also includes external sensors which allow the car to communicate with its environment.

The near future will see the introduction of connected vehicles onto the roads. This will create high demand for control and interaction technology, and this is where the IoT comes in. For example, the IoT will be capable of providing information on the traffic, on what routes to follow and helping in controlling and reducing road congestions (Foschini et al., 2011). The IoT system will also control car speed depending on roads and traffic conditions. The IoT system will be capable of showing engine diagnostics, and other car features, in terms of their conditions and functionality. The fuel and lubricant levels, mechanical part statuses and conditions can be controlled and monitored by the IoT system and

Table 3. General requirements for IoT smart grid applications

Category	Comment
Environment type	Urban, sub-urban, rural, home
Location	Indoor and Outdoor
Mobility requirement	Stationary
Actors	Meter devices (electricity, gas, water), automation and control devices
Devices Mobility Requirement	Stationary
Device to AP Communication	Bidirectional (sending metered data; and control)
Traffic type	Varies from: • Continuous • Periodic • Burst
Coverage needed	Indoor (High), Outdoor (Low -depends on the app's design)
Reliability requirement	High
Security Requirement	Commercial-grade

communicated to the car's owner or the relevant party. This enhances car longevity by avoiding engine knocks and other forms of system failures (MacGillivray et al., 2014). Also, the car system will be controlled via audio-visual enhancements, including voice recognition to enhance in-car safety. The IoT can be used to prevent car thefts (J. Liu & Yang, 2011). The technology will enhance the tracking and retrieval of stolen vehicles, and will be able to communicate with all the concerned parties.

Vehicle-to-X Technology

As the IoT revolution unfolds, automotive innovation and value creation will be shifting to the boundaries with other IoT applications such as home automation, smart grids, smart cities, healthcare and retail. Vehicle-to-Infrastructure (V2I) (Chou, Li, Chien, & Lan, 2009), and Vehicle-to-Retail (V2R) (Siddiqui 2014) are projected to be the dominant segments with respectively 459 and 406 million vehicles featuring smart car IoT applications by 2030, followed by V2H (Vehicle-to-Home) and V2P (Vehicle-to-Person) with 163 and 239 million vehicles, respectively. Meanwhile, Vehicle-to-Grid (V2G) services will be offered on 50 million vehicles in 2030 (Staff, 2014).

Therefore, the IoT is promising to revolute the connected and driverless car industry. The IoT offers the capabilities of connecting cars not only to the Internet, but also to their surroundings. Therefore, an IoT smart car may interact with surrounding roads, buildings, traffic lights, pedestrians, emergency and police vehicles and personnel. Also, it interacts with other vehicles and people, in order to provide real time information for better self-car maneuvering. In addition to optimizing routes and fuel consumption, minimizing traffic congestions, the IoT in this space plays a role in reducing noise and air pollutions, and ideally improving roads safety. The IoT will find its way in accommodating services related to green energy and sustainable energy resources as well. For instance, in the case of a smart electric connected car, the IoT will be able to provide information regarding nearby electric recharging stations (Hess et al., 2012) and the rate at which the solar panel are harvesting energy (assuming solar energy plays a role in powering the electric car). The IoT can provide information regarding the number of sunny hours on a particular day, in a particular location or during a journey of travel such as in the study presented in (Nwogu, 2015).

Nevertheless, the opportunities offered by integrating the IoT with smart vehicles are endless. The IoT opens the door to various technological innovations which will transform not only the way we perceive the car industry, but also the way cars are integrated in future smart cities. For instance, Figure 3 shows how smart cars, using the IoT, can communicate with other cars, traffic lights, and pedestrians.

Smart Parking

Smart parking is one of the emerging enablers for smart cities. A smart parking system operating as part of the IoT network can be used to enhance parking efficiency such as the study presented in (Pala & Inanc, 2007). It provides information on various parking areas, security levels and available parking spaces in a given area. It works by collecting and distributing real-time information about where parking is available to smart cars which are already connected to the IoT infrastructure. The power of an IoT smart parking system lies in its ability to track the movements of vehicles and availability of parking spaces in real-time such as the system proposed in (Lu, Lin, Zhu, & Shen, 2009). Thus, the system will be able to automatically direct a driverless car to an allocated parking space. It does that using an automated allocation system which analyzes in real-time information relating to traffic conditions, availability of

Figure 3. Vehicle to X connectivity

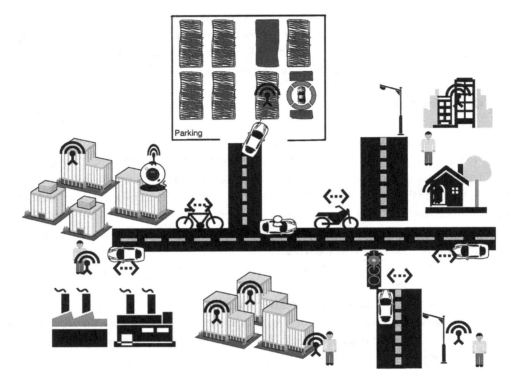

parking spaces in nearby car parks, among others. Apart from saving fuel, time and making life easier for the user, the technology helps reducing emissions and road congestions. From the government perspective, the IoT helps with law enforcement such as the enforcement of parking limits. Another application of smart parking in the IoT is linking a smart parking system with dynamic pricing platforms, where prices scale based on parking supply and demand (Polycarpou, Lambrinos, & Protopapadakis, 2013). It can also offer drivers parking options based on the price and proximity of their intended destination. Additionally, the data provided and generated from smart parking systems can be leveraged by retailers in a mall or store to predict the rush and accordingly manage workforce allocation. This will result in an improved quality of life in the city. This will also help in keeping the records on the levels of emissions in a city, making it possible for local authorities to apply pollution control measures with enough prior knowledge.

Other Smart City Applications

Smart Lighting

Smart lighting entails the provision of automated lights in public streets that change dynamically according to street activities or weather conditions (Castro, Jara, & Skarmeta, 2013). Smart lighting is also known as intelligent street lighting (Yue, Changhong, Xianghong, & Wei, 2010) and adaptive street lighting (Dramsvik, 2009). A smart lighting system controls lighting based on the weather condition, day and night cycle and movements of road users, e.g., vehicles, pedestrians, motorcyclists and cyclists.

Smart lights dim when no activity is detected, but brighten when movement is detected. This type of lighting mechanism is different from traditional, stationary illumination, or dimmable street lighting systems that dim at a pre-determined time. Smart lightings are turned on automatically by sensors that detect when lighting is required. Thus, the IoT enables street lights to communicate with one another. For example, when a passer-by is detected by a sensor, the smart lighting system communicates this information to neighboring street lights. These lights will then brighten providing people with light along their path (Carrington, 2013).

Obviously, smart lighting applications contribute to better approaches of saving energy. Additionally, it reduces chances of thefts and accidents by providing visibility in sensitive areas or by detecting certain motions. The motion detectors will be capable of controlling individual street lights in various areas of a city (Perandones et al., 2014). Smart lighting systems also could be combined with other IoT applications such as air quality monitoring systems (Zanella, Bui, Castellani, Vangelista, & Zorzi, 2014). An urban IoT system may provide a service to monitor the energy consumption of the whole city. Thus, it enables the authorities and individuals to get a clear and detailed view of the amount of energy required for particular services such as public lighting, transportation, traffic lights, control cameras, and heating/cooling of public buildings. Additionally, the system can be used to provide features such as identifying the main energy consumption sources. This feature allows the optimization of energy consumption by setting priorities among different devices and applications (Zanella et al., 2014). Accordingly, smart lighting systems play an important role in smart grid applications as well (Güngör et al., 2011).

Structural Health

Structural Health Monitoring (SHM) systems are used to monitor the conditions of buildings and other physical structures such as bridges (Farrar & Worden, 2007). SHM systems implement damage detection plans and characterize strategies for engineering structures. SHM systems involve the process of observing and monitoring a physical structure over time. A typical SHM system uses an array of sensors which periodically collect measurements from a monitored physical structure. The system samples the collected data and extracts related damage-sensitive information. It then uses statistical analysis methods to determine the structural health status of a physical structure (Dawson, 1976). The Rio-Antirrio Bridge in Greece is an example of an SHM system (Tselentis et al., 2007). It uses more than 100 sensors. These sensors monitor traffic and the bridge structure condition in real time (Parcharidis, Foumelis, Kourkouli, & Wegmuller, 2009). Other examples of SHM systems is the Hong Kong Wind and Structural Health Monitoring System (WASHMS) (S. Kim et al., 2007). WASHMS has four different levels of operation: sensory systems, data acquisition systems, local centralized computer systems, and a global central computer system. The WASHMS system measures the structural behavior of the bridges continuously. Both the WASHMS and Rio-Antirrio systems provide an early warning system for structural health of the relevant monitored bridges.

Recent researches on IoT structural health monitoring systems can be classified into two categories. The first category involves sensor technologies for collecting measurements such as in (S. Kim et al., 2007). The second type of research is centered on developing theoretical algorithms which process the data collected by sensors. The frequency response method has often been used for the analysis of data in these systems (Huang, Xu, Li, Su, & Liu, 2012). Significantly, the IoT contributes to SHM systems by providing Internet connectivity and real-time monitoring features. The IoT connects SHM systems with other areas of the IoT such as driverless car systems, environmental monitoring systems, road congestion systems and forecast systems among many others.

Smart Environment

The IoT can be used to detect noise which goes above a given level of decibels in various parts of the city especially in bars and restaurants. This will ensure efficiency in dealing with noise pollution and making it possible for authorities to react to too much noise in real-time. This is in addition to monitoring noise produced by cars in the city, and residential and industrial areas. This helps in the better planning of residential and industrial areas. An example of noise monitoring system in the IoT is the study presented in (Su, Shao, Vause, & Tang, 2013).

There are many ways through which the IoT technology will be able to help in the environmental management. Some of these applications have already been discussed such as monitoring leakages in rivers, flood control and water pollution. However, there are several other ways through which the technology could enhance the conservation of natural resources such as:

- **Detecting Forest Fires:** The IoT can be used to monitor the presence of combustion gases, and provide information on forest fires as soon as possible. This ensures that the response unit can act early to prevent a disaster (Debnath, Chin, Haque, & Yuen, 2014). Forest fires have been known to spread very fast and widely, with adverse environmental and economic effects. The IoT promises an easier job for the authorities in terms of responding to fires in the forest ecosystems around the country.
- **Monitoring Snow Level:** This enhances the provision of important information concerning skiing and also it makes it possible for the authorities to detect potential avalanche risks in real-time (Debnath et al., 2014). This information will be used to enhance the efficiency of the skiing sport as well.
- **Earthquake Detection:** One of the most devastating natural disasters are earth quakes. When they do occur, they leave behind a trail of huge destructions, including loss of life and property. The IoT technology can be used for the early detection of earthquakes using reliable sophisticated sensors. The IoT enhances earthquake early detection systems such as in (Chi, Chen, Chao, & Kuo, 2011). The future will see the application of IoT to detect earthquakes even hours before they occur. This will make it possible for the authorities to communicate with the people early enough to facilitate evacuation of the most vulnerable neighborhoods.

Waste Management

The technology of connecting things to the Internet will also make it possible for cities to control waste disposal (Debnath et al., 2014). From a logistics perspective, the waste-management process requires tremendous organization. The key objective is in collecting, sorting, and processing waste as efficiently as possible. With the introduction of the IoT in this area, multiple wastes related sites, whether collection companies, recycling plants or power companies that handle waste, can seamlessly schedule deliveries, with one part of the process feeding the next. Research and industry leaders are already working on new IoT solutions for waste management such as smart connected bins. For instance, in (Hong et al.,

2014) an IoT-based smart garbage system (SGS) composed of a number of smart garbage bins (SGBs), routers, and servers has been proposed. Each SGB, which plays a role in collecting food waste, is battery operated for mobility, and considering the convenience to residents, performs various operations through wireless communications. Pollution control is another area relating to waste management. The IoT provides information about pollutants, polluters and the levels of pollution in real time in a given area; thus, contributing to the overall management strategies of rubbish, recyclable and biodegradable waste.

Enhanced Security

The IoT will see the introduction of an increased number of vigilance and highly informed alert systems, which will be capable of fully securing homes, cars, workplaces, recreational places and other properties (Vlacheas et al., 2013). IoT security systems offer a myriad of features including door and window sensors, motion detectors, and video recording mechanisms. The IoT will facilitate access control and ensure that a person has the right permission to access authorized information at the right time and location. Biometric and facial recognition will enhance the automate access to services and resources. The IoT also contributes towards fighting crime, thefts and terrorist activities.

IoT Smart City Requirements

The previous sections provided a vision of a holistic smart city consisting of numerous heterogeneous applications which include various smart city scenarios and related applications. The growth of smart cities within the IoT encompasses the development and connection of several urban and rural geographical areas together. Ultimately, the IoT interconnects a wide range of applications including emergency services, healthcare, smart home, smart metering, and smart roads among others. However, each of these applications delivers a range of complex services to individuals, businesses, and governments within a variety of national, regional, and state administrative structures. This poses numerous integration challenges in the IoT.

Therefore, within this diversified system, it is a tremendous task to define the requirements for smart cities in the IoT. For the realization of a true vision of a smart city in the IoT, several incremental processes of developments and technologies are needed. They include revolutionary advancements in communication technologies, device hardware and software development, and new service architectures. For instance, in many of the smart city applications surveyed in this chapter, there is a need for a wireless technology with a simplified architecture that supports low energy consumption. However, in many other applications, the requirement of having a higher data rate is more important than energy requirement. Consequently, in the context of this mounting complexity and platformization, interoperability between the different facets of IoT is exceptionally vital and can be considered as the crucial requirement for smart cities in the IoT. No matter what technology, topology or device is being used, interoperability has to be achieved for the realization of the IoT. Additionally, one particular challenge in the context of smart cities relates to the open data business model. As services become pervasive and ubiquitous, the matter of making databases accessible by IoT applications and services will become more important. Transparency towards the end user on how his/her information is being used, with clear opt-in options and secured environments, has to be the starting point when providing services that leverage personal data.

CONCLUSION

This chapter provides a survey of some of the interesting applications projected in the IoT. It explores applications in many areas of health, smart homes, and smart cities. The çhapter illustrates how the various applications of the IoT enhance the overall quality of life. The IoT becomes fruitful when various IoT applications are connected together. Thus, the chapter provides examples on compound IoT applications that emerge from combining smart services from different areas. It shows that the IoT sponsors the move from standalone closed systems towards open systems and platforms that support multiple applications and services. Hence, several IoT scenarios are reported. These scenarios combine data from different sources, linking several things, including devices, peoples and the environment to deliver and share information, enhancing business value, quality of life, and creating new business opportunities.

Nevertheless, to realize the unique and futuristic characteristics of the IoT, many challenges need to be overcome. There is a need to maintain scalable, private, secure and trustworthy operations in the IoT. With billions of things equipped with sensors and actuators entering the digital word using a vast array of technologies, incorporated into devices like lights, electric appliances, home automation systems and a vast number of other integrated machinery devices, transport vehicles, and equipment, as shown in this chapter, management of things become very challenging. Moreover, the growth in connected devices to the communication networks translates into increased security risks and poses new challenges to security and privacy. A device which connects to the Internet, whether it is a constraint or a more powerful device, inherits the security risks of today's computer devices. Therefore, it is essential that things are securely connected to their designated network(s), securely controlled and accessed by authorized entities. Many IoT applications require that data generated by things to be collected, analyzed, stored, dispatched and presented in a secure manner. Furthermore, there are security and privacy risks associated with things to things communications as well. This is in addition to the risks relating to things-to-person communications. For instance, the chapter describes many interaction scenarios where things are accessed by other things independently from the user. This highlights the need for end-to-end security and privacy protection solutions. As such security and privacy solutions should guarantee that things are accessed only by authorized entities in a secure manner. They should ensure that things are not leaking information or disclosing private information about their operations or their users to unauthorized entities. They also need to ensure that things are not used miscellaneously to impinge on the privacy of users.

REFERENCES

Ashton, K. (22 July 2009). That 'Internet of Things' Thing. *RFID Journal*. Retrieved from http://www.rfidjournal.com/article/view/4986

Atzori, L., Iera, A., & Morabito, G. (2010). The internet of things: A survey. *Computer Networks*, *54*(15), 2787–2805. doi:10.1016/j.comnet.2010.05.010

Baig, M., & Gholamhosseini, H. (2013). Smart Health Monitoring Systems: An Overview of Design and Modeling. *Journal of Medical Systems*, *37*(2), 1–14. doi:10.1007/s10916-012-9898-z PMID:23321968

Basu, D., Moretti, G., Gupta, G. S., & Marsland, S. (2013). Wireless sensor network based smart home: Sensor selection, deployment and monitoring. *Paper presented at the2013 IEEE Sensors Applications Symposium (SAS)*, Galveston, USA. doi:doi:10.1109/SAS.2013.6493555 doi:10.1109/SAS.2013.6493555

Benzi, F., Anglani, N., Bassi, E., & Frosini, L. (2011). Electricity smart meters interfacing the households. *IEEE Transactions on Industrial Electronics*, *58*(10), 4487–4494. doi:10.1109/TIE.2011.2107713

Bohli, J.-M., Skarmeta, A., Victoria Moreno, M., Garcia, D., & Langendorfer, P. (2015). SMARTIE project: Secure IoT data management for smart cities. *Paper presented at the2015 International Conference on Recent Advances in Internet of Things (RIoT)*, Singapore. doi:doi:10.1109/RIOT.2015.7104906 doi:10.1109/RIOT.2015.7104906

Boulos, M. N. K., & Al-Shorbaji, N. M. (2014). On the Internet of Things, smart cities and the WHO Healthy Cities. *International Journal of Health Geographics*, *13*(10). PMID:24669838

Braun, A., Neumann, S., Schmidt, S., Wichert, R., & Kuijper, A. (2014). Towards interactive car interiors: the active armrest. *Paper presented at the8th Nordic Conference on Human-Computer Interaction: Fun, Fast, Foundational*, Helsinki, Finland. doi:doi:10.1145/2639189.2670191 doi:10.1145/2639189.2670191

Carrington, D. (2013). Tvilight: The 'talking' streetlamps that will lighten your heart (but not your wallet). *CNN*. Retrieved from http://edition.cnn.com/2013/07/18/tech/innovation/tvilight-street-lamps-roosegarde/

Castro, M., Jara, A. J., & Skarmeta, A. F. (2013). Smart lighting solutions for smart cities. *Paper presented at the27th International Conference on Advanced Information Networking and Applications Workshops (WAINA)*, Barcelona, Spain.

Chan, M., Campo, E., Estève, D., & Fourniols, J.-Y. (2009). Smart homes—current features and future perspectives. *Maturitas*, *64*(2), 90–97. doi:10.1016/j.maturitas.2009.07.014 PMID:19729255

Chi, T.-Y., Chen, C.-H., Chao, H.-C., & Kuo, S.-Y. (2011). An Efficient Earthquake Early Warning Message Delivery Algorithm Using an in Time Control-Theoretic Approach. In C.-H. Hsu, L. Yang, J. Ma, & C. Zhu (Eds.), Ubiquitous Intelligence and Computing (Vol. 6905, pp. 161-173): Springer Berlin Heidelberg. doi:doi:10.1007/978-3-642-23641-9_15 doi:10.1007/978-3-642-23641-9_15

Chong, Z., Qin, B., Bandyopadhyay, T., Wongpiromsarn, T., Rebsamen, B., Dai, P., & Ang, M. H. Jr. (2013). *Autonomy for mobility on demand Intelligent Autonomous Systems 12* (pp. 671–682). Springer. doi:10.1007/978-3-642-33926-4_64

Chou, C.-M., Li, C.-Y., Chien, W.-M., & Lan, K.-c. (2009). A feasibility study on vehicle-to-infrastructure communication: WiFi vs. WiMAX. *Paper presented at theTenth International Conference on Mobile Data Management: Systems, Services and Middleware*, Taipei, Taiwan. doi:doi:10.1109/MDM.2009.127 doi:10.1109/MDM.2009.127

Chowdhury, N., Bhuiyan, M. M. H., & Islam, S. (2013). IOT: Detection of Keys, Controlling Machines and Wireless Sensing Via Mesh Networking Through Internet. *Global Journal of Researches In Engineering*, 13(13).

Clarke, R. Y. (2013). *Smart Cities and the Internet of Everything: The Foundation for Delivering Next-Generation Citizen Services*. Alexandria, VA: Tech. Rep.

Clendenin, M. (2010). China's 'Internet Of Things' Overblown, Says Exec. *Information Week*. Retrieved from http://www.informationweek.com/news/storage/virtualization/225700966?subSection=News

Connected Car Forecast: Global Connected Car Market to Grow Threefold Within Five Years. (2014). Retrieved from www.gsma.com

Da Xu, L., He, W., & Li, S. (2014). Internet of things in industries: A survey. *IEEE Transactions on Industrial Informatics*, *10*(4), 2233–2243. doi:10.1109/TII.2014.2300753

Dawson, B. (1976). Vibration condition monitoring techniques for rotating machinery. *The shock and vibration digest*, 8, 12.

Debnath, A. K., Chin, H. C., Haque, M. M., & Yuen, B. (2014). A methodological framework for benchmarking smart transport cities. *Cities (London, England)*, *37*, 47–56. doi:10.1016/j.cities.2013.11.004

Dlodlo, N., & Kalezhi, J. (2015). The internet of things in agriculture for sustainable rural development. *Paper presented at the2015 International Conference on Emerging Trends in Networks and Computer Communications (ETNCC)*, Namibia. doi:doi:10.1109/ETNCC.2015.7184801 doi:10.1109/ETNCC.2015.7184801

Domingo, M. C. (2012). An overview of the internet of underwater things. *Journal of Network and Computer Applications*, *35*(6), 1879–1890. doi:10.1016/j.jnca.2012.07.012

Dramsvik, B. (2009). Adaptive Street Lighting: A Way Forward to Improve ITS-Implementation as Well as Increase Road Safety and to Save Energy. *Paper presented at the16th ITS World Congress and Exhibition on Intelligent Transport Systems and Services*.

Duan, X. J. (2014). Research on IOT-Based Smart Garden Project. *Paper presented at the Applied Mechanics and Materials*. doi:doi:10.4028/www.scientific.net/AMM.608-609.321 doi:10.4028/www.scientific.net/AMM.608-609.321

Elkhodr, M., Shahrestani, S., & Cheung, H. (2011a). An approach to enhance the security of remote health monitoring systems. *Paper presented at the4th international conference on Security of information and networks*, Sydney, Australia. doi:doi:10.1145/2070425.2070458 doi:10.1145/2070425.2070458

Elkhodr, M., Shahrestani, S., & Cheung, H. (2011b). Ubiquitous health monitoring systems: Addressing security concerns. *Journal of Computer Science*, *7*(10), 1465–1473. doi:10.3844/jcssp.2011.1465.1473

Elkhodr, M., Shahrestani, S., & Cheung, H. (2013). A contextual-adaptive location disclosure agent for general devices in the internet of things. *Paper presented at the EEE 38th Conference on Local Computer Networks Workshops (LCN Workshops)*, Sydney, Australia. doi:doi:10.1109/LCNW.2013.6758522 doi:10.1109/LCNW.2013.6758522

Elkhodr, M., Shahrestani, S., & Cheung, H. (2014). A semantic obfuscation technique for the Internet of Things. *Paper presented at theIEEE International Conference on Communications Workshops (ICC)*, Sydney, Australia. doi:doi:10.1109/ICCW.2014.6881239 doi:10.1109/ICCW.2014.6881239

Elkhodr, M., Shahrestani, S., & Cheung, H. (2016). *Wireless Enabling Technologies for the Internet of Things Innovative Research and Applications in Next-Generation High Performance Computing*. Hershey, PA, USA: IGI Global.

Erol-Kantarci, M., & Mouftah, H. T. (2011). Wireless sensor networks for cost-efficient residential energy management in the smart grid. *IEEE Transactions on Smart Grid, 2*(2), 314–325. doi:10.1109/TSG.2011.2114678

Evans, D. (2012). The internet of everything: How more relevant and valuable connections will change the world. *Cisco IBSG.*

Fan, W., & Bifet, A. (2013). Mining big data: current status, and forecast to the future. *ACM sIGKDD Explorations Newsletter, 14*(2), 1-5.

Farbotko, C., Walton, A., Mankad, A., & Gardner, J. (2014). Household rainwater tanks: Mediating changing relations with water? *Ecology and Society, 19*(2), 62. doi:10.5751/ES-06632-190262

Farrar, C. R., & Worden, K. (2007). An introduction to structural health monitoring. *Philosophical Transactions of the Royal Society of London A: Mathematical, Physical and Engineering Sciences, 365*(1851), 303-315.

Foschini, L., Taleb, T., Corradi, A., & Bottazzi, D. (2011). M2M-based metropolitan platform for IMS-enabled road traffic management in IoT. *IEEE Communications Magazine, 49*(11), 50–57. doi:10.1109/MCOM.2011.6069709

Francesco, M. D., Li, N., Raj, M., & Das, S. K. (2012). A storage Infrastructure for Heterogeneous and Multimedia Data in the Internet of Things. *Paper presented at theIEEE International Conference on Green Computing and Communications (GreenCom)*, Besançon, France. doi:doi:10.1109/GreenCom.2012.15 doi:10.1109/GreenCom.2012.15

Fries, J. F., Koop, C. E., Sokolov, J., Beadle, C. E., & Wright, D. (1998). Beyond health promotion: Reducing need and demand for medical care. *Health Affairs, 17*(2), 70–84. doi:10.1377/hlthaff.17.2.70 PMID:9558786

Gubbi, J., Buyya, R., Marusic, S., & Palaniswami, M. (2013). Internet of Things (IoT): A vision, architectural elements, and future directions. *Future Generation Computer Systems, 29*(7), 1645–1660. doi:10.1016/j.future.2013.01.010

Güngör, V. C., Sahin, D., Kocak, T., Ergüt, S., Buccella, C., Cecati, C., & Hancke, G. P. (2011). Smart grid technologies: Communication technologies and standards. *IEEE Transactions on Industrial Informatics, 7*(4), 529–539. doi:10.1109/TII.2011.2166794

Hess, A., Malandrino, F., Reinhardt, M. B., Casetti, C., Hummel, K. A., & Barceló-Ordinas, J. M. (2012). Optimal deployment of charging stations for electric vehicular networks. *Paper presented at theThe first workshop on Urban networking*, Nice, France. doi:doi:10.1145/2413236.2413238 doi:10.1145/2413236.2413238

Hong, I., Park, S., Lee, B., Lee, J., Jeong, D., & Park, S. (2014). IoT-Based Smart Garbage System for Efficient Food Waste Management. *TheScientificWorldJournal*, 2014. PMID:25258730

Hoy, M. B. (2015). The "Internet of Things": What It Is and What It Means for Libraries. *Medical Reference Services Quarterly, 34*(3), 353–358. doi:10.1080/02763869.2015.1052699 PMID:26211795

Huang, Q., Xu, Y., Li, J., Su, Z., & Liu, H. (2012). Structural damage detection of controlled building structures using frequency response functions. *Journal of Sound and Vibration*, *331*(15), 3476–3492. doi:10.1016/j.jsv.2012.03.001

ITU. (2005). *ITU Internet Reports 2005: The internet of things*. Retrieved from https://www.itu.int/wsis/tunis/newsroom/stats/The-Internet-of-Things-2005.pdf

Jaykumar, J., & Blessy, A. (2014). Secure Smart Environment Using IOT based on RFID. *International Journal of Computer Science & Information Technologies*, *5*(2).

Kalra, D., & Ingram, D. (2006). *Electronic health records Information technology solutions for healthcare* (pp. 135–181). Springer. doi:10.1007/1-84628-141-5_7

Kar, A., & Kar, A. (2015). A novel design of a portable double beam-in-time spectrometric sensor platform with cloud connectivity for environmental monitoring applications. *Paper presented at the Third International Conference on Computer, Communication, Control and Information Technology (C3IT)*, Hooghly, India. doi:doi:10.1109/C3IT.2015.7060228 doi:10.1109/C3IT.2015.7060228

Kawamoto, Y., Nishiyama, H., Yoshimura, N., & Yamamoto, S. (2014). Internet of Things (IoT): Present State and Future Prospects. *IEICE Transactions on Information and Systems*, *97*(10), 2568–2575. doi:10.1587/transinf.2013THP0009

Kim, S., Pakzad, S., Culler, D., Demmel, J., Fenves, G., Glaser, S., & Turon, M. (2007). Health monitoring of civil infrastructures using wireless sensor networks. *Paper presented at the 6th International Symposium on Information Processing in Sensor Networks*, Cambridge, USA. doi:doi:10.1109/IPSN.2007.4379685 doi:10.1109/IPSN.2007.4379685

Kim, S. A., Shin, D., Choe, Y., Seibert, T., & Walz, S. P. (2012). Integrated energy monitoring and visualization system for Smart Green City development: Designing a spatial information integrated energy monitoring model in the context of massive data management on a web based platform. *Automation in Construction*, *22*, 51–59. doi:10.1016/j.autcon.2011.07.004

Kim, Y., Suh, J., Cho, J., Singh, S., & Seo, J. (2015). Development of Real-Time Pipeline Management System for Prevention of Accidents. *International Journal of Control and Automation*, *8*(1), 211–226. doi:10.14257/ijca.2015.8.1.19

Kinnunen, M., Mian, S. Q., Oinas-Kukkonen, H., Riekki, J., Jutila, M., Ervasti, M., & Alasaarela, E. et al. (2016). Wearable and mobile sensors connected to social media in human well-being applications. *Telematics and Informatics*, *33*(1), 92–101. doi:10.1016/j.tele.2015.06.008

Lara, A. M., Kigozi, J., Amurwon, J., Muchabaiwa, L., Wakaholi, B. N., Mota, R. E. M., & Reid, A. et al. (2012). Cost effectiveness analysis of clinically driven versus routine laboratory monitoring of antiretroviral therapy in Uganda and Zimbabwe. *PLoS ONE*, *7*(4). PMID:22545079

Laranjo, I., Macedo, J., & Santos, A. (2012). Internet of things for medication control: Service implementation and testing. *Procedia Technology*, *5*, 777–786. doi:10.1016/j.protcy.2012.09.086

Li, C., Suna, L., & Hua, X. (2012). A context-aware lighting control system for smart meeting rooms. *Systems Engineering Procedia*, *4*, 314–323. doi:10.1016/j.sepro.2011.11.081

Liu, J., & Yang, L. (2011). Application of Internet of Things in the community security management. *Paper presented at theThird International Conference on Computational Intelligence, Communication Systems and Networks (CICSyN)*, Bali, Indonesia. doi:doi:10.1109/CICSyN.2011.72 doi:10.1109/CICSyN.2011.72

Liu, W.-H. E. (2010). Analytics and information integration for smart grid applications. *Paper presented at the2010 IEEE Power and Energy Society General Meeting*, Minneapolis, USA. doi:doi:10.1109/PES.2010.5589898 doi:10.1109/PES.2010.5589898

Lomas, N. (2009). Online gizmos could top 50 billion in 2020. *Business Week*. Retrieved from http://www.businessweek.com/globalbiz/content/jun2009/gb20090629_492027.htm

Lu, R., Lin, X., Zhu, H., & Shen, X. S. (2009). SPARK: a new VANET-based smart parking scheme for large parking lots. *Paper presented at theIEEE INFOCOM '09*, Rio de Janeiro, Brazil. doi:doi:10.1109/INFCOM.2009.5062057 doi:10.1109/INFCOM.2009.5062057

Lundqvist, J., de Fraiture, C., & Molden, D. (2008). Saving water: from field to fork: curbing losses and wastage in the food chain. Retrieved from http://dlc.dlib.indiana.edu/dlc/handle/10535/5088

MacGillivray, C., Turner, V., Lund, D., Dugar, A., Dunbrack, L. A., Salmeron, A., . . . Clarke, R. Y. (2014). Worldwide Internet of Things 2014 Top 10 Predictions: Nascent Market Shakes Up Vendor Strategies.

Mainetti, L., Patrono, L., & Vilei, A. (2011). Evolution of wireless sensor networks towards the internet of things: A survey. *Paper presented at the19th International Conference on Software, Telecommunications and Computer Networks (SoftCOM)*, Split, Croatia.

Melo, V. A. Z. C., Sakurai, C. A., Fontana, C. F., Tosta, J. A., Silva, W. S., & Dias, E. M. (2011). Technological Model for Application of Internet of Things to Monitor Pharmaceutical Goods Transportation. *Paper presented at the18th ITS World Congress*, Orlando, USA.

Misra, P., Simmhan, Y., & Warrior, J. (2015). Towards a Practical Architecture for the Next Generation Internet of Things. *arXiv preprint arXiv:1502.00797*.

Mohsenian-Rad, A.-H., Wong, V. W., Jatskevich, J., Schober, R., & Leon-Garcia, A. (2010). Autonomous demand-side management based on game-theoretic energy consumption scheduling for the future smart grid. *IEEE Transactions on Smart Grid*, *1*(3), 320–331. doi:10.1109/TSG.2010.2089069

Muhic, I., & Hodzic, M. (2014). Internet of Things: Current Technological Review. *Periodicals of Engineering and Natural Sciences (PEN)*, *2*(2).

Mylonas, G., & Theodoridis, E. (2015). Developments and challenges ahead in smart city frameworks-lessons from SmartSantander. *International Journal of Intelligent Engineering Informatics*, *3*(2-3), 95–119. doi:10.1504/IJIEI.2015.069882

Neil, G. (2000). *When things start to think*. Holt Paperbacks.

Nelson, G. (2015). *Where is Google's car going?: a vision emerges in Silicon Valley*. Automotive News.

Neuhaeuser, J., & D'Angelo, L. (2013). Collecting and distributing wearable sensor data: an embedded personal area network to local area network gateway server. *Paper presented at the35th Annual International Conference of the IEEE Engineering in Medicine and Biology Society (EMBC)*, Osaka, Japan. doi:doi:10.1109/EMBC.2013.6610584 doi:10.1109/EMBC.2013.6610584

Nwogu, K. (2015). *Energy Harvesting And Storage: The Catalyst To The Power Constraint For Leveraging Internet Of Things (IoT) On Trains. (Master of Science)*. University of Nebraska-Lincoln.

Open Aquarium - Aquaponics and Fish Tank Monitoring for Arduino. (2014). Retrieved from http://www.cooking-hacks.com/documentation/tutorials/open-aquarium-aquaponics-fish-tank-monitoring-arduino

Ozkul, T., & Sevin, A. (2014). Survey of Popular Networks used for Biosensors. *Biosens. J.*, *3*(110), 2.

Pala, Z., & Inanc, N. (2007). Smart parking applications using RFID technology. *Paper presented at the 2007 1st Annual RFID Eurasia*, Istanbul, Turkey. doi:doi:10.1109/RFIDEURASIA.2007.4368108 doi:10.1109/RFIDEURASIA.2007.4368108

Pang, Z., Zheng, L., Tian, J., Kao-Walter, S., Dubrova, E., & Chen, Q. (2015). Design of a terminal solution for integration of in-home health care devices and services towards the Internet-of-Things. *Enterprise Information Systems*, *9*(1), 86–116. doi:10.1080/17517575.2013.776118

Parcharidis, I., Foumelis, M., Kourkouli, P., & Wegmuller, U. (2009). Persistent Scatterers InSAR to detect ground deformation over Rio-Antirio area (Western Greece) for the period 1992–2000. *Journal of Applied Geophysics*, *68*(3), 348–355. doi:10.1016/j.jappgeo.2009.02.005

Parwekar, P. (2011). From Internet of Things towards cloud of things. *Paper presented at the2nd International Conference on Computer and Communication Technology (ICCCT)*, Allahabad, India. doi:doi:10.1109/ICCCT.2011.6075156 doi:10.1109/ICCCT.2011.6075156

Pearce, R. (2009). IoT tech to drive water treatment in Queensland. *Computerworld*. Retrieved from http://www.computerworld.com.au/article/528602/iot_tech_drive_water_treatment_queensland/

Perandones, J. M., del Campo Jiménez, G., Rodríguez, J. C., Jie, S., Sierra, S. C., García, R. M., & Santamaría, A. (2014). Energy-saving smart street lighting system based on 6LoWPAN. *Paper presented at theThe First International Conference on IoT in Urban Space*, Rome, Italy. doi:doi:10.4108/icst.urb-iot.2014.257221 doi:10.4108/icst.urb-iot.2014.257221

Pereira, T., & Santos, H. (2015). *Child Abuse Monitor System Model: A Health Care Critical Knowledge Monitor System. In Internet of Things. User-Centric IoT* (pp. 255–261). Springer.

Polycarpou, E., Lambrinos, L., & Protopapadakis, E. (2013). Smart parking solutions for urban areas. *Paper presented at the IEEE 14th International Symposium and Workshops on a World of Wireless, Mobile and Multimedia Networks (WoWMoM)*, Boston, USA. doi:doi:10.1109/WoWMoM.2013.6583499 doi:10.1109/WoWMoM.2013.6583499

Qin, Z., Denker, G., Giannelli, C., Bellavista, P., & Venkatasubramanian, N. (2014). A Software Defined Networking Architecture for the Internet-of-Things. *Paper presented at the2014 IEEE Network Operations and Management Symposium (NOMS)*, Krakow, Poland. doi:doi:10.1109/NOMS.2014.6838365 doi:10.1109/NOMS.2014.6838365

Robles, T., Alcarria, R., Martin, D., Morales, A., Navarro, M., Calero, R., . . . Lopez, M. (2014). An internet of things-based model for smart water management. *Paper presented at the 2014 28th International Conference on Advanced Information Networking and Applications Workshops (WAINA)*, Barcelona, Spain. doi:doi:10.1109/WAINA.2014.129 doi:10.1109/WAINA.2014.129

Rost, S., & Balakrishnan, H. (2006). Memento: A health monitoring system for wireless sensor networks. *Paper presented at the 3rd Annual IEEE Communications Society on Sensor and Ad Hoc Communications and Networks*, Reston, USA. doi:doi:10.1109/SAHCN.2006.288514 doi:10.1109/SAHCN.2006.288514

Rumbaugh, J., Blaha, M., Premerlani, W., Eddy, F., & Lorensen, W. E. (1991). *Object-oriented modeling and design* (Vol. 199). Prentice-hall Englewood Cliffs.

Sanchez, L., Muñoz, L., Galache, J. A., Sotres, P., Santana, J. R., Gutierrez, V., & Theodoridis, E. et al. (2014). SmartSantander: IoT experimentation over a smart city testbed. *Computer Networks, 61*, 217–238. doi:10.1016/j.bjp.2013.12.020

Savola, R. M., Abie, H., & Sihvonen, M. (2012). Towards metrics-driven adaptive security management in e-health IoT applications. *Paper presented at the The 7th International Conference on Body Area Networks*. doi:doi:10.4108/icst.bodynets.2012.250241 doi:10.4108/icst.bodynets.2012.250241

Schneps-Schneppe, M., Namiot, D., Maximenko, A., & Malov, D. (2012). Wired Smart Home: energy metering, security, and emergency issues. *Paper presented at the 4th International Congress on Ultra Modern Telecommunications and Control Systems and Workshops (ICUMT)*, St. Petersburg, Russia. doi:doi:10.1109/ICUMT.2012.6459700 doi:10.1109/ICUMT.2012.6459700

Scurlock, C., & D'Ambrosio, C. (2015). Telemedicine in the Intensive Care Unit: State of the Art. *Critical Care Clinics, 31*(2), 187–195. doi:10.1016/j.ccc.2014.12.001 PMID:25814449

Siddiqui, A. (2014). An Emperical Study of Consumer Perception Regarding Organised Retail In Tier Three Cities. *Journal of Business and Management, 1*, 91–105.

Staff, A. (2014). Connected Car Technology Shifts Internet of Things Boundaries. *PubNub.com*. Retrieved from http://www.pubnub.com/blog/connected-car-technology-shifts-internet-things-boundaries/

Su, X., Shao, G., Vause, J., & Tang, L. (2013). An integrated system for urban environmental monitoring and management based on the Environmental Internet of Things. *International Journal of Sustainable Development and World Ecology, 20*(3), 205–209. doi:10.1080/13504509.2013.782580

Sula, A., Spaho, E., Matsuo, K., Barolli, L., Xhafa, F., & Miho, R. (2013). *An IoT-Based Framework for Supporting Children with Autism Spectrum Disorder Information Technology Convergence* (pp. 193–202). Springer.

Tai, H., Celesti, A., Fazio, M., Villari, M., & Puliafito, A. (2015). An integrated system for advanced water risk management based on cloud computing and IoT. *Paper presented at the 2nd World Symposium on Web Applications and Networking (WSWAN)*, Tunisia. doi:doi:10.1109/WSWAN.2015.7210305 doi:10.1109/WSWAN.2015.7210305

Taylor, D. (2014). RFID in the pharmaceutical industry: Addressing counterfeits with technology. *Journal of Medical Systems, 38*(11), 1–5. doi:10.1007/s10916-014-0141-y PMID:25308613

Tiwari, G. (2011). Hardware/Software Based a Smart Sensor Interface Device for Water Quality Monitoring in IoT Environment. *International Journal of Technology and Science*, *3*(1), 5–9.

TongKe, F. (2013). Smart Agriculture Based on Cloud Computing and IOT. *Journal of Convergence Information Technology*, *8*(2).

Tselentis, G.-A., Serpetsidaki, A., Martakis, N., Sokos, E., Paraskevopoulos, P., & Kapotas, S. (2007). Local high-resolution passive seismic tomography and Kohonen neural networks—Application at the Rio-Antirio Strait, central Greece. *Geophysics*, *72*(4), B93–B106. doi:10.1190/1.2729473

Vermesan, O., & Friess, P. (2013). *Internet of things: converging technologies for smart environments and integrated ecosystems*. River Publishers.

Vermesan, O., Friess, P., Guillemin, P., Gusmeroli, S., Sundmaeker, H., Bassi, A., & Eisenhauer, M. et al. (2011). Internet of things strategic research roadmap. *Internet of Things: Global Technological and Societal Trends*, *1*, 9–52.

Vlacheas, P., Giaffreda, R., Stavroulaki, V., Kelaidonis, D., Foteinos, V., Poulios, G., & Moessner, K. et al. (2013). Enabling smart cities through a cognitive management framework for the internet of things. *IEEE Communications Magazine*, *51*(6), 102–111. doi:10.1109/MCOM.2013.6525602

Wilson, C., Hargreaves, T., & Hauxwell-Baldwin, R. (2015). Smart homes and their users: A systematic analysis and key challenges. *Personal and Ubiquitous Computing*, *19*(2), 463–476. doi:10.1007/s00779-014-0813-0

Wu, Y., Chen, Y., & Lei, P. (2012). Analysis on Water Quality Monitoring Technologies and Application of Internet of Things. *China Water & Wastewater*, *28*(22), 9–13.

Yue, W., Changhong, S., Xianghong, Z., & Wei, Y. (2010). Design of new intelligent street light control system. *Paper presented at the 2010 8th IEEE International Conference on Control and Automation (ICCA)*, Xiamen, China.

Zanella, A., Bui, N., Castellani, A. P., Vangelista, L., & Zorzi, M. (2014). *Internet of things for smart cities*. IEEE Internet of Things Journal.

Zhao, W., Wang, C., & Nakahira, Y. (2011). Medical application on Internet of Things. *Paper presented at theIET Conference*, Beijing, China.

ZHU, X.-y., & PAN, Y. (2015). Research on the Identification of Real-time Water Leakage Based on Internet-based Smart Water Meters and Complex Event Processing. *Group Technology & Production Modernization*, *1*, 006.

Zorzi, M., Gluhak, A., Lange, S., & Bassi, A. (2010). From today's intranet of things to a future internet of things: A wireless-and mobility-related view. *IEEE Wireless Communications*, *17*(6), 44–51. doi:10.1109/MWC.2010.5675777

KEY TERMS AND DEFINITIONS

eHealth: Also written e-health, eHealth, and E-health, is an acronym for Electronic health and a term used for managing health information in the digital world during their digital storage, electronic process and communication.

EHR: Stands for Electronic Health Record. EHR is also known as EPR (Electronic Patient Record) and EMR (electronic medical record). The term represents a patient's health record or his or her information in digital format.

Interoperability: The ability of devices to communicate on the Internet of Things regardless of their make, model or the communication technology in use.

Internet of Things: The future Internet. It can be described as a heterogeneous network that combines several devices, services, people, and wired and wireless technologies together.

Low Power Wireless Technologies: Wireless technologies that consume low energy. Typically, devices that use low power wireless technologies are characterized by their low cost as well.

M2M: Machine to Machine communications is a term used to describe communication between two devices with minimal human interference.

Smart Cities: The city of the future where technology and communications plays a vital role in everyday activities.

428

Compilation of References

3D. FFT. (n. d.). Retrieved from http://charm.cs.uiuc.edu/cs498lvk/projects/kunzman/index.htm

Abdallah, Z. S., Gaber, M. M., Srinivasan, B., & Krishnaswamy, S. (2015). Adaptive mobile activity recognition system with evolving data streams. *Neurocomputing*, *150*, 304–317. doi:10.1016/j.neucom.2014.09.074

Adame, T., Bel, A., Bellalta, B., Barcelo, J., Gonzalez, J., & Oliver, M. (2013). *Capacity analysis of IEEE 802.11 ah WLANs for M2M communications*. Springer.

Adame, T., Bel, A., Bellalta, B., Barcelo, J., & Oliver, M. (2014). IEEE 802.11 AH: The WiFi approach for M2M communications. *IEEE Wireless Communications*, *21*(6), 144–152. doi:10.1109/MWC.2014.7000982

Advanced RISC Machines Limited (ARM) Inc. (1996). *ARM Software Development Toolkit*.

Advanced Synchronization Facility. (n. d.). *Wikipedia, the free encyclopedia*. Retrieved from https://en.wikipedia.org/w/index.php?title=Advanced_Synchronization_Facility&oldid=680636378

Aguilera, M. K., Chen, W., & Toueg, S. (1997). Heartbeat: A timeout-free failure detector for quiescent reliable communication. In Distributed Algorithms (pp. 126-140). Springer Berlin Heidelberg.

Agullo, E., Coti, C., Dongarra, J., Herault, T., & Langou, J. (2010, April). QR factorization of tall and skinny matrices in a grid computing environment.*Proceedings of the IEEE International Symposium on Parallel & Distributed Processing (IPDPS)*,(pp. 1-11). IEEE. doi:10.1109/IPDPS.2010.5470475

Ahmed, E., Khan, S., Yaqoob, I., Gani, A., & Salim, F. (2013). Multi-objective optimization model for seamless application execution in mobile cloud computing. *Paper presented at the 2013 5th International Conference on Information & Communication Technologies (ICICT)*. doi:doi:10.1109/ICICT.2013.6732790 doi:10.1109/ICICT.2013.6732790

Ahmed, E., Akhunzada, A., Whaiduzzaman, M., Gani, A., Ab Hamid, S. H., & Buyya, R. (2015). Network-centric performance analysis of runtime application migration in mobile cloud computing. *Simulation Modelling Practice and Theory*, *50*, 42–56.

Ahmed, H. (2013). *Study on the trade off between throughput and power consumption in the design of Bluetooth Low Energy applications*. The University of Tennessee At Chattanooga.

Aho, A. V., Sethi, R., & Ullman, J. D. (1986). *Compilers: principles, techniques, and tools*. Boston, MA: Addison-Wesley Longman Publishing Co., Inc.

Ahrens, J., Rogers, D., & Springmeyer, B. (2010). Visualization and data analysis at the exascale (Technical Report LLNL-TR-474731).

Aidemark, J., Vinter, J., Folkesson, P., & Karlsson, J. (2001). Goofi: generic object-oriented fault injection tool.*Proceedings of International conference on dependable systems and networks (DSN)*.IEEE. doi:10.1109/DSN.2001.941394

Akidau, T., Balikov, A., Bekiroğlu, K., Chernyak, S., Haberman, J., Lax, R., & Whittle, S. et al. (2013). MillWheel: Fault-tolerant stream processing at internet scale. *Proceedings of the VLDB Endowment, 6*(11), 1033–1044. doi:10.14778/2536222.2536229

Akkary, H. H., Adl-Tabatabai, A.-R., Saha, B., & Rajwar, R. (2014). *Unbounded transactional memory systems*. Google Patents.

Akutsu, T., Miyano, S., & Kuhara, S. (2000). Algorithms for identifying boolean networks and related biological networks based on matrix multiplication and fingerprint function.*Proceedings of ACM international conference on computational molecular biology*. ACM. doi:10.1145/332306.332317

Akyildiz, I. F., Su, W., Sankarasubramaniam, Y., & Cayirci, E. (2002). Wireless sensor networks: A survey. *Computer Networks, 38*(4), 393–422. doi:10.1016/S1389-1286(01)00302-4

Alessandrini, V. (2015). *Shared Memory Application Programming: Concepts and strategies in multicore application programming*. Morgan Kaufmann.

Alexandrov, A., Ionescu, M. F. K., Schauser, E., & Scheiman, C. (1997). LogGP: Incorporating long messages into the logp model for parallel computation. *Journal of Parallel and Distributed Computing, 44*(1), 71–79. doi:10.1006/jpdc.1997.1346

Alfeld, P. (2015). N-queens problem. Retrieved from http://www.math.utah.edu/~alfeld/queens/queens.html

Ali, H., & Ahmed, M. (2012, October). HPRDG: A scalable framework hypercube-P2P-based for resource discovery in computational Grid. *Proceedings of the 2012 22nd International Conference on Computer Theory and Applications (ICCTA)* (pp. 2-8). IEEE.

Alizadeh, M., Greenberg, A., Maltz, D. A., Padhye, J., Patel, P., Prabhakar, B., & Sridharan, M. (2011). Data center tcp (dctcp). *Computer Communication Review, 41*(4), 63–74.

Almeida, J., Almeida, V., Ardagna, D., Cunha, ´. I., Francalanci, C., & Trubian, M. (2010). Joint admission control and resource allocation in virtualized servers. *Journal of Parallel and Distributed Computing, 70*(4), 344–362. doi:10.1016/j.jpdc.2009.08.009

Alnuaimi, M., Shuaib, K., & Jawhar, I. (2006). Performance evaluation of IEEE 802.15. 4 physical layer using MatLab/simulink. *Paper presented at the Innovations in Information Technology*, Dubai, UAE.

Alverson, G., Alverson, R., Callahan, D., Koblenz, B., Porterfield, A., & Smith, B. (1990). The tera computer system. *Proceedings of the Fourth international Conference on Supercomputing* (pp 1-6) doi:10.1145/77726.255132

Alverson, G., Alverson, R., Callahan, D., Koblenz, B., Porterfield, A., & Smith, B. (1992). Exploiting heterogeneos parallelism on a multithreading multiproccesor.*Processing of the Sixth International Conference on Supercomputing* (pp. 188-197). doi:10.1145/143369.143408

Alvisi, L., & Marzullo, K. (1995, May). Message logging: Pessimistic, optimistic, and causal.*Proceedings of the 15th International Conference on Distributed Computing Systems* (pp. 229-236). IEEE. doi:10.1109/ICDCS.1995.500024

Alvisi, L., Rao, S., Husain, S. A., De Mel, A., & Elnozahy, E. (1999, June). An analysis of communication-induced checkpointing.*Proceedings of the Twenty-Ninth Annual International Symposium on Fault-Tolerant Computing, Digest of Papers.* (pp. 242-249). IEEE. doi:10.1109/FTCS.1999.781058

Amazon. (2015). Amazon Elastic Compute Cloud (EC2). Retrieved from http://www.amazon.com/ec2/

Amdahl, M. G. (1967). Validity of the single processor approach to achieving large scale computing capabilities. In *Proceedings of the Spring Joint Computer Conference* (pp. 483-485). ACM Press. doi:10.1145/1465482.1465560

Amini, A., Wah, T. Y., & Saboohi, H. (2014). On density-based data streams clustering algorithms: A survey. *Journal of Computer Science and Technology*, *29*(1), 116–141. doi:10.1007/s11390-014-1416-y

Angskun, T., Bosilca, G., & Dongarra, J. (2007). Binomial graph: A scalable and fault-tolerant logical network topology. In *Parallel and Distributed Processing and Applications* (pp. 471–482). Springer Berlin Heidelberg. doi:10.1007/978-3-540-74742-0_43

Angskun, T., Fagg, G., Bosilca, G., Pješivac-Grbović, J., & Dongarra, J. (2010). Self-healing network for scalable fault-tolerant runtime environments. *Future Generation Computer Systems*, *26*(3), 479–485. doi:10.1016/j.future.2009.04.001

Anitha, P., & Chandrasekar, C. (2011). Energy Aware Routing Protocol For Zigbee Networks. *Journal of Computer Applications*, *4*(3), 92–94.

Annavaram, M. (2011). A case for guarded power gating for multi-core processors. *Proceedings of the 2011 IEEE 17th International Symposium on High Performance Computer Architecture (HPCA)* (pp. 291–300).

Appel, A. W. (1997). *Modern Compiler Implementation in C: Basic Techniques*. New York: Cambridge University Press. doi:10.1017/CBO9781139174930

Apple. (2015a). iCloud. Retrieved from http://www.apple.com/icloud/

Apple. (2015b). Siri. Retrieved from http://www.apple.com/ios/siri/

Araiza Leon, J. C. (2015). *Evaluation of IEEE 802.11 ah Technology for Wireless Sensor Network Applications* [Master's thesis]. Tampere University of Technology.

Arcas, O., Kirchhofer, P., Sönmez, N., Schindewolf, M., Unsal, O. S., Karl, W., & Cristal, A. (2012). A low-overhead profiling and visualization framework for Hybrid Transactional Memory. *Proceedings of the 2012 IEEE 20th Annual International Symposium on In Field-Programmable Custom Computing Machines (FCCM)* (pp. 1–8). IEEE.

Armbrust, M., Fox, A., Griffith, R., Joseph, A. D., Katz, R., Konwinski, A., & Stoica, I. et al. (2010). A view of cloud computing. *Communications of the ACM*, *53*(4), 50–58. doi:10.1145/1721654.1721672

Arora, M., Manne, S., Eckert, Y., Paul, I., Jayasena, N., & Tullsen, D. (2014). A comparison of core power gating strategies implemented in modern hardware. Proceedings of the 2014 ACM international conference on Measurement and modeling of computer systems (pp. 559–560). ACM. doi:doi:10.1145/2591971.2592017 doi:10.1145/2591971.2592017

Asha, M. M. (2012). Analysis of PS Protocols Using Markov and Cluster Model in 802.11 WLANS. *Analysis*, *2*(2), 298–305.

Ashton, K. (22 July 2009). That 'Internet of Things' Thing. *RFID Journal*. Retrieved from http://www.rfidjournal.com/article/view/4986

Assunc̣, M. D., Calheiros, R. N., Bianchi, S., Netto, M. A., & Buyya, R. (2014). Big data computing and clouds: Trends and future directions. *Journal of Parallel and Distributed Computing*, *79-80*, 3–15. doi:10.1016/j.jpdc.2014.08.003

Atzori, L., Iera, A., & Morabito, G. (2010). The internet of things: A survey. *Computer Networks*, *54*(15), 2787–2805. doi:10.1016/j.comnet.2010.05.010

Aust, S., Prasad, R. V., & Niemegeers, I. G. (2012). IEEE 802.11 ah: Advantages in standards and further challenges for sub 1 GHz Wi-Fi. *Paper presented at the IEEE International Conference on Communications (ICC)*, Ottawa, Canada.

Awan, A., Ferreira, R. A., Jagannathan, S., & Grama, A. (2005). Unstructured Peer-to-Peer Networks for Sharing Processor Cycles. *Parallel Computing, 32*(2), 115–135. doi:10.1016/j.parco.2005.09.002

Azodolmolky, S., Wieder, P., & Yahyapour, R. (2013). Cloud computing networking: Challenges and opportunities for innovations. *Communications Magazine, IEEE, 51*(7), 54–62. doi:10.1109/MCOM.2013.6553678

Baccarelli, E., & Biagi, M. (2003a). Optimized power allocation and signal shaping for interference-limited multi-antenna "ad hoc" networks. In Personal Wireless Communications, LNCS (Vol. 2775, pp. 138-152). Springer Verlag.

Baccarelli, E., & Biagi, M. (2003b). Error resistant space-time coding for emerging 4G-WLANs. Proceedings of WCNC'03 (pp.72-77).

Baccarelli, E., & Biagi, M. (2004). Power–allocation policy and optimized design of multiple-antenna systems with imperfect channel estimation. *IEEE Transactions on Vehicular Technology, 52*(1), 136–145. doi:10.1109/TVT.2003.822025

Baccarelli, E., Biagi, M., Bruno, R., Conti, M., & Gregori, E. (2005). Broadband wireless access networks: a road map on emerging trends and standards. In *Broadband services: business models and technologies for community networks* (pp. 215–240). John Wiley & Sons. doi:10.1002/0470022515.ch14

Baccarelli, E., Cordeschi, N., & Patriarca, T. (2012). Jointly optimal source-flow, transmit-power, and sending-rate control for maximum-throughput delivery of VBR traffic over faded links. *IEEE Transactions on Mobile Computing, 11*(3), 390–401. doi:10.1109/TMC.2011.68

Baig, M., & Gholamhosseini, H. (2013). Smart Health Monitoring Systems: An Overview of Design and Modeling. *Journal of Medical Systems, 37*(2), 1–14. doi:10.1007/s10916-012-9898-z PMID:23321968

Bailey, D., Harris, T., Saphir, W., Wijngaart, R. V. D., Woo, A., & Yarrow, M. (1995). *The NAS Parallel Benchmarks 2.0*. Moffett Field, CA: NAS Systems Division, NASA Ames Research Center.

Baker, N. (2005). ZigBee and Bluetooth: Strengths and weaknesses for industrial applications. *Computing & Control Engineering Journal, 16*(2), 20–25. doi:10.1049/cce:20050204

Balart, J., Duran, A., Gonzàlez, M., Martorell, X., Ayguadé, E., & Labarta, J. (2004). Nanos mercurium: a research compiler for OpenMP. *Proceedings of the European Workshop on OpenMP* 8, 103-109.

Balasangameshwara, J., & Raju, N. (2012). A hybrid policy for fault tolerant load balancing in grid computing environments. *Network and Computer Applications, 35*(1), 412–422. doi:10.1016/j.jnca.2011.09.005

Baliga, J., Ayre, R. W., Hinton, K., & Tucker, R. (2011). Green cloud computing: Balancing energy in processing, storage, and transport. *Proceedings of the IEEE, 99*(1), 149–167. doi:10.1109/JPROC.2010.2060451

Ballani, H., Costa, P., Karagiannis, T., & Rowstron, A. (2011). Towards predictable datacenter networks. *Computer Communication Review, 41*(4), 242–253. doi:10.1145/2043164.2018465

Bandara, H. D., & Jayasumana, A. P. (2013). Distributed, multi-user, multi-application, and multi-sensor data fusion over named data networks. *Computer Networks, 57*(16), 3235–3248. doi:10.1016/j.comnet.2013.07.033

Banning, J. (1979). An efficient way to find side effects of procedure calls and aliases of variables.*Proceedings of ACM SIGACT/SIGPLAN Symposium on Principles of Programming Languages (POPL'79)*, San Antonio, Texas, USA. ACM. doi:10.1145/567752.567756

Barcelona Supercomputing Center. (2015, June 15). *Extrae*. Retrieved from http://www.bsc.es/computer-sciences/extrae

Barcelona Supercomputing Center. (2015, June 15). *Nanos++*. Retrieved from https://pm.bsc.es/projects/nanox

Barcelona Supercomputing Center. (2015, June 15). *Paraver.* Retrieved from http://www.bsc.es/computer-sciences/performance-tools/paraver

Barnes, B. J., Rountree, B., Lowenthal, D. K., & Reeves, J., B. Supinski de, & Schulz M. (2008). A regression-based approach to scalability prediction. *Proceedings of International Conference on Supercomputing (ICS'08),* Island of Kos, Aegean Sea, Greece, USA. ACM.

Barnes, G. H., Brown, R. M., Kato, M., Kuck, D. J., Slotnick, D. L., & Stokes, R. A. (1968). The ILLIAC IV Computer. *IEEE Transactions on Computers, C-17*(8), 746–757. doi:10.1109/TC.1968.229158

Barros, R. C., Basgalupp, M. P., De Carvalho, A. C., & Freitas, A. (2012). A survey of evolutionary algorithms for decision-tree induction. *Systems, Man, and Cybernetics, Part C: Applications and Reviews. IEEE Transactions on, 42*(3), 291–312.

Basu, D., Moretti, G., Gupta, G. S., & Marsland, S. (2013). Wireless sensor network based smart home: Sensor selection, deployment and monitoring. *Paper presented at the 2013 IEEE Sensors Applications Symposium (SAS),* Galveston, USA. doi:doi:10.1109/SAS.2013.6493555 doi:10.1109/SAS.2013.6493555

Bejarano, O., Knightly, E. W., & Park, M. (2013). IEEE 802.11 ac: From channelization to multi-user MIMO. *IEEE Communications Magazine, 51*(10), 84–90. doi:10.1109/MCOM.2013.6619570

Bellard, F. (2005). Qemu, a fast and portable dynamic translator. *Proceedings of usenix annual technical conference.* ACM.

Benzi, F., Anglani, N., Bassi, E., & Frosini, L. (2011). Electricity smart meters interfacing the households. *IEEE Transactions on Industrial Electronics, 58*(10), 4487–4494. doi:10.1109/TIE.2011.2107713

Bernaschi, M., Fatica, M., Melchiona, S., Succi, S., & Kaxiras, E. (2010). A flexible high- performance lattice boltzmann gpu code for the simulations of fluid flows in complex geometries. *Concurrency Computa.: Pract. Exper., 22*(1), 1–14. doi:10.1002/cpe.1466

Binkert, N., Beckmann, B., Black, G., Reinhardt, S. K., Saidi, A., Basu, A., & Wood, D. A. (2011, August). The gem5 simulator. *SIGARCH Comput. Archit. News, 39*(2), 1–7. doi:10.1145/2024716.2024718

Blagov, M. (n.d.). *DDoS Attack Glossary.* Retrieved November 13, 2015, from www.incapsula.com

Bluetooth SIG. (2001). Bluetooth specification version 1.1. Retrieved from http://www.bluetooth.com

Bluetooth Smart Technology. (2015). Powering the Internet of Things. Retrieved from http://www.bluetooth.com/Pages/Bluetooth-Smart.aspx

Bluetooth, S. I. G. (2012). Bluetooth Core Version 4.0. Retrieved from https://www.bluetooth.org/Technical/Specifications/adopted.htm

Bobba, J., Goyal, N., Hill, M. D., Swift, M. M., & Wood, D. A. (2008). Tokentm: Efficient execution of large transactions with hardware transactional memory. ACM SIGARCH Computer Architecture News, 36(3), pp. 127–138. IEEE Computer Society.

Bobba, J., Moore, K. E., Volos, H., Yen, L., Hill, M. D., Swift, M. M., & Wood, D. A. (2007). Performance pathologies in hardware transactional memory. In *ACM SIGARCH Computer Architecture News* (Vol. 35, pp. 81–91). ACM.

Bohli, J.-M., Skarmeta, A., Victoria Moreno, M., Garcia, D., & Langendorfer, P. (2015). SMARTIE project: Secure IoT data management for smart cities. *Paper presented at the 2015 International Conference on Recent Advances in Internet of Things (RIoT),* Singapore. doi:doi:10.1109/RIOT.2015.7104906 doi:10.1109/RIOT.2015.7104906

Bonabeau, E. (2002). Agent-based modeling: Methods and techniques for simulating human systems. Proceedings of the National Academy of Sciences of the United States of America, 99(Suppl. 3), 7280–7287. PubMed PMID:12011407

Bos, J. W., Osvik, D. A., & Stefan, D. (2009). *Fast Implementations of AES on Various Platforms.* IACR Cryptology ePrint ArchiveR.

Bosilca, G., Bouteiller, A., Cappello, F., Djilali, S., Fedak, G., Germain, C., Selikhov, A. (2002, November). MPICH-V: Toward a scalable fault tolerant MPI for volatile nodes. *Proceedings of Supercomputing, ACM/IEEE 2002 Conference* (pp. 29-29). IEEE.

Bosilca, G., Coti, C., Herault, T., Lemarinier, P., & Dongarra, J. (2009). *Constructing Resiliant Communication Infrastructure for Runtime Environments* (pp. 441–451). PARCO.

Bosilca, G., Delmas, R., Dongarra, J., & Langou, J. (2009). Algorithm-based fault tolerance applied to high performance computing. *Journal of Parallel and Distributed Computing*, 69(4), 410–416. doi:10.1016/j.jpdc.2008.12.002

Boulos, M. N. K., & Al-Shorbaji, N. M. (2014). On the Internet of Things, smart cities and the WHO Healthy Cities. *International Journal of Health Geographics*, 13(10). PMID:24669838

Bouteiller, A., Cappello, F., Herault, T., Krawezik, G., Lemarinier, P., & Magniette, F. (2003, November). MPICH-V2: a fault tolerant MPI for volatile nodes based on pessimistic sender based message logging.*Proceedings of the 2003 ACM/IEEE conference on Supercomputing* (p. 25). ACM. doi:10.1145/1048935.1050176

Bouteiller, A., Collin, B., Herault, T., Lemarinier, P., & Cappello, F. (2005, April). Impact of event logger on causal message logging protocols for fault tolerant mpi.*Proceedings of the 19th IEEE International Conference on Parallel and Distributed Processing Symposium* (pp. 97-97). IEEE. doi:10.1109/IPDPS.2005.249

Bouteiller, A., Herault, T., Krawezik, G., Lemarinier, P., & Cappello, F. (2006). MPICH-V project: A multiprotocol automatic fault-tolerant MPI. *International Journal of High Performance Computing Applications*, 20(3), 319–333. doi:10.1177/1094342006067469

Bouteiller, A., Lemarinier, P., Krawezik, G., & Cappello, K. (2003, December). Coordinated checkpoint versus message log for fault tolerant MPI.*Proceedings of the 2003 IEEE International Conference on Cluster Computing* (pp. 242-250). IEEE. doi:10.1109/CLUSTR.2003.1253321

Brandt, J., Schneider, K., Ahuja, S., & Shukla, S. K. (2010). The model checking view to clock Sgating and operand isolation. *Proceedings of the 2010 10th International Conference on Application of Concurrency to System Design (ACSD)* (pp. 181–190). IEEE.

Branover, A., Foley, D., & Steinman, M. (2012). AMD fusion APU: Llano. *IEEE Micro*, 32(2), 28–37. doi:10.1109/MM.2012.2

Braun, A., Neumann, S., Schmidt, S., Wichert, R., & Kuijper, A. (2014). Towards interactive car interiors: the active armrest. *Paper presented at the8th Nordic Conference on Human-Computer Interaction: Fun, Fast, Foundational*, Helsinki, Finland. doi:doi:10.1145/2639189.2670191 doi:10.1145/2639189.2670191

Brunner, R., Caminero, A. C., Rana, O. F., Freitag, F., & Navarro, L. (2012). Network-aware summarisation for resource discovery in P2P-content networks.*Future Generation Computer Systems*, 28(3), 563–572. doi:10.1016/j.future.2011.03.004

Buntinas, D., Coti, C., Herault, T., Lemarinier, P., Pilard, L., Rezmerita, A., & Cappello, F. et al. (2008). Blocking vs. non-blocking coordinated checkpointing for large-scale fault tolerant MPI protocols. *Future Generation Computer Systems*, 24(1), 73–84. doi:10.1016/j.future.2007.02.002

Butler, R., Gropp, W., & Lusk, E. (2001). Components and interfaces of a process management system for parallel programs. *Parallel Computing*, 27(11), 1417–1429. doi:10.1016/S0167-8191(01)00097-7

Cai, M., Frank, M., Chen, J., & Szekely, P. (2004). MAAN: A multi-attribute addressable network for grid information services. *Journal of Grid Computing*, 2(1), 3–14. doi:10.1007/s10723-004-1184-y

Cambell, S., & Mellander, J. (2011). Experiences with Intrusion Detection in High Performance Computing. In *Proceedings of the Cray User Group (CUG)*. Fairbanks, AK.

Caminero, A. C., Robles-Gómez, A., Ros, S., Hernández, R., & Tobarra, L. (2013). P2P-based resource discovery in dynamic grids allowing multi-attribute and range queries. *Parallel Computing*, 39(10), 615–637. doi:10.1016/j.parco.2013.08.003

Canalys. (2013). Mobile device market to reach 2.6 billion units by 2016. Retrieved from http://www.canalys.com/newsroom/mobile-device-market-reach-26-billion-units-2016

Cao, Z., Li, K., & Liu, Y. (2008). A Multi-Level Super Peer Based P2P Architecture. *In proceeding of the International Conference on Information Networking* (ICOIN), Busan. IEEE.

Caputo, D., Mainetti, L., Patrono, L., & Vilei, A. (2012). Implementation of the EXI schema on wireless sensor nodes using Contiki. *Paper presented at the 2012 Sixth International Conference on Innovative Mobile and Internet Services in Ubiquitous Computing (IMIS)*, Palermo, Italy.

Carrington, D. (2013). Tvilight: The 'talking' streetlamps that will lighten your heart (but not your wallet). *CNN*. Retrieved from http://edition.cnn.com/2013/07/18/tech/innovation/tvilight-street-lamps-roosegarde/

Castro, M., Jara, A. J., & Skarmeta, A. F. (2013). Smart lighting solutions for smart cities. *Paper presented at the 27th International Conference on Advanced Information Networking and Applications Workshops (WAINA)*, Barcelona, Spain.

Cederman, D., & Tsigas, P. (2008, June). On dynamic load balancing on graphics processors. *Proceedings of the 23rd ACM SIGGRAPH/EUROGRAPHICS symposium on Graphics hardware* (pp. 57-64). Aire-la-Ville, Switzerland: Eurographics Association.

Ceze, L., Tuck, J., Torrellas, J., & Cascaval, C. (2006). Bulk disambiguation of speculative threads in multiprocessors. ACM SIGARCH Computer Architecture News, 34(2), 227–238. ACM. doi:doi:10.1109/ISCA.2006.13 doi:10.1109/ISCA.2006.13

Chakraborty, A., Homayoun, H., Khajeh, A., Dutt, N., Eltawil, A., & Kurdahi, F. (2010). E< MC2: less energy through multi-copy cache. *Proceedings of the 2010 international conference on Compilers, architectures and synthesis for embedded systems* (pp. 237–246). ACM.

Chambers, C., Raniwala, A., Perry, F., Adams, S., Henry, R. R., Bradshaw, R., & Weizenbaum, N. (2010). FlumeJava: easy, efficient data-parallel pipelines. *Paper presented at the ACM Sigplan Notices*.

Chandler, C. F., Leangsuksun, C., & DeBardeleben, N. (2009). Towards Resilient High Performance Applications Through Real Time Reliability Metric Generation and Autonomous Failure Correction. In *Proceedings of the 2009 Workshop on Resiliency in High Performance (Resilience '09)*. Munich, Germany. doi:10.1145/1552526.1552527

Chandra, T. D., Griesemer, R., & Redstone, J. (2007). Paxos made live: an engineering perspective. *Paper presented at the Proceedings of the twenty-sixth annual ACM symposium on Principles of distributed computing*. doi:doi:10.1145/1281100.1281103 doi:10.1145/1281100.1281103

Chandra, R., Dagum, L., Kohr, D., Maydan, D., McDonald, J., & Menon, R. (2001). *Parallel programming in OpenMP*. San Francisco, CA: Morgan Kaufmann.

Chandy, K. M., & Lamport, L. (1985). Distributed snapshots: Determining global states of distributed systems. *ACM Transactions on Computer Systems, 3*(1), 63–75. doi:10.1145/214451.214456

Chang, C.-Y., Tso, P.-C., Huang, C.-H., & Yang, P.-H. (2012). A fast wake-up power gating technique with inducing a balanced rush current. *Proceedings of the 2012 IEEE International Symposium on Circuits and Systems (ISCAS)* (pp. 3086–3089). IEEE. doi:doi:10.1109/ISCAS.2012.6271972 doi:10.1109/ISCAS.2012.6271972

Chan, M., Campo, E., Estève, D., & Fourniols, J.-Y. (2009). Smart homes—current features and future perspectives. *Maturitas, 64*(2), 90–97. doi:10.1016/j.maturitas.2009.07.014 PMID:19729255

Chen, G. K., Fojtik, M., Kim, D., Fick, D., Park, J., Seok, M., . . . Blaauw, D. (2010). Millimeter-scale nearly perpetual sensor system with stacked battery and solar cells. Proceedings of ISSCC (Vol. 10, pp. 288–289). doi:doi:10.1109/ISSCC.2010.5433921 doi:10.1109/ISSCC.2010.5433921

Chen, W.-H., Chang, H.-H., Hung, J.-H., & Hsieh, T.-M. (2012). Clock tree construction using gated clock cloning. *Proceedings of the 2012 4th Asia Symposium on Quality Electronic Design (ASQED)* (pp. 54–58). IEEE.

Chen, D., Nixon, M., & Mok, A. (2010). *WirelessHART*. Springer. doi:10.1007/978-1-4419-6047-4

Chen, H., Chen, W., Huang, J., Robert, B., & Kuhn, H. (2006). MPIPP: an automatic profile-guided parallel process placement toolset for SMP clusters and multi-clusters.*Proceedings of International Conference on Supercomputing (ICS'06)*. Cairns, Australia. doi:10.1145/1183401.1183451

Chen, S. H., & Pollino, C. A. (2012). Good practice in Bayesian network modelling. *Environmental Modelling & Software, 37*, 134–145. doi:10.1016/j.envsoft.2012.03.012

Chen, S., Zhang, Z., Chen, S., & Shi, B. (2008). Efficient file search in non-DHT P2P networks. *Computer Communications, 31*(2), 304–317. doi:10.1016/j.comcom.2007.08.011

Chen, T. M., & Jamil, N. (2006). Effectiveness of Quarantine in Worm Epidemic, In *Proceedings of the IEEE International Conference on Communications*.

Chen, T. M., Zhang, X.-, Li, H.-, Wang, D., & Wu, Y. (2013). Propagation Modeling of Active P2P Worms Based On Ternary Matrix. *Journal of Network and Computer Applications, 36*(5), 1387–1394. doi:10.1016/j.jnca.2013.02.032

Chen, T., Zhang, X., & Wu, Y. (2014). FPM: Four-Factors Propagation Model for Passive P2P Worms. *Future Generation Computer Systems, 36*, 133–141. doi:10.1016/j.future.2013.06.025

Chen, X.-W., & Lin, X. (2014). Big data deep learning: Challenges and perspectives. *Access, 2*, 514–525. doi:10.1109/ACCESS.2014.2325029

Chen, Z., & Dongarra, J. (2009). Algorithm-based Fault Tolerance for Fail-Stop Failures. *IEEE Transactions on Parallel and Distributed Systems, 9*(12).

Che, S., Boyer, M., Meng, J., Tarjan, D., Sheaffer, J. W., Lee, S.-H., & Skadron, K. (2009). Rodinia: A benchmark suite for heterogeneous computing.*Proceedings of IEEE international symposium on workload characterization (IISWC)*. IEEE. doi:10.1109/IISWC.2009.5306797

Che, S., Sheaffer, J. W., & Skadron, K. (2011, November). Dymaxion: optimizing memory access patterns for heterogeneous systems.*Proceedings of the 2011 International Conference for High Performance Computing, Networking, Storage, and Analysis*. ACM. doi:10.1145/2063384.2063401

Chi, T.-Y., Chen, C.-H., Chao, H.-C., & Kuo, S.-Y. (2011). An Efficient Earthquake Early Warning Message Delivery Algorithm Using an in Time Control-Theoretic Approach. In C.-H. Hsu, L. Yang, J. Ma, & C. Zhu (Eds.), Ubiquitous Intelligence and Computing (Vol. 6905, pp. 161-173): Springer Berlin Heidelberg. doi:doi:10.1007/978-3-642-23641-9_15 doi:10.1007/978-3-642-23641-9_15

Chodnekar, S., Srinivasan, V., Vaidya, A. S., Sivasubramaniam, A., & Das, C. R. (1997). Towards a communication characterization methodology for parallel applications. *Proceedings of High-Performance Computer Architecture HPCA '97,* San Antonio, TX, USA. IEEE. doi:10.1109/HPCA.1997.569693

Cholvi, V., Felber, P., & Biersack, E. (2004). Efficient search in unstructured peer-to-peer networks. *Euroapen Transection on Telecomunications, 15*(6), 535–548. doi:10.1002/ett.1017

Chong, Z., Qin, B., Bandyopadhyay, T., Wongpiromsarn, T., Rebsamen, B., Dai, P., & Ang, M. H. Jr. (2013). *Autonomy for mobility on demand Intelligent Autonomous Systems 12* (pp. 671–682). Springer. doi:10.1007/978-3-642-33926-4_64

Chou, C.-M., Li, C.-Y., Chien, W.-M., & Lan, K.-c. (2009). A feasibility study on vehicle-to-infrastructure communication: WiFi vs. WiMAX. *Paper presented at theTenth International Conference on Mobile Data Management: Systems, Services and Middleware,* Taipei, Taiwan. doi:doi:10.1109/MDM.2009.127 doi:10.1109/MDM.2009.127

Choudhury, N., Mehta, Y., Wlmarth, T. L., Bohm, E. J., & Kalé, L. V. (2005). Scaling an optimistic parallel simulation of large-scale interconnection networks.*Proceedings of the 2005 Winter Simulation Conference (WSC'05),* Huntington Beach. IEEE. doi:10.1109/WSC.2005.1574299

Chowdhury, N., Bhuiyan, M. M. H., & Islam, S. (2013). IOT: Detection of Keys, Controlling Machines and Wireless Sensing Via Mesh Networking Through Internet. *Global Journal of Researches In Engineering, 13*(13).

Chun, B.-G., Ihm, S., Maniatis, P., & Naik, M. (2010). Clonecloud: boosting mobile device applications through cloud clone execution. *arXiv preprint arXiv:1009.3088.*

Cinlar, E. (2013). *Introduction to Stochastic Processes.* Dover.

Clarke, R. Y. (2013). *Smart Cities and the Internet of Everything: The Foundation for Delivering Next-Generation Citizen Services.* Alexandria, VA: Tech. Rep.

Clendenin, M. (2010). China's 'Internet Of Things' Overblown, Says Exec. *Information Week.* Retrieved from http://www.informationweek.com/news/storage/virtualization/225700966?subSection=News

Click, C. (2009). Azul's experiences with hardware transactional memory. *Proceedings of theTransactional Memory Workshop.*

CompuGreen. (2015, June). *Green500 list.* Retrieved from http://green500.org/news/green500-list-june-2015

Connected Car Forecast: Global Connected Car Market to Grow Threefold Within Five Years. (2014). Retrieved from www.gsma.com

Conte, S. D., & de Boor, C. (1976). *Elementary Numerical Analysis.* New York: McGraw-Hill.

Cordeschi, N., Amendola, D., & Baccarelli, E. (2014a). Primary-secondary resource-management on vehicular networks under soft and hard collision constraints.*Proceedings of the fourth ACM international symposium on Development and analysis of intelligent vehicular networks and applications* (pp. 161-168). ACM. doi:10.1145/2656346.2656362

Cordeschi, N., Polli, V., & Baccarelli, E. (2012). Traffic engineering for wireless connectionless access networks supporting QoS-demanding media applications. *Computer Networks, 56*(1), 186–197. doi:10.1016/j.comnet.2011.08.016

Cordeschi, N., Shojafar, M., Amendola, D., & Baccarelli, E. (2014b). Energy-efficient adaptive networked datacenters for the QoS support of real-time applications. *The Journal of Supercomputing*, *71*(2), 448–478. doi:10.1007/s11227-014-1305-8

Cordeschi, N., Shojafar, M., Amendola, D., & Baccarelli, E. (2015). Energy-Saving QoS Resource Management of Virtualized Networked Data Centers for Big Data Stream Computing. In S. Bagchi (Ed.), *Emerging Research in Cloud Distributed Computing Systems* (pp. 122–155). Hershey, PA, USA: IGI Global. doi:10.4018/978-1-4666-8213-9.ch004

Cordeschi, N., Shojafar, M., & Baccarelli, E. (2013). Energy-saving self-configuring networked data centers. *Computer Networks*, *57*(17), 3479–3491. doi:10.1016/j.comnet.2013.08.002

Coti, C. (2015). Exploiting Redundant Computation in Communication-Avoiding Algorithms for Algorithm-Based Fault Tolerance. *arXiv preprint arXiv:1511.00212.*

Coti, C., Herault, T., Lemarinier, P., Pilard, L., Rezmerita, A., Rodriguez, E., & Cappello, F. (2006, November). Blocking vs. non-blocking coordinated checkpointing for large-scale fault tolerant MPI.*Proceedings of the 2006 ACM/IEEE conference on Supercomputing* (p. 127). ACM. doi:10.1145/1188455.1188587

Crespo, A., & Garcia-Molina, H. (2002). Routing indices for peer-to-peer systems.*Proceeding of the International Conference on Distributed Computing SystemsICDCS,*Vienna, Austria. IEEE. doi:10.1109/ICDCS.2002.1022239

Crowd Studios. (2015, June 15). *Golaem.* Retrieved from http://www.golaem.com

Cuervo, E., Balasubramanian, A., Cho, D.-k., Wolman, A., Saroiu, S., Chandra, R., & Bahl, P. (2010). MAUI: making smartphones last longer with code offload. *Paper presented at theProceedings of the 8th international conference on Mobile systems, applications, and services.* doi:doi:10.1145/1814433.1814441 doi:10.1145/1814433.1814441

cuFFT. (n. d.). Retrieved from http://developer.nvidia.com/cuda/cufft

Cugola, G., & Margara, A. (2012). Processing flows of information: From data stream to complex event processing. *ACM Computing Surveys*, *44*(3), 15. doi:10.1145/2187671.2187677

Culler, D. E., Gupta, A., & Singh, J. P. (1997). *Parallel Computer Architecture: A Hardware/Software Approach.* San Francisco, CA, USA: Morgan Kaufmann Publishers Inc.

Czesla, S., Schroter, S., Schneider, C. P., Huber, K. F., & Pfeifer, F. (2015)*Pyastronomy.* from http://www.hs.uni-hamburg.de/DE/Ins/Per/Czesla/PyA/PyA/index.html

D. Tarjan, S. Thoziyoor, & N. P. Jouppi. (2006). CACTI 4.0. *HP Laboratories Palo Alto.*

Da Xu, L., He, W., & Li, S. (2014). Internet of things in industries: A survey. *IEEE Transactions on Industrial Informatics*, *10*(4), 2233–2243. doi:10.1109/TII.2014.2300753

Daemen, J., & Rijmen, V. (1999). *AES proposal: Rijndael.* Retrieved from http://www.science.upm.ro/~apetrescu/OLD/public_html/Tehnologia%20Informatiei/Securitatea%20informatiei/Laborator/AES/rijndael%20doc%20V2.pdf

Daghighi, B., Kiah, M. L. M., Shamshirband, S., & Rehman, M. H. (2015). Toward secure group communication in wireless mobile environments: Issues, solutions, and challenges. *Journal of Network and Computer Applications*, *50*, 1–14. doi:10.1016/j.jnca.2014.11.001

Daliri, Z. S., Shamshirband, S., & Besheli, M. A. (2011). Railway security through the use of wireless sensor networks based on fuzzy logic. *Int. J. Phys. Sci*, *6*(3), 448–458.

Dally, W. J., Labonte, F., Das, A., Hanrahan, P., Ahn, J., Gummaraju, J., & Kapasi, U. J. et al. (2003). Supercomputing with streams.*Proceedings of the ACM/IEEE Conference on Supercomputing* (pp. 35).

Daly, J. (2006). A Higher Order Estimate of the Optimum Checkpoint Interval for Restart Dumps. *Future Generation Computer Systems*, *22*(3), 303–312. doi:10.1016/j.future.2004.11.016

Daly, J., Pritchett, L., & Michalak, S. (2008). Application MTTFE vs. Platform MTBF: A Fresh Perspective on System Reliability and Application Throughput for Computations at Scale. In *Proceedings of the IEEE Symposium on Cluster Computing and the Grid*. Lyon, France. doi:10.1109/CCGRID.2008.103

Das, T., & Sivalingam, K. M. (2013). TCP improvements for data center networks. *Proceedings of the 2013 fifth international conference on Communication systems and networks* (pp. 1–10). doi:doi:10.1109/COMSNETS.2013.6465539 doi:10.1109/COMSNETS.2013.6465539

Data, S., & Wang, H. (2005). The Effectiveness of Vaccinations on the Spread of Email-Borne Computer Viruses. In *Proceedings of the IEEE Canadian Conference on Electrical and Computer Engineering*. Saskatoon, Canada. doi:10.1109/CCECE.2005.1556914

Daud, S., Ahmad, R. B., & Lynn, O. B. (2014). CPU Power Prediction on Modern Multicore Embedded Processor. *International journal of Computer Science and Mobile Computing*, *3*(2), 709–715. IJCSMC.

Davidson, A. A., Zhang, Y., & Owens, J. D. (2011). An Auto-tuned Method for Solving Large Tridiagonal Systems on the GPU.*Proceedings of the 25th IEEE International Symposium on Parallel and Distributed Processing* (pp. 956-965). doi:10.1109/IPDPS.2011.92

Dawson, B. (1976). Vibration condition monitoring techniques for rotating machinery. *The shock and vibration digest*, *8*, 12.

De Vegt, R. (2008). 802.11 ac Usage Models Document. *IEEE 802.11-09/0161r2*.

DeBardeleben, N., Blanchard, S., Guan, Q., Zhang, Z., & Fu, S. (2011). *Experimental framework for injecting logic errors in a virtual machine to profile applications for soft error resilience*. *Proceedings of Euro-par workshops*. ACM.

DeBardeleben, N., Laros, J., Daly, J. T., Scott, S. L., Engelmann, C., & Harrod, B. (2009). *High-end computing resilience: Analysis of issues facing the HEC community and path-forward for research and development (Whitepaper)*. DOE.

DeBarteleben, N., Laros, J., Daly, J., Scott, S., Engelmann, C., & Harrod, W. (2009). *High-End Computing Resilience: Analysis of Issues facing the HEC Community and Path Forward for Research and Development. (Whitepaper)*. Oak Ridge, TN: Oak Ridge National Laboratory.

Debnath, A. K., Chin, H. C., Haque, M. M., & Yuen, B. (2014). A methodological framework for benchmarking smart transport cities. *Cities (London, England)*, *37*, 47–56. doi:10.1016/j.cities.2013.11.004

Delen, D., & Demirkan, H. (2013). Data, information and analytics as services. *Decision Support Systems*, *55*(1), 359–363. doi:10.1016/j.dss.2012.05.044

Dementyev, A., Hodges, S., Taylor, S., & Smith, J. (2013). Power Consumption Analysis of Bluetooth Low Energy, ZigBee and ANT Sensor Nodes in a Cyclic Sleep Scenario. *Microsoft Research*.

Demmel, J., Grigori, L., Hoemmen, M., & Langou, J. (2008). Communication-avoiding parallel and sequential QR factorizations. *CoRR abs/0806.2159*.

Deng, Y., Wang, F., & Ciura, A. (2009). Ant colony optimization in spired resource discovery in P2P Grid systems. *The Journal of Supercomputing*, *49*(1), 4–21. doi:10.1007/s11227-008-0214-0

Dennard, R. H., Gaensslen, F. H., Rideout, V. L., Bassous, E., & LeBlanc, A. R. (1974). Design of ion-implanted mosfet's with very small physical dimensions. *IEEE Journal of Solid-State Circuits*, *9*(5), 256–268. doi:10.1109/JSSC.1974.1050511

Denning, J. P., & Dennis, B. J. (2010). The resurgence of parallelism. *Communications of the ACM*, *53*(6), 30–32. doi:10.1145/1743546.1743560

Desilles, G. (1998). *Differential Kolmogorov Equations for Transiting Processes.* (Masters thesis). Massachusetts Institute of Technology, Boston, MA.

Dice, D., Lev, Y., Moir, M., Nussbaum, D., & Olszewski, M. (2009). *Early experience with a commercial hardware transactional memory implementation.* Sun Microsystems. doi:10.1145/1508244.1508263

Dillen, S. J., Priore, D., Horiuchi, A. K., & Naffziger, S. D. (2012, September). Design and implementation of soft-edge flip-flops for x86-64 AMD microprocessor modules. *Proceedings of theCustom Integrated Circuits Conference CICC'12* (pp. 1-4). IEEE. doi:doi:10.1109/CICC.2012.6330707 doi:10.1109/CICC.2012.6330707

Dlodlo, N., & Kalezhi, J. (2015). The internet of things in agriculture for sustainable rural development. *Paper presented at the2015 International Conference on Emerging Trends in Networks and Computer Communications (ETNCC)*, Namibia. doi:doi:10.1109/ETNCC.2015.7184801 doi:10.1109/ETNCC.2015.7184801

Domingo, M. C. (2012). An overview of the internet of underwater things. *Journal of Network and Computer Applications*, *35*(6), 1879–1890. doi:10.1016/j.jnca.2012.07.012

Donfack, S., Grigori, L., & Gupta, A. K. (2010, April). Adapting communication-avoiding LU and QR factorizations to multicore architectures.*Proceedings of the International Symposium on Parallel & Distributed Processing (IPDPS)* (pp. 1-10). IEEE. doi:10.1109/IPDPS.2010.5470348

Donno, M., Ivaldi, A., Benini, L., & Macii, E. (2003). Clock-tree power optimization based on RTL clock-gating. Proceedings of the Design Automation Conference (pp. 622–627). IEEE.

Dramsvik, B. (2009). Adaptive Street Lighting: A Way Forward to Improve ITS-Implementation as Well as Increase Road Safety and to Save Energy. *Paper presented at the16th ITS World Congress and Exhibition on Intelligent Transport Systems and Services.*

Draper, N. R., & Smith, H. (2014). *Applied regression analysis.* John Wiley & Sons.

DropBox. (2015). Retrieved from www.dropbox.com/android

Drugarin, C. V. A., Ahmad, M. A., Ahmad, N. A., & Lyashenko, V. (2015). Algorithmic Research and Application Using the Rayleigh Method. *Int. Journal of Science & Research*, *4*(4), 1669–1671.

Duan, X. J. (2014). Research on IOT-Based Smart Garden Project. *Paper presented at the Applied Mechanics and Materials.* doi:doi:10.4028/www.scientific.net/AMM.608-609.321 doi:10.4028/www.scientific.net/AMM.608-609.321

Duran, A., Ayguadé, E., Badia, R. M., Labarta, J., Martinell, L., Martorell, X., & Planas, J. (2011). OmpSs: A proposal for programming heterogeneous multi-core architectures. Parallel Processing Letters, 21(2), 173–193.

Duta, C. L., Michiu, G., Stoica, S., & Gheorghe, L. (2013, May). Accelerating encryption algorithms using parallelism. *Proceedings of the 2013 19th International Conference on Control Systems and Computer Science* (pp. 549-554). IEEE. doi:10.1109/CSCS.2013.92

Dwarkadas, S., Shriraman, A., & Scott, M. (2014). *Mechanism to support flexible decoupled transactional memory.* Google Patents.

Ebadi, S., & Mohammad Khanli, L. (2011). A new distributed and hierarchical mechanism for service discovery in a grid environment. *Future Generation Computer Systems*, *19*(5), 836–842. doi:10.1016/j.future.2010.11.011

Elahi, A., & Gschwender, A. (2009). *ZigBee wireless sensor and control network.* Pearson Education.

Elkhodr, M., Shahrestani, S., & Cheung, H. (2011a). An approach to enhance the security of remote health monitoring systems. *Paper presented at the 4th international conference on Security of information and networks*, Sydney, Australia. doi:doi:10.1145/2070425.2070458 doi:10.1145/2070425.2070458

Elkhodr, M., Shahrestani, S., & Cheung, H. (2013). A contextual-adaptive location disclosure agent for general devices in the internet of things. *Paper presented at the EEE 38th Conference on Local Computer Networks Workshops (LCN Workshops)*, Sydney, Australia. doi:doi:10.1109/LCNW.2013.6758522 doi:10.1109/LCNW.2013.6758522

Elkhodr, M., Shahrestani, S., & Cheung, H. (2013). The Internet of Things: Vision & Challenges. *Paper presented at the IEEE Tencon*, Sydney, Australia. doi:doi:10.1109/TENCONSpring.2013.6584443 doi:10.1109/TENCONSpring.2013.6584443

Elkhodr, M., Shahrestani, S., & Cheung, H. (2014). A semantic obfuscation technique for the Internet of Things. *Paper presented at the IEEE International Conference on Communications Workshops (ICC)*, Sydney, Australia. doi:doi:10.1109/ICCW.2014.6881239 doi:10.1109/ICCW.2014.6881239

Elkhodr, M., Shahrestani, S., & Cheung, H. (2011b). Ubiquitous health monitoring systems: Addressing security concerns. *Journal of Computer Science*, 7(10), 1465–1473. doi:10.3844/jcssp.2011.1465.1473

Elkhodr, M., Shahrestani, S., & Cheung, H. (2016). *Wireless Enabling Technologies for the Internet of Things Innovative Research and Applications in Next-Generation High Performance Computing*. Hershey, PA, USA: IGI Global.

Elnozahy, E. N., Alvisi, L., Wang, Y. M., & Johnson, D. B. (1996). A Survey of Rollback-Recovery Protocols in Message-Passing Systems (Technical Report CMU-CS-96-181). Carnegie Mellon Univ.

Elnozahy, E. N., Alvisi, L., Wang, Y. M., & Johnson, D. B. (2002). A survey of rollback-recovery protocols in message-passing systems. *ACM Computing Surveys*, 34(3), 375–408. doi:10.1145/568522.568525

Englemann, C., Vallee, G., Naughton, T., & Scott, S. (2009). Proactive Fault Tolerance Using Preemptive Migration. In *Proceedings of 17th Euromicro International Conference on Parallel, Distributed, and Network-Based Processing*.

Enriquez, P., Brown, A., & Patterson, D. A. (2002). Lessons from the PSTN for Dependable Computing. In *Proceedings of the Workshop on Self-Healing, Adaptive and Self-Managed Systems*.

Erdil, D. C. (2012). Simulating peer-to-peer cloud resource scheduling. *Peer-to-Peer Networking and Applications*, 5(3), 219–230. doi:10.1007/s12083-011-0112-8

Erol-Kantarci, M., & Mouftah, H. T. (2011). Wireless sensor networks for cost-efficient residential energy management in the smart grid. *IEEE Transactions on Smart Grid*, 2(2), 314–325. doi:10.1109/TSG.2011.2114678

Esmaeilzadeh, H., Blem, E., St. Amant, R., Sankaralingam, K., & Burger, D. (2011). Dark silicon and the end of multicore scaling. *Proceedings of the 38th Annual International Symposium on Computer Architecture* (pp 365-376). ACM press. doi:10.1145/2000064.2000108

Esser, R., & Knecht, R. (1993). Intel paragon xp/s - architecture and software environment. In *Proceedings of Supercomputer* (pp. 121–141). Springer Berlin Heidelberg. doi:10.1007/978-3-642-78348-7_13

Evans, D. (2012). The internet of everything: How more relevant and valuable connections will change the world. *Cisco IBSG*.

Fagg, G. E., & Dongarra, J. J. (2000). FT-MPI: Fault tolerant MPI, supporting dynamic applications in a dynamic world. In Recent advances in parallel virtual machine and message passing interface (pp. 346-353). Springer Berlin Heidelberg.

Fagg, G. E., Gabriel, E., Bosilca, G., Angskun, T., Chen, Z., Pjesivac-Grbovic, J., & Dongarra, J. J. et al. (2004, June). Extending the MPI specification for process fault tolerance on high performance computing systems.*Proceedings of the International Supercomputer Conference (ICS)* (pp. 97-104).

Fagg, G. E., Gabriel, E., Chen, Z., Angskun, T., Bosilca, G., Pjesivac-Grbovic, J., & Dongarra, J. J. (2005). Process fault tolerance: Semantics, design and applications for high performance computing. *International Journal of High Performance Computing Applications, 19*(4), 465–477. doi:10.1177/1094342005056137

Faissol, G., & Gallagher, B. (2014). *The Price of Anarchy and Malice: A Game Theoretic Study of Targeted Failures in HPC Systems. (Technical report)*. Livermore, CA: Lawrence Livermore National Laboratory.

Fan, W., & Bifet, A. (2013). Mining big data: current status, and forecast to the future. *ACM sIGKDD Explorations Newsletter, 14*(2), 1-5.

Fan, W., & Yeung, K. (2013). Virus Propagation Modeling in Facebook. In *The Influence of Technology on Social Network Analysis and Mining*. Springer. doi:10.1007/978-3-7091-1346-2_8

Farahani, S. (2011). *ZigBee wireless networks and transceivers*. Newnes.

Farbotko, C., Walton, A., Mankad, A., & Gardner, J. (2014). Household rainwater tanks: Mediating changing relations with water? *Ecology and Society, 19*(2), 62. doi:10.5751/ES-06632-190262

Farkas, R. K. K., Jouppi, N. P., Ranganathan, P., & Tullsen, D. M. (2015). A Multi-Core Approach to Addressing the Energy-Complexity Problem in Microprocessors.*Proceedings of Workshop on Complexity-Effective Design*.

Farrar, C. R., & Worden, K. (2007). An introduction to structural health monitoring. *Philosophical Transactions of the Royal Society of London A: Mathematical, Physical and Engineering Sciences, 365*(1851), 303-315.

Fatica, M. (2009, March). Accelerating Linpack with CUDA on heterogenous clusters.*Proceedings of the 2nd Workshop on General Purpose Processing on Graphics Processing Units* (pp. 46-51). ACM. doi:10.1145/1513895.1513901

Favier, J., Revell, A., & Pinelli, A. (2014). A Lattice Boltzmann–Immersed Boundary method to simulate the fluid interaction with moving and slender flexible object. *Journal of Computational Physics, 261*(0), 145–161. doi:10.1016/j.jcp.2013.12.052

Feinleib, D. (2014). The Intersection of Big Data, Mobile, and Cloud Computing. In Big Data Bootcamp (pp. 85-101). Springer.

Ferrante, J., Ottenstein, K. J., & Warren, J. D. (1987). The program dependence graph and its use in optimization. *ACM Transactions on Programming Languages and Systems, 9*(3), 319–349. doi:10.1145/24039.24041

Ferro, L., Pierre, L., Amor, Z. B. H., Lachaize, J., & Lefftz, V. (2011). Runtime Verification of Typical Requirements for a Space Critical SoC Platform. In *Formal Methods for Industrial Critical Systems* (pp. 21–36). Springer. doi:10.1007/978-3-642-24431-5_4

FFT OpenMP. (n. d.). Retrieved from http://people.sc.fsu.edu/~jburkardt/c_src/fft_openmp/fft_openmp.html

FIPS. P. (2001, November). *Specification for the Advanced Encryption Standard*. Retrieved from http://csrc.nist.gov/publications/fips/fips197/fips-197.pdf

Firoozshahian, A. (2009). *Smart memories: A reconfigurable memory system architecture*. ProQuest.

Fisher, D. H. (1987). Knowledge acquisition via incremental conceptual clustering. *Machine Learning, 2*(2), 139–172. doi:10.1007/BF00114265

FISHPACK. (n. d.). Netlib. Retrieved from http://www.netlib.org/fishpack/

Ford, D., Labelle, F., Popovici, F. I., Stokely, M., Truong, V. A., Barroso, L., & Quinlan, S. et al. (2010, October). *Availability in Globally Distributed Storage Systems* (pp. 61–74). OSDI.

Foschini, L., Taleb, T., Corradi, A., & Bottazzi, D. (2011). M2M-based metropolitan platform for IMS-enabled road traffic management in IoT. *IEEE Communications Magazine, 49*(11), 50–57. doi:10.1109/MCOM.2011.6069709

Francesco, M. D., Li, N., Raj, M., & Das, S. K. (2012). A storage Infrastructure for Heterogeneous and Multimedia Data in the Internet of Things. *Paper presented at theIEEE International Conference on Green Computing and Communications (GreenCom)*, Besançon, France. doi:doi:10.1109/GreenCom.2012.15 doi:10.1109/GreenCom.2012.15

Fries, J. F., Koop, C. E., Sokolov, J., Beadle, C. E., & Wright, D. (1998). Beyond health promotion: Reducing need and demand for medical care. *Health Affairs, 17*(2), 70–84. doi:10.1377/hlthaff.17.2.70 PMID:9558786

Fung, W. W., Singh, I., Brownsword, A., & Aamodt, T. M. (2011). Hardware transactional memory for GPU architectures.*Proceedings of the 44th Annual IEEE/ACM International Symposium on Microarchitecture* (pp. 296–307). ACM.

Fung, W. W., Singh, I., Brownsword, A., & Aamodt, T. M. (2012). *Kilo tm: Hardware transactional memory for gpu architectures* (Vol. 3, pp. 7–16). IEEE Micro.

Gaber, M. M., Gomes, J. B., & Stahl, F. (2014). *Pocket data mining* (Vol. 2). Springer. doi:10.1007/978-3-319-02711-1

Gani, A., Siddiqa, A., Shamshirband, S., & Hanum, F. (2015). A survey on indexing techniques for big data: Taxonomy and performance evaluation. *Knowledge and Information Systems, 46*(2), 241-284.

Gaona, E., Titos-Gil, R., Acacio, M. E., & Fernández, J. (2012). Dynamic Serialization: Improving Energy Consumption in Eager-Eager Hardware Transactional Memory Systems. *Proceedings of the 2012 20th Euromicro International Conference on Parallel, Distributed and Network-Based Processing (PDP)* (pp. 221–228). IEEE.

Garbacki, P., Epema, D. H. J., & van Steen, M. (2007). Optimizing peer relationships in a super-peer network. *Proceeding of27th International Conference on Distributed Computing Systems ICDCS '07*, Toronto: IEEE. doi:doi:10.1109/ICDCS.2007.126 doi:10.1109/ICDCS.2007.126

Garbacki, P., Epema, D. H. J., & Steen, M. (2010). The design and evaluation of a self-organizing super-peer network. *Computers. IEEE Transactions., 59*(3), 317–331.

Gardiner, C. W. (1985). *Handbook of Stochastic Methods for Physics, Chemistry, and the Natural Sciences*. Springer-Verlag. doi:10.1007/978-3-662-02452-2

Gardner, E. (2014). *What public disclosures has Intel made about Knights Landing?* Intel Corporation.

Garland, M., & Kirk, D. B. (2010). Understanding throughput-oriented architectures. *Communications of the ACM, 53*(11), 58–66. doi:10.1145/1839676.1839694

Garlasu, D., Sandulescu, V., Halcu, I., Neculoiu, G., Grigoriu, O., Marinescu, M., & Marinescu, V. (2013). A big data implementation based on Grid computing. *Paper presented at the 2013 11th Roedunet International Conference (RoEduNet)*. doi:doi:10.1109/RoEduNet.2013.6511732 doi:10.1109/RoEduNet.2013.6511732

Geer, D. (2005). Chip makers turn to multicore processors. *Computer, 38*(5), 11–13. doi:10.1109/MC.2005.160

Geier, E. (2014). What's next for Wi-Fi? A second wave of 802.11ac devices, and then: 802.11ax. *PC World.* Retrieved from http://www.pcworld.com/article/2366929/what-s-next-for-wi-fi-a-second-wave-of-802-11ac-devices-and-then-802-11ax.html

Giurgiu, I., Riva, O., Juric, D., Krivulev, I., & Alonso, G. (2009). *Calling the cloud: enabling mobile phones as interfaces to cloud applications Middleware 2009* (pp. 83–102). Springer.

Gnumeric. (2012). Gnumeric spreadsheet. Retrieved from http://freecode.com/projects/gnumeric

Gomes, J. B., Krishnaswamy, S., Gaber, M. M., Sousa, P. A., & Menasalvas, E. (2012). Mars: a personalised mobile activity recognition system. *Paper presented at the 2012 IEEE 13th International Conference on Mobile Data Management (MDM).* doi:doi:10.1109/MDM.2012.33 doi:10.1109/MDM.2012.33

Gomez, C., Oller, J., & Paradells, J. (2012). Overview and evaluation of bluetooth low energy: An emerging low-power wireless technology. *Sensors (Basel, Switzerland), 12*(9), 11734–11753.

González, A., Aliagas, C., & Valero, M. (2014, June). A data cache with multiple caching strategies tuned to different types of locality. *Proceedings of the 25th Anniversary International Conference on Supercomputing Anniversary* (pp. 217-226). ACM. doi:doi:10.1145/2591635.2667170 doi:10.1145/2591635.2667170

Google. (2015a). Google App Engine Retrieved from http://appengine.google.com

Google. (2015b). Google App Frontend Instance Class. Retrieved from https://developers.google.com/appengine/docs/adminconsole/performancesettings

Google. (2015c). Google Apps for Business. Retrieved from http://www.google.com/enterprise/apps/business/

Graham, S. L., Kessler, P. B., & Mckusick, M. K. (1982). Gprof: A call graph execution profiler. *Proceedings of symposium on compiler construction.* ACM.

Gray, J. (1986). Why do computers stop and what can be done about it? In *Proceedings of the 5th Symposium on Reliability in Distributed Software and Database Systems.* Los Alamitos, CA.

Gray, J. (1990). A Census of Tandem System Availability between 1985 and 1990. *IEEE Transactions on Reliability, 39*(4), 409–418. doi:10.1109/24.58719

Gregg, C., Dorn, J., Hazelwood, K., & Skadron, K. (2012, June). Fine-grained resource sharing for concurrent GPGPU kernels. *Paper Presented at the 4th USENIX conference on Hot Topics in Parallelism*, Berkeley, CA, USA.

Gronqvist, J., & Lokhmotov, A. (2014). Optimising OpenCL kernels for the ARM Mali tm-t600 GPUs. In W. Engel (Ed.), *GPU Pro 5: Advanced Rendering Techniques.* CRC Press. doi:10.1201/b16721-25

GSMArena. (2015). Sony Xperia S. Retrieved from http://www.gsmarena.com/sony_xperia_s-4369.php

Guan, Q., DeBardeleben, N., Blanchard, S., & Fu, S. (2014). Towards exploring the soft error susceptibility of heapsort algorithms. *Proceedings of the 44th annual IEEE/IFIP international conference on dependable systems and networks (DSN).* IEEE.

Guan, Q., Fu, S., DeBardeleben, N., & Blanchard, S. (2014). F-SEFI: A fine-grained soft error fault injection tool for profiling application vulnerability. *Proceedings of IEEE 28th international symposium on parallel distributed processing (IPDPS).* IEEE. doi:10.1109/IPDPS.2014.128

Gubbi, J., Buyya, R., Marusic, S., & Palaniswami, M. (2013). Internet of Things (IoT): A vision, architectural elements, and future directions. *Future Generation Computer Systems, 29*(7), 1645–1660. doi:10.1016/j.future.2013.01.010

Guerraoui, R., & Romano, P. (2014). *Transactional Memory. Foundations, Algorithms, Tools, and Applications, LCNS* (Vol. 8913). Springer.

Guerraoui, R., & Schiper, A. (1997). Software-based replication for fault tolerance. *Computer*, *30*(4), 68–74. doi:10.1109/2.585156

Guevara, M., Gregg, C., Hazelwood, K., & Skadron, K. (2009, September). Enabling task parallelism in the CUDA scheduler.*Proceedings of the First Workshop on Programming Models for Emerging Architectures* (pp. 69-76). IEEE.

Gulati, A., Merchant, A., & Varman, P. J. (2010). mclock: handling throughput variability for hypervisor io scheduling. *Proceedings of the 9th usenix conference on operating systems design and implementation* (pp. 1–7).

Güngör, V. C., Sahin, D., Kocak, T., Ergüt, S., Buccella, C., Cecati, C., & Hancke, G. P. (2011). Smart grid technologies: Communication technologies and standards. *IEEE Transactions on Industrial Informatics*, *7*(4), 529–539. doi:10.1109/TII.2011.2166794

Guo, C., Lu, G., Wang, H. J., Yang, S., Kong, C., Sun, P., & Zhang, Y. (2010). Secondnet: a data center network virtualization architecture with bandwidth guarantees.*Proceedings of the 6th international conference* (p. 15). doi:10.1145/1921168.1921188

Guo, Z., Zheng, C., & Shi, B. (2002). An extrapolation method for boundary conditions in lattice Boltzmann method. *Physics of Fluids*, *14*(6), 2007–2010. doi:10.1063/1.1471914

Gustafson, J. L. (1988). Reevaluating Amdahl's Law. *Communications of the ACM*,31(5), 532-533.

Hassan, Q.F., Riad, A.M., & Hassan, A.E. (2012). Understanding Cloud Computing. In H. Yang, & X. Liu (Eds.), *Software Reuse in the Emerging Cloud Computing Era* (pp. 204-227). Hershey, PA, USA: IGI Global.

Hackmann, G. (2006). *802.15 Personal Area Networks*. Department of Computer Science and Engineering, Washington University.

Hadri, B., Ltaief, H., Agullo, E., & Dongarra, J. (2009, September). Tall and Skinny QR Matrix Factorization Using Tile Algorithms on Multicore Architectures. *LAPACK Working Note*, *222*, ICL.

Hager, G., Treibig, J., Habich, J., & Wellein, G. (2014). Exploring performance and power properties of modern multicore chips via simple machine models. *Concurrency and Computation*.

Haghighi, P. D., Krishnaswamy, S., Zaslavsky, A., Gaber, M. M., Sinha, A., & Gillick, B. (2013). Open mobile miner: A toolkit for building situation-aware data mining applications. *Journal of Organizational Computing and Electronic Commerce*, *23*(3), 224–248. doi:10.1080/10919392.2013.807713

Hall, M., Frank, E., Holmes, G., Pfahringer, B., Reutemann, P., & Witten, I. H. (2009). The WEKA data mining software: an update. *ACM SIGKDD explorations newsletter*, 11(1), 10-18.

Hammond, L., Wong, V., Chen, M., Carlstrom, B. D., Davis, J. D., Hertzberg, B., & Olukotun, K. (2004). Transactional memory coherence and consistency. In *ACM SIGARCH Computer Architecture News* (Vol. 32, p. 102). IEEE Computer Society.

Han, I., & Shin, Y. (2012). Synthesis of clock gating logic through factored form matching. *Proceedings of the 2012 IEEE International Conference on IC Design & Technology (ICICDT)* (pp. 1–4). IEEE. doi:doi:10.1109/ICICDT.2012.6232835 doi:10.1109/ICICDT.2012.6232835

Hanumaiah, V., & Vrudhula, S. (2014). Energy-efficient operation of multicore processors by DVFS, task migration, and active cooling. *IEEE Transactions on Computers*, *63*(2), 349–360. doi:10.1109/TC.2012.213

Hardware Approaches for Transactional Memory. (n. d.). Retrieved from http://arco.e.ac.upc.edu/wiki/images/e/e3/Mlupon_msc.pdf

Hashem, I. A. T., Yaqoob, I., Anuar, N. B., Mokhtar, S., Gani, A., & Khan, S. U. (2015). The rise of "big data" on cloud computing: Review and open research issues. *Information Systems*, *47*, 98–115. doi:10.1016/j.is.2014.07.006

Hassan, Q. (2011). Demystifying Cloud Computing. *The Journal of Defense Software Engineering*, 2011, 16-21.

Hastie, T., Tibshirani, R., & Friedman, J. (2001). *The elements of statistical learning*. New York, NY, USA: Springer New York Inc. doi:10.1007/978-0-387-21606-5

Hawa, M., As-Sayid-Ahmad, L., & Khalaf, L. (2013). On enhancing reputation management using peer-to-peer interaction history. *Peer-to-Peer Networking and Applications*, *6*(1), 101–113. doi:10.1007/s12083-012-0142-x

He, Y., Yuan, R., Ma, X., & Li, J. (2008). The IEEE 802.11 power saving mechanism: An experimental study. *Paper presented at theIEEE Wireless Communications and Networking Conference*, Las Vegas, USA. doi:doi:10.1109/WCNC.2008.245 doi:10.1109/WCNC.2008.245

Heer, T., Garcia-Morchon, O., Hummen, R., Keoh, S. L., Kumar, S. S., & Wehrle, K. (2011). Security Challenges in the IP-based Internet of Things. *Wireless Personal Communications*, *61*(3), 527–542. doi:10.1007/s11277-011-0385-5

Hélary, J. M., Mostéfaoui, A., & Raynal, M. (1997). *Virtual precedence in asynchronous systems: Concept and applications*. Springer Berlin Heidelberg.

Hélary, J. M., Mostefaoui, A., & Raynal, M. (1999). Communication-induced determination of consistent snapshots. *IEEE Transactions on Parallel and Distributed Systems*, *10*(9), 865–877. doi:10.1109/71.798312

Helbing, D., & Molnar, P. (1995). Social force model for pedestrian dynamics. Physical Review E: Statistical Physics, Plasmas, Fluids, and Related Interdisciplinary Topics, 51(5), 42–82. PubMed PMID:9963139

Henderson, A., Prakash, A., Yan, L. K., Hu, X., Wang, X., Zhou, R., & Yin, H. (2013). make it work, make it right, make it fast, building a platform-neutral whole-system dynamic binary analysis platform.*Proceedings of the international symposium on software testing and analysis (ISSTA)*. ACM.

Hennessy, J. L., & Patterson, D. A. (2011). Computer Architecture: A Quantitative Approach (5th ed.). San Francisco, CA, USA: Morgan Kaufmann Publishers Inc.

Hennessy, J. L., & Patterson, D. A. (2011). *Computer architecture: a quantitative approach*. Elsevier.

Herlihy, M. (2014). Fun with hardware transactional memory.*Proceedings of the 2014 ACM SIGMOD international conference on Management of data* (pp. 575–575). ACM. doi:10.1145/2588555.2602132

Herlihy, M., & Moss, J. E. B. (1993). *Transactional memory: Architectural support for lock-free data structures* (Vol. 21). ACM. doi:10.1145/165123.165164

Hernández, B., & Rudomin, I. (2011). A rendering pipeline for real-time crowds. GPU Pro, 2, 369–383.

Hernandez, B., Pérez, H., Rudomin, I., Ruiz, S., de Gyves, O., & Toledo, L. (2014). Simulating and Visualizing Real-Time Crowds on GPU Clusters. Computación y Sistemas, 18(4), 651–664.

Hess, A., Malandrino, F., Reinhardt, M. B., Casetti, C., Hummel, K. A., & Barceló-Ordinas, J. M. (2012). Optimal deployment of charging stations for electric vehicular networks. *Paper presented at theThe first workshop on Urban networking*, Nice, France. doi:doi:10.1145/2413236.2413238 doi:10.1145/2413236.2413238

Hirzel, M., Soule´, R., Schneider, S., Gedik, B., & Grimm, R. (2014). A catalog of stream processing optimizations. *ACM Computing Surveys*, *46*(4), 46. doi:10.1145/2528412

Hong, I., Park, S., Lee, B., Lee, J., Jeong, D., & Park, S. (2014). IoT-Based Smart Garbage System for Efficient Food Waste Management. *TheScientificWorldJournal*, 2014. PMID:25258730

Hong, S., & Kim, H. (2010). An integrated GPU power and performance model. In *ACM SIGARCH Computer Architecture News* (Vol. 38, pp. 280–289). ACM. doi:10.1145/1815961.1815998

Horwitz, S., Reps, T., & Binkley, D. (1990). Interprocedural slicing using dependence graphs. *ACM Transactions on Programming Languages and Systems*, *12*(1), 26–60. doi:10.1145/77606.77608

Hosseinabadi, A. A. R., Siar, H., Shamshirband, S., Shojafar, M., & Nasir, M. H. N. M. (2014). Using the gravitational emulation local search algorithm to solve the multi-objective flexible dynamic job shop scheduling problem in Small and Medium Enterprises. *Annals of Operations Research*, *229*(1), 451–474. doi:10.1007/s10479-014-1770-8

Hoy, M. B. (2015). The "Internet of Things": What It Is and What It Means for Libraries. *Medical Reference Services Quarterly*, *34*(3), 353–358. doi:10.1080/02763869.2015.1052699 PMID:26211795

Hsu, S.-J., & Lin, R.-B. (2011). Clock gating optimization with delay-matching. Proceedings of the Design, Automation & Test in Europe Conference & Exhibition (pp. 1–6). IEEE.

Huang, J., Yeluri, S., Frailong, J. M., Libby, J. G., Gupta, A. P., & Coelho, P. (2014). *U.S. Patent No. 8,627,007*. Washington, DC: U.S. Patent and Trademark Office.

Huang, K.-H., & Abraham, J. (1984). Algorithm-based fault tolerance for matrix operations. *IEEE Transactions on Computers*, *C-33*(6), 518–528.

Huang, Q., Xu, Y., Li, J., Su, Z., & Liu, H. (2012). Structural damage detection of controlled building structures using frequency response functions. *Journal of Sound and Vibration*, *331*(15), 3476–3492. doi:10.1016/j.jsv.2012.03.001

Huang, S.-H., Tu, W.-P., & Li, B.-H. (2012). High-level synthesis for minimum-area low-power clock gating. *Journal of Information Science and Engineering*, *28*(5), 971–988.

Hursey, J., Mattox, T. I., & Lumsdaine, A. (2009, June). Interconnect agnostic checkpoint/restart in Open MPI. *Proceedings of the 18th ACM international symposium on High performance distributed computing* (pp. 49-58). ACM. doi:10.1145/1551609.1551619

Iamnitchi, A., & Foster, I. (2004). A peer-to-peer approach to resource location in grid environments. In J. Nabrzyski, J. M. Schopf, & J. Węglarz (Eds.), *Grid Resource Management* (pp. 413–429). Springer, US. doi:10.1007/978-1-4615-0509-9_25

IBM Sequoia. (2015, August 18). Wikipedia, the free encyclopedia. Retrieved from https://en.wikipedia.org/w/index.php?title=IBM_Sequoia&oldid=676692785

IBM. (2010). Developer Works survey. Retrieved from http://public.dhe.ibm.com/software/dw/survey/2010surveyresults/2010surveresults-pdf.pdf

IDC. (2013). More Smartphones Were Shipped in Q1 2013 Than Feature Phones, An Industry First According to IDC. Retrieved from http://www.idc.com/getdoc.jsp?containerId=prUS24085413

IEEE 802.11 Working Group. (2010). IEEE Standard for Information Technology–Telecommunications and information exchange between systems–Local and metropolitan area networks–Specific requirements–Part 11: Wireless LAN Medium Access Control (MAC) and Physical Layer (PHY) specifications Amendment 6: Wireless Access in Vehicular Environments. *IEEE Std, 802*, 11.

IEEE Transactional memory. (n. d.). *Wikipedia, the free encyclopedia*. Retrieved from https://en.wikipedia.org/w/index. php?title=Transactional_memory

IEEE802.org. (2015). IEEE P802.11 Sub 1GHz Study Group. Retrieved from http://www.ieee802.org/11/Reports/ tgah_update.htm

Intel Corporation. (2009). Intel 5520 chipset and Intel 5500 chipset-datasheet.

Intel Ltd. Intel trace analyzer & collector (2009). Retrieved from: http://www.intel.com/cd/software/products/asmo-na/ eng/244171.htm

Ishihara, S., Hariyama, M., & Kameyama, M. (2011). A low-power FPGA based on autonomous fine-grain power gating. *IEEE Transactions on Very Large Scale Integration (VLSI) Systems*, *19*(8), 1394–1406.

ITU. (2005). *ITU Internet Reports 2005: The internet of things*. Retrieved from https://www.itu.int/wsis/tunis/newsroom/ stats/The-Internet-of-Things-2005.pdf

Iwai, K., Kurokawa, T., & Nisikawa, N. (2010, November). AES encryption implementation on CUDA GPU and its analysis.*Proceedings of the 2010 First International Conference on Networking and Computing* (pp. 209-214). IEEE. doi:10.1109/IC-NC.2010.49

Iyer, R. K., Rossetti, D. J., & Hsueh, M. C. (1986). Measurement and Modeling of Computer Reliability as Affected by System Activity. *ACM Transactions on Computer Systems*, *4*(3), 214–237. doi:10.1145/6420.6422

Jackson, J. C., Vijayakumar, V., Quadir, M. A., & Bharathi, C. (2015). Survey on Programming Models and Environments for Cluster, Cloud, and Grid Computing that Defends Big Data. *Procedia Computer Science*, *50*, 517–523.

Jacob, B., Ng, S., & Wang, D. (2010). *Memory systems: cache, DRAM, disk*. Morgan Kaufmann.

Jain, R. (2014). Wireless Protocols for Internet of Things: Part II–ZigBee. Retrieved from www.cse.wustl.edu/~jain/ cse574-14/j_13zgb.htm

Jain, A. K. (2010). Data clustering: 50 years beyond K-means. *Pattern Recognition Letters*, *31*(8), 651–666. doi:10.1016/j. patrec.2009.09.011

Januszewski, M., & Kostur, M. (2014). Sailfish: A flexible multi-GPU implementation of the lattice Boltzmann method. *Computer Physics Communications*, *185*(9), 2350–2368. doi:10.1016/j.cpc.2014.04.018

Javanmardi, S., Shojafar, M., Amendola, D., Cordeschi, N., Liu, H., & Abraham, A. (2014, January). Hybrid job scheduling algorithm for cloud computing environment.*Proceedings of the Fifth International Conference on Innovations in Bio-Inspired Computing and Applications IBICA 2014* (pp. 43-52). Springer International Publishing. doi:10.1007/978-3-319-08156-4_5

Javanmardi, S., Shojafar, M., Shariatmadari, S., Abawajy, J. H., & Singhal, M. (2014). PGSW-OS: A novel approach for resource management in a semantic web operating system based on a P2P grid architecture. *The Journal of Supercomputing*, *69*(2), 955–975. doi:10.1007/s11227-014-1221-y

Jayaraman, P. P., Perera, C., Georgakopoulos, D., & Zaslavsky, A. (2014). MOSDEN: A scalable mobile collaborative platform for opportunistic sensing applications. arXiv preprint arXiv:1405.5867.

Jaykumar, J., & Blessy, A. (2014). Secure Smart Environment Using IOT based on RFID. *International Journal of Computer Science & Information Technologies*, *5*(2).

Jeff, B. (2012). Big.LITTLE system architecture from ARM: saving power through heterogeneous multiprocessing and task context migration. In P. Groeneveld, D. Sciuto, & S. Hassoun (Eds.), *DAC* (pp. 1143–1146). ACM. doi:10.1145/2228360.2228569

Jeffers, J., & Reinders, J. (2013). *Intel Xeon Phi Coprocessor High Performance Programming*. San Francisco, CA, USA: Morgan Kaufmann Publishers Inc.

Jelasity, M., Montresor, A., & Babaoglu, O. (2009). T-Man: Gossip-based fast overlay topology construction. *Computer Network Elsevier*, *53*(13), 2321–2339. doi:10.1016/j.comnet.2009.03.013

Jeong, K., Kahng, A. B., Kang, S., Rosing, T. S., & Strong, R. (2012). MAPG: Memory access power gating.*Proceedings of the Conference on Design, Automation and Test in Europe* (pp. 1054–1059). EDA Consortium.

Jian, X., Duwe, H., Sartori, J., Sridharan, V., & Kumar, R. (2013). Low-power, low-storage-overhead chipkill correct via multi line error correction.*Proceedings of the international conference on high performance computing, networking, storage and analysis* (pp. 24:1–24:12). New York, NY, USA: ACM. doi:10.1145/2503210.2503243

Jiménez, V. J., Vilanova, L., Gelado, I., Gil, M., Fursin, G., & Navarro, N. (2009). Predictive runtime code scheduling for heterogeneous architectures. In *High Performance Embedded Architectures and Compilers* (pp. 19–33). Springer Berlin Heidelberg. doi:10.1007/978-3-540-92990-1_4

Jin, X., & Chan, S.-H. G. (2010). Unstructured peer-to-peer network architectures. In X. Shen, H. Yu, J. Buford, & M. Akon (Eds.), *Handbook of Peer-to-Peer Networking* (pp. 117–142). Springer. doi:10.1007/978-0-387-09751-0_5

Johnson, C., Allen, D.H., Brown, J., Vanderwiel, S., Hoover, R., Achilles, H., Cher, CY., May, G.A., Franke, H., Xenidis, J. & Basso, C. (2010). 5.5 A Wire-Speed PowerTM Processor: 2.3 GHz 45nm SOI with 16 Cores and 64 Threads.

Jones, W., Daly, J., & DeBarteleben, N. (2008). Application Resilience: Making Progress In Spite of Failures. In *Proceedings of the IEEE Symposium on Cluster Computing and the Grid*. Lyon, France. doi:10.1109/CCGRID.2008.99

Jotwani, R., Sundaram, S., Kosonocky, S., Schaefer, A., Andrade, V., Constant, G., & Naffziger, S. (2010). An x86-64 core implemented in 32nm SOI CMOS. *Proceedings of the 2010 IEEE International Solid-State Circuits Conference-(ISSCC)*. IEEE.

Jou, J.-Y., & Abraham, J. (1986, May). Fault-tolerant matrix arithmetic and signal processing on highly concurrent computing structures. *Proceedings of the IEEE*, *74*(5), 732–741. doi:10.1109/PROC.1986.13535

Kalra, D., & Ingram, D. (2006). *Electronic health records Information technology solutions for healthcare* (pp. 135–181). Springer. doi:10.1007/1-84628-141-5_7

Kalyanakrishnam, M., Kalbarczyk, Z., & Iyer, R. (1999). Failure Data Analysis of a LAN of Windows NT based computers. In *Proceedings of the 18th IEEE Symposium on Reliable Distributed Systems*. doi:10.1109/RELDIS.1999.805094

Kamble, M. B., & Ghose, K. (1998). Modeling energy dissipation in low power caches. *Proceedings of theInternational Symposium on Low Power Electronics and Design* (pp. 143–148).

Kang, K., Kim, J., Yoo, S., & Kyung, C.-M. (2010). Temperature-aware integrated DVFS and power gating for executing tasks with runtime distribution. *IEEE Transactions on Computer-Aided Design of Integrated Circuits and Systems*, *29*(9), 1381–1394. doi:10.1109/TCAD.2010.2059290

Kapasi, U., Dally, W. J., Rixner, S., Owens, J. D., & Khailany, B. (2002). The imagine stream processor. *Proceedings of the 2002 IEEE International Conference on Computer Design: VLSI in Computers and Processors* (pp. 282-288). IEEE Computer Society. doi:doi:10.1109/ICCD.2002.1106783 doi:10.1109/ICCD.2002.1106783

Kappadia, M., Pelechano, N., Guy, S., Allbeck, J., & Chrysanthou, Y. (2014). Simulating heterogeneous crowds with interactive behaviors. *Eurographics 2014 - Tutorials.*

Kar, A., & Kar, A. (2015). A novel design of a portable double beam-in-time spectrometric sensor platform with cloud connectivity for environmental monitoring applications. *Paper presented at the Third International Conference on Computer, Communication, Control and Information Technology (C3IT)*, Hooghly, India. doi:doi:10.1109/C3IT.2015.7060228 doi:10.1109/C3IT.2015.7060228

Kaul, H., Anders, M., Hsu, S., Agarwal, A., Krishnamurthy, R., & Borkar, S. (2012). Near-threshold voltage (ntv) design: opportunities and challenges. *Proceedings of the 49th annual design automation conference.* ACM.

Kawamoto, Y., Nishiyama, H., Yoshimura, N., & Yamamoto, S. (2014). Internet of Things (IoT): Present State and Future Prospects. *IEICE Transactions on Information and Systems*, 97(10), 2568–2575. doi:10.1587/transinf.2013THP0009

Keller, A., & Martin-Flatin, J.-P. (2006). *Self-Managed Networks, Systems, and Services.* Springer. doi:10.1007/11767886

Kemp, R., Palmer, N., Kielmann, T., & Bal, H. (2012). *Cuckoo: a computation offloading framework for smartphones Mobile Computing, Applications, and Services* (pp. 59–79). Springer. doi:10.1007/978-3-642-29336-8_4

Kerbyson, D. J., Alme, H. J., Hoisie, A., Petrini, F., Wasserman, H. J., & Gittings, M. (2001). Predictive performance and scalability modeling of a large-scale application.*Proceedings of International Conference on High Performance Computing, Networking, Storage and Analysis (SC'01)*, Denver, Colorado, USA. IEEE. doi:10.1145/582034.582071

Kermack, W., & McKendrick, A. (1927). Contributions to the Mathematical Theory of Epidemics I. In *Proceedings of the Royal Society of London, Series A.*

Kermack, W., & McKendrick, A. (1932). Contributions to the Mathematical Theory of Epidemics II: The Problem of Endemicity. In *Proceedings of the Royal Society of London, Series A.*

Kermack, W., & McKendrick, A. (1933). Contributions to the mathematical theory of epidemics III: Further studies of the problem of endemicity. In *Proceedings of the Royal Society of London, Series A.*

Khailany, B. K., Williams, T., Lin, J., Long, E. P., Rygh, M., Tovey, D. W., & Dally, W. J. (2008). A programmable 512 GOPS stream processor for signal, image, and video processing. *IEEE Journal of Solid-State Circuits*, 43(1), 202–213. doi:10.1109/JSSC.2007.909331

Khan, A. N., Mat Kiah, M., Khan, S. U., Madani, S. A., & Khan, A. R. (2013). A Study of Incremental Cryptography for Security Schemes in Mobile Cloud Computing Environments. *Paper presented at theIEEE Symposium on Wireless Technology and Applications (ISWTA).* doi:doi:10.1109/ISWTA.2013.6688818 doi:10.1109/ISWTA.2013.6688818

Khan, A. N., Kiah, M. M., Ali, M., Madani, S. A., & Shamshirband, S. (2014). BSS: Block-based sharing scheme for secure data storage services in mobile cloud environment. *The Journal of Supercomputing*, 70(2), 946–976. doi:10.1007/s11227-014-1269-8

Khan, A. N., Kiah, M. M., Madani, S. A., Ali, M., & Shamshirband, S. (2014). Incremental proxy re-encryption scheme for mobile cloud computing environment. *The Journal of Supercomputing*, 68(2), 624–651. doi:10.1007/s11227-013-1055-z

Khan, A. R., Othman, M., Ali, M., Khan, A. N., & Madani, S. A. (2014). Pirax: Framework for application piracy control in mobile cloud environment. *The Journal of Supercomputing*, 68(2), 753–776. doi:10.1007/s11227-013-1061-1

Khan, A. R., Othman, M., Khan, A. N., Abid, S. A., & Madani, S. A. (2015). MobiByte: An Application Development Model for Mobile Cloud Computing. *Journal of Grid Computing*, 13(4), 6005-628. doi:10.1007/s10723-015-9335-x

Khan, A. R., Othman, M., Madani, S. A., & Khan, S. U. (2014). A Survey of Mobile Cloud Computing Application Models. *IEEE Communications Surveys and Tutorials*, *16*(1), 393–413. doi:10.1109/SURV.2013.062613.00160

Khan, A. R., Othman, M., Xia, F., & Khan, A. N. (2015). Context-Aware Mobile Cloud Computing and Its Challenges. *IEEE Cloud Computing*, *2*(3), 42–49. doi:10.1109/MCC.2015.62

Khan, A., Mat Kiah, M. L., Ali, M., Shamshirband, S., & Khan, A. R. (2015). A Cloud-Manager-Based Re-Encryption Scheme for Mobile Users in Cloud Environment: A Hybrid Approach. *Journal of Grid Computing*. doi:10.1007/s10723-015-9352-9

Khan, B., Horsnell, M., Rogers, I., Luján, M., Dinn, A., & Watson, I. (2008). A first insight into object-aware hardware transactional memory.*Proceedings of the twentieth annual symposium on Parallelism in algorithms and architectures* (pp. 107–109). ACM. doi:10.1145/1378533.1378552

Khorov, E., Lyakhov, A., Krotov, A., & Guschin, A. (2014). A survey on IEEE 802.11 ah: An enabling networking technology for smart cities. *Computer Communications*, *2014*, 53–69.

Kim, J., & Lilja, D. J. (1998). Characterization of communication patterns in message-passing parallel scientific application programs. In P.K. Dhabaleswar, & C.B. Stunkel (Ed.), Network-Based Parallel Computing Communication, Architecture, and Applications (pp. 202-216). New York, NY: Springer. doi:doi:10.1007/BFb0052218 doi:10.1007/BFb0052218

Kim, J., Radhakrishnan, S., & Jang, J. (2006). Cost Optimization in SIS Model of Worm Infection. ETRI Journal, 28(5).

Kim, S., Pakzad, S., Culler, D., Demmel, J., Fenves, G., Glaser, S., & Turon, M. (2007). Health monitoring of civil infrastructures using wireless sensor networks. *Paper presented at the6th International Symposium on Information Processing in Sensor Networks*, Cambridge, USA. doi:doi:10.1109/IPSN.2007.4379685 doi:10.1109/IPSN.2007.4379685

Kim, H.-S., Wu, S., Chang, L.-W., & Hwu, W.-W. (2011). A Scalable Tridiagonal Solver for GPUs.*Proceedings of the 40nd International Conference on Parallel Processing* (pp. 444-453).

Kim, K. H., Buyya, R., & Kim, J. (2007). *Power aware scheduling of bag-of-tasks applications with deadline constraints on dvs-enabled clusters* (Vol. 7, pp. 541–548). Ccgrid. doi:10.1109/CCGRID.2007.85

Kim, S. A., Shin, D., Choe, Y., Seibert, T., & Walz, S. P. (2012). Integrated energy monitoring and visualization system for Smart Green City development: Designing a spatial information integrated energy monitoring model in the context of massive data management on a web based platform. *Automation in Construction*, *22*, 51–59. doi:10.1016/j.autcon.2011.07.004

Kimura, H., Sato, M., Hotta, Y., Boku, T., & Takahashi, D. (2006). Empirical study on reducing energy of parallel programs using slack reclamation by dvfs in a power-scalable high performance cluster. Proceedings of the 2006 IEEE international conference on Cluster computing (pp. 1–10).

Kim, Y., Suh, J., Cho, J., Singh, S., & Seo, J. (2015). Development of Real-Time Pipeline Management System for Prevention of Accidents. *International Journal of Control and Automation*, *8*(1), 211–226. doi:10.14257/ijca.2015.8.1.19

Kin, J., Gupta, M., & Mangione-Smith, W. H. (1997). The filter cache: an energy efficient memory structure.*Proceedings of the 30th annual ACM/IEEE international symposium on Microarchitecture* (pp. 184–193). IEEE Computer Society. doi:10.1109/MICRO.1997.645809

Kinnunen, M., Mian, S. Q., Oinas-Kukkonen, H., Riekki, J., Jutila, M., Ervasti, M., & Alasaarela, E. et al. (2016). Wearable and mobile sensors connected to social media in human well-being applications. *Telematics and Informatics*, *33*(1), 92–101. doi:10.1016/j.tele.2015.06.008

Kiran, M., Richmond, P., Holcombe, M., Chin, L. S., Worth, D., & Greenough, C. (2010). FLAME: simulating large populations of agents on parallel hardware architectures. *In Proceedings of the 9th International Conference on Autonomous Agents and Multiagent Systems*, 1(1), 1633-1636.

Kirk, P. (n. d). *RFC-Gnutella 0.6*. Retrieved from http://rfc-gnutella.sourceforge.net/index.html

Kitchin, R. (2014). The real-time city? Big data and smart urbanism. *GeoJournal, 79*(1), 1–14. doi:10.1007/s10708-013-9516-8

Klecka, J. S., Bruckert, W. F., & Jardine, R. L. (2002). *U.S. Patent No. 6,393,582*. Washington, DC: U.S. Patent and Trademark Office.

Knight, T. (1986). An architecture for mostly functional languages.*Proceedings of the 1986 ACM conference on LISP and functional programming* (pp. 105–112). ACM. doi:10.1145/319838.319854

Kocak, T., & Lacks, D. (2012). Design and analysis of a distributed grid resource discovery Protocol. *Cluster Computing, 15*(1), 37–52. doi:10.1007/s10586-010-0147-2

Kogge, P., Bergman, K., Borkar, S., Campbell, D., Carlson, W., Dally, W., . . . Yelick, K. (2008). ExaScale Computing Study: Technology Challenges in Achieving Exascale Systems. (Technical report). Defense Advanced Research Projects Agency Information Processing Techniques Office. Washington, DC: DARPA IPTO.

Kongetira, P., Aingaran, K., & Olukotun, K. (2005). Niagara: A 32-way multithreaded SPARC processor. *IEEE Micro, 25*(2), 21–29. doi:10.1109/MM.2005.35

Koppanalil, J., Yeung, G., Driscoll, D. O., Householder, S., & Hawkins, C. (2011). A 1.6 GHz dual-core ARM Cortex A9 implementation on a low power high-K metal gate 32nm process. Proceedings of the 2011 International Symposium on VLSI Design, Automation and Test (VLSI-DAT) (pp. 1–4). IEEE.

Koutsoupias, E., & Papadimitriou, C. (2009). Worst-Case Equilibria. *Computer Science Review, 3*(2), 65–69. doi:10.1016/j.cosrev.2009.04.003

Koyuturk, M., Szpankowski, W., & Grama, A. (2004). Biclustering gene-feature matrices for statistically significant dense patterns.*Proceedings of IEEE computational systems bioinformatics conference*. IEEE. doi:10.1109/CSB.2004.1332467

Krauss, L. M., & Starkman, G. D. (2004). Universal Limits of Computation.

Kreps, J., Narkhede, N., & Rao, J. (2011). Kafka: A distributed messaging system for log processing. *Paper presented at theProceedings of the NetDB*.

Krishnan, S., & Gonzalez, J. U. (2015). Building Your Next Big Thing with Google Cloud Platform: A Guide for Developers and Enterprise Architects.

Kuhn, D. R. (1997). Sources of failure in the public switched telephone network. *IEEE Computer, 30*(4).

Labarta, J., Girona, S., Pillet, V., Cortes, T., & Gregoris, L. (1996). DiP: A parallel program development environment. *Proceedings of International Conference on Euro-Par Parallel Processing (Euro-Par'96)*, Lyon, France. Springer.

Lamport, L. (1978). Time, clocks, and the ordering of events in a distributed system. *Communications of the ACM, 21*(7), 558–565. doi:10.1145/359545.359563

Landau, R. H. (n.d). *A beginner's guide to high performance computing*. Retrieved June 9, 2015, from http://www.shodor.org/petascale/resources/search/view/2594/

Lange, J., Pedretti, K., Hudson, T., Dinda, P., Cui, Z., Xia, L., & Brightwell, R. (2010). Palacios and kitten: New high performance operating systems for scalable virtualized and native supercomputing.*Proceedings of IEEE international symposium on parallel distributed processing (IPDPS)*. IEEE. doi:10.1109/IPDPS.2010.5470482

Langou, J. (2010). Computing the R of the QR factorization of tall and skinny matrices using MPI_Reduce. *arXiv preprint arXiv:1002.4250*.

Lara, A. M., Kigozi, J., Amurwon, J., Muchabaiwa, L., Wakaholi, B. N., Mota, R. E. M., & Reid, A. et al. (2012). Cost effectiveness analysis of clinically driven versus routine laboratory monitoring of antiretroviral therapy in Uganda and Zimbabwe. *PLoS ONE, 7*(4). PMID:22545079

Laranjo, I., Macedo, J., & Santos, A. (2012). Internet of things for medication control: Service implementation and testing. *Procedia Technology, 5*, 777–786. doi:10.1016/j.protcy.2012.09.086

Lattner, C., & Adve, V. (2004). Llvm: a compilation framework for lifelong program analysis transformation.*Proceedings of International symposium on generation and optimization (CGO)*. ACM. doi:10.1109/CGO.2004.1281665

LaValle, S., Lesser, E., Shockley, R., Hopkins, M. S., & Kruschwitz, N. (2013). Big data, analytics and the path from insights to value. *MIT sloan management review, 21*.

Le, H. Q., Guthrie, G. L., Williams, D. E., Michael, M. M., Frey, B. G., Starke, W. J., Nakaike, T. (2015). Transactional memory support in the IBM POWER8 processor. *IBM Journal of Research and Development, 59*(1), pp. 8:1–8:14.

Lee, I., & Iyer, R. (1995). Software Dependability in the Tandem GUARDIAN System. *IEEE Transactions on Software Engineering, 21*(5).

Lee, J. S. (2006). Performance evaluation of IEEE 802.15. 4 for low-rate wireless personal area networks. *IEEE Transactions on Consumer Electronics, 52*(3), 742–749. doi:10.1109/TCE.2006.1706465

Lee, J., Chapin, S., & Taylor, S. (2003). Reliable Heterogeneous Applications. *IEEE Transactions on Reliability, 52*(3), 330–339. doi:10.1109/TR.2003.819502

Lee, M. C. (2009). A Divide-and-Conquer Strategy and PVM Computation Environment for the Matrix Multiplication. *Proceedings of the 9th International Conference on Algorithms and Architectures for Parallel Processing* (pp. 535-544). doi:10.1007/978-3-642-03095-6_51

Leis, V., Kemper, A., & Neumann, T. (2014). Exploiting hardware transactional memory in main-memory databases. *Proceedings of the 2014 IEEE 30th International Conference on Data Engineering (ICDE)* (pp. 580–591). IEEE. doi:doi:10.1109/ICDE.2014.6816683 doi:10.1109/ICDE.2014.6816683

Lemarinier, P., Bouteiller, A., Herault, T., Krawezik, G., & Cappello, F. (2004, September). Improved message logging versus improved coordinated checkpointing for fault tolerant MPI.*Proceedings of the 2004 IEEE International Conference on Cluster Computing*, (pp. 115-124). IEEE. doi:10.1109/CLUSTR.2004.1392609

Lemstra, W., Hayes, V., & Groenewegen, J. (2010). *The innovation journey of Wi-Fi: The road to global success*. Cambridge University Press. doi:10.1017/CBO9780511666995

Lev, Y., & Maessen, J.-W. (2008). Split hardware transactions: true nesting of transactions using best-effort hardware transactional memory. *Proceedings of the 13th ACM SIGPLAN Symposium on Principles and practice of parallel programming* (pp. 197–206). ACM.

Leveugle, R., Calvez, A., Maistri, P., & Vanhauwaert, P. (2009). Statistical fault injection: Quantified error and confidence. *Proceedings of design, automation test in Europe conference exhibition* (pp. 502-506). IEEE

Levy, S., Dosanjh, M. G. F., Bridges, P. G., & Ferreira, K. B. (2013). Using unreliable virtual hardware to inject errors in extreme-scale systems.*Proceedings of the 3rd workshop on fault tolerance for HPC at extreme scale.* IEEE. doi:10.1145/2465813.2465820

Li, L., Wang, W., Choi, K., Park, S., & Chung, M.-K. (2010). SeSCG: Selective sequential clock gating for ultra-low-power multimedia mobile processor design. *Proceedings of the 2010 IEEE International Conference on Electro/Information Technology (EIT)* (pp. 1–6). IEEE.

Li, S., Ahn, J. H., Strong, R. D., Brockman, J. B., Tullsen, D. M., & Jouppi, N. P. (2009). McPAT: an integrated power, area, and timing modeling framework for multicore and manycore architectures. *Proceedings of the 42nd Annual IEEE/ ACM International Symposium on Microarchitecture MICRO-42* (pp. 469–480). IEEE. doi:doi:10.1145/1669112.1669172 doi:10.1145/1669112.1669172

Liang, J., Kumar, R., & Ross, K. (2004). The KaZaa overlay: A measurement study.*Proceedings of the 19th IEEE Annual Computer Communications Workshop*, Bonita Springs, Florida, USA.

Liang, Y., Zhang, Y., Sivasubramaniam, A., Sahoo, R., Moreira, J., & Gupta, M. (2005). Filtering Failure Logs for a BlueGene/L Prototype. In *Proceedings of the International Conference on Dependable Systems and Networks (DSN '05).* Yokohama, Japan.

Li, C., Suna, L., & Hua, X. (2012). A context-aware lighting control system for smart meeting rooms. *Systems Engineering Procedia, 4*, 314–323. doi:10.1016/j.sepro.2011.11.081

Li, D., Vetter, J., & Yu, W. (2012). Classifying soft error vulnerabilities in extreme-scale scientific applications using a binary instrumentation tool.*Proceedings of IEEE/ACM international conference on high performance computing, networking, storage and analysis (SC).* IEEE. doi:10.1109/SC.2012.29

Li, K., Yang, W., & Li, K. (2015). Performance analysis and optimization for SpMV on GPU using probabilistic modeling. *IEEE Transactions on Parallel and Distributed Systems, 26*(1), 196–205. doi:10.1109/TPDS.2014.2308221

Lindholm, E., Nickolls, J., Oberman, S., & Montrym, J. (2008). NVIDIA tesla: A unified graphics and computing architecture. *Micro, IEEE, 28*(2), 39–55. doi:10.1109/MM.2008.31

Lipmaa, H., Wagner, D., & Rogaway, P. (2000). Comments to NIST concerning AES modes of operation: CTR-mode encryption. *Paper presented at the2000 Symmetric Key Block Cipher Modes of Operation Workshop*, Baltimore, MD.

Li, Q., Zhong, C., Zhao, K., Mei, X., & Chu, X. (2012, June). Implementation and analysis of AES encryption on GPU. *Proceedings of the 2012 IEEE 14th International Conference on High Performance Computing and Communication & the 2012 IEEE 9th International Conference on Embedded Software and Systems* (pp. 843-848). IEEE. doi:10.1109/ HPCC.2012.119

Litzkow, M., Tannenbaum, T., Basney, J., & Livny, M. (1997). *Checkpoint and migration of UNIX processes in the Condor distributed processing system.* Computer Sciences Department, University of Wisconsin.

Liu, J., & Yang, L. (2011). Application of Internet of Things in the community security management. *Paper presented at theThird International Conference on Computational Intelligence, Communication Systems and Networks (CICSyN)*, Bali, Indonesia. doi:doi:10.1109/CICSyN.2011.72 doi:10.1109/CICSyN.2011.72

Liu, W.-H. E. (2010). Analytics and information integration for smart grid applications. *Paper presented at the2010 IEEE Power and Energy Society General Meeting*, Minneapolis, USA. doi:doi:10.1109/PES.2010.5589898 doi:10.1109/ PES.2010.5589898

Liu, G., An, H., Han, W., Xu, G., Yao, P., Xu, M., & Wang, Y. et al. (2009, December). A program behavior study of block cryptography algorithms on GPGPU.*Proceedings of the 2009 Fourth International Conference on Frontier of Computer Science and Technology* (pp. 33-39). IEEE. doi:10.1109/FCST.2009.13

Liu, P., Chen, Y., Tang, W., & Yue, Q. (2012). *Mobile weka as data mining tool on android Advances in Electrical Engineering and Automation* (pp. 75–80). Springer. doi:10.1007/978-3-642-27951-5_11

Liu, Q., Zhou, S., & Giannakis, G. B. (2004). Cross-layer combining of adaptive modulation and coding with truncated arq over wireless links. *IEEE Transactions on Wireless Communications*, *3*(5), 1746–1755. doi:10.1109/TWC.2004.833474

Li, Y., & Henkel, J. (1998). A framework for estimation and minimizing energy dissipation of embedded HW/SW systems.*Proceedings of the 35th annual Design Automation Conference* (pp. 188–193). ACM. doi:10.1145/277044.277097

LLNL. (2014). ASCI purple benchmark. Retrieved from: https://asc.llnl.gov/computing_resources/purple/archive/benchmarks/

Lomas, N. (2009). Online gizmos could top 50 billion in 2020. *Business Week*. Retrieved from http://www.businessweek.com/globalbiz/content/jun2009/gb20090629_492027.htm

Lomet, D. B. (1985). *Process structuring, synchronization, and recovery using atomic actions*. Springer. doi:10.1007/978-3-642-82470-8_21

Loser, A., Naumann, F., Siberski, W., Nejdl, W., & Thaden, U. (2004). Semantic Overlay Clusters within Super-Peer Networks. In K. Aberer et al (Ed.), *Databases, Information Systems, and Peer-to-Peer Computing: proceeding of the First International Workshop, DBISP2P (LNCS)* (Vol. 2944, pp. 33-47). Berlin Heidelberg, Germany: Springer.

Lu, C.-W., Li, S.-C., & Wu, Q. (2011). Interconnecting ZigBee and 6LoWPAN wireless sensor networks for smart grid applications. *Paper presented at theFifth International Conference on Sensing Technology (ICST)*, Palmerston North, New Zealand.

Lu, R., Lin, X., Zhu, H., & Shen, X. S. (2009). SPARK: a new VANET-based smart parking scheme for large parking lots. *Paper presented at theIEEE INFOCOM '09*, Rio de Janeiro, Brazil. doi:doi:10.1109/INFCOM.2009.5062057 doi:10.1109/INFCOM.2009.5062057

Lua, E. K., Zhou, X., Crowcroft, J., & Mieghem, P. V. (2008). Scalable multicasting with network-aware geometric overlay. *Computer Communication Elsevier*, *31*(3), 464–488. doi:10.1016/j.comcom.2007.08.046

Luk, C.-K., Cohn, R., Muth, R., Patil, H., & Klauser, A., Lowney, Hazelwood, K. (2005). Pin: building customized program analysis tools with dynamic instrumentation. *Proceedings of acm conference on programming language design and implementation (PLDI)*. ACM. doi:doi:10.1145/1065010.1065034 doi:10.1145/1065010.1065034

Luk, C. K., Hong, S., & Kim, H. (2009, December). Qilin: exploiting parallelism on heterogeneous multiprocessors with adaptive mapping.*Proceedings of the 42nd Annual IEEE/ACM International Symposium on Microarchitecture* (pp. 45-55). IEEE. doi:10.1145/1669112.1669121

Lundqvist, J., de Fraiture, C., & Molden, D. (2008). Saving water: from field to fork: curbing losses and wastage in the food chain. Retrieved from http://dlc.dlib.indiana.edu/dlc/handle/10535/5088

Lu, T., Chen, M., & Andrew, L. L. (2013). Simple and effective dynamic provisioning for power-proportional data centers. *Parallel and Distributed Systems. IEEE Transactions on*, *24*(6), 1161–1171.

Lyons, R. E., & Vanderkulk, W. (1962). The use of triple-modular redundancy to improve computer reliability. *IBM Journal of Research and Development*, *6*(2), 200–209. doi:10.1147/rd.62.0200

Lysenko, M., & D'Souza, R. M. (2008). A framework for megascale agent based model simulations on graphics processing units. Journal of Artificial Societies and Social Simulation, 11(4), 10.

Ma, K. L. (2009). In situ visualization at extreme scale: Challenges and opportunities. IEEE Computer Graphics and Applications, 29(6), 14–19. PubMed PMID:24806775

Ma, R. K., Lam, K. T., & Wang, C.-L. (2011). eXCloud: Transparent runtime support for scaling mobile applications in cloud. *Paper presented at the 2011 International Conference on Cloud and Service Computing (CSC).*

MacGillivray, C., Turner, V., Lund, D., Dugar, A., Dunbrack, L. A., Salmeron, A., . . . Clarke, R. Y. (2014). Worldwide Internet of Things 2014 Top 10 Predictions: Nascent Market Shakes Up Vendor Strategies.

Mackensen, E., Lai, M., & Wendt, T. M. (2012). Bluetooth low energy (ble) based wireless sensors. *Paper presented at the IEEE Sensors*, Taipei, Taiwan.

Madan, N., Buyuktosunoglu, A., Bose, P., & Annavaram, M. (2012). Guarded power gating in a multi-core setting. In *Computer Architecture* (pp. 198–210). Springer.

Magnusson, P. S., Christensson, M., Eskilson, J., Forsgren, D., Hallberg, G., Hogberg, J., & Werner, B. et al. (2002). Simics: A full system simulation platform. *IEEE Computer*, *35*(2), 50–58. doi:10.1109/2.982916

Mahajan, R., Wetherall, D., & Anderson, T. (2002). *Understanding BGP Misconfiguration.* In *Proceedings of SIGCOMM.* Pittsburgh, PA.

Mahdy, A. M., Deogun, J. S., & Wang, J. (2007). A Dynamic Approach for the Selection of Super Peers in Ad Hoc Networks.*proceeding of the Sixth International Conference on Networking (ICN).* Martinique: IEEE. doi:10.1109/ICN.2007.1

Mainetti, L., Patrono, L., & Vilei, A. (2011). Evolution of wireless sensor networks towards the internet of things: A survey. *Paper presented at the19th International Conference on Software, Telecommunications and Computer Networks (SoftCOM)*, Split, Croatia.

Maistri, P., Masson, F., & Leveugle, R. (2011, September). Implementation of the Advanced Encryption Standard on GPUs with the NVIDIA CUDA framework.*Proceedings of the 2011 IEEE Symposium on Industrial Electronics and Applications* (pp. 213-217). IEEE. doi:10.1109/ISIEA.2011.6108701

Manavski, S. (2007, November). CUDA compatible GPU as an efficient hardware accelerator for AES cryptography. *Proceedings of the 2007 IEEE International Conference on Signal Processing and Communications* (pp. 65-68). IEEE. doi:10.1109/ICSPC.2007.4728256

Marathe, V. J., & Dice, D. (2014). *Lock-clustering compilation for software transactional memory.* Google Patents.

March, V., Gu, Y., Leonardi, E., Goh, G., Kirchberg, M., & Lee, B. S. (2011). μCloud: Towards a new paradigm of rich mobile applications. *Procedia Computer Science*, *5*, 618–624. doi:10.1016/j.procs.2011.07.080

Marz, N. (2014). *History of Apache Storm and lessons learned.* Thoughts from the Red Planet.

Mastroianni, C., Talia, D., & Verta, O. (2005a). Advances in Grid Computing. In P. M. A. Sloot et al (Ed.), *A Super-Peer Model for Building Resource Discovery Services in Grids: Design and Simulation Analysis:Proceeding of the 2005 European Grid Conference,* Amsterdam, LCNS (*Vol. 3470*, pp. 132-143). Springer Berlin Heidelberg.

Mastroianni, C., Talia, D., & Verta, O. (2005b). A super-peer model for resource discovery services in large-scale Grids. *Future Generation Computer Systems*, *21*(8), 1235–1248. doi:10.1016/j.future.2005.06.001

Mathew, V., Sitaraman, R. K., & Shenoy, P. (2012). Energy-aware load balancing in content delivery networks. Proceedings of IEEE INFOCOM '12 (pp. 954–962). doi:doi:10.1109/INFCOM.2012.6195846 doi:10.1109/INFCOM.2012.6195846

McDermott-Wells, P. (2004). What is bluetooth? *IEEE Potentials*, *23*(5), 33–35. doi:10.1109/MP.2005.1368913

McDonald, A. (2009). *Architectures for Transactional Memory* [Ph.D. Dissertation]. Stanford University, Stanford, USA. Retrieved from http://csl.stanford.edu/~christos/publications/2009.austen_mcdonald.phd_thesis.pdf

Melo, V. A. Z. C., Sakurai, C. A., Fontana, C. F., Tosta, J. A., Silva, W. S., & Dias, E. M. (2011). Technological Model for Application of Internet of Things to Monitor Pharmaceutical Goods Transportation. *Paper presented at the18th ITS World Congress*, Orlando, USA.

Meshkova, E., Riihijarvi, J., Petrova, M., & Mähönen, P. (2008). A survey on resource discovery mechanisms, peer-to-peer and service discovery framework. *Computer Networks*, *52*(11), 2097–2128. doi:10.1016/j.comnet.2008.03.006

Message Passing Interface Forum (2004). MPI: A message-passing interface standard *(Technical Report UT-CS-94-230)*. Department of Computer Science, University of Tennessee.

Microsoft. (2015). Microsoft Azure. Retrieved from http://www.windowsazure.com

Minh, C. C. (2008). *Designing an effective hybrid transactional memory system*. ProQuest.

Mirkovic, J., & Reiher, P. (2004). A taxonomy of DDoS attack and DDoS defense mechanisms. *Computer Communication Review*, *34*(2), 39–53. doi:10.1145/997150.997156

Mishra, B., & Prajapati. (2014). A Mathematical Model on Attack by Malicious Objects Leading to Cyber War. *International Journal of Nonlinear Science, 17*(2).

Mishra, A., Jain, R., & Durresi, A. (2012). Cloud computing: Networking and communication challenges. *IEEE Communications Magazine*, *50*(9), 24–25. doi:10.1109/MCOM.2012.6295707

Mishra, B., & Jha, N. (2007). Fixed Period of Temporary Immunity after run of Anti-Malicious Software on Computer Nodes. *Applied Mathematics and Computation*, *190*(2), 1207–1212. doi:10.1016/j.amc.2007.02.004

Mishra, B., & Jha, N. (2010). SEIRS Model for the Transmission of Malicious Objects in Computer Network. *Applied Mathematical Modelling*, *34*(3), 710–715. doi:10.1016/j.apm.2009.06.011

Mishra, B., & Pandey, S. (2013). Dynamic Model of Worm Propagation in Computer Network. *Applied Mathematical Modelling*, *38*(7).

Misra, P., Simmhan, Y., & Warrior, J. (2015). Towards a Practical Architecture for the Next Generation Internet of Things. *arXiv preprint arXiv:1502.00797*.

Misra, S., Krishna, P. V., Agarwal, H., Saxena, A., & Obaidat, M. S. (2011). A learning automata based solution for preventing distributed denial of service in Internet of things. *Paper presented at the International Conference on Internet of Things (iThings)*, Dalian, China. doi:doi:10.1109/iThings/CPSCom.2011.84 doi:10.1109/iThings/CPSCom.2011.84

Mittal, M. (1998). *Computer system and method of allocating cache memories in a multilevel cache hierarchy utilizing a locality hint within an instruction*. Google Patents.

Mohapatra, S. K., Choudhury, R. R., & Das, P. (2014). The Future Directions in Evolving WI-FI: Technologies, Applications, and Services. *International Journal of Next-Generation Networks*, *6*(3), 13–22. doi:10.5121/ijngn.2014.6302

Mohr, B., & Wolf, F. (2003). KOJAK-A tool set for automatic performance analysis of parallel programs.*Proceedings of International Conference on Euro-Par Parallel Processing (Euro-Par'03)*, Klagenfurt, Austria. Springer. doi:10.1007/978-3-540-45209-6_177

Mohsenian-Rad, A.-H., Wong, V. W., Jatskevich, J., Schober, R., & Leon-Garcia, A. (2010). Autonomous demand-side management based on game-theoretic energy consumption scheduling for the future smart grid. *IEEE Transactions on Smart Grid, 1*(3), 320–331. doi:10.1109/TSG.2010.2089069

Moir, M., Moore, K., & Nussbaum, D. (2007). The Adaptive Transactional Memory Test Platform: A tool for experimenting with transactional code for Rock. *Proceedings of the Workshop on Transactional Computing (Transact)*. Sun Microsystems.

Molnar, S., Cox, M., Ellsworth, D., & Fuchs, H. (1994). A sorting classification of parallel rendering. IEEE Computer Graphics and Applications, 14(4), 23–32.

Mont-Blanc Project, from http://www.montblanc-project.eu/

Moore, K. E., Bobba, J., Moravan, M. J., Hill, M. D., & Wood, D. A. (2006, February). LogTM: log-based transactional memory. Proceedings of HPCA '06 (pp. 254-265). doi:doi:10.1109/HPCA.2006.1598134 doi:10.1109/HPCA.2006.1598134

Moore, G. E. (1965). Cramming more components onto integrated circuits. *Electronics, 38*(8), 56–59.

Moore, K. E., & Grossman, D. Log-based transactional memory. *Proc. of the Twelfth International Symposium on High-Performance Computer Architecture* (pp. 11–15).

Moravan, M. J., Bobba, J., Moore, K. E., Yen, L., Hill, M. D., Liblit, B., & Wood, D. A. (2006). Supporting nested transactional memory in LogTM. In *ACM Sigplan Notices* (Vol. 41, pp. 359–370). ACM.

Moreland, K.D. (2013). Oh %24%23*%40! Exascale! The Effect of Emerging Architectures on Scientific Discovery. In *High Performance Computing, Networking, Storage and Analysis (SCC)* (pp. 224 – 231).

Moreland, K. D. (2012). Oh, $#*@! Exascale! The Effect of Emerging Architectures on Scientific Discovery. High Performance Computing, Networking. *Storage and Analysis, 224*(231), 10–16.

Moscibroda, T., Schmid, S., & Wattenhofer, R. (2006). When selfish meets evil: Byzantine players in a virus inoculation game. In *Proceedings of the 25th Annual ACM Symposium on Principles of Distributed Computing.* doi:10.1145/1146381.1146391

Moss, J. E. B., & Hosking, A. L. (2006). Nested transactional memory: Model and architecture sketches. *Science of Computer Programming, 63*(2), 186–201. doi:10.1016/j.scico.2006.05.010

Moussaïd, M., Helbing, D., & Theraulaz, G. (2011). How simple rules determine pedestrian behavior and crowd disasters. Proceedings of the National Academy of Sciences of the United States of America, 108(17), 6884–6888. PubMed PMID:21502518

Muchnick, S. S. (1997). *Advanced Compiler Design and Implementation*. San Francisco, CA: Morgan Kaufmann Publishers Inc.

Muhammad Yasir, Q., Klaus D, M.-M. (2010). Data cache-energy and throughput models: design exploration for embedded processors. *EURASIP Journal on Embedded Systems*. EURASIP.

Muhic, I., & Hodzic, M. (2014). Internet of Things: Current Technological Review. *Periodicals of Engineering and Natural Sciences (PEN), 2*(2).

Murphy, B., & Gent, T. (1995). Measuring System and Software Reliability Using an Automated Data Collection Process. *Quality and Reliability Engineering International, 11*(5), 341–353. doi:10.1002/qre.4680110505

Murphy, D. B., & Davidson, M. W. (2012). *Fundamentals of light microscopy and electronic imaging*. John Wiley and Sons, Inc. doi:10.1002/9781118382905

Mustafa, S., Nazir, B., Hayat, A., Khan, A. R., & Madani, S. A. Resource management in cloud computing: Taxonomy, prospects, and challenges. *Computers & Electrical Engineering*. doi:10.1016/j.compeleceng.2015.07.021

Mylonas, G., & Theodoridis, E. (2015). Developments and challenges ahead in smart city frameworks-lessons from Smart-Santander. *International Journal of Intelligent Engineering Informatics*, *3*(2-3), 95–119. doi:10.1504/IJIEI.2015.069882

Nagarajan, A. B., & Mueller, F. (2007). Proactive Fault Tolerance for HPC with Xen Virtualization. In *Proceedings of the 21st Annual International Conference on Supercomputing*. doi:10.1145/1274971.1274978

Nagel W. E., Arnold A., Weber M., Hoppe H. C., & Solchenbach K. (1996). VAMPIR: Visualization and analysis of MPI resources. *Supercomputer*, 12(1).

Nagel, K., & Rickert, M. (2001). Parallel implementation of the TRANSIMS micro-simulation. Parallel Computing, 27(12), 1611–1639.

Nagendra, M., & Sekhar, M. C. (2014). Performance Improvement of Advanced Encryption Algorithm using Parallel Computation. *International Journal of Software Engineering and Its Applications*, *8*(2), 287–296.

Navalgund, S. S., Desai, A., Ankalgi, K., & Yamanur, H. (2013). Parallelization of AES Algorithm Using OpenMP. *Lecture Notes on Information Theory*, *1*(4), 144–147. doi:10.12720/lnit.1.4.144-147

Navarro, C. A., Hitschfeld-Kahler, N., & Mateu, L. (2014). A survey on parallel computing and its applications in data-parallel problems using GPU architectures.Communications in Computational Physics, 15(2), 285–329.

Navimipour, N. J., Rahmani, A. M., Navin, A. H., & Hosseinzadeh, M. (2014). Resource discovery mechanisms in grid systems: A survey. *Journal of Network and Computer Applications*, *41*, 389–410. doi:10.1016/j.jnca.2013.09.013

Navimpour, N. J., & Milani, F. S. (2014). A comprehensive study of the resource discovery techniques in peer-to-peer networks. *Peer–to-Peer Networking and Applications*, *8*(3), 474–492. doi:10.1007/s12083-014-0271-5

Negi, A., Titos-Gil, R., Acacio, M. E., Garcia, J. M., & Stenstrom, P. (2012). π-TM: Pessimistic invalidation for scalable lazy hardware transactional memory. *Proceedings of the 2012 IEEE 18th International Symposium on High Performance Computer Architecture (HPCA)* (pp. 1–12). IEEE.

Neil, G. (2000). *When things start to think*. Holt Paperbacks.

Nejdl, W., Wolpers, W., Siberski, W., Schmitz, C. H., Schlosser, M., Brunkhorst, I., & Loser, A. (2003). Super-peer-based routing strategies for RDF-based peer-to-peer networks. *Web Semantics: Science, Services, and Agents on the World Wide Web*, *1*(2), 177–186. doi:10.1016/j.websem.2003.11.004

Nelson, G. (2015). *Where is Google's car going?: a vision emerges in Silicon Valley*. Automotive News.

Nemirovsky, M., & Tullsen, M. D. (2013). *Multithreading Architecture. Synthesis Lectures on Computer Architecture*. Morgan and Claypool Publishers.

Neuhaeuser, J., & D'Angelo, L. (2013). Collecting and distributing wearable sensor data: an embedded personal area network to local area network gateway server. *Paper presented at the 35th Annual International Conference of the IEEE Engineering in Medicine and Biology Society (EMBC)*, Osaka, Japan. doi:doi:10.1109/EMBC.2013.6610584 doi:10.1109/EMBC.2013.6610584

Newman, M. E., Forrest, S., & Balthrop, J. (2002). Email Networks and the Spread of Computer Viruses. *Physical Review E: Statistical, Nonlinear, and Soft Matter Physics*, *66*(3), 035101. doi:10.1103/PhysRevE.66.035101

NVIDIA Corporation. (2004). NVIDIA NVLink High-Speed Interconnect: Application Performance.

NVIDIA Corporation. (2013). Just the facts.

NVIDIA Corporation. (2014). NVIDIA Next Generation CUDA Compute Architecture: Kepler GK110/210 (Whitepaper version 1.1).

NVIDIA. (2015a). *CUDA C best practices guide*. Retrieved from http://docs.nvidia.com/cuda/cuda-c-best-practices-guide/index.html

NVIDIA. (2015b). *CUDA C programming guide*. Retrieved from http://docs.nvidia.com/cuda/cuda-c-programming-guide/index.html

Nwogu, K. (2015). *Energy Harvesting And Storage: The Catalyst To The Power Constraint For Leveraging Internet Of Things (IoT) On Trains. (Master of Science)*. University of Nebraska-Lincoln.

Nyland, L. S., Prins, J. F., Goldberg, A., & Mills, P. H. (2000). A Design Methodology for Data-Parallel Applications. *IEEE Transactions on Software Engineering, 26*(4), 293–314. doi:10.1109/32.844491

Ogata, Y., Endo, T., Maruyama, N., & Matsuoka, S. (2008, April). An efficient, model-based CPU-GPU heterogeneous FFT library. *Proceedings of the 22nd IEEE International Symposium on Parallel and Distributed Processing* (pp. 1-10). IEEE.

Oliver, J. P., Curto, J., Bouvier, D., Ramos, M., & Boemo, E. (2012). Clock gating and clock enable for FPGA power reduction. *Proceedings of the 2012 VIII Southern Conference on Programmable Logic (SPL)* (pp. 1–5). IEEE. doi:doi:10.1109/SPL.2012.6211782 doi:10.1109/SPL.2012.6211782

Olukotun, K. (2007). *Chip Multiprocessor Architecture: Techniques to Improve Throughput and Latency. Synthesis Lectures on Computer Architecture*. Morgan and Claypool Publishers.

Olyaei, B. B., Pirskanen, J., Raeesi, O., Hazmi, A., & Valkama, M. (2013). Performance comparison between slotted IEEE 802.15. 4 and IEEE 802.1 lah in IoT based applications. *Paper presented at the IEEE 9th International Conference on Wireless and Mobile Computing, Networking and Communications (WiMob)*, Lyon, France.

Ondřej, J., Pettré, J., Olivier, A. H., & Donikian, S. (2010). A synthetic-vision based steering approach for crowd simulation. ACM Transactions on Graphics, 29(4), 123.

Open Aquarium - Aquaponics and Fish Tank Monitoring for Arduino. (2014). Retrieved from http://www.cooking-hacks.com/documentation/tutorials/open-aquarium-aquaponics-fish-tank-monitoring-arduino

OpenACC, from http://www.openacc-standard.org/

Oppenheimer, D., Ganapathi, A., & Patterson, D. A. (2003). Why do Internet Services Fail, and What Can Be Done About It? In *Proceedings of the 4th Usenix Symposium on Internet Technologies and Systems*. Seattle, WA.

Ortega, J., Trefftz, H., & Trefftz, C. (2011, May). Parallelizing AES on multicores and GPUs. *Proceedings of the 2011 IEEE International Conference on Electro/Information Technology* (pp. 15-17). IEEE.

Ozen, G., Ayguadé, E., & Labarta, J. (2014). On the roles of the programmer, the compiler and the runtime system when programming accelerators in OpenMP. In Using and Improving OpenMP for Devices (pp. 215–229).

Ozkul, T., & Sevin, A. (2014). Survey of Popular Networks used for Biosensors. *Biosens. J., 3*(110), 2.

Pakbaznia, E., & Pedram, M. (2012). Design of a tri-modal multi-threshold CMOS switch with application to data retentive power gating. *IEEE Transactions on Very Large Scale Integration Systems, 20*(2), 380–385.

Pala, Z., & Inanc, N. (2007). Smart parking applications using RFID technology. *Paper presented at the 2007 1st Annual RFID Eurasia*, Istanbul, Turkey. doi:doi:10.1109/RFIDEURASIA.2007.4368108 doi:10.1109/RFIDEURASIA.2007.4368108

Pal, A., Mehta, A., Mirshekar-Syahkal, D., Deo, P., & Nakano, H. (2014). Dual-Band Low-Profile Capacitively Coupled Beam-Steerable Square-Loop Antenna. *IEEE Transactions on Antennas and Propagation, 62*(3), 1204–1211. doi:10.1109/TAP.2013.2294866

Palankar, M. R., Iamnitchi, A., Ripeanu, M., & Garfinkel, S. (2008). Amazon S3 for science grids: a viable solution? *Paper presented at theProceedings of the 2008 international workshop on Data-aware distributed computing.* doi:doi:10.1145/1383519.1383526 doi:10.1145/1383519.1383526

Pang, Z., Zheng, L., Tian, J., Kao-Walter, S., Dubrova, E., & Chen, Q. (2015). Design of a terminal solution for integration of in-home health care devices and services towards the Internet-of-Things. *Enterprise Information Systems, 9*(1), 86–116. doi:10.1080/17517575.2013.776118

Parasyris, K., Tziantzoulis, G., Antonopoulos, C. D., & Bellas, N. (2014). Gemfi: A fault injection tool for studying the behavior of applications on unreliable substrates.*Proceedings of IEEE 28th international symposium on parallel distributed processing (IPDPS).* IEEE. doi:10.1109/DSN.2014.96

Parcharidis, I., Foumelis, M., Kourkouli, P., & Wegmuller, U. (2009). Persistent Scatterers InSAR to detect ground deformation over Rio-Antirio area (Western Greece) for the period 1992–2000. *Journal of Applied Geophysics, 68*(3), 348–355. doi:10.1016/j.jappgeo.2009.02.005

Paris, S., Pettré, J., & Donikian, S. (2007). Pedestrian reactive navigation for crowd simulation: A predictive approach. Computer Graphics Forum, 26(3), 665–674.

Parwekar, P. (2011). From Internet of Things towards cloud of things. *Paper presented at the2nd International Conference on Computer and Communication Technology (ICCCT)*, Allahabad, India. doi:doi:10.1109/ICCCT.2011.6075156 doi:10.1109/ICCCT.2011.6075156

Patel, A., Afram, F., & Ghose, K. (2011). Marss-x86: A qemu-based micro-architectural and systems simulator for x86 multicore processors. Proceedings of the 1st International Qemu Users' Forum (pp. 29–30).

Pearce, R. (2009). IoT tech to drive water treatment in Queensland. *Computerworld.* Retrieved from http://www.computerworld.com.au/article/528602/iot_tech_drive_water_treatment_queensland/

Pelechano, N., Allbeck, J. M., & Badler, N. I. (2008). Virtual crowds: Methods, simulation, and control. Synthesis Lectures on Computer Graphics and Animation, 3(1), 1–176.

Perahia, E., & Stacey, R. (2013). *Next Generation Wireless LANs: 802.11 n and 802.11 ac.* Cambridge university press. doi:10.1017/CBO9781139061407

Perandones, J. M., del Campo Jiménez, G., Rodríguez, J. C., Jie, S., Sierra, S. C., García, R. M., & Santamaría, A. (2014). Energy-saving smart street lighting system based on 6LoWPAN. *Paper presented at theThe First International Conference on IoT in Urban Space*, Rome, Italy. doi:doi:10.4108/icst.urb-iot.2014.257221 doi:10.4108/icst.urb-iot.2014.257221

Pereira, T., & Santos, H. (2015). *Child Abuse Monitor System Model: A Health Care Critical Knowledge Monitor System. In Internet of Things. User-Centric IoT* (pp. 255–261). Springer.

Perera, C., Zaslavsky, A., Christen, P., & Georgakopoulos, D. (2014). Sensing as a service model for smart cities supported by internet of things. *Transactions on Emerging Telecommunications Technologies, 25*(1), 81–93. doi:10.1002/ett.2704

PGI Compilers & Tools, (n. d.) Retrieved from http://www.pgroup.com/

Pinelli, A., Naqavi, I., Piomelli, U., & Favier, J. (2010). Immersed-Boundary methods for general finite- differences and finite-volume Navier-Stokes solvers. *Journal of Computational Physics, 229*(24), 9073–9909. doi:10.1016/j.jcp.2010.08.021

Pioro, M., & Medhi, D. (2004). *Routing, flow, and capacity design in communication and computer networks. Elsevier.*

Plank, J. S., Beck, M., Kingsley, G., & Li, K. (1995, January). Libckpt: transparent checkpointing under Unix.*Proceedings of the USENIX 1995 Technical Conference Proceedings* (pp. 18-18). USENIX Association.

Plank, J. S., Kim, Y., & Dongarra, J. J. (1995, June). Algorithm-based diskless checkpointing for fault tolerant matrix operations. In *Proceedings of the Twenty-Fifth International Symposium on Fault-Tolerant Computing, (FTCS-25). Digest of Papers.*,(pp. 351-360). IEEE. doi:10.1109/FTCS.1995.466964

Plank, J. S., Li, K., & Puening, M. (1998). Diskless checkpointing. *IEEE Transactions on Parallel and Distributed Systems, 9*(10), 972–986. doi:10.1109/71.730527

Polycarpou, E., Lambrinos, L., & Protopapadakis, E. (2013). Smart parking solutions for urban areas. *Paper presented at the IEEE 14th International Symposium and Workshops on a World of Wireless, Mobile and Multimedia Networks (WoWMoM),* Boston, USA. doi:doi:10.1109/WoWMoM.2013.6583499 doi:10.1109/WoWMoM.2013.6583499

Portnoy, M. (2012). *Virtualization essentials.* John Wiley & Sons.

Pothuganti, K., & Chitneni, A. (2014). A Comparative Study of Wireless Protocols: Bluetooth, UWB, ZigBee, and Wi-Fi. In *Advance in Electronic and Electric Engineering* (pp. 2231-1297).

Pourqasem, J., Karimi, S., & Edalatpanah, S. A. (2014). Comparison of Cloud and Grid Computing. *American Jornal of Software Engineering, 2*(1), 8–12.

Pousa, A., Sanz, V., & De Giusti, A. (2012). Performance Analysis of a Symmetric Cryptographic Algorithm on Multicore Architectures.*Proceedings of the 2012 Computer Science & Technology Series-XVII Argentine Congress of Computer Science-Selected Papers* (pp. 57-66). La Plata, Argentina: Edulp.

Preissl, R., Kockerbauer, T., Schulz, M., Kranzlmuler, D., Supinski, B. R., & Quinlan, D. J. (2008). Detecting patterns in MPI communication traces.*Proceedings of International Conference on Parallel Processing (ICPP'08),* Portland, OR, USA. IEEE. doi:10.1109/ICPP.2008.71

Preissl, R., Schulz, M., Kranzlmuller, D., Supinski, B. R., & Quinlan, D. J. (2008). Using MPI communication patterns to guide source code transformations. In M. Bubak, G. D. Albada, J. Dongarra, & P. M. A. Sloot (Eds.), *Network-Based Parallel Computing Communication, Architecture, and Applications* (pp. 253–260). New York, NY: Springer. doi:10.1007/978-3-540-69389-5_29

Przybylski, S. A. (1990). *Cache and memory hierarchy design: a performance-directed approach.* Morgan Kaufmann.

Puppin, D., Moncelli, S., Baraglia, R., & Tonellotto, N. (2005). A grid information service based on peer-to-peer. *Proceedings of the 11th international Euro-Par conference on parallel processing* (ISTI CNR), Lisbon, Portugal. Springer Berlin Heidelberg. doi:doi:10.1007/11549468_52 doi:10.1007/11549468_52

Qadri, M. Y., & McDonald-Maier, K. D. (2010). Analytical Evaluation of Energy and Throughput for Multilevel Caches. *Proceedings of the 2010 12th International Conference on Computer Modelling and Simulation (UKSim)* (pp. 598–603). IEEE. doi:doi:10.1109/UKSIM.2010.114 doi:10.1109/UKSIM.2010.114

Qadri, M. Y., & McDonald-Maier, K. D. (2010, March). Analytical Evaluation of Energy and Throughput for Multilevel Caches. *Proceedings of the 2010 12th International Conference on Computer Modelling and Simulation (UKSim)* (pp. 598-603). IEEE. doi:10.1109/UKSIM.2010.114

Qadri, M. Y., Gujarathi, H. S., & McDonald-Maier, K. D. (2009). Low Power Processor Architectures and Contemporary Techniques for Power Optimization–A Review. *Journal of Computers, 4*(10), 927–942. doi:10.4304/jcp.4.10.927-942

Qian, Z., He, Y., Su, C., Wu, Z., Zhu, H., Zhang, T., & Zhang, Z. et al. (2013). Timestream: Reliable stream computation in the cloud. *Proceedings of the 8th ACM European conference on computer systems* (pp. 1–14). doi:10.1145/2465351.2465353

Qiao, Y., & Bustamante, F. E. (2006). Structured and unstructured overlays under the microscope: a measurement-based view of two P2P systems that people use. *Proceedings of the annual conference on USENIX' 06 annual technical conference.* Berkeley, CA, USA: ACM.

Qin, Z., Denker, G., Giannelli, C., Bellavista, P., & Venkatasubramanian, N. (2014). A Software Defined Networking Architecture for the Internet-of-Things. *Paper presented at the 2014 IEEE Network Operations and Management Symposium (NOMS)*, Krakow, Poland. doi:doi:10.1109/NOMS.2014.6838365 doi:10.1109/NOMS.2014.6838365

Qualcomm. (2012). IEEE802.11ac: The Next Evolution of Wi-FiTM Standards. Retrieved from www.qualcomm.com/documents/qualcomm-research-ieee80211ac-next-evolution-wi-fi

Qualcomm. (2014). Improving whole home coverage and power efficiency. Retrieved from www.qualcomm.com/invention/research/projects/wi-fi-evolution/80211ah

Rababah, A. (2008). Bivariate orthogonal polynomials on triangular domains. *Mathematics and Computers in Simulation*, *78*(1), 107–111. doi:10.1016/j.matcom.2007.06.006

Rababah, A., & Alqudah, M. (2005). Jacobi-weighted orthogonal polynomials on triangular domains. *Journal of Applied Mathematics*, *2005*(3), 205–217. doi:10.1155/JAM.2005.205

Rabbah, R., & Agarwal, A. (2004). Versatility and versabench: A new metric and a benchmark suite for flexible architectures. *Proceedings of international conference on architectural support for programming language and operating systems (ASPLOS), the wild and crazy idea session.* ACM.

Rackspace. (2015). Rackspace Cloud. Retrieved from http://www.rackspace.com/

Raicu, I., Foster, I., & Zhao, Y. (2008). Many-Task Computing: Bridging the Gap Between High Throughput Computing and High Performance Computing. In *Proceedings of the Workshop on Many-Task Computing on Clouds, Grids, and Supercomputers (MTAGS)*. Austin, TX.

Rajwar, R., & Goodman, J. R. (2001). Speculative lock elision: Enabling highly concurrent multithreaded execution. *Proceedings of the 34th annual ACM/IEEE international symposium on Microarchitecture* (pp. 294–305). IEEE Computer Society.

Rajwar, R., & Goodman, J. R. (2002). Transactional lock-free execution of lock-based programs. *Operating Systems Review*, *36*(5), 5–17. doi:10.1145/635508.605399

Rajwar, R., Herlihy, M., & Lai, K. (2005). Virtualizing transactional memory. *Proceedings of 32nd International Symposium on Computer Architecture ISCA '05* (pp. 494–505). IEEE. doi:10.1109/ISCA.2005.54

Ramadan, H. E., Rossbach, C. J., Porter, D. E., Hofmann, O. S., Bhandari, A., & Witchel, E. (2007). Metatm/tx-linux: Transactional memory for an operating system. *ACM SIGARCH Computer Architecture News*, *35*(2), 92–103. doi:10.1145/1273440.1250675

Ratnasamy, S., Francis, P., Handley, M., Karp, R., & Shenker, S. (2001). A scalable content-addressable network. *Proceedings of the 2001 conference on applications, technologies, architectures, and protocols for computer communications (SIGCOMM).* San Diego, California: ACM. doi:doi:10.1145/383059.383072 doi:10.1145/383059.383072

Ravichandran, D., Pantel, P., & Hovy, E. (2004). The Terascale Challenge. In *Proceedings of the KDD Workshop on Mining for and from the Semantic Web.*

Reed, D. A., Lu, C.-D., & Mendes, C. L. (2006). Reliability challenges in large systems. *Future Generation Computer Systems*, *22*(3), 293–302. doi:10.1016/j.future.2004.11.015

Rehman, M. H., Liew, C. S., & Wah, T. Y. (2014a). Frequent pattern mining in mobile devices: A feasibility study. *Paper presented at the 2014 International Conference on Information Technology and Multimedia (ICIMU)*. doi:doi:10.1109/ICIMU.2014.7066658 doi:10.1109/ICIMU.2014.7066658

Rehman, M. H., Liew, C. S., & Wah, T. Y. (2014b). UniMiner: Towards a unified framework for data mining. *Paper presented at the 2014 Fourth World Congress on Information and Communication Technologies (WICT)*.

Rehman, M. H., & Batool, A. (2015). The Concept of Pattern based Data Sharing in Big Data Environments. *International Journal of Database Theory and Application*, *8*(4), 11–18. doi:10.14257/ijdta.2015.8.4.02

Rehman, M. H., Liew, C. S., Wah, T. Y., Shuja, J., & Daghighi, B. (2015). Mining Personal Data Using Smartphones and Wearable Devices: A Survey. *Sensors (Basel, Switzerland)*, *15*(2), 4430–4469. doi:10.3390/s150204430 PMID:25688592

Reynolds, C. W. (1987). Flocks, herds and schools: A distributed behavioral model. Computer Graphics, 21(4), 25–34.

Richmond, P., Coakley, S., & Romano, D. M. (2009, May). A high performance agent based modelling framework on graphics card hardware with CUDA. *Proceedings of the 8th International Conference on Autonomous Agents and Multiagent Systems* (Vol. 2, pp. 1125-1126).

Rinaldi, P. R., Dari, E. A., Vénere, M. J., & Clausse, A. (2012). A Lattice-Boltzmann solver for 3D fluid simulation on GPU. *Simulation Modelling Practice and Theory*, *25*, 163–171. doi:10.1016/j.simpat.2012.03.004

Rivas, J. I. R., Gyves, O. D., Rudomín, I., & Pelechano, N. (2014). Coupling Camera-tracked Humans with a Simulated Virtual Crowd. *Proceedings of GRAPP Conference 2014* (pp. 312-321).

River, W. (2006). Simics Full System Simulator.

Robinson, D., & Stearly, J. (2011). *Resilience of High Performance Computing Systems. (Technical report)*. Albuquerque, NM: Sandia National Laboratories.

Robles, T., Alcarria, R., Martin, D., Morales, A., Navarro, M., Calero, R., . . . Lopez, M. (2014). An internet of things-based model for smart water management. *Paper presented at the 2014 28th International Conference on Advanced Information Networking and Applications Workshops (WAINA)*, Barcelona, Spain. doi:doi:10.1109/WAINA.2014.129 doi:10.1109/WAINA.2014.129

Rojas, R. (2013). *Neural networks: a systematic introduction*. Springer Science & Business Media.

Roman, E., Duell, J., & Hargrove, P. (2003). *The design and implementation of Berkeley Lab's Linux Checkpoint/Restart. Technical Report publication LBNL-54941*. Berkeley Lab.

Rosenthal, J. S. (2006). *A First Look at Rigorous Probability Theory*. World Scientific Publishing. doi:10.1142/6300

Rost, S., & Balakrishnan, H. (2006). Memento: A health monitoring system for wireless sensor networks. *Paper presented at the 3rd Annual IEEE Communications Society on Sensor and Ad Hoc Communications and Networks*, Reston, USA. doi:doi:10.1109/SAHCN.2006.288514 doi:10.1109/SAHCN.2006.288514

Roy, S., Ranganathan, N., & Katkoori, S. (2011). State-retentive power gating of register files in multicore processors featuring multithreaded in-order cores. *IEEE Transactions on Computers*, *60*(11), 1547–1560. doi:10.1109/TC.2010.249

Rubio-Campillo, X. (2014). Pandora: A Versatile Agent-Based Modelling Platform for Social Simulation. *Proceedings of the SIMUL 2014: The Sixth International Conference on Advances in System Simulation* (pp. 29-34).

Rudomin, I., Hernández, B., deGyves, O., Toledo, L., Rivalcoba, I., & Ruiz, S. (2013). GPU generation of large varied animated crowds. Computación y Sistemas, 17(3), 365–380.

Rudomín, I., Millán, E., & Hernández, B. (2005). Fragment shaders for agent animation using finite state machines. Simulation Modelling Practice and Theory, 13(8), 741–751.

Ruiz, S., Hernández, B., Alvarado, A., & Rudomín, I. (2013). Reducing memory requirements for diverse animated crowds. Proceedings of Motion on Games (pp. 77-86).

Rumbaugh, J., Blaha, M., Premerlani, W., Eddy, F., & Lorensen, W. E. (1991). *Object-oriented modeling and design* (Vol. 199). Prentice-hall Englewood Cliffs.

Russell, R. M. (1978). The cray-1 computer system. *Communications of the ACM, 21*(1), 63–72. doi:10.1145/359327.359336

Saha, A., Chatterjee, A., Pal, N., Ghosh, A., & Chaki, N. (2015). A Lightweight Implementation of Obstruction-Free Software Transactional Memory. In *Applied Computation and Security Systems* (pp. 67–84). Springer. doi:10.1007/978-81-322-1988-0_5

Saha, B., Adl-Tabatabai, A.-R., Hudson, R. L., Minh, C. C., & Hertzberg, B. (2006). McRT-STM: a high performance software transactional memory system for a multi-core runtime. *Proceedings of the eleventh ACM SIGPLAN symposium on Principles and practice of parallel programming* (pp. 187–197). ACM. doi:10.1145/1122971.1123001

Sahoo, R. K., Sivasubramaniam, A., Squillante, M. S., & Zhang, Y. (2004). Failure Data Analysis of a Large-Scale Heterogeneous Server Environment. In *Proceedings of the International Conference on Dependable Systems and Networks (DSN)*. Florence, Italy. doi:10.1109/DSN.2004.1311948

Sakaryan, G., Wulff, M., & Unger, H. (2004). Search methods in P2P networks: a Survey. In T. Böhme et al (Ed.), Innovative Internet Community Systems. Proceedings of I2CS-Innovative Internet Community Systems, Guadalajara, Mexico. Springer Berlin Heidelberg.

Sakharnykh, N. (2010). Tridiagonal solvers on the GPU and applications to fluid simulation. *Proceedings of the NVIDIA GPU Technology Conference*.

Salesforce. (2015). Salesforce Cloud Computing. Retrieved from http://www.salesforce.com/cloudcomputing/

Sanaei, Z., Abolfazli, S., Gani, A., & Buyya, R. (2014). Heterogeneity in mobile cloud computing: Taxonomy and open challenges. *IEEE Communications Surveys and Tutorials, 16*(1), 369–392. doi:10.1109/SURV.2013.050113.00090

Sánchez, D., Michelogiannakis, G., & Kozyrakis, C. (2010). An analysis of on-chip interconnection networks for large-scale chip multiprocessors. *ACM Transactions on Architecture and Code Optimization, 7*(1), 1–4. doi:10.1145/1736065.1736069

Sanchez, L., Muñoz, L., Galache, J. A., Sotres, P., Santana, J. R., Gutierrez, V., & Theodoridis, E. et al. (2014). Smart-Santander: IoT experimentation over a smart city testbed. *Computer Networks, 61*, 217–238. doi:10.1016/j.bjp.2013.12.020

Sanders, J., & Kandrot, E. (2010). *CUDA by example: an introduction to general-purpose GPU programming*. Addison-Wesley Professional.

Sankaran, S., Squyres, J. M., Barrett, B., Sahay, V., Lumsdaine, A., Duell, J., & Roman, E. et al. (2005). The LAM/MPI checkpoint/restart framework: System-initiated checkpointing. *International Journal of High Performance Computing Applications, 19*(4), 479–493. doi:10.1177/1094342005056139

Sarkar, D. (2014). *Introducing hdinsight Pro Microsoft HDInsight* (pp. 1–12). Springer. doi:10.1007/978-1-4302-6056-1_1

Sastry Hari, S., Adve, S., Naeimi, H., & Ramachandran, P. (2013). *Relyzer: Application resiliency analyzer for transient faults. Proceedings of Micro*. IEEE.

Sathya, S. S., & Babu, K. S. (2010). Survey of fault tolerant techniques for grid. *Computer Science Review, 4*(2), 101–120. doi:10.1016/j.cosrev.2010.02.001

Sato, K. (2012). An inside look at google bigquery (White paper). Retrieved from https://cloud.google.com/files/Big-QueryTechnicalWP.pdf

Satyanarayanan, M., Bahl, P., Caceres, R., & Davies, N. (2009). The case for vm-based cloudlets in mobile computing. *Pervasive Computing, 8*(4), 14–23. doi:10.1109/MPRV.2009.82

Savola, R. M., Abie, H., & Sihvonen, M. (2012). Towards metrics-driven adaptive security management in e-health IoT applications. *Paper presented at theThe 7th International Conference on Body Area Networks.* doi:doi:10.4108/icst.bodynets.2012.250241 doi:10.4108/icst.bodynets.2012.250241

Schneps-Schneppe, M., Namiot, D., Maximenko, A., & Malov, D. (2012). Wired Smart Home: energy metering, security, and emergency issues. *Paper presented at the4th International Congress on Ultra Modern Telecommunications and Control Systems and Workshops (ICUMT)*, St. Petersburg, Russia. doi:doi:10.1109/ICUMT.2012.6459700 doi:10.1109/ICUMT.2012.6459700

Schroeder, B., & Gibson, G. (2007). Understanding Failures in Petascale Computers. *Journal of Physics: Conference Series 78*, No. 1. IOP Publishing.

Schroeder, B., & Gibson, G. (2005). *A Large-Scale Study of Failures in High Performance Computing Systems. (Technical report).* Pittsburgh, PA: Carnegie Mellon University.

Scott, M. (2015). Transactional Memory Today. *ACM SIGACT News, 46*(2), 96–104. doi:10.1145/2789149.2789166

Scott, S. L. (1996). Synchronization and communication in the T3E multiprocessor. *SIGPLAN Not., 31*(9), 26–36. doi:10.1145/248209.237144

Scurlock, C., & D'Ambrosio, C. (2015). Telemedicine in the Intensive Care Unit: State of the Art. *Critical Care Clinics, 31*(2), 187–195. doi:10.1016/j.ccc.2014.12.001 PMID:25814449

Segars, S. (2001). *Low power design techniques for microprocessors.* Tutorial Note of the ISSCC.

Seiler, L., Carmean, D., Sprangle, E., Forsyth, T., Abrash, M., Dubey, P., & Hanrahan, P. et al. (2008). Larrabee: A many-core x86 architecture for visual computing.*Proceedings of the 35th International Conference and Exhibition on Computer Graphics and Interactive Techniques* (Vol. 18, pp. 1-15), New York, NY: ACM Press. doi:10.1145/1399504.1360617

Seok, M., Hanson, S., Blaauw, D., & Sylvester, D. (2012). Sleep Mode Analysis and Optimization with Minimal-Sized Power Gating Switch for Ultra-Low Operation. *IEEE Transactions on Very Large Scale Integration Systems, 20*(4), 605–615.

Seomun, J., Shin, I., & Shin, Y. (2010). Synthesis and implementation of active mode power gating circuits. *Proceedings of the 2010 47th ACM/IEEE Design Automation Conference (DAC)* (pp. 487–492). IEEE. doi:doi:10.1145/1837274.1837395 doi:10.1145/1837274.1837395

SGI. Open64 compiler and tools. (2008). Retrieved from http://www.open64.net

Shah, N. A., & Ahir, D. H. (2013). Power Consumption Reduction using Microarchitecture Techniques for Modern Multicore Microprocessors. *Current Trends in Information Technology, 3*(3), 16–20.

Shamshirband, S., Petković, D., Ćojbašić, Ž., Nikolić, V., Anuar, N. B., Shuib, N. L. M., & Akib, S. et al. (2014). Adaptive neuro-fuzzy optimization of wind farm project net profit. *Energy Conversion and Management, 80*, 229–237.

Shamshirband, S., Petkovic, D., Javidnia, H., & Gani, A. (2015). Sensor Data Fusion by Support Vector Regression Methodology—A Comparative Study. *Sensors Journal, IEEE, 15*(2), 850–854. doi:10.1109/JSEN.2014.2356501

Shamshirband, S., Shojafar, M., Hosseinabadi, A. R., Kardgar, M., Nasir, M. M., & Ahmad, R. (2015). OSGA: Genetic-based open-shop scheduling with consideration of machine maintenance in small and medium enterprises. *Annals of Operations Research, 229*(1), 743–758. doi:10.1007/s10479-015-1855-z

Shao, F., Chang, Z., & Zhang, Y. (2010, February). AES encryption algorithm based on the high performance computing of GPU.*Proceedings of the 2010 Second International Conference on Communication Software and Networks* (pp. 588-590). IEEE. doi:10.1109/ICCSN.2010.124

Sharma, V. C., Haran, A., Rakamari'c, Z., & Gopalakrishnan, G. (2013). Towards formal approaches to system resilience. *Proceedings of the 19th IEEE pacific rim international symposium on dependable computing (PRDC)*. IEEE.

Shelar, R. S. (2012). A fast and near-optimal clustering algorithm for low-power clock tree synthesis. *IEEE Transactions on Computer-Aided Design of Integrated Circuits and Systems, 31*(11), 1781–1786.

Shende, S., & Malony, A. D. (2006). TAU: The tau parallel performance system. *International Journal of High Performance Computing Applications, 20*(2), 2006. doi:10.1177/1094342006064482

Sherchan, W., Jayaraman, P. P., Krishnaswamy, S., Zaslavsky, A., Loke, S., & Sinha, A. (2012). Using on-the-move mining for mobile crowdsensing. *Paper presented at the 2012 IEEE 13th International Conference on Mobile Data Management (MDM)*. doi:doi:10.1109/MDM.2012.58 doi:10.1109/MDM.2012.58

Shet, A. G., Siddharth, K., Sorathiya, S. H., Deshpande, A. M., Sher-lekar, S. D., Kaul, B., & Ansumali, S. (2013). On Vectorization for Lattice Based Simulations. *International Journal of Modern Physics C, 24*(12).

Shoaib, M., Bosch, S., Incel, O. D., Scholten, H., & Havinga, P. J. (2014). Fusion of smartphone motion sensors for physical activity recognition. *Sensors (Basel, Switzerland), 14*(6), 10146–10176. doi:10.3390/s140610146 PMID:24919015

Shojafar, M., Abawajy, J. H., Delkhah, Z., Ahmadi, A., Pooranian, Z., & Abraham, A. (2015). An efficient and distributed file search in unstructured peer-to-peer networks. *Peer-to-Peer Networking and Applications, 8*(1), 120–136. doi:10.1007/s12083-013-0236-0

Shojafar, M., Cordeschi, N., Amendola, D., & Baccarelli, E. (2015a). Energy-saving adaptive computing and traffic engineering for real-time-service data centers.*Proceedings of IEEE ICC Workshop on Cloud Computing Systems, Networks, and Applications* (pp. 1800-1806). doi:10.1109/ICCW.2015.7247442

Shojafar, M., Javanmardi, S., Abolfazli, S., & Cordeschi, N. (2015b). FUGE: A joint meta-heuristic approach to cloud job scheduling algorithm using fuzzy theory and a genetic method. *Cluster Computing, 18*(2), 829–844. doi:10.1007/s10586-014-0420-x

Shreve, S. E. (2004). *Stochastic Calculus for Finance II: Continuous-Time Models*. Springer. doi:10.1007/978-1-4757-4296-1

Siddiqui, A. (2014). An Emperical Study of Consumer Perception Regarding Organised Retail In Tier Three Cities. *Journal of Business and Management, 1*, 91–105.

Siddiqui, F., Zeadally, S., & Salah, K. (2015). Gigabit Wireless Networking with IEEE 802.11 ac: Technical Overview and Challenges. *Journal of Networks, 10*(3), 164–171. doi:10.4304/jnw.10.3.164-171

Silvano, C., Fornaciari, W., & Villar, E. (2014). *Multi-objective Design Space Exploration of Multiprocessor SoC Architectures*. Springer.

Šimunić, T., Benini, L., & De Micheli, G. (1999). Cycle-accurate simulation of energy consumption in embedded systems.*Proceedings of the 36th annual ACM/IEEE Design Automation Conference* (pp. 867–872). ACM. doi:10.1109/DAC.1999.782199

Singh, H., Agarwal, K., Sylvester, D., & Nowka, K. J. (2007). Enhanced leakage reduction techniques using intermediate strength power gating. *IEEE Transactions on Very Large Scale Integration Systems, 15*(11), 1215–1224.

Singh, J. P., Hennessy, J. L., & Gupta, A. (1995). Implications of hierarchical N-body methods for multiprocessor architectures. *ACM Transactions on Computer Systems, 13*(2), 141–202. doi:10.1145/201045.201050

Singh, J. P., Holt, C., Hennessy, J. L., & Gupta, A. (1993). A parallel adaptive fast multipole method.*Proceedings of the 1993 ACM/IEEE conference on Supercomputing* (pp. 54–65). ACM. doi:10.1145/169627.169651

Sivasubramanian, S. (2012). Amazon dynamoDB: a seamlessly scalable non-relational database service. *Paper presented at the2012 ACM SIGMOD International Conference on Management of Data.* doi:doi:10.1145/2213836.2213945 doi:10.1145/2213836.2213945

Själander, M., Martonosi, M., & Kaxiras, S. (2014). *Power-Efficient Architectures: Recent Advances. Synthesis Lectures on Computer Architecture.* Morgan and Claypool Publishers.

Smith R. (2014). Intel's Knights Landing Xeon Phi coprocessor.

Smith, A. J. (1982). Cache memories.[CSUR]. *ACM Computing Surveys, 14*(3), 473–530. doi:10.1145/356887.356892

Smith, B. J. (1982). Architecture and applications of the HEP multiprocessor computer system.*Proceedings of the International Society for Optical Engineering* (Vol. 298, pp 241-248).

Snavely, A., Carrington, L., Wolter, N., Labarta, J., Badia, R., & Purkayastha, A. (2002). A framework for application performance modeling and prediction.*Proceedings of International Conference on High Performance Computing, Networking, Storage and Analysis (SC'02)*, Baltimore, USA. IEEE.

Snir, M., Wisniewski, R. W., Abraham, J. A., Adve, S. V., Bagchi, S., Balaji, P., & Hensbergen, E. V. (2014). Addressing failures in exascale computing. *International Journal of High Performance Computing Applications, 28*(2), 129–173. doi:10.1177/1094342014522573

Song, D., Brumley, D., Yin, H., Caballero, J., Jager, I., Kang, M., & Gxena, P. (2008). BitBlaze: A new approach to computer security via binary analysis. *Proceedings of international conference on information systems security (ICISS).* Springer Berlin Heidelberg. doi:doi:10.1007/978-3-540-89862-7_1 doi:10.1007/978-3-540-89862-7_1

Song, F., Tomov, S., & Dongarra, J. (2012, June). Enabling and scaling matrix computations on heterogeneous multicore and multi-GPU systems.*Proceedings of the 26th ACM international conference on Supercomputing* (pp. 365-376). ACM. doi:10.1145/2304576.2304625

Sridharan, V., Stearley, J., DeBardeleben, N., Blanchard, S., & Gurumurthi, S. (2013). Feng shui of supercomupter positional effects in dram and sram faults.*Proceedings of International conference for high performance computing, networking, storage and analysis (SC).* IEEE. doi:10.1145/2503210.2503257

Staff, A. (2014). Connected Car Technology Shifts Internet of Things Boundaries. *PubNub.com.* Retrieved from http://www.pubnub.com/blog/connected-car-technology-shifts-internet-things-boundaries/

Sterling, T., Becker, D. J., Savarese, D., Dorband, J. E., Ranawake, U. A., & Packer, C. V. (1995). Beowulf: A parallel workstation for scientific computation.*Proceedings of the 24th International Conference on Parallel Processing* (pp. 11-14). CRC Press.

Still, G. K. (2000). Crowd dynamics [Doctoral dissertation]. University of Warwick.

Stoica, I., Morris, R., Karger, D., Kaashoek, M. F., & Balakrishnan, H. (2001). Chord: A scalable peer-to-peer lookup service for internet applications. *Computer Communication Review, 31*(4), 149–160. doi:10.1145/964723.383071

Stroud, F. (2015). 802.11ac. *Webpedia*. Retrieved from http://www.webopedia.com/TERM/8/802_11ac.html

Su, C.-L., & Despain, A. M. (1995). Cache design trade-offs for power and performance optimization: a case study. *Proceedings of the 1995 international symposium on Low power design* (pp. 63–68). ACM. doi:10.1145/224081.224093

Succi, S. (2001). *The lattice Boltzmann equation: for fluid dynamics and beyond*. New York: Oxford university press.

Sula, A., Spaho, E., Matsuo, K., Barolli, L., Xhafa, F., & Miho, R. (2013). *An IoT-Based Framework for Supporting Children with Autism Spectrum Disorder Information Technology Convergence* (pp. 193–202). Springer.

Sullivan, M. S., & Chillarege, R. (1992). A Comparison of Software Defects in Database Management Systems and Operating Systems. In *Proceedings of the 22nd International Symposium on Fault-Tolerant Computing*. Boston, MA. doi:10.1109/FTCS.1992.243586

Susukita, R., Ando, H., Ando, M., ... (2008). Performance prediction of large-scale parallell system and application using macro-level simulation. *Proceedings of International Conference on High Performance Computing, Networking, Storage and Analysis (SC'08)*, Austin, Texas, USA. IEEE.

Sutter, H. (2005). The free lunch is over: A fundamental turn toward concurrency in software. *Dr. Dobb's journal*, 30(3), 202-210.

Su, X., Shao, G., Vause, J., & Tang, L. (2013). An integrated system for urban environmental monitoring and management based on the Environmental Internet of Things. *International Journal of Sustainable Development and World Ecology*, 20(3), 205–209. doi:10.1080/13504509.2013.782580

Swarztrauber, P. N. (1974). A direct Method for the Discrete Solution of Separable Elliptic Equations. *SIAM Journal on Numerical Analysis*, 11(6), 1136–1150. doi:10.1137/0711086

Tai, H., Celesti, A., Fazio, M., Villari, M., & Puliafito, A. (2015). An integrated system for advanced water risk management based on cloud computing and IoT. *Paper presented at the 2nd World Symposium on Web Applications and Networking (WSWAN)*, Tunisia. doi:doi:10.1109/WSWAN.2015.7210305 doi:10.1109/WSWAN.2015.7210305

Takahashi, D. (2001). An extended split-radix fft algorithm. *Signal Processing Letters, IEEE*, 8(5), 145–147. doi:10.1109/97.917698

Takeda, S., Miwa, S., Usami, K., & Nakamura, H. (2012a). Efficient leakage power saving by sleep depth controlling for Multi-mode Power Gating. *Proceedings of the 2012 13th International Symposium on Quality Electronic Design (ISQED)* (pp. 625–632). IEEE. doi:doi:10.1109/ISQED.2012.6187558 doi:10.1109/ISQED.2012.6187558

Takeda, S., Miwa, S., Usami, K., & Nakamura, H. (2012b). Stepwise sleep depth control for run-time leakage power saving. *Proceedings of the great lakes symposium on VLSI* (pp. 233–238). ACM. doi:10.1145/2206781.2206838

Talia, D. (2013). Toward Cloud-based Big-data Analytics. *IEEE Computer Science*, 2013, 98-101.

Talia, D., & Trunfio, P. (2005). Peer-to-Peer protocols and Grid services for resource discovery on Grids. *Advances in Parallel Computing*, 14, 83–103. doi:10.1016/S0927-5452(05)80007-3

Tamm, O., Hermsmeyer, C., & Rush, A. M. (2010). Eco-sustainable system and network architectures for future transport networks. *Bell Labs Technical Journal*, 14(4), 311–327. doi:10.1002/bltj.20418

Tang, D., & Iyer, R. (1991). Impact of Correlated Failures on Dependability in a VAX Cluster System. In *Proceedings of the IFIP Working Conference on Dependable Computing for Critical Applications*.

Tang, D., & Iyer, R. (1992). Analysis and Modeling of Correlated Failures in Multicomputer Systems. *IEEE Transactions on Computers*, 41(5), 567–577. doi:10.1109/12.142683

Tang, D., Iyer, R., & Subramani, S. (1990). Failure Analysis and Modeling of a VAX Cluster System. In *Proceedings of the International Symposium on Fault-Tolerant Computing.*

Tan, Y. H., Lü, K., & Lin, Y. P. (2012). Organisation and management of shared documents in super-peer networks based semantic hierarchical cluster trees. *Peer-to-Peer Networking and Applications, 5*(3), 292–308. doi:10.1007/s12083-012-0123-0

Tatourian, A. (2013). *NVIDIA GPU architecture & CUDA programming environment.* Retrieved from http://tatourian.com/2013/09/03/nvidia-gpu-architecture-cuda-programming-environment/

Taylor, D. (2014). RFID in the pharmaceutical industry: Addressing counterfeits with technology. *Journal of Medical Systems, 38*(11), 1–5. doi:10.1007/s10916-014-0141-y PMID:25308613

Texas Instruments. (2013). Texas Instruments CC2540/41 Bluetooth® Low Energy Software Developer's Guide v1. 4.0. *SWRU271F Version.* Retrieved from http://www.ti.com/lit/ug/swru271f/swru271f.pdf

Thakur, A., & Iyer, R. (1996). Analyze NOW: An Environment for Collection and Analysis of Failures in a Network of Workstations. *IEEE Transactions on Reliability, 46*(4).

The International Technology Roadmap for Semiconductors. (2013). *Technical report.* ITRS.

Thomas, A., & Pattabiraman, K. (2013). Error detector placement for soft computation.*Proceedings of IEEE/IFIP International Conference on Dependable Systems and Networks (DSN).* IEEE.

Thompson, K. M. (2006). Scale, Spectacle and Movement: Massive Software and Digital Special Effects in The Lord of the Rings. Cap, 16, 283–299.

Titos-Gil, R., Negi, A., Acacio, M. E., Garcia, J. M., & Stenstrom, P. (2013). Eager beats lazy: Improving store management in eager hardware transactional memory. *IEEE Transactions on Parallel and Distributed Systems, 24*(11), 2192–2201. doi:10.1109/TPDS.2012.315

Tiwari, G. (2011). Hardware/Software Based a Smart Sensor Interface Device for Water Quality Monitoring in IoT Environment. *International Journal of Technology and Science, 3*(1), 5–9.

TongKe, F. (2013). Smart Agriculture Based on Cloud Computing and IOT. *Journal of Convergence Information Technology, 8*(2).

TOP500 List. (n. d.). Retrieved from http://www.top500.org/

TOP500.org. (2015, June). *Top500 list.* Retrieved from http://www.top500.org/list/2015/06/

Torkestani, J. A. (2012). A distributed resource discovery algorithm for P2P grids. *Journal of Network and Computer Applications, 35*(6), 28–36.

Toscano, E., & Bello, L. L. (2012). Comparative assessments of IEEE 802.15. 4/ZigBee and 6LoWPAN for low-power industrial WSNs in realistic scenarios. *Paper presented at the9th IEEE International Workshop on Factory Communication Systems (WFCS),* Lemgo, Germany.

Transmeta. (n. d.). *Wikipedia, the free encyclopedia.* Retrieved from https://en.wikipedia.org/w/index.php?title=Transmeta&oldid=680746415

Trunfio, P., Talia, D., Papadakis, H., Fragopoulou, P., Mordacchini, M., Pennanen, M., & Haridi, S. et al. (2007). Peer-to-Peer resource discovery in Grids: Models and systems. *Future Generation Computer Systems, 23*(7), 864–878. doi:10.1016/j.future.2006.12.003

Tselentis, G.-A., Serpetsidaki, A., Martakis, N., Sokos, E., Paraskevopoulos, P., & Kapotas, S. (2007). Local high-resolution passive seismic tomography and Kohonen neural networks—Application at the Rio-Antirio Strait, central Greece. *Geophysics*, *72*(4), B93–B106. doi:10.1190/1.2729473

Ungerer, T., Robic, B., & Silc, J. (2003). A survey of processors with explicit multithreading. *ACM Computing Surveys*, *35*(1), 29–63. doi:10.1145/641865.641867

United States Department of Defense. (1998). *Military Handbook: Electronic Reliability Design Handbook*. Washington, D.C.: Author.

Urgaonkar, R., Kozat, U. C., Igarashi, K., & Neely, M. J. (2010). Dynamic resource allocation and power management in virtualized data centers. Proceedings of the Network operations and management symposium NOMS '10 (pp. 479–486). IEEE. doi:doi:10.1109/NOMS.2010.5488484 doi:10.1109/NOMS.2010.5488484

Vajda, A. (2011). *Programming Many-Core Chips*. Springer. doi:10.1007/978-1-4419-9739-5

Valerio, P. (2014). *Can Sub-1GHz WiFi Solve The IoT Connectivity Issues?* The New Global Enterprise.

Valero-Lara P., Igual F. D., Prieto-Matías M., Pinelli A., & Favier J. (2015). Accelerating fluid–solid simulations (Lattice-Boltzmann & Immersed-Boundary) on heterogeneous architectures. *Journal of Computational Science*. Doi:10.1016/j.jocs.2015.07.002.

Valero-Lara, P., & Pelayo, F. L. (2013). Analysis in performance and new model for multiple kernels executions on many-core architectures. *Proceedings of the IEEE 12th International Conference on Cognitive Informatics and Cognitive Computing* (pp. 189-194). doi:doi:10.1109/ICCI-CC.2013.6622243 doi:10.1109/ICCI-CC.2013.6622243

Valero-Lara, P. (2014). Accelerating solid-fluid interaction based on the immersed boundary method on multicore and GPU architectures. *The Journal of Supercomputing*, *70*(2), 799–815. doi:10.1007/s11227-014-1262-2

Valero-Lara, P., & Pelayo, F. L. (2011). Towards a More Efficient Use of GPUs.*Proceedings of International Conference on Computational Science and Its Applications Workshops* (pp. 3-9).

Valero-Lara, P., & Pelayo, F. L. (2013, July). Analysis in performance and new model for multiple kernels executions on many-core architectures.*Proceedings of the 12th IEEE International Conference on Cognitive Informatics & Cognitive Computing* (pp. 189-194). IEEE. doi:10.1109/ICCI-CC.2013.6622243

Valero-Lara, P., & Pelayo, F. L. (2015). Full-Overlapped Concurrent Kernels.*Proceedings of the 28th International Conference on Architecture of Computing Systems* (pp. 1-8).

Valero-Lara, P., Pinelli, A., Favier, J., & Prieto-Matías, M. (2012). Block Tridiagonal Solvers on Heterogeneous Architectures.*Proceedings of 10th IEEE International Symposium on Parallel and Distributed Processing with Applications Workshop* (pp. 609-616).

Valero-Lara, P., Pinelli, A., & Prieto-Matías, M. (2014a). Fast finite difference Poisson solvers on heterogeneous architectures. *Computer Physics Communications*, *185*(4), 1265–1272. doi:10.1016/j.cpc.2013.12.026

Valero-Lara, P., Pinelli, A., & Prieto-Matías, M. (2014b). Accelerating Solid-fluid Interaction using Lattice-boltzmann and Immersed Boundary Coupled Simulations on Heterogeneous Platforms.*Proceedings of the International Conference on Computational Science* (pp. 50-61). doi:10.1016/j.procs.2014.05.005

Valero, P., & Pelayo, F. L. (2011, June). Towards a more efficient use of GPUs.*Proceedings of the 2011 International Conference on Computational Science and Its Applications* (pp. 3-9). IEEE. doi:10.1109/ICCSA.2011.55

van Dam, H. J. J., Vishnu, A., & de Jong, W. A. (2013). A case for soft error detection and correction in computational chemistry. *Journal of Chemical Theory and Computation*, *9*(9), 3995–4005. doi:10.1021/ct400489c PMID:26592395

Van Den Berg, J., Guy, S. J., Lin, M., & Manocha, D. (2011). Reciprocal n-body collision avoidance. In Robotics Research (pp. 3-19).

Van den Berg, J., Patil, S., Sewall, J., Manocha, D., & Lin, M. (2008). Interactive navigation of multiple agents in crowded environments. *Proceedings of the 2008 symposium on Interactive 3D graphics and games* (pp. 139-147).

Van Kampen, N. G. (Ed.). (2007). *Stochastic Processes in Physics and Chemistry*. Elsevier.

Varia, J., & Mathew, S. (2013). Overview of amazon web services. *Jan-2014*.

Vecchio, M., Giaffreda, R., & Marcelloni, F. (2014). Adaptive Lossless Entropy Compressors for Tiny IoT Devices. *IEEE Transactions on Wireless Communications*, *13*(2), 1088–1100. doi:10.1109/TWC.2013.121813.130993

Vermesan, O., & Friess, P. (2013). *Internet of things: converging technologies for smart environments and integrated ecosystems*. River Publishers.

Vermesan, O., Friess, P., Guillemin, P., Gusmeroli, S., Sundmaeker, H., Bassi, A., & Eisenhauer, M. et al. (2011). Internet of things strategic research roadmap. *Internet of Things: Global Technological and Societal Trends*, *1*, 9–52.

Vetter, J. S., & McCracken, M. O. (2001). Statistical scalability analysis of communication operations in distributed applications.*Proceedings of ACM SIGPLAN Symposium on Principles and Practice of Parallel (PPoPP'01)*, Snowbird, Utah, USA. ACM. doi:10.1145/568014.379590

Vetter, J. S., & Mueller, F. (2002). Communication characteristics of large-scale scientific applications for contemporary cluster architectures.*Proceedings of International Parallel and Distributed Processing Symposium (IPDPS'02)*, Florida, USA. IEEE. doi:10.1109/IPDPS.2002.1015504

Victoria, A. D. C., Ahmad, M. A., Ahmad, N. A., & Silviu, D. (2015). The Mathematical Study of Data Transmission in Digital Electronics. *Int. J. of Advanced Research*, *3*(3), 697–702.

Vlacheas, P., Giaffreda, R., Stavroulaki, V., Kelaidonis, D., Foteinos, V., Poulios, G., & Moessner, K. et al. (2013). Enabling smart cities through a cognitive management framework for the internet of things. *IEEE Communications Magazine*, *51*(6), 102–111. doi:10.1109/MCOM.2013.6525602

Von Laszewski, G., Wang, L., Younge, A. J., & He, X. (2009). Power-aware scheduling of virtual machines in dvfs-enabled clusters. Proceedings of the IEEE international conference on Cluster computing and workshops Cluster '09 (pp. 1–10). doi:doi:10.1109/CLUSTR.2009.5289182 doi:10.1109/CLUSTR.2009.5289182

Walker, R. C., & Betz, R. M. (2013). An investigation of the effects of error correcting code on gpu-accelerated molecular dynamics simulations. *Proceedings of the conference on extreme science and engineering discovery environment: Gateway to discovery* (pp. 8:1–8:3). New York, NY, USA: ACM. doi:doi:10.1145/2484762.2484774 doi:10.1145/2484762.2484774

Waller, M. A., & Fawcett, S. E. (2013). Data science, predictive analytics, and big data: A revolution that will transform supply chain design and management. *Journal of Business Logistics*, *34*(2), 77–84. doi:10.1111/jbl.12010

Walraed-Sullivan, M., Vahdat, A., & Marzullo, K. (2013, December). Aspen trees: balancing data center fault tolerance, scalability and cost.*Proceedings of the ninth ACM conference on Emerging networking experiments and technologies* (pp. 85-96). ACM. doi:10.1145/2535372.2535383

Wang, W., Ohta, Y., Ishii, Y., Usami, K., & Amano, H. (2012). Trade-off analysis of fine-grained power gating methods for functional units in a CPU. Proceedings of IEEE 2012 Cool Chips XV (COOL Chips), (pp. 1–3). IEEE. doi:doi:10.1109/COOLChips.2012.6216587 doi:10.1109/COOLChips.2012.6216587

Wang, A., & Naffziger, S. (2008). *Adaptive techniques for dynamic processor optimization: theory and practice.* Springer Science & Business Media. Springer. doi:10.1007/978-0-387-76472-6

Wang, L., Zhang, F., Arjona Aroca, J., Vasilakos, A. V., Zheng, K., Hou, C., & Liu, Z. (2014). Greendcn: A general framework for achieving energy efficiency in data center networks. *IEEE Journal on Selected Areas in Communications*, *32*(1), 4–15. doi:10.1109/JSAC.2014.140102

Wang, P., González, M. C., Menezes, R., & Barabási, A.-L. (2013). Understanding the Spread of Malicious Mobile-Phone Programs and their Damage Potential. *International Journal of Information Security*, *12*(5), 383–392. doi:10.1007/s10207-013-0203-z

Wanner, L., El Malaki, S., Lai, L., Gupta, P., & Srivastava, M. (2013). Varemu: An emulation testbed for variability-aware software. *Proceedings of the international conference on hardware/software co-design and system synthesis.* IEEE.

Warneke, D., & Kao, O. (2011). Exploiting dynamic resource allocation for efficient parallel data processing in the cloud. *IEEE Transactions on Parallel and Distributed Systems*, *22*(6), 985–997. doi:10.1109/TPDS.2011.65

Wei, H., Shao, Z., Huang, Z., Chen, R., Guan, Y., Tan, J., & Shao, Z. (2016). RT-ROS: A real-time ROS architecture on multi-core processors. *Future Generation Computer Systems*, *56*, 171–178. doi:10.1016/j.future.2015.05.008

Weiser, M. (1984). Program slicing. *IEEE Transactions on Software Engineering*, *10*(4), 352–357. doi:10.1109/TSE.1984.5010248

Wellein, G., Zeiser, T., Hager, G., & Donath, S. (2006, September). On the single processor performance of simple lattice Boltzmann kernels. *Computers & Fluids*, *35*(8-9), 910–919. doi:10.1016/j.compfluid.2005.02.008

Whitham, J., Audsley, N. C., & Davis, R. I. (2014). Explicit reservation of cache memory in a predictable, preemptive multitasking real-time system. *ACM Transactions on Embedded Computing Systems*, *13*(4s), 120. doi:10.1145/2523070

Wilson, A. W. Jr, & Frank, S. J. (1988). *Hierarchical cache memory system and method.* Google Patents.

Wilson, C., Hargreaves, T., & Hauxwell-Baldwin, R. (2015). Smart homes and their users: A systematic analysis and key challenges. *Personal and Ubiquitous Computing*, *19*(2), 463–476. doi:10.1007/s00779-014-0813-0

Winter, S., Tretter, M., Sattler, B., & Suri, N. (2013). simfi: From single to simultaneous software fault injections.*Proceedings of International conference on dependable systems and networks (DSN)*. IEEE. doi:10.1109/DSN.2013.6575310

Wolstenholme, L. (1999). *Reliability Modeling: A Statistical Approach.* Chapman & Hall/CRC Press.

Woo, S. C., Ohara, M., Torrie, E., Singh, J. P., & Gupta, A. (1995). The SPLASH-2 programs: Characterization and methodological considerations. In ACM SIGARCH Computer Architecture News (Vol. 23, pp. 24–36). ACM.

Wu, Y., Chen, Y., & Lei, P. (2012). Analysis on Water Quality Monitoring Technologies and Application of Internet of Things. *China Water & Wastewater*, *28*(22), 9–13.

Xia, L., Cui, Z., Lange, J. R., Tang, Y., Dinda, P. A., & Bridges, P. G. (2012). Vnet/p: Bridging the cloud and high performance computing through fast overlay networking.*Proceedings of the 21st international symposium on high-performance parallel and distributed computing* (pp. 259–270). doi:10.1145/2287076.2287116

Xiao, L., Zhuang, Z., & Liu, Y. (2005). Dynamic layer management in super-peer architectures. *IEEE Transactions on Parallel and Distributed Systems*, *16*(11), 1078–1091.

Xue, R., Liu, X., Wu, M., Guo, Z., Chen, W., Zheng, W., & Voelker, G. M. et al. (2009). MPIWiz: subgroup reproducible replay of mpi applications. *Proceedings of ACM SIGPLAN Symposium on Principles and Practice of Parallel (PPoPP '09)*, North Carolina, USA. ACM. doi:10.1145/1594835.1504213

Xu, J., Kalbarczyk, Z., & Iyer, R. (1999). Networked Windows NT System Field Failure Data Analysis. In *Proceedings of the IEEE Pacific Rim International Symposium on Dependable Computing*. Hong Kong, China.

Xu, T., Zhang, Z., Yu, P. S., & Long, B. (2012). Generative models for evolutionary clustering. *ACM Transactions on Knowledge Discovery from Data*, 6(2), 7. doi:10.1145/2297456.2297459

Xu, X., & Li, M.-L. (2012). Understanding soft error propagation using efficient vulnerability-driven fault injection. *Proceeding of IEEE/IFIP international conference on dependable systems and networks (DSN)*. IEEE.

Yang, B. (2009). Study on security of wireless sensor network based on ZigBee standard. *Paper presented at the International Conference on Computational Intelligence and Security*, Beijing, China doi:doi:10.1109/CIS.2009.208 doi:10.1109/CIS.2009.208

Yang, F., Zhan, S. H., & Shen, F. (2004). Maintaining and self-recovering global state in a super-peer overlay for service discovery. In M. Li & X. Sun & Q. Deng & J. Ni (Eds.), *Grid and Cooperative Computing: proceeding of Second International Workshop (GCC)*. Springer Berlin Heidelberg. doi:doi:10.1007/978-3-540-30208-7_120 doi:10.1007/978-3-540-30208-7_120

Yang, Y., Li, C.-T., Sun, X., & Yang, H. (2008). Removable visible image watermarking algorithm in the discrete cosine transform domain. *Journal of Electronic Imaging*, 17(3).

Yang, B., & Garcia-m, H. (2003). Designing a super-peer network. *Proceedings of the 2003 19th international conference on the data engineering (ICDE)*. IEEE.

Yang, B., & Garcia-Molina, H. (2002). Improving search in peer-to-peer systems. *Proceedings of the 22nd International Conference on Distributed Computing Systems (ICDSC)*, Vienna, Austria. IEEE. doi:10.1109/ICDCS.2002.1022237

Yang, C., Wang, F., Du, Y., Chen, J., Liu, J., Yi, H., & Lu, K. (2010, September). Adaptive optimization for petascale heterogeneous CPU/GPU computing. *Proceedings of the 2010 IEEE International Conference on Cluster Computing* (pp. 19-28). IEEE. doi:10.1109/CLUSTER.2010.12

Yang, W., Li, K., Liu, Y., Shi, L., & Wan, L. (2014). Optimization of quasi-diagonal matrix–vector multiplication on GPU. *International Journal of High Performance Computing Applications*, 28(2), 183–195. doi:10.1177/1094342013501126

Yang, W., Li, K., Mo, Z., & Li, K. (2015). Performance Optimization Using Partitioned SpMV on GPUs and Multicore CPUs. *IEEE Transactions on Computers*, 64(9), 2623–2636. doi:10.1109/TC.2014.2366731

Yen, L., Bobba, J., Marty, M. R., Moore, K. E., Volos, H., Hill, M. D., & Wood, D. (2007, February). LogTM-SE: Decoupling hardware transactional memory from caches. *Proceedings of the IEEE 13th International Symposium on In High Performance Computer Architecture* (pp. 261-272). IEEE.

Yibo, C., Hou, K.-m., Zhou, H., Shi, H.-l., Liu, X., Diao, X., . . . De Vaulx, C. (2011). 6LoWPAN stacks: a survey. *Paper presented at the 7th International Conference on Wireless Communications, Networking and Mobile Computing (WiCOM)*, Wuhan, China.

Yip, M., & Chandrakasan, A. P. (2013). A resolution-reconfigurable 5-to-10-bit 0.4-to-1 V power scalable SAR ADC for sensor applications. *IEEE Journal of Solid-State Circuits*, 48(6), 1453–1464. doi:10.1109/JSSC.2013.2254551

Yourst, M. T. (2007). PTLsim: A cycle accurate full system x86-64 microarchitectural simulator. *Proceedings of the IEEE International Symposium on Performance Analysis of Systems & Software ISPASS '07* (pp. 23–34). IEEE. doi:doi:10.1109/ISPASS.2007.363733 doi:10.1109/ISPASS.2007.363733

Yu, H., Wang, C., Grout, R. W., Chen, J. H., & Ma, K. L. (2010). In situ visualization for large-scale combustion simulations. IEEE Computer Graphics and Applications, 3, 45–57. PubMed PMID:20650717

Yu, T., Dou, M., & Zhu, M. (2015). A data parallel approach to modelling and simulation of large crowd. Cluster Computing, 18(3), 1307-1316.

Yuan, H., & Chen, G. (2008). Network Virus-Epidemic Model with the Point-to-Group Information Propagation. *Applied Mathematics and Computation, 206*(1), 357–367. doi:10.1016/j.amc.2008.09.025

Yue, W., Changhong, S., Xianghong, Z., & Wei, Y. (2010). Design of new intelligent street light control system. *Paper presented at the 2010 8th IEEE International Conference on Control and Automation (ICCA)*, Xiamen, China.

Yu, J., & Li, M. (2008). CBT: A proximity-aware peer clustering system in large scale Bit Torrent-like Peer-to-Peer networks. *Computer Communications, 31*(3), 591–602. doi:10.1016/j.comcom.2007.08.020

Zaharia, M., Chowdhury, M., Franklin, M. J., Shenker, S., & Stoica, I. (2010). Spark: cluster computing with working sets. *Paper presented at theProceedings of the 2nd USENIX conference on Hot topics in cloud computing.*

Zaharia, M., Das, T., Li, H., Hunter, T., Shenker, S., & Stoica, I. (2013). Discretized streams: Fault-tolerant streaming computation at scale.*Proceedings of the twenty-fourth ACM symposium on operating systems principles* (pp. 423– 438). doi:10.1145/2517349.2522737

Zanella, A., Bui, N., Castellani, A. P., Vangelista, L., & Zorzi, M. (2014). *Internet of things for smart cities.* IEEE Internet of Things Journal.

Zhai, J., Hu, J., Tang, X., Ma, X., & Chen, W. (2014). CYPRESS: Combining Static and Dynamic Analysis for Top-Down Communication Trace Compression.*Proceedings of International Conference on High Performance Computing, Networking, Storage and Analysis (SC'14)*, New Orleans, LA, USA. IEEE. doi:10.1109/SC.2014.17

Zhang, J., Li, Z., Sandoval, O., Xin, N., Ren, Y., Martin, R., & Cao, J. (2013). Supporting Personizable Virtual Internet of Things. *Paper presented at the Ubiquitous Intelligence and Computing, 2013 IEEE 10th International Conference on and 10th International Conference on Autonomic and Trusted Computing (UIC/ATC)*. doi:doi:10.1109/UIC-ATC.2013.48 doi:10.1109/UIC-ATC.2013.48

Zhang, Y., Cohen, J., & Owens, J. D. (2010). Fast tridiagonal solvers on the GPU. *Proceedings of the 20th ACM SIGPLAN Symposium on Principles and Practice of Parallel Programming* (pp. 127-136).

Zhang, Y., Tong, Q., Li, L., Wang, W., Choi, K., Jang, J. E., . . . Ahn, S. Y. (2012). Automatic Register Transfer level CAD tool design for advanced clock gating and low power schemes. *Proceedings of the 2012 International SoC Design Conference (ISOCC)* (pp. 21–24). IEEE.

Zhang, Z., Kavousianos, X., Chakrabarty, K., & Tsiatouhas, Y. (2011). A robust and reconfigurable multi-mode power gating architecture. *Proceedings of the 2011 24th International Conference on VLSI Design (VLSI Design)* (pp. 280–285). IEEE. doi:doi:10.1109/VLSID.2011.29 doi:10.1109/VLSID.2011.29

Zhang, J., Zhai, J., Chen, W., & Zheng, W. (2009). Process mapping for mpi collective communications.*Proceedings of International Conference on Euro-Par Parallel Processing (Euro-Par'09)*, Delft, Netherlands. Springer.

Zhang, K., & Wu, B. (2013, May). Task Scheduling Greedy Heuristics for GPU Heterogeneous Cluster Involving the Weights of the Processor.*Proceedings of the 27th IEEE International Parallel and Distributed Processing Symposium Workshops & PhD Forum* (pp. 1817-1827). IEEE. doi:10.1109/IPDPSW.2013.38

Zhang, X., Jeong, S., Kunjithapatham, A., & Gibbs, S. (2010). *Towards an elastic application model for augmenting computing capabilities of mobile platforms In Mobile wireless middleware, operating systems, and applications* (pp. 161–174). Springer. doi:10.1007/978-3-642-17758-3_12

Zhao, W., Wang, C., & Nakahira, Y. (2011). Medical application on Internet of Things. *Paper presented at theIET Conference*, Beijing, China.

Zheng, G., Shi, L., & Kalé, L. V. (2004, September). FTC-Charm++: an in-memory checkpoint-based fault tolerant runtime for Charm++ and MPI.*Proceedings of the 2004 IEEE International Conference on Cluster Computing* (pp. 93-103). IEEE. doi:10.1109/CLUSTR.2004.1392606

Zhong, Z., Rychkov, V., & Lastovetsky, A. (2012, September). Data partitioning on heterogeneous multicore and multi-GPU systems using functional performance models of data-parallel applications.*proceedings of the 2012 IEEE International Conference on Cluster Computing* (pp. 191-199). IEEE. doi:10.1109/CLUSTER.2012.34

Zhou, Y., Peng, X., Hou, L., Wan, P., & Lin, P. (2014). Clock gating-A power optimization technique for smart card. *Proceedings of the 2014 12th IEEE International Conference on Solid-State and Integrated Circuit Technology (ICSICT)* (pp. 1–3). IEEE. doi:doi:10.1109/ICSICT.2014.7021594 doi:10.1109/ICSICT.2014.7021594

ZHU, X.-y., & PAN, Y. (2015). Research on the Identification of Real-time Water Leakage Based on Internet-based Smart Water Meters and Complex Event Processing. *Group Technology & Production Modernization*, 1, 006.

ZigBee Alliance. (2006). Zigbee specification. Retrieved from http://www.zigbee.org/zigbee-for-developers/network-specifications/

ZigBee Alliance. (2014). ZigBee architecture and specifications overview. Retrieved from http://www.zigbee.org/zigbee-for-developers/network-specifications/zigbeeip/

Zilles, C., & Rajwar, R. (2007). Transactional memory and the birthday paradox.*Proceedings of the nineteenth annual ACM symposium on Parallel algorithms and architectures* (pp. 303–304). ACM. doi:10.1145/1248377.1248428

Zorzi, M., Gluhak, A., Lange, S., & Bassi, A. (2010). From today's intranet of things to a future internet of things: A wireless-and mobility-related view. *IEEE Wireless Communications*, 17(6), 44–51. doi:10.1109/MWC.2010.5675777

Zou, C. C., Gong, W., & Towsley, D. (2003). Worm Propagation Modeling and Analysis Under Dynamic Quarantine Defense. In *Proceedings of the ACM CCS Workshop on Rapid Malcode*. doi:10.1145/948187.948197

Zyuban, V., Friedrich, J., Gonzalez, C. J., Rao, R., Brown, M. D., Ziegler, M. M., & Culp, J. A. (2011). Power optimization methodology for the IBM POWER7 microprocessor. *IBM Journal of Research and Development*, 55(3), 7–11. doi:10.1147/JRD.2011.2110410

About the Contributors

Qusay F. Hassan received his Ph.D. from Mansoura University in computer science and information systems, in 2015. His research interests are varied which include SOA, high-performance computing, grid computing, cloud computing, and IoT. Qusay has authored and co-authored a number of journal and conference papers as well as book chapters. Moreover, he is currently editing/authoring a number of new books including "Internet of Things: Technologies, Applications, and Implementations" and "Networks of the Future: Architectures, Technologies, and Implementation", to be released in 2017. Dr. Hassan is a senior IEEE member, and a member of the editorial board of a number of associations including IEEE and AICIT. Moreover, he has many years of practical experience in ICT and software engineering. Qusay currently works as a systems analyst for the United States Agency for International Development (USAID) in Cairo, Egypt, where he deals with large-scale and complex systems.

* * *

Jameel Ahmed received his BS and MS degrees respectively in Electronic Engineering and Electrical Engineering from NED University of Engineering & Technology, Karachi and National University of Sciences & Technology, Pakistan. He secured his doctorate degree in Communication Engineering from Pakistan and Nanyang Technological University (NTU), Singapore. Subsequently, he pursued Post Doctorate Fellowship and Visiting Professor at School of Electrical & Electronic Engineering (EEE), Nanyang Technological University (NTU), Singapore. Dr Jameel has twenty four years of professional experience in his credit in the field of teaching & research at undergraduate and graduate level. He is writer of five books including two by Springer-Verlag. He has published more than 40 research publications at both the national and international level. Dr Jameel is member of IEEE, USA and its three societies. Currently, he is carrying out research on a Rs 27.16 Million funded research project as a Principal Investigator. Dr Jameel has been on the panel of Pakistan Engineering Council (PEC) as a convener and expert and visited so far almost all the leading universities from Karachi to Kashmir. In addition, he is also a member of the Nation Curriculum Revision Committee (NCRC), of HEC for Electrical and Telecommunication curriculum. Presently, Dr Jameel is serving as a Professor and Chairman, Department of Electrical Engineering, HITEC University, Taxila-Islamabad.

Saad Arif is currently a PhD candidate in the Department of Robotics and Intelligent Machines Engineering, School of Mechanical and Manufacturing Engineering, National University of Sciences and Technology, Islamabad, Pakistan. He received his Master of Mechatronics Engineering from the National University of Sciences and Technology, Islamabad, Pakistan in 2012 and Bachelor of Mechatronics Engineering from Air University, Islamabad, Pakistan, in 2009. He has 6 years of experience in engineering research and undergraduate teaching. His research interests include Motion Planning Algorithm development for Mobile Robots, the Design of Embedded Control Systems and Intelligent Automotive Systems.

Eduard Ayguadé received the Engineering degree in Telecommunications in 1986 and the Ph.D. degree in Computer Science in 1989, both from the Universitat Politècnica de Catalunya (UPC), Spain. Since 1987, Prof. Ayguadé has been lecturing at the Computer Science School (FIB) and Telecommunications Engineering (ETSETB) both in Barcelona. Since 1997, he has been a full professor of the Computer Architecture Department at UPC. Prof. Ayguadé has lectured a number of (undergraduate and graduate) courses related with computer organization and architecture, parallel programming models and their implementation. Prof. Ayguadé is also involved in the Computer Architecture and Technology PhD Program at UPC, where he has (co-)advised 15 PhD thesis, in topics related with his research interests: multicore architectures, parallel programming models and their architectural support and compilers for HPC architectures. In these research topics, Prof. Ayguadé has published around 300 papers and participated in several research projects in the framework of the European Union and research collaborations with companies related with HPC technologies (IBM, Intel, Nvidia and Microsoft). Currently, Prof. Ayguadé is the associated director for research in the Computer Sciences Department at the Barcelona Supercomputing Center (BSC-CNS), part of the National Center for Supercomputing located in Barcelona, Spain.

Enzo Baccarelli received a Laurea degree (summa cum laude) in electronic engineering and a Ph.D. degree in Communication Theory and Systems, both from the University Sapienza in 1989 and 1992, respectively. In 1995, he received a Post-Doctorate degree in Information Theory and Applications from the INFOCOM Dept., University "La Sapienza" where he also served as a Research Scientist from 1996 to 1998. Since 1998, he has been an Associate Professor in the signal processing and radio communications at the University "La Sapienza". Since 2003, he is a full Professor in data communications at the University "La Sapienza". He has authored/co-authored more than 250 publications (Citations: 1100+, h-index=18) in well-known conferences and journals such as IEEE transactions (40+ papers) and Elsevier publishers.

Aisha Batool is a MS student in the Department of Computing and Technologies, Iqra University, Islamabad, Pakistan. She is working on data analysis methods using artificial intelligence theories. Her research covers multiple disciplines within computer science and software engineering, including mobile computing, image processing, artificial intelligences, and big data. She has two journal publications and three years of experience in research organizations.

Sean Blanchard works on kernel-level system support in research and production at the Los Alamos National Laboratory. He researches soft-error resilience and scalable system software.

Hon Cheung is a Senior Lecturer in the School of Computing, Engineering and Mathematics, University of Western Sydney. He graduated from The University of Western Australia in 1984 with First Class Honours in Electrical Engineering. He received his PhD degree from the same university in 1988. He was a lecturer in the Department of Electronic Engineering, Hong Kong Polytechnic from 1988 to 1990. From 1990 to 1999, he was a lecturer of Computer Engineering at Edith Cowan University, Western Australia. Dr Cheung has research experience in a number of areas, including conventional methods in artificial intelligence, fuzzy sets, artificial neural networks, digital signal processing, image processing, and network security and forensics.

A. Don Clark obtained his Bachelor of Science degree in Electrical Engineering from the Illinois Institute of Technology (IIT). He later received his Masters and Doctorate degrees in Applied Mathematics from Rensselaer Polytechnic Institute (RPI). Currently, Dr. Clark is a Research Scientist at the Laboratory for Physical Sciences (LPS) -- a Government affiliated laboratory with the University of Maryland and an Associate Research Professor with West Virginia University (WVU). His research interests include biometrics, biological processes, and high performance computing (HPC).

Nicola Cordeschi received a Laurea degree (bachelor) in Communication Engineering from the University of Rome "La Sapienza" in 2004. He received his Ph.D. degree in Information and Communication Engineering in 2008. His Ph.D. dissertation was on the adaptive QoS Transport of Multimedia over Wireless Connections via cross-layer approaches based on the Calculus of Variations. He is currently a Contractor-Researcher with the DIET Dept., University of Rome "La Sapienza". His research activity is focused on wireless communications and deals with the design and optimization of high performance transmission systems for wireless multimedia applications. Nicola published more 70+ papers in several well-known IEEE Transaction and Elsevier journals in his research.

Camille Coti is an Ass. Professor at Univ. Paris 13 since 2010. Prior, was a post-doctoral research associate at Iowa State University (2009-2010), Graduate research assistant at Univ. Paris Sud and INRIA (2006-2009), graduated with a PhD in Computer Science from Univ. Paris Sud in 2009. Graduated with a MSc in Telecommunication Engineering from Telecom INT (now Telecom SudParis) in 2006, formerly a research assistant at King's College, London in 2005.

Claude H. Davis IV is an undergraduate student majoring in Computer Science at Clemson University who is expected to graduate on May 2016. He is planning to pursue graduate studies in computer science upon graduation. Proud member of Phi Sigma Pi National Honor Fraternity and enjoys playing jazz guitar.

Nathan DeBardeleben received his Ph.D. in Computer Engineering from Clemson University in 2004 and has been at Los Alamos National Laboratory since. His specialty is in high performance computing (HPC) and supercomputing resilience, fault-tolerance, and dependability. Nathan studies U.S. Department of Energy supercomputers for reliability trends to prepare the agency for next-generation reliability challenges. He also focuses on studying scientific applications fault-tolerance and methodologies to make them more resilient.

S.A. Edalatpanah is an academic member of Islamic Azad University of Lahijan and University of Guilan. His research interests are numerical linear algebra, operation research computer science and computational mathematics. He is on the editorial boards of more than 30 refereed journals.

Mahmoud Elkhodr is currently completing his PhD on the Internet of Things with Western Sydney University. He is a Lecturer with the School of Computing, Engineering and Mathematics at Western Sydney University and an academic coordinator with Victoria University. He is the founding Chair of the UWS IEEE Chapter, and an executive committee member of IEEE NSW section.

Erich L Foster received his PhD in Applied Mathematics from Virginia Tech, where he studied "Finite Elements for the Quasigeostrophic Equations of the Ocean." After receiving his PhD, he went on to a 2-year postdoc with the Basque Center for Applied Mathematics, where his main research focus was on adaptive finite elements, and creating a new layer of abstraction for FEniCS/DOLFIN. After completing his postdoc with the Basque Center for Applied Mathematics, Erich joined the Institute of Computational Science at the Universita della Svizzera italiana as a postdoc, where his main focus is on building a model for the entire heart.

Song Fu is currently an Assistant Professor in the Department of Computer Science and Engineering and the Director of the Dependable Computing Systems Laboratory at the University of North Texas. He was an Assistant Professor in Computer Science and Engineering at New Mexico Institute of Mining and Technology from 2008 to 2010. He received his Ph.D. degree in Computer Engineering from Wayne State University in 2008. His research interests include distributed, parallel and cloud systems, particularly in system resilience, failure detection and prediction, resource management, power saving, high-performance computing, and virtualization. His research projects have been sponsored by the U.S. National Science Foundation, Los Alamos National Laboratory, Amazon, NVidia, and the University of North Texas. He is a senior member of the IEEE and a member of the ACM.

Qiang Guan is a postdoctoral researcher in the Ultra-scale System Research Center (USRC), HPC-5, Los Alamos National Laboratory. He is mentored by Dr. Nathan DeBardeleben and Sean Blanchard. He obtained his Ph.D. degree in Computer Science and Engineering from University of North Texas, Denton, Texas, in 2014 (Ph.D. advisor: Dr. Song Fu.). He received a M.S. degree in Information Engineering from Myongji University, Seoul, South Korea, in 2008 and a B.S. degree in Communication Engineering from Northeastern University, Shenyang, China, in 2005. Respectively, he worked as a firmware/software Engineer at Techsphere Co., Ltd and Yullin Technology Co.

Benjamin Hernandez works at OLCF at the Oak Ridge National Laboratory.

Johan Jansson (male), received his PhD in computational mathematical modelling at Chalmers University in 2006, was postdoc at KTH (2007-2009) and became an assistant professor at KTH in 2014 (tenure track). Since 2012, he has been a research line leader at the Basque Center for Applied Mathematics (BCAM) in Bilbao, Spain (taking leave of absence from KTH). His research focus is in automated computational mathematical modelling based on the finite element method: mathematical methods, algorithms and massively parallel software implementations with applications in computational mechanics. He was a part of starting the FEniCS open source software project in 2004 with a group of colleagues, and has been a developer and maintainer since. In 2015, he won first prize for best poster at the Bilbao Marine Energy Week for his work on adaptive hydrodynamics computation in FEniCS. In 2014, he was given an excellent written review of his research by the BCAM Scientific Advisory Committee composed of world-leading mathematicians (P-L Lions, J Ball, A Bermudez de Castro, A Makowski, J-P Puel, A Stevens). He is the principal investigator and participant of several academic and industrial projects in Sweden and Spain, for example an EU PRACE Tier-0 (highest level) supercomputing project based on FEniCS, a Spanish national research project in mathematics for adaptive methods, the EU FP7 EUNISON FET-Open project, and several academic-industrial collaboration projects in Sweden and Spain based on FEniCS. He is the author of 25 peer-reviewed journal/conference papers.

William M. Jones is an associate professor and chair of the Department of Computer Science and Information Systems at Coastal Carolina University. He is also an adjunct assistant professor of Electrical and Computer Engineering at Clemson University. He attended Clemson University, where he obtained a BS ('99), a MS ('00) and a PhD ('05), each in Computer Engineering. His research interests include parallel computing, parallel file systems, computational grids, job scheduling, resilience, fault injection, performance evaluation and modeling, and discrete event simulation.

Bilal Khalid is a student of BS in Electrical Engineering. He has experience as a Research Assistant in a project on multi-core reconfigureable processors funded by ICT R&D fund, Ministry of IT, Pakistan. He is also a member of an organization Emwi-tech, where he is working on Embedded Benchmarking. He has interests in Hard Real Time programming, Advanced Computer Architecture and Embedded Systems.

Keqin Li is a SUNY Distinguished Professor of computer science. His current research interests include parallel computing and high-performance computing, distributed computing, energy-efficient computing and communication, heterogeneous computing systems, cloud computing, big data computing, CPU-GPU hybrid and cooperative computing, multicore computing, storage and file systems, wireless communication networks, sensor networks, peer-to-peer file sharing systems, mobile computing, service computing, Internet of things and cyber-physical systems. He has published over 370 journal articles, book chapters, and refereed conference papers, and has received several best paper awards. He is currently or has served on the editorial boards of IEEE Transactions on Parallel and Distributed Systems, IEEE Transactions on Computers, IEEE Transactions on Cloud Computing, Journal of Parallel and Distributed Computing. He is an IEEE Fellow.

Yan Li is a research scientist at Intel Labs China. He received a Ph.D. degree in computer science from the University of Chinese Academy of Science in 2013, and joined the PACMAN group at the Department of Computer Science and Technology in Tsinghua University as a postdoctoral researcher in 2014. His research is focusing on high performance computing, GPU computing and large-scale deep learning.

Saba Munawar is currently a PhD candidate at Department of Electrical Engineering, University of Engineering and Technology, Taxila, Pakistan. She received her Master of Electrical Engineering from HITEC University, Taxila, Pakistan in 2013 and Bachelor of Electrical Engineering from University of Engineering and Technology, Taxila, Pakistan in 2009. She has 6 years of experience in engineering research and teaching at undergraduate level. Her research interests include multi-threaded architectures, electronics system design and control system design.

Maryam Murad have recently completed her MS in Electrical Engineering from HITEC University, Taxila Cantt, Pakistan. She has also obtained her Bachelor's degree in Electrical Engineering from HITEC University, Taxila Cantt, Pakistan. She has worked as a Research assistant and design Engineer in a research project on Multicore Reconfigurable Processor. Her interest areas are Embedded System and Computer Architecture.

Abdul Nasir Khan received his Ph.D from the University of Malaya, Malaysia in 2014. He received his MCS and MS(CS) degrees from COMSATS Institute of Information Technology, Abbottabad, Pakistan in 2005 and 2008, respectively. Currently, he is serving as an Assistant Professor in the Department of Computer Science, COMSATS Institute of Information Technology. He has published 13 research papers in reputed journals and conferences. His research interests include various aspects of network security and distributed computing.

Abel Paz-Gallardo received his B.S. degree in Computer Engineer from the University of Extremadura (Spain, 2007) and his M.Sc. and Ph.D. degrees in Computer Science from the Univ. of Extremadura (Spain, 2009 and 2011) being one of the youngest Ph.Ds in the University. His Ph.D. and main research interests comprise remotely sensed hyperspectral image analysis, signal processing, and efficient implementations of large-scale scientific problems on high performance computing architectures such as clusters & graphical processing units (GPUs). During 2006 and 2007, he was a Research Assistant in the Computer Architecture Dept. at the University of Extremadura, where he became Assistant Professor in 2008. At the same time he started working in the Minimally Invasive Surgery Center Jesús Usón in Cáceres. In 2010, he started working for Bull Spain S.A. to deploy at CETA-Ciemat (Trujillo, Spain), the biggest GPGPU Cluster in Spain and one of the biggest ones in Europe. Since November 2010, he is also working as an Associate Professor in the Computer Architecture Dept. Since October 2011, he has been the IT Manager (CIO) of CETA-Ciemat. Dr. Paz has authored more than 40 publications, including 11 journal citation report (JCR) papers (most of them published by IEEE journals) and over 30 peer-reviewed international conference papers.

Hugo Perez has a BSc. in Electrical Electronic Engineering from the National University of Mexico, an MSc. in Computer Architectures, Networks and Systems from the Polytechnic University of Catalonia. Currently, he is studying a PhD. in Computer Architectures at the Polytechnic University of Catalonia in conjunction with the Barcelona Supercomputing Center. His research interests are real-time crowd simulation and in situ visualization using high-performance computing.

Javad Pourqasem is a MA. He has studied Distributed Systems since 2013. His articles have been published in several journals, the American Journal of Software Engineering, Science and Education Publishing, and IJCMSA. He is also a musician and plays the santoor. He completed his BA at the University of Ramsar, and he did his MA in computer networks at Guilan. He did the MCITP course at the Tehran Engineering Institution. Javad pourqasem lives in Mazandaran, Iran.

Manuel Prieto-Matías received a PhD degree in computer science from the Complutense University of Madrid (UCM) in 2000. He is now associate professor in the Department of Computer Architecture at UCM and serves as vice-dean for External Relations and Research at the School of Computer Science and Engineering. His research interests include areas of parallel computing and computer architecture. Most of his activities have focused on leveraging parallel computing platforms and on complexity-effective micro-architecture design. His current research addresses emerging issues related to asymmetric processors, heterogeneous systems and energy-aware computing, with a special emphasis on the interaction between the system software and the underlying architecture. He has co-written numerous articles in journals and for international conferences in the field of parallel computing and computer architecture. He is a member of the ACM and IEEE Computer Society.

Nadia N. Qadri is an Associate Professor and Program Coordinator in Department of Electrical Engineering at COMSATS Institute of Information Technology, Wah Campus. Dr. Qadri obtained her PhD degree in Electronics Systems Engineering from University of Essex, UK. She has more than 13 years of teaching and research experience at renowned universities of Pakistan. She is also leading a research group of Wireless Networks. She published her research work in more than 34 journals/conferences and in various international books. She has also edited a book for IGI global. Her research interests include video streaming, mobile ad hoc and vehicular ad hoc networks, P2P networks, wireless sensor networks, smart grids, self-organized networks, embedded systems, image and video processing. She is also a Professional member of IEEE. She has served on the program committee of more than 20 international conferences.

Atta ur Rehman Khan is an Assistant Professor and a freelance ICT consultant having over nine years of research, teaching, and industry experience at various positions. Dr. Khan has completed renowned projects and published research articles in reputed journals and conferences. He is an editor of a journal, Technical Program Committee (TPC) member of international conferences, and a domain expert of international project proposal evaluation committees. Dr. Khan has received multiple awards, scholarships, and research grants. His areas of research interest include mobile computing, cloud computing, ad hoc networks, distributed systems, and security.

Muhammad Habib ur Rehman is a PhD student at the Department of Computer Systems and Technology, University of Malaya, Kuala Lumpur, Malaysia. He is working on big data mining systems for Internet of Things. His research covers a wide spectrum of application areas including smart cities, mobile social networks, Quantified self, mHealth and wearable assistive technologies among many others. The key research areas of his interest include mobile computing, edge-cloud computing, Internet of Things, data mining, machine learning, and mobile distributed analytics. He has published 10 articles in reputed journals and conferences. Moreover, he is a reviewer of top tier journals, TPC member of reputed conferences, and a student member of IEEE. He has over 10 years of experience in multiple organizations.

Isaac Rudomin completed his PhD in 1990 at the University of Pennsylvania with Dr. Norman Badler as his advisor. He worked as a professor at the Instituto Tecnologico de Monterrey (ITESM) Campus Estado de Mexico from 1991 to 2012 and is now a senior Researcher at Barcelona Supercomputing Center. His interests are in Computer Graphics, with an emphasis on real-time Crowd simulation, generation, animation and rendering using High Performance Computing.

Arsalan Shahid is a student of BE Electrical Engineering in HITEC University Taxila Cantt., Pakistan. He is working as a research associate at EmwiTech, Pakistan where he is leading a research team of 17 members. As a team lead, he is working on hard-real-Time embedded processor benchmarks. He has a previous research experience of more than 2 years as a research assistant in a funded research project on multicore reconfigurable processor platform by ICT R&D fund, Ministry of IT, Pakistan. He has interests in real-time programming, parallel computing/programming, advanced computer architecture, processor benchmarking and embedded systems.

Seyed Shahrestani completed his PhD degree in Electrical and Information Engineering at the University of Sydney. He joined UWS in 1999, where he is currently a Senior Lecturer. He is also the head of the Networking, Security and Cloud Research (NSCR) group at UWS. Seyed has established collaborations with several researchers and groups around the globe. He has been a Visiting Scholar at the University of California, Berkeley. Seyed's research in complex systems has resulted in the establishment of a framework for global control of complex nonlinear, and possibly chaotic, systems. In addition to introducing new concepts and strategies, the framework utilizes established methods for analysis and control of complex nonlinear systems but with new intent. In computer networking, Seyed's research has provided some original solutions to problems in two important aspects of the Internet, namely: network security and management. These works include novel approaches and the use of AI and particularly fuzzy logic and soft computing to enhance modeling and management of large networks and enterprises.

Mohammad Shojafar is currently a 3rd year Ph.D. student in Information and Communication Engineering in the DIET Dept. of the Sapienza University of Rome. He received his Msc in Software Engineering in Qazvin Islamic Azad University, Qazvin, Iran in 2010. Also, he received his Bsc in Computer Engineering-Software major in Iran University Science and Technology, Tehran, Iran in 2006. His current research focuses on wireless communications, distributed computing and mathematical and AI optimization. He is an author/co-author of 40+ peer-reviewed publications (h-index=8) in well-known conferences (e.g., IEEE ICC, GLOBECOM, PIMRC, HIS, ISDA) and journals in IEEE, Elsevier, IOS press and Springer publishers. Since 2013, he is a member of the IEEE Systems Man and Cybernetics Society Technical Committee on Soft Computing and a Distinguished Lecturer of the IEEE Computer Society representing Europe. He has served as a reviewer and PC member for international conferences (e.g., HPCC, HIS, WCI, NaBIC, WICT, FSDM) and international journals (e.g., IEEE Transaction on Fuzzy Systems, JPDC, COMNET, SUPE, ASC, WPC). In addition, Mohammad was a Programmer and Analyzer in Exploration Directorate Section at N.I.O.C in Iran from 2012-2013.

Pedro Valero-Lara received his B.S. and M.Sc. degrees in Computer Engineer from the University of Castilla-La Mancha (Spain, 2009 and 2010). He defended his Ph.D. degree in Computer Science at the Univ. Complutense of Madrid (Spain, 2015). His Ph.D. comprises heterogeneous computing and efficient implementations of large-scale scientific problems. He is an Associate Researcher in the Linear Algebra Group, University of Manchester. Although his experience includes several fields, such as Image Processing or Data Retrieval, his main research line is High-Performance Computing applied to Computational Fluid Dynamics. His work covers the use of different parallel systems, such as NVIDIA GPUs, Intel MIC, multicore, and Cray, among others. He is the main developer of the LBM-HPC software framework for fluid simulations based on Lattice-Boltzmann Method. He has authored over 30 publications, including journal citation report (JCR) papers and more than 20 peer-reviewed international conference papers.

Muhammad Yasir Qadri has obtained his PhD in Electronic Systems Engineering from University of Essex, UK. He has over ten years of practical experience in the development of high-end embedded systems and FPGAs. He is an Approved PhD Supervisor by the Higher Education Commission of Pakistan, and is currently a visiting researcher at University of Essex, UK. He is also a Visiting Faculty Member at HITEC University, Taxila. Dr. Yasir is the editor of a recently published book on Multicore Technology by CRC Press, USA, and has two US patent applications in the area of computer architecture. He is also the recipient of a research grant by National ICT R&D Fund, and is the Co-Principal Investigator for the project of development of a reconfigurable multicore architecture. His area of specialization is energy/performance optimization in reconfigurable MPSoC architectures.

Jidong Zhai received the BS degree in computer science from the University of Electronic Science and Technology of China in 2003 and the PhD degree in computer science from Tsinghua University in 2010. He is now an assistant professor in the Department of Computer Science and Technology, Tsinghua University. His research interests include high-performance computing, compilers and performance analysis, and optimization of parallel applications.

Index

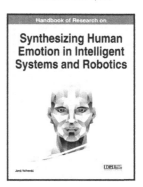

Printed in the United States
By Bookmasters